INTERNATIONAL MACROECONOMICS

Fifth Edition

INTERNATIONAL MACROECONOMICS

Robert C. Feenstra
University of California, Davis

Alan M. Taylor
University of California, Davis

 worth publishers
Macmillan Learning

New York

To Gail and Claire

Senior Vice President, Content Strategy: Charles Linsmeier
Program Director: Shani Fisher
Program Manager: Carolyn Merrill
Senior Development Editors: Jane Tufts and Valerie Raymond
Assessment Editor: Kristyn Brown
Marketing Manager: Clay Bolton
Marketing Assistant: Steven Huang
Senior Media Editor: Lindsay Neff
Media Project Manager: Jason Perkins
Assistant Editor: Amanda Gaglione
Director, Content Management Enhancement: Tracey Kuehn
Senior Managing Editor: Lisa Kinne
Senior Content Project Manager: Edgar Doolan
Director of Design, Content Management: Diana Blume
Design Services Manager: Natasha Wolfe
Interior Design: Lumina Datamatics, Inc.
Cover Design: John Callahan
Permissions Manager: Jennifer MacMillan
Photo Researcher: Krystyna Borgen, Lumina Datamatics, Inc.
Media Permissions Manager: Christine Buese
Text Permissions Manager: Michael McCarty
Senior Workflow Project Manager: Paul W. Rohloff
Production Supervisor: Robert Cherry
Composition: Lumina Datamatics, Inc.
Printing and Binding: LSC Communications
Cover Image: Roydee/Getty Images
Banner: Juls Dumanska/Shutterstock

Library of Congress Control Number: 2020909269

ISBN-13: 978-1-319-21842-3
ISBN-10: 1-319-21842-3

1 2 3 4 5 6   25 24 23 22 21 20

Worth Publishers
One New York Plaza
Suite 4600
New York, NY 10004-1562
www.macmillanlearning.com

About the Authors

Bud Harmon

Robert C. Feenstra and **Alan M. Taylor** are Professors of Economics at the University of California, Davis. They each began their studies abroad: Feenstra received his B.A. in 1977 from the University of British Columbia, in Canada, and Taylor received his B.A. in 1987 from King's College, Cambridge, in England. They trained as professional economists in the United States, where Feenstra earned his Ph.D. in economics from MIT in 1981 and Taylor earned his Ph.D. in economics from Harvard University in 1992. Feenstra has been teaching international trade at the undergraduate and graduate levels at the University of California, Davis, since 1986, where he holds the C. Bryan Cameron Distinguished Chair in International Economics. Taylor teaches international finance and macroeconomics at the University of California, Davis, where he also holds appointments as Director of the Center for the Evolution of the Global Economy and Professor of Finance in the Graduate School of Management.

Both Feenstra and Taylor are active in research and policy discussions in international economics. They are research associates of the National Bureau of Economic Research, where Feenstra directed the International Trade and Investment research program from 1992 to 2016. They have published monographs in international economics: *Offshoring in the Global Economy* and *Product Variety and the Gains from International Trade* (MIT Press, 2010) by Robert C. Feenstra, and *Global Capital Markets: Integration, Crisis, and Growth* (Cambridge University Press, 2004) by Maurice Obstfeld and Alan M. Taylor. Feenstra received the Bernhard Harms Prize from the Institute for World Economics, Kiel, Germany, in 2006, and he delivered the Ohlin Lectures at the Stockholm School of Economics in 2008. Taylor was awarded a Guggenheim Fellowship in 2004 and was a Houblon-Norman/George Fellow at the Bank of England in 2009–10.

Feenstra lives in Davis, California, with his wife, Gail. They have two grown children, Heather and Evan, and two grandchildren, Grant and Lily. Taylor also lives in Davis, with his wife, Claire, and their two children, Olivia and Sebastian.

Brief Contents

INTERNATIONAL MACROECONOMICS

Preface

A Course That's More Important Than Ever

As the writing of this book draws to a close in April 2020, the world economy is experiencing what is likely to be its biggest adverse macroeconomic shock since World War II. The 2019–20 coronavirus pandemic has already tipped most countries into recession—starting in China, where the virus originated, and then spreading outwards to East Asia, Australasia, Europe, the United States, and beyond. This event is unfolding barely a decade after what was the previous largest postwar economic shock, the Global Financial Crisis of 2008. Both crises caused great damage to aggregate economic activity—contracting output, trade, investment, and consumption and causing the levels of unemployment around the world to rapidly increase. The damage was only slowly repaired after 2008, and we might be in for an equally slow recovery after this latest shock.

These two recent crises, and the patchy economic recovery that fell between them, illustrate the importance of international linkages in today's globalized world. Obviously, the transmission of a virus pays no heed to international borders, absent intervention measures to limit travel or impose quarantines. But economic transactions also cross borders, and those links have served for decades, or even centuries, as ways for events in faraway places to cause sudden disruptions to our own economic conditions at home. In 2008, the global economy was tied together by financial transactions, some of which fell under suspicion of being very risky; countries were also connected via trade flows, which often collapsed as trouble in an importing country spilled over into reduced demand for the products of the exporting country, government debts dramatically expanded, central banks made extraordinary interventions, and currency values moved this way and that with every piece of news. After the crisis, growth took new forms and different trade patterns emerged. Some groups in society fared better or worse than others, amplifying distributional concerns, and protectionist trade policies caused further disruption in the global economy, particularly so under U.S. president Donald Trump. Many of the same tensions continue to simmer and could well flare up again.

We saw huge shocks and policy responses emerge and propagate throughout the global economy a decade ago, and we see similar phenomena yet again today. The magnitude of the economic, political, and social impacts is hard to overstate, and they are felt across the entire globe, from the richest advanced economies to the upcoming emerging markets and the poorest developing nations. Arguably, looking at this fraught landscape, it has never been clearer that a sound grasp of international economics is essential knowledge if we are to better understand the world we inhabit.

Why Our Book?

Since the first edition of our text, it has been our goal to present the theories of international economics and bring its models alive through applications that draw on world events. All students want to understand the events they see described on their mobile screens, and our book helps them do just that. We draw on the very latest research—presented at a level appropriate to undergraduate students—to put solid numbers on the models we discuss. Our applications deal not only with the economics behind world events but also with the political economy underlying policy decisions.

Emphasis on Applications

How do you bring theories and models to life? You pair them with real life stories, so most of our chapters include a story, either told directly or taken from a media report. Examples include the tumult at the beginning stages of the coronavirus pandemic (Chapter 1), tariffs used by U.S. presidents (including and before President Trump, Chapter 8), the influence of the Swedish teenager and environmental activist Greta Thunberg (Chapter 11), the suffering in Iceland during the Great Recession (Chapter 12), or in contrast the successful policy followed by Chile (Chapter 17). In each case, the story is meant to draw the student into the theme of the chapter by using a current or historical event. But it's not just these stories that will engage the students: our textbook is unique in that it integrates empirical applications throughout the chapters. Students are asked to think critically about the theory and how it holds up in reality by applying it to historical and current examples. We accomplish these goals by integrating special features throughout:

Applications are integrated into the main text because they are an essential part of our approach to seamlessly blend theory and empirical data with real-world policies, events, and evidence.

Headlines present excerpts from current and historic media stories that further illustrate how topics in the main text relate directly to media coverage of the global economy.

Side Bars illuminate topics that, while not essential, nonetheless provide deeper understanding of the issues under discussion.

To see all Applications, Headlines, and Side Bars, please go to the Detailed Table of Contents.

Emphasis on Empirical Studies

In addition to expanding our coverage to include up-to-date theory and policy applications, our other major goal is to present all the material—both new and old—in the most teachable way. To do this, we ensure that all of the material presented rests on firm and up-to-the-minute empirical evidence. We believe this approach is the right way to study economics, and it is our experience, shared by many instructors, that teaching is more effective and more enlivened when students can see not just an elegant derivation in theory but, right next to it, some persuasive evidence of the economic mechanisms under investigation.

Balanced Coverage of Emerging and Advanced Economies

In our view, emerging markets and developing countries deserve more attention in the curriculum because of their substantial and growing importance in the global economy. For example, in the sections on international trade we discuss in detail the evolving factor endowments in China, including both capital and human capital, the effect of free trade within North America on Mexico, and the migration flows into the United States from Mexico and neighboring countries to the south. In the sections on international macroeconomics, we examine fixed exchange rates in Peru and Argentina, austerity in Poland and Latvia, sudden stops in emerging markets, and the importance of foreign aid in developing countries.

Broadening Learning with Practice

Each chapter concludes with exercises that ask students to think critically about the core concepts in each chapter.

- **Discovering Data** problems at the end of each chapter ask students to seek out, analyze, and interpret real-world data related to chapter topics.

- **Work It Out** problems at the end of each chapter provide students with step-by-step assistance, thus helping develop analytical skills. Each of these problems has a live, online counterpart in *Achieve*, Macmillan's new digital platform, available with this edition.

Introducing *Achieve*: Engage Every Student

Achieve is a comprehensive set of interconnected teaching and assessment tools. It incorporates the most effective elements from Macmillan's market-leading solutions into a single, easy-to-use platform.

Everything Your Students Need in a Single Learning Path

Achieve supports students and instructors at every step, from the first point of contact with new content to demonstrating mastery of concepts and skills. Powerful multimedia resources with an integrated e-book, robust homework, and a variety of interactivities create an extraordinary learning resource for students. *LearningCurve* is adaptive quizzing with a game-like interface, offering students a low-stakes way to brush up on concepts and help identify knowledge gaps. LearningCurve's design nudges students to reference the e-book, providing both the incentive to read and a framework for an efficient reading experience. In addition to *Discovering Data* and *Work It Out* problems, each chapter includes curated *End of Chapter* problems. These multistep questions are adapted from problems found in the text. Each problem is paired with rich feedback for incorrect and correct responses that guide students through the process of problem solving. These questions also feature graphing problems designed so that the student's entire focus is on shading the correct areas or moving the appropriate curves in the correct directions, virtually eliminating grading issues for instructors.

The best place for pricing and bundle options is the Macmillan Learning Online Student Store.

Everything Instructors Need

Achieve's Instructor's Resource Section includes the following:

Instructor's Resource Manual provides summaries and teaching tips for the text's content, along with suggested in-class problems and answers.

Solutions Manual includes answers to end-of-chapter questions.

Test Bank includes expansive multiple-choice and essay-assessment questions.

Lecture Slides include chapter notes and figures, as well as clicker questions and data exercises that can be used in class.

Multiple Formats Support Classroom Needs

The International Economics course is sometimes taught as two separate courses, so this text is issued in multiple formats to allow instructors to tailor the content to their needs and keep costs down for their students:

■ A combined edition (*International Economics*)
■ Two split editions (*International Trade* and *International Macroeconomics*)

What's New in This Edition (Combined and Split Versions)

Below is a brief list including some of the major updates made to this edition of the text:

A new opening example in **Chapter 1, Trade in the Global Economy**, covers the effects of the coronavirus pandemic on international trade.

Chapter 2, Trade and Technology: The Ricardian Model, includes a heavily revised application on "Labor Productivity and Wages" and a new figure showing the impact of different deflators for real wages in the United States.

Chapter 3, Gains and Losses from Trade in the Specific-Factors Model, features two new applications, both of which include new figures. "The 'China Shock' and Employment in the United States" examines whether jobs lost within import-competing industries are made up for by jobs gained in export industries, as the international trade models typically assume. "Can Losses to Factors of Production Be Offset?" discusses policies that encourage the movement of factors of production between sectors when changing international prices cause losses in a given sector.

Chapter 4, Trade and Resources: The Heckscher–Ohlin Model, includes several new sections and a heavily revised section now titled "Evolution of Factor Endowments in China and the United States." The new coverage looks at "effective" endowments in China and in the United States over several years and tells an interesting story about growth in China as compared with the United States.

Chapter 5, Movement of Labor and Capital Between Countries, contains a new application, "The Political Economy of Migration," that discusses extensively the economics of and policies concerning immigrants in the United States and Europe.

Chapter 6, Increasing Returns to Scale and Monopolistic Competition, contains new extensive coverage of the differences between NAFTA and USMCA.

The chapters dealing with trade policy, including **Chapter 8** (Import Tariffs and Quotas Under Perfect Competition), **Chapter 9** (Import Tariffs and Quotas Under Imperfect Competition), and **Chapter 10** (Export Policies in Resource-Based and High-Technology Industries), have been thoroughly revised. All chapters have extensive new coverage of President Trump's tariffs applied on imports from China and other countries, as well as retaliatory tariffs against the United States, and also the U.S. attempt to compensate its farmers.

Chapter 11, International Agreements on Trade and the Environment, has been thoroughly revised to reflect recent events, including the U.S. withdrawal from the Trans-Pacific Partnership, the trade war with China, Brexit, the USMCA, and the Green Deal.

Chapter 12 (Chapter 1), The Global Macroeconomy, contains a new introduction about the post-coronavirus pandemic international macroeconomic environment.

Chapter 17 (Chapter 6), Balance of Payments I: The Gains from Financial Globalization, is redesigned and now contains a chapter appendix titled "Can Poor Countries Gain from Financial Globalization?"

Chapter 18 (Chapter 7), Balance of Payments II: Output, Exchange Rates, and Macroeconomic Policies in the Short Run, has a new application about monetary policy at the zero lower bound after the Global Financial Crisis and the coronavirus pandemic recession.

Chapter 21 (Chapter 10), The Euro: Economics and Politics, has been updated thoroughly to reflect the most recent changes in the EU and the Eurozone, including Brexit, and includes a new figure (21-8) showing how often EU members violate the fiscal rules.

Topics and Approaches

The hundreds of instructors using our book have enthusiastically supported the topics we have included and the approach we have taken in our presentation. Topics covered in international trade (Chapters 1–11 in *International Economics* and in the *International Trade* split volume) include the offshoring of goods and services (Chapter 6); tariffs and quotas under imperfect competition (Chapter 9); and international agreements on trade and the environment (Chapter 11). These topics are in addition to core chapters on the Ricardian model (Chapter 2), the specific-factors model (Chapter 3), the Heckscher–Ohlin model (Chapter 4), trade with increasing returns to scale and imperfect competition (Chapter 6), import tariffs and quotas under perfect competition (Chapter 8), and export subsidies (Chapter 10).

Topics covered in international macroeconomics (Chapters 12–21 in *International Economics* and Chapters 1–10 in the *International Macroeconomics* split volume) include the gains from financial globalization (Chapter 17/Chapter 6), fixed versus floating regimes (Chapter 19/Chapter 8), exchange rate crises (Chapter 20/Chapter 9), and the euro (Chapter 21/Chapter 10). These topics are in addition to core chapters on foreign exchange markets and exchange rates in the short run and the long run (Chapters 13–15/Chapters 2–4), the national and international accounts (Chapter 16/Chapter 5), and the open economy IS–LM model (Chapter 18/Chapter 7). In addition, an online chapter, Topics in International Macroeconomics, covers applied topics of current interest (Exchange Rates in the Long Run: Deviations from Purchasing Power Parity; Exchange Rates in the Short Run: Deviations from Uncovered Interest Parity; Debt and Default; and Case Study: The Global Macroeconomy and the Global Financial Crisis).

In writing our chapters we have made every effort to link them analytically. For example, although immigration and foreign direct investment are sometimes treated as an afterthought in international economics books, we integrate these topics into the discussion of the trade models by covering the movement of labor and capital between countries in Chapter 5. Specifically, we analyze the movement of labor and capital between countries in the short run using the specific-factors model, and we explore the long-run implications using the Heckscher–Ohlin model. Chapter 5 therefore builds on the models that the student has learned in Chapters 3 and 4 and applies them to issues at the forefront of policy discussion.

In the macroeconomics section, this analytical linking is seen in the parallel development of fixed and floating exchange rate regimes, from the opening introductory tour in Chapter 12/Chapter 1, through the workings of exchange rates in Chapters 13–15/Chapters 2–4 and the discussion of policy in the IS–LM model of Chapter 18/Chapter 7, to the discussion of regime choice in Chapter 19/Chapter 8. Many textbooks discuss fixed and floating regimes separately, with fixed regimes often treated as an afterthought. But given the widespread use of fixed rates in many countries, the rising macro weight of fixed regimes, and the collapse of fixed rates during crises, we think it is more helpful for the student to grapple with the different workings and cost-benefit trade-offs of the two regimes by studying them side by side. This approach also allows us to address numerous policy issues, such as the implications of the trilemma and the optimal choice of exchange rate regime.

Acknowledgments

A book like this would not be possible without the assistance of many people, whom we gratefully acknowledge.

First, the renowned team at Worth has spared no effort to help us; their experience and skill in publishing economics textbooks were invaluable. Numerous individuals have been involved with this project, but we must give special mention to a few: the project has been continually and imaginatively guided by program manager Carolyn Merrill, program director Shani Fisher, and development editor Valerie Raymond. The online portion of the book has been brought to fruition by Lindsay Neff, senior media editor, and Kristyn Brown, assessment editor. Through it all, the manuscript was improved endlessly by our primary development editor, Jane Tufts. We would also like to thank our content project manager, Edgar Doolan, who worked tirelessly on this edition. We are greatly in their debt.

We have also relied on the assistance of a number of graduate students in collecting data for applications, preparing problems, and proofreading material. We would like to thank Leticia Arroyo Abad, Felipe Benguria, Chang Hong, Anna Ignatenko, David Jacks, Joseph Kopecky, Alyson Ma, Ahmed Rahman, Seema Sangita, Radek Szulga, and Yingying Xu for their assistance.

We are grateful to Benjamin Mandel, who worked on many of the international trade chapters in the first edition; Philip Luck, who worked on all the chapters in the second edition; Mingzhi Xu and Joseph Kopecky, who worked on the trade and the macro chapters, respectively, in the fourth edition; and especially to Charles Liao, who worked on the trade chapters in the fourth and fifth editions. Thanks for advice on the fifth and earlier editions also go to Christian Broda, Colin Carter, Michele Cavallo, Menzie Chinn, Sebastian Edwards, Ann Harrison, Mervyn King, Philip Lane, Judith Lavin, Karen Lewis, Christopher Meissner, Gian Maria Milesi-Ferretti, Michael Pakko, Ugo Panizza, Giovanni Peri, Eswar Prasad, Andrés Rodríguez-Clare, Katheryn Russ, Jay Shambaugh, Deborah Swenson, and Martin Wolf, many of whom provided data used in applications and examples.

We have taught the chapters of this book ourselves many times and have benefited from the feedback of colleagues. For this fifth edition, we received valuable input from the following instructors:

Adina Ardelean—Santa Clara University

Brian Bethune—Tufts University

Geoffrey Carliner—Boston University, Boston

Xiaofen Chen—Truman State University

Jonathan Conning—CUNY, Hunter College

Anthony Delmond—The University of Tennessee, Martin

Kacey Douglas—Arizona State University, Tempe

Stefania Garetto—Boston University, Boston

William Hauk—University of South Carolina, Columbia

Denise Hazlett—Whitman College

Ralf Hepp—Fordham University, Bronx

Aldo Sandoval Hernandez—University of Western Ontario

Alex Hohmann—Rutgers University, New Brunswick

Jason Jones—Furman University

Young Cheol Jung—Mount Royal University

Ayse Kabukcuoglu Dur—North Carolina State University

Evan Kraft—American University, Washington

Moshe Lander—Concordia University, Montreal, Sir G. William Campus

Xuepeng Liu—Kennesaw State University

Beyza Ural Marchand—University of Alberta, Edmonton

Sandeep Mazumder—Wake Forest University, Winston-Salem

Karl Pinno—University of British Columbia, Kelowna

Jennifer Poole—American University, Washington

Pau Pujolas—McMaster University, Hamilton

Carlos Pulido—Arizona State University, Tempe

Dhimitri Qirjo—SUNY College, Plattsburgh

Dina Rady—George Washington University

Mark Scanlan—Stephen F. Austin State University

Krishnakali SenGupta—McMaster University, Hamilton

Arjun Sondhi—Bloomsburg University of Pennsylvania

Richard Stahl—Louisiana State University and A&M College

Andrey Stoyanov—York University, North York

Bedassa Tadesse—University of Minnesota, Duluth

Mark Tendall—Stanford University

Kasaundra Tomlin—Oakland University

Russell Triplett—University of North Florida

Michael Vaney—University of British Columbia, Vancouver

Mary Jane Waples—Memorial University, St. John's

Pinar Cebi Wilber—Georgetown University

George Zestos—Christopher Newport University

Kevin Zhang—Illinois State University

For the fourth edition, we benefited from the suggestions of the following instructors:

Bradley Andrew—Juniata College

Damir Cosic—Brooklyn College

Lane Eckis—Troy University

Gerald Fox—High Point University

Fuad Hasanov—Georgetown University

Viktoria Hnatkovska—University of British Columbia

Kathy Kelly—University of Texas at Arlington

Paul Kubik—DePaul University

James McDermott—George Mason University

Thomas Mondschean—DePaul University

Braimoh Oseghale—Fairleigh Dickinson University

Masha Rahnama—Texas Tech University

Stefania Scandizzo—University of Maryland, College Park

Brandon Sheridan—North Central College

Till Schreiber—College of William & Mary

Scott Siegel—San Francisco State

Edward Stuart—Loyola University of Chicago

Miao Wang—Marquette University

Yanling Wang—Carleton University

Derrill Watson—Tarleton State University

Diana Weymark—Vanderbilt University

Janice Yee—Worcester State University

For the third edition, we benefited from the suggestions of the following instructors:

Basil Al-Hashimi—Mesa Community College

Sam Andoh—Southern Connecticut State University

Adina Ardelean—Santa Clara University

Joel Auerbach—Florida Atlantic University

Mohsen Bahmani-Oskooee—University of Wisconsin, Milwaukee

Jeremy Baker—Owens Community College

Rita Balaban—University of North Carolina, Chapel Hill

Jim Bruehler—Eastern Illinois University

Thomas Chaney—Toulouse School of Economics

John Chilton—Virginia Commonwealth University

Reid Click—George Washington University

Catherine Co—University of Nebraska at Omaha

Antoinette Criss—University of South Florida

Judith Dean—Brandeis University

James Devault—Lafayette College

Asif Dowla—St. Mary's College of Maryland

Justin Dubas—Texas Lutheran University

Lee Erickson—Taylor University

Xin Fang—Hawaii Pacific University

Stephen Grubaugh—Bentley University

Ronald Gunderson—Northern Arizona University

Chang Hong—Clark University

Carl Jensen—Rutgers University

Jeff Konz—University of North Carolina, Asheville

Robert Krol—California State University, Northridge

Dave LaRivee—United States Air Force Academy

Daniel Lee—Shippensburg University

Yu-Feng (Winnie) Lee—New Mexico State University

James Lehman—Pitzer College

Carlos Liard-Muriente—Central Connecticut State University

Rita Madarassy—Santa Clara University

Margaret Malixi—California State University, Bakersfield

Diego Mendez-Carbajo—Illinois Wesleyan University

Kathleen Odell—Dominican University

Kerry Pannell—DePauw University

Elizabeth Perry-Sizemore—Randolph College

Diep Phan—Beloit College

Reza Ramazani—Saint Michael's College

Artatrana Ratha—St. Cloud State University

Raymond Riezman—University of Iowa

Helen Roberts—University of Illinois, Chicago

Mari L. Robertson—University of Cincinnati

Margaretha Rudstrom—University of Minnesota, Crookston

Fred Ruppel—Eastern Kentucky University

Farhad Saboori—Albright College

Jeff Sarbaum—University of North Carolina, Greensboro

Mark Scanlan—Stephen F. Austin State University

Katherine Schmeiser—Mount Holyoke College

Annie Voy—Gonzaga University

Linda Wilcox Young—Southern Oregon University

Zhen Zhu—University of Central Oklahoma

Sixth-grade class with their teacher in La Carreta #2 school in Ciudad Darío, Nicaragua.

We would also like to thank our families, especially Gail and Claire, for their sustained support during the time we have devoted to writing this book.

Finally, you will see an accompanying picture of children in Ciudad Darío, Nicaragua, with their teacher in the classroom of a small schoolhouse that was built for them by Seeds of Learning (www.seedsoflearning.org), a nonprofit organization dedicated to improving educational opportunities in rural Latin America. A portion of the royalties from this book go toward supporting the work of Seeds of Learning.

Robert C. Feenstra

Alan M. Taylor
Davis, California
April 2020

Contents

PART 3   **The Balance of Payments**

1

The Global Macroeconomy

So much of barbarism, however, still remains in the transactions of most civilized nations, that almost all independent countries choose to assert their nationality by having, to their inconvenience and that of their neighbors, a peculiar currency of their own.

John Stuart Mill

Neither a borrower nor a lender be; / For loan oft loseth both itself and friend. / And borrowing dulls the edge of husbandry.

Polonius, in William Shakespeare's *Hamlet*

History, in general, only informs us of what bad government is.

Thomas Jefferson

Questions to Consider

1 Why do exchange rates matter, and what explains their behavior?

2 Why do countries borrow from and lend to each other, and with what effects?

3 How do government policy choices affect macroeconomic outcomes?

Not in recent memory has there been a more compelling time to study international macroeconomics. The world is experiencing its biggest adverse economic shock since World War II. The coronavirus pandemic of 2019–20 has already pushed most countries into recession—starting in China, where the virus originated, and spreading outwards to East Asia, Australasia, Europe, the United States, and beyond—and the persistent impacts will be widely but unequally felt. More than ever, global macroeconomics events are acutely relevant for our lives, livelihoods, and societies.

International macroeconomics is devoted to the study of large-scale economic interactions among interdependent economies. It is international because a deeper exploration of the interconnections among nations is essential to understanding how the global economy works. It is macroeconomic because it focuses on key economy-wide variables, such as exchange rates, prices, interest rates, income, wealth, and the current account. In the chapters that follow, we use familiar macroeconomic ideas to examine the main features of the global macroeconomy.

In keeping with the chapter-opening quotations, the broad range of topics and issues we study can be reduced to three key elements: the world has many monies (not one), countries are financially integrated (not isolated), and economic policy choices are made in this context (but not always very well).

1

- **Money** John Stuart Mill echoes the complaints of many exasperated travelers and traders when he bemoans the profusion of different monies around the world. Why do all these monies exist, and what purposes do they serve? How do they affect the global economy? What are the causes and consequences of the changing value of one currency against another? Do the benefits of having a national currency outweigh the costs?

- **Finance** William Shakespeare's Polonius might be distressed by the sight of mounting debts, public and private, in the United States and other countries. For him, happiness meant financial isolation, with income equal to expenditure. But this has always been a minority view. Today, debts loom large and capital is mobile internationally. Why do these transactions occur? Who lends to whom, and why? Does the free flow of finance have costs as well as benefits?

- **Policy** Thomas Jefferson's pessimism seems extreme, but it surely contains a germ of truth. If government policies were always optimal, recessions never happened, currencies never crashed, and debts were never in default . . . well, that would be a nice world. In reality policymaking often errs, and in the worst-run countries, poverty, hyperinflation, and crises are common. How can we formulate better policies? What are the trade-offs for monetary, fiscal, and other policy choices? Is there a single "right" approach to the complex economic problems facing interdependent nations?

Many fundamental questions like these must be addressed if we are to better understand the economic world around us. To that end, the chapters that follow combine clear economic theory with compelling empirical evidence to explain the workings of today's global macroeconomy. This introductory chapter briefly explains the road ahead.

1 Foreign Exchange: Currencies and Crises

In most branches of economics, and even in the study of international trade, it is common to assume either that all goods are priced in a common, single currency, or sometimes that no money is used at all. Despite unrealistic assumptions, such analyses can deliver important insights into many economic problems.

In the real world, however, countries have different currencies, and a complete understanding of how a country's economy works in a global setting requires that we study the *exchange rate*, the price of foreign currency. Because products and investments move across borders, fluctuations in exchange rates can have significant effects on the relative prices of home and foreign goods (such as autos and clothing), services (such as insurance and tourism), and assets (such as equities and bonds). We start our analysis of the global economy with the theory of exchange rates, and learn how and why they fluctuate. In later chapters, we'll see why exchange rates matter for economic outcomes and why they are an important focus of economic policymaking.

How Exchange Rates Behave

In studying exchange rates, it is important to understand the types of behavior that any theory of exchange rate determination must explain. Figure 1-1 illustrates some basic facts about exchange rates. Panel (a) shows the exchange rate of China with the United States, in yuan per U.S. dollar ($).[1] Panel (b) shows the exchange rate of the United States with the Eurozone, in U.S. dollars per euro.

---

[1] The Chinese yuan is also known as the *renminbi* ("people's currency").

The behavior of the two exchange rates is very different. The yuan–dollar rate is at times almost flat. In fact, in the period shown up to mid-2005 it was literally unchanged, day after day, at 8.28 yuan/$. On July 23, 2005, it dropped exactly 2%, then followed a fairly smooth, slow downward trend for a while. By September 2008 (when the global financial crisis began), it had fallen a further 15%. After the crisis, it remained stable at 6.83 yuan/$ until mid-2010, then it resumed a gradual slow decline, before starting to rise again in 2014. During the period shown, the daily average absolute change in the exchange rate was slightly more than five-hundredths of one percent (0.074%).

In contrast, the euro–dollar exchange rate experienced much wider and more frequent fluctuations over the same period. On a *daily* basis, the average absolute change in this exchange rate was about four-tenths of one percent (0.402%), about five or six times as large as the average absolute change in the yuan–dollar rate.

Based on such clearly visible differences in exchange rate behavior, economists divide the world into two groups of countries: those with **fixed** (or *pegged*) **exchange rates** and those with **floating** (or *flexible*) **exchange rates**. In Figure 1-1, China's exchange rate with the United States would be considered strictly fixed for long periods. It was officially set at a fixed exchange rate with the dollar until July 2005, and again in 2008–10, but even at other times its very limited range of movement was so controlled that it has been seen as effectively "fixed" to a moving target.[2] In contrast, the euro–dollar exchange rate has been more volatile: it is seen as a floating exchange rate, one that moves up and down over a much wider range, even on a weekly or daily basis, with no outward sign of control.

FIGURE 1-1

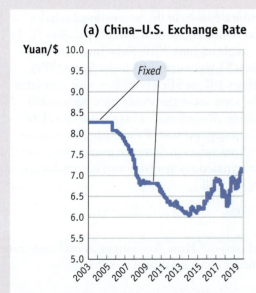

Major Exchange Rates The chart shows two key exchange rates from 2003 to 2019. The China–U.S. exchange rate varies relatively little and was usually considered a fixed exchange rate, despite some periods when it followed a gradual trend. The U.S.–Eurozone exchange rate varies a lot and often was considered a floating exchange rate.

Note: For comparative purposes, the two vertical scales have the same proportions: the maximum is twice the minimum.

Data from: FRED (Federal Reserve Economic Data).

___
[2] At the time of writing, in late 2019, the yuan–dollar exchange rate has started to rise amid a U.S. trade war with China and signs of a global economic slowdown.

100 Chinese yuan, U.S. dollars, Eurozone euros

Key Topics How are exchange rates determined? Why do some exchange rates fluctuate sharply in the short run, while others remain almost constant? What explains why exchange rates rise, fall, or stay flat in the long run?

Why Exchange Rates Matter

Changes in exchange rates affect an economy in two ways:

- Changes in exchange rates cause a change in the international relative prices of goods. That is, one country's goods and services become more or less expensive relative to another's when expressed in a common unit of currency. For example, in 2011 the German newspaper *Der Spiegel* interviewed one Swiss cheesemaker:

   > When Hans Stadelmann talks about currency speculators, it seems like two worlds are colliding. . . . Five men are working at the boilers, making the most popular Swiss cheese in Germany according to a traditional recipe . . . then there are the international financial markets, that abstract global entity whose actors have decided that the Swiss franc is a safe investment and, in doing so, have pushed the currency's value to record levels. . . . A year back, one euro was worth 1.35 francs. Two weeks ago, the value was 1-to-1. This presents a problem for Stadelmann. About 40% of his products are exported, most of them to EU countries. In order to keep his earnings level in francs, he's being forced to charge higher prices in euros—and not all of his customers are willing to pay them. "I'm already selling less, and I'm afraid it's going to get much worse," Stadelmann says. And it's not just his company he's worried about. "I get my milk from 50 small family farmers," he says. "If I close up shop, I'd be destroying the livelihoods of 50 families."[3]

- Changes in exchange rates can cause a change in the international relative prices of assets. These fluctuations in wealth can then affect firms, governments, and individuals. For example, in June 2010, Swiss investors held $397 billion of U.S. securities, when $1 was worth 1.05 Swiss francs (SFr). So these assets were worth 1.05 times 397, or SFr 417 billion. One year later $1 was worth only SFr 0.85, so the same securities would have been worth just 0.85 times 397 or SFr 337 billion, all else equal. That capital loss of SFr 80 billion (about 20%) came about purely because of exchange rate changes. Although other factors affect securities values in domestic transactions with a single currency, all cross-border transactions involving two currencies are strongly affected by exchange rates as well.[4]

Key Topics How do exchange rates affect the real economy? How do changes in exchange rates affect international prices, the demand for goods from different countries, and hence the levels of national output? How do changes in exchange rates affect the values of foreign assets, and hence change national wealth?

When Exchange Rates Misbehave

Even after studying how exchange rates behave and why they matter, we still face the challenge of explaining one type of event that is almost guaranteed to put exchange rates front and center in the news: an **exchange rate crisis**. In such a crisis, a currency experiences a sudden and pronounced loss of value against another currency, following a period in which the exchange rate had been fixed or relatively stable.

---

[3] Christian Teevs, "The Surging Franc: Swiss Fear the End of Economic Paradise," *Spiegel Online* (http://www.spiegel.de), August 25, 2011.
[4] Data for this example are from the U.S. Treasury TIC report, June 30, 2011.

One of the most dramatic currency crises in recent history occurred in Argentina from December 2001 to January 2002. For a decade, the Argentine peso had been fixed to the U.S. dollar at a one-to-one rate of exchange. But in January 2002, the fixed exchange rate became a floating exchange rate. A few months later, one Argentine peso, which had been worth one U.S. dollar prior to 2002, had fallen in value to just $0.25 (equivalently, the price of a U.S. dollar rose from one peso to almost four pesos).

The drama was not confined to the foreign exchange market. The Argentine government declared a then-record **default** (i.e., a suspension of payments) on its $155 billion of debt, the financial system was in a state of near closure for months, inflation climbed, output collapsed and unemployment soared, and more than 50% of Argentine households fell below the poverty line. At the height of the crisis, violence flared and the country had five presidents in the space of two weeks.

Argentina's experience was extreme but hardly unique. Exchange rate crises are fairly common. Figure 1-2 lists 37 exchange rate crises in the 21-year period from 1997 to 2018. In almost all cases, a fairly stable exchange rate experienced a large and sudden change. The year 1997 was especially eventful, with seven crises, five of them in East Asia. The Indonesian rupiah lost 49% of its U.S. dollar value, but severe collapses also occurred in Thailand, Korea, Malaysia, and the Philippines. Other notable crises during this period included Liberia in 1998, Russia in 1998, and Brazil in 1999. More recently, Iceland and Ukraine saw their exchange rates crash during the global financial crisis of 2008 (see **Headlines: Economic Crisis in Iceland**). More recent examples include Iran in 2013 and Russia in 2014. Venezuela also appears several times on the list, although there, as in other cases, the parallel "black market" exchange rates often lost even more value than the official rates shown here.

FIGURE 1-2

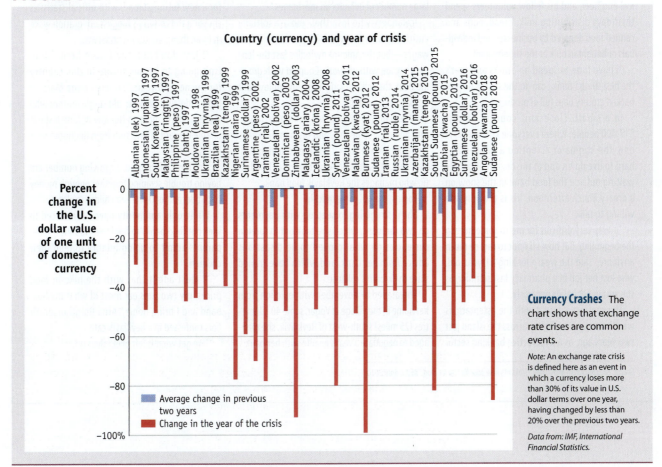

Currency Crashes The chart shows that exchange rate crises are common events.

Note: An exchange rate crisis is defined here as an event in which a currency loses more than 30% of its value in U.S. dollar terms over one year, having changed by less than 20% over the previous two years.

Data from: IMF, *International Financial Statistics.*

HEADLINES

Economic Crisis in Iceland

International macroeconomics can often seem like a dry and abstract subject, but it must be remembered that societies and individuals can be profoundly shaken by the issues we will study. This article was written just after the start of the severe economic crisis that engulfed Iceland in 2008, following the collapse of its exchange rate, a financial crisis, and a government fiscal crisis. Real output per person shrank by more than 10%, and unemployment rose from 1% to 9%. In the long run, years or decades later, economies typically recover from crises, as full employment is restored and growth rebounds, and indeed this happened in Iceland. Output eventually surpassed its 2008 level—but not until 2015. In the short run, these events can impose an enormous human toll.

The crisis that brought down Iceland's economy in late 2008 threw thousands of formerly well-off families into poverty, forcing people like Iris to turn to charity to survive.

Each week, up to 550 families queue up at a small white brick warehouse in Reykjavik to receive free food from the Icelandic Aid to Families organisation, three times more than before the crisis.

Rutur Jonsson, a 65-year-old retired mechanical engineer, and his fellow volunteers spend their days distributing milk, bread, eggs and canned food donated by businesses and individuals or bought in bulk at the supermarket.

"I have time to spend on others and that's the best thing I think I can do," he said as he pre-packed grocery bags full of produce.

In a small, close-knit country of just 317,000 people, where everyone knows everyone, the stigma of accepting a hand-out is hard to live down and of the dozens of people waiting outside the food bank in the snow on a dreary March afternoon, Iris is the only one willing to talk.

"It was very difficult for me to come here in the beginning. But now I try not to care so much anymore," said the weary-looking 41-year-old, who lost her job in a pharmacy last summer, as she wrung her hands nervously.

The contrast is brutal with the ostentatious wealth that was on display across the island just two years ago, as a hyperactive banking sector flooded the small, formerly fishing-based economy with fast cash.

Back then, the biggest worry for many Icelanders was who had the nicest SUV, or the most opulent flat.

But today visible signs of poverty are quickly multiplying in the Nordic island nation, despite its generous welfare state, as the middle class is increasingly hit by unemployment, which is up from one to nine per cent in about a year, and a large number of defaults on mortgages.

Icelanders who lose their job are initially entitled to benefits worth 70 per cent of their wages—but the amount dwindles fast the longer they are without work. Coupled with growing debt, the spike in long-term unemployment is taking a heavy toll.

"The 550 families we welcome here represent about 2,700 people, and the number keeps going up. And we think it will keep growing until next year, at least," said Asgerdur Jona Flosadottir, who manages the Reykjavik food bank.

For Iris, the fall came quickly.

She is struggling to keep up with payments on two car loans, which she took out in foreign currencies on what proved to be disastrous advice from her bank, and which have tripled since the kronur's collapse.

Threatened in November with eviction from her home in the village of Vogar, some 40 kilometres (25 miles) south-west of Reykjavik, she managed to negotiate a year's respite with her bank.

"I feel very bad and I am very worried," she said, running her fingers through her long, brown hair.

"I've thought about going abroad, but decided to stay because friends have come forward to guarantee my loans," she added sadly, before leaving with a friend who was driving her back home.

To avoid resorting to charity, many other Icelanders are choosing to pack their bags and try for a new future abroad, with official statistics showing the country's biggest emigration wave in more than a century is underway.

"I just don't see any future here. There isn't going to be any future in this country for the next 20 years," laments Anna Margret Bjoernsdottir, a 46-year-old single mother who is preparing to move to Norway in June if she is unable to ward off eviction from her home near Reykjavik.

For those left behind, a growing number are having trouble scraping together enough money to put decent food on their children's plates.

While only a minority have been forced to seek out food banks to feed their families, some parents admit to going hungry to feed their children.

"I must admit that with the hike in food prices, my two sons eat most of what my husband and I bring home," Arna Borgthorsdottir Cors confessed in a Reykjavik cafe.

"We get what is left over," she says.

Source: Excerpted from Marc Preel, "Iceland's new poor line up for food," AFP, 8 April 2010.

Crisis episodes display some regular patterns. Output typically falls, banking and debt problems emerge, households and firms suffer. In addition, political turmoil often ensues. Government finances worsen and embarrassed authorities may appeal for external help from international organizations, such as the **International Monetary Fund (IMF)** or **World Bank** or other entities. The economic setbacks are often more pronounced in poorer countries. Although we could confine our study of exchange rates to normal times, the frequent and damaging occurrence of crises obliges us to pay attention to these abnormal episodes, too.

Key Topics Why do exchange rate crises occur? Are they an inevitable consequence of deeper fundamental problems in an economy, or are they an avoidable result of "animal spirits"—irrational forces in financial markets? Why are these crises so economically and politically costly? What steps might be taken to prevent crises, and at what cost?

Summary and Plan of Study

International macroeconomists frequently refer to the exchange rate as "the single most important price in an open economy." If we can accept this statement as more than self-promotion, we should perhaps learn why it might be true. In our course of study, we will explore the factors that determine the exchange rate, how the exchange rate affects the economy, and how crises occur.

Our study of exchange rates proceeds as follows: in Chapter 2, we learn about the structure and operation of the markets in which foreign currencies are traded. Chapters 3 and 4 present the theory of exchange rates. Chapter 5 discusses how exchange rates affect international transactions in assets. We examine the short-run impact of exchange rates on the demand for goods in Chapter 7, and with this understanding Chapter 8 examines the trade-offs governments face as they choose between fixed and floating exchange rates. Chapter 9 covers exchange rate crises in detail, and Chapter 10 covers the euro, a common currency used in many countries.

2 Globalization of Finance: Debts and Deficits

Financial development is a defining characteristic of modern economies. Households' use of financial instruments such as credit cards, savings accounts, and mortgages is taken for granted, as is the ability of firms and governments to use the products and services offered by banks and financial markets. A few years ago, very little of this financial activity spilled across international borders; countries were very nearly closed from a financial standpoint. Today, many countries are more open: financial globalization has taken hold around the world, starting in the economically advanced countries and spreading to many emerging market countries.

Although you might expect that you need many complex and difficult theories to begin to understand the financial transactions between countries, such analysis starts with the application of familiar household accounting concepts such as income, expenditure, and wealth. We develop these concepts at the national level to understand how flows of goods, services, income, and capital make the global macroeconomy work. We can then see how the smooth functioning of international finance can make countries better off by allowing them to lend and borrow. Along the way, we also find that financial interactions are not always so smooth. Defaults, risks, and other problems in global financial markets can mean that the potential gains from globalization are not so easily realized in practice.

Deficits and Surpluses: The Balance of Payments

Do you keep track of your finances? If so, you probably follow two important figures: your income and your expenditure. The difference between the two is an important number: if it is positive, you have a surplus; if it is negative, you have a deficit. The number tells you if you are living within or beyond your means. What would you do with a surplus? The extra money could be added to savings or used to pay down debt. How would you handle a deficit? You could run down your savings or borrow and go into deeper debt. Thus, imbalances between income and expenditure require you to engage in financial transactions with the world outside your household.

At the national level, we can make the same kinds of economic measurements of **income**, **expenditure**, **deficit**, and **surplus**, and these important indicators of economic performance are the subject of heated policy debate. For example, Table 1-1 shows measures of U.S. national income and expenditure since 1990 in billions of U.S. dollars. At the national level, the income measure is called *gross national disposable income*; the expenditure measure is called *gross national expenditure*. The difference between the two is a key macroeconomic aggregate called the *current account*.

TABLE 1-1

Income, Expenditure, and the Current Account The table shows data for the United States from 1990 to 2019 in billions of U.S. dollars. During this period, in all but one year U.S. expenditure exceeded income, with the U.S. current account in deficit. The last (small) surplus was in 1991.

	Income Gross National Disposable Income	Expenditure Gross National Expenditure	Difference Current Account
1990	$5,966	$6,041	−$75
1991	6,195	6,187	8
1992	6,509	6,555	−46
1993	6,844	6,924	−79
1994	7,264	7,380	−116
1995	7,624	7,730	−106
1996	8,055	8,170	−115
1997	8,550	8,680	−130
1998	9,020	9,226	−205
1999	9,608	9,887	−278
2000	10,231	10,627	−396
2001	10,567	10,950	−383
2002	10,919	11,362	−443
2003	11,448	11,961	−513
2004	12,208	12,833	−625
2005	13,021	13,758	−737
2006	13,784	14,586	−802
2007	14,460	15,170	−711
2008	14,753	15,436	−683
2009	14,473	14,845	−372
2010	15,069	15,506	−437
2011	15,657	16,122	−466
2012	16,318	16,766	−448
2013	16,907	17,276	−369
2014	17,659	18,035	−376
2015	18,321	18,745	−424
2016	18,792	19,234	−441
2017	19,628	20,095	−467
2018	20,709	21,218	−510
2019	21,557	22,060	−503

Data from: U.S. National Income and Product Accounts, Tables 1.1.5 and 4.1 (rev. March 26, 2020), bea.gov.

Since posting a small surplus in 1991, the U.S. deficit on the current account (a negative number) has grown much larger, and at times it has approached $1 trillion per year, although it fell markedly during and after the Great Recession of 2008. That is, U.S. income has not been high enough to cover U.S. expenditure in these years. How did the United States bridge this deficit? It engaged in financial transactions with the outside world and borrowed the difference, just as households do.

Because the world *as a whole* is a closed economy (we can't borrow from outer space, as yet), it is impossible for the world to run a deficit. If the United States is a net borrower, running a current account deficit with income less than expenditure, then the rest of the world must be a net lender to the United States, running surpluses with expenditure less than income. Globally, the world's finances must balance in this way, even if individual countries and regions have surpluses or deficits. Figure 1-3 shows the massive scale of some of these recent imbalances, dramatically illustrating the impact of financial globalization.

FIGURE 1-3

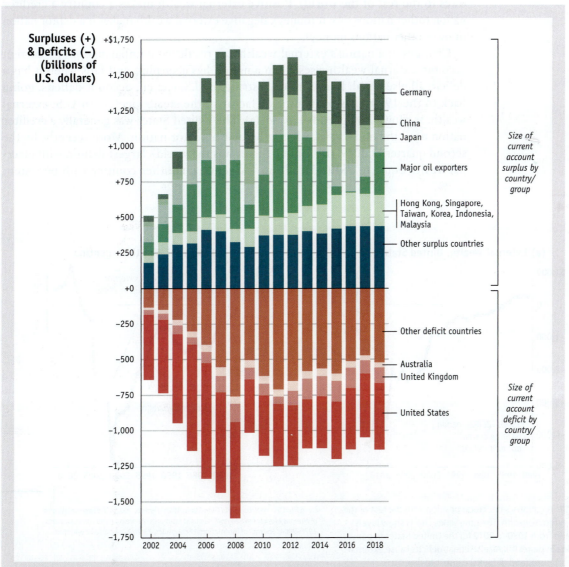

Global Imbalances For almost two decades, the current account deficit in the United States has accounted for between a third and a half of all deficits globally. Major offsetting surpluses have been seen in Germany, China, Japan, some smaller Asian economies, and in oil-exporting countries. Imbalances shrank in the wake of the 2008 global financial crisis but have risen again since.

Data from: IMF, World Economic Outlook, April 2019.

Key Topics How do different international economic transactions contribute to current account imbalances? How are these imbalances financed? How long can they persist? Why are some countries in surplus and others in deficit? What role do current account imbalances perform in a well-functioning economy? Why are these imbalances the focus of so much policy debate?

Debtors and Creditors: External Wealth

To understand the role of wealth in international financial transactions, we revisit our household analogy. Your total **wealth** or net worth is equal to your assets (what others owe you) minus your liabilities (what you owe others). When you run a surplus, and save money (buying assets or paying down debt), your total wealth, or net worth, tends to rise. Similarly, when you have a deficit and borrow (taking on debt or running down savings), your wealth tends to fall. We can use the same type of analysis to understand the behavior of nations. From an international perspective, a country's net worth is called its *external wealth*, and it equals the difference between its foreign assets (what it is owed by the rest of the world) and its foreign liabilities (what it owes to the rest of the world). Positive external wealth makes a country a creditor nation (other nations owe it money); negative external wealth makes it a debtor nation (it owes other nations money).

Changes in a nation's external wealth can result from imbalances in its current account: external wealth rises when a nation has a surplus, and falls when it has a deficit, all else equal. For example, a string of U.S. current account deficits, going back to the 1980s, has been a major factor in the steady decline in U.S. external wealth, as shown in Figure 1-4, panel (a). The United States was generally a creditor nation until the mid-1980s, when it became a debtor nation. More recently, by the second quarter of 2019, the United States was the world's largest debtor, with external wealth equal to –$10,555 billion.[5] Argentina, another country with persistent

FIGURE 1-4

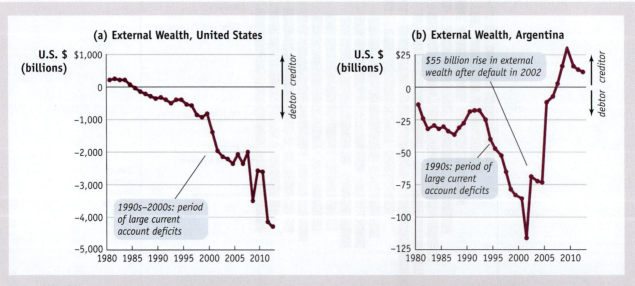

External Wealth A country's net credit position with the rest of the world is called external wealth. The time series charts show levels of external wealth from 1980 to 2012 for the United States in panel (a) and Argentina in panel (b). All else equal, deficits cause external wealth to fall; surpluses (and defaults) cause it to rise.

Data from: Philip R. Lane and Gian Maria Milesi-Ferretti, 2007, "The External Wealth of Nations Mark II: Revised and Extended Estimates of Foreign Assets and Liabilities, 1970–2004," Journal of International Economics, 73(2), 223–250 (and updates).

[5] Based on data released by bea.gov on September 30, 2019.

current account deficits in the 1990s, also saw its external wealth decline, as panel (b) in Figure 1-4 shows.

A closer look at these figures shows that there must be other factors that affect external wealth besides expenditure and income. For example, in years in which the United States ran deficits, its external wealth sometimes went up, not down. How can this be? Let us return to the household analogy. If you have ever invested in the stock market, you may know that even in a year when your expenditure exceeds your income, you may still end up wealthier because the value of your stocks has risen. For example, if you run a deficit of $1,000, but the value of your stocks rises by $10,000, then, on net, you are $9,000 wealthier. If the stocks' value falls by $10,000, your wealth will fall by $11,000. Again, what is true for households is true for countries: their external wealth can be affected by valuation changes known as **capital gains** (or, if negative, capital losses) on investments, so we need to think carefully about the complex causes and consequences of external wealth.

We also have to remember that a country can gain not only by having the value of its assets rise but also by having the value of its liabilities fall. Sometimes, liabilities fall because of market fluctuations; at other times they fall as a result of a deliberate action, such as a nation deciding to default on its debts. For example, in 2002 Argentina announced a record default on its government debt by offering to pay about 30¢ for each dollar of debt in private hands. The foreigners who held most of this debt lost about $55 billion. At the same time, Argentina gained about $55 billion in external wealth, as shown by the sudden jump in Figure 1-4, panel (b). Thus, you don't have to run a surplus to increase external wealth—external wealth rises not only when creditors are paid off but also when they are blown off.

Key Topics What forms can a nation's external wealth take, and does the composition of wealth matter? What explains the level of a nation's external wealth, and how does it change over time? How important is the current account as a determinant of external wealth? How does it relate to the country's present and future economic welfare?

Darlings and Deadbeats: Defaults and Other Risks

The 2002 Argentine government's debt default was by no means unusual. The following countries (among many others) have defaulted (sometimes more than once) on private creditors since 1980: Argentina (three times), Chile, Dominican Republic (twice), Ecuador, Greece, Indonesia, Mexico, Nigeria, Pakistan, Peru (twice), Philippines, Russia (twice), South Africa (twice), Ukraine (twice), and Uruguay (twice).[6] Dozens more countries could be added to the list if we expanded the definition of default to include the inability to make payments on loans from international financial institutions like the World Bank. (These debts may be continually rolled over, thus avoiding default by a technicality. In some cases, such loans are eventually forgiven, so they do not fall into the "default" category.)

Defaults highlight a peculiar risk of international finance: creditors may be poorly protected in foreign jurisdictions. Almost by definition, a sovereign government can usually default on its debt, if it so chooses, and without legal penalty; it can also hurt creditors in other ways, such as by taking away their assets or changing laws or regulations after investments have already been made.

International investors try to avoid these risks as much as possible by carefully assessing and monitoring debtors. For example, any financial misbehavior by a nation or firm usually ends up on a credit report: a "grade A" credit score means easy access

---

[6] The list is limited to privately issued bond and bank debts since 1980. Data from Eduardo Levy Yeyati and Ugo G. Panizza, January 2011, "The Elusive Costs of Sovereign Defaults," *Journal of Development Economics*, 94(1), 95–105, with author's updates to include the more recent cases of Greece, Argentina, and Ukraine.

to low-interest loans; a "grade C" score means more limited credit and very high interest rates. Advanced countries typically have good credit ratings, but emerging markets often find themselves subject to lower ratings.

In one important type of credit rating, countries are also rated on the quality of the bonds they issue to raise funds. Such bonds are rated by agencies such as Standard & Poor's (S&P): bonds rated BBB– or higher are considered high-grade or *investment-grade* bonds, and bonds rated BB+ and lower are called *junk bonds*. Poorer ratings tend to go hand in hand with higher interest rates. The difference between the interest paid on a safe "benchmark" U.S. Treasury bond and the interest paid on a bond issued by a nation associated with greater risk is called **country risk**. Thus, if U.S. bonds pay 3% and another country pays 5% per annum on its bonds, the country risk is +2%.

For example, on January 8, 2016, the *Financial Times* reported that relatively good investment-grade governments such as Poland (grade A–) and Mexico (BBB+) carried a country risk of +1.48% and +0.44%, respectively, relative to U.S. Treasuries, a small penalty. Governments with lower grades like Brazil (grade BB+) and Turkey (BBB–) had to pay higher interest rates, with a country risk of 4.62% and 3.38%, respectively, a much larger penalty.

Key Topics Why do countries default? And what happens when they do? What are the determinants of risk premiums? How do risk premiums affect macroeconomic outcomes such as output, wealth, and exchange rates?

Summary and Plan of Study

International flows of goods, services, income, and capital allow the global macro-economy to operate. In our course of study, we build up our understanding gradually, starting with basic accounting and measurement, then moving on to the causes and consequences of imbalances in the flows and the accumulations of debts and credits. Along the way, we learn about the gains from financial globalization, as well as some of its potential risks.

In Chapter 5, we learn how international transactions enter into a country's national income accounts. Chapter 6 considers the helpful functions that imbalances can play in a well-functioning economy in the long run and shows us the potential long-run benefits of financial globalization. Chapter 7 then explores how imbalances play a role in short-run macroeconomic adjustment and in the workings of the monetary and fiscal policies that are used to manage a nation's aggregate demand. In Chapter 8, we learn that assets traded internationally are often denominated in different currencies and see how wealth can be sensitive to exchange rate changes and what macroeconomic effects this might have. Chapter 9 examines the implications of risk premiums for exchange rates and discusses how exchange rate crises and default crises are linked.

3 Government and Institutions: Policies and Performance

In theory, one could devise a course of study in international economics without reference to government, but the result might not shed much light on reality. As we know from other courses in economics, and as we have already started to see in this chapter, government actions influence economic outcomes in many ways by making decisions about exchange rates, macroeconomic policies, whether to pay (or not pay) their debts, and so on.

To gain a deeper understanding of the global macroeconomy, we can look at government activity on several levels. We will study **policies**, direct government actions, including familiar textbook topics like monetary and fiscal policy. However, economists also consider the broader context of rules and norms, or the **regimes** in which policy choices are made. At the broadest level, research also focuses on **institutions**, a term that refers to the overall legal, political, cultural, and social structures that influence economic and political actions.

To conclude this brief introduction to international macroeconomics, we highlight three important features of the broad macroeconomic environment that play an important role in the remainder of this book: the rules that a government decides to apply to restrict or allow capital mobility; the decision that a government makes between a fixed and a floating exchange rate regime; and the institutional foundations of economic performance, such as the quality of governance that prevails in a country.

Integration and Capital Controls: The Regulation of International Finance

The United States is seen as one of the most financially open countries in the world, fully integrated into the global capital market. This is mostly true, but in recent years the U.S. government has blocked some foreign investment in ports, oil, and airlines. These are rare cases in the United States, but in many countries there can be pervasive and severe restrictions on cross-border financial transactions.

It is important to remember that globalization does not occur in a political vacuum. Globalization is often viewed as a technological phenomenon, an unstoppable process driven by innovations in transport and communications such as container shipping and the Internet. But international economic integration has also occurred because some governments have allowed it to happen. In the past 60 years, international trade has grown as trade barriers have been slowly dismantled. More recently, many nations have encouraged international capital movement by lifting restrictions on financial transactions.

Figure 1-5 documents some of the important features of the trend toward financial globalization since 1970. Panel (a) employs an index of financial openness, where

FIGURE 1-5

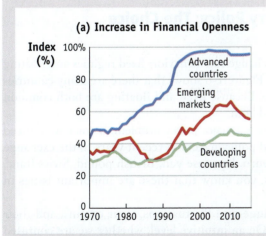

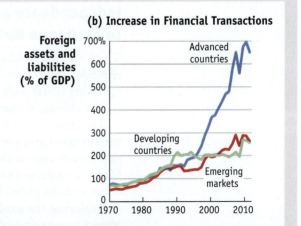

Financial Globalization Since the 1970s, many restrictions on international financial transactions have been lifted, as shown by the time series chart in panel (a). The volume of transactions has also increased dramatically, as shown in panel (b). These trends have been strongest in the advanced countries, followed by the emerging markets and the developing countries.

Data from: Philip R. Lane and Gian Maria Milesi-Ferretti, 2007, "The External Wealth of Nations Mark II: Revised and Extended Estimates of Foreign Assets and Liabilities, 1970–2004," Journal of International Economics 73(2), 223–250 (and updates); Menzie D. Chinn and Hiro Ito, 2006, "What Matters for Financial Development? Capital Controls, Institutions, and Interactions," Journal of Development Economics, 81(1), 163–192 (and updates); country classifications are an extended version of those developed by M. Ayhan Kose, Eswar Prasad, Kenneth S. Rogoff, and Shang-Jin Wei, 2006, "Financial Globalization: A Reappraisal," NBER Working Paper No. 12484.

0% means fully closed with tight capital controls and 100% means fully open with no controls. The index is compiled from measures of restriction on cross-border financial transactions. The average value of the index is shown for three groups of countries that will play an important role in our analysis:

- **Advanced countries**—countries with high levels of income per person that are well integrated into the global economy
- **Emerging markets**—middle-income countries that are growing and becoming more integrated into the global economy
- **Developing countries**—low-income countries that are not yet well integrated into the global economy

Using these data to gauge policy changes over the past three decades, we can see that the trend toward financial openness started first, and went the furthest, in the advanced countries, with a rapid shift toward openness evident in the 1980s, when many countries abolished capital controls that had been in place since World War II. We can also see that in the 1990s, emerging markets also started to become more financially open and, to a lesser degree, so did some developing countries.

Evading control: For years, Zimbabwe imposed capital controls. In theory, U.S. dollars could be traded for Zimbabwe dollars only through official channels at an official rate. On the street, the reality was different.

REUTERS/Howard Burditt/Newscom

What were the consequences of these policy changes? Panel (b) shows that as the world became more financially open, the extent of cross-border financial transactions (total foreign assets and liabilities expressed as a fraction of output) increased by a factor of about 10. As one might expect, this trend has gone the furthest in the more financially open advanced countries, but the emerging markets and developing countries follow a similar path.

Key Topics Why have so many countries made the choice to pursue policies of financial openness? What are the potential economic benefits of removing capital controls and encouraging openness? If there are benefits, why has this policy change been so slow to occur since the 1970s? Are there any costs that offset the benefits? If so, can capital controls benefit the country that imposes them?

Independence and Monetary Policy: The Choice of Exchange Rate Regimes

There are two broad categories of exchange rate behavior: fixed regimes and floating regimes. How common is each type? Figure 1-6 shows that there are many countries operating under each kind of regime. Because fixed and floating are both common regime choices, we have to understand both.

The choice of exchange rate regime is a major policy problem. If you have noticed the attention given by journalists and policymakers in recent years to the exchange rate movements of the U.S. dollar, euro, Japanese yen, British pound, Swiss franc, Chinese yuan, and other currencies, you know that these are important issues in debates on the global economy.

Exploring the evidence on exchange rate fluctuations, their origins, and their impact is a major goal of this book. On an intuitive level, whether we are confused travelers fumbling to change money at the airport kiosk or importers and exporters trying to conduct business in a predictable way, we have a sense that exchange rate fluctuations, especially if drastic, can impose real economic costs. If every country fixed its exchange rate, we could avoid those costs. Or, taking the argument to an extreme, if we had a single world currency, we might think that all currency-related transaction costs could be avoided. With more than 150 different currencies in existence today, however, we are very far from such a monetary utopia!

FIGURE 1-6

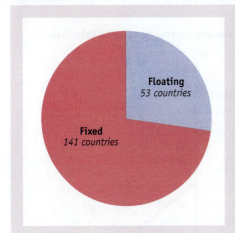

Exchange Rate Regimes The pie chart shows a classification of exchange rate regimes around the world using the most recent data from the year 2010.

Notes: The fixed category includes: no separate legal tender, pre-announced peg or currency board arrangement, pre-announced horizontal band that is narrower than or equal to +/− 2%, de facto peg, pre-announced crawling peg, pre-announced crawling band that is narrower than or equal to +/− 2%, de facto crawling peg, and de facto crawling band that is narrower than or equal to +/− 2%.

The floating category includes: pre-announced crawling band that is wider than or equal to +/− 2%, de facto crawling band that is narrower than or equal to +/− 5%, moving band that is narrower than or equal to +/− 2% (i.e., allows for both appreciation and depreciation over time), managed floating, freely floating, freely falling, and dual market in which parallel market data are missing.

Data from: Ethan Ilzetzki, Carmen M. Reinhart, and Kenneth S. Rogoff, 2019, "Exchange Rate Arrangements Entering the 21st Century: Which Anchor Will Hold?" Quarterly Journal of Economics, 134(2), 599–646. See the next chapter for more details.

The existence of multiple currencies in the world dates back centuries, and for a country to possess its own currency has long been viewed as an almost essential aspect of sovereignty. Without control of its own national currency, a government's freedom to pursue its own monetary policy is sacrificed automatically. However, it still remains to be seen how beneficial monetary independence is.

Despite the profusion of currencies, we also see newly emerging forms of monetary organization. Some groups of countries have sought to simplify their transactions through the adoption of a **common currency** with shared policy responsibility. The most notable example is the Eurozone, a subset of the European Union, which at the time of writing in 2019 comprised 19 member countries, with more countries expected to join in the future. Still other countries have chosen to use currencies over which they have no policy control; for example, Ecuador and El Salvador have adopted the U.S. dollar, a radical monetary shift known as **dollarization**.

Key Topics Why do so many countries insist on the "barbarism" of having their own currency (as John Stuart Mill put it)? Why do some countries create a common currency or adopt another nation's currency as their own? Why do some of the countries that have kept their own currencies maintain a fixed exchange rate with another currency? And why do others permit their exchange rate to fluctuate over time, making a floating exchange rate their regime choice?

Institutions and Economic Performance: The Quality of Governance

Going beyond specific policy choices, economists also consider the broader institutional context in which such choices are made. The legal, political, social, cultural, ethical, and religious structures of a society can influence the environment for economic prosperity and stability, or poverty and instability.

Figure 1-7 shows evidence on the importance of the quality of a nation's institutions or "governance" using an average or composite of measures on six dimensions: voice and accountability, political stability, government effectiveness, regulatory quality, rule of law, and control of corruption. The figure shows that, across countries, institutional quality is strongly correlated with economic outcomes.

First, we see that better-quality institutions are correlated with higher levels of **income per capita** in panel (a). A government that is unaccountable, unstable, ineffective, unpredictable, corrupt, and not based on laws is unlikely to encourage

FIGURE 1-7

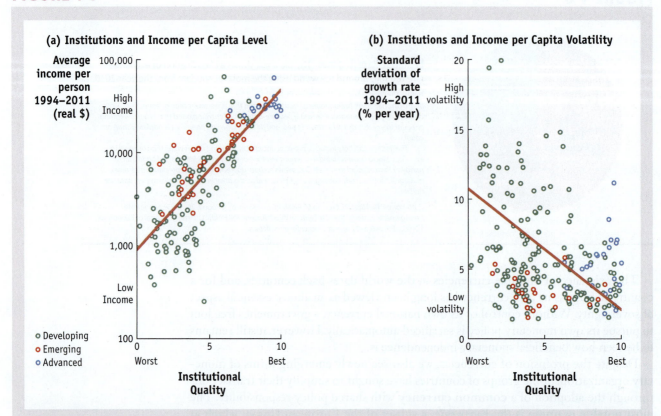

(a) Institutions and Income per Capita Level

Average income per person 1994–2011 (real $)

(b) Institutions and Income per Capita Volatility

Standard deviation of growth rate 1994–2011 (% per year)

○ Developing
○ Emerging
○ Advanced

Institutions and Economic Performance The scatterplots show how the quality of a country's institutions is positively correlated with the level of income per capita (panel a), and inversely correlated with the volatility of income per capita (panel b). In each case, the line of best fit is shown.

Data from: Real GDP per capita from Penn World Tables. Institutional quality from Daniel Kaufmann, Aart Kraay, and Massimo Mastruzzi, September 2015, "The Worldwide Governance Indicators, 2015 Update," World Bank Policy Research.

commerce, business, investment, or innovation. The effects of institutions on economic prosperity are very large. In the advanced countries at the top right of the figure, income per person is more than 50 times larger than in the poorest developing countries at the bottom left, probably the largest gap between rich and poor nations we have ever seen in history. Economists refer to this unequal outcome as "The Great Divergence."

We also see that better-quality institutions are correlated with lower levels of **income volatility** (i.e., smaller fluctuations in the growth of income per capita, measured by the standard deviation). This result is shown in panel (b) and may also reflect the unpredictability of economic activity in poorly governed economies. There may be periodic shifts in political power, leading to big changes in economic policies. Or there may be internal conflict between groups that sporadically breaks out and leads to conflict over valuable economic resources. Or the state may be too weak to ensure that essential policies to stabilize the economy (such as bank regulation) are carried out.

Recent research has documented these patterns and has sought to show that causality runs from institutions to outcomes and to explore the possible sources of institutional variation. Institutional change is typically very slow, taking decades or even centuries, because vested interests may block efficiency-enhancing reforms. Thus, as the institutional economist Thorstein Veblen famously pointed out, "Institutions are products of the past process, are adapted to past circumstances, and are therefore never in full accord with the requirements of the present." Consequently, influential recent research seeks to find the roots of institutional (and income) divergence in factors such as:

- Actions of colonizing powers (helpful in setting up good institutions in areas settled by Europeans but harmful in tropical areas where Europeans did not transplant their own institutions, but instead supported colonizers and local elites with a strong interest in extracting revenue or resources);

- Types of legal codes that different countries developed (British common law generally resulted in better outcomes than codes based on continental civil law);

- Resource endowments (tropical regions being more suitable for slave-based economies, elite rule, and high inequality; temperate regions being more suited to small-scale farming, decentralized democracy, and better governance).[7]

Key Topics The quality of governance can help explain large differences in countries' economic outcomes. Poor governance generally means that a country is poorer, is subject to more damaging macroeconomic and political shocks, and cannot conduct policy in a reliable and consistent way. These characteristics force us to think carefully about how to formulate optimal policies and policy regimes in rich and poor countries. One size may not fit all, and policies that work well in a stable, well-governed country may be less successful in an unstable, developing country with poor governance.

Summary and Plan of Study

The functioning of the global macroeconomy is affected in many ways by the actions of governments. Throughout this book, we must pay attention to the possible actions that governments might take and try to understand their possible causes and consequences.

Chapter 4 explores the finding that if a country is financially open, then a fixed exchange rate is incompatible with monetary policy autonomy. Because both goals may be desirable, policymakers are often reluctant to face up to the difficult trade-offs implied by financial globalization. Chapter 6 explores the economic rationales for financial liberalization: If financial openness has clear economic benefits, why are countries slow to liberalize? We explore exchange rate regime choice in detail in Chapter 8 and study the trade-offs involved. Then, in Chapter 9, we study crises, and find that if a country's policymakers cling to fixed exchange rates, there is a risk of suffering costly crises. The remarkable euro project, discussed in Chapter 10, throws these issues into sharper perspective in the one region of the world where economic integration has arguably progressed the furthest in recent decades—but where the aftereffects of the Great Recession have been the most severe and persistent. The main lessons of our study are that policymakers need to acknowledge trade-offs, formulate sensible goals, and exercise careful judgment when deciding when and how to financially open their economies. Sadly, history shows that, all too often, they don't.

---

[7] Daron Acemoglu, Simon Johnson, and James A. Robinson, December 2001, "The Colonial Origins of Comparative Development: An Empirical Investigation," *American Economic Review*, 91(5), 1369–1401; Stanley L. Engerman and Kenneth L. Sokoloff, 1997, "Factor Endowments, Institutions, and Differential Paths of Growth Among New World Economies: A View from Economic Historians of the United States," in Stephen Haber, ed., *How Latin America Fell Behind* (Stanford, Calif.: Stanford University Press); Rafael La Porta, Florencio Lopez-de-Silanes, Andrei Shleifer, and Robert Vishny, April 1999, "The Quality of Government," *Journal of Law, Economics and Organization*, 15(1), 222–279.

4 Conclusions

Today's global macroeconomy is an economic system characterized by increasingly integrated markets for goods, services, and capital. To effectively study macroeconomic outcomes in this context, we must understand the economic linkages between different countries—their currencies, their trade, their capital flows, and so on. Only then can we begin to understand some of the most important economic phenomena in the world today, such as the fluctuations in currencies, the causes of crises, the determinants of global imbalances, the problems of economic policymaking, and the origins of the growing gap between rich and poor countries.

KEY POINTS

1. Countries have different currencies, and the price at which these currencies trade is known as the exchange rate. In learning what determines this exchange rate and how the exchange rate is linked to the rest of the economy, we confront various questions: Why do some countries have fixed exchange rates and others floating? Why do some go from one to the other, often in response to a crisis? Why do some countries have no currency of their own?

2. When countries are financially integrated, they are able to decouple their level of income from their level of expenditure; the difference between the two is the current account. An important goal is to understand what determines the current account and how the current account is linked to the rest of

a nation's economy. Along the way, we learn how a country's current account affects its wealth, how its credits and debts are settled, and how the current account changes.

3. Countries differ in the quality of their policy choices and in the quality of the deeper institutional context in which policies are made. In studying international macroeconomic interactions and events, it is essential to understand how policy regimes and institutions affect policy choices and economic outcomes. How does quality of governance affect economic outcomes? Why might some policies, such as a fixed exchange rate, work better in some contexts than others? Do country characteristics affect the costs and benefits of financial globalization?

KEY TERMS

fixed exchange rate, p. 3
floating exchange rate, p. 3
exchange rate crisis, p. 4
default, p. 5
International Monetary Fund (IMF),
  p. 7
World Bank, p. 7
income, p. 8

expenditure, p. 8
deficit, p. 8
surplus, p. 8
wealth, p. 10
capital gain, p. 11
country risk, p. 12
policies, p. 12
regimes, p. 13

institutions, p. 13
advanced countries, p. 14
emerging markets, p. 14
developing countries, p. 14
common currency, p. 15
dollarization, p. 15
income per capita, p. 15
income volatility, p. 16

PROBLEMS

1. **Discovering Data** In this problem you will use data from the Bureau of Economic Analysis (BEA) to investigate the dependence of the United States on foreign markets over time. Go to the BEA website at www.bea.gov and under the "Tools" tab open "Interactive Data," then "National Data," and

then "GDP & Personal Income." Open Section 4, Table 4.1, for "Foreign Transactions in the National Income and Product Accounts" and download all the annual data going back to 1969. (*Hint:* Modify the displayed table to get the appropriate frequency and range of years.)

a. The current account is the difference between "current payments to the rest of the world" and "current receipts from the rest of the world." What is the latest estimate of the current account?

b. Create a graph that shows: current receipts, current payments, and current account over time.

c. In what year was the current account largest? How would you characterize its trend over time? How would you characterize the trends in receipts and payments?

d. The U.S. current account deficit grew significantly from the 1990s up until the financial crisis of 2008. In principle, this growth could have occurred because of falling receipts from abroad, increasing payments to foreign countries, or both. Which factor appears to have driven the growth in the current account deficit in this period?

e. What does the evolution of the three trends you plotted in part (b) tell you about the reliance of the United States on foreign markets? Does the country appear to be growing more open or more closed over time?

2. The data in Figure 1-1 end in 2019. Visit https://research.stlouisfed.org/fred2/series/DEXCHUS and https://research.stlouisfed.org/fred2/series/DEXUSEU (or another site with daily exchange rate data) and download data on the same exchange rates (yuan per dollar and dollar per euro) for the past 12 months. What are the rates today? What were they a year ago? By what percentage amount did the rates change? Do you think the rates are floating or fixed? Why?

WORK IT OUT ≋ Achieve | interactive activity

3. The data in Figure 1-3 end in the year 2018. Find the IMF's World Economic Outlook Databases. (*Hint:* Try searching "imf weo database.") Use this interactive tool to obtain the latest data on current accounts in U.S. dollars for all countries (actual data or IMF estimates). Which countries had the 10 largest deficits last year? Which countries had the 10 largest surpluses last year?

4. The following charts show the growth of real GDP per capita in three pairs of geographically adjacent countries: North and South Korea, Argentina and Chile, Zimbabwe and Botswana (using data from the Penn World Table).

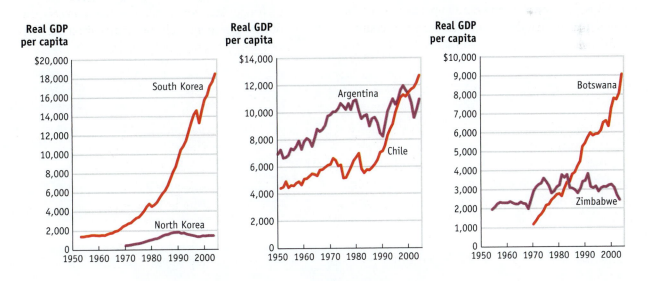

	Control of Corruption	Government Effectiveness	Political Stability and Absence of Violence	Rule of Law	Regulatory Quality	Voice and Accountability
South Korea	0.37	0.63	0.49	0.64	0.47	0.76
North Korea	−0.93	−1.10	−0.66	−1.08	−1.70	−2.02
Chile	1.56	1.34	0.85	1.31	1.38	0.56
Argentina	−0.34	0.28	0.48	0.17	0.45	0.44
Botswana	1.02	0.98	0.90	0.67	0.79	0.78
Zimbabwe	−0.87	−1.13	−1.21	−0.74	−1.61	−0.97

a. Which country in each pair experienced faster growth in GDP per capita? Which one is now richest?

b. The World Bank's World Governance Indicators for each country in 2000 were as shown in the table (higher is better):

Based on these data, do you think institutions can explain the divergent outcomes in these countries? Explain. Why do you think it helps to compare countries that are physically contiguous?

5. Visit one of the many websites that lists all of the current exchange rates between different currencies around the world. Try a financial newspaper's site such as ft.com, or try websites devoted to foreign exchange market data such as oanda.com or xe.com (dig down; don't just look at the major currency tables). According to these lists, how many distinct currencies exist around the world today? Are some currencies used in more than one country?

2

Introduction to Exchange Rates and the Foreign Exchange Market

The chapter on the Fall of the Rupee you may omit. It is somewhat too sensational.

Miss Prism, in Oscar Wilde's *The Importance of Being Earnest*, 1895

The people who benefit from roiling the world currency market are speculators and as far as I am concerned they provide not much useful value.

Paul O'Neill, U.S. Secretary of the Treasury, 2002

Questions to Consider

1 What features of exchange rates do we need to understand?

2 How does the foreign exchange market operate?

3 Why do arbitrage and expectations matter for exchange rates?

Every few years, George, an American, considers taking a vacation in Paris. To make purchases in Paris, he buys foreign currency, or *foreign exchange*. He can purchase euros, the currency used in France, by trading his U.S. dollars for euros in the *market for foreign exchange* at the prevailing market *exchange rate*. In 2011, 1 euro could be purchased for $1.40, so the €100 he'd spend on a night at his favorite hotel cost $140 in U.S. currency. By 2019, the cost of 1 euro had fallen to $1.10, so each night at the same hotel (where the room price hadn't changed) only made a $110 dent in his vacation budget. In 2011, the high prices made George think seriously about vacationing in northern California, where he might enjoy good hotels, restaurants, food, and wine at more affordable prices. But in 2019, the lower prices saw him happily back on the Left Bank enjoying croissants, café au lait, escargots, and vin rouge.

Tourists like George are not the only people affected by exchange rates. Exchange rates affect large flows of international trade by influencing the prices in different currencies of the imported goods and services we buy and the exported goods and services we sell. Foreign exchange also facilitates massive flows of international investment, which include the direct investments made by multinationals in overseas firms as well as the stock and bond trades individual investors and fund managers make as they allocate funds in their portfolios.

Individual foreign exchange transactions may seem far removed from macroeconomic and political consequences. In the aggregate, however, activity in the foreign exchange market can be responsible for "sensational" events (and we are not being ironic as was Oscar Wilde in the chapter opening quote) and can arouse strong passions (the quote from Paul O'Neill is only one of many to criticize the activities of currency traders). Trillions of dollars are traded each day in the foreign exchange market, and the economic implications of shifts in this market can be dramatic. In times of crisis, the fates of nations and their leaders can hang, in part, on the state of the currency market. Why is that so?

In this chapter, we begin our study of the foreign exchange market. We first survey exchange rate basics: the key definitions of exchange rates and related concepts. We then examine the evidence to see how exchange rates behave in the real world and establish some basic facts about exchange rate behavior that require explanation. We next look at the workings of the foreign exchange market, including the role of private participants, as well as interventions by governments. Finally, we look in detail at how foreign exchange markets work, emphasizing two key market mechanisms: *arbitrage* and *expectations*.

1 Exchange Rate Essentials

An **exchange rate** (E) is the price of some foreign currency expressed in terms of a home (or domestic) currency. Because an exchange rate is the relative price of two currencies, it may be quoted in either of two ways:

1. The number of home currency units that can be exchanged for one unit of foreign currency. For example, if the United States is considered home, the dollar–euro exchange rate can be expressed as $1.15 per euro (or 1.15 $/€). To buy one euro, you would have to pay $1.15.

2. The number of foreign currency units that can be exchanged for one unit of home currency. For example, the 1.15 $/€ exchange rate can also be expressed as €0.87 per U.S. dollar (or 0.87 €/$). To buy one dollar, you would have to pay €0.87.

Knowing the format, and units, in which exchange rates are quoted is essential to avoid confusion, so international economists follow a systematic rule, or convention, even if it is arbitrary.

Defining the Exchange Rate

It is common practice to quote the prices of items traded, whether goods or assets, as *units of home currency per units of the item being purchased*. In the United States, coffee might be sold at 10 dollars per pound ($/lb); in France, at 20 euros per kilogram (€/kg).[1]

For us, the same rule will apply when quoting the price of foreign currency: *the exchange rate is the units of home currency per unit of foreign currency*. Confusion may arise because the price then depends on the perspective of the observer. Consider the dollar–euro exchange rate. For the U.S. citizen, who is accustomed to prices expressed as $/unit, the price of a foreign currency (say, the euro) is in terms of $/€. For someone in the Eurozone, however, the strict use of the convention would mean quoting prices as €/unit, so the price would be in €/$.

To avoid confusion, we must specify which country is the home country and which is the foreign country. Throughout the remaining chapters of this book, when we

---

[1] Coffee prices could also be quoted as 0.1 lb/$ or 0.05 kg/€, but this format is not the norm.

refer to a particular country's exchange rate, we will quote it in terms of units of home currency per unit of foreign currency. From now on, $E_{1/2}$ will denote the exchange rate of country 1, in units of country 1's currency per unit of country 2's currency; it is the rate at which country 1's currency can be exchanged for one unit of country 2's currency. For example, $E_{\$/€}$ is the U.S. exchange rate (against the euro) in U.S. dollars per euro. In our previous example, $E_{\$/€}$ was 1.15 $/€.

All that being said, we can encounter different expressions of the same exchange rate all the time, some of which do not follow the strict economists' convention described above—even on the same page in the same publication! So it is important to keep things straight and keep track of the units. For example, Table 2-1 presents a typical display of exchange rate information as one might see it in the financial press or online.[2] Column (1) shows the reported price of U.S. dollars in various currencies (e.g., €/$); columns (2) and (3) show, respectively, the price of euros (e.g., $/€) and British pounds sterling (e.g., $/£) on the date November 15, 2019.[3] Thus, the first three entries in row 1 show the Canadian dollar's exchange rate against the U.S. dollar, the euro, and the pound. For comparison, columns (4) to (6) show the same rates one year earlier.

The four bold entries in this table correspond to the dollar–euro exchange rate. On November 15, 2019, for example, the euro was quoted at $1.1045 per euro. According to our convention, this is the price from the U.S. perspective, and it is sometimes called the *American terms*. Conversely, the exchange rate of €0.9054 per dollar (row 3, column 1) is called the *European terms*.

TABLE 2-1

Exchange Rate Quotations This table shows major exchange rates as they might appear in the financial media. Columns (1) to (3) show rates on November 15, 2019. For comparison, columns (4) to (6) show rates on November 15, 2018. For example, column (1) shows that in 2019, one U.S. dollar was worth 1.3230 Canadian dollars, 6.7661 Danish krone, 0.9054 euros, and so on. The euro–dollar rates appear in bold type.

Country (currency)	Currency Symbol	EXCHANGE RATES ON NOVEMBER 15, 2019			EXCHANGE RATES ON NOVEMBER 15, 2018 ONE YEAR PREVIOUSLY		
		(1) Per $	(2) Per €	(3) Per £	(4) Per $	(5) Per €	(6) Per £
Canada (dollar)	C$	1.3230	1.4613	1.7067	1.3192	1.4940	1.6825
Denmark (krone)	DKr	6.7661	7.4731	8.7285	6.5890	7.4619	8.4035
Eurozone (euro)	€	**0.9054**	—	1.1680	**0.8830**	—	1.1262
Japan (yen)	¥	108.81	120.17	140.36	113.45	128.48	144.69
Norway (krone)	NKr	9.0870	10.0366	11.7226	8.4790	9.6023	10.8140
Sweden (krona)	SKr	9.6489	10.6572	12.4474	9.0519	10.2511	11.5446
Switzerland (franc)	SFr	0.9904	1.0939	1.2776	1.0056	1.1388	1.2825
United Kingdom (pound)	£	0.7752	0.8562	—	0.7841	0.8880	—
United States (dollar)	$	—	**1.1045**	1.2900	—	**1.1325**	1.2754

Data from: xe.com.

---

[2] These are typically *midrange* or *central* interbank rates—an end-of-day average of buying and selling rates by banks in the market. As we discuss later in the chapter, such rates do not allow for the differences, or *spreads*, between the prices at which currencies are bought and sold. In any market in which intermediaries are present, commissions and fees push buying prices above selling prices.
[3] The currency's price in terms of itself equals 1 and is omitted.

We will write these exchange rates using mathematical symbols as follows, taking care to spell out the relevant units:

$$E_{\$/\euro} = 1.1045 = \text{U.S. exchange rate (American terms)}$$
$$E_{\euro/\$} = 0.9054 = \text{U.S. exchange rate (European terms)}$$

Just as there is complete equivalence when we express the relative price of coffee and dollars at 10 \$/lb or 0.1 lb/\$, the price of the euro in terms of dollars always equals the reciprocal (or inverse) of the price of dollars in terms of euros. Hence,

$$E_{\$/\euro} = \frac{1}{E_{\euro/\$}}$$

In our example,

$$1.1045 = \frac{1}{0.9054}$$

Similar calculations and notations apply to any pair of currencies.

Appreciations and Depreciations

Like many financial tables, Table 2-1 includes information on how prices have changed over time. Over the previous 12 months, the Eurozone exchange rate *increased* from $E_{\euro/\$} = 0.8830$ a year before to $E_{\euro/\$} = 0.9054$ on November 15, 2019. The value of the euro relative to the dollar went down—more euros were needed to buy one dollar. This change is often described by saying that the euro got "weaker" or "weakened" against the dollar.

Symmetrically, the value of the dollar in euro terms also changed. We see this by computing the reciprocal American terms. Over the same year, the U.S. exchange rate *decreased* from $E_{\$/\euro} = 1/0.8830 = 1.1325$ a year before to $E_{\$/\euro} = 1/0.9054 = 1.1045$ on November 15, 2019. The value of the dollar relative to the euro went up—fewer dollars were needed to buy one euro. This change is often described by saying that the dollar got "stronger" or "strengthened" against the euro.

If one currency buys more of another currency over a certain period, we say it has experienced an **appreciation**—its value has *risen, appreciated,* or *strengthened*. If a currency buys less of another currency over a certain period, we say it has experienced a **depreciation**—its value has *fallen, depreciated,* or *weakened*.

In our example, we can understand appreciation and depreciation from both the U.S. and European perspective, but the same lesson applies to all other currency pairs.

In U.S. terms, the following holds true:

- When the U.S. exchange rate $E_{\$/\euro}$ *rises*, more dollars are needed to buy one euro. The price of one euro goes up in dollar terms, and the U.S. dollar depreciates.

- When the U.S. exchange rate $E_{\$/\euro}$ *falls*, fewer dollars are needed to buy one euro. The price of one euro goes down in dollar terms, and the U.S. dollar appreciates.

Similarly, in European terms, the following holds true:

- When the Eurozone exchange rate $E_{\euro/\$}$ *rises*, the price of one dollar goes up in euro terms and the euro depreciates.

- When the Eurozone exchange rate $E_{\euro/\$}$ *falls*, the price of one dollar goes down in euro terms and the euro appreciates.

If the dollar appreciates against the euro, the euro must simultaneously depreciate against the dollar. Because the two exchange rates are the reciprocal of each other, changes in $E_{\$/€}$ and $E_{€/\$}$ must always move in opposite directions.

It may seem confusing or counterintuitive that a *fall* in the U.S. exchange rate means the dollar is *appreciating*. Yet on reflection it will seem reasonable because we express the price of foreign currency in dollars, just as we express the prices of other goods. When the price of coffee falls from $10 to $9 per pound, it seems sensible to say that coffee is depreciating or falling in value—but relative to what? To the dollars—the currency in which the price is denominated. Conversely, we would say that dollars are *appreciating* against coffee because it takes fewer dollars to buy the same amount of coffee! If we keep this analogy in mind, it makes sense that when the dollar price of a euro falls, the dollar has appreciated against the euro.

Exchange rate humor.

In addition to knowing whether a currency has appreciated or depreciated, we are often interested in knowing the size of an appreciation or depreciation. To do this, we can calculate the proportional or fractional change in the foreign-currency value of the home currency. This proportional change is usually expressed in percentage terms.

In the previous example, we would describe these changes as follows:

- In 2018, at time t, the dollar value of the euro was $E_{\$/€,t} = \$1.1325$.
- In 2019, at time $t+1$, the dollar value of the euro was $E_{\$/€,t+1} = \$1.1045$.
- The change in the dollar value of the euro was
  $\Delta E_{\$/€,t} = 1.1045 - 1.1325 = -\$0.0280$.
- The percentage change was $\Delta E_{\$/€,t}/E_{\$/€,t} = -0.0280/1.1325 = -2.47\%$.
- Thus, the euro *depreciated* against the dollar by 2.47%.

Similarly, over the same year:

- In 2018, at time t, the euro value of the dollar was $E_{€/\$,t} = €0.8830$.
- In 2019, at time $t+1$, the euro value of the dollar was $E_{€/\$,t+1} = €0.9054$.
- The change in the euro value of the dollar was
  $\Delta E_{€/\$,t} = 0.9054 - 0.8830 = +€0.0224$.
- The percentage change was $\Delta E_{€/\$,t}/E_{€/\$,t} = 0.9054/0.8830 = +2.53\%$.
- Thus, the dollar *appreciated* against the euro by 2.53%.

Note that the size of one country's appreciation (here 2.53%) does not exactly equal the size of the other country's depreciation (here 2.47%). For small changes, however, the opposing movements are *approximately* equal. For example, if the U.S. terms move slightly from $1.00 to $1.01 per euro, the European terms move from €1.00 to €0.99099; a 1% euro appreciation is approximately a 1% dollar depreciation.[4]

---

[4] In general, suppose that the home exchange rate is a, so one unit of home currency buys $1/a$ units of foreign currency. Now the home exchange rate depreciates to $b > a$, and one unit of home currency buys $1/b$ units of foreign currency, with $1/b < 1/a$. The size of the depreciation D of the home currency is

$$D = \left(\frac{1}{a} - \frac{1}{b}\right) \bigg/ \left(\frac{1}{a}\right) = \left(1 - \frac{a}{b}\right) = \left(\frac{b-a}{b}\right)$$

Symmetrically, the foreign currency was initially worth a units of home currency but is now worth b. Thus, the size of the appreciation A of the foreign currency is

$$A = \frac{(b-a)}{a} = \frac{b}{a}D$$

Thus, the percentage appreciation A will be approximately equal to the percentage depreciation D when b/a is close to 1, which is when b is approximately equal to a, that is, when the change in the exchange rate is small.

Multilateral Exchange Rates

So far, our discussion of exchange rates has focused on the exchange rate between two countries or currencies, which economists refer to as a *bilateral* exchange rate. In reality, we live in a world of many countries and many currencies, so it is important to be able to gauge whether a particular currency has strengthened or weakened not just against one other currency, but against other currencies in general. This is an important concept in the financial media, among policymakers, and for some issues that we study later in this book.

The answer is not always obvious. It is often the case that the U.S. dollar may be depreciating against some currencies, while remaining fixed or appreciating against others. To aggregate different trends in bilateral exchange rates into one measure, economists calculate *multilateral* exchange rate changes for baskets of currencies using *trade weights* to construct an average of all the bilateral changes for each currency in the basket. The resulting measure is called the change in the **effective exchange rate**.

For example, suppose 40% of Home trade is with country 1 and 60% is with country 2; Home's currency appreciates 10% against 1 but depreciates 30% against 2. To calculate the change in Home's effective exchange rate, we multiply each exchange rate change by the corresponding trade share and then add up: $(-10\% \times 40\%) + (30\% \times 60\%) = (-0.1 \times 0.4) + (0.3 \times 0.6) = -0.04 + 0.18 = 0.14 = +14\%$. In this example, Home's effective exchange rate has depreciated by 14%.

In general, suppose there are N currencies in the basket, and Home's trade with the N partners is $\text{Trade} = \text{Trade}_1 + \text{Trade}_2 + \cdots + \text{Trade}_N$. Applying trade weights to each bilateral exchange rate change, the home country's effective exchange rate ($E_{\text{effective}}$) will change according to the following weighted average:

$$\frac{\Delta E_{\text{effective}}}{E_{\text{effective}}} = \underbrace{\frac{\Delta E_1}{E_1} \frac{\text{Trade}_1}{\text{Trade}} + \frac{\Delta E_2}{E_2} \frac{\text{Trade}_2}{\text{Trade}} + \cdots + \frac{\Delta E_N}{E_N} \frac{\text{Trade}_N}{\text{Trade}}}_{\text{Trade-weighted average of bilateral nominal exchange rate changes}}$$

An especially contentious topic in recent years has been the path of the United States' effective exchange rate, shown in Figure 2-1. From 2002 to 2008, the U.S. dollar steadily fell in value against two baskets of other currencies. During the financial crisis of 2008, its value rebounded temporarily and later rose steadily in the 2010s, reversing the trend of the 2000s. During these swings, the U.S. dollar lost quite a lot of value against many well-known major currencies, such as the euro, the pound sterling, the Canadian dollar, and the Swiss franc. But on average, the weakening of the dollar was not as pronounced when measured against a broad basket of U.S. trading partners. The reason for this was the fact that Japan and China, along with several other developing countries in Asia, sought to peg or control their exchange rates to limit their appreciation against the dollar. Thus, in the figure the downward move for the broad basket of currencies was not as steep as that for the basket of seven major currencies.

Example: Using Exchange Rates to Compare Prices in a Common Currency

To make comparisons of prices across nations, we must convert prices to a common currency. The following examples show how we use exchange rates to accomplish this task.

James Bond is back from another mission and, what with all the explosions and shootouts, his wardrobe is looking ragged. He needs a new tuxedo. Bond will be in numerous cities on Her Majesty's Secret Service in the next few days, so he can shop around the globe. Although style is important, price is a key factor in Bond's choice,

FIGURE 2-1

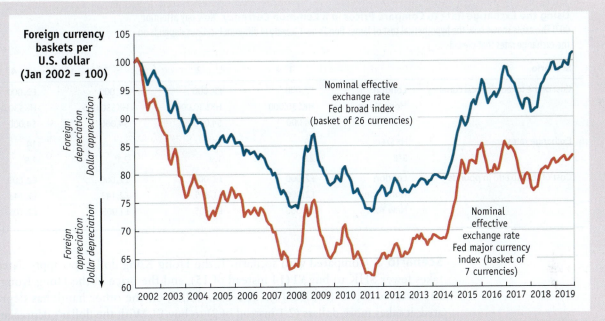

Effective Exchange Rates: Change in the Value of the U.S. Dollar, 2002–19 The chart shows the value of the dollar measured by the U.S. Federal Reserve using two different baskets of foreign currencies, starting with the index set to 100 foreign baskets in January 2002. Against a basket of 7 major currencies, the dollar had depreciated by more than 25% by late 2004, and 35% by early 2008. But against a broad basket of 26 currencies, the dollar had lost only 15% of its value by 2004, and 25% by 2008. This is because the dollar was floating against the major currencies, but the broad basket included important U.S. trading partners (such as China and other Asian economies) that maintained fixed or tightly managed exchange rates against the dollar. These trends only briefly reversed during the global financial crisis of 2008 before continuing up to 2019.

Data from: FRED (Federal Reserve Economic Data).

given the meager MI6 clothing allowance. Should he visit a new tailor in Manhattan? Go back to his favorite cutter in Hong Kong? Or simply nip around the corner to Savile Row in London?

The London tailor sells a tux for £2,000; the Hong Kong shop is asking HK$30,000; and in New York, the going rate is $4,000. In the near future, when the decision must be made, these prices are fixed in their respective home currencies. Which tux will 007 choose?

To choose among goods priced in different currencies, Bond must first convert all the prices into a common currency; for this he uses the exchange rate (and a calculator disguised as a toothbrush). Table 2-2 shows the prices, in local currency and converted into pounds, under different hypothetical exchange rates.

Scenario 1 In the first column, the Hong Kong suit costs HK$30,000 and the exchange rate is HK$15 per £. Dividing HK$30,000 by 15, we find that this suit costs £2,000 in British currency. The U.S. suit has a price of $4,000, and at an exchange rate of $2 per pound we obtain a British currency price of £2,000. Here the exchange rates are such that all prices are the same when measured in a common currency (pounds). Bond faces a difficult choice.

Scenario 2 Moving to the next column, the Hong Kong dollar has depreciated against the pound compared with scenario 1: it takes more HK$ (16 instead of 15) to buy £1. In contrast, the U.S. dollar has appreciated against the pound: it takes fewer dollars (1.9 instead of 2.0) to buy £1. At the new exchange rates, the cost of the New York tux has gone up to £2,105 (4,000/1.9), and the Hong Kong tux has fallen to £1,875 (30,000/16). Hong Kong now has the lowest price.

TABLE 2-2

Using the Exchange Rate to Compare Prices in a Common Currency Now pay attention, 007! This table shows how the hypothetical cost of James Bond's next tuxedo in different locations depends on the exchange rates that prevail.

Scenario		1	2	3	4
Cost of the tuxedo in local currency	London	£2,000	£2,000	£2,000	£2,000
	Hong Kong	HK$30,000	HK$30,000	HK$30,000	HK$30,000
	New York	$4,000	$4,000	$4,000	$4,000
Exchange rates	HK$/£	15	16	14	14
	$/£	2.0	1.9	2.1	1.9
Cost of the tuxedo in pounds	London	£2,000	£2,000	£2,000	£2,000
	Hong Kong	£2,000	£1,875	£2,143	£2,143
	New York	£2,000	£2,105	£1,905	£2,105

Scenario 3 Compared with scenario 1, the Hong Kong dollar has appreciated: it takes fewer $HK to buy £1 (14 instead of 15), and the price of the Hong Kong tux has risen to £2,143 (30,000/14). The U.S. dollar, on the other hand, has depreciated: it takes more dollars (2.1 instead of 2) to buy £1. With the dollar's depreciation, New York now has the best price of £1,905 (4,000/2.1).

Scenario 4 In this case, compared with scenario 1, the pound has depreciated against both of the other currencies, and they have each appreciated against the pound. It takes fewer Hong Kong dollars (14 instead of 15) and fewer U.S. dollars (1.9 instead of 2.0) to buy £1. Now London has the bargain price of £2,000 and the other cities have higher prices.

This example emphasizes a key point. We assumed that while exchange rates may change, the prices of goods in each country are fixed in the short run (in domestic-currency terms). An economist would say the prices are *sticky* in the short run, and, as we see later, this is not an unreasonable assumption. Given that assumption, changes in exchange rates will cause changes in the common-currency prices of goods from different countries.

Generalizing The same logic applies to any exchange rate. All else equal, when the prices of goods are constant in each country, the following conclusions will apply:

- *Changes in the exchange rate cause changes in prices of foreign goods expressed in the home currency.*

- *Changes in the exchange rate cause changes in the relative prices of goods produced in the home and foreign countries.*

- *When the home country's exchange rate depreciates, home exports become less expensive as imports to foreigners, and foreign exports become more expensive as imports to home residents.*

- *When the home country's exchange rate appreciates, home exports become more expensive as imports to foreigners, and foreign exports become less expensive as imports to home residents.*

2 Exchange Rates in Practice

Now that you have seen the data in Table 2-1, it might be tempting to use the same figures as a guide to today's exchange rates between countries. This would be a big mistake. Exchange rates fluctuate. They depreciate and appreciate. A lot. On a single day, in a matter of hours or even minutes, they can change substantially. Over a year, they may move considerably in one direction or another. Any complete theory of exchange rate determination must account for the various exchange rate movements and patterns we see in different times and places, so we now take some time to get familiar with these phenomena.

Exchange Rate Regimes: Fixed Versus Floating

Economists group different patterns of exchange rate behavior into categories known as **exchange rate regimes**. These outcomes reflect choices made by governments, and the causes and consequences of exchange rate regimes are a major focus of our study.

There are two major regime types:

- **Fixed** (or **pegged**) **exchange rate regimes** are those in which a country's exchange rate fluctuates in a narrow range (or not at all) against some *base currency* over a sustained period, usually a year or longer. A country's exchange rate can remain rigidly fixed for long periods only if the government intervenes in the foreign exchange market in one or both countries.

- **Floating** (or **flexible**) **exchange rate regimes** are those in which a country's exchange rate fluctuates in a wider range, and the government makes no attempt to fix it against any base currency. Appreciations and depreciations may occur from year to year, each month, by the day, or every minute.

For example, earlier in the book we saw data for two of the most talked-about exchange rates in the world today: the U.S. dollar–euro and the Chinese yuan–U.S. dollar rates. The dollar–euro rate fluctuated considerably and was said to be floating; the yuan–dollar rate held steady or changed very slowly and was said to be fixed.

However, the "fixed versus floating" classification is not without its problems. First, to classify a regime as fixed or floating, we have to decide where to draw a somewhat arbitrary line between "narrow" and "wide" fluctuations. One rule of thumb is to use the size of annual variations (say, within ±2% or ±1%) as the sign of a fixed regime. Second, using just two categories (fixed and floating) offers only a very broad description of exchange rate regimes. In reality, the distinctions are not so cut and dried. Fixed and floating provide important benchmarks throughout this book and deliver great insights, but we sometimes need more precise ways of describing *intermediate regimes*, as the following application illustrates.

APPLICATION

Recent Exchange Rate Experiences

If we spend a moment looking at recent exchange rate experiences in a variety of countries, we see not only some helpful illustrations of the differences between floating and fixed rate regimes but also some of the different varieties of fixed and floating behavior. We also see examples of regime change, in which one type of regime gives way to another, either smoothly or catastrophically.

Evidence from Developed Countries Figure 2-2 shows the daily exchange rates from 1996 to 2019 for various currency pairs. The top row shows the U.S. dollar exchange rate against two major currencies (the Japanese yen, the British pound sterling) and against the currency of a neighboring country (the Canadian dollar, also called the *loonie*, because it bears the image of a common loon). The bottom row shows the exchange rate of the euro against the yen, the pound, and the Danish krone. In all six charts, the vertical scale varies by a factor of 2 from maximum to

FIGURE 2-2

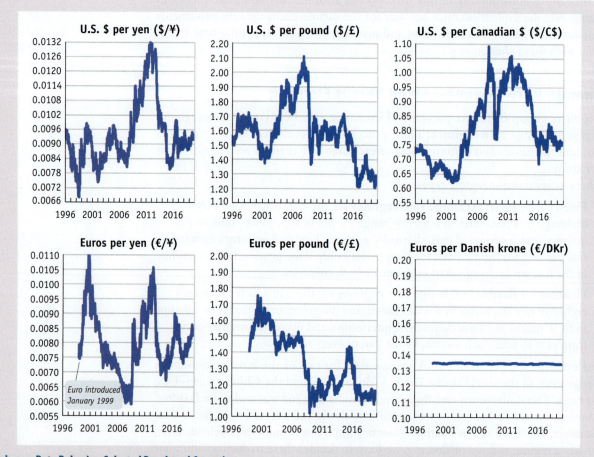

Exchange Rate Behavior: Selected Developed Countries, 1996–2019 This figure shows exchange rates of three currencies against the U.S. dollar and three against the euro. The euro rates begin in 1999 when the currency was introduced. The yen, pound, and Canadian dollar all float against the U.S. dollar. The pound and yen float against the euro. The Danish krone is fixed against the euro. The vertical scale ranges by a factor of 2 on all charts.

Data from: FRED (Federal Reserve Economic Data); European Central Bank.

minimum, so all of these charts are comparable in terms of their representation of these exchange rates' volatility.

We can clearly see that the U.S. dollar is in a floating relationship with all three foreign currencies shown in the top row—the yen, pound, and loonie. How volatile are the exchange rates? The range of variation in each case is about the same, with the maximum being about one and a half times the minimum: the yen ranges from $0.007 to $0.013, the pound from $1.2 to $2.1, and the loonie from $0.6 to about $1.1. The movements between these peaks and troughs may take many months or years to occur, but the exchange rate also shows much short-run volatility, with lots of up-and-down movement from day to day. A floating regime of this sort is called a **free float**. Similarly, the bottom row of Figure 2-2 shows that the euro floats against the yen and the pound.

In the sixth and final chart, the Danish krone provides a clear contrast—an example of a fixed exchange rate in a developed country. Denmark is part of the European Union, but it has kept its own national currency, at least for now, and does not use the euro as its currency. However, Denmark has fixed its exchange rate against the euro, keeping it very close to 7.44 krone per euro (0.134 euro per krone). There is only a tiny variation around this rate, well within plus or minus 2%. This type of fixed regime is known as a **band**.

Evidence from Developing Countries Figure 2-3 shows the daily exchange rates against the U.S. dollar from 1996 to 2019 for some developing countries. Exchange rates in developing countries can be much more volatile than those in developed countries. The charts in the top row illustrate exchange rate behavior in three Asian countries (India, Thailand, and South Korea); the maximum on the vertical axis is three times the minimum.

India had what looked like a fixed rate of about 35 rupees per dollar until a depreciation in 1997; there was then a period of pronounced movement more like a float. However, the government still acted to prevent abrupt currency movements even after 1997. This middle ground, somewhere between a fixed rate and a free float, is called a **managed float** (also known as a *dirty float*, or a policy of *limited flexibility*).

Thailand and South Korea show more extreme versions of the same pattern, except that in these cases the depreciation in 1997 was large and sudden, with the baht and the won exchange rates more than doubling in a matter of weeks. Such dramatic depreciations are called **exchange rate crises**, and they are more common in developing

FIGURE 2-3

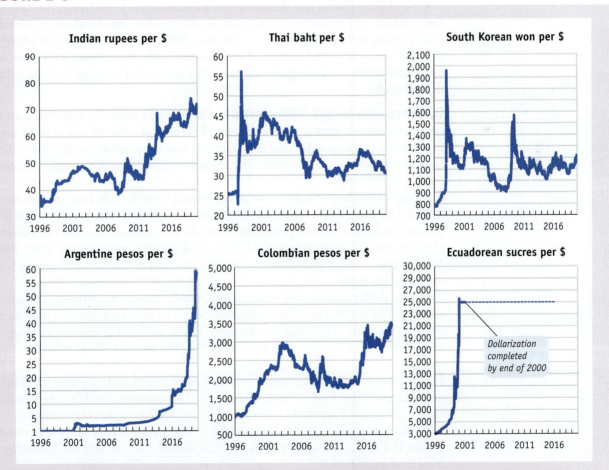

Exchange Rate Behavior: Selected Developing Countries, 1996–2019 Exchange rates in developing countries show a wide variety of experiences and greater volatility. Pegging is common but is punctuated by periodic crises (you can see the effects of these crises in graphs for Thailand, South Korea, and Argentina). Rates that are unpegged may show some flexibility (India). Some rates crawl gradually (Colombia). Dollarization can occur (Ecuador). The vertical scale ranges by a factor of 3 on the upper charts and by a factor of 10 on the lower-right two charts, and by a factor of 60 on the lower-left Argentina chart.

Data from: FRED (Federal Reserve Economic Data); Banco Central de la República Argentina; Banco de la República; IMF, International Financial Statistics.

countries than in developed countries. Indeed, South Korea had another mini-crisis in 2008. But outside of crisis periods both exchange rates are fairly stable.

The bottom row of Figure 2-3 shows some Latin American countries and more varieties of exchange rate experience. The maximum on the vertical scale is now 10 times the minimum (or 60 in the case of Argentina), a change made necessary by the even more volatile exchange rates in this region.

Argentina initially had a fixed rate (of one peso per dollar), followed in 2001 by an exchange rate crisis. After a period of limited flexibility, Argentina returned to an almost fixed rate with a band that appeared to be centered at about 3 pesos per dollar, before the exchange rate drifted higher after 2008, slowly at first, and then rapidly in the later years after 2013.

Colombia presents an example of a different kind of fixed exchange rate. Here the authorities did not target the level of the Colombian peso but allowed it to steadily depreciate at an almost constant rate for several years from 1996 to 2002 (before then switching to a managed float). This type of fixed arrangement is called a **crawl** (if the exchange rate follows a simple trend, it is a *crawling peg*; if some variation about the trend is allowed, it is termed a *crawling band*).

In the bottom right corner, Ecuador displays a different crisis pattern. Here a period of floating was followed by a fixed rate rather than the other way around. Episodes of very rapid depreciation like this represent a distinct form of exchange rate behavior; some economists have suggested, not jokingly, that these regimes be identified separately as *freely falling* exchange rate regimes.[5] The Ecuadorean currency stabilized at a fixed rate of 25,000 sucres per dollar, but then the sucre ceased to be. Ecuador took the remarkable step of dollarizing: abolishing its own national currency and adopting the U.S. dollar as its legal tender.

Currency Unions and Dollarization   Almost every economy issues its own currency and jealously guards this sovereign right. There are only two exceptions: groups of economies that agree to form a currency or monetary union and adopt a common currency, and individual economies that dollarize by adopting the currency of another country as their own.

Under a **currency union** (or **monetary union**), there is some form of transnational structure such as a single central bank or monetary authority that is accountable to the member nations. The most prominent example of a currency union is the Eurozone. Other currency unions include the CFA and CFP Franc zones (among some former French colonies in Africa and the Pacific) and the Eastern Caribbean Currency Union of six member states.

Under **dollarization** one country unilaterally adopts the currency of another country. The reasons for this choice can vary. The adopting country may be very small, so the costs of running its own central bank and issuing its own currency may be prohibitive. Such is the case, for example, for the 60 or so Pitcairn Islanders (who use the New Zealand dollar as their standard currency). Other countries may have a poor record of managing their own monetary affairs and may end up "importing" a better policy from abroad. The currency changeover could be a de jure policy choice; or it may happen de facto if people are so fed up that they stop using the national currency and switch en masse to an alternative. Many of these economies use the U.S. dollar, but other popular choices include the euro and the Australian and New Zealand dollars.

Exchange Rate Regimes of the World   To move beyond specific examples, Figure 2-4 shows a classification of exchange rate regimes around the world, which

---

[5] Carmen M. Reinhart and Kenneth S. Rogoff, 2004, "The Modern History of Exchange Rate Arrangements: A Reinterpretation," *Quarterly Journal of Economics*, 119(1), 1–48.

allows us to see the prevalence of different regime types across the whole spectrum from fixed to floating.[6]

The classification covers 182 economies, and regimes are ordered from the most rigidly fixed to the most freely floating. The first 52 countries are those that have no currency of their own—they are either dollarized or in a currency union. Next are six countries using an ultra-hard peg called a **currency board**, a type of fixed regime that has special legal and procedural rules designed to make the peg "harder"—that is, more

FIGURE 2-4

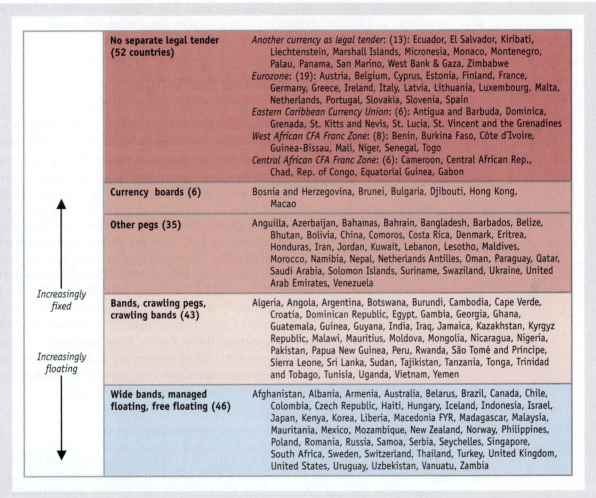

No separate legal tender (52 countries)	*Another currency as legal tender*: (13): Ecuador, El Salvador, Kiribati, Liechtenstein, Marshall Islands, Micronesia, Monaco, Montenegro, Palau, Panama, San Marino, West Bank & Gaza, Zimbabwe	
	Eurozone: (19): Austria, Belgium, Cyprus, Estonia, Finland, France, Germany, Greece, Ireland, Italy, Latvia, Lithuania, Luxembourg, Malta, Netherlands, Portugal, Slovakia, Slovenia, Spain	
	Eastern Caribbean Currency Union: (6): Antigua and Barbuda, Dominica, Grenada, St. Kitts and Nevis, St. Lucia, St. Vincent and the Grenadines	
	West African CFA Franc Zone: (8): Benin, Burkina Faso, Côte d'Ivoire, Guinea-Bissau, Mali, Niger, Senegal, Togo	
	Central African CFA Franc Zone: (6): Cameroon, Central African Rep., Chad, Rep. of Congo, Equatorial Guinea, Gabon	
Currency boards (6)	Bosnia and Herzegovina, Brunei, Bulgaria, Djibouti, Hong Kong, Macao	
Other pegs (35)	Anguilla, Azerbaijan, Bahamas, Bahrain, Bangladesh, Barbados, Belize, Bhutan, Bolivia, China, Comoros, Costa Rica, Denmark, Eritrea, Honduras, Iran, Jordan, Kuwait, Lebanon, Lesotho, Maldives, Morocco, Namibia, Nepal, Netherlands Antilles, Oman, Paraguay, Qatar, Saudi Arabia, Solomon Islands, Suriname, Swaziland, Ukraine, United Arab Emirates, Venezuela	
Bands, crawling pegs, crawling bands (43)	Algeria, Angola, Argentina, Botswana, Burundi, Cambodia, Cape Verde, Croatia, Dominican Republic, Egypt, Gambia, Georgia, Ghana, Guatemala, Guinea, Guyana, India, Iraq, Jamaica, Kazakhstan, Kyrgyz Republic, Malawi, Mauritius, Moldova, Mongolia, Nicaragua, Nigeria, Pakistan, Papua New Guinea, Peru, Rwanda, São Tomé and Príncipe, Sierra Leone, Sri Lanka, Sudan, Tajikistan, Tanzania, Tonga, Trinidad and Tobago, Tunisia, Uganda, Vietnam, Yemen	
Wide bands, managed floating, free floating (46)	Afghanistan, Albania, Armenia, Australia, Belarus, Brazil, Canada, Chile, Colombia, Czech Republic, Haiti, Hungary, Iceland, Indonesia, Israel, Japan, Kenya, Korea, Liberia, Macedonia FYR, Madagascar, Malaysia, Mauritania, Mexico, Mozambique, New Zealand, Norway, Philippines, Poland, Romania, Russia, Samoa, Serbia, Seychelles, Singapore, South Africa, Sweden, Switzerland, Thailand, Turkey, United Kingdom, United States, Uruguay, Uzbekistan, Vanuatu, Zambia	

Increasingly fixed

Increasingly floating

A Spectrum of Exchange Rate Regimes The chart shows a recent classification of exchange rate regimes around the world.

Data from: With the major exception of Estonia and Lithuania, which have since joined the Eurozone and are re-classified as such, all classifications are based on the
year 2010 using the data from Ethan Ilzetzki, Carmen M. Reinhart, and Kenneth S. Rogoff, 2010, "Exchange Rate Arrangements Entering the 21st Century: Which Anchor Will Hold?" and updates based on the author's calculations. See the next chapter for more details.

---

[6] Up until 2008 the IMF provided an unofficial classification based on observed exchange rate behavior. Most economists prefer this type of classification to the often misleading official classifications that were based on countries' official policy announcements. For example, as we saw in Figure 2-3, Thailand pegged to the dollar before the 1997 crisis, even though official statements denied this and the Thai authorities claimed the baht was floating. On unofficial or de facto classifications, see Carmen M. Reinhart and Kenneth S. Rogoff, 2004, "The Modern History of Exchange Rate Arrangements: A Reinterpretation," *Quarterly Journal of Economics*, 119(1), 1–48; Jay C. Shambaugh, 2004, "The Effect of Fixed Exchange Rates on Monetary Policy," *Quarterly Journal of Economics*, 119(1), 301–52; and Eduardo Levy Yeyati and Federico Sturzenegger, 2005, "Classifying Exchange Rate Regimes: Deeds vs. Words," *European Economic Review*, 49(6), 1603–35.

durable. Then come 35 other pegs, with variations of less than ±1%, some fixed to a single currency and a few pegging against a basket of currencies. These are followed by 43 bands, crawling pegs, and crawling bands. We then encounter the more flexible regimes: 46 cases of wide bands, managed floating rates, and freely floating regimes.

Looking Ahead This brief look at the evidence motivates the analysis in the remainder of this book. First, the world is divided into fixed and floating rate regimes, so we need to understand how *both* types of regime work. Studying fixed and floating regimes side by side will occupy much of our attention for the next few chapters. Second, when we look at who is fixed and who is floating, we start to notice patterns. Most of the floaters are advanced countries, and most of the fixers are developing countries (the major exception is the euro area). The important question of why some countries fix while others float is covered in more detail in later chapters.

3 The Market for Foreign Exchange

Day by day, and minute by minute, exchange rates the world over are set in the **foreign exchange market** (or **forex** or **FX** market), which, like any market, is a collection of private individuals, corporations, and some public institutions that buy and sell. When two currencies are traded for each other in a market, the exchange rate is the price at which the trade was done, a price that is determined by market forces.

The forex market is not an organized exchange: each trade is conducted "over the counter" between two parties at numerous interlinked locations around the world. The forex market is massive and has grown dramatically in recent years. According to the Bank for International Settlements, in April 2019 the global forex market traded $6.6 trillion per day in currency; this was 29% more than in 2016, over three times more than in 2004, and over six times more than in 1992. The four major foreign exchange centers—the United Kingdom ($3,576 billion per day, almost all in London), the United States ($1,370 billion, mostly in New York), Singapore ($633 billion), and Hong Kong ($632 billion)—played home to more than 70% of the trade.[7] Other important centers for forex trade include Tokyo, Zurich, Paris, and Frankfurt. Thanks to time-zone differences, when smaller trading centers are included, there is not a moment in the day when foreign exchange is not being traded somewhere in the world. This section briefly examines the basic workings of this market.

The Spot Contract

The simplest forex transaction is a contract for the immediate exchange of one currency for another between two parties. This is known as a **spot contract** because it happens "on the spot." Accordingly, the exchange rate for this transaction is often called the **spot exchange rate**. In this book, the use of the term "exchange rate" always refers to the spot rate. Spot trades are now essentially riskless: technology permits settlement for most trades in real time, so that the risk of one party failing to deliver on its side of the transaction (*default risk* or *settlement risk*) is essentially zero.[8]

Most of our personal transactions in the forex market are small spot transactions via retail channels, but this represents just a tiny fraction of the activity in the forex market each day. The vast majority of trading involves commercial banks in major financial centers around the world. But even there the spot contract is the most common

---

[7] Data from BIS, *Triennial Central Bank Survey: Foreign exchange turnover in April 2019* (Basel, Switzerland: Bank for International Settlements, September 2019).

[8] Spot trades formerly took two days for settlement. If a bank failed in that period, spot trades could suffer occasional settlement failure. However, since 1997 a *continuously linked settlement* system has been used by the major trading banks and now covers a substantial majority of cross-currency transactions all over the world.

type of trade and appears in more than 80% of all forex transactions, either on its own as a single contract or in trades where it is combined with other forex contracts.

Transaction Costs

When individuals buy a little foreign currency through a retail channel (such as a bank), they pay a higher price than the midrange quote typically seen in the press; when they sell, they are paid a lower price. The difference, or **spread**, between the "buy at" and "sell for" prices may be large, perhaps 2% to 5%. These fees and commissions go to the many middlemen who stand between the person on the street and the forex market. But when a big firm or a bank needs to exchange millions of dollars, the spreads and commissions are very small. Spreads are usually less than 0.10% (10 basis points), and for actively traded major currencies, they are approximately 0.01% to 0.03% (1 to 3 basis points).

Spreads are an important example of **market frictions** or **transaction costs**. These frictions create a wedge between the price paid by the buyer and the price received by the seller. Although spreads are potentially important for any microeconomic analysis of the forex market, macroeconomic analysis usually proceeds on the assumption that, in today's world of low-cost trading, the transaction-cost spreads in markets are so low for the key investors that they can be ignored for most purposes.

Derivatives

The spot contract is undoubtedly the most important contract in the forex market, but there are many other related forex contracts. These contracts include *forwards*, *swaps*, *futures*, and *options*. Collectively, all these related forex contracts are called **derivatives** because the contracts and their pricing are derived from the spot rate.

The most important of the derivatives is the **forward** contract. A forward contract differs from a spot contract in that the two parties make the contract today, but the *settlement date* for the delivery of the currencies is in the future, or forward. The time to delivery, or *maturity*, varies—30 days, 90 days, six months, a year, or even longer—depending on the contract. However, because the price is fixed as of today, the contract carries no risk.

With the exception of forwards, the forex derivatives market is small relative to the entire global forex market. According to the most recent April 2013 survey data from the Bank for International Settlements, the trade in spot contracts amounted to $2,046 billion per day (38% of trades), the trade in forward contracts was $680 billion per day (13% of trades), and the trade in swaps (which combine a spot and a forward) accounted for $2,282 billion per day (43% of trades). The remaining derivative trades amounted to $337 billion per day (6% of trades).

For the rest of this chapter, we focus on the two most important contracts—the spot and the forward. Figure 2-5 shows an example of trends in the spot and forward rates in the dollar–euro market during the year 2008. The forward rate tends to track the spot rate fairly closely, and we will explore this relationship further in a moment.

The full study of derivative markets requires an in-depth analysis of risk that is beyond the scope of this book. Such topics are reserved for advanced courses in finance that explore derivative contracts in great detail.

FIGURE 2-5

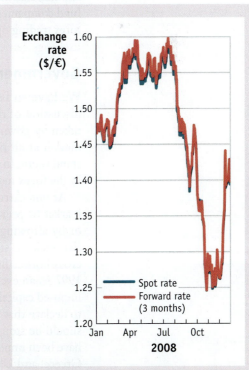

Spot and Forward Rates The chart shows typical movements in the U.S. spot and three-month forward exchange rates for the euro in dollars per euro using the year 2008 as an example. The spot and forward rates closely track each other.

Data from: Federal Reserve Bank of New York.

Private Actors

The key actors in the forex market are the traders. Most forex traders work for **commercial banks**. These banks trade for themselves in search of profit and also serve clients who want to import or export goods, services, or assets. Such transactions usually involve a change of currency, and commercial banks are the principal financial intermediaries that provide this service.

For example, suppose Apple Computer Inc. has sold €1 million worth of computers to a German distributor and wishes to receive payment for them in U.S. dollars (with the spot rate at $1.30 per euro). The German distributor informs its commercial bank, Deutsche Bank, which then debits €1 million from the distributor's bank account. Deutsche Bank then sells the €1 million bank deposit in the forex market in exchange for a $1.3 million deposit and credits that $1.3 million to Apple's bank in the United States, which, in turn, deposits $1.3 million into Apple's account.

This is an example of **interbank trading**. This business is highly concentrated: more than half of all forex market transactions globally are handled by just 10 banks, led by names such as JPMorgan, UBS, Bank of America, Citi, HSBC, Goldman Sachs, and Deutsche Bank. The vast majority of forex transactions are profit-driven interbank trades, and it is the exchange rates for these trades that underlie quoted market exchange rates. Consequently, we focus on profit-driven trading as the key force in the forex market that affects the determination of the spot exchange rate.

Other actors are increasingly participating directly in the forex market. Some **corporations** may trade in the market if they are engaged in extensive transactions either to buy inputs or to sell products in foreign markets. It may be costly for them to do this, but by doing so, they can bypass the fees and commissions charged by commercial banks. Similarly, some **nonbank financial institutions** such as mutual fund companies may invest so much overseas that they can justify setting up their own forex trading operations.

Government Actions

We have so far described the forex market in terms of the private actors. Our discussion of the forex market is incomplete, however, without mention of actions taken by government authorities. Such activities are by no means present in every market at all times, but they are sufficiently frequent that we need to fully understand them. In essence, there are two primary types of actions taken by governments in the forex market.

At one extreme, it is possible for a government to try to completely control the market by preventing its free operation, by restricting trading or movement of forex, or by allowing the trading of forex only through government channels. A policy that seeks to stop, or substantially limit, foreign exchange transactions and restricts cross-border financial transactions is known as a **capital control**. In the wake of the 1997 Asian exchange rate crisis, for example, the Malaysian government temporarily imposed capital controls, an event that prompted Prime Minister Mahathir Mohamad to declare that "currency trading is unnecessary, unproductive and totally immoral. It should be stopped, it should be made illegal."[9] In more recent years capital controls have been imposed in countries such as China, Argentina, Venezuela, Iceland, Cyprus, Greece, and Ukraine.

---

[9] From a speech at the World Bank meeting in Hong Kong, September 20, 1997, in which Mr. Mohamad also referred to the legendary currency trader George Soros as a "moron." See Edward A. Gargan, "Premier of Malaysia Spars with Currency Dealer; Mahathir Says Soros and His Ilk Are 'Impoverishing Others' for Profit," *New York Times*, September 22, 1997, p. A1.

Capital controls are never 100% successful, however. Illegal trades will inevitably occur and are almost impossible to stop. The government may set up an **official market** for foreign exchange and issue a law requiring people to buy and sell in that market at officially set rates. But illicit dealings can persist "on the street" in **black markets** or *parallel markets* where individuals may trade at exchange rates determined by market forces and not set by the government. For example, in Italy in the 1930s, the Mussolini regime set harsh punishments for trading in foreign currency that gradually rose to include the death penalty, but trading still continued on the black market.

A less drastic action taken by government authorities is to let the private market for forex function but to fix or control forex prices in the market through **intervention**, a job typically given to a nation's central bank.

How do central banks intervene in the forex market? Indeed, how can a government control a price in any market? This is an age-old problem. Consider the issue of food supply in medieval and premodern Europe, one of the earliest examples of government intervention to fix prices in markets. Rulers faced a problem because droughts and harvest failures often led to food shortages, even famines—and sometimes political unrest. Governments reacted by establishing state-run granaries, where wheat would be stored up in years of plenty and then released to the market in years of scarcity. The price could even be fixed if the government stood ready to buy or sell grain at a preset price *and if the government always had enough grain in reserve to do so*. Some authorities successfully followed this strategy for many years. Others failed when they ran out of grain reserves. Once a reserve is gone, market forces take over. If there is a heavy demand that is no longer being met by the state, a rapid price increase will inevitably follow.

Government intervention in the forex market works in a similar manner. To maintain a fixed or pegged exchange rate, the central bank must stand ready to buy or sell its own currency, in exchange for the base foreign currency to which it pegs, at a fixed price. In practice, this means keeping some foreign currency reserves as a buffer, but having this buffer raises many problems. For one thing, it is costly—resources are tied up in foreign currency when they could be invested in more profitable activities. Second, these reserves are not an unlimited buffer, and if they run out, then market forces will take over and determine the exchange rate. In later chapters, we explore why countries peg, how a peg is maintained and reserves are used, and under what circumstances pegs fail, leading to an exchange rate crisis.

So, as we've seen, the extent of government intervention can vary. However, even with complete capital controls, including the suppression of the black market, private actors are always present in the market. Our first task is therefore to understand how private economic motives and actions affect the forex market.

Forex traders at their desks in London and money changers on the street in Kabul.

4 Arbitrage and Spot Exchange Rates

The most basic of activities pursued by private actors in any market is **arbitrage**, a trading strategy that exploits any profit opportunities arising from price differences. Understanding arbitrage is one of the keys to thinking like an economist in any situation and is essential in studying exchange rates.

In the simplest terms, arbitrage means to buy low and sell high for a profit. If such profit opportunities exist in a market, then it is considered to be out of equilibrium. If no such profit opportunities exist, there will be no arbitrage; the market is in **equilibrium** and satisfies a **no-arbitrage condition**.

Arbitrage with Two Currencies

Suppose you trade dollars and pounds for a bank with branches in New York and London. You can electronically transfer the funds cost free between the two branch locations. Forex trading commissions are the same in each city and so small as to be negligible. Suppose the exchange rate in New York is $E_{£/\$}^{N.Y.} = £0.50$ per dollar, in London $E_{£/\$}^{London} = £0.55$ per dollar. Can you make a profit for the bank?

Yes. You can buy \$1 for £0.50 in New York and sell it for £0.55 in London for an instant, riskless profit. Indeed, everyone would buy in New York and sell in London.

In general, one of three outcomes can occur in the forex market. The spot rate can be higher in London: $E_{£/\$}^{N.Y.} < E_{£/\$}^{London}$; the spot rate can be higher in New York: $E_{£/\$}^{N.Y.} > E_{£/\$}^{London}$; or the spot rate can be the same in both locations: $E_{£/\$}^{N.Y.} = E_{£/\$}^{London}$. Arbitrage occurs in the first two cases. Only in the last case, in which spot rates are equal, does no arbitrage occur. Hence, the no-arbitrage condition for spot rates is

$$E_{£/\$}^{N.Y.} = E_{£/\$}^{London}$$

Figure 2-6 shows the no-arbitrage condition. Following both sets of arrows (AB and ACDB), we see that on each path we start with a dollar and end up with pounds, but we are indifferent between these paths only when the end result is identical. This situation would be an equilibrium, in which no arbitrage is possible.

If the market is out of equilibrium, arbitrage would drive up the price in the low-price market and drive down the price in the high-price market. In our example, everyone buying dollars in New York and selling in London would bid up the spot rate in New York from £0.50 and would bid down the spot rate in London from £0.55. This process would continue until the prices converged, arbitrage ceased, and equilibrium was reached. In forex markets, these adjustments happen nearly instantaneously, whether in the high-tech electronics markets of world financial centers or in the markets on street corners in the developing world.

FIGURE 2-6

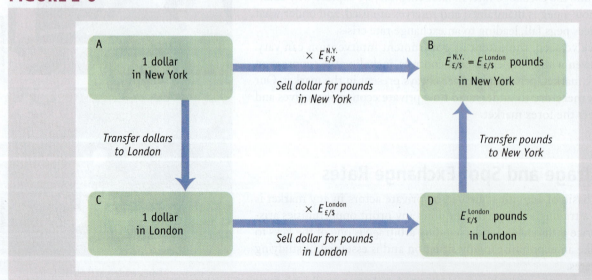

Arbitrage and Spot Rates Arbitrage ensures that the trade of currencies in New York along the path AB occurs at the same exchange rate as via London along path ACDB. At B the pounds received must be the same. Regardless of the route taken to get to B, $E_{£/\$}^{N.Y.} = E_{£/\$}^{London}$.

Arbitrage with Three Currencies

The same logic that we just applied to transactions between two currencies can also be applied to transactions involving three currencies. Again, as the trader in New York, you are considering trading dollars and pounds, but you also consider indirect or "triangular" trade via a third currency, say, the euro. Triangular arbitrage works as follows: you sell dollars in exchange for euros, then immediately sell the same euros in exchange for pounds. This roundabout way to acquire pounds is feasible, but is it sensible? Perhaps.

For example, suppose euros can be obtained at $E_{\text{€}/\$} = \text{€}0.8$ per dollar, and pounds can be obtained at $E_{\text{£}/\text{€}} = \text{£}0.7$ per euro. Starting with \$1, you can obtain 0.8 euros, and with those 0.8 euros, you can obtain 0.7×0.8 pounds. Thus, setting aside the negligibly small commissions, the resulting pound–dollar exchange rate on the combined trade is $E_{\text{£}/\text{€}} \times E_{\text{€}/\$} = 0.7 \times 0.8 = 0.56$ pounds per dollar. If, say, the exchange rate on the direct trade from dollars to pounds is a less favorable $E_{\text{£}/\$} = 0.5$, we can trade \$1 for £0.56 via the euro, and then trade the £0.56 for \$1.12 by way of a direct trade (because $1.12 = 0.56/0.5$), a riskless profit of 12 cents.

In general, three outcomes are again possible. The direct trade from dollars to pounds has a better rate: $E_{\text{£}/\$} > E_{\text{£}/\text{€}}E_{\text{€}/\$}$; the indirect trade has a better rate: $E_{\text{£}/\$} < E_{\text{£}/\text{€}}E_{\text{€}/\$}$; or the two trades have the same rate and yield the same result: $E_{\text{£}/\$} = E_{\text{£}/\text{€}}E_{\text{€}/\$}$. Only in the last case are there no profit opportunities. This no-arbitrage condition can be written in two ways:

$$\underbrace{E_{\text{£}/\$}}_{\substack{\text{Direct} \\ \text{exchange rate}}} = E_{\text{£}/\text{€}}E_{\text{€}/\$} = \underbrace{\frac{E_{\text{£}/\text{€}}}{E_{\$/\text{€}}}}_{\text{Cross rate}}$$

The right-hand expression, a ratio of two exchange rates, is called a **cross rate**. Examine the units carefully and notice how the two € cancel out. This no-arbitrage condition applies to all currency combinations and is illustrated by the paths AB and ACB in Figure 2-7 (you can see why it is called *triangular arbitrage*).

The cross-rate formula is very convenient. It means that we do not need to keep track of the exchange rate of every currency at all times. For example, if we know the

FIGURE 2-7

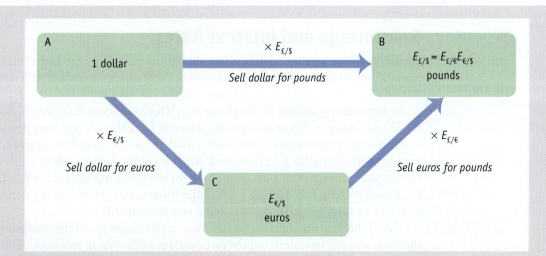

Arbitrage and Cross Rates Triangular arbitrage ensures that the direct trade of currencies along the path AB occurs at the same exchange rate as via a third currency along path ACB. The pounds received at B must be the same on both paths, and $E_{\text{£}/\$} = E_{\text{£}/\text{€}}E_{\text{€}/\$}$.

exchange rates against, say, the dollar, for every currency, then for *any* pair of currencies A and B we can use the dollar rates of each currency and the cross-rate formula to work out the rate at which the two currencies will trade: $E_{A/B} = E_{A/\$}/E_{B/\$}$. In practice, this is how most exchange rates are calculated.

Cross Rates and Vehicle Currencies

The study of cross rates is not a meaningless exercise because the vast majority of currency pairs are exchanged for each other through a third currency. There are 180 distinct currencies in the world at the time of writing. Based on that, if you wrote down every possible currency pair, then counted them up, there would be 16,110 active forex markets in operation. In reality, however, there is only a tiny fraction of this number. Why?

The vast majority of the world's currencies trade directly with only one or two of the major currencies, such as the dollar, euro, yen, or pound, and perhaps a few other currencies from neighboring countries. This is not too surprising. After all, to take some obscure examples, how often does somebody want to trade a Kenyan shilling for a Paraguayan guaraní? Or a Mauritanian ouguiya for a Tongan pa'anga? These are small, far-apart countries between which there is very little international trade or investment. It is hard to find counterparties for forex trade in these currencies—so hard that the costs of trading become prohibitive. And there is no need to bear these costs because, to continue our example, Kenya, Paraguay, Mauritania, and Tonga conduct a lot of business in major currencies such as the U.S. dollar, so individuals always have the option to engage in a triangular trade at the cross rate to convert shillings to dollars to guaranís (or ouguiyas to dollars to pa'angas), all for a reasonable commission.

When a third currency, such as the U.S. dollar, is used in these transactions, it is called a **vehicle currency** because it is not the home currency of either of the parties involved in the trade. Market data illustrate the importance of vehicle currencies. According to the 2013 survey data from the Bank for International Settlements, the most common vehicle currency is the U.S. dollar, which appears on one side of 87% of all global trades. The euro is next, playing a role in 33% of all trades (many of them with the U.S. dollar). The yen appears in 23% of all trades and the British pound in 12%.

5 Arbitrage and Interest Rates

So far, our discussion of arbitrage has shown how actors in the forex market—for example, the banks—exploit profit opportunities if currencies trade at different prices. But this is not the only type of arbitrage activity affecting the forex market.

An important question for investors is in which currency they should hold their liquid cash balances. Their cash can be placed in bank deposit accounts denominated in various currencies where it will earn a modest interest rate. For example, a trader working for a major bank in New York could leave the bank's cash in a euro deposit for one year earning a 2% euro interest rate or she could put the money in a U.S. dollar deposit for one year earning a 4% dollar interest rate. How can she decide which asset, the euro or the dollar deposit, is the best investment?

This is the final problem that we address in this chapter, and this analysis provides the tools we need to understand the forex market in the rest of this book. The analysis again centers on arbitrage. Would selling euro deposits and buying dollar deposits make a profit for the banker? Decisions like these drive the demand for dollars versus euros and the exchange rate between the two currencies.

The Problem of Risk A key issue for the trader is the exchange rate risk. The trader is in New York, and her bank cares about returns in U.S. dollars. The dollar deposit pays a known return, in dollars. But the euro deposit pays a return in euros, and one year from now we cannot know for sure what the dollar–euro exchange rate will be. Thus, how we analyze arbitrage in the sections that follow depends on how exchange rate risk is handled by the investor.

As we know from our discussion of derivatives, an investor may elect to cover or hedge their exposure to exchange rate risk by using a forward contract, and their decision then simplifies to a case of *riskless arbitrage*. On the other hand, an investor may choose not to use a forward, and instead wait to use a spot contract when their investment matures, whereupon their decision is a case of *risky arbitrage*. These two ways of doing arbitrage lead to two important implications, called *parity conditions*, which describe equilibria in the forward and spot markets. We now examine each one in turn.

Riskless Arbitrage: Covered Interest Parity

Suppose that forward contracts to exchange euros for dollars in one year's time carry an exchange rate of $F_{\$/€}$ dollars per euro. This is known as the **forward exchange rate**, and it allows investors to be absolutely sure of the price at which they can trade forex in the future.

Assume you are trading for the bank in New York, and you have to decide whether to invest \$1 for one year in either a dollar or euro bank deposit that pays interest. The interest rate offered in New York on dollar deposits is $i_\$$ and in Europe the interest rate offered on euro deposits is $i_€$. Which investment offers the higher return?

If you invest in a dollar deposit, your \$1 placed in a U.S. bank account will be worth $(1+i_\$)$ dollars in one year's time. The dollar value of principal and interest for the U.S. dollar bank deposit is called the *dollar return*. Note that we explicitly specify in what currency the return is measured, so that we may compare returns.

If you invest in a euro deposit, you first need to convert the dollar to euros. Using the spot exchange rate, \$1 buys $1/E_{\$/€}$ euros today. These $1/E_{\$/€}$ euros would be placed in a euro account earning $i_€$, so in a year's time they would be worth $(1+i_€)/E_{\$/€}$ euros. You would then convert the euros back into dollars, but you cannot know for sure what the future spot rate will be. To avoid that risk, you engage in a forward contract today to make the future transaction at a forward rate $F_{\$/€}$. The $(1+i_€)/E_{\$/€}$ euros you will have in one year's time can then be exchanged for $(1+i_€)F_{\$/€}/E_{\$/€}$ dollars, the dollar value of principal and interest, or the dollar return on the euro bank deposit.[10]

Three outcomes are possible when you compare the dollar returns from the two deposits: the U.S. deposit has a higher dollar return, the euro deposit has a higher dollar return, or both deposits have the same dollar return. In the first case, you would advise your bank to sell its euro deposits and buy dollar deposits; in the second case, you would advise the bank to sell its dollar deposits and buy euro deposits. Only in the third case is there no expected profit from arbitrage, so the corresponding no-arbitrage condition can be written as follows:

$$\text{Covered interest parity (CIP):}\quad \underbrace{(1+i_\$)}_{\substack{\text{Dollar return on}\\\text{dollar deposits}}} = \underbrace{(1+i_€)\frac{F_{\$/€}}{E_{\$/€}}}_{\substack{\text{Dollar return on}\\\text{euro deposits}}} \qquad (2\text{-}1)$$

---

[10] Note that this arbitrage strategy requires a spot and a forward contract. The two can be combined in a swap contract, and this helps explain the prevalence of swaps in the forex market.

FIGURE 2-8

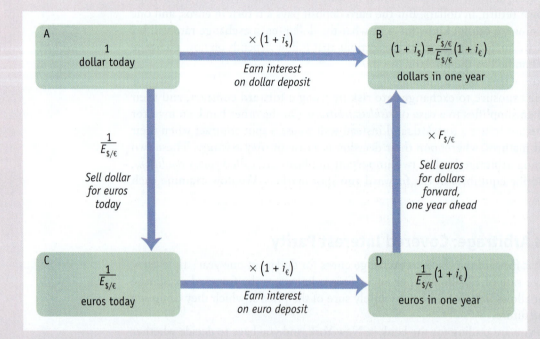

Arbitrage and Covered Interest Parity Under CIP, returns to holding dollar deposits accruing interest going along the path AB must equal the returns from investing in euros going along the path ACDB with risk removed by use of a forward contract. Hence, at B, the riskless payoff must be the same on both paths, and

$$(1 + i_\$) = \frac{F_{\$/€}}{E_{\$/€}}(1 + i_€).$$

This expression is called **covered interest parity (CIP)** because all exchange rate risk on the euro side has been "covered" by use of the forward contract. We say that such a trade employs *forward cover*. The condition is illustrated in Figure 2-8.

What Determines the Forward Rate? Covered interest parity is a no-arbitrage condition that describes an equilibrium in which investors are indifferent between the returns on interest-bearing bank deposits in two currencies and exchange risk has been eliminated by the use of a forward contract. Because one of the returns depends on the forward rate, covered interest parity can be seen as providing us with a theory of what determines the forward exchange rate. We can rearrange the Equation 2-1 and solve for the forward rate:

$$F_{\$/€} = E_{\$/€}\frac{1 + i_\$}{1 + i_€}$$

Thus, if covered interest parity holds, we can calculate the forward rate if we know all three right-hand-side variables: the spot rate $E_{\$/€}$, the dollar interest rate $i_\$$, and the euro interest rate $i_€$. For example, suppose the euro interest rate is 3%, the dollar interest rate is 5%, and the spot rate is $1.30 per euro. Then the preceding equation says the forward rate would be $1.30 \times (1.05)/(1.03) = 1.3252 per euro.

In practice, this is exactly how the forex market works and how the price of a forward contract is set. Traders at their computers all around the world can see the interest rates on bank deposits in each currency, and the spot exchange rate. We can now also see why the forward contract is called a "derivative" contract: to establish the price of the forward contract (the forward rate F), we first need to know the price of the spot contract (the spot rate E). That is, the pricing of the forward contract is derived from the pricing of the underlying spot contract, using additional information on interest rates.

This result raises a new question: How are the interest rates and the spot rate determined? We return to that question in a moment, after looking at some evidence to verify that covered interest parity does indeed hold.

APPLICATION

Evidence on Covered Interest Parity

Does covered interest parity hold? We expect returns to be equalized only if arbitrage is possible. But if governments impose capital controls, there is no way for traders to exploit profit opportunities and no reason for the returns on different currencies to equalize. Historical examples of such policies can provide illustration.

For example, Figure 2-9 shows that covered interest parity held for the United Kingdom and Germany after the two countries abolished their capital controls in the period from 1979 to 1981. (The German deposits shown here were denominated in marks prior to 1999; after 1999, the euro replaced the mark as the German currency.)

The chart shows the profit that could have been made (measured in percent per annum in British currency, before transaction costs) if the investor had been able to move funds from the United Kingdom to Germany with forward cover (or, when the line is in negative territory, the profit from moving funds from Germany to the

FIGURE 2-9

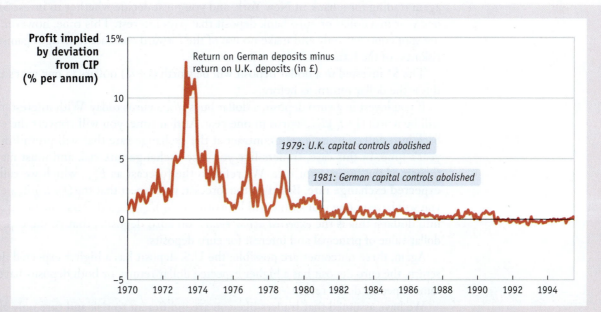

Financial Liberalization and Covered Interest Parity: Arbitrage Between the United Kingdom and Germany The chart shows the difference in monthly pound returns on deposits in British pounds and German marks using forward cover from 1970 to 1995. In the 1970s, the difference was positive and often large: traders would have profited from arbitrage by moving money from pound deposits to mark deposits, but capital controls prevented them from freely doing so.

After financial liberalization, these profits essentially vanished, and no arbitrage opportunities remained. The CIP condition held, aside from small deviations resulting from transactions costs and measurement errors.

Data from: Maurice Obstfeld and Alan M. Taylor, 2004, Global Capital Markets: Integration, Crisis, and Growth, Japan-U.S. Center Sanwa Monographs on International Financial Markets (Cambridge, U.K.: Cambridge University Press).

United Kingdom). From Equation (2-1), and using the symbol DM to denote the German mark, we know that the profit from this riskless arbitrage would be

$$\text{Profit} = \underbrace{(1 + i_{DM})\frac{F_{\pounds/DM}}{E_{\pounds/DM}}}_{\substack{\text{Pound return on} \\ \text{German deposits}}} - \underbrace{(1 + i_{\pounds})}_{\substack{\text{Pound return on} \\ \text{U.K. deposits}}}$$

This profit would be zero only if covered interest parity held. In the 1960s and 1970s, the *hypothetical* profits implied by this expression were large—or would have been had arbitrage been allowed. Instead, capital controls in both countries prevented arbitrage. Covered interest parity therefore failed to hold. Following the financial liberalization from 1979 to 1981, arbitrage became possible. From that time until the present, profits have been essentially zero (not exactly zero because of regulations, fees, other transaction costs, and measurement error). Once we allow for these factors, there are no profit opportunities left. Covered interest parity generally holds when capital markets are open, although since the global financial crisis of 2008, deviations have occasionally reappeared (but on a smaller scale than was seen in the 1970s) as banks' capacity to engage in international currency arbitrage has been more limited by tighter regulation of the risks they can take.

Risky Arbitrage: Uncovered Interest Parity

As we noted above, the second way to engage in arbitrage is to use spot contracts and accept that the future exchange rate is then subject to risk. We now examine this case, and by doing so, we will arrive at an understanding of how the exchange rate is determined in the spot market.

To keep things simple, let us suppose, for now, that investors focus *exclusively* on the expected dollar return of the two bank deposits and not on any other characteristics of the investment. (See **Side Bar: Assets and Their Attributes**.) Imagine you are once again trading for a bank in New York, and you must decide whether to invest $1 for one year in a dollar or euro bank deposit that pays interest. This time, however, you use spot contracts only and make no use of the forward contract to hedge against the riskiness of the future exchange rate.

The $1 invested in a dollar deposit will be worth $(1 + i_{\$})$ dollars in one year's time; this is the dollar return, as before.

If you invest in a euro deposit, a dollar buys $1/E_{\$/€}$ euros today. With interest, these will be worth $(1 + i_{€})/E_{\$/€}$ euros in one year. At that time, you will convert the euros back into dollars using a spot contract at the exchange rate that will prevail in one year's time. In this case, traders like you face exchange rate risk and must make a *forecast* of the future spot rate. We refer to the forecast as $E_{\$/€}^{e}$, which we call the **expected exchange rate**. Based on the forecast, you expect that the $(1 + i_{€})/E_{\$/€}$ euros you will have in one year's time will be worth $(1 + i_{€})E_{\$/€}^{e}/E_{\$/€}$ dollars when converted into dollars; this is the *expected dollar return* on euro deposits, that is, the expected dollar value of principal and interest for euro deposits.

Again, three outcomes are possible: the U.S. deposit has a higher expected dollar return, the euro deposit has a higher expected dollar return, or both deposits have the same expected dollar return.

We have assumed that traders like you are indifferent to risk and care only about expected returns. Thus, in the first two cases, you have expected profit opportunities and risky arbitrage is possible: you would sell the deposit with the low expected return and buy the deposit with the higher expected return. Only in the third case is there no expected profit from arbitrage. This no-arbitrage condition can be written as follows:

$$\text{Uncovered interest parity (UIP):} \quad \underbrace{(1 + i_{\$})}_{\substack{\text{Dollar return on} \\ \text{dollar deposits}}} = \underbrace{(1 + i_{€})\frac{E_{\$/€}^{e}}{E_{\$/€}}}_{\substack{\text{Expected dollar return} \\ \text{on euro deposits}}} \tag{2-2}$$

Assets and Their Attributes

The bank deposits traded in the forex market pay interest and are part of the wider portfolio of assets held by banks and other private actors. As we have argued, the forex market is heavily influenced by the demand for these deposits as assets.

An investor's entire portfolio of assets may include stocks, bonds, real estate, art, bank deposits in various currencies, and so on. What influences the demand for all these different kinds of assets? Viewed from a financial viewpoint (i.e., setting aside the beauty of a painting or seaside mansion), all assets have three key attributes that influence demand: return, risk, and liquidity.

An asset's **rate of return** is the total net fractional increase in wealth (measured in a given currency) resulting from holding the asset for a specified period, typically one year. For example, you start the year by buying one share of DotBomb Inc., a hot Internet stock, for $100. At year's end, the share is worth $150 and has paid you a dividend of $5. Your total return is $55: a $50 capital gain from the change in the stock price plus a $5 dividend. Your total annual rate of return is 55/100, or 55%. The next year, the stock falls from $150 to $75 and pays no dividend. You lose half of your money in the second year: your rate of return for that year equals −75/150, or −50%. All else equal, investors prefer investments with high returns.

The **risk** of an asset refers to the volatility of its rate of return. The **liquidity** of an asset refers to the ease and speed with which it can be liquidated, or sold. A stock may seem to have high risk because its rate of return bounces up and down a lot, but its risk must be considered in relation to the riskiness of other investments. Its degree of risk could be contrasted with the rate of interest your bank offers on a money market deposit, a return that is usually very stable over time. You will lose your bank deposit only if your bank fails, which is unlikely. Your bank deposit is also very liquid. You can go to a cash machine or write a check to instantly access that form of wealth. In contrast, a work of art, say, is much less liquid. To sell the art for the greatest amount, you usually need the services of an auctioneer. Art is also risky. Works by different artists go in and out of fashion. All else equal, investors prefer assets with low risk and high liquidity.

This discussion of an asset's attributes allows us to make two observations. First, because all else is never equal, investors are willing to trade off among these attributes. You may be willing to hold a relatively risky and illiquid asset if you expect it will pay a relatively high return. Second, what you expect matters. Most investments, like stocks or art, do not have a fixed, predictable, guaranteed rate of return. As a result, all investors have to forecast. We refer to the forecast of the rate of return as the **expected rate of return**.

This expression is called **uncovered interest parity (UIP)** because exchange rate risk has been left "uncovered" by the decision not to hedge against exchange rate risk by using a forward contract and instead simply wait to use a spot contract in a year's time. The condition is illustrated in Figure 2-10.

What Determines the Spot Rate? Uncovered interest parity is a no-arbitrage condition that describes an equilibrium in which investors are indifferent between the returns on unhedged interest-bearing bank deposits in two currencies (where forward contracts are not employed). Because one of the returns depends on the spot rate, uncovered interest parity can be seen as providing us with a theory of what determines the spot exchange rate. We can rearrange the above equation and solve for the spot rate:

$$E_{\$/€} = E_{\$/€}^e \, \frac{1+i_€}{1+i_\$}$$

Thus, if uncovered interest parity holds, we can calculate today's spot rate if we know all three right-hand-side variables: the expected future exchange rate $E_{\$/€}^e$; the dollar interest rate $i_\$$; and the euro interest rate $i_€$. For example, suppose the euro interest rate is 2%, the dollar interest rate is 4%, and the expected future spot rate is $1.40 per euro. Then the preceding equation says today's spot rate would be $1.40 \times (1.02)/(1.04) = \$1.3731$ per euro.

However, this result raises more questions: How can the expected future exchange rate $E_{\$/€}^e$ be forecast? And, as we asked in the case of covered interest parity, how are the two interest rates determined?

In the next two chapters, we address these unanswered questions, as we continue to develop the building blocks needed for a complete theory of exchange

FIGURE 2-10

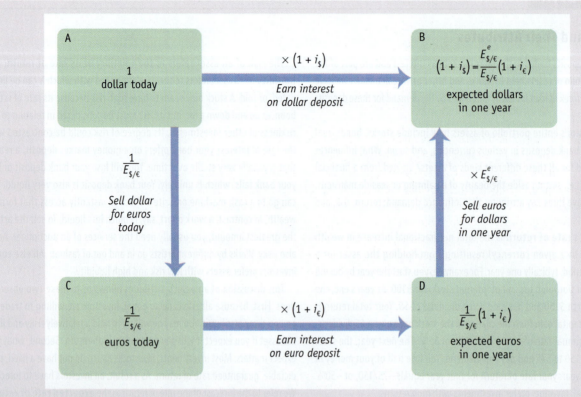

Arbitrage and Uncovered Interest Parity Under UIP, returns to holding dollar deposits accruing interest going along the path AB must equal the *expected* returns from investing in euros going along the risky path ACDB. Hence, at B, the expected payoff must be the same on both paths, and $(1+i_\$) = \dfrac{E^e_{\$/€}}{E_{\$/€}}(1+i_€)$.

rate determination. We start by looking at the determinants of the expected future exchange rate $E^e_{\$/€}$, and developing a model of exchange rates in the long run, and then by looking at the determinants of the interest rates $i_\$$ and $i_€$. We will soon learn that future expectations make the solution of forward-looking economic problems tricky: we have to solve backward from the future to the present, and this motivates the order of the material in this textbook—we must understand exchange rates in the long run before we can understand them in the short run.

APPLICATION

Evidence on Uncovered Interest Parity

Does uncovered interest parity hold? The two interest parity equations seen previously are very similar. Equation (2-1), the CIP equation, uses the forward rate; Equation (2-2), the UIP equation, uses the expected future spot rate:

$$\text{CIP: } (1+i_\$) = (1+i_€)\frac{F_{\$/€}}{E_{\$/€}}$$

$$\text{UIP: } (1+i_\$) = (1+i_€)\frac{E^e_{\$/€}}{E_{\$/€}}$$

To allow us to see what this implies about the relationship between the expected future spot rate and the forward rate, we divide the second equation by the first, to obtain

$$1 = E^e_{\$/\euro}/F_{\$/\euro}, \text{ or}$$
$$F_{\$/\euro} = E^e_{\$/\euro}$$

The expected future spot rate and the forward rate are distinct concepts. They are also the instruments employed in two different forms of arbitrage—risky and riskless. But, in equilibrium, *under the assumptions we have made*, we now see that they should not differ at all; they should be exactly the same!

Thus, if *both* covered interest parity *and* uncovered interest parity hold, an important relationship emerges: *the forward rate $F_{\$/\euro}$ must equal the expected future spot rate $E^e_{\$/\euro}$*. The result is intuitive. In equilibrium, and *if investors do not care about risk* (as we have assumed in our presentation of UIP), then they have no reason to prefer to avoid risk by using the forward rate, or to embrace risk by awaiting the future spot rate; for them to be indifferent, as market equilibrium requires, the two rates must be equal.

With this result we can find an approach to testing UIP that is fairly easy to describe and implement. Because the evidence in favor of CIP is strong, as we have seen, we may assume that it holds. In that case, the previous equation then provides a test for whether UIP holds. But if the forward rate equals the expected spot rate, then we can also express this equivalence relative to today's spot rate, to show that the **expected rate of depreciation** (between today and the future period) equals the **forward premium** (the proportional difference between the forward and spot rates):

$$\underbrace{\frac{F_{\$/\euro}}{E_{\$/\euro}} - 1}_{\substack{\text{Forward} \\ \text{premium}}} = \underbrace{\frac{E^e_{\$/\euro}}{E_{\$/\euro}} - 1}_{\substack{\text{Expected rate} \\ \text{of depreciation}}}$$

For example, if the spot rate is $1.00 per euro, and the forward rate is $1.05, the forward premium is 5%. But if $F_{\$/\euro} = E^e_{\$/\euro}$, the expected future spot rate is also $1.05, and there is a 5% expected rate of depreciation.

We can easily observe the left-hand side of the preceding equation, the forward premium, because both the current spot and forward rates are data we can collect in the market. The difficulty is on the right-hand side: we typically cannot observe expectations. Still, the test can be attempted using surveys in which traders are asked to report their expectations. Using data from one such test, Figure 2-11 shows a strong correlation between expected rates of depreciation and the forward premium, with a slope close to 1. Because expected depreciation does not always equal the interest differential, the points do not lie exactly on the 45-degree line. Does this mean that arbitrage is not working? Not necessarily. The deviations may be caused by sampling errors or noise (differences in opinion of individual traders). In addition, there may be limits to risky arbitrage in the real world because of various factors such as transactions costs (market frictions) and aversion to risk, which we have so far neglected, but which we discuss in more detail in later chapters. That the slope "on average" is close to 1 provides some support for UIP.

Uncovered Interest Parity: A Useful Approximation

Because it provides a theory of how the spot exchange rate is determined, the uncovered interest parity equation (2-2) is one of the most important conditions in international macroeconomics. Yet for most purposes, a simpler and more convenient concept can be used.

The intuition behind the approximation is as follows. Holding dollar deposits rewards the investor with dollar interest. Holding euro deposits rewards investors in two ways: they receive euro interest, but they also receive a gain (or loss) on euros equal

FIGURE 2-11

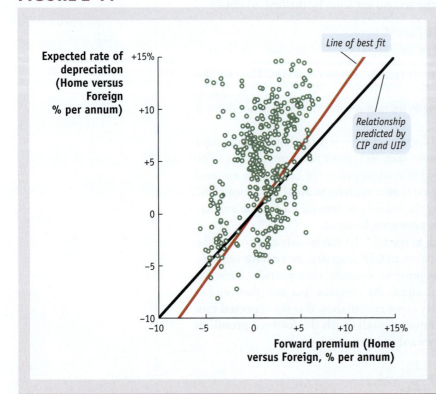

Expected rate of depreciation (Home versus Foreign % per annum)

Forward premium (Home versus Foreign, % per annum)

Evidence on Interest Parity When UIP and CIP hold, the 12-month forward premium should equal the 12-month expected rate of depreciation. A scatterplot showing these two variables should be close to the diagonal 45-degree line. Using evidence from surveys of individual forex traders' expectations over the period 1988 to 1993, UIP finds some support, as the line of best fit is close to the diagonal.

Notes: Line of best fit is through the origin. Data are monthly for the German mark, Swiss franc, Japanese yen, British pound, and Canadian dollar against the U.S. dollar from February 1988 to October 1993.

Data from: Menzie Chinn and Jeffrey A. Frankel, 2002, "Survey Data on Exchange Rate Expectations: More Currencies, More Horizons, More Tests," in W. Allen and D. Dickinson, eds., Monetary Policy, Capital Flows and Financial Market Developments in the Era of Financial Globalisation: Essays in Honour of Max Fry (London: Routledge), pp. 145–67.

to the rate of euro appreciation that approximately equals the rate of dollar depreciation. Thus, for UIP to hold, and for an investor to be indifferent between dollar deposits and euro deposits, any interest shortfall (excess) on the euro side must be offset by an expected gain (loss) in the form of euro appreciation or dollar depreciation.

We can write the approximation formally as follows:

$$\text{UIP approximation:} \quad \underbrace{i_\$}_{\substack{\text{Interest rate} \\ \text{on dollar} \\ \text{deposits} = \\ \text{Dollar rate} \\ \text{of return on} \\ \text{dollar deposits}}} = \underbrace{\underbrace{i_\euro}_{\substack{\text{Interest rate} \\ \text{on euro deposits}}} + \underbrace{\frac{\Delta E^e_{\$/\euro}}{E_{\$/\euro}}}_{\substack{\text{Expected rate of} \\ \text{depreciation of the} \\ \text{dollar}}}}_{\substack{\text{Expected dollar rate of} \\ \text{return on euro deposits}}} \qquad (2\text{-}3)$$

There are three terms in this equation. The left-hand side is the interest rate on dollar deposits. The first term on the right is the interest rate on euro deposits. The second term on the right can be expanded as $\Delta E^e_{\$/\euro}/E_{\$/\euro} = (E^e_{\$/\euro} - E_{\$/\euro})/E_{\$/\euro}$ and is the expected fractional change in the euro's value, or the expected rate of appreciation of the euro. As we have seen, this expression equals the appreciation of the euro exactly, but for small changes it approximately equals the expected rate of depreciation of the dollar.[11]

---

[11] To derive Equation (2-3), we can write $E^e_{\$/\euro}/E_{\$/\euro} = (1 + \Delta E^e_{\$/\euro}/E_{\$/\euro})$, so Equation (2-2) becomes

$$1 + i_\$ = (1 + i_\euro)\left(1 + \frac{\Delta E^e_{\$/\euro}}{E_{\$/\euro}}\right) = 1 + i_\euro + \frac{\Delta E^e_{\$/\euro}}{E_{\$/\euro}} + \left[i_\euro \frac{\Delta E^e_{\$/\euro}}{E_{\$/\euro}}\right]$$

When the euro interest rate and the expected rate of depreciation are small, the last term in brackets is very small and may be neglected in an approximation. We can then cancel out the 1 that appears in the first and third terms of the above equation to obtain Equation (2-3).

The UIP approximation equation, Equation (2-3), says that the home interest rate equals the foreign interest rate plus the expected rate of depreciation of the home currency.

A numerical example illustrates the UIP approximation formula. Suppose the dollar interest rate is 4% per year and the euro interest rate is 3% per year. If UIP is to hold, then the expected rate of dollar depreciation over a year must be 1%. In that case, a dollar investment put into euros for a year will grow by 3% because of euro interest and in dollar terms will grow by an extra 1% because of euro appreciation, so the total dollar return on the euro deposit is approximately equal to the 4% that is offered by dollar deposits.[12]

To sum up, the uncovered interest parity condition, whether in its exact form (2-2) or its approximate form (2-3), states that there must be parity between expected returns, *expressed in a common currency*, in the two markets.

Summary

All economic models produce an output (some unknown or *endogenous* variable to be explained) and require a set of inputs (some known or *exogenous* variables that are treated as given). The two interest parity conditions provide us with models that explain how the prices of the two most important forex contracts are determined in market equilibrium with no arbitrage possibilities. Uncovered interest parity applies to the spot market and determines the spot rate, based on interest rates and exchange rate expectations. Covered interest parity applies to the forward market and determines the forward rate based on interest rates and the spot rate. Figure 2-12 sums up what we have learned.

FIGURE 2-12

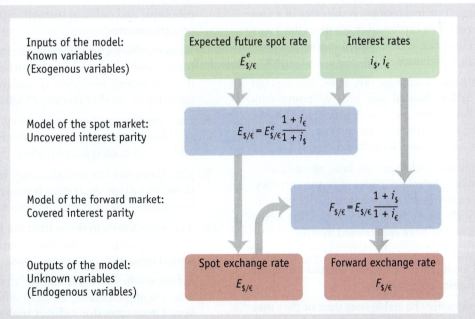

How Interest Parity Relationships Explain Spot and Forward Rates In the spot market, UIP provides a model of how the spot exchange rate is determined. To use UIP to find the spot rate, we need to know the expected future spot rate and the prevailing interest rates for the two currencies. In the forward market, CIP provides a model of how the forward exchange rate is determined. When we use CIP, we derive the forward rate from the current spot rate (from UIP) and the interest rates for the two currencies.

---

[12] Note that the $1 investment in euros will be worth $(1.03) \times (1.01) = \$1.0403$ after one year, which is very close to $1.04, the value of the dollar deposit after one year. The difference is just the approximation error. See the previous footnote.

6 Conclusions

The forex market has a long and often tumultuous record, and, in today's globalized world, exchange rates matter more than ever. They affect the prices of international transactions, can be a focus of government policy, and often play a major role in economic and political crises.

This chapter has set the stage for our study of exchange rates. We learned what exchange rates are and how they are used. We have also seen how they have behaved in reality under different exchange rate regimes. History shows a vast range of past experiences, and this experimentation continues.

These observations underscore the importance of understanding different regimes and their causes and consequences. We have prepared ourselves by examining the workings of the forex market in some detail. Government intervention (or its absence) in this market determines the nature of the exchange rate regime in operation, from fixed to floating. The workings of actors in the forex market then ultimately determine equilibrium values of exchange rates.

How is forex market equilibrium determined? We have learned that there are two key economic forces at work in the forex market: expectations and arbitrage. Through expectations, news about the future can affect expected returns. Through arbitrage, differences in expected returns are equalized, as summed up by the two important interest parity conditions, covered interest parity and uncovered interest parity. In the next two chapters, we build on these ideas to develop a complete theory of exchange rates.

KEY POINTS

1. The exchange rate in a country is the price of a unit of foreign currency expressed in terms of the home currency. This price is determined in the spot market for foreign exchange.

2. When the home exchange rate rises, less foreign currency is bought/sold per unit of home currency; the home currency has depreciated. If home currency buys $x\%$ less foreign currency, the home currency is said to have depreciated by $x\%$.

3. When the home exchange rate falls, more foreign currency is bought/sold per unit of home currency; the home currency has appreciated. If home currency buys $x\%$ more foreign currency, the home currency is said to have appreciated by $x\%$.

4. The exchange rate is used to convert the prices of goods and assets into a common currency to allow meaningful price comparisons.

5. Exchange rates may be stable over time or they may fluctuate. History supplies examples of the former (fixed exchange rate regimes) and the latter (floating exchange rate regimes), as well as a number of intermediate regime types.

6. An exchange rate crisis occurs when the exchange rate experiences a sudden and large depreciation. These events are often associated with broader economic and political turmoil, especially in developing countries.

7. Some countries may forgo a national currency to form a currency union with other nations (e.g., the Eurozone), or they may unilaterally adopt the currency of another country ("dollarization").

8. Looking across all countries today, numerous fixed and floating rate regimes are observed, so we must understand both types of regime.

9. The forex market is dominated by spot transactions, but many derivative contracts exist, such as forwards, swaps, futures, and options.

10. The main actors in the market are private investors and (frequently) government authorities, represented usually by the central bank.

11. Arbitrage on currencies means that spot exchange rates are approximately equal in different forex markets. Cross rates (for indirect trades) and spot rates (for direct trades) are also approximately equal.

12. Riskless interest arbitrage leads to the covered interest parity (CIP) condition. CIP says that the dollar return on dollar deposits must equal the dollar return on euro deposits, where forward contracts are used to cover exchange rate risk.

13. Covered interest parity says that the forward rate is determined by home and foreign interest rates and the spot exchange rate.

14. Risky interest arbitrage leads to the uncovered interest parity (UIP) condition. UIP says that when spot contracts are used and exchange rate risk is not covered, the dollar return on dollar deposits must equal the expected dollar returns on euro deposits.

15. Uncovered interest parity explains how the spot rate is determined by the home and foreign interest rates and the expected future spot exchange rate.

KEY TERMS

exchange rate, p. 22
appreciation, p. 24
depreciation, p. 24
effective exchange rate, p. 26
exchange rate regimes, p. 29
fixed (or pegged) exchange rate regime, p. 29
floating (or flexible) exchange rate regime, p. 29
free float, p. 30
band, p. 30
managed float, p. 31
exchange rate crises, p. 31
crawl, p. 32
currency (or monetary) union, p. 32
dollarization, p. 32
currency board, p. 33

foreign exchange (forex or FX) market, p. 34
spot contract, p. 34
spot exchange rate, p. 34
spread, p. 35
market friction, p. 35
transaction cost, p. 35
derivatives, p. 35
forward, p. 35
commercial banks, p. 36
interbank trading, p. 36
corporations, p. 36
nonbank financial institutions, p. 36
capital control, p. 36
official market, p. 37
black market, p. 37
intervention, p. 37

arbitrage, p. 37
equilibrium, p. 38
no-arbitrage condition, p. 38
cross rate, p. 39
vehicle currency, p. 40
forward exchange rate, p. 41
covered interest parity (CIP), p. 42
expected exchange rate, p. 44
rate of return, p. 45
risk, p. 45
liquidity, p. 45
expected rate of return, p. 45
uncovered interest parity (UIP), p. 45
expected rate of depreciation, p. 47
forward premium, p. 47

PROBLEMS

1. **Discovering Data** Not all pegs are created equal! In this question you will explore trends in exchange rates. Go to the St. Louis Federal Reserve's Economic Data (FRED) website at https://research.stlouisfed.org/fred2/ and access the United States exchange rates with Venezuela, India, and Hong Kong from 1990 to present. These can be found most easily by searching for the country names and "daily exchange rate." (*Hint*: Most of the answers in this question can be gleaned from the interactive chart tool, without staring at the raw numbers.)

    a. Plot the Indian rupee to U.S. dollar exchange rate over this period. For what years does the rupee appear to be pegged to the dollar? Does this peg break? If so, how many times?

    b. How would you characterize the relationship between the rupee and the dollar from 1998 to 2008? Does it appear to be fixed, crawling, or floating during this period? How would you characterize it from 2008 onward?

    c. The Hong Kong dollar has maintained its peg with the United States dollar since 1983. Over the course of the period you have downloaded, what are the highest and lowest values for this exchange rate?

    d. Venezuela has been less successful in its attempts to fix its official exchange rate against the dollar. Since 1995 how many times has the Venezuelan bolívar peg to the dollar broken? What is the average length of a peg? What is roughly the average size of a devaluation in the 12 months following each peg break?

2. Refer to the exchange rates given in the following table:

Country (currency)	January 20, 2016		January 20, 2015	
	FX per $	FX per £	FX per €	FX per $
Australia (dollar)	1.459	2.067	1.414	1.223
Canada (dollar)	1.451	2.056	1.398	1.209
Denmark (krone)	6.844	9.694	7.434	6.430
Eurozone (euro)	0.917	1.299	1.000	0.865
Hong Kong (dollar)	7.827	11.086	8.962	7.752
India (rupee)	68.05	96.39	71.60	61.64
Japan (yen)	116.38	164.84	136.97	118.48
Mexico (peso)	18.60	26.346	16.933	14.647
Sweden (krona)	8.583	12.157	9.458	8.181
United Kingdom (pound)	0.706	1.000	0.763	0.660
United States (dollar)	1.000	1.416	1.156	1.000

Data from: U.S. Federal Reserve Board of Governors, H.10 release: Foreign Exchange Rates.

Based on the table provided, answer the following questions:

a. Compute the U.S. dollar–yen exchange rate $E_{\$/¥}$ and the U.S. dollar–Canadian dollar exchange rate $E_{\$/C\$}$ on January 20, 2016, and January 20, 2015.

b. What happened to the value of the U.S. dollar relative to the Japanese yen and Canadian dollar between January 20, 2015, and January 20, 2016? Compute the percentage change in the value of the U.S. dollar relative to each currency using the U.S. dollar–foreign currency exchange rates you computed in (a).

c. Using the information in the table for January 20, 2016, compute the Danish krone–Canadian dollar exchange rate $E_{krone/C\$}$.

d. Visit the website of the Board of Governors of the Federal Reserve System at http://www.federalreserve.gov/. Click on "Data" and then "Foreign Exchange Rates - H.10/G.5" for the latest weekly data. What has happened to the value of the U.S. dollar relative to the Canadian dollar, Japanese yen, and Danish krone since January 20, 2016?

e. Using the information from (d), what has happened to the value of the U.S. dollar relative to the British pound and the euro? *Note:* The H.10 release quotes these exchange rates as U.S. dollars per unit of foreign currency in line with long-standing market conventions.

3. Consider the United States and the countries it trades with the most (measured in trade volume): Canada, Mexico, China, and Japan. For simplicity, assume these are the only four countries with which the United States trades. Trade shares (trade weights) and U.S. nominal exchange rates for these four countries are as follows:

Country (currency)	Share of Trade	$ per FX in 2015	$ per FX in 2016
Canada (dollar)	36%	0.8271	0.6892
Mexico (peso)	28%	0.0683	0.0538
China (yuan)	20%	0.1608	0.1522
Japan (yen)	16%	0.0080	0.0086

a. Compute the percentage change from 2015 to 2016 in the four U.S. bilateral exchange rates (defined as U.S. dollars per unit of foreign exchange, or FX) in the table provided.

b. Use the trade shares as weights to compute the percentage change in the nominal effective exchange rate for the United States between 2015 and 2016 (in U.S. dollars per foreign currency basket).

c. Based on your answer to (b), what happened to the value of the U.S. dollar against this basket between 2015 and 2016? How does this compare with the change in the value of the U.S. dollar relative to the Mexican peso? Explain your answer.

4. Go back to the FRED website: https://research.stlouisfed.org/fred2/. Locate the monthly exchange rate data for the following:

a. Canada (dollar), 1980–2012

b. China (yuan), 1999–2004, 2005–09, and 2009–10

c. Mexico (peso), 1993–95 and 1995–2012

d. Thailand (baht), 1986–97 and 1997–2012

e. Venezuela (bolivar), 2003–12

Look at the graphs and make your own judgment as to whether each currency was fixed (peg or band), crawling (peg or band), or floating relative to the U.S. dollar during each time frame given.

5. Describe the different ways in which the government may intervene in the forex market. Why does the government have the ability to intervene in this way, while private actors do not?

6. Suppose quotes for the dollar–euro exchange rate $E_{\$/€}$ are as follows: in New York $1.05 per euro, and in Tokyo $1.15 per euro. Describe how investors use arbitrage to take advantage of the difference in exchange rates. Explain how this process will affect the dollar price of the euro in New York and Tokyo.

WORK IT OUT  Achieve | interactive activity

7. Consider a Dutch investor with 1,000 euros to place in a bank deposit in either the Netherlands or Great Britain. The (one-year) interest rate on bank deposits is 1% in Britain and 5% in the Netherlands. The (one-year) forward euro–pound exchange rate is 1.65 euros per pound, and the spot rate is 1.5 euros per pound. Answer the following questions, using the *exact* equations for uncovered interest parity (UIP) and covered interest parity (CIP) as necessary.

a. What is the euro-denominated return on Dutch deposits for this investor?

b. What is the (riskless) euro-denominated return on British deposits for this investor using forward cover?

c. Is there an arbitrage opportunity here? Explain why or why not. Is this an equilibrium in the forward exchange rate market?

d. If the spot rate is 1.5 euros per pound, and interest rates are as stated previously, what is the equilibrium forward rate, according to CIP?

e. Suppose the forward rate takes the value given by your answer to (d). Compute the forward premium on the British pound for the Dutch investor (where exchange rates are in euros per pound). Is it positive or negative? Why do investors require this premium/discount in equilibrium?

f. If UIP holds, what is the expected depreciation of the euro (against the pound) over one year?

g. Based on your answer to (f), what is the expected euro–pound exchange rate one year ahead?

8. You are a financial adviser to a U.S. corporation that expects to receive a payment of 60 million Japanese yen in 180 days for goods exported to Japan. The current spot rate is 100 yen per U.S. dollar ($E_{\$/¥} = 0.01000$). You are concerned that the U.S. dollar is going to appreciate against the yen over the next six months.

a. Assuming the exchange rate remains unchanged, how much does your firm expect to receive in U.S. dollars?

b. How much would your firm receive (in U.S. dollars) if the dollar appreciated to 110 yen per U.S. dollar ($E_{\$/¥} = 0.00909$)?

c. Describe how you could use a forward contract to hedge against the risk of losses associated with the potential appreciation in the U.S. dollar.

9. Consider how transactions costs affect foreign currency exchange. Rank each of the following foreign exchanges according to their probable spread (between the "buy at" and "sell for" bilateral exchange rates) and justify your ranking.

a. An American returning from a trip to Turkey wants to exchange his Turkish lira for U.S. dollars at the airport.

b. Citigroup and HSBC, both large commercial banks located in the United States and United Kingdom, respectively, need to clear several large checks drawn on accounts held by each bank.

c. Honda Motor Company needs to exchange yen for U.S. dollars to pay American workers at its Ohio manufacturing plant.

d. A Canadian tourist in Germany pays for her hotel room using a credit card.

3

Exchange Rates I: The Monetary Approach in the Long Run

Our willingness to pay a certain price for foreign money must ultimately and essentially be due to the fact that this money possesses a purchasing power as against commodities and services in that foreign country.

Gustav Cassel, of the Swedish school of economics, 1922

The fundamental things apply / As time goes by.

Herman Hupfeld, songwriter, 1931 (featured in the film *Casablanca*, 1942)

Questions to Consider

1 In the long run, how does goods market arbitrage link the purchasing power of currencies and their exchange rates?

2 How does the supply and demand for money in turn affect the purchasing power of currencies?

3 Given how these forces work, what factors influence the monetary and exchange rate choices made by policymakers?

The cost of living is usually rising, but it rises in some places more than others. From 1990 to 2010, for example, a standardized Canadian basket of consumer goods rose in price. Suppose that in 1990 a Canadian would have spent C$116 (116 Canadian dollars, or "loonies") to purchase this basket; by 2010 the same basket cost C$173. Thus, Canadian prices rose by 49%. Over the same period, in the United States, a standardized U.S. basket of goods that cost $100 in 1990 had risen in cost to $167 by 2010. Thus, U.S. prices saw a much larger increase of 67%. Both countries witnessed inflation, but U.S. prices rose more.

Did these price changes cause U.S. goods to appear relatively expensive? Would they have caused Canadians to start spending less on U.S. goods, or Americans to spend more on Canadian goods?

The answer to these questions is no. In 1990 $1 was worth C$1.16. So in 1990 both baskets cost the same *when their cost was expressed in a common currency*, namely C$116 = $100. By 2010, however, the Canadian dollar had appreciated relative to its 1990 value and only C$1.04 was needed to buy $1.00. Thus, the $167 U.S. basket in 2010 would actually have cost only $167 × 1.04 = C$174 when expressed in Canadian currency—almost the same price as the C$173 Canadian basket! (Expressed in U.S. currency, the Canadian basket cost about 173/1.04 = $166, almost the same as the $167 U.S. basket.)

In this example, although U.S. prices rose about 12% more than Canadian prices, Canadian residents also found that each of their loonies could buy about 12% more

U.S. dollars. Equivalently, Canadian prices rose about 12% less than U.S. prices, but U.S. consumers found that their dollars bought 12% fewer Canadian dollars. From either point of view, the cost of the baskets in each country *expressed in U.S. dollars* rose by about the same amount; the same was true with prices expressed in Canadian dollars. Economists (such as Gustav Cassel, quoted at the opening of this chapter) would say that the relative *purchasing power* of each currency (in terms of U.S. versus Canadian goods) had remained the same.

Was it just a pure coincidence that the changes in prices and exchange rates turned out that way? Perhaps not. Indeed, one of the oldest and most fundamental macroeconomic theories, dating back to the sixteenth century, asserts that this outcome is *not* a coincidence at all—and predicts that *in the long run*, prices and exchange rates will always adjust so that the purchasing power of each currency remains comparable over baskets of goods in different countries (as here, where U.S. and Canadian dollars could purchase comparable amounts of goods in 1990, and also in 2010). This hypothesis, which we explore in this chapter, provides another key building block in the theory of how exchange rates are determined. In the last chapter, uncovered interest parity provided us with a theory of how the spot exchange rate is determined, given knowledge of three variables: the expected future exchange rate, the home interest rate, and the foreign interest rate. In this chapter we look at the long run to see how the expected future exchange rate is determined; then, in the next chapter, we turn to the short run and discuss how interest rates are determined in each country. When all the pieces are put together, we will have a complete theory of how exchange rates are determined in the short run and in the long run.

If investors are to make forecasts of future exchange rates, they need a plausible theory of how exchange rates are determined in the long run. The theory we develop in this chapter has two parts. The first part involves the theory of purchasing power, which links the exchange rate to price levels in each country in the long run. This theory provides a partial explanation of the determinants of long-run exchange rates, but it raises another question: How are price levels determined? In the second part of the chapter, we explore how price levels are related to monetary conditions in each country. Combining the monetary theory of price level determination with the purchasing power theory of exchange rate determination, we emerge with a *long-run* theory known as the **monetary approach to exchange rates**. The goal of this chapter is to set out the long-run relationships between money, prices, and exchange rates.

1 Exchange Rates and Prices in the Long Run: Purchasing Power Parity and Goods Market Equilibrium

Just as arbitrage occurs in the international market for financial assets, it also occurs in the international markets for goods. An implication of complete goods market arbitrage would be that the prices of goods in different countries expressed in a common currency must be equalized. When applied to a single good, this property is called the *law of one price*. When applied to an entire basket of goods, this property is called *purchasing power parity*.

Why should these "laws" hold? If the price of a good is not the same in two locations, buyers will rush to buy at the cheap location (forcing prices up there) and avoid buying from the expensive location (forcing prices down there). Some factors, such as the costs of transporting goods between locations, may hinder the process of arbitrage, and more refined models take such *frictions* into account. For now our goal is to develop a simple yet useful theory based on an idealized world of *frictionless trade* where transaction costs can be neglected. We start at the microeconomic level with single goods and the law of one price. We then move to the macroeconomic level to consider baskets of goods and purchasing power parity.

The Law of One Price

The **law of one price (LOOP)** states that in the absence of trade frictions (such as transport costs and tariffs), and under conditions of free competition and price flexibility (where no individual seller or buyer has the power to manipulate prices and prices can freely adjust), identical goods sold in different locations must sell for the same price *when prices are expressed in a common currency.*

To see how the law of one price operates, consider the trade in diamonds that takes place between the United States and the Netherlands. Suppose that a diamond of a given quality is priced at €5,000 in the Amsterdam market, and the exchange rate is $1.20 per euro. If the law of one price holds, the same-quality diamond should sell in New York for (€5,000 per diamond) × (1.20 $/€) = $6,000 per diamond.

Why will the prices be the same? Under competitive conditions and frictionless trade, arbitrage will ensure this outcome. If diamonds were more expensive in New York, arbitragers would buy at a low price in Amsterdam and sell at a high price in Manhattan. If Dutch prices were higher, arbitragers would profit from the reverse trade. *By definition*, in a market equilibrium there are no arbitrage opportunities. If diamonds can be freely moved between New York and Amsterdam, both markets must offer the same price. Economists refer to this situation in the two locations as an *integrated market*.

We can mathematically state the law of one price as follows, for the case of any good g sold in two locations, say, Europe (EUR, meaning the Eurozone) and the United States (US). The *relative price* of good g (denoted $q^g_{US/EUR}$) is the ratio of the good's price in Europe relative to the good's price in the United States where both prices are expressed in a common currency.

Using subscripts to indicate locations and currencies, the relative price can be written

$$\underbrace{q^g_{US/EUR}}_{\substack{\text{Relative price of good } g \text{ in} \\ \text{Europe versus United States}}} = \underbrace{(E_{\$/€} P^g_{EUR})}_{\substack{\text{European price} \\ \text{of good } g \text{ in } \$}} / \underbrace{P^g_{US}}_{\substack{\text{U.S. price} \\ \text{of good } g \text{ in } \$}}$$

where P^g_{US} is the good's price in the United States, P^g_{EUR} is the good's price in Europe, and $E_{\$/€}$ is the dollar–euro exchange rate used to convert euro prices into dollar prices.

Notice that $q^g_{US/EUR}$ expresses the rate at which goods can be exchanged: it tells us how many units of the U.S. good are needed to purchase one unit of the same good in Europe (hence, the subscript uses the notation *US/EUR*). This contrasts with the nominal exchange rate $E_{\$/€}$ which expresses the rate at which currencies can be exchanged ($/€).

The law of one price may or may not hold. Recall from Chapter 2 that there are three possibilities in an arbitrage situation of this kind: the ratio exceeds 1 and the good is costlier in Europe; the ratio is less than 1 and the good is cheaper in Europe; or $E_{\$/€} P^g_{EUR} = P^g_{US}$, the ratio is $q^g_{US/EUR} = 1$, and the good is the same price in both locations. Only in the final case is there no arbitrage, the condition that defines market equilibrium. In equilibrium, European and U.S. prices, expressed in the same currency, are equal; the relative price q equals 1, and the law of one price holds.

How does the law of one price further our understanding of exchange rates? We can rearrange the equation for price equality, $E_{\$/€} P^g_{EUR} = P^g_{US}$, to show that if the law of one price holds, then the exchange rate must equal the ratio of the goods' prices expressed in the two currencies:

$$\underbrace{E_{\$/\euro}}_{\substack{\text{Exchange} \\ \text{rate}}} = \underbrace{P_{US}^{g}/P_{EUR}^{g}}_{\substack{\text{Ratio of} \\ \text{goods' prices}}}$$

One final word of caution: given our concerns in the previous chapter about the right way to define the exchange rate, we must take care when using expressions that are ratios to ensure that the units on each side of the equation correspond. In the last equation, we know we have it right because the left-hand side is expressed in dollars per euro and the right-hand side is also a ratio of dollars to euros ($ per unit of goods divided by € per unit of goods).

Purchasing Power Parity

The principle of **purchasing power parity (PPP)** is the macroeconomic counterpart to the microeconomic law of one price. The law of one price relates exchange rates to the relative prices of an individual good, while purchasing power parity relates exchange rates to the relative prices of a basket of goods. In studying international macroeconomics, purchasing power parity is the more relevant concept.

We can define a *price level* (denoted P) in each location as a weighted average of the prices of all goods g in a basket, using the same goods and weights in both locations. Let P_{US} be the basket's price in the United States and P_{EUR} the basket's price in Europe. *If the law of one price holds for each good in the basket, it will also hold for the price of the basket as a whole.*[1]

To express PPP algebraically, we can compute the relative price of the two baskets of goods in each location, denoted $q_{US/EUR}$:

$$\underbrace{q_{US/EUR}}_{\substack{\text{Relative price} \\ \text{of basket} \\ \text{in Europe} \\ \text{versus United States}}} = \underbrace{(E_{\$/\euro}P_{EUR})}_{\substack{\text{European price} \\ \text{of basket} \\ \text{expressed} \\ \text{in \$}}} / \underbrace{P_{US}}_{\substack{\text{U.S. price} \\ \text{of basket} \\ \text{expressed} \\ \text{in \$}}}$$

Just as there were three possible outcomes for the law of one price, there are three possibilities for PPP: the basket is cheaper in United States; the basket is cheaper in Europe; or $E_{\$/\euro}P_{EUR} = P_{US}$, the basket is the same price in both locations, and $q_{US/EUR} = 1$. In the first two cases, the basket is cheaper in one location and profitable arbitrage on the baskets is possible. Only in the third case is there no arbitrage. PPP holds *when price levels in two countries are equal when expressed in a common currency*. This statement about equality of price levels is also called **absolute PPP**.

For example, suppose the European basket costs €100, and the exchange rate is $1.20 per euro. For PPP to hold, the U.S. basket would have to cost $1.20 \times 100 = \$120$.

The Real Exchange Rate

The relative price of the two countries' baskets (denoted q) is the macroeconomic counterpart to the microeconomic relative price of individual goods (q^g). The relative

---

[1] For example, if the law of one price holds and $P_{US}^{g} = (E_{\$/\euro}) \times (P_{EUR}^{g})$ for all goods g, this implies that for N goods, the *arithmetic* weighted average satisfies $\sum_{g=1}^{N} \omega^g P_{US}^{g} = (E_{\$/\euro}) \times \sum_{g=1}^{N} \omega^g P_{EUR}^{g}$ for any set of weights ω^g that sum to 1, so PPP holds. The same is also true for *geometric* averages. Technically speaking, this follows for *any* price index definition that satisfies the usually required property that the index be homogeneous of degree 1 in the individual goods' prices.

price of the baskets is one of the most important variables in international macro-economics, and it has a special name: it is known as the **real exchange rate**. The real exchange rate $q_{US/EUR} = E_{\$/€}P_{EUR}/P_{US}$ tells us how many U.S. baskets are needed to purchase one European basket.

As with the nominal exchange rate, we need to be careful about what is in the numerator of the real exchange rate and what is in the denominator. According to our definition (based on the case we just examined), we will refer to $q_{US/EUR} = E_{\$/€}P_{EUR}/P_{US}$ as the home country, or the U.S. real exchange rate: it is the price of the European basket in terms of the U.S. basket (or, if we had a home–foreign example, the price of a foreign basket in terms of a home basket).

To avoid confusion, it is essential to understand the difference between nominal exchange rates (which we have studied so far) and real exchange rates. The exchange rate for currencies is a *nominal* concept; it says how many dollars can be exchanged for one euro. The real exchange rate is a *real* concept; it says how many U.S. baskets of goods can be exchanged for one European basket.

The real exchange rate has some terminology similar to that used with the nominal exchange rate:

- If the real exchange rate rises (more home goods are needed in exchange for foreign goods), we say Home has experienced a **real depreciation**.

- If the real exchange rate falls (fewer home goods are needed in exchange for foreign goods), we say Home has experienced a **real appreciation**.

Absolute PPP and the Real Exchange Rate

We can restate absolute PPP in terms of real exchange rates: *purchasing power parity states that the real exchange rate is equal to 1*. Under absolute PPP, all baskets have the same price when expressed in a common currency, so their relative price is 1.

It is common practice to use the absolute PPP-implied level of 1 as a benchmark or reference level for the real exchange rate. This leads naturally to some new terminology:

- If the real exchange rate $q_{US/EUR}$ is below 1 by $x\%$, then foreign goods are relatively cheap: $x\%$ cheaper than home goods. In this case, the home currency (the dollar) is said to be *strong*, the euro is *weak*, and we say the euro is **undervalued** by $x\%$.

- If the real exchange rate $q_{US/EUR}$ is above 1 by $x\%$, then foreign goods are relatively expensive: $x\%$ more expensive than home goods. In this case, the home currency (the dollar) is said to be *weak*, the euro is *strong*, and we say the euro is **overvalued** by $x\%$.

For example, if a European basket costs $E_{\$/€}P_{EUR} = \$550$ in dollar terms, and a U.S. basket costs only $P_{US} = \$500$, then $q_{US/EUR} = E_{\$/€}P_{EUR}/P_{US} = \$550/\$500 = 1.10$, the euro is strong, and the euro is 10% overvalued against the dollar.

Absolute PPP, Prices, and the Nominal Exchange Rate

Finally, just as we did with the law of one price, we can rearrange the no-arbitrage equation for the equality of price levels, $E_{\$/€}P_{EUR} = P_{US}$, to allow us to solve for the exchange rate that would be implied by absolute PPP:

$$\text{Absolute PPP}: \quad \underbrace{E_{\$/€}}_{\text{Exchange rate}} = \underbrace{P_{US}/P_{EUR}}_{\text{Ratio of price levels}} \quad \text{(3-1)}$$

This is one of the most important equations in our course of study because it shows how PPP (or absolute PPP) makes a clear prediction about exchange rates: *Purchasing*

FIGURE 3-1

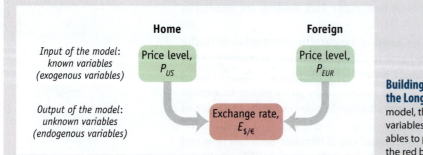

Building Block: Price Levels and Exchange Rates in the Long Run According to the PPP Theory In this model, the price levels are treated as known exogenous variables (in the green boxes). The model uses these variables to predict the unknown endogenous variable (in the red box), which is the exchange rate.

power parity implies that the exchange rate at which two currencies trade equals the relative price levels of the two countries.

For example, if a basket of goods costs $500 in the United States and the same basket costs €400 in Europe, the theory of PPP predicts an exchange rate of $500/€400 = $1.25 per euro.

Thus, if we know the price levels in different locations, we can use PPP to determine an implied exchange rate, subject to all of our earlier assumptions about frictionless trade, flexible prices, free competition, and identical goods. The PPP relationship between the price levels in two countries and the exchange rate is therefore a key building block in our theory of how exchange rates are determined, as shown in Figure 3-1. Moreover, the theory is not tied to any point in time: if we can forecast future price levels, then we can also use PPP to forecast the expected future exchange rate implied by those forecasted future price levels, which is the main goal of this chapter.

Relative PPP, Inflation, and Exchange Rate Depreciation

PPP in its absolute form involves price levels, but in macroeconomics we are often more interested in the rate at which price levels change than we are in the price levels themselves. The rate of growth of the price level is known as the *rate of inflation*, or simply **inflation**. For example, if the price level today is 100, and one year from now it is 103.5, then the rate of inflation is 3.5% (per year). Because inflation is such an important variable in macroeconomics, we examine the implications of PPP for the study of inflation.

To consider changes over time, we introduce a subscript t to denote the time period, and calculate the rate of change of both sides of Equation (3-1) from period t to period $t+1$. On the left-hand side, the rate of change of the exchange rate in Home is the rate of exchange rate depreciation in Home given by[2]

$$\frac{\Delta E_{\$/€,t}}{E_{\$/€,t}} = \underbrace{\frac{E_{\$/€,t+1} - E_{\$/€,t}}{E_{\$/€,t}}}_{\text{Rate of depreciation of the nominal exchange rate}}$$

On the right of Equation (3-1), the rate of change of the ratio of two price levels requires us to use the formula for the rate of change of a fraction; that is, the rate of

---

[2] The rate of depreciation in Home and the rate of appreciation in Foreign are approximately equal, as we saw in the previous chapter.

change of the numerator minus the rate of change of the denominator. Here this is given by the rate of change of home prices minus the rate of change of foreign prices:[3]

$$\frac{\Delta(P_{US}/P_{EUR})}{(P_{US}/P_{EUR})} = \frac{\Delta P_{US,t}}{P_{US,t}} - \frac{\Delta P_{EUR,t}}{P_{EUR,t}}$$

$$= \underbrace{\left(\frac{P_{US,t+1} - P_{US,t}}{P_{US,t}}\right)}_{\substack{\text{Rate of inflation in U.S.} \\ \pi_{US,t}}} - \underbrace{\left(\frac{P_{EUR,t+1} - P_{EUR,t}}{P_{EUR,t}}\right)}_{\substack{\text{Rate of inflation in Europe} \\ \pi_{EUR,t}}} = \pi_{US,t} - \pi_{EUR,t}$$

where the terms in brackets are the inflation rates in each location, denoted π_{US} and π_{EUR}, respectively, since the rate of change of the price level is, by definition, the inflation rate.

The result of all this is that if Equation (3-1) holds for levels of exchange rates and prices, then it must also hold for rates of change in these variables. By combining the last two expressions, we obtain

$$\text{Relative PPP :} \qquad \underbrace{\frac{\Delta E_{\$/€,t}}{E_{\$/€,t}}}_{\substack{\text{Rate of depreciation} \\ \text{of the nominal exchange rate}}} = \underbrace{\pi_{US,t} - \pi_{EUR,t}}_{\text{Inflation differential}} \qquad (3\text{-}2)$$

Equation (3-2) provides a new and slightly different way of describing PPP in rates of change, and it is called **relative PPP**. It *implies that the rate of depreciation of the nominal exchange rate equals the difference between the inflation rates of two countries (the inflation differential)*.

Does this sound familiar? We actually saw relative PPP in action in the example at the very start of this chapter, as a back-of-the-envelope calculation shows. Over 20 years, from 1990 to 2010, Canadian prices rose 12% less than U.S. prices (look back at the price level changes: 1.67/1.49 = 1.12), and over the same period the Canadian dollar appreciated 12% against the U.S. dollar (look back at the exchange rate change: 1.16/1.04 = 1.12). Converting these to annual rates, Canadian prices rose by 0.6% per year less than U.S. prices (the inflation differential), and the loonie appreciated by 0.6% per year against the dollar. Thus, we see that relative PPP did indeed hold true in this case.[4]

Two points should be kept in mind about relative PPP. First, unlike absolute PPP, relative PPP predicts a relationship between *changes* in prices and *changes* in exchange rates, rather than a relationship between their levels. Second, remember that relative PPP is *derived from* absolute PPP. Hence, the latter always implies the former: *if absolute PPP holds, this implies that relative PPP must hold also.* But the converse need not be true: *relative PPP does not necessarily imply absolute PPP* (if relative PPP holds, absolute PPP can hold or fail). For example, imagine that all goods consistently cost 20% more in country A than in country B, so absolute PPP fails; however, it still can be the case that the inflation differential between A and B (say, 5%) is always equal to the rate of depreciation (say, 5%), so relative PPP will still hold.

Summary

The purchasing power parity theory, whether in absolute or relative form, suggests that price levels in different countries and exchange rates are tightly linked, either in their absolute levels or in the rates at which they change. To assess how useful this theory is, let's look at some empirical evidence to see how well the theory matches reality. We can then reexamine the workings of PPP and reassess its underlying assumptions.

---

[3] This expression is exact for small changes and otherwise holds true as an approximation.

[4] Note that the rates of change are approximate, with $1.0060^{20} \approx 1.12$.

APPLICATION

Evidence for PPP in the Long Run and Short Run

Is there evidence for PPP? The data offer some support for relative PPP most clearly over the long run, when even moderate inflation mounts and leads to large cumulative changes in price levels and, hence, substantial cumulative inflation differentials.

The scatterplot in Figure 3-2 shows average rates of depreciation and inflation differentials for a sample of countries compared with the United States over three decades from 1975 to 2005. If relative PPP were true, then the depreciation of each country's currency would exactly equal the inflation differential, and the data would line up on the 45-degree line. We see that this is not literally true, but the correlation is close. Relative PPP is an approximate, useful guide to the relationship between prices and exchange rates in the long run, over horizons of many years or decades.

But the purchasing power theory turns out to be a fairly useless theory in the short run, over horizons of just a few years. This is easily seen by examining the time series of relative price ratio and exchange rates for any pair of countries, and looking at the behavior of these variables from year to year and not just over a long period. If absolute PPP held at all times, then the exchange rate would always equal the relative price ratio. Figure 3-3 shows 42 years of data for the United States and United Kingdom from 1975 to 2017. This figure confirms the relevance of absolute and relative PPP in the long run because the price-level ratio and the exchange rate have similar levels and drift together along a common trend. In the short run, however, the two series show substantial and persistent differences. In any given year the differences can be 10%, 20%, or more. These differences in levels and changes show that absolute and

FIGURE 3-2

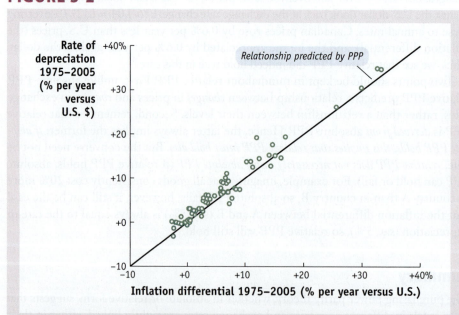

Inflation Differentials and the Exchange Rate, 1975–2005 This scatterplot shows the relationship between the rate of exchange rate depreciation against the U.S. dollar (the vertical axis) and the inflation differential against the United States (horizontal axis) over the long run, based on data for a sample of 82 countries. The correlation between the two variables is strong and bears a close resemblance to the theoretical prediction of PPP that all data points would appear on the 45-degree line.

Data from: IMF, International Financial Statistics.

FIGURE 3-3

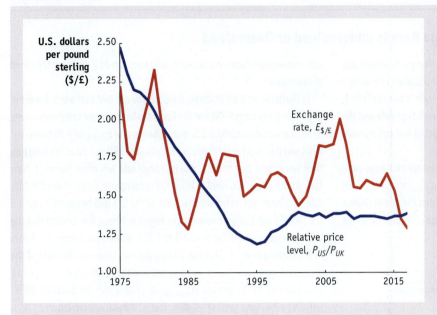

Exchange Rates and Relative Price Levels Data for the United States and United Kingdom for 1975 to 2017 show that the exchange rate and relative price levels do not always move together in the short run. Relative price levels tend to change slowly and have a small range of movement; exchange rates move more abruptly and experience large fluctuations. Therefore, relative PPP does *not* hold in the short run. However, it is a better guide to the long run, and we can see that the two series do tend to drift together over the decades.

Data from: Penn World Table, version 9.1.

relative PPP fail in the short run from year to year, and the same failure is seen even over periods of several years. For example, from 1980 to 1985, the pound depreciated by 45% (from $2.32 to $1.28 per pound), but the cumulative inflation differential over these five years was only 20%.

How Slow Is Convergence to PPP?

If PPP were taken as a strict proposition for the short run, then price adjustment via arbitrage would occur fully and instantaneously, rapidly closing the gap between common-currency prices in different countries for all goods in the basket. This doesn't happen. The evidence suggests that PPP works better in the long run. But how long is the long run?

Research shows that price differences—the deviations from PPP—can be persistent. Estimates suggest that these deviations may die out at a rate of about 15% per year. This kind of measure is often called a *speed of convergence*: in this case, it implies that after one year, 85% (0.85) of an initial price difference persists; compounding, after two years, 72% of the gap persists ($0.72 = 0.85^2$); and after four years, 52% ($0.52 = 0.85^4$). Thus, approximately half of any PPP deviation still remains after four years: economists would refer to this as a four-year *half-life*.

Such estimates provide a rule of thumb that is useful as a guide to forecasting real exchange rates. For example, suppose the home basket costs $100 and the foreign basket $90, in home currency. Here, Home's real exchange rate is 0.900, and the home currency is overvalued, with foreign goods less expensive than home goods. The deviation of the real exchange rate from the PPP-implied level of 1 is now −10% (or −0.1). Our rule of thumb tells us that next year we expect that 15% of this deviation will have disappeared (i.e., 0.015), so the new forecast deviation will be only −0.085; thus, Home's real exchange rate would be forecast to be 0.915 after one year and thus end up a little bit closer to 1, after a small depreciation. Similarly, after four years, all else being equal, 52% of the deviation (or 0.052) would have

SIDE BAR

Forecasting When the Real Exchange Rate Is Undervalued or Overvalued

When relative PPP holds, forecasting exchange rate changes is simple: just compute the inflation differential. But how do we forecast when PPP doesn't hold, as is often the case? Even if the real exchange rate is not equal to 1, having an estimate of the current level of the real exchange rate and the convergence speed can allow us to construct a forecast of real and nominal exchange rates.

To see how, let's start with the definition of the real exchange rate: $q_{US/EUR} = E_{\$/€}P_{EUR}/P_{US}$. Rearranging, we find $E_{\$/€} = q_{US/EUR} \times (P_{US}/P_{EUR})$. By taking the rate of change of that expression, we find that the rate of change of the nominal exchange rate equals the rate of change of the real exchange rate plus home inflation minus foreign inflation:

$$\underbrace{\frac{\Delta E_{\$/€,t}}{E_{\$/€,t}}}_{\substack{\text{Rate of depreciation of the}\\ \text{nominal exchange rate}}} = \underbrace{\frac{\Delta q_{US/EUR,t}}{q_{US/EUR,t}}}_{\substack{\text{Rate of depreciation of the}\\ \text{real exchange rate}}} + \underbrace{\pi_{US,t} - \pi_{EUR,t}}_{\text{Inflation differential}}$$

When the real exchange rate q is constant, the first term on the right is zero and we are back to the simple world of relative PPP and Equation (3-2). In that case, for forecasting purposes, the predicted nominal depreciation is then just the second term on the right, the inflation differential. For example, if the forecast is for U.S. inflation to be 3% next year and for European inflation to be 1%, then the inflation differential is +2% and we would forecast a U.S. dollar depreciation, or rise in $E_{\$/€}$, of +2% next year.

What if q isn't constant and PPP fails? If there is currently a deviation from absolute PPP, but we still think that there will be convergence to absolute PPP in the long run, the first term on the right of the above formula is not

zero and we then have to estimate it, which we can do if we know the speed of convergence.

To illustrate with an example, suppose you are told that a U.S. basket of goods currently costs $100, but the European basket of the same goods costs $130. You would compute a U.S. real exchange rate $q_{US/EUR}$ of 1.30 today. But what will it be next year? If you expect absolute PPP to hold in the long run, then you expect that the U.S. real exchange rate will move toward 1. How fast? At this point, you need to know the convergence speed. Using the 15% rule of thumb, you estimate that 15% of the 0.3 gap between 1 and 1.3 (i.e., 0.045) will dissipate over the coming year. Hence, you forecast that the U.S. real exchange will fall from 1.3 to 1.255, implying a change of −3.46% in the coming year. In this case, adding the two terms on the right of the expression given previously, you forecast that the approximate change in E next year will be the change in $q_{US/EUR}$ of −3.46% plus the inflation differential of +2%, for a total of −1.46%; that is, a dollar appreciation of 1.46% against the euro.

The intuition for the result is as follows: the U.S. dollar is undervalued against the euro. If convergence to PPP is to happen, then some of that undervaluation will dissipate over the course of the year through a real appreciation of the dollar (predicted to be 3.46%). That real appreciation can be broken down into two components:

1. U.S. goods will experience higher inflation than European goods (we have predicted that the inflation differential will be +2%).

2. The remainder of the real appreciation will be accomplished via a 1.46% nominal dollar appreciation (predicted based on a convergence speed of 15% per year).

---

been erased, and the real exchange rate would by then be 0.952, only −4.8% from the PPP level. (See **Side Bar: Forecasting When the Real Exchange Rate Is Undervalued or Overvalued.**)

What Explains Deviations from PPP?

If it takes four years for even half of any given price difference to dissipate, as research has indicated, it is no surprise that PPP does not hold in the short run. But how can arbitrage take so long to eliminate price differences? Economists have found a variety of reasons why PPP fails in the short run.

- *Transaction costs.* Trade is not frictionless as we have assumed thus far because the costs of international transportation are significant for most goods and because some goods also bear additional costs, such as tariffs and duties, when they cross borders. By some recent estimates, transportation costs may add about 20% on average to the price of goods moving internationally, while tariffs (and other policy barriers) may add another 10%.[5] Other costs arise due to the time it takes to ship goods, and the costs and time delays associated with developing distribution networks and satisfying legal and regulatory requirements in foreign markets.

■ *Nontraded goods.* Some goods are inherently nontradable; one can think of them as having infinitely high transaction costs. Most goods and services fall somewhere between tradable and nontradable. Consider a restaurant meal; it includes traded goods, such as some raw foods, and nontraded goods, such as the work of the chef. As a result, PPP may not hold. (See **Headlines: The Big Mac Index**.)

■ *Imperfect competition and legal obstacles.* Many goods are not simple undifferentiated commodities, as LOOP and PPP assume, but are differentiated products with brand names, copyrights, and legal protection. For example, consumers have the choice of cheaper generic acetaminophen or a pricier brand-name product such as Tylenol, but these are not seen as perfect substitutes. Such differentiated goods create conditions of *imperfect competition* because firms have some power to set the price of their good. With this kind of *market power*, firms can charge different prices not just across brands but also across countries (pharmaceutical companies, e.g., charge different prices for drugs in different countries). This practice is possible because arbitrage can be shut down by legal threats or regulations. For example, if you try to import large quantities of a firm's pharmaceutical drugs and resell them as an unauthorized distributor, you will probably hear very quickly from the firm's lawyers and/or from the government regulators. The same would apply to many other goods such as automobiles and consumer electronics.

■ *Price stickiness.* One of the most common assumptions of macroeconomics is that prices are "sticky" in the short run—that is, they do not or cannot adjust quickly and flexibly to changes in market conditions. PPP assumes that arbitrage can force prices to adjust, but adjustment will be slowed down by price stickiness. Empirical evidence shows that many goods' prices do not adjust quickly in the short run. For example, in Figure 3-3, we saw that the nominal exchange rate moves up and down in a very dramatic fashion but that price levels are much more sluggish in their movements and do not fully match exchange rate changes.

Despite these problems, the evidence suggests that as a long-run theory of exchange rates, PPP is still a useful approach.[6] And PPP may become even more relevant in the future as arbitrage becomes more efficient and more goods and services are traded. Years ago we might have taken it for granted that certain goods and services (such as pharmaceuticals, customer support, and health-care services) were strictly nontraded and thus not subject to arbitrage at the international level. Today, many consumers shop for pharmaceuticals overseas to save money. If you dial a U.S. software support call center, you may find yourself being assisted by an operator in another country. In some countries, citizens motivated by cost considerations may travel overseas for dental treatment, eye care, hip replacements, and other health services (so-called medical tourism or health tourism). These globalization trends may well continue.

---

[5] There is also evidence of other significant border-related barriers to trade. See James Anderson and Eric van Wincoop, 2004, "Trade Costs," *Journal of Economic Literature*, 42, 691–751.

[6] Alan M. Taylor and Mark P. Taylor, 2004, "The Purchasing Power Parity Debate," *Journal of Economic Perspectives*, 8, 135–158.

TABLE 3-1

The Big Mac Index The table shows the price of a Big Mac in July 2019 in local currency (column 1) and converted to U.S. dollars (column 2) using the actual exchange rate (column 4). The dollar price can then be compared with the average price of a Big Mac in the United States ($5.74 in column 1, row 1). The difference (column 5) is a measure of the overvaluation (+) or undervaluation (−) of the local currency against the U.S. dollar. The exchange rate against the dollar implied by PPP (column 3) is the hypothetical price of dollars in local currency that would have equalized burger prices, which may be compared with the actual observed exchange rate (column 4).

	Big Mac Prices		Exchange Rate (Local Currency per U.S. Dollar)		Overvaluation (+)/ Undervaluation (−) Against U.S. Dollar, %
	In Local Currency (1)	In U.S. Dollars (2)	Implied by PPP (3)	Actual, July 25th (4)	(5)
United States	5.74 USD	$5.74	—	—	—
Argentina	120 ARS	$2.87	20.91	41.80	−50
Australia	6.15 AUD	$4.26	1.07	1.44	−25.8
Azerbaijan	3.95 AZN	$2.33	0.69	1.70	−59.4
Bahrain	1.4 BHD	$3.71	0.24	0.38	−35.3
Brazil	17.5 BRL	$4.60	3.05	3.81	−19.9
Britain	3.29 GBP	$4.10	0.57	0.80	−28.5
Canada	6.77 CAD	$5.16	1.18	1.31	−10.2
Chile	2640 CLP	$3.83	459.93	689.75	−33.3
China	21 CNY	$3.05	3.66	6.88	−46.9
Colombia	11900 COP	$3.69	2073.17	3227.00	−35.8
Costa Rica	2290 CRC	$3.94	398.95	581.94	−31.4
Croatia	22 HRK	$3.33	3.83	6.60	−41.9
Czech Republic	85 CZK	$3.73	14.81	22.80	−35
Denmark	30 DKK	$4.50	5.23	6.66	−21.5
Egypt	42 EGP	$2.53	7.32	16.62	−56
Euro area	4.08 EUR	$4.57	0.71	0.89	−20.3
Guatemala	25 GTQ	$3.26	4.36	7.68	−43.3
Honduras	86 HNL	$3.51	14.98	24.48	−38.8
Hong Kong	20.5 HKD	$2.62	3.57	7.81	−54.3
Hungary	900 HUF	$3.10	156.79	290.54	−46
India	183 INR	$2.67	31.88	68.55	−53.5
Indonesia	32000 IDR	$2.26	5574.91	14130.00	−60.5
Israel	17 ILS	$4.77	2.96	3.57	−17
Japan	390 JPY	$3.59	67.94	108.77	−37.5
Jordan	2.3 JOD	$3.24	0.40	0.71	−43.5
Kuwait	1.1 KWD	$3.61	0.19	0.30	−37.1
Lebanon	6500 LBP	$4.31	1132.40	1507.00	−24.9
Malaysia	8.85 MYR	$2.14	1.54	4.14	−62.8
Mexico	50 MXN	$2.65	8.71	18.90	−53.9
Moldova	43 MDL	$2.41	7.49	17.81	−57.9
New Zealand	6.4 NZD	$4.23	1.11	1.51	−26.3
Nicaragua	110 NIO	$3.32	19.16	33.16	−42.2
Norway	42 NOK	$4.85	7.32	8.65	−15.4
Oman	1.21 OMR	$3.14	0.21	0.39	−45.2
Pakistan	480 PKR	$3.05	83.62	157.45	−46.9
Peru	10.5 PEN	$3.19	1.83	3.29	−44.3
Philippines	142 PHP	$2.77	24.74	51.32	−51.8
Poland	10.8 PLN	$2.84	1.88	3.81	−50.6
Qatar	13 QAR	$3.57	2.26	3.64	−37.8
Romania	9.3 RON	$2.20	1.62	4.22	−61.6
Russia	130 RUB	$2.04	22.65	63.84	−64.5
Saudi Arabia	13 SAR	$3.47	2.26	3.75	−39.6
Singapore	5.8 SGD	$4.26	1.01	1.36	−25.8
South Africa	31 ZAR	$2.19	5.40	14.18	−61.9
South Korea	4500 KRW	$3.81	783.97	1180.55	−33.6
Sri Lanka	640 LKR	$3.64	111.50	175.68	−36.5
Sweden	51 SEK	$5.38	8.89	9.48	−6.2
Switzerland	6.5 CHF	$6.54	1.13	0.99	14
Taiwan	72 TWD	$2.31	12.54	31.17	−59.8
Thailand	119 THB	$3.86	20.73	30.83	−32.7
Turkey	13.99 TRY	$2.44	2.44	5.72	−57.4
Ukraine	57 UAH	$2.22	9.93	25.65	−61.3
United Arab Emirates	14.75 AED	$4.02	2.57	3.67	−30
Uruguay	164 UYU	$4.66	28.57	35.17	−18.8
Vietnam	65000 VND	$2.80	11324.04	23231.00	−51.3

Data from: economist.com.

HEADLINES

The Big Mac Index

For more than 30 years, *The Economist* newspaper has engaged in a whimsical attempt to judge PPP theory based on a well-known, globally uniform consumer good: McDonald's Big Mac. The over- or undervaluation of a currency against the U.S. dollar is gauged by comparing the relative prices of a burger in a common currency, and expressing the difference as a percentage deviation from one:

$$\text{Big Mac Index} = q^{\text{Big Mac}} - 1 = \left(\frac{E_{\$/\text{local currency}} P_{\text{local}}^{\text{Big Mac}}}{P_{\text{US}}^{\text{Big Mac}}} \right) - 1$$

Home of the undervalued burger?

Table 3-1 shows the July 2019 survey results, and some examples will illustrate how the calculations work. Row 1 shows the average U.S. dollar price of the Big Mac of $5.74. An example of undervaluation appears in the entry for Argentina, in row 2, where we see that the Buenos Aires correspondent found the same burger cost 120 pesos (symbol: ARS), which, at an actual exchange rate of 41.80 pesos per dollar, worked out to be only $2.87 in U.S. currency, or exactly 50% less than the U.S. price. Therefore, the peso was 50% undervalued against the U.S. dollar according to this measure, and Argentina's exchange rate would have had to appreciate to 20.91 pesos per dollar to attain the level implied by a burger-based PPP theory. In 2019, a rare example of overvaluation appears in the entry for Switzerland. There a Big Mac cost 6.50 Swiss francs (symbol: CHF), or $6.54 in U.S. currency at the prevailing exchange rate of 0.99 Swiss francs per dollar, making the Swiss burgers 14% more expensive than their U.S. counterparts. To get to its PPP-implied level, and put the burgers at parity, the Swiss currency would have needed to depreciate to 1.13 Swiss francs per dollar. Looking through the table, burger disparity is typical, with only a few countries within ±10% of PPP. Note also that most of entries in the final column are negative: the year 2019 was a period of unusual dollar strength against most of the other currencies in the world.

2 Money, Prices, and Exchange Rates in the Long Run: Money Market Equilibrium in a Simple Model

It is time to take stock of the theory developed so far in this chapter. Up to now, we have concentrated on PPP, which says that in the long run the exchange rate is determined by the ratio of the price levels in two countries. But this prompts a question: What determines those price levels?

Monetary theory supplies an answer: according to this theory, in the long run, price levels are determined in each country by the relative demand and supply of money. You may recall this theory from previous macroeconomics courses in the context of a closed economy. This section recaps the essential elements of monetary theory and shows how they fit into our theory of exchange rates in the long run.

What Is Money?

Let's recall the distinguishing features of this peculiar asset that is so central to our everyday economic life. Economists think of **money** as performing three key functions in an economy:

1. Money is a *store of value* because, as with any asset, money held from today until tomorrow can still be used to buy goods and services in the future. Money's rate of return is low compared with many other assets. Because we earn no interest on it, there is an opportunity cost to holding money. If this cost is low, we hold money more willingly than other assets (stocks, bonds, etc.).

2. Money is a *unit of account* in which all prices in the economy are quoted. When we enter a store in France, we expect to see the prices of goods to read something like "100 euros"—not "10,000 Japanese yen" or "500 bananas," even though, in principle, the yen or the banana could also function as a unit of account in France (bananas would, however, be a poor store of value).

3. Money is a *medium of exchange* that allows us to buy and sell goods and services without the need to engage in inefficient barter (direct swaps of goods). The ease with which we can convert money into goods and services is a measure of how *liquid* money is compared with the many illiquid assets in our portfolios (such as real estate). Money is the most liquid asset of all.

The Measurement of Money

What counts as money? Clearly, currency (coins and bills) in circulation is money. But do checking accounts count as money? What about savings accounts, mutual funds, and other securities? Figure 3-4 depicts the most widely used measures of the money supply and illustrates their relative magnitudes with recent data from the United States. The most basic concept of money is currency in circulation (i.e., in the hands of the nonbank public). After that, M0 is typically the narrowest definition of money (also called "base money"), and it includes both currency in circulation and the reserves of commercial banks (liquid cash held in their vaults or on deposit at the Fed). Normally, in recent years, banks' reserves have been very small and so M0 has been virtually identical to currency in circulation. This changed dramatically after the financial crisis of 2008 gave rise to liquidity problems, and banks began to maintain huge reserves at the Fed as a precaution. (When and how this unprecedented hoard of cash will be unwound remains to be seen, and this is a matter of some concern to economists and policymakers.)

FIGURE 3-4

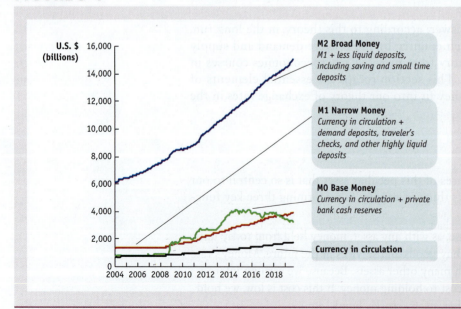

The Measurement of Money This figure shows the major kinds of monetary aggregates (currency, M0, M1, and M2) for the United States from 2004 to 2019. Normally, bank reserves are very close to zero, so M0 and currency are virtually identical. But reserves spiked up during the financial crisis in 2008, as private banks sold securities to the Fed and stored up the cash proceeds in their Fed reserve accounts as a precautionary hoard of liquidity, a situation that persisted.

Data from: Federal Reserve Economic Data (FRED).

A different narrow measure of money, M1, includes currency in circulation plus highly liquid instruments such as demand deposits in checking accounts and traveler's checks, but it *excludes* bank's reserves, and thus may be a better gauge of money available for transactions purposes. A much broader measure of money, M2, includes slightly less liquid assets such as savings and small time deposits.[7]

For our purposes, money is defined as the *stock of liquid assets that are routinely used to finance transactions*, as implied by the "medium of exchange" function of money. So, in this book, when we speak of money (denoted M), we will generally mean M1 (currency in circulation plus demand deposits). Many important assets are excluded from M1, including longer-term assets held by individuals and the voluminous interbank deposits used in the foreign exchange market discussed in the previous chapter. These assets do not count as money in the sense we use the word because they are relatively illiquid and not used routinely for transactions.

The Supply of Money

How is the supply of money determined? In practice, a country's **central bank** controls the **money supply**. Strictly speaking, by issuing notes, coins, and private bank reserves the central bank controls directly only the level of M0, or base money, the amount of currency and reserves in the economy. However, it can *indirectly* control the level of M1 by using monetary policy to influence the behavior of the private banks that are responsible for checking deposits. The intricate mechanisms by which monetary policy affects M1 are beyond the scope of this book. For our purposes, we make the simplifying assumption that the central bank's policy tools are sufficient to allow it to control the level of M1 indirectly, but accurately.[8]

The Demand for Money: A Simple Model

A simple theory of household money demand is motivated by the assumption that the need to conduct transactions is in proportion to an individual's income. For example, if an individual's income doubles from $20,000 to $40,000, we expect their demand for money (expressed in dollars) to double also.

Moving from the individual or household level up to the aggregate or macroeconomic level, we can infer that the aggregate **money demand** will behave similarly. *All else equal, a rise in national dollar income (nominal income) will cause a proportional increase in transactions and, hence, in aggregate money demand.*

This insight suggests a simple model in which the demand for money is proportional to dollar income. This model is known as the **quantity theory of money**:

$$\underset{\substack{\text{Demand} \\ \text{for money (\$)}}}{M^d} = \underset{\substack{\text{A constant}}}{\bar{L}} \times \underset{\substack{\text{Nominal} \\ \text{income (\$)}}}{PY}$$

---

[7]There is little consensus on the right broad measure of money. Until 2006 the U.S. Federal Reserve collected data on M3, which included large time deposits, repurchase agreements, and money market funds. This was discontinued because the data were costly to collect and thought to be of limited use to policymakers. In the United Kingdom, a slightly different broad measure, M4, is still used. Some economists now prefer a money aggregate called MZM, or "money of zero maturity," as the right broad measure, but its use is not widespread.

[8] A full treatment of this topic may be found in a textbook on money and banking. See Laurence M. Ball, 2012, *Money, Banking, and Financial Markets*, 2nd edition (New York: Worth).

Here, PY measures the total nominal dollar value of income in the economy, equal to the price level P times real income Y. The term $\bar{L}$ is a constant that measures how much demand for liquidity is generated for each dollar of nominal income. To emphasize this point, we assume for now that every \$1 of nominal income requires \$$\bar{L}$ of money for transactions purposes and that this relationship is constant. (Later, we relax this assumption.)

The intuition behind the last equation is as follows: If the price level rises by 10% and real income is fixed, we are paying a 10% higher price for all goods, so the dollar cost of transactions rises by 10%. Similarly, if real income rises by 10% but prices stay fixed, the dollar amount of transactions will rise by 10%. Hence, the *demand for nominal money balances*, M^d, is proportional to the *nominal* income PY.

Another way to look at the quantity theory is to convert all quantities into real quantities by dividing the previous equation by P, the price level (the price of a basket of goods). Quantities are then converted from nominal dollars to real units (specifically, into units of baskets of goods). These conversions allow us to derive the *demand for real money balances*:

$$\underbrace{\frac{M^d}{P}}_{\substack{\text{Demand} \\ \text{for real} \\ \text{money}}} = \underbrace{\bar{L}}_{\text{A constant}} \times \underbrace{Y}_{\text{Real income}}$$

Real money balances measure the purchasing power of the stock of money in terms of goods and services. The expression just given says that the demand for real money balances is proportional to real income. The more real income we have, the more real transactions we have to perform, and the more real money we need.

Equilibrium in the Money Market

The condition for equilibrium in the money market is that the demand for money M^d must equal the supply of money M, which we assume to be under the control of the central bank. Imposing this condition on the last two equations, we find that nominal money supply equals nominal money demand:

$$M = \bar{L}PY$$

and, equivalently, that real money supply equals real money demand:

$$\frac{M}{P} = \bar{L}Y$$

A Simple Monetary Model of Prices

We are now in a position to put together a simple model of the exchange rate, using two building blocks. The first building block, the quantity theory, is a model that links prices to monetary conditions. The second building block, PPP, is a model that links exchange rates to prices.

We consider two locations, or countries, as before; the United States will be the home country and we will treat the Eurozone as the foreign country. We will refer to the Eurozone, or more simply Europe, as a country in this and later examples. The model generalizes to any pair of countries or locations.

Let's consider the last equation given and apply it to the United States, adding U.S. subscripts for clarity. We can rearrange this formula to obtain an expression for the U.S. price level:

$$P_{US} = \frac{M_{US}}{\overline{L}_{US}Y_{US}}$$

Note that the price level is determined by how much nominal money is issued relative to the demand for real money balances: the numerator on the right-hand side M_{US} is the total supply of *nominal* money; the denominator $\overline{L}_{US}Y_{US}$ is the total demand for *real* money balances.

The analogous expression for the European price level is:

$$P_{EUR} = \frac{M_{EUR}}{\overline{L}_{EUR}Y_{EUR}}$$

The last two equations are examples of the **fundamental equation of the monetary model of the price level**. Two such equations, one for each country, give us another important building block for our theory of prices and exchange rates as shown in Figure 3-5.

In the long run, we assume prices are flexible and will adjust to put the money market in equilibrium. For example, if the amount of money in circulation (the nominal money supply) rises, say, by a factor of 100, and real income stays the same, then there will be "more money chasing the same quantity of goods." This leads to inflation, and in the long run, the price level will rise by a factor of 100. In other words, we will be in the same economy as before except that all prices will have two zeros tacked on to them.

A Simple Monetary Model of the Exchange Rate

A long-run model of the exchange rate is close at hand. If we take the last two equations, which use the monetary model to find the price level in each country, and plug them into Equation (3-1), we can use absolute PPP to solve for the exchange rate:

$$\underset{\text{Exchange rate}}{E_{\$/€}} = \underset{\text{Ratio of price levels}}{\frac{P_{US}}{P_E}} = \frac{(\frac{M_{US}}{\overline{L}_{US}Y_{US}})}{(\frac{M_{EUR}}{\overline{L}_{EUR}Y_{EUR}})} = \underset{\substack{\text{Relative nominal money supplies} \\ \text{divided by} \\ \text{relative real money demands}}}{\frac{(M_{US}/M_{EUR})}{(\overline{L}_{US}Y_{US}/\overline{L}_{EUR}Y_{EUR})}} \quad (3\text{-}3)$$

FIGURE 3-5

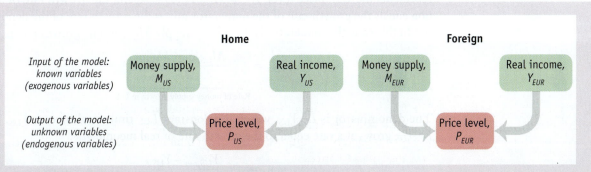

Building Block: The Monetary Theory of the Price Level According to the Long-Run Monetary Model In these models, the money supply and real income are treated as known exogenous variables (in the green boxes). The models use these variables to predict the unknown endogenous variables (in the red boxes), which are the price levels in each country.

This is the **fundamental equation of the monetary approach to exchange rates**. By substituting the price levels from the monetary model into PPP, we have put together the two building blocks from Figures 3-1 and 3-5. The implications of this equation are as follows:

- Suppose the U.S. money supply increases, all else equal. The right-hand side increases (the U.S. nominal money supply increases relative to Europe), causing the exchange rate to increase (the U.S. dollar depreciates against the euro). For example, if the U.S. money supply doubles, then all else equal, the U.S. price level doubles. That is, a bigger U.S. supply of money leads to a weaker dollar. That makes sense—there are more dollars around, so you expect each dollar to be worth less.

- Now suppose the U.S. real income level increases, all else equal. Then the right-hand side decreases (the U.S. real money demand increases relative to Europe), causing the exchange rate to decrease (the U.S. dollar appreciates against the euro). For example, if the U.S. real income doubles, then all else equal, the U.S. price level falls by a factor of one-half. That is, a stronger U.S. economy leads to a stronger dollar. That makes sense—there is more demand for the same quantity of dollars, so you expect each dollar to be worth more.

Money Growth, Inflation, and Depreciation

The model just presented uses absolute PPP to link the level of the exchange rate to the level of prices and uses the quantity theory to link prices to monetary conditions in each country. But as we have said before, macroeconomists are often more interested in rates of change of variables (e.g., inflation) rather than levels.

Can we extend our theory to this purpose? Yes, but this task takes a little work. We convert Equation (3-3) into growth rates by taking the rate of change of each term.

The first term of Equation (3-3) is the exchange rate $E_{\$/\euro}$. Its rate of change is the rate of depreciation $\Delta E_{\$/\euro}/E_{\$/\euro}$. When this term is positive, say, 1%, the dollar is depreciating at 1% per year; if negative, say, –2%, the dollar is appreciating at 2% per year.

The second term of Equation (3-3) is the ratio of the price levels P_{US}/P_{EUR}, and as we saw when we derived relative PPP at Equation (3-2), its rate of change is the rate of change of the numerator (U.S. inflation) minus the rate of change of the denominator (European inflation), which equals the inflation differential $\pi_{US,t} - \pi_{EUR,t}$.

What is the rate of change of the third term in Equation (3-3)? The numerator represents the U.S. price level, $P_{US} = M_{US}/\bar{L}_{US}Y_{US}$. Again, the growth rate of a fraction equals the growth rate of the numerator minus the growth rate of the denominator. In this case, the numerator is the money supply M_{US}, and its growth rate is μ_{US}:

$$\mu_{US,t} = \underbrace{\frac{M_{US,t+1} - M_{US,t}}{M_{US,t}}}_{\text{Rate of money supply growth in U.S.}}$$

The denominator is $\bar{L}_{US}Y_{US}$, which is a constant $\bar{L}_{US}$ times real income Y_{US}. Thus, $\bar{L}_{US}Y_{US}$ grows at a rate equal to the growth rate of real income g_{US}:

$$g_{US,t} = \underbrace{\frac{Y_{US,t+1} - Y_{US,t}}{Y_{US,t}}}_{\text{Rate of real income growth in U.S.}}$$

Putting all the pieces together, the growth rate of $P_{US} = M_{US}/\bar{L}_{US}Y_{US}$ equals the money supply growth rate μ_{US} minus the real income growth rate g_{US}. We have already seen that the growth rate of P_{US} on the left-hand side is the inflation rate π_{US}. Thus, we know that

$$\pi_{US,t} = \mu_{US,t} - g_{US,t} \tag{3-4}$$

The denominator of the third term of Equation (3-3) represents the European price level, $P_{EUR} = M_{EUR}/\overline{L}_{EUR}Y_{EUR}$, and its rate of change is calculated similarly:

$$\pi_{EUR,t} = \mu_{EUR,t} - g_{EUR,t} \tag{3-5}$$

The intuition for these last two expressions echoes what we said previously: when money growth is higher than real income growth, we have "more money chasing fewer goods" and this leads to inflation.

Combining Equation (3-4) and Equation (3-5), we can now solve for the inflation differential in terms of monetary fundamentals and finish our task of computing the rate of depreciation of the exchange rate:

$$\underbrace{\frac{\Delta E_{\$/\euro,t}}{E_{\$/\euro,t}}}_{\substack{\text{Rate of depreciation} \\ \text{of the nominal exchange rate}}} = \underbrace{\pi_{US,t} - \pi_{EUR,t}}_{\text{Inflation differential}} = (\mu_{US,t} - g_{US,t}) - (\mu_{EUR,t} - g_{EUR,t})$$

$$= \underbrace{(\mu_{US,t} - \mu_{EUR,t})}_{\substack{\text{Differential in} \\ \text{nominal money supply} \\ \text{growth rates}}} - \underbrace{(g_{US,t} - g_{EUR,t})}_{\substack{\text{Differential in} \\ \text{real output} \\ \text{growth rates}}} \tag{3-6}$$

The last term here is the rate of change of the fourth term in Equation (3-3).

Equation (3-6) is the fundamental equation of the monetary approach to exchange rates expressed in rates of change, and much of the same intuition we applied in explaining Equation (3-3) carries over here.

- If the United States runs a looser monetary policy in the long run measured by a faster money growth rate, the dollar will depreciate more rapidly, all else equal. For example, suppose Europe has a 5% annual rate of change of money and a 2% rate of change of real income; then its inflation would be the difference: 5% minus 2% equals 3%. Now suppose the United States has a 6% rate of change of money and a 2% rate of change of real income; then its inflation would be the difference: 6% minus 2% equals 4%. And the rate of depreciation of the dollar would be U.S. inflation minus European inflation, 4% minus 3%, or 1% per year.

- If the U.S. economy grows faster in the long run, the dollar will appreciate more rapidly, all else equal. In the last numerical example, suppose the U.S. growth rate of real income in the long run increases from 2% to 5%, all else equal. U.S. inflation equals the money growth rate of 6% minus the new real income growth rate of 5%, so inflation is just 1% per year. Now the rate of dollar depreciation is U.S. inflation minus European inflation, that is, 1% minus 3%, or –2% per year (meaning the U.S. dollar would now appreciate at 2% per year against the euro).

With a change of notation to make the United States the foreign country, the same lessons could be derived for Europe and the euro.

3 The Monetary Approach: Implications and Evidence

The monetary approach is the workhorse model in the study of long-run exchange rate movements. In this section, we look at some applications and empirical evidence.

Exchange Rate Forecasts Using the Simple Model

An important application of the monetary approach to exchange rate determination is to provide a forecast of the future exchange rate. Remember from the previous chapter that foreign exchange (forex) market arbitragers need such a forecast to be able to make arbitrage calculations using uncovered interest parity. Using Equation (3-3), we can see that a forecast of future exchange rates (the left-hand side) can be constructed as long as we know how to forecast future money supplies and real income (the right-hand side).

In practice, this is why expectations about money and real income in the future attract so much attention in the financial media, and especially in the forex market. The discussion returns with obsessive regularity to two questions. The first question—What are central banks going to do?—leads to relentless attempts to decode the statements of central bank officials. The second question—How is the economy expected to grow in real terms?—leads to a keen interest in any economic indicators, such as productivity or investment, that might hint at changes in the rate of income growth.

Any such forecasts come with at least two major caveats. First, there is great uncertainty in trying to answer these questions, and forecasts of economic variables years in the future are inevitably subject to large errors. Nonetheless, this is one of the key tasks of financial markets. Second, whenever one uses the monetary model for forecasting, one is answering a hypothetical question: What path would exchange rates follow from now on *if prices were flexible and PPP held*? As forecasters know, in the short run there might be deviations from this prediction about exchange rate changes, but in the longer run, we expect the prediction will supply a more reasonable guide.

Forecasting Exchange Rates: An Example

To see how forecasting might work, let's look at a simple scenario and focus on what would happen under flexible prices. Assume that U.S. and European real income growth rates are identical and equal to zero (0%) so that real income levels are constant. Assume also that the European money supply is constant. If the money supply and real income in Europe are constant, then the European price level is constant, and European inflation is zero, as we can see from Equation (3-5). These assumptions allow us to perform a controlled thought-experiment, and focus on changes on the U.S. side of the model, all else equal. Let's look at two cases.

Case 1: A one-time unanticipated increase in the money supply. In the first, and simpler, case, suppose at some time T that the U.S. money supply rises by a fixed proportion, say, 10%, all else equal. Assuming that prices are flexible, what does our model predict will happen to the level of the exchange rate after time T? To spell out the argument in detail, we look at the implications of our model for some key variables.

a. There is a 10% increase in the money supply M.

b. Real money balances M/P remain constant, because real income is constant.

c. These last two statements imply that price level P and money supply M must move in the same proportion, so there is a 10% increase in the price level P.

d. PPP implies that the exchange rate E and price level P must move in the same proportion, so there is a 10% increase in the exchange rate E; that is, the dollar depreciates by 10%.

A quicker solution uses the fundamental equation of the monetary approach at Equation (3-3): the price level and exchange rate are proportional to the money supply, all else equal.

Case 2: An unanticipated increase in the rate of money growth. The model also applies to more complex scenarios. Consider a second case in which the U.S. money supply is not constant, but grows at a steady fixed rate μ. Then suppose we learn at time T that the United States will raise the rate of money supply growth from some previously fixed rate μ to a slightly higher rate $\mu + \Delta\mu$. How would people expect the exchange rate to behave, assuming price flexibility? Let's work through this case step by step:

a. Money supply M is growing at a constant rate.

b. Real money balances M/P remain constant, as before.

c. These last two statements imply that price level P and money supply M must move in the same proportion, so P is always a constant multiple of M.

d. PPP implies that the exchange rate E and price level P must move in the same proportion, so E is always a constant multiple of P (and hence of M).

Corresponding to these four steps, the four panels of Figure 3-6 illustrate the path of the key variables in this example. This figure shows that if we can forecast

FIGURE 3-6

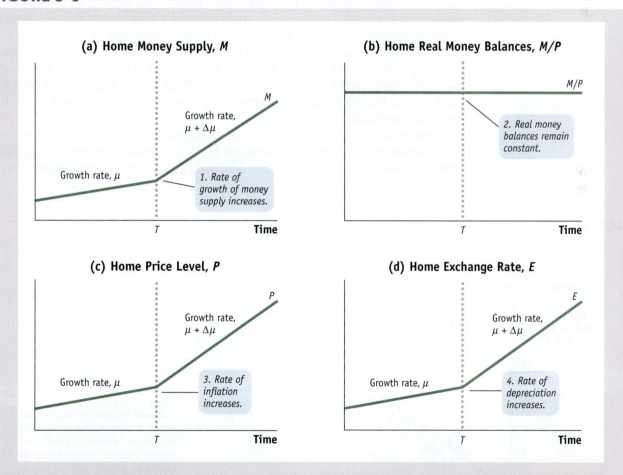

An Increase in the Growth Rate of the Money Supply in the Simple Model Before time T, money, prices, and the exchange rate all grow at rate μ. Foreign prices are constant. In panel (a), we suppose at time T that there is an increase $\Delta\mu$ in the rate of growth of home money supply M. In panel (b), the quantity theory assumes that the level of real money balances remains unchanged. After time T, if real money balances (M/P) are constant, then money M and prices P still grow at the same rate, which is now $\mu + \Delta\mu$, so the rate of inflation rises by $\Delta\mu$, as shown in panel (c). PPP and an assumed stable foreign price level imply that the exchange rate will follow a path similar to that of the domestic price level, so E also grows at the new rate $\mu + \Delta\mu$, and the rate of depreciation rises by $\Delta\mu$, as shown in panel (d).

the money supply at any future period as in (a), and if we know real money balances remain constant as in (b), then we can forecast prices as in (c) and exchange rates as in (d). These forecasts are good in any future period, under the assumptions of the monetary approach. Again, Equation (3-3) supplies the answer more quickly; under the assumptions we have made, money, prices, and exchange rates all move in proportion to one another.

APPLICATION

Evidence for the Monetary Approach

The monetary approach to prices and exchange rates suggests that, all else equal, increases in the rate of money supply growth should be the same size as increases in the rate of inflation and the rate of exchange rate depreciation. Looking for evidence of this relationship in real-world data is one way to put this theory to the test.

The scatterplots in Figure 3-7 and Figure 3-8 show data from 1975 to 2005 for a large sample of countries. The results offer fairly strong support for the monetary theory. All else equal, Equation (3-6) predicts that an $x\%$ difference in money growth rates (relative to the United States) should be associated with an $x\%$ difference in inflation rates (relative to the United States) and an $x\%$ depreciation of the home exchange rate (against the U.S. dollar). If this association were literally true in the data, then each country in the scatterplot would be on the 45-degree line. This is not exactly true, but the actual relationship is very close and offers some support for the monetary approach.

One reason the data do not sit on the 45-degree line is that all else is *not* equal in this sample of countries. In Equation (3-6), countries differ not only in their relative money supply growth rates but also in their real income growth rates.

FIGURE 3-7

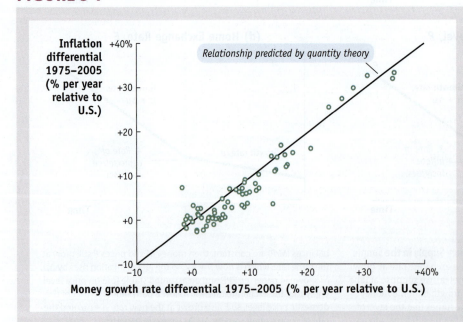

Inflation Rates and Money Growth Rates, 1975–2005 This scatterplot shows the relationship between the rate of inflation and the money supply growth rate over the long run, based on data for a sample of 76 countries. The correlation between the two variables is strong and bears a close resemblance to the theoretical prediction of the monetary model that all data points would appear on the 45-degree line.

Data from: IMF, International Financial Statistics.

FIGURE 3-8

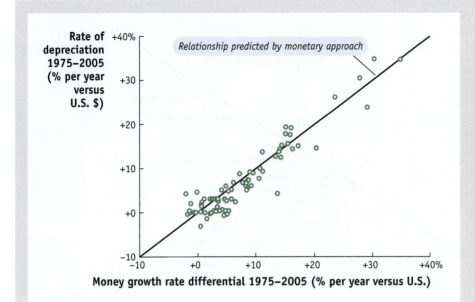

Money Growth Rates and the Exchange Rate, 1975–2005 This scatterplot shows the relationship between the rate of exchange rate depreciation against the U.S. dollar and the money growth rate differential versus the United States over the long run, based on data for a sample of 82 countries. The data show a strong correlation between the two variables and a close resemblance to the theoretical prediction of the monetary approach to exchange rates, which would predict that all data points would appear on the 45-degree line.

Data from: IMF, International Financial Statistics.

Another explanation is that we have been assuming that the money demand parameter L is constant, and this may not be true in reality. This is an issue we must now confront.[9]

APPLICATION

Hyperinflations

The monetary approach assumes long-run PPP, which has some support, as we saw in Figure 3-2. But we have been careful to note, again, that PPP generally works poorly in the short run. However, there is one notable exception to this general failure of PPP in the short run: hyperinflations.

Economists traditionally define a **hyperinflation** as occurring when the inflation rate exceeds 50% *per month* for a sustained period (which means that prices are doubling every 51 days). In common usage, some lower-inflation episodes are also called hyperinflations; for example, an inflation rate of 1,000% *per year* is a common rule of thumb (when inflation is "only" 22% per month).

There have been many hyperinflations worldwide since the early twentieth century. They usually occur when governments face a budget crisis, are unable to borrow to finance a deficit, and instead choose to print money to cover their financing needs. The situation is not sustainable and usually leads to economic, social, or political crisis, which is eventually resolved with a return to price stability. (For more discussion of hyperinflations and their consequences, see **Side Bar: Currency Reform**.)

[9] Economists can use sophisticated statistical techniques to address these issues and still find results favorable to the monetary approach in the long run. See David E. Rapach and Mark E. Wohar, 2002, "Testing the Monetary Model of Exchange Rate Determination: New Evidence from a Century of Data," *Journal of International Economics*, 58(2), 359–385.

FIGURE 3-9

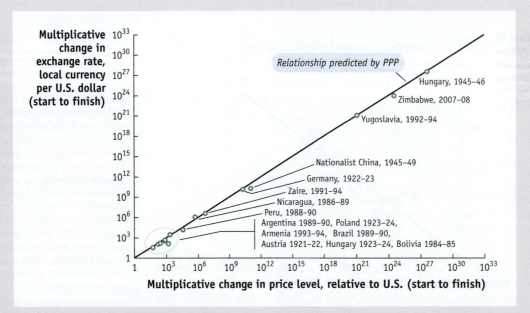

Purchasing Power Parity During Hyperinflations The scatterplot shows the relationship between the cumulative start-to-finish exchange rate depreciation against the U.S. dollar and the cumulative start-to-finish rise in the local price level for hyperinflations since the early twentieth century. Note the use of logarithmic scales. The data show a strong correlation between the two variables and a *very* close resemblance to the theoretical prediction of PPP that all data points would appear on the 45-degree line.

Data from: IMF, International Financial Statistics; Phillip Cagan, 1956, "The Monetary Dynamics of Hyperinflation," in Milton Friedman, ed., Studies in the Quantity Theory

of Money (Chicago: University of Chicago Press), pp. 25–117; Pavle Petrovic and Zorica Mladenovic, 2000, "Money Demand and Exchange Rate Determination Under Hyperinflation: Conceptual Issues and Evidence from Yugoslavia," Journal of Money, Credit and Banking, 32, 785–806; Teh-Wei Hu, 1971, "Hyperinflation and the Dynamics of the Demand for Money in China, 1945–1949," Journal of Political Economy, 79(1), 186–195; Jason Lim II, 2012, "Observations of the Political and Economic Situation in China by the British Mercantile Community During the Civil War, 1945–1949," in Anne-Marie Brady and Douglas Brown, eds., Foreigners and Foreign Institutions in Republican China (Abingdon, U.K.: Routledge), pp. 109–127; Zimbabwe estimate based on author's calculations and Steve H. Hanke and Alex K. F. Kwok, 2009, "On the Measurement of Zimbabwe's Hyperinflation," Cato Journal, 29(2), 353–364.

SIDE BAR

Currency Reform

Hyperinflations help us understand how some currencies become extinct if they cease to function well and lose value rapidly. Dollarization in Ecuador is a recent example. Other currencies survive such traumas, only to be reborn. But the low-denomination bills—the ones, fives, tens—usually become essentially worthless, and normal transactions can require you to be a millionaire. The elimination of a few pesky zeros might then be a good idea. A government may then *redenominate* a new unit of currency equal to 10^N (10 raised to the power N) old units.

Sometimes N can get quite large. In the 1980s, Argentina suffered hyperinflation. On June 1, 1983, the *peso argentino* replaced the (old) peso at a rate of 10,000 to 1. Then on June 14, 1985, the *austral* replaced the peso argentino at 1,000 to 1. Finally, on January 1, 1992, the *convertible peso* replaced the austral at a rate of 10,000 to 1 (i.e., 10,000,000,000 old pesos). After all

this, if you had owned 1 new peso in 1983 (and had changed it into the later monies), it would have lost 99.99997% of its U.S. dollar value by 2003.

In 1946 the Hungarian *pengö* became so worthless that the authorities no longer printed the denomination on each note in numbers, but only in words—perhaps to avert distrust (unsuccessful), to hide embarrassment (also unsuccessful), or simply because there wasn't room to print all those zeros. By July 15, 1946, there were 76,041,000,000,000,000,000,000,000 pengö in circulation. A stable new currency, the *forint*, was finally introduced on July 26, 1946, with each forint worth 400,000 quadrillion pengö ($4 \times 10^{20} = 400,000,000,000,000,000,000$ pengö). The dilution of the Zimbabwean dollar from 2005 to 2009 was even more extreme, as the authorities lopped off 25 zeros in a series of reforms before the currency finally vanished from use.

PPP in Hyperinflations Each of these crises provides a unique laboratory for testing the predictions of the PPP theory. The scatterplot in Figure 3-9 looks at the data using changes in levels (from start to finish, expressed as multiples). The change in the exchange rate (with the United States) is on the vertical axis and the change in the price level (compared with the United States) is on the horizontal axis. Because of the huge changes involved, both axes use log scales in powers of 10. For example, 10^{12} on the vertical axis means the exchange rate rose (the currency depreciated) by a factor of a trillion against the U.S. dollar during the hyperinflation.

If PPP holds, changes in prices and exchange rates should be equal and all observations would be on the 45-degree line. The changes follow this pattern very closely, providing support for PPP. What the hyperinflations have in common is that a very large depreciation was about equal to a very large inflation differential. In an economy with fairly stable prices and exchange rates, large changes in exchange rates and prices only develop over the very long run of years and decades; in a hyperinflation, large inflations and large depreciations are compressed into the short run of years or months, so this is one case where PPP holds quite well even in the short run.

Some price changes were outrageously large. Austria's hyperinflation of 1921 to 1922 was the first one on record, and prices rose by a factor of about 100 (10^2). In Germany from 1922 to 1923, prices rose by a factor of about 20 billion (2×10^{10}); in the worst month, prices were doubling on average every two days. In Hungary from 1945 to 1946, pengö prices rose by a factor of about 4 septillion (4×10^{27}), the current record, and in July 1946, prices were doubling on average every 15 hours. Serbia's inflation from 1992 to 1994 came close to breaking the record for cumulative price changes, as did the most recent case in Zimbabwe. In comparison, Argentina's 700-fold inflation and Brazil's 200-fold inflation from 1989 to 1990 look modest.

Money Demand in Hyperinflations There is one other important lesson to be learned from hyperinflations. In our simple monetary model, the money demand parameter L was assumed to be *constant* and equal to $\bar{L}$. This implied that real money balances were proportional to real income, with $M/P = \bar{L}Y$ as shown in Equation (3-5). Is this assumption of stable real money balances justified?

The evidence shown in Figure 3-10 suggests this assumption is not justified, based on a subset of the hyperinflations. For each point on the horizontal axis of this figure,

Above top to bottom are an Argentine 500,000 austral bill of 1990; a 1923 one billion German mark note (1 German billion = 1 U.S. trillion); and a Hungarian 100 Million B-pengö of 1946, with the "B" denoting the Hungarian billion, or a million million: this 100,000,000,000,000,000,000 pengö note is the highest denomination of currency ever issued by any country.

FIGURE 3-10

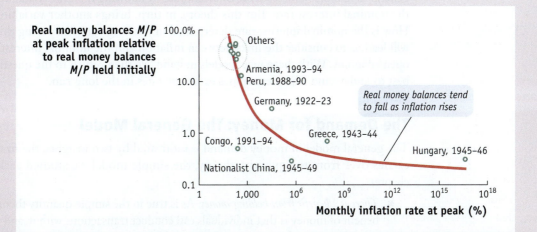

The Collapse of Real Money Balances During Hyperinflations This figure shows that real money balances tend to collapse in hyperinflations as people economize by reducing their holdings of rapidly depreciating notes. The horizontal axis shows the peak monthly inflation rate (%), and the vertical axis shows the ratio of real money balances in that peak month relative to real money balances at the start of the hyperinflationary period. Logarithmic scales are used for clarity.

Data from: IMF, International Financial Statistics; Phillip Cagan, 1956, "The Monetary Dynamics of Hyperinflation," in Milton Friedman, ed., Studies in the Quantity Theory of Money (Chicago: University of Chicago Press), pp. 25–117; Teh-Wei Hu, 1971, "Hyperinflation and the Dynamics of the Demand for Money in China, 1945-1949," Journal of Political Economy, 79(1), 186–195.

we see the peak monthly inflation rate (the moment when prices were rising most rapidly); on the vertical axis, we see the level of real money balances in that month relative to their initial level (in the month just before the hyperinflation began). If real money balances were stable, there should be no variation in the vertical dimension aside from fluctuations in real income. But there is variation, and with a clear pattern: the higher the level of inflation, the lower the level of real money balances. These declines are far too severe to be explained by just the fall in real incomes experienced during hyperinflations, though such income declines did occur.

This finding may not strike you as very surprising. If prices are doubling every few days (or every few hours), the money in people's pockets is rapidly turning into worthless pieces of paper. They will try to minimize their money holdings—and will do so even more as inflation rises higher and higher, just as the figure shows. It becomes just too costly to hold very much money, despite one's need to use it for transactions.

If you thought along these lines, you have an accurate sense of how people behave during hyperinflations to avoid the cost of holding money. But the point is more general and anticipates the extensions to the simple model that we make in the next section so it is more realistic. Even during "normal" inflations—situations that are less pathological than a hyperinflation—it is implausible to assume that real money balances are perfectly stable. In our extension of the simple model, we will assume that people make the trade-off highlighted previously: comparing the benefits of holding money for transactions purposes with the costs of holding money as compared with other assets.

4 Money, Interest Rates, and Prices in the Long Run: A General Model

So far we have a long-run theory that links exchange rates to the price levels in each country: PPP. We also have a simple long-run monetary model that links price levels in each country to money supply and demand: the *quantity theory*.

These building blocks provide some basic intuition for the links between price levels, money, and exchange rates. The trouble is that the quantity theory's assumption—that the demand for money is stable—is implausible. In this section, we explore a more general model that addresses this shortcoming by allowing money demand to vary with the nominal interest rate. But this theory, in turn, brings another variable into play: How is the nominal interest rate determined in the long run? Answering this question will lead us to consider the links between inflation and the nominal interest rate in an open economy. With these new models in hand, we then return to the question of how best to understand what determines exchange rates in the long run.

The Demand for Money: The General Model

The general model of money demand is motivated by two insights, the first of which carries over from the quantity theory, the simple model we studied earlier in this chapter.

- *There is a benefit from holding money.* As is true in the simple quantity theory, the benefit of money is that individuals can conduct transactions with it, and we continue to assume that transactions demand is in proportion to income, all else equal.

- *There is a cost to holding money.* The nominal interest rate on money is zero, $i_{money} = 0$. By holding money and not earning interest, people incur the opportunity cost of holding money. For example, an individual could hold an interest-earning asset paying $i_\$$. The difference in nominal returns between this asset and money would be $i_\$ - i_{money} = i_\$ > 0$. This is one way of expressing the opportunity cost.

Moving from the individual or household level up to the macroeconomic level, we can infer that aggregate money demand in the economy as a whole will behave similarly:

All else equal, a rise in national dollar income (nominal income) will cause a proportional increase in transactions and, hence, in aggregate money demand.

All else equal, a rise in the nominal interest rate will cause the aggregate demand for money to fall.

Thus, we arrive at a general model in which money demand is proportional to nominal income, and is a decreasing function of the nominal interest rate:

$$\underbrace{M^d}_{\substack{\text{Demand} \\ \text{for money (\$)}}} = \underbrace{L(i)}_{\substack{\text{A} \\ \text{decreasing} \\ \text{function}}} \times \underbrace{P \times Y}_{\substack{\text{Nominal} \\ \text{income (\$)}}}$$

Recall that, formerly, in the quantity theory, the parameter L (the liquidity ratio, the amount of money needed for transactions per dollar of nominal GDP) was a constant. In this general model, we assume that L is a decreasing function of the nominal interest rate i. Dividing by P, we can derive the demand for real money balances:

$$\underbrace{\frac{M^d}{P}}_{\substack{\text{Demand} \\ \text{for real money}}} = \underbrace{L(i)}_{\substack{\text{A} \\ \text{decreasing} \\ \text{function}}} \times \underbrace{Y}_{\substack{\text{Real} \\ \text{income}}}$$

Figure 3-11(a) shows a typical **real money demand function** of this form, with the quantity of real money balances demanded on the horizontal axis and the nominal interest rate on the vertical axis. The downward slope of the demand curve reflects the inverse relationship between the demand for real money balances and the nominal interest rate *at a given level of real income* (Y).

Figure 3-11(b) shows what happens when real income increases from Y_1 to Y_2. When real income increases (by $x\%$), the demand for real money balances increases (by $x\%$) at each level of the nominal interest rate and the curve shifts.

FIGURE 3-11

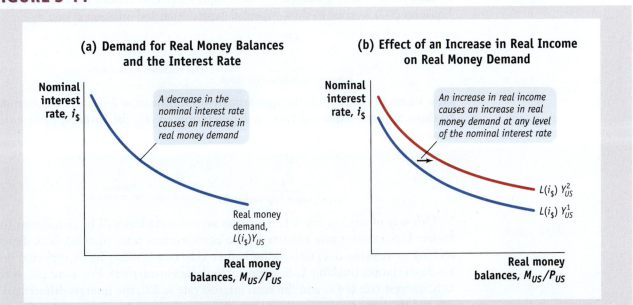

The Standard Model of Real Money Demand Panel (a) shows the real money demand function for the United States. The downward slope implies that the quantity of real money demand rises as the nominal interest rate $i_\$$ falls. Panel (b) shows that an increase in real income from Y_{US}^1 to Y_{US}^2 causes real money demand to rise at all levels of the nominal interest rate $i_\$$.

Long-Run Equilibrium in the Money Market

The money market is in equilibrium when the real money supply (determined by the central bank) equals the demand for real money balances (determined by the nominal interest rate and real income):

$$\underbrace{\frac{M}{P}}_{\text{Real money supply}} = \underbrace{L(i)Y}_{\text{Real money demand}} \tag{3-7}$$

We will continue to assume that prices are flexible in the long run and that they adjust to ensure that equilibrium is maintained.

We now have a model that describes equilibrium in the money market that will help us on the way to understanding the determination of the exchange rate. Before we arrive at the long-run exchange rate, however, we need one last piece to the puzzle. Under the quantity theory, the nominal interest rate was ignored. Now, in our general model, it is a key variable in the determination of money demand. So we need a theory to tell us what the level of the nominal interest rate i will be in the long run. Once we have solved this problem, we will be able to apply this new, more complex but more realistic, model of the money market to the analysis of exchange rate determination in the long run.

Inflation and Interest Rates in the Long Run

The tools we need to determine the nominal interest rate in an open economy are already at hand. So far in this chapter, we have developed the idea of purchasing power parity (PPP), which links prices and exchange rates. In the last chapter, we developed another parity idea, uncovered interest parity (UIP), which links exchange rates and interest rates. With only these two relationships in hand, PPP and UIP, we can derive a powerful and striking result concerning interest rates that has profound implications for our study of open economy macroeconomics.

Relative PPP, as indicated in Equation (3-2), states that the rate of depreciation equals the inflation differential at time t. When market actors use this equation to forecast future exchange rates, we use a superscript e to denote such expectations. Equation (3-2) is recast to show expected depreciation and inflation at time t:

$$\underbrace{\frac{\Delta E^e_{\$/€}}{E_{\$/€}}}_{\text{Expected rate of dollar depreciation}} = \underbrace{\pi^e_{US} - \pi^e_{EUR}}_{\text{Expected inflation differential}}$$

Next we recall that UIP in the approximate form (Equation 2-3) can be rearranged to show that the expected rate of depreciation equals the interest differential at time t:

$$\underbrace{\frac{\Delta E^e_{\$/€}}{E_{\$/€}}}_{\text{Expected rate of dollar depreciation}} = \underbrace{i_{\$}}_{\substack{\text{Net dollar} \\ \text{interest rate}}} - \underbrace{i_{€}}_{\substack{\text{Net euro} \\ \text{interest rate}}}$$

This way of writing the UIP equation says that traders will be indifferent to a higher U.S. interest rate relative to the euro interest rates (making U.S. deposits look more attractive) only if the higher U.S. rate is offset by an expected dollar depreciation (making U.S. deposits look less attractive). For example, if the U.S. interest rate is 4% and the euro interest rate is 2%, the interest differential is 2% and the forex market can be in equilibrium only if traders expect a 2% depreciation of the U.S. dollar against the euro, which would exactly offset the higher U.S. interest rate.

The Fisher Effect

Because the left sides of the previous two equations are equal, the right sides must also be equal. Thus, the nominal interest differential equals the expected inflation differential:

$$\underbrace{i_\$ - i_\€}_{\text{Nominal interest rate differential}} = \underbrace{\pi^e_{US} - \pi^e_{EUR}}_{\substack{\text{Nominal inflation rate differential} \\ \text{(expected)}}} \qquad (3\text{-}8)$$

What does this important result say? To take an example, suppose expected inflation is 4% in the United States and 2% in Europe. The inflation differential on the right is then +2% (4% − 2% = +2%). If interest rates in Europe are 3%, then to make the interest differential the same as the inflation differential, +2%, the interest rate in the United States must equal 5% (5% − 3% = +2%).

Now suppose expected inflation in the United States changes, rising by one percentage point to 5%. If nothing changes in Europe, then the U.S. interest rate must also rise by one percentage point to 6% for the equation to hold. In general, this equation predicts that changes in the expected rate of inflation will be fully incorporated (one for one) into changes in nominal interest rates.

All else equal, a rise in the expected inflation rate in a country will lead to an equal rise in its nominal interest rate.

This result is known as the **Fisher effect**, named for the American economist Irving Fisher (1867–1947). Note that because this result depends on an assumption of PPP, it is therefore likely to hold only in the long run.

The Fisher effect makes clear the link between inflation and interest rates under flexible prices, a finding that is widely applicable. For a start, it makes sense of the evidence we just saw on money holdings during hyperinflations (see Figure 3-10). As inflation rises, the Fisher effect tells us that the nominal interest rate i must rise by the same amount; the general model of money demand then tells us that $L(i)$ must fall because it is a decreasing function of i. Thus, for a given level of real income, real money balances must fall as inflation rises.

In other words, the Fisher effect predicts that the change in the opportunity cost of money is equal not just only to the change in the nominal interest rate but also to the change in the inflation rate. In times of very high inflation, people should, therefore, want to reduce their money holdings—and they do.

Real Interest Parity

As just described, the Fisher effect tells us something about nominal interest rates, but we can quickly derive the implications for real interest rates, too. Rearranging the last equation, we find

$$i_\$ - \pi^e_{US} = i_\€ - \pi^e_{EUR}$$

The expressions on either side of this equation might look familiar from previous courses in macroeconomics. When the inflation rate (π) is subtracted from a *nominal* interest rate (i), the result is a **real interest rate** (r), the inflation-adjusted return on an interest-bearing asset. Given this definition, we can simplify the last equation further. On the left is the expected real interest rate in the United States ($r^e_{US} = i_\$ - \pi^e_{US}$). On the right is the expected real interest rate in Europe ($r^e_{EUR} = i_\€ - \pi^e_{EUR}$).

Thus, using only two assumptions, PPP and UIP, we have shown that

$$r^e_{US} = r^e_{EUR} \qquad (3\text{-}9)$$

This remarkable result states the following: *if PPP and UIP hold, then expected real interest rates are equalized across countries.*

This powerful condition is called **real interest parity**, and because it depends on an assumption of PPP, it is therefore likely to hold only in the long run.[10]

We have arrived at a strong conclusion about the potential for globalization to cause convergence in economic outcomes, because real interest parity implies the following: *arbitrage in goods and financial markets alone is sufficient, in the long run, to cause the equalization of real interest rates across countries.*

We have considered two locations, but this argument applies to all countries integrated into the global capital market. In the long run, they will all share a common expected real interest rate, the long-run expected **world real interest rate** denoted r^*, so

$$r_{US}^e = r_{EUR}^e = r^*$$

From now on, unless indicated otherwise, we treat r^* as a given, exogenous variable, something outside the control of a policymaker in any particular country.[11]

Under these conditions, the Fisher effect is even clearer, because, by definition,

$$i_\$ = r_{US}^e + \pi_{US}^e = r^* + \pi_{US}^e \qquad\qquad i_\euro = r_{EUR}^e + \pi_{EUR}^e = r^* + \pi_{EUR}^e$$

Thus, in each country, the long-run expected nominal interest rate is the long-run world real interest rate plus that country's expected long-run inflation rate. For example, if the world real interest rate is $r^* = 2\%$, and the country's long-run expected inflation rate goes up by two percentage points from 3% to 5%, then its long-run nominal interest rate also goes up by two percentage points from the old level of $2 + 3 = 5\%$ to a new level of $2 + 5 = 7\%$.

APPLICATION

Evidence on the Fisher Effect

Are the Fisher effect and real interest parity supported by empirical evidence? One might expect a problem here. We derived both of these results using an assumption of purchasing power parity. The evidence we have seen on PPP offers some support in the long run, but not in the short run. Thus, we should not expect the Fisher effect and real interest parity to hold in the short run either; however, we might expect them to hold (at least approximately) in the long run.

Figure 3-12 shows that the Fisher effect is close to reality in the long run: on average, countries with higher inflation rates tend to have higher nominal interest rates, and the data line up fairly well with the predictions of the theory. Figure 3-13 shows that, for three developed countries, real interest parity holds fairly well in the long run: real interest differentials are not always zero, but they tend to fluctuate around zero in the long run. This could be seen as evidence in favor of long-run real interest parity.

---

[10] You may have encountered other theories in which real interest rates are equalized across countries by other means. Countries may share common technologies (because of technology diffusion) or might have similar saving behavior (because of similar preferences). Such assumptions could lead to identical real interest rates even in two *closed* economies. But here we have derived the real interest parity condition *only* from UIP and PPP, meaning that, in *open* economies, these are *sufficient* conditions for real interest rates to be equalized. No other assumptions are needed!

[11] Advanced economic theories explore the determinants of the world real interest rate, with reference to consumption preferences of households and the extent to which they discount the future.

FIGURE 3-12

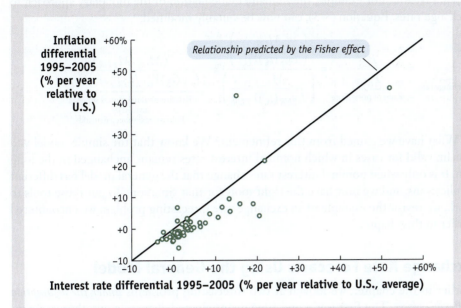

Inflation Rates and Nominal Interest Rates, 1995–2005 This scatterplot shows the relationship between the average annual nominal interest rate differential and the annual inflation differential relative to the United States over a 10-year period for a sample of 62 countries. The correlation between the two variables is strong and bears a close resemblance to the theoretical prediction of the Fisher effect that all data points would appear on the 45-degree line.

Data from: IMF, International Financial Statistics.

FIGURE 3-13

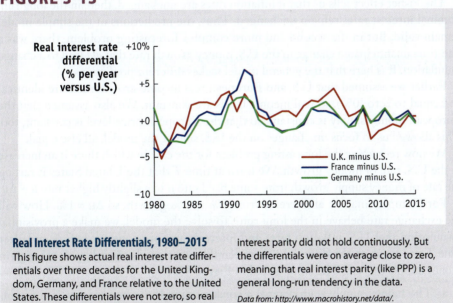

Real Interest Rate Differentials, 1980–2015 This figure shows actual real interest rate differentials over three decades for the United Kingdom, Germany, and France relative to the United States. These differentials were not zero, so real interest parity did not hold continuously. But the differentials were on average close to zero, meaning that real interest parity (like PPP) is a general long-run tendency in the data.

Data from: http://www.macrohistory.net/data/.

The Fundamental Equation Under the General Model

Now that we understand how the nominal interest rate is determined in the long run, our general model is complete. This model differs from the simple model (the quantity theory) *only* by allowing L to vary as a function of the nominal interest rate i.

We can therefore update our fundamental equations to allow for this change in how we treat L. For example, the fundamental equation of the monetary approach to exchange rates, Equation (3-3), can now be suitably modified:

$$\underbrace{E_{\$/€}}_{\text{Exchange rate}} = \underbrace{\frac{P_{US}}{P_{EUR}}}_{\text{Ratio of price levels}} = \frac{\left(\dfrac{M_{US}}{L_{US}(i_\$)Y_{US}}\right)}{\left(\dfrac{M_{EUR}}{L_{EUR}(i_€)Y_{EUR}}\right)} = \underbrace{\frac{(M_{US}/M_{EUR})}{(L_{US}(i_\$)Y_{US}/L_{EUR}(i_€)Y_{EUR})}}_{\substack{\text{Relative nominal money supplies} \\ \text{divided by} \\ \text{Relative real money demands}}} \quad (3\text{-}10)$$

What have we gained from this refinement? We know that the simple model will remain valid for cases in which nominal interest rates remain unchanged in the long run. It is only when nominal interest rates change that the general model has different implications, and we now have the right tools for that situation. To put those tools to work, we revisit the example of an exchange rate forecasting problem we encountered earlier in this chapter.

Exchange Rate Forecasts Using the General Model

Earlier in the chapter, we looked at two forecasting problems *under the assumption of flexible prices*. The first was a one-time unanticipated change in an otherwise constant U.S. money supply. Under the assumptions we made (stable real income in both countries and stable European money supply), this change caused a one-time increase in the U.S. price level but did not lead to a change in U.S. inflation (which was zero before and after the event).

The Fisher effect tells us that if inflation rates are unchanged, then, in the long run, nominal interest rates remain unchanged. Thus, the predictions of the simple model remain valid. But in the second and more complex forecasting problem, there was a one-time unanticipated change in the U.S. money growth rate that *did* lead to a change in inflation. It is here that the general model makes different predictions.

Earlier we assumed that U.S. and European real income growth rates are identical and equal to zero (0%), so real income levels are constant. We also assumed that the European money supply is constant, so that the European price level is constant, too. This allowed us to focus on changes on the U.S. side of the model, all else equal.

We now reexamine the forecasting problem for the case in which there is an increase in the U.S. rate of money growth. We learn at time T that the United States is raising the rate of money supply growth from some fixed rate μ to a slightly higher rate $\mu + \Delta\mu$.

For example, imagine an increase from 2% to 3% growth, so $\Delta\mu = 1\%$. How will the exchange rate behave in the long run? To solve the model, we make a provisional assumption that U.S. inflation rates and interest rates are constant before and after time T and focus on the differences between the two periods caused by the change in money supply growth. The story is told in Figure 3-14:

a. The money supply is growing at a constant rate. If the interest rate is constant in each period, then real money balances M/P remain constant, by assumption, because $L(i)Y$ is then a constant. If real money balances are constant, then M and P grow at the same rate. Before T that rate is $\mu = 2\%$; after T that rate is $\mu + \Delta\mu = 3\%$. That is, the U.S. inflation rate rises by an amount $\Delta\mu = 1\%$ at time T.

b. As a result of the Fisher effect, U.S. interest rates also rise by $\Delta\mu = 1\%$ at time T. Consequently, real money balances M/P must fall at time T because $L(i)Y$ will decrease as i increases.

c. In (a) we have described the path of M. In (b) we found that M/P is constant up to T, then drops suddenly, and then is constant after time T. What path must the price level P follow? Up to time T, it is a constant multiple of M; the

FIGURE 3-14

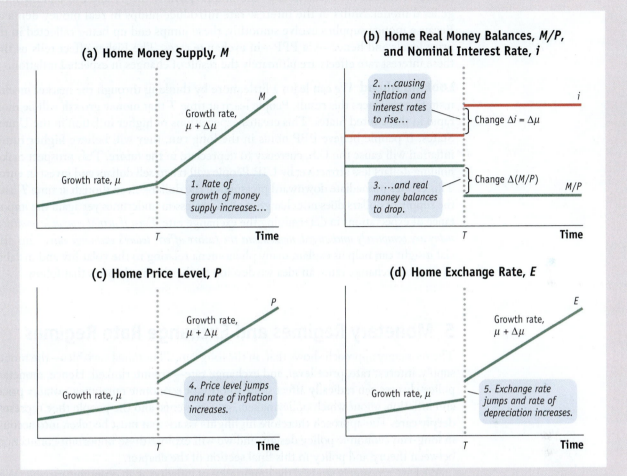

(a) Home Money Supply, M

Growth rate, $\mu + \Delta\mu$

Growth rate, μ

1. Rate of growth of money supply increases...

T   **Time**

(b) Home Real Money Balances, M/P, and Nominal Interest Rate, i

2. ...causing inflation and interest rates to rise...

Change $\Delta i = \Delta\mu$ *i*

Change $\Delta(M/P)$

3. ...and real money balances to drop.   *M/P*

T   **Time**

(c) Home Price Level, P

P

Growth rate, $\mu + \Delta\mu$

Growth rate, μ

4. Price level jumps and rate of inflation increases.

T   **Time**

(d) Home Exchange Rate, E

E

Growth rate, $\mu + \Delta\mu$

Growth rate, μ

5. Exchange rate jumps and rate of depreciation increases.

T   **Time**

An Increase in the Growth Rate of the Money Supply in the Standard Model Before time *T*, money, prices, and the exchange rate all grow at rate μ. Foreign prices are constant. In panel (a), we suppose at time *T* that there is an increase $\Delta\mu$ in the rate of growth of home money supply *M*. This causes an increase $\Delta\mu$ in the rate of inflation; the Fisher effect means that there will be a $\Delta\mu$ increase in the nominal interest rate; as a result, as shown in panel (b), real money demand falls with a discrete jump at *T*. If real money balances are to fall when the nominal money supply expands continuously, then the domestic price level must make a discrete jump up at time *T*, as shown in panel (c). Subsequently, prices grow at the new higher rate of inflation; and given the stable foreign price level, PPP implies that the exchange rate follows a similar path to the domestic price level, as shown in panel (d).

same applies after time *T*, but the constant has increased. Why? The nominal money supply grows smoothly, without a jump. So if real money balances drop down discontinuously at time *T*, the price level must jump up discontinuously at time *T*. The intuition for this is that the rise in inflation and interest rates at time *T* prompts people to instantaneously demand less real money, but because the supply of nominal money is unchanged, the price level has to jump up. Apart from this jump, *P* grows at a constant rate; before *T* that rate is $\mu = 2\%$; after *T* that rate is $\mu + \Delta\mu = 3\%$.

d. PPP implies that *E* and *P* must move in the same proportion, so *E* is always a constant multiple of *P*. Thus, *E* jumps like *P* at time *T*. Apart from this jump, *E* grows at a constant rate; before *T* that rate is $\mu = 2\%$; after *T* that rate is $\mu + \Delta\mu = 3\%$.

Corresponding to these four steps, Figure 3-14 illustrates the path of the key variables in this example. (Our provisional assumption of constant inflation rates and interest rates in each period is satisfied, so the proposed solution is internally consistent.)

Comparing Figure 3-14 with Figure 3-6, we can observe the subtle qualitative differences between the predictions of the simple quantity theory and those of the more general model. Shifts in the interest rate introduce jumps in real money demand. Because money supplies evolve smoothly, these jumps end up being reflected in the price levels and hence—via PPP—in exchange rates. The Fisher effect tells us that these interest rate effects are ultimately the result of changes in expected inflation.

Looking Ahead We can learn a little more by thinking through the market mechanism that produces this result. People learn at time T that money growth will be more rapid in the United States. This creates expectations of higher inflation in the United States. If people believe PPP holds in the long run, they will believe higher future inflation will cause the U.S. currency to depreciate in the future. This prospect makes holding dollars less attractive, by UIP. People will try to sell dollars and invest in euros. This creates immediate downward pressure on the dollar—even though at time T itself the supply of dollars does not change at all! This lesson underlines yet again the importance of expectations in determining the exchange rate. *Even if actual economic conditions today are completely unchanged, news about the future affects today's exchange rate.* This crucial insight can help us explain many phenomena relating to the volatility and instability in spot exchange rates, an idea we develop further in the chapters that follow.

5 Monetary Regimes and Exchange Rate Regimes

The monetary approach shows that, in the long run, all nominal variables—the money supply, interest rate, price level, and exchange rate—are interlinked. Hence, monetary policy choices can radically affect some important economic outcomes, notably prices and inflation, about which policymakers, governments, and the people they represent deeply care. The approach therefore highlights issues that must be taken into account in long-run economic policy design, and we will explore these important connections between theory and policy in this final section of the chapter.

We have repeatedly stressed the importance of inflation as an economic variable. Why is it so important? High or volatile inflation rates are considered undesirable. They may destabilize an economy or retard its growth.[12] Economies with low and stable inflation generally grow faster than those with high or volatile inflation. Inflationary crises, in which inflation jumps to a high or hyperinflationary level, are very damaging indeed.[13]

Thus, an overarching aspect of a nation's economic policy is the desire to keep inflation within certain bounds. The achievement of such an objective requires that policymakers be subject to (or subject themselves to) some kind of constraint in the long run. Such constraints are called **nominal anchors** because they attempt to tie down a nominal variable that is potentially under the policymakers' control.

Policymakers cannot directly control prices, so the attainment of price stability in the *short run* is not feasible. The question is what policymakers can do to promote price stability in the long run and what types of flexibility, if any, they will allow themselves

---

[12] Macroeconomists can list numerous potential costs of inflation. Expected inflation generates a cost of holding money, a tax on transactions that adds friction to the economy; firms and workers use nominal contracts for prices and would have to change prices and rewrite contracts more often; inflation also distorts the economy when a tax system has significant nominal provisions (e.g., fixed deductions and exemptions). Unexpected inflation creates arbitrary redistributions from creditors to debtors, and this introduces risk into borrowing and lending, making interest rates and investment more costly. In short, if inflation is other than low and stable, economic life becomes at best inconvenient and at worst (as in a hyperinflation) dysfunctional. See N. Gregory Mankiw, 2013, *Macroeconomics*, 8th edition, Chap. 5 (New York: Worth).

[13] This evidence is merely suggestive: high inflation and slow growth may each be caused by other factors, such as weak institutions. Some studies have used sophisticated econometrics to address this problem. See Stanley Fischer, 1993, "The Role of Macroeconomic Factors in Growth," *Journal of Monetary Economics*, 32, 485–511; Robert J. Barro, 1997, *Determinants of Economic Growth* (Cambridge, Mass.: MIT Press); Michael Bruno and William Easterly, 1998, "Inflation Crises and Long-Run Growth," *Journal of Monetary Economics*, 41, 3–26.

in the short run. Long-run nominal anchoring and short-run flexibility are the characteristics of the policy framework that economists call the **monetary regime**. In this section, we examine different types of monetary regimes and what they mean for the exchange rate.

The Long Run: The Nominal Anchor

Which variables could policymakers use as anchors to achieve an inflation objective in the long run? To answer this key question, all we have to do is go back and rearrange the equations for relative PPP at Equation (3-2), the quantity theory in rates of change at Equation (3-6), and the Fisher effect at Equation (3-8), to obtain alternative expressions for the rate of inflation in the home country. To emphasize that these findings apply generally to all countries, we re-label the countries Home (H) and Foreign (F) instead of United States and Europe.

The three main nominal anchor choices that emerge are as follows:

- **Exchange rate target:** Relative PPP at Equation (3-2) says that the rate of depreciation equals the inflation differential, or $\Delta E_{H/F}/E_{H/F} = \pi_H - \pi_F$. Rearranging this expression suggests that one way to anchor inflation is as follows:

$$\underbrace{\pi_H}_{\text{Inflation}} = \underbrace{\frac{\Delta E_{H/F}}{E_{H/F}}}_{\substack{\text{Rate of} \\ \text{depreciation}}} + \underbrace{\pi_F}_{\substack{\text{Foreign} \\ \text{inflation}}}$$

Anchor variable

Relative PPP says that home inflation equals the rate of depreciation plus foreign inflation. A simple rule would be to set the rate of depreciation equal to a constant. Under a fixed exchange rate, that constant is set at zero (a peg). Under a crawl, it is a nonzero constant. Alternatively, there may be room for movement about a target (a band). Or there may be a vague goal to allow the exchange rate "limited flexibility." Such policies can deliver stable home inflation if PPP works well and if policymakers keep their commitment. The drawback is the final term in the equation: PPP implies that over the long run the home country "imports" inflation from the foreign country over and above the chosen rate of depreciation. For example, under a peg, if foreign inflation rises by 1% per year, then so, too, does home inflation. Thus, countries almost invariably peg to a country with a reputation for price stability (e.g., the United States). This is a common policy choice: fixed exchange rates of some form are in use in more than half of the world's countries.

- **Money supply target:** The quantity theory suggests another way to anchor because the fundamental equation for the price level in the monetary approach says that inflation equals the excess of the rate of money supply growth over and above the rate of real income growth:

$$\underbrace{\pi_H}_{\text{Inflation}} = \underbrace{\mu_H}_{\text{Money supply growth}} - \underbrace{g_H}_{\text{Real output growth}}$$

Anchor variable

A simple rule of this sort is: set the growth rate of the money supply equal to a constant, say, 2% a year. The printing presses should be put on automatic pilot, and no human interference should be allowed. Essentially, the central bank is run by robots. This would be difficult to implement. Again the drawback is the final term in the previous equation: real income growth can be unstable. In periods of high growth, inflation will be below the desired level. In periods of low growth, inflation will be above the desired level. For this reason, money supply targets are waning in popularity or are used in conjunction with other targets. For example, the European Central Bank claims to use monetary growth rates as a partial guide to policy, but nobody is quite sure how serious it is.

- **Inflation target plus interest rate policy:** The Fisher effect suggests yet another anchoring method:

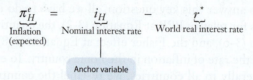

$$\underbrace{\pi_H^e}_{\substack{\text{Inflation}\\\text{(expected)}}} = \underbrace{i_H}_{\substack{\text{Nominal interest rate}\\|\\\boxed{\text{Anchor variable}}}} - \underbrace{r^*}_{\text{World real interest rate}}$$

The Fisher effect says that home inflation is the home nominal interest rate minus the foreign real interest rate. If the latter can be assumed to be constant, then as long as the average home nominal interest rate is kept stable, inflation can also be kept stable. This type of nominal anchoring framework is an increasingly common policy choice. Assuming a stable world real interest rate is not a bad assumption. (And in principle, the target level of the nominal interest rate could be adjusted if necessary.) More or less flexible versions of inflation targeting can be implemented. A central bank could in theory set the nominal interest rate at a fixed level at all times, but such rigidity is rarely seen, and central banks usually adjust interest rates in the short run to meet other goals. For example, if the world real interest rate is $r^* = 2.5\%$, and the country's long-run inflation target is 2%, then its long-run nominal interest rate ought to be on average equal to 4.5% (because $2.5\% = 4.5\% - 2\%$). This would be termed the *neutral* level of the nominal interest rate. But in the short run, the central bank might desire to use some flexibility to set interest rates above or below this neutral level. How much flexibility is a matter of policy choice, as is the question of what economic objectives should drive deviations from the neutral rate (e.g., inflation performance alone, or other factors like output and employment that we shall consider in later chapters).

The Choice of a Nominal Anchor and Its Implications

Under the assumptions we have made, any of the three nominal anchor choices are valid. If a particular long-run inflation objective is to be met, then, all else equal, the first equation says it will be consistent with one particular rate of depreciation; the second equation says it will be consistent with one particular rate of money supply growth; the third equation says it will be consistent with one particular rate of interest. But if policymakers announced targets for all three variables, they would be able to match all three consistently only by chance. Two observations follow.

First, using more than one target may be problematic. Under a fixed exchange rate regime, policymakers cannot employ any target other than the exchange rate. However, they may be able to use a mix of different targets if they adopt an intermediate regime, such as managed floating. Table 3-2 illustrates the ways in which the choice of a target as a nominal anchor affects the choice of exchange rate regime. Obviously, these are not independent choices. But a variety of choices do exist. Thus, *nominal anchoring is possible with a variety of exchange rate regimes.*

Second, whatever target choice is made, a country that commits to a target as a way of nominal anchoring is committing itself to set future money supplies and interest rates in such a way as to meet the target. Only one path for future policy will be compatible with the target in the long run. Thus, *a country with a nominal anchor sacrifices monetary policy autonomy in the long run.*

TABLE 3-2

Exchange Rate Regimes and Nominal Anchors This table illustrates the possible exchange rate regimes that are consistent with various types of nominal anchors. Countries that are dollarized or in a currency union have a "superfixed" exchange rate target. Pegs, bands, and crawls also target the exchange rate. Managed floats have no preset path for the exchange rate, which allows other targets to be employed. Countries that float freely or independently are judged to pay no serious attention to exchange rate targets; if they have anchors, they will involve monetary targets or inflation targets with an interest rate policy. The countries with "freely falling" exchange rates have no serious target and have high rates of inflation and depreciation. It should be noted that many countries engage in implicit targeting (e.g., inflation targeting) without announcing an explicit target and that some countries may use a mix of more than one target.

Type of Nominal Anchor	Compatible Exchange Rate Regimes				
	Countries Without a Currency of Their Own	Pegs/ Bands/ Crawls	Managed Floating	Freely Floating	Freely Falling (rapid depreciation)
Exchange rate target	✓	✓	✓		
Money supply target			✓	✓	
Inflation target (plus interest rate policy)			✓	✓	
None				✓	✓

APPLICATION

Nominal Anchors in Theory and Practice

An appreciation of the importance of nominal anchors has transformed monetary policymaking and inflation performance throughout the global economy in recent decades.

In the 1970s, most of the world was struggling with high inflation. An economic slowdown prompted central banks everywhere to loosen monetary policy. In advanced countries, a move to floating exchange rates allowed great freedom for them to loosen their monetary policy. Developing countries had already proven vulnerable to high inflation, and now many of them were exposed to even worse inflation. Those who were pegged to major currencies imported high inflation via PPP. Those who weren't pegged struggled to find a credible nominal anchor as they faced economic downturns of their own. High oil prices everywhere contributed to inflationary pressure.

In the 1980s, inflationary pressure continued in many developed countries, and in many developing countries high levels of inflation, and even hyperinflations, were not uncommon. Governments were forced to respond to public demands for a more stable inflation environment. In the 1990s, policies designed to create effective nominal anchors were put in place in many countries, and these have endured to the present.

One study found that the use of explicit targets grew markedly in the 1990s, replacing regimes in which there had previously been no explicit nominal anchor. The number of countries in the study with exchange rate targets increased from 30 to 47. The number with money targets increased from 18 to 39. The number with inflation targets increased most dramatically, almost sevenfold, from 8 to 54. Many countries had more than one target in use: in 1998, 55% of the sample announced an explicit target (or monitoring range) for more than one of: the exchange rate, money, and inflation. These shifts have persisted. As of 2010, more than a decade later, there were still more than 50 inflation-targeting countries (many now part of the single Eurozone bloc),

TABLE 3-3

Global Disinflation Cross-country data from 1980 to 2015 show the gradual reduction in the annual rate of inflation around the world. This disinflation process began in the advanced economies in the early 1980s. The emerging markets and developing countries suffered from even higher rates of inflation, although these finally began to fall in the 1990s.

	Annual Inflation Rate (%)						
	1980–84	1985–89	1990–94	1995–99	2000–04	2005–09	2010–14
World	14.1	15.5	30.4	8.4	3.9	4.0	4.1
Advanced economies	8.7	3.9	3.8	2.0	1.8	2.0	1.6
Emerging markets and developing countries	31.4	48.0	53.2	13.1	5.6	6.5	6.0

Data from: Kenneth Rogoff, 2003, "Globalization and Global Disinflation," Economic Review, Federal Reserve Bank of Kansas City, IV, 45–78. Updated for the years 2005 to 2014 using the IMF World Economic Outlook database.

and there were more than 80 countries pursuing some kind of exchange rate target via a currency board, peg, band, or crawl type of arrangement.[14]

Looking back from the present we can see that most, but not all, of those policies have turned out to be credible, too, thanks to political developments in many countries that have fostered **central bank independence**. Independent central banks stand apart from the interference of politicians: they have operational freedom to try to achieve the inflation target, and they may even play a role in setting that target.

Overall, these efforts are judged to have achieved some success, although in many countries inflation had already been brought down substantially in the early to mid-1980s before inflation targets and institutional changes were implemented. Table 3-3 shows a steady decline in average levels of inflation since the early 1980s. The lowest levels of inflation are seen in the advanced economies, although developing countries have also started to make some limited progress. In the industrial countries, central bank independence is now commonplace (it was not in the 1970s), but in developing countries it is still relatively rare.

Still, one can have too much of a good thing, and the crisis of 2008–2010 prompted some second thoughts about inflation targets. Typically, such targets have been set at about 2% in developed countries, and with a world real interest rate of 2% this implies a neutral nominal interest rate of 4%. In terms of having room to maneuver, this rate permits central banks to temporarily cut their interest rates up to four percentage points below the neutral level. Prior to the crisis this range was considered ample room for central banks to take short-run actions as needed (e.g., to stimulate output or the rate of inflation if either fell too low). In the crisis, however, central banks soon hit the lower bound of zero interest rates and could not prevent severe output losses and declines in rates of inflation to low levels below their targets—and, at times, even negative rates of inflation (i.e., *deflation*). As Irving Fisher famously noted, deflation is very damaging economically—it drives up real interest rates when nominal rates can fall no further as an offset, and falling prices make the real burden of nominal debts higher. These problems led some economists, among them the IMF's Chief Economist at the time, Olivier Blanchard, to question whether inflation targets should be set higher (e.g., at 4% rather than 2%).[15] The idea received a lukewarm reception,

---

[14] On the 1990s see Gabriel Sterne, 1999, "The Use of Explicit Targets for Monetary Policy: Practical Experiences of 91 Economies in the 1990s," *Bank of England Quarterly Bulletin*, 39(3), 272–281. Data for circa 2010 from www.centralbanknews.info and from exchange rate classifications in the previous chapter.

[15] Olivier Blanchard, Giovanni Dell'Ariccia, and Paolo Mauro, 2010, "Rethinking Macroeconomic Policy," *IMF Staff Position Note*, SPN/10/03.

however: moving to a higher inflation target is easy in principle, but many feared its potential abuse would risk the hard-won credibility gains that central banks have earned for themselves in the last three decades. Indeed, even as inflation rates fell almost to zero in major economies like the United States and Eurozone, many central bankers continued to speak of their vigilance in guarding against inflation.

6 Conclusions

This chapter emphasized the determinants of exchange rates in the long run using the monetary approach. We employed purchasing power parity and a simple monetary model (the quantity theory) to study an equilibrium in which goods are arbitraged and prices are flexible. Under these assumptions, in the home country, changes in the money supply pass through into proportional changes in the price level and the exchange rate.

We also found that uncovered interest parity and purchasing power parity implied that real interest rates are equalized across countries. This helped us develop a monetary model that was more complex—and more realistic—because it allowed money demand to fluctuate in response to changes in the interest rate. In that setting, increases in money growth lead to higher inflation and a higher nominal interest rate and, hence, via decreases in money demand, to even higher price levels. Still, the same basic intuition holds, and one-time changes in the money supply still lead to proportional changes in prices and exchange rates.

The monetary approach to exchange rates provides a basis for certain kinds of forecasting and policy analysis using the flexible-price model in the long run. But such forecasts matter even in the short run because today's spot exchange rate depends, like all asset prices, on the exchange rate expected to prevail in the future. To make these connections clear, in the next chapter we bring together the key ideas of arbitrage (from the previous chapter) and expectations (from this chapter) to form a complete model of the exchange rate.

KEY POINTS

1. Purchasing power parity (PPP) implies that the exchange rate should equal the relative price level in the two countries, and the real exchange rate should equal 1.

2. Evidence for PPP is weak in the short run but more favorable in the long run. In the short run, deviations are common and changes in the real exchange rate do occur. The failure of PPP in the short run is primarily the result of market frictions, imperfections that limit arbitrage, and price stickiness.

3. A simple monetary model (the quantity theory) explains price levels in terms of money supply levels and real income levels. Because PPP can explain exchange rates in terms of price levels, the two together can be used to develop a monetary approach to the exchange rate.

4. If we can forecast money supply and income, we can use the monetary approach to forecast the level of the exchange rate at any time in the future. However, the monetary approach is valid only under the assumption that prices are flexible. This assumption is more likely to hold in the long run, so the monetary approach is not useful in the short-run forecast. Evidence for PPP and the monetary approach is more favorable in the long run.

5. PPP theory, combined with uncovered interest parity, leads to the strong implications of the Fisher effect (interest differentials between countries should equal inflation differentials). The Fisher effect says that changes in local inflation rates pass through one for one into changes in local nominal interest rates. The result implies real interest parity (expected real interest rates should be equalized

across countries). Because these results rest on PPP, they should be viewed only as long-run results, and the evidence is somewhat favorable.

6. We can augment the simple monetary model (quantity theory) to allow for the demand for real money balances to decrease as the nominal interest rate rises. This leads to the general monetary model. Its predictions are similar to those of the simple model, except that a one-time rise in money growth rates leads to a one-time rise in inflation, which leads to a one-time drop in real money

demand, which in turn causes a one-time jump in the price level and the exchange rate.

7. The monetary approach to exchange rate determination in the long run has implications for economic policy. Policymakers and the public generally prefer a low-inflation environment. Various policies based on exchange rates, money growth, or interest rates have been proposed as nominal anchors. Recent decades have seen a worldwide decline in inflation thanks to the explicit recognition of the need for nominal anchors.

KEY TERMS

monetary approach to exchange rates, p. 56
law of one price (LOOP), p. 57
purchasing power parity (PPP), p. 58
absolute PPP, p. 58
real exchange rate, p. 59
real depreciation, p. 59
real appreciation, p. 59
undervalued, p. 59
overvalued, p. 59
inflation, p. 60

relative PPP, p. 61
money, p. 67
central bank, p. 69
money supply, p. 69
money demand, p. 69
quantity theory of money, p. 69
fundamental equation of the monetary model of the price level, p. 71
fundamental equation of the monetary approach to exchange rates, p. 72
hyperinflation, p. 77

real money demand function, p. 81
Fisher effect, p. 83
real interest rate, p. 83
real interest parity, p. 84
world real interest rate, p. 84
nominal anchors, p. 88
monetary regime, p. 89
exchange rate target, p. 89
money supply target, p. 89
inflation target plus interest rate policy, p. 90
central bank independence, p. 92

PROBLEMS

1. **▢ Discovering Data** In recent years China has been routinely accused of currency manipulation. In this question you are asked to use the freely available *finder.com* Starbucks Index to investigate these claims. Go to https://www.finder.com/star-bucks-index to access the most recent version of their data.

   a. What is the most recent price of a Starbucks tall latte in China? What is the price in the United States? What is the implied yuan/dollar exchange rate based on these prices?

   b. Does this measure suggest that the Chinese yuan is overvalued or undervalued relative to the dollar? Why might this be beneficial to the Chinese economy?

   c. The fundamental assumption of this index is that the cost of producing a Starbucks tall latte is identical across countries. Why might this assumption be violated? How might this violation affect your answer in part (b)?

   d. Which three countries are most undervalued relative to the U.S. dollar in the most recent year? Which three are most overvalued?

   e. Optional for extra credit: compare these Starbucks Index PPP measures with the Big Mac Index PPP measures for a few countries in the same year (Big Mac data can be found at https://github.com/TheEconomist/big-mac-data). Do the two PPP indices agree?

2. Suppose that two countries, Vietnam and Côte d'Ivoire, produce coffee. The currency unit used in Vietnam is the dong (VND). Côte d'Ivoire is

a member of the *Communauté Financière Africaine* (CFA), a currency union of West African countries that use the CFA franc (XOF). In Vietnam, coffee sells for 4,500 dong (VND) per pound. The exchange rate is 40 VND per 1 CFA franc, $E_{VND/XOF} = 30$.

a. If the law of one price holds, what is the price of coffee in Côte d'Ivoire, measured in CFA francs?

b. Assume the price of coffee in Côte d'Ivoire is actually 160 CFA francs per pound of coffee. Compute the relative price of coffee in Côte d'Ivoire versus Vietnam. Where will coffee traders buy coffee? Where will they sell coffee in this case? How will these transactions affect the price of coffee in Vietnam? In Côte d'Ivoire?

3. Consider each of the following goods and services. For each, identify whether the law of one price will hold, and state whether the relative price $q^g_{US/Foreign}$ is greater than, less than, or equal to 1. Explain your answer in terms of the assumptions we make when using the law of one price.

a. Rice traded freely in the United States and Canada

b. Sugar traded in the United States and Mexico; the U.S. government imposes a quota on sugar imports into the United States

c. The McDonald's Big Mac sold in the United States and Japan

d. Haircuts in the United States and the United Kingdom

4. Use the table that follows to answer this question. Treat the country listed as the home country, and treat the United States as the foreign country. Suppose the cost of the market basket in the United States is $P_{US} = \$190$. Check to see whether PPP holds for each of the countries listed, and determine whether we should expect a real appreciation or real depreciation for each country (relative to the United States) in the long run. For the answer, create a table similar to the one shown and fill in the blank cells. (*Hint:* Use a spreadsheet application such as Excel.)

Country (currency measured in FX units)	Per $, $E_{FX/\$}$	Price of Market Basket (in FX)	Price of U.S. Basket in FX (P_{US} times $E_{FX/\$}$)	Real Exchange Rate, $q_{COUNTRY/US}$	Does PPP Hold? (yes/no)	Is FX Currency Overvalued or Undervalued?	Is FX Currency Expected to Have Real Appreciation or Depreciation?
Brazil (real)	4.07	520					
India (rupee)	68.51	12,000					
Mexico (peso)	18.89	1,800					
South Africa (rand)	15.78	800					
Zimbabwe (Z$)	101,347	4,000,000					

5. Table 3-1 in the text shows the percentage undervaluation or overvaluation in the Big Mac, based on exchange rates in July 2019. Go to the main data repository for the BigMac dataset at https://github.com/TheEconomist/big-mac-data and download the complete dataset. Locate the worksheets showing all data for July 2019 as in Table 3-1, and the corresponding worksheets for July 2018 (one year prior) and July 2014 (five years prior). Focus on the data for nine countries only: Brazil, Canada, Denmark, Eurozone, India, Japan, Mexico, Sweden, and the United States (the base country).

a. Make a table with three columns. In the first column write the first eight country names, excluding the United States. In the second column write the percentage deviation from PPP versus the U.S. dollar in 2018. In the third column report the percentage change in the nominal exchange rate versus the U.S. dollar from 2018 to 2019. How well did PPP deviations in 2018 predict the one-year nominal exchange rate change from 2018 to 2019?

b. Now repeat the exercise using 2014 as the start year; report 2014 PPP percentage deviations, and report the percentage change in the nominal exchange rate from 2014 to 2019. How well did PPP deviations in 2014 predict the five-year nominal exchange rate change from 2018 to 2019?

c. Why might the latter prediction work better than the former?

WORK IT OUT   Achieve | interactive activity

6. You are given the following information. The current dollar–pound exchange rate is $1.5 per pound. A U.S. basket that costs $100 would cost $120 in the United Kingdom. For the next year, the Fed is predicted to keep U.S. inflation at 2% and the Bank of England is predicted to keep U.K. inflation at 3%. The speed of convergence to absolute PPP is 15% per year.

   a. What is the expected U.S. minus U.K. inflation differential for the coming year?

   b. What is the current U.S. real exchange rate $q_{US/UK}$ with the United Kingdom?

   c. How much is the dollar overvalued/undervalued?

   d. What do you predict the U.S. real exchange rate with the United Kingdom will be in one year's time?

   e. What is the expected rate of real depreciation for the United States (versus the United Kingdom)?

   f. What is the expected rate of nominal depreciation for the United States (versus the United Kingdom)?

   g. What do you predict will be the dollar price of one pound a year from now?

7. Describe how each of the following factors might explain why PPP is a better guide for exchange rate movements in the long run versus the short run: (i) transactions costs, (ii) nontraded goods, (iii) imperfect competition, (iv) price stickiness. As markets become increasingly integrated, do you suspect PPP will become a more useful guide in the future? Why or why not?

8. Consider two countries: Japan and South Korea. In 1996 Japan experienced relatively slow output growth (1%), while South Korea had relatively robust output growth (6%). Suppose the Bank of Japan allowed the money supply to grow by 2% each year, while the Bank of Korea chose to maintain relatively high money growth of 15% per year.

   For the following questions, use the simple monetary model (where L is constant). You will find it easiest to treat South Korea as the home country and Japan as the foreign country.

   a. What is the inflation rate in South Korea? In Japan?

   b. What is the expected rate of depreciation in the Korean won relative to the Japanese yen (¥)?

   c. Suppose the Bank of Korea decreases the money growth rate from 15% to 12%. If nothing in Japan changes, what is the new inflation rate in South Korea?

   d. Using time series diagrams, illustrate how this decrease in the money growth rate affects the money supply M_K, South Korea's interest rate, prices P_K, real money supply, and $E_{won/¥}$ over time. (Plot each variable on the vertical axis and time on the horizontal axis.)

   e. Suppose the Bank of Korea wants to maintain an exchange rate peg with the Japanese yen. What money growth rate would the Bank of Korea have to choose to keep the value of the won fixed relative to the yen?

   f. Suppose the Bank of Korea sought to implement policy that would cause the Korean won to appreciate relative to the Japanese yen. What ranges of the money growth rate (assuming positive values) would allow the Bank of Korea to achieve this objective?

9. This question uses the general monetary model, where L is no longer assumed constant, and money demand is inversely related to the nominal interest rate. Consider the same scenario described at the beginning of the previous question. In addition, the bank deposits in Japan pay a 3% interest rate, $i_¥ = 3\%$.

   a. Compute the interest rate paid on South Korean won deposits.

   b. Using the definition of the real interest rate (nominal interest rate adjusted for inflation), show that the real interest rate in South Korea is equal to the real interest rate in Japan. (Note that the inflation rates you computed in the previous question will be the same in this question.)

   c. Suppose the Bank of Korea decreases the money growth rate from 15% to 12% and the inflation rate falls proportionately (one for one) with this decrease. If the nominal interest rate in Japan remains unchanged, what happens to the interest rate paid on Korean won deposits?

   d. Using time series diagrams, illustrate how this decrease in the money growth rate affects the money supply M_K; South Korea's interest rate; prices P_K; real money supply; and $E_{won/¥}$ over time. (Plot each variable on the vertical axis and time on the horizontal axis.)

10. Both advanced economies and developing countries have experienced a decrease in inflation since the 1980s (see Table 3-3 in the text). This question considers how the choice of policy regime has

influenced such global disinflation. Use the monetary model to answer this question.

a. Consider a period when the Swiss Central Bank targeted its money growth rate to achieve policy objectives. Suppose Switzerland has output growth of 2% and money growth of 3% each year. What is Switzerland's inflation rate in this case? Describe how the Swiss Central Bank could achieve an inflation rate of 2% in the long run through the use of a nominal anchor.

b. Consider a period when the Reserve Bank of New Zealand used an interest rate target. Suppose the Reserve Bank of New Zealand maintains a 5% interest rate target and the world *real* interest rate is 1.5%. What is the New Zealand inflation rate in the long run? In 1997 New Zealand adopted a policy agreement that required the bank to maintain an inflation rate no higher than 2.5%. What interest rate targets would achieve this objective?

c. Consider a period when, prior to euro entry, the central bank of Lithuania maintained an exchange rate band relative to the euro—at the time this was a prerequisite for joining the Eurozone. The rules said that Lithuania had to keep its exchange rate within ±15% of the central parity of 3.4528 litas per euro. Compute the exchange rate values corresponding to the upper and lower edges of this band. Suppose PPP holds. Assuming Eurozone inflation was 2% per year and inflation in Lithuania was 6%, compute the PPP-implied rate of depreciation of the lita. Could Lithuania maintain the band requirement? For how long? Does your answer depend on where in the band the exchange rate currently sits? A primary objective of the European Central Bank is price stability (low inflation) in the current and future Eurozone. Is an exchange rate band a necessary or sufficient condition for the attainment of this objective?

11. Several countries that have experienced hyperinflation adopt dollarization as a way to control domestic inflation. For example, Ecuador has used the U.S. dollar as its domestic currency since 2000. What does dollarization imply about the exchange rate between Ecuador and the United States? Why might countries experiencing hyperinflation adopt dollarization? Why might they do this rather than just fixing their exchange rate?

12. You are the central banker for a country that is considering the adoption of a new nominal anchor. When you take the position as chairperson, the inflation rate is 5% and your position as the central bank chairperson requires that you achieve a 2.5% inflation target within the next year. The economy's growth in real output is currently 1%. The world real interest rate is currently 1.5%. The currency used in your country is the lira. *Assume prices are flexible.*

a. Why is having a nominal anchor important for you to achieve the inflation target? What is the drawback of using a nominal anchor?

b. What is the growth rate of the money supply in this economy? If you choose to adopt a money supply target, which money supply growth rate will allow you to meet your inflation target?

c. Suppose the inflation rate in the United States is currently 2% and you adopt an exchange rate target relative to the U.S. dollar. Compute the percentage appreciation/depreciation in the lira needed for you to achieve your inflation target. Will the lira appreciate or depreciate relative to the U.S. dollar?

d. Your final option is to achieve your inflation target using interest rate policy. Using the Fisher equation, compute the current nominal interest rate in your country. What nominal interest rate will allow you to achieve the inflation target?

4

Exchange Rates II: The Asset Approach in the Short Run

The long run is a misleading guide to current affairs. In the long run we are all dead. Economists set themselves too easy, too useless a task if in tempestuous seasons they can only tell us that when the storm is past the ocean is flat again.

John Maynard Keynes, *A Tract on Monetary Reform*, 1923

Questions to Consider

1 In the short run, how do expectations and interest rate arbitrage determine the exchange rate?

2 How do money market conditions, including central bank policy choices, determine interest rates?

3 What can the theory of exchange rates tell us about the difference between floating and fixed exchange rate regimes?

As we saw in the last chapter, the monetary approach to exchange rates may work in the long run, but it is a poor guide to what happens in the short run. To recap this distinction, let's return to the Canada–U.S. comparison with which we opened the last chapter—only this time we'll focus on developments in the short run.

As an example, consider the one-year period from March 2005 to March 2006, when the Canadian price level (measured by the consumer price index) rose from 126.5 to 129.3, an increase of 2.2%. The U.S. price level rose from 193.3 to 199.8, an increase of 3.4%. U.S. prices therefore increased 1.2% more than Canadian prices. But over the same period, the Canadian dollar rose in value from $0.8267 to $0.8568, an appreciation of 3.6%.[1]

Because Canadian baskets cost 2.2% more in Canadian dollar terms, *and* because each Canadian dollar cost 3.6% more in U.S. dollar terms, the change in the U.S. dollar price of the Canadian basket was about 5.8%, the sum of these two changes. Over the same period, however, the U.S. dollar price of U.S. baskets rose only 3.4%. Thus, Canadian baskets were 2.4% more expensive than U.S. baskets, meaning that the U.S. *real* exchange rate with Canada rose by 2.4%, a real depreciation of the U.S. dollar. This pattern was not unusual. In the previous year from March 2004 to March 2005, the real depreciation of the U.S. dollar was 7.5%, so over the two years Canadian goods rose in price by about 10% compared with U.S. goods.

As we have already noted, evidence of this kind suggests that substantial deviations from purchasing power parity (PPP) regularly occur in the short run: the same basket of goods generally does *not* cost the same everywhere at all times. These short-run failures of the monetary approach prompted economists to develop an alternative theory to explain exchange rates in the short run: the **asset approach to exchange rates**, the subject of this chapter.

---

[1] Data for this example are taken from the Bank of Canada and U.S. Bureau of Labor Statistics.

The asset approach is based on the idea that currencies are assets. The price of the asset in this case is the spot exchange rate, the price of one unit of foreign exchange. To explain the determination of exchange rates in the short run, we can draw on what we learned about arbitrage. Recall from Chapter 2 that arbitrage plays a major role in the foreign exchange (forex or FX) market by forcing the expected returns of two assets in different currencies to be equal. This insight led us to derive the uncovered interest parity (UIP) condition. Because it characterizes the forex market equilibrium in the short run, UIP will be further explored and extensively applied in this chapter.

The asset approach differs from the monetary approach in its time frame and assumptions. The monetary approach applies more to a long run of several years or even decades; the asset approach applies more to a short run of a few weeks or months, or maybe a year or so at most. In the monetary approach, we treat goods prices as perfectly flexible, a plausible assumption in the long run; in the asset approach, we assume that goods prices are sticky, a more appropriate assumption in the short run. Each theory is valid but only in the right context. Thus, rather than supplanting the monetary approach, the asset approach complements it, and provides us with the final building blocks necessary to construct a complete theory of exchange rates.

So far, we have assumed that exchange rates are determined by market forces in the goods, money, and forex markets—so our theory is relevant when the exchange rate floats and the authorities leave it to find its own market-determined level. Can our theory tell us anything about fixed exchange rates? Yes. At the end of this chapter, we see how the same theoretical framework can be applied to a fixed exchange rate regime.

1 Exchange Rates and Interest Rates in the Short Run: UIP and FX Market Equilibrium

To begin our study of exchange rates in the short run, let's recap the crucial equilibrium condition for the forex market. In our earlier presentation, we considered a U.S. investor with two alternative investment strategies: a one-year investment in a U.S. dollar account with an interest rate $i_\$$, or a one-year investment in a euro account with an interest rate $i_\mathbb{\euro}$. Here are the essentials.

Risky Arbitrage

For the case of risky arbitrage, we saw that the forex market is in equilibrium when there is no expected difference in the rates of return on each type of currency investment in the two countries or locations. As before, we assume Home is the United States (U.S.) and Foreign is Europe (EUR, meaning the Eurozone). According to the approximate uncovered interest parity condition—seen before at Equation (2-3), and repeated here as Equation (4-1)—this outcome requires that the dollar rate of return on the home investment (the dollar deposit) equal the expected dollar rate of return on the foreign investment (the euro deposit),

$$
\underbrace{\underset{\substack{\text{Interest rate} \\ \text{on dollar deposits} \\ = \\ \text{Dollar rate of return} \\ \text{on dollar deposits}}}{i_\$}} = \underbrace{\underset{\substack{\text{Interest rate} \\ \text{on euro deposits}}}{i_\mathbb{\euro}} + \underbrace{\frac{(E^e_{\$/\mathbb{\euro}} - E_{\$/\mathbb{\euro}})}{E_{\$/\mathbb{\euro}}}}_{\substack{\text{Expected rate of depreciation} \\ \text{of the dollar}}}}_{\substack{\text{Expected dollar rate of return} \\ \text{on euro deposits}}}
\tag{4-1}
$$

where each interest rate is an annual rate, $E_{\$/\mathbb{\euro}}$ is today's exchange rate (the spot rate), and $E^e_{\$/\mathbb{\euro}}$ is the expected future exchange rate that will prevail one year ahead.

The uncovered interest parity (UIP) equation is the **fundamental equation of the asset approach to exchange rates**, and from now on, we use it in the form of Equation (4-1). As we have seen, by rearranging this equation, we can solve it for the spot exchange rate, *if we know all of the other variables*. Thus, the asset approach employs the UIP equation to determine today's spot exchange rate, as illustrated in Figure 4-1. *Note that the theory is useful only if we know the future expected exchange rate and the short-term interest rates*. Where does that knowledge come from?

Short-Term Interest Rates The first assumption in the asset approach is that we know today's interest rates on deposit accounts in each currency, the dollar interest rate $i_\$$, and the euro account interest rate $i_\euro$. It is a fact that market participants can observe these key variables in the theory. But this fact provokes a deeper question: how are these interest rates determined, and, in particular, what is their relation to economic policy? In the next section, we address that question to develop a fuller understanding of how exchange rates are determined.

Exchange Rate Expectations The second assumption in the asset approach is that we know the forecast of the future level of the exchange rate $E^e_{\$/\euro}$. The asset approach itself does not tell us how one might determine the expected exchange rate. To determine this other key variable in the theory, we must look to the long-run monetary approach to the exchange rate presented in Chapter 3. Bringing in that long-run approach here shows us how the asset approach and monetary approach fit together.

Equilibrium in the FX Market: An Example

To get familiar with the concepts we have just outlined, let's work through a numerical example to show how equilibrium in the forex market is determined.

Suppose that the current European interest rate $i_\euro$ is 3%, and the current U.S. interest rate $i_\$$ is 5%. Suppose also that we have made a forecast (using the long-run monetary model of exchange rates) that the expected future exchange rate $E^e_{\$/\euro}$ (in one year's time) is 1.224 dollars per euro.

We can now examine Table 4-1 to see how, for various values of the spot exchange rate $E_{\$/\euro}$, we can calculate the domestic rate of return and expected foreign rate of return in U.S. dollars. (Remember the notation that 5% = 0.05, 3% = 0.03, etc.) As you work through the table, remember that the foreign returns have two components: one due to the European interest rate $i_\euro$ and the other due to the expected rate of depreciation of the dollar, as in Equation (4-1).

FIGURE 4-1

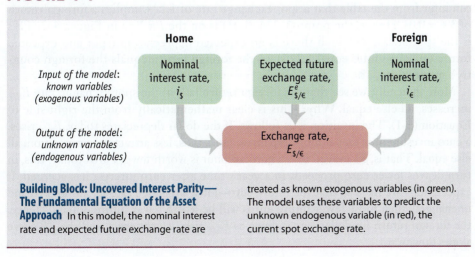

Building Block: Uncovered Interest Parity—The Fundamental Equation of the Asset Approach In this model, the nominal interest rate and expected future exchange rate are treated as known exogenous variables (in green). The model uses these variables to predict the unknown endogenous variable (in red), the current spot exchange rate.

TABLE 4-1

Interest Rates, Exchange Rates, Expected Returns, and FX Market Equilibrium: A Numerical Example The foreign exchange (FX) market is in equilibrium when the domestic and foreign returns are equal. In the example shown in this table, the dollar interest rate is 5% (column 1), the euro interest rate is 3% (column 2), and the expected future exchange rate (one year ahead) is $E^e_{\$/€} = 1.224$ $/€ (column 4). The rows in the table correspond to a range of possible spot exchange rates shown in column 3, and these spot rates in turn imply the expected depreciation rates in column 5 and the expected foreign returns in column 6. The unique equilibrium is highlighted, where both domestic and expected foreign returns are 5% in annual dollar terms, and the spot rate is 1.20 $/€. Figures are rounded in the table. Figure 4-2 plots the domestic and foreign returns (columns 1 and 6) against the spot exchange rate (column 3).

(1)	(2)	(3)	(4)	(5)	(6) = (2)+(5)
Interest Rate on Dollar Deposits (annual)	Interest Rate on Euro Deposits (annual)	Spot Exchange Rate (today)	Expected Future Exchange Rate (in 1 year)	Expected Euro Appreciation against Dollar (in 1 year)	Expected Dollar Return on Euro Deposits (annual)
Domestic Return ($)					Foreign Expected Return ($)
$i_\$$	$i_€$	$E_{\$/€}$	$E^e_{\$/€}$	$\dfrac{E^e_{\$/€} - E_{\$/€}}{E_{\$/€}}$	$i_€ + \dfrac{E^e_{\$/€} - E_{\$/€}}{E_{\$/€}}$
0.05	0.03	1.16	1.224	0.0552	0.0852
0.05	0.03	1.18	1.224	0.0373	0.0673
0.05	0.03	1.20	1.224	0.02	0.05
0.05	0.03	1.22	1.224	0.0033	0.0333
0.05	0.03	1.24	1.224	−0.0129	0.0171

Market equilibrium (row: 0.05 | 0.03 | 1.20 | 1.224 | 0.02 | 0.05)

Figure 4-2 presents an **FX market diagram**, a graphical representation of these returns in the forex market. We plot the expected domestic and foreign returns (on the vertical axis) against today's spot exchange rate (on the horizontal axis). The domestic dollar return (*DR*) (which is Home's nominal interest rate) is fixed at 5% = 0.05 and is independent of the spot exchange rate.

According to Equation (4-1), the foreign expected dollar return (*FR*) depends on the spot exchange rate, and it varies as shown in Table 4-1. For example, we can infer from the table that a spot exchange rate of 1.224 implies a foreign return of 3% = 0.03. Hence, the point (1.224, 0.03) is on the *FR* line in Figure 4-2. This is the special case in which there is no expected depreciation (spot and expected future exchange rates equal 1.224), so the foreign return equals the foreign country's interest rate, 3%.

More generally, we see that the foreign return falls as the spot exchange rate $E_{\$/€}$ increases, all else equal. Why? This is clear mathematically from the right side of Equation (4-1). The intuition is as follows. If the dollar depreciates today, $E_{\$/€}$ rises; a euro investment is then a more expensive (and, thus, less attractive) proposition, all else equal. That is, $1 moved into a euro account is worth fewer euros today; this, in turn, leaves fewer euro proceeds in a year's time after euro interest has accrued. If expectations are fixed so that the future euro–dollar exchange rate $E^e_{\$/€}$ is known and unchanged, then those fewer future euros will be worth fewer future dollars. Hence, the foreign return (in dollars) goes down as $E_{\$/€}$ rises, *all else equal*, and the *FR* curve slopes downward.

FIGURE 4-2

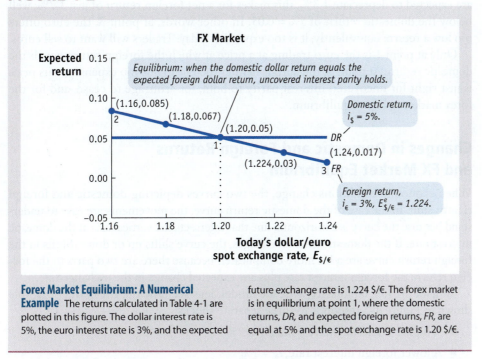

Forex Market Equilibrium: A Numerical
Example The returns calculated in Table 4-1 are
plotted in this figure. The dollar interest rate is
5%, the euro interest rate is 3%, and the expected
future exchange rate is 1.224 $/€. The forex market
is in equilibrium at point 1, where the domestic
returns, *DR*, and expected foreign returns, *FR*, are
equal at 5% and the spot exchange rate is 1.20 $/€.

What is the equilibrium level of the spot exchange rate? According Table 4-1, the
equilibrium exchange rate is 1.20 $/€. Only at that exchange rate are domestic returns
and foreign returns equalized. To illustrate the solution graphically, domestic and foreign returns are plotted in Figure 4-2. The FX market is in equilibrium, and foreign
and domestic returns are equal, at point 1 where the *FR* and *DR* curves intersect.

Adjustment to Forex Market Equilibrium

Our forex market equilibrium condition and its graphical representation should now
be clear. But how is this equilibrium reached? It turns out that arbitrage automatically
pushes the level of the exchange rate toward its equilibrium value.

To see this, suppose that the market is initially out of equilibrium, with the spot
$E_{\$/€}$ exchange rate at a level too low, so that the foreign return—the right-hand side
of Equation (4-1)—exceeds the domestic return (the left-hand side).

At point 2 in Figure 4-2, foreign returns are well above domestic returns. With the
spot exchange rate of 1.16 $/€ and (from Table 4-1) an expected future exchange rate as
high as 1.224 $/€, the euro is expected to *appreciate* by 5.5% = 0.055 [=(1.224/1.16) − 1].
In addition, euros earn at an interest rate of 3%, for a whopping foreign expected return
of 5.5% + 3% = 8.5% = 0.085, which far exceeds the domestic return of 5%. At point 2,
in other words, the euro offers too high a return; equivalently, it is too cheap. Traders
want to sell dollars and buy euros. These market pressures bid up the price of a euro:
the dollar starts to depreciate against the euro, causing $E_{\$/€}$ to rise, which moves foreign
and domestic returns into equality and forces the exchange rate back toward equilibrium at point 1.

The same idea applies to a situation in which the spot exchange rate $E_{\$/€}$ is initially
too high. At point 3 in Figure 4-2, foreign and domestic returns are not equal: the
exchange rate is 1.24 $/€. Given where the exchange rate is expected to be in a year's
time (1.224 $/€), paying a high price of 1.24 $/€ today means the euro is expected to

depreciate by about 1.3% = 0.013 [=1.224/1.24 − 1]. If euro deposits pay 3%, and euros are expected to depreciate 1.3%, this makes for a net foreign return of just 1.7%, well below the domestic return of 5% = 0.05. In other words, at point 3, the euro offers too low a return; equivalently, it is too expensive today. Traders will want to sell euros.

Only at point 1 is the euro trading at a price at which the foreign return equals the domestic return. At point 1, the euro is neither too cheap nor too expensive—its price is just right for uncovered interest parity to hold, for arbitrage to cease, and for the forex market to be in equilibrium.

Changes in Domestic and Foreign Returns and FX Market Equilibrium

When economic conditions change, the two curves depicting domestic and foreign returns shift. In the case of the domestic return curve, the movements are easy to understand because the curve is a horizontal line that intersects the vertical axis at the domestic interest rate. If the domestic interest changes, the curve shifts up or down. Shifts in the foreign return curve are a bit more complicated because there are two parts to the foreign return: the foreign interest rate plus any expected change in the exchange rate.

To gain greater familiarity with the model, let's see how the FX market example shown in Figure 4-2 responds to three separate shocks:

- A higher domestic interest rate, $i_\$ = 7\%$
- A lower foreign interest rate, $i_\text{€} = 1\%$
- A lower expected future exchange rate, $E^e_{\$/\text{€}} = 1.20$ \$/€

These three cases are shown in Figure 4-3, panels (a), (b), and (c). In all three cases, the shocks make dollar deposits more attractive than euro deposits, but for different reasons. Regardless of the reason, however, the shocks we examine all lead to dollar appreciations.

A Change in the Domestic Interest Rate In Figure 4-3, panel (a), when $i_\$$ rises to 7%, the domestic return is increased by 2% so the domestic return curve *DR* shifts up by 2% = 0.02 from DR_1 to DR_2. The foreign return is unaffected. Now, at the initial equilibrium spot exchange rate of 1.20 \$/€, the domestic return (point 4) is higher than the foreign return. Traders sell euros and buy dollars; the dollar appreciates to 1.177 \$/€ at the new equilibrium, point 5. The foreign return and domestic return are equal once again and UIP holds once more.

A Change in the Foreign Interest Rate In Figure 4-3, panel (b), when $i_\text{€}$ falls to 1%, euro deposits now pay a lower interest rate (1% versus 3%). The foreign return curve *FR* shifts down by 2% = 0.02 from FR_1 to FR_2. The domestic return is unaffected. Now, at the old equilibrium rate of 1.20 \$/€, the foreign return (point 6) is lower than the domestic return. Traders sell euros and buy dollars; the dollar appreciates to 1.177 \$/€ at the new equilibrium, point 7, and UIP holds once more.

A Change in the Expected Future Exchange Rate In Figure 4-3, panel (c), a decrease in the expected future exchange rate $E^e_{\$/\text{€}}$ lowers the foreign return because a future euro is expected to be worth fewer dollars in the future. The foreign return curve *FR* shifts down from FR_1 to FR_2. The domestic return is unaffected. At the old equilibrium rate of 1.20 \$/€, the foreign return (point 6) is lower than the domestic return. Again, traders sell euros and buy dollars, causing the dollar to appreciate and the spot exchange rate to fall to 1.177 \$/€. The new equilibrium is point 7.

FIGURE 4-3

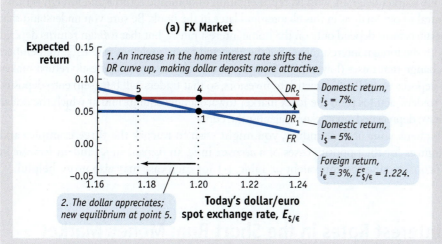

(a) A Change in the Home Interest Rate
A rise in the dollar interest rate from 5% to 7% increases domestic returns, shifting the DR curve up from DR_1 to DR_2. At the initial equilibrium exchange rate of 1.20 $/€ on DR_2, domestic returns are above foreign returns at point 4. Dollar deposits are more attractive and the dollar appreciates from 1.20 $/€ to 1.177 $/€. The new equilibrium is at point 5.

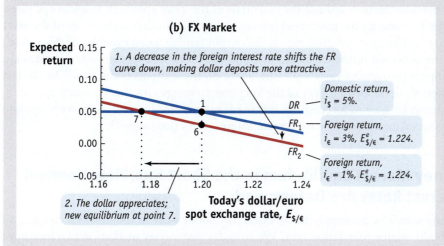

(b) A Change in the Foreign Interest Rate
A fall in the euro interest rate from 3% to 1% lowers foreign expected dollar returns, shifting the FR curve down from FR_1 to FR_2. At the initial equilibrium exchange rate of 1.20 $/€ on FR_2, foreign returns are below domestic returns at point 6. Dollar deposits are more attractive and the dollar appreciates from 1.20 $/€ to 1.177 $/€. The new equilibrium is at point 7.

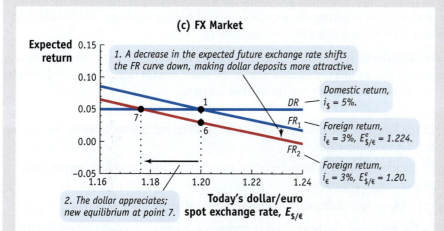

(c) A Change in the Expected Future Exchange Rate A fall in the expected future exchange rate from 1.224 to 1.20 lowers foreign expected dollar returns, shifting the FR curve down from FR_1 to FR_2. At the initial equilibrium exchange rate of 1.20 $/€ on FR_2, foreign returns are below domestic returns at point 6. Dollar deposits are more attractive and the dollar appreciates from 1.20 $/€ to 1.177 $/€. The new equilibrium is at point 7.

Summary

The FX market diagram, with its representation of domestic returns and foreign returns, is central to our analysis in this chapter and later in the book. Be sure you understand that domestic returns depend only on the home interest rate $i_\$$, but that foreign returns depend on both the foreign interest rate $i_\euro$ *and* the expected future exchange rate $E^e_{\$/\euro}$. Remember: any change that raises (lowers) the foreign return relative to the domestic return makes euro deposits more (less) attractive to investors, so that traders will buy (sell) euro deposits. The traders' actions push the forex market toward a new equilibrium at which the dollar will have depreciated (appreciated) against the euro.

To check your understanding, you might wish to rework the three examples and the figures for the opposite cases of a *decrease* in $i_\$$, an *increase* in $i_\euro$, and an *increase* in $E^e_{\$/\euro}$; constructing the equivalent of Table 4-1 for each case may also prove helpful.

2 Interest Rates in the Short Run: Money Market Equilibrium

The previous section laid out the essentials of the asset approach to exchange rates. Figure 4-1 sums up the uncovered interest parity relationship at the heart of the asset approach. The spot exchange rate is the output (endogenous variable) of this model, and the expected future exchange rate and the home and foreign interest rates are the inputs (exogenous variables). But where do these inputs come from? In the last chapter, we developed a theory of the long-run exchange rate, the monetary approach, which can be used to forecast the future exchange rate. That leaves us with just one unanswered question: How are current interest rates determined?

Money Market Equilibrium in the Short Run: How Nominal Interest Rates Are Determined

Having seen how the supply and demand for money work in the previous chapter, we can build on that foundation here. We consider two money markets in two locations: the United States and Europe. Both markets are in equilibrium with money demand equal to money supply. In both locations, the money supply is controlled by a central bank and is taken as given; the demand for real money balances $M/P = L(i)Y$ is a function of the interest rate i and real income Y.

The Assumptions It is important to understand the key difference between the way we approach money market equilibrium in the short run (in this chapter) and the way we approached it in the long run (in the last chapter).

In the last chapter, we made the following *long-run* assumptions:

- In the long run, the price level P is fully flexible and adjusts to bring the money market to equilibrium.

- In the long run, the nominal interest rate i equals the world real interest rate plus domestic inflation.

In this chapter, we make *short-run* assumptions that are quite different:

- In the short run, the price level is sticky; it is a known predetermined variable, fixed at $P = \bar{P}$ (the bar indicates a fixed value).

- In the short run, the nominal interest rate i is fully flexible and adjusts to bring the money market to equilibrium.

Why do we make different assumptions in the short run?

First, why assume prices are now sticky? The assumption of sticky prices, also called **nominal rigidity**, is common to the study of macroeconomics in the short run. Economists have many explanations for price stickiness. Nominal wages may be sticky because of long-term labor contracts. Nominal product prices may be sticky because of contracts, and also due to *menu costs*; that is, firms may find it costly to frequently change their output prices. Thus, although it is reasonable to assume that all prices are flexible in the long run, the evidence shows that this is not true in the short run.

Second, why assume that interest rates are now flexible? In the previous chapter, we showed that nominal interest rates are pinned down by the Fisher effect (or real interest parity) in the long run: in that case, the home nominal interest rate was equal to the world real interest rate plus the home rate of inflation. However, recall that this result does not apply in the short run because it is derived from purchasing power parity—which, as we know, only applies in the long run. Indeed, the evidence shows that in the short run real interest rates fluctuate in ways that deviate from real interest parity.

The Model With these explanations of our short-run assumptions in hand, we can now use the same general monetary model of the previous chapter and write down expressions for money market equilibrium in the two locations as follows:

$$\underbrace{\frac{M_{US}}{\bar{P}_{US}}}_{\substack{\text{U.S. supply of} \\ \text{real money balances}}} = \underbrace{L(i_\$) \times Y_{US}}_{\substack{\text{U.S. demand for} \\ \text{real money balances}}} \tag{4-2}$$

$$\underbrace{\frac{M_{EUR}}{\bar{P}_{EUR}}}_{\substack{\text{European supply of} \\ \text{real money balances}}} = \underbrace{L(i_\euro) \times Y_{EUR}}_{\substack{\text{European demand for} \\ \text{real money balances}}} \tag{4-3}$$

To recap: In the long run, prices adjust to clear the money market and bring money demand and money supply into line. In the short run, when prices are sticky, such adjustment is not possible. However, nominal interest rates *are* free to adjust. In the short run, the nominal interest rate in each location adjusts to bring money supply and money demand into equilibrium.

Money Market Equilibrium in the Short Run: Graphical Solution

Figure 4-4 represents the U.S. money market (a similar diagram applies to the European market). On the horizontal axis is the quantity of U.S. real money balances M_{US}/P_{US} and on the vertical axis is the U.S. nominal interest rate $i_\$$. The vertical line represents the supply of real money balances; this supply is fixed by the central bank at the level $M_{US}^1/\bar{P}_{US}^1$ and is independent of the level of the interest rate. The downward-sloping line represents the demand for real money balances, $L(i_\$) \times Y_{US}$. Demand decreases as the U.S. nominal interest rate increases because the opportunity cost of holding money rises and people don't want to hold high money balances. The money market is in equilibrium at point 1: the demand and supply of real money balances are equal at $M_{US}^1/\bar{P}_{US}^1$ and at a nominal interest rate $i_\$^1$.

Adjustment to Money Market Equilibrium in the Short Run

If interest rates are flexible in the short run, as we assume they are, there is nothing to prevent them from adjusting to clear the money market. But how do market forces ensure that a nominal interest rate $i_\$^1$ is attained? The adjustment process works as follows.

FIGURE 4-4

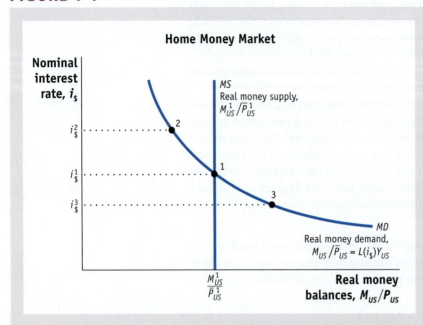

Home Money Market

Nominal interest rate, $i_\$$

MS
Real money supply,
$M_{US}^1/\bar{P}_{US}^1$

$i_\$^2$ 2

$i_\$^1$ 1

$i_\$^3$ 3

MD
Real money demand,
$M_{US}/\bar{P}_{US} = L(i_\$)Y_{US}$

$\dfrac{M_{US}^1}{\bar{P}_{US}^1}$

Real money balances, M_{US}/P_{US}

Equilibrium in the Home Money Market
The supply and demand for real money balances determine the nominal interest rate. The money supply curve (*MS*) is vertical at $M_{US}^1/\bar{P}_{US}^1$ because the quantity of money supplied does not depend on the interest rate. The money demand curve (*MD*) is downward sloping because an increase in the interest rate raises the cost of holding money, thus lowering the quantity demanded. The money market is in equilibrium when the nominal interest rate $i_\$^1$ is such that real money demand equals real money supply (point 1). At points 2 and 3, demand does not equal supply and the interest rate will adjust until the money market returns to equilibrium.

Suppose instead that the interest rate was $i_\$^2$, so that we were at point 2 on the real money demand curve. At this interest rate, real money demand is less than real money supply. In the aggregate, the central bank has put more money in the hands of the public than the public wishes to hold. The public will want to reduce its cash holdings by exchanging money for interest-bearing assets such as bonds, saving accounts, and so on. That is, they will save more and seek to lend their money to borrowers. But borrowers will not want to borrow more unless the cost of borrowing falls. So the interest rate will be driven down as eager lenders compete to attract scarce borrowers. As this happens, back in the money market, in Figure 4-4, we move from point 2 back toward equilibrium at point 1.

A similar story can be told if the money market is initially at point 3, where there is an excess demand for money. In this case, the public wishes to reduce their savings in the form of interest-bearing assets and turn them into cash. Now fewer loans are extended. The loan market will suffer an excess demand. But borrowers will not want to borrow less unless the cost of borrowing rises. So the interest rate will be driven up as eager borrowers compete to attract scarce lenders. These adjustments end only when point 1 is reached and there is no excess supply of real money balances.

Another Building Block: Short-Run Money Market Equilibrium

This model of the money market may be familiar from previous courses in macroeconomics. The lessons that are important for our theory of exchange rates are summed up in Figure 4-5. We treat the price level in each country as fixed and known in the short run. We also assume that the money supply and real income in each country are known. The equilibrium equations for the money market, Equations (4-2) and (4-3), then tell us the interest rates in each country. Once these are known, we can put them to use in another building block seen earlier: the interest rates can be plugged into the fundamental equation of the asset approach to exchange rate determination, Equation (4-1), along with the future expected exchange rate derived from a forecast

FIGURE 4-5

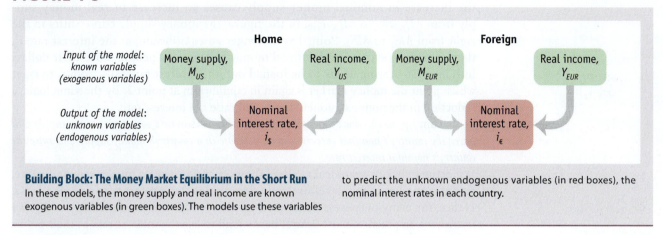

Building Block: The Money Market Equilibrium in the Short Run
In these models, the money supply and real income are known exogenous variables (in green boxes). The models use these variables to predict the unknown endogenous variables (in red boxes), the nominal interest rates in each country.

based on the long-run monetary model of the previous chapter. In that way, the spot exchange rate can finally be determined.

Changes in Money Supply and the Nominal Interest Rate

Money market equilibrium depends on money supply and money demand. If either changes, the equilibrium will change. To help us better understand how exchange rates are determined, we need to understand how these changes occur.

Figure 4-6, panel (a), shows how the money market responds to a monetary policy change consisting of an increase in home (U.S.) nominal money supply from M_{US}^1

FIGURE 4-6

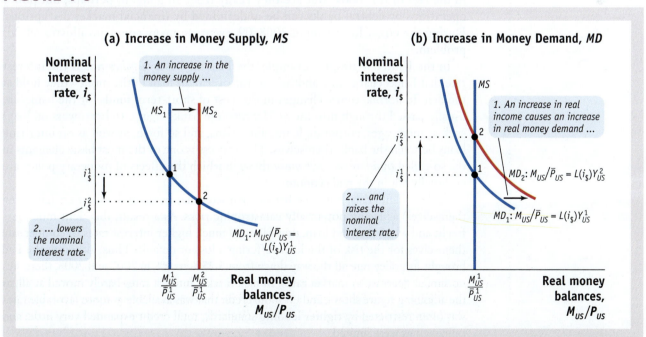

Home Money Market with Changes in Money Supply and Money Demand In panel (a), with a fixed price level $\bar{P}_{US}^1$, an increase in nominal money supply from M_{US}^1 to M_{US}^2 causes an increase in real money supply from $M_{US}^1/\bar{P}_{US}^1$ to $M_{US}^2/\bar{P}_{US}^1$. The nominal interest rate falls from $i_\$^1$ to $i_\$^2$ to restore equilibrium at point 2. In panel (b), with a fixed price level $\bar{P}_{US}^1$, an increase in real income from Y_{US}^1 to Y_{US}^2 causes real money demand to increase from MD_1 to MD_2. To restore equilibrium at point 2, the interest rate rises from $i_\$^1$ to $i_\$^2$.

to M_{US}^2. Because, by assumption, the U.S. price level is fixed in the short run at $\bar{P}_{US}^1$, the increase in nominal money supply causes an increase in real money supply from $M_{US}^1/\bar{P}_{US}^1$ to $M_{US}^2/\bar{P}_{US}^1$. In the figure, the money supply curve shifts to the right from MS_1 to MS_2. Point 1 is no longer an equilibrium; at the interest rate $i_\$^1$, there is now an excess supply of real money balances. As people move their dollars into interest-bearing assets to be loaned out, the interest rate falls from $i_\$^1$ to $i_\$^2$, at which point the money market is again in equilibrium at point 2. By the same logic, a reduction in the nominal money supply will raise the interest rate.

To sum up, *in the short run, all else equal, an increase in a country's money supply will lower the country's nominal interest rate; a decrease in a country's money supply will raise the country's nominal interest rate.*

Fortunately, our graphical analysis shows that, for a *given* money demand curve, setting a money supply level uniquely determines the interest rate and vice versa. Hence, for many purposes, *the money supply or the interest rate may be used as a policy instrument*. In practice, most central banks tend to use the interest rate as their policy instrument because the money demand curve may not be stable, and the fluctuations caused by this instability would lead to unstable interest rates if the money supply were set at a given level as the policy instrument.

APPLICATION

Can Central Banks Always Control the Interest Rate? A Lesson from the Crisis of 2008–09

In our analyses so far, we have assumed that central banks can control the money market interest rate, and that they can effectively do so whether they set the interest rate or the money supply. These assumptions are critical in this chapter and in the rest of this book. But are they really true? In general, perhaps, but policy operations by central banks can be undermined by financial market disruptions. During the Great Recession of 2008–09, events in many countries illustrated this problem.

In the United States, for example, the Federal Reserve *policy rate* is the interest rate that banks charge one another for the overnight loan of the money they hold at the Fed. In normal times, changes in this cost of short-term funds for the banks are usually passed through into the *market rates* the banks charge to borrowers on loans such as mortgages, corporate loans, auto loans, and so forth, as well as on interbank loans between the banks themselves. This process is one of the most basic elements in the so-called *transmission mechanism* through which the effects of monetary policy are eventually felt in the real economy.

In the recent crisis, however, banks regarded other banks and borrowers (and even themselves) as facing potentially catastrophic risks. As a result, they lent much less freely, and when they did loan, they charged much higher interest rates to compensate themselves for the risk of the loan suffering a loss or default. Thus, although the Fed brought its policy rate all the way down from 5.25% to 0% in 2007 and 2008, there was no similar decrease in market rates. In fact, market interest rates barely moved at all, as the adjoining figure shows, and even the credit that was available at more favorable rates was often restricted by tighter lending standards; total credit expanded very little, and refinancings were limited.

A second problem arose once policy rates hit the *zero lower bound* (ZLB). At that point, the central banks' capacity to lower the policy rate further was exhausted. However, many central banks wanted to keep applying downward pressure to market rates to calm financial markets. The Fed's response was a policy of *quantitative easing*.

Usually, the Fed expands base money M0 by either lending to banks that put up safe government bonds as collateral, or by buying government bonds outright in open-market operations—although these actions are taken only in support of the Fed's interest rate target. But in the crisis, and with interest rates stuck at a floor, the Fed engaged in a number of extraordinary policy actions to push more money out more quickly:

1. It expanded the range of credit securities it would accept as collateral to include lower-grade, private-sector bonds.

2. It expanded the range of securities that it would buy outright to include private-sector credit instruments such as commercial paper and mortgage-backed securities.

3. It expanded the range of counterparties from whom it would buy securities to include some nonbank institutions such as primary dealers and money market funds.

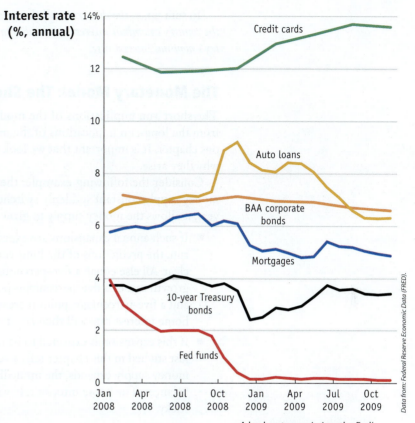

A broken transmission: the Fed's extraordinary interventions did little to change private credit market interest rates from 2008 through 2009.

As a result of massive asset purchases along these lines, M0 in the United States more than doubled to over a trillion dollars. However, there was very little change in M1 or M2, indicating that banks had little desire to translate the cash they were receiving from the Fed into the new loans and new deposits that would expand the broad money supply.

Similar crisis actions were taken by the Bank of England and, eventually, by the European Central Bank (ECB); both expanded their collateral rules, although their outright purchase programs were more narrowly focused on aggressive use of open-market operations to purchase large quantities of U.K. and Eurozone government bonds (though in the ECB's case this included low-grade bonds from crisis countries such as Greece and Portugal).

To sum up, with the traditional transmission mechanism broken, central banks had to find different tools. In the Fed's case, by directly intervening in markets for different types of private credit at different maturities, policymakers hoped to circumvent the impaired transmission mechanism. Would matters have been much worse if the central banks had done nothing at all? It's hard to say. However, if the aim was to lower market interest rates in a meaningful way and expand broader monetary aggregates, it is not clear that these policies had significant economic effects.

Changes in Real Income and the Nominal Interest Rate

Figure 4-6, panel (b), shows how the money market responds to an increase in home (U.S.) real income from Y_{US}^1 to Y_{US}^2. The increase in real income causes real money demand to increase as reflected in the shift from MD_1 to MD_2. At the initial interest rate $i_\$^1$, there is now an excess demand for real money balances. To restore equilibrium at point 2, the interest rate rises from $i_\$^1$ to $i_\$^2$ to encourage people to hold lower dollar balances. Similarly, a reduction in real income will lower the interest rate.

To sum up, *in the short run, all else equal, an increase in a country's real income will raise the country's nominal interest rate; a decrease in a country's real income will lower the country's nominal interest rate*.

The Monetary Model: The Short Run Versus the Long Run

The short-run implications of the model we have just developed differ profoundly from the long-run implications of the monetary approach we presented in the previous chapter. It is important that we look at these differences, and understand how and why they arise.

Consider the following example: the home central bank that previously kept the money supply constant suddenly switches to an expansionary policy. In the following year, it allows the money supply to grow at a rate of 5%.

- If such annual expansions are expected to be a permanent policy in the long run, the predictions of the long-run monetary approach and Fisher effect are clear. All else equal, a five-percentage-point increase in the rate of home money growth causes a five-percentage-point increase in the rate of home inflation and a five-percentage-point increase in the home nominal interest rate. The home interest rate will then *rise* in the long run when prices are flexible.

- If this expansion is expected to be temporary, then the short-run model we have just studied in this chapter tells a very different story. All else equal, if the home money supply expands, the immediate effect is an excess supply of real money balances. The home interest rate will then *fall* in the short run when prices are sticky.

These different outcomes illustrate the importance of the assumptions we make about price flexibility. They also point out the importance of the nominal anchor in monetary policy formulation and the constraints that central banks have to confront.

The different outcomes also explain some apparently puzzling linkages among money, interest rates, and exchange rates. In both of the previous cases, an expanded money supply leads to a weaker currency. However, in the short run, low interest rates and a weak currency go together, whereas in the long run, high interest rates and a weak currency go together.

What is the intuition for these findings? In the short run, when we study the impact of a lower interest rate and we say "all else equal," we have assumed that expectations have not changed concerning future exchange rates (or money supply or inflation). In other words, we assume (implicitly) a temporary policy that does not tamper with the nominal anchor. In the long run, if the policy turns out to be permanent, this assumption is inappropriate; prices are flexible and money growth, inflation, and expected depreciation now all move in concert—in other words, the "all else" is no longer equal.

A good grasp of these key differences between the short- and long-run approaches is essential to understanding how exchange rates are determined. To cement our understanding, in the rest of the chapter we explore the different implications of temporary and permanent policy changes. To make our exploration a bit easier, we now lay out the short-run model in a succinct, graphical form.

3 The Asset Approach: Applications and Evidence

To simplify the graphical presentation of the asset approach, we focus on conditions in the home economy; a similar approach can be used for the foreign economy. For illustration we again assume that Home is the United States and Foreign is Europe, meaning the Eurozone.

The Asset Approach to Exchange Rates: Graphical Solution

Figure 4-7 shows two markets: panel (a) shows the home money market (for the United States), and panel (b) shows the FX market diagram (for the dollar–euro market). This figure summarizes the asset approach in the short run.

The U.S. Money Market Panel (a) depicts equilibrium in the U.S. money market. The horizontal axis shows the quantity of U.S. real money balances demanded or supplied, M_{US}/P_{US}. The vertical axis shows the U.S. nominal interest rate $i_\$$. Two relationships are shown:

1. The vertical line MS represents the U.S. real money supply. The line is vertical because (i) the nominal U.S. money supply M_{US} is treated as exogenous (known), because it is set by the home central bank, and (ii) the U.S. price level $\bar{P}_{US}$ is treated as exogenous (known) in the short run because prices are sticky.

2. The curve MD on the diagram represents the U.S. demand for real money balances, $L(i_\$)Y_{US}$. It slopes down because, when the home nominal interest rate $i_\$$ rises, the opportunity cost of holding money increases, and demand falls. For now, we also assume that the U.S. real income level Y_{US} is exogenous (given) and fixed in the short run.

In equilibrium, money demand equals money supply; the quantity of real money demanded and supplied is $M^1_{US}/\bar{P}^1_{US}$, and the nominal interest rate is $i^1_\$$ (point 1).

The Market for Foreign Exchange Panel (b) depicts equilibrium in the FX market. The horizontal axis shows the spot exchange rate, $E_{\$/€}$. The vertical axis shows U.S. dollar returns on home and foreign deposits. Two relationships are shown:

1. The downward-sloping foreign return curve FR shows the relationship between the exchange rate and the expected dollar rate of return on foreign

FIGURE 4-7

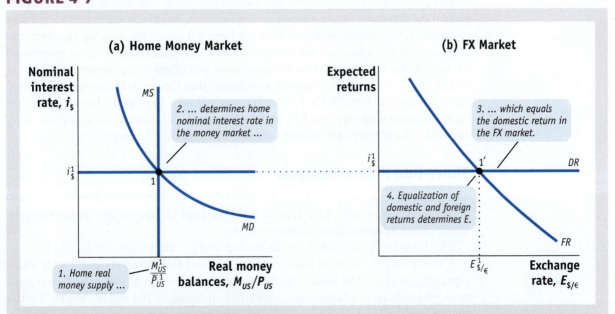

(a) Home Money Market

(b) FX Market

1. *Home real money supply ...*

2. *... determines home nominal interest rate in the money market ...*

3. *... which equals the domestic return in the FX market.*

4. *Equalization of domestic and foreign returns determines E.*

Equilibrium in the Money Market and the FX Market The figure summarizes the equilibria in the two asset markets in one diagram. In panel (a), in the home (U.S.) money market, the home nominal interest rate $i^1_\$$ is determined by the home levels of real money supply MS and demand MD with equilibrium at point 1. In panel (b), in the dollar–euro FX market, the spot exchange rate $E^1_{\$/€}$ is determined by foreign and domestic expected returns, with equilibrium at point 1′. Arbitrage forces the domestic and foreign returns in the FX market to be equal, a result that depends on capital mobility.

deposits $[i_{\unicode{0x20AC}} + (E^e_{\$/\unicode{0x20AC}} - E_{\$/\unicode{0x20AC}})/E_{\$/\unicode{0x20AC}}]$. The European interest rate $i_{\unicode{0x20AC}}$ is treated as exogenous (given); it is determined in the European money market, which is not shown in this figure. The expected future exchange rate $E^e_{\$/\unicode{0x20AC}}$ is treated as exogenous (given); it is determined by a forecast obtained from the long-run model we developed in the previous chapter.

2. The horizontal domestic return line DR shows the dollar rate of return on U.S. deposits, which is the U.S. nominal interest rate $i_{\$}$. It is horizontal at $i^1_{\$}$ because this is the U.S. interest rate determined in the home money market in panel (a), and it is the same regardless of the spot exchange rate.

In equilibrium, foreign and domestic returns are equal (uncovered interest parity holds) and the FX market is in equilibrium at point 1'.

Capital Mobility Is Crucial We assume that the FX market is subject to the arbitrage forces we have studied and that uncovered interest parity will hold. But this is true only if there are no capital controls: as long as capital can move freely between home and foreign capital markets, domestic and foreign returns will be equalized. Our assumption that DR equals FR depends on capital mobility. If capital controls are imposed, there is no arbitrage and no reason why DR has to equal FR.

Putting the Model to Work With this graphical apparatus in place, it is relatively straightforward to solve for the exchange rate given knowledge of all the known (exogenous) variables we have just specified.

To solve for the exchange rate, we start in the home money market in panel (a) on the horizontal axis, at the level of real money supply $M^1_{US}/\bar{P}^1_{US}$; we trace upward along MS to MD at point 1, to find the current home interest rate $i^1_{\$}$. We then trace right and move across from the home money market to the FX market in panel (b), since the home interest rate is the same as domestic return DR in the FX market. We eventually meet the FR curve at point 1'. We then trace down and read off the equilibrium exchange rate $E^1_{\$/\unicode{0x20AC}}$.

Our graphical treatment shows that solving the model is as simple as tracing a path around the diagrams. While we gain in simplicity, we also lose some generality because one market, the foreign money market, has been left out of the analysis. However, the same analysis also applies to the foreign country. As a quick check that you understand the logic of the asset approach to exchange rates, you might try to construct the equivalent of Figure 4-7 under an opposite assumption that Europe is Home and the United States is Foreign. (*Hint:* In the FX market, you will need to treat the home [European] expected future exchange rate $E^e_{\unicode{0x20AC}/\$}$ and the foreign [U.S.] interest rate $i_{\$}$ as given. Take care with the currency units of every variable when making the switch.)

Short-Run Policy Analysis

The graphical exposition in Figure 4-7 shows how the asset approach works to determine the exchange rate. This approach can be used to analyze the impacts of economic policy or other shocks to the economy.

The most straightforward shocks we can analyze are temporary shocks because they affect only the current state of the money and forex markets and do not affect expectations about the future. In this section, we use the model to see what happens when there is a temporary, short-run increase in the money supply by the central bank.

A Temporary Shock to the Home Money Supply We take the model of Figure 4-7 and assume that, apart from the home money supply, all exogenous variables remain unchanged and fixed at the same level. Thus, foreign money supply, home and foreign real income and price levels, and the expected future exchange rate are all fixed.

The initial state of all markets is shown in Figure 4-8. The home money market is in equilibrium at point 1 where home money supply MS and money demand MD are equal at the home nominal interest rate $i_\$^1$. The forex market is in equilibrium at point 1′, where domestic return DR equals foreign return FR, where $i_\$^1 = i_\epsilon^1 + (E_{\$/\epsilon}^e - E_{\$/\epsilon}^1)/E_{\$/\epsilon}^1$, and the spot exchange rate is $E_{\$/\epsilon}^1$.

Suppose the U.S. money supply is increased temporarily from M_{US}^1 to M_{US}^2. Under the assumption of sticky prices, $\bar{P}_{US}^1$ does not change, so the U.S. real money supply will increase to M_{US}^2/P_{US}^1, and the real money supply curve shifts from MS_1 to MS_2 in panel (a). U.S. real money demand is unchanged, so the money market equilibrium shifts from point 1 to point 2 and the nominal interest rate falls from $i_\$^1$ to $i_\$^2$. The expansion of the U.S. money supply causes the U.S. nominal interest rate to fall.

A *temporary* monetary policy shock leaves the long-run expected exchange rate $E_{\$/\epsilon}^e$ unchanged. Assuming all else equal, European monetary policy is also unchanged, and the euro interest rate remains fixed at i_ϵ. If $E_{\$/\epsilon}^e$ and i_ϵ are unchanged, then the foreign return FR curve in panel (b) is unchanged and the new FX market equilibrium is at point 2′. The lower domestic return $i_\$^2$ is matched by a lower foreign return. The foreign return is lower because the U.S. dollar has depreciated from $E_{\$/\epsilon}^1$ to $E_{\$/\epsilon}^2$.

The result is intuitive, and we have seen each of the steps previously. We now just put them all together: a home monetary expansion lowers the home nominal interest rate, which is also the domestic return in the forex market. This makes foreign deposits more attractive and makes traders wish to sell home deposits and buy foreign deposits. This, in turn, makes the home exchange rate increase (depreciate). However, this depreciation makes foreign deposits less attractive (all else equal). Eventually, the equality of foreign and domestic returns is restored, uncovered interest parity holds again, and the forex market reaches a new short-run equilibrium.

FIGURE 4-8

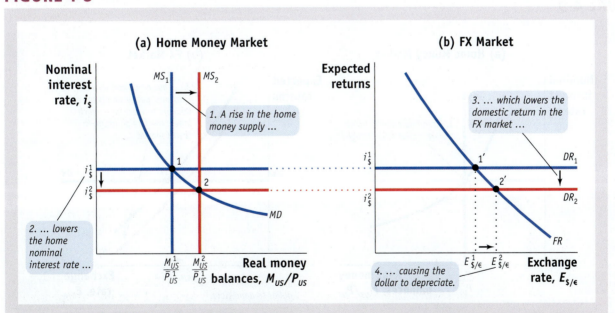

Temporary Expansion of the Home Money Supply In panel (a), in the home money market, an increase in home money supply from M_{US}^1 to M_{US}^2 causes an increase in real money supply from $M_{US}^1/\bar{P}_{US}^1$ to $M_{US}^2/\bar{P}_{US}^1$. To keep real money demand equal to real money supply, the interest rate falls from $i_\$^1$ to $i_\$^2$, and the new money market equilibrium is at point 2. In panel (b), in the FX market, to maintain the equality of domestic and foreign expected returns, the exchange rate rises (the dollar depreciates) from $E_{\$/\epsilon}^1$ to $E_{\$/\epsilon}^2$, and the new FX market equilibrium is at point 2′.

A Temporary Shock to the Foreign Money Supply We now repeat the previous analysis for a shock to the *foreign* money supply. All other exogenous variables remain unchanged and fixed at their initial levels. Thus, home money supply, home and foreign real income and price levels, and the expected future exchange rate are all fixed. The initial state of all markets is shown in Figure 4-9: the home money market is in equilibrium at point 1 and the FX market is in equilibrium at point 1'.

Let's see what happens when the foreign money supply increases temporarily. Because changes in the foreign money supply have no effect on the home money market in panel (a), equilibrium remains at point 1 and the home nominal interest rate stays at $i_\$^1$.

The shock is temporary, so long-run expectations are unchanged, and the expected exchange rate $E_{\$/€}^e$ stays fixed in panel (b). However, because the foreign money supply has expanded temporarily, the euro interest rate falls from $i_€^1$ to $i_€^2$. Foreign returns are diminished, all else equal, by a fall in euro interest rates, so the foreign return curve *FR* shifts downward from FR_1 to FR_2. On the horizontal axis in panel (b), we can see that at the new FX market equilibrium (point 2') the home exchange rate has decreased (the U.S. dollar has appreciated) from $E_{\$/€}^1$ to $E_{\$/€}^2$.

This result is also intuitive. A foreign monetary expansion lowers the foreign nominal interest rate, which lowers the foreign return in the forex market. This makes foreign deposits less attractive and makes traders wish to buy home deposits and sell foreign deposits. This, in turn, makes the home exchange rate decrease (appreciate). However, this appreciation makes foreign deposits more attractive (all else equal). Eventually, the equality of foreign and domestic returns is restored, uncovered interest parity holds again, and the forex market reaches a new short-run equilibrium.

To ensure you have grasped the model fully, you might try two exercises. First, derive the predictions of the model for temporary *contractions* in the home or foreign money supplies. Second, go back to the version of Figure 4-7 that you constructed

---

FIGURE 4-9

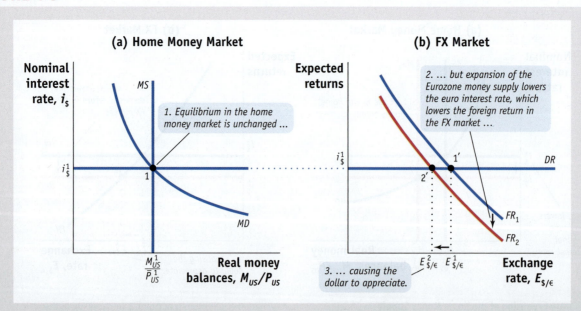

(a) Home Money Market

(b) FX Market

1. Equilibrium in the home money market is unchanged ...

2. ... but expansion of the Eurozone money supply lowers the euro interest rate, which lowers the foreign return in the FX market ...

3. ... causing the dollar to appreciate.

Temporary Expansion of the Foreign Money Supply In panel (a), there is no change in the home money market. In panel (b), an increase in the foreign money supply causes the foreign (euro) interest rate to fall from $i_€^1$ to $i_€^2$. For a U.S. investor, this lowers the foreign return $i_€ + (E_{\$/€}^e - E_{\$/€})/E_{\$/€}$, all else equal. To maintain the equality of domestic and foreign returns in the FX market, the exchange rate falls (the dollar appreciates) from $E_{\$/€}^1$ to $E_{\$/€}^2$, and the new FX market equilibrium is at point 2'.

from the European perspective and generate predictions using that version of the model, first for a temporary expansion of the money supply in Europe and then for a temporary expansion in the United States. Do you get the same answers?

APPLICATION

The Rise and Fall of the Dollar, 1999–2004

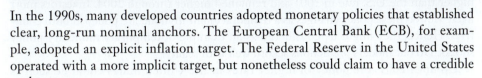

In the 1990s, many developed countries adopted monetary policies that established clear, long-run nominal anchors. The European Central Bank (ECB), for example, adopted an explicit inflation target. The Federal Reserve in the United States operated with a more implicit target, but nonetheless could claim to have a credible anchor, too.

The Fisher effect tells us that nominal anchoring of this kind ought to keep nominal interest rate differentials between the United States and the Eurozone roughly constant in the long run. But in the short run, this constraint does not apply, so central banks have some freedom to temporarily change their monetary policies. In the years 1999 to 2004, such flexibility was put to use and interest rates in the United States and Europe followed very different tracks.

In later chapters, we study in more detail why central banks alter monetary policy in the short run, but for now we focus on how such changes affect exchange rates. As Figure 4-10 shows, the Fed raised interest rates from 1999 to 2001 faster than the ECB (the Fed was more worried about the U.S. economy "overheating" with higher inflation). In this period of global economic boom, the ECB's policy also tightened over time, as measured by changes in the euro interest rate—the refinancing rate set by the ECB. But the changes were more restrained and slower in coming.

FIGURE 4-10

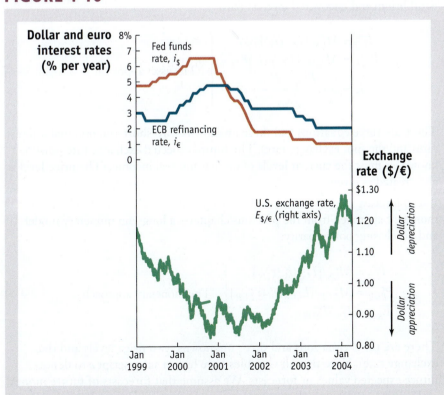

U.S.-Eurozone Interest Rates and Exchange Rates, 1999–2004 From the euro's birth in 1999 until 2001, the dollar steadily appreciated against the euro, as interest rates in the United States were raised well above those in Europe. In early 2001, however, the Federal Reserve began a long series of interest rate reductions. By 2002 the Fed funds rate was well below the ECB's refinancing rate. Theory predicts a dollar appreciation (1999–2001) when U.S. interest rates were relatively high, followed by a U.S. dollar depreciation (2001–04) when U.S. interest rates were relatively low. Looking at the figure, you can see that this occurred.

Data from: Websites of central banks; oanda.com.

As Figure 4-10 also shows, the Fed then lowered interest rates aggressively from 2001 to 2004, with rates falling as low as 1% in 2003 to 2004 (the U.S. economy had slowed after the boom and the Fed hoped that lower interest rates would avert a recession; the terrorist attacks of September 11, 2001, led to fears of a more serious economic setback and encouraged further monetary easing). The ECB also acted similarly to lower interest rates, but again the ECB did not move rates as far or as fast as the Fed.

As a result, the ECB's interest rate, previously lower than the Fed's rate, was soon higher than the U.S. rate in 2001 and remained higher through 2004. Investors most likely viewed these policy changes as a temporary shift in monetary policy in both countries. Hence, they might be considered as an example of temporary monetary policy shocks. Do our model's predictions accord well with reality?

Up until 2001, the policy of higher rates in the United States could be seen as a temporary home monetary contraction (relative to foreign), and our model would predict a dollar appreciation in the short run. After 2001, the aggressive reductions in U.S. interest rates could be seen as a temporary home monetary expansion (relative to foreign), and our model predicts a dollar depreciation in the short run. Looking at the path of the dollar–euro exchange rate in the figure, we can see that the model accords well with reality.

4 A Complete Theory: Unifying the Monetary and Asset Approaches

In this section, we extend our analysis from the short run to the long run, and examine permanent as well as temporary shocks. To do this, we put together a complete theory of exchange rates that couples the long-run and short-run approaches, as shown schematically in Figure 4-11:

- We need the asset approach (this chapter)—short-run money market equilibrium and uncovered interest parity:

$$\left.\begin{array}{l} \bar{P}_{US} = M_{US}/[L_{US}(i_\$)Y_{US}] \\ \bar{P}_{EUR} = M_{EUR}/[L_{EUR}(i_\euro)Y_{EUR}] \\ i_\$ = i_\euro + \dfrac{E^e_{\$/\euro} - E_{\$/\euro}}{E_{\$/\euro}} \end{array}\right\} \quad \text{The asset approach} \qquad (4\text{-}4)$$

- There are three equations and three unknowns (two short-run nominal interest rates and the spot exchange rate). The future expected exchange rate must be known, as must the current levels of money and real income. (The price level is also treated as given.)

- But to forecast the future expected exchange rate, we also need the long-run monetary approach from the previous chapter—a long-run monetary model and purchasing power parity:

$$\left.\begin{array}{l} P^e_{US} = M^e_{US}/[L_{US}(i^e_\$)Y^e_{US}] \\ P^e_{EUR} = M^e_{EUR}/[L_{EUR}(i^e_\euro)Y^e_{EUR}] \\ E^e_{\$/\euro} = P^e_{US}/P^e_{EUR} \end{array}\right\} \quad \text{The monetary approach} \qquad (4\text{-}5)$$

- There are three equations and three unknowns (two price levels and the exchange rate). Note that all variables here have a superscript *e* to denote future expected values or forecasts. We assume that forecasts of future money, real income, and nominal interest rates are known. This model can then be

FIGURE 4-11

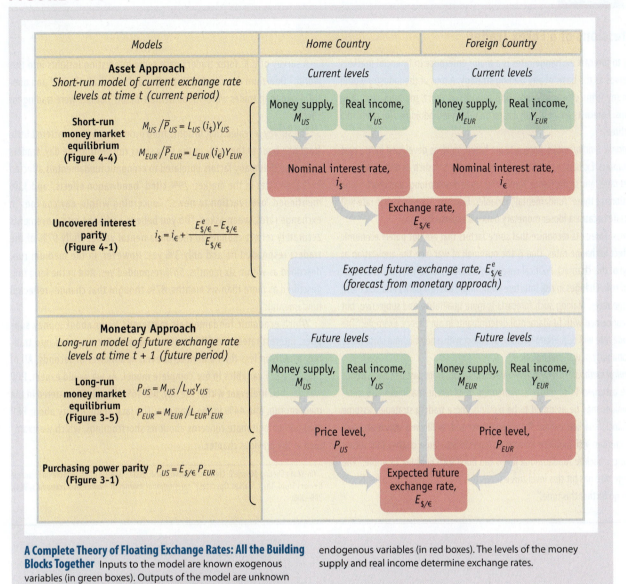

A Complete Theory of Floating Exchange Rates: All the Building Blocks Together Inputs to the model are known exogenous variables (in green boxes). Outputs of the model are unknown endogenous variables (in red boxes). The levels of the money supply and real income determine exchange rates.

applied to obtain price forecasts and, hence, a forecast of the future expected exchange rate.[2]

Figure 4-11 sums up all the theory we have learned so far in the past two chapters. It shows how all the pieces fit together. In total we have six equations and six unknowns.

It is only now, with all the building blocks in place, that we can fully appreciate how the two key mechanisms of *expectations* and *arbitrage* operate in a variety of ways to determine

---

[2] Recall that the previous chapter also showed us how real interest parity can be used to solve for the long-run nominal interest rate i in each country, the so-called *neutral level* of the nominal interest rate. For example, restricting our attention to the case of a stable long-run inflation rate (e.g., under nominal anchoring in which an announced inflation target is expected to be hit in each country), we have

$$\left. \begin{array}{l} i_\$ = \pi_{US,\text{target}} + r^* \\ i_\euro = \pi_{EUR,\text{target}} + r^* \end{array} \right\} \text{ Real interest parity}$$

Confessions of a Forex Trader

Trying to forecast exchange rates is a major enterprise in financial markets and serves as the basis of any trading strategy. A tour of the industry would find many firms offering forecasting services at short, medium, and long horizons. Forecasts are generally based on three methodologies (or some mix of all three):

1. *Economic fundamentals.* Forecasts are based on ideas developed in the past two chapters. Exchange rates are determined by factors such as money, output, interest rates, and so on; hence, forecasters try to develop long- and short-range predictions of these "fundamental" variables. Example: "The exchange rate will depreciate because a looser monetary policy is expected."

2. *Politics.* Forecasts recognize that some factors that are not purely economic can affect exchange rates. One is the outbreak of war (see the application at the end of this chapter). Political crises might matter, too, if they affect perceptions of risk. Changes in risk interfere with simple interest parity and can move exchange rates. Making such forecasts is more qualitative and subjective, but is still concerned with fundamental determinants in our theory. Example: "The exchange rate will depreciate because a conflict with a neighboring state raises the probability of war and inflation."

3. *Technical methods.* Forecasts rely on extrapolations from past behavior. Trends may be assumed to continue ("momentum"), or recent maximum and minimum values may be assumed to be binding. These trading strategies assume that financial markets exhibit some persistence and, if followed, may make such an assumption self-fulfilling for a time. Nonetheless, large crashes that return asset prices back to fundamental levels can burst such bubbles. Example: "The exchange rate has hit this level three times this year but never gone further; it will not go further this time."

A survey of U.K. forex traders gave some interesting insights into this world.[*] One-third described their trading as "technically based," and one-third said their trades were "fundamentals-based"; others were trading for clients.

The survey revealed that insights from economic theory mattered little from one hour to the next. In the very short run, within the day, traders confessed that many factors unrelated to economic fundamentals affected exchange rates in the market: 29% cited "bandwagon effects," and 33% mentioned "overreaction to news." Concerning within-day changes in exchange rates, when asked, "Do you believe exchange rate movements accurately reflect changes in the fundamental value?" fully 97% of the traders responded no and only 3% yes. However, in the medium run, described as within six months, 58% responded yes. And in the long run, described as more than six months, 87% thought that changes reflected fundamentals.

Which economic fundamentals mattered? News about money supplies, interest rates, and GDP levels was quickly incorporated into trading, usually in less than a minute or even in a matter of seconds. All of these are key variables in our complete model. As we would expect, PPP was deemed irrelevant within the day, but 16% thought it mattered in the medium run, and 44% in the long run. The lack of unanimity about PPP may reflect legitimate concerns about its shortcomings, which we examined in the previous chapter.

---

[*] Yin-Wong Cheung, Menzie D. Chinn, and Ian W. Marsh, 2004, "How Do UK-Based Foreign Exchange Dealers Think Their Market Operates?" *International Journal of Finance and Economics*, 9(4), 289–306.

---

exchange rates in both the short run and the long run. Ensure you are comfortable with all of the building blocks—how they work individually and how they connect.

After all our hard work, we have arrived at a complete theory to explain exchange rates in the short run and the long run. The model incorporates all of the key economic fundamentals that affect exchange rates, and, in practice, although forex markets exhibit a great deal of turbulence and uncertainty, there is evidence that these fundamentals play a major role in shaping traders' decisions (see **Side Bar: Confessions of a Forex Trader**).

Long-Run Policy Analysis

When and how can we apply the complete model? The downside of working with the complete model is that we have to keep track of multiple mechanisms and variables; the upside is that the theory is fully developed and can be applied to short-run and long-run policy shocks.

The temporary shocks we saw in the last section represent only one kind of monetary policy change, one that does not affect the long-run nominal anchor. The fact that these shocks were temporary allowed us to conduct all of the analysis under the assumption that the long-run expected level of the exchange rate remained unchanged.

When the monetary authorities decide to make a *permanent* change, however, this assumption of unchanged expectations is no longer appropriate. Under such a change, the authorities would cause an enduring change in all nominal variables; that is, they would be electing to change their nominal anchor policy in some way. Thus, when a monetary policy shock is permanent, the long-run expectation of the level of the exchange rate has to adjust. This change will, in turn, cause the exchange rate predictions of the short-run model to differ from those made when the policy shock was only temporary.

These insights guide our analysis of permanent policy shocks. They also tell us that we cannot approach such analysis chronologically. Before we can figure out what happens in the short run, we have to know expectations, that is, what is going to happen in the long run. Thus, we have to use a technique that is common in forward-looking economic problems: we must *solve backward* from the future to the present. (This ordering mirrors the presentation of the material in this textbook—we must understand the long run before we can understand the short run.)

A Permanent Shock to the Home Money Supply
We start our analysis of the home (U.S.) and foreign (Europe) economies with each economy currently at a long-run equilibrium in which all variables are steady. In this equilibrium, we assume that each country has a fixed real income, a fixed money supply, and a zero rate of inflation. Hence, there is a zero rate of depreciation because the equilibrium is characterized by purchasing power parity, and interest rates in each country are the same because the equilibrium is characterized by uncovered interest parity.

Our analysis is shown in Figure 4-12. Panels (a) and (b) show the short-run impacts of a permanent increase in the money supply in the home (U.S.) money and FX markets; panels (c) and (d) show the long-run impacts and the adjustment from the short run to the long run.

As shown in panels (a), (b), (c), and (d), we suppose the home economy starts with initial equilibria in the home money and FX markets shown by points 1 and 1', respectively. In the money market, in panels (a) and (c), at point 1, the home money market is initially in equilibrium: MS_1 corresponds to an initial real money supply of $M^1_{US}/\bar{P}^1_{US}$; given real money demand MD, the nominal interest rate is $i^1_\$$. In the FX market, in panels (b) and (d), at point 1', the domestic return DR_1 is the nominal interest rate $i^1_\$$. Given the foreign return curve FR_1, the equilibrium exchange rate is $E^1_{\$/€}$. If both economies are at a long-run equilibrium with zero depreciation, then this is also the expected future exchange rate $E^{e1}_{\$/€} = E^1_{\$/€}$.

We now start to figure out what happens after the policy shock hits today, working backward from the future to the present.

The Long Run
Refer to panels (c) and (d) of Figure 4-12. In the long run, we know from the monetary approach that an increase in the money supply will eventually lead to a proportionate increase in the price level and the exchange rate. If the money supply increases from M^1_{US} to M^2_{US} today, then the price level will *eventually* increase by the same proportion from P^1_{US} to P^2_{US}, and, to maintain PPP, the exchange rate will *eventually* rise by the same proportion (and the dollar will depreciate) from $E^1_{\$/€}$ to its long-run level $E^4_{\$/€}$, in panel (d), where $E^4_{\$/€}/E^1_{\$/€} = P^2_{US}/P^1_{US} = M^2_{US}/M^1_{US} > 1$. (We use "4" to denote long-run exchange rate values because there will be some short-run responses to consider in just a moment.)

Thus, in the long run, in panel (c), if money and prices both rise in the same proportion, then the real money supply will be unchanged at its original level $M^1_{US}/\bar{P}^1_{US} = M^2_{US}/\bar{P}^2_{US}$, the real money supply curve will revert to its original position MS_1, and the nominal interest rate will again be $i^1_\$$. In the long run, the money market returns to where it started: long-run equilibrium is at point 4 (which is the same as point 1).

FIGURE 4-12

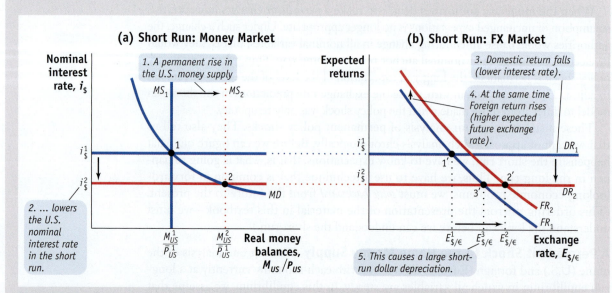

(a) Short Run: Money Market

Nominal interest rate, $i_\$$

1. A permanent rise in the U.S. money supply

MS_1 → MS_2

$i_\$^1$ — 1

$i_\$^2$ — 2

MD

2. ... lowers the U.S. nominal interest rate in the short run.

$\dfrac{M_{US}^1}{\overline{P}_{US}^1}$ $\dfrac{M_{US}^2}{\overline{P}_{US}^1}$ **Real money balances, M_{US}/P_{US}**

(b) Short Run: FX Market

Expected returns

3. Domestic return falls (lower interest rate).

4. At the same time Foreign return rises (higher expected future exchange rate).

$i_\$^1$ — 1'

$i_\$^2$ — 3'   2'

DR_1

DR_2

FR_2

FR_1

$E_{\$/€}^1$ $E_{\$/€}^3$ $E_{\$/€}^2$ **Exchange rate, $E_{\$/€}$**

5. This causes a large short-run dollar depreciation.

Permanent Expansion of the Home Money Supply: Short-Run Impact: In panel (a), the home price level is fixed, but the supply of dollar balances increases and real money supply shifts out. To restore equilibrium at point 2, the interest rate falls from $i_\$^1$ to $i_\$^2$. In panel (b), in the FX market, the home interest rate falls, so the domestic return decreases and DR shifts down. In addition, the permanent change in the home money supply implies a permanent, long-run depreciation of the dollar. Hence, there is also a permanent rise in $E_{\$/€}^e$, which causes a permanent increase in the foreign return $i_€ + (E_{\$/€}^e - E_{\$/€})/E_{\$/€}$, all else equal; FR shifts up from FR_1 to FR_2. The simultaneous fall in DR and rise in FR cause the home currency to depreciate steeply, leading to a new equilibrium at point 2' (and not at 3', which would be the equilibrium if the policy were temporary).

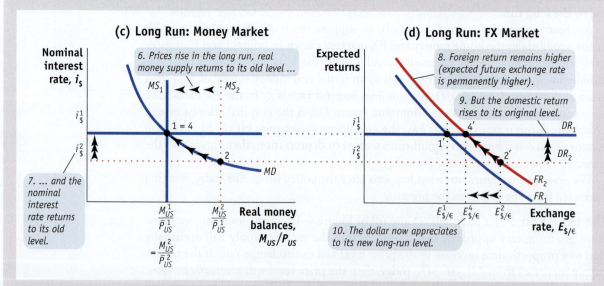

(c) Long Run: Money Market

Nominal interest rate, $i_\$$

6. Prices rise in the long run, real money supply returns to its old level ...

MS_1 ← ← ← MS_2

$i_\$^1$ — 1 = 4

$i_\$^2$ — 2

MD

7. ... and the nominal interest rate returns to its old level.

$\dfrac{M_{US}^1}{\overline{P}_{US}^1}$ $\dfrac{M_{US}^2}{\overline{P}_{US}^1}$ **Real money balances, M_{US}/P_{US}**

$= \dfrac{M_{US}^2}{\overline{P}_{US}^2}$

(d) Long Run: FX Market

Expected returns

8. Foreign return remains higher (expected future exchange rate is permanently higher).

9. But the domestic return rises to its original level.

$i_\$^1$ — 1'   4'

$i_\$^2$ — 2'

DR_1

DR_2

FR_2

FR_1

$E_{\$/€}^1$ $E_{\$/€}^4$ $E_{\$/€}^2$ **Exchange rate, $E_{\$/€}$**

10. The dollar now appreciates to its new long-run level.

Long-Run Adjustment: In panel (c), in the long run, prices are flexible, so the home price level and the exchange rate both rise in proportion with the money supply. Prices rise to $\overline{P}_{US}^2$, and real money supply returns to its original level $M_{US}^1/\overline{P}_{US}^1$. The money market gradually shifts back to equilibrium at point 4 (the same as point 1). In panel (d), in the FX market, the domestic return DR, which equals the home interest rate, gradually shifts back to its original level. The foreign return curve FR does not move at all: there are no further changes in the foreign interest rate or in the future expected exchange rate. The FX market equilibrium shifts gradually to point 4'. The exchange rate falls (and the dollar appreciates) from $E_{\$/€}^2$ to $E_{\$/€}^4$. Arrows in both graphs show the path of gradual adjustment.

In the FX market, however, a permanent money supply shock causes some permanent changes in the long run. One thing that does not change is the domestic return DR_1, since in the long run it returns to $i_\$^1$. But the exchange rate will rise from the initial long-run exchange rate $E_{\$/€}^1$ to a new long-run level $E_{\$/€}^4$. Because $E_{\$/€}^4$ is a long-run stable level, it is also the new expected level of the exchange rate $E_{\$/€}^{4e}$ that will prevail in the future. That is, the future will look like the present, under our assumptions, except that the exchange rate will be sitting at $E_{\$/€}^4$ instead of $E_{\$/€}^1$. What does this change do to the foreign return curve FR? As we know, when the expected exchange rate increases, foreign returns are higher, so the FR curve shifts up, from FR_1 to FR_2. Because in the long run $E_{\$/€}^4$ is the new stable equilibrium exchange rate, and $i_\$^1$ is the interest rate, the new FX market equilibrium is at point 4′ where FR_2 intersects DR_1.

The Short Run Only now that we have changes in expectations worked out can we work back through panels (a) and (b) of Figure 4-12 to see what will happen in the short run.

Look first at the FX market in panel (b). Because expectations about the future exchange rate have changed with today's policy announcement, the FX market is affected immediately. Everyone knows that the exchange rate will be $E_{\$/€}^4$ in the future. The foreign return curve shifts when the expected exchange rate changes; it rises from FR_1 to FR_2. This is the same shift we just saw in the long-run panel (d). The dollar is expected to depreciate to $E_{\$/€}^4$ (relative to $E_{\$/€}^1$) in the future, so euro deposits are more attractive today.

Now consider the impact of the change in monetary policy in the short run. Look at the money market in panel (a). In the short run, if the money supply increases from M_{US}^1 to M_{US}^2 but prices are sticky at P_{US}^1, then real money balances rise from $M_{US}^1/\bar{P}_{US}^1$ to $M_{US}^2/\bar{P}_{US}^1$. The real money supply shifts from MS_1 to MS_2 and the home interest rate falls from $i_\$^1$ to $i_\$^2$, leading to a new short-run money market equilibrium at point 2.

Now look back to the FX market in panel (b). If this were a *temporary* monetary policy shock, expectations would be unchanged, and the FR_1 curve would still describe foreign returns, but domestic returns would fall from DR_1 to DR_2 as the interest rate fell, and the home currency would depreciate to the level $E_{\$/€}^3$. The FX market equilibrium, after a temporary money supply shock, would be at point 3′, as we have seen before.

But this is not the case now. This time we are looking at a permanent shock to money supply. It has *two* effects on today's FX market. One impact of the money supply shock is to lower the home interest rate, decreasing domestic returns in today's FX market from DR_1 to DR_2. The other impact of the money supply shock is to increase the future expected exchange rate, increasing foreign returns in today's FX market from FR_1 to FR_2. Hence, the FX market equilibrium in the short run is where DR_2 and FR_2 intersect, now at point 2′, and the exchange rate depreciates all the way to $E_{\$/€}^2$.

Note that the short-run equilibrium level of the exchange rate $(E_{\$/€}^2)$ is higher than the level that would be observed under a temporary shock $(E_{\$/€}^3)$ and also higher than the level that will be observed in the long run $(E_{\$/€}^4)$. To sum up, *in the short run, the permanent shock causes the exchange rate to depreciate more than it would under a temporary shock and more than it will end up depreciating in the long run.*

Adjustment from Short Run to Long Run The arrows in panels (c) and (d) of Figure 4-12 trace what happens as we move from the short run to the long run. Prices that were initially sticky in the short run become unstuck. The price level rises from

P_{US}^1 to P_{US}^2, and this pushes the real money supply back to its initial level, from MS_2 back to MS_1. Money demand MD is unchanged. Hence, in the home money market of panel (c), the economy moves from the short-run equilibrium at point 2 to the long-run equilibrium, which is again at point 1, following the path shown by the arrows. Hence, the interest rate gradually rises from $i_\$^2$ back to $i_\$^1$. This raises the domestic returns over in the FX market of panel (d) from DR_2 back to DR_1. So the FX market moves from the short-run equilibrium at point 2′ to the long-run equilibrium, which is again at point 4′.

An Example Let's make this very tricky experiment a bit more concrete with a numerical example. Suppose you are told that, all else equal, (i) the home money supply permanently increases by 5% today; (ii) prices are sticky in the short run, so this also causes an increase in real money supply that lowers domestic interest rates by four percentage points from 6% to 2%; (iii) prices will fully adjust in one year's time to today's monetary expansion and PPP will hold again. Based on this information, can you predict what will happen to prices and the exchange rate today and in a year's time?

Yes. Work backward from the long run to the short run, as before. In the long run, a 5% increase in M means a 5% increase in P that will be achieved in one year. By PPP, this 5% increase in P implies a 5% rise in E (a 5% depreciation in the dollar's value) over the same period. In other words, over the next year E will rise at 5% per year, which will be the rate of depreciation. Finally, in the short run, UIP tells us what happens to the exchange rate today: to compensate investors for the four-percentage-point decrease in the domestic interest rate, arbitrage in the FX market requires that the value of the home currency be expected to appreciate at 4% per year; that is, E must fall 4% in the year ahead. However, if E has to fall 4% in the next year and still end up 5% above its level at the start of today, then it must jump up 9% today: it overshoots its long-run level.

Overshooting

Compared with the temporary expansion of money supply we studied before, the permanent shock has a much greater impact on the exchange rate in the short run.

Under the temporary shock, domestic returns go down; traders want to sell the dollar for one reason only—temporarily lower dollar interest rates make dollar deposits less attractive. Under the permanent shock, domestic returns go down and foreign returns go up; traders want to sell the dollar for two reasons—temporarily lower dollar interest rates and an expected dollar depreciation make dollar deposits *much* less attractive. In the short run, the interest rate and exchange rate effects combine to create an instantaneous "double whammy" for the dollar, which gives rise to a phenomenon that economists refer to as exchange rate **overshooting**.

To better visualize the overshooting phenomenon, we show in Figure 4-13 the time path over which the key economic variables change after the permanent shock we just studied using Figure 4-12. We see the following:

a. The nominal money supply is subject to a one-time increase at time T.

b. Real money balances rise instantaneously but revert to their initial level in the long run; the nominal interest rate falls instantaneously but reverts to its initial level in the long run.

c. The price level is sticky in the short run but rises to a new higher level in the long run, increasing in the same proportion as the nominal money supply.

FIGURE 4-13

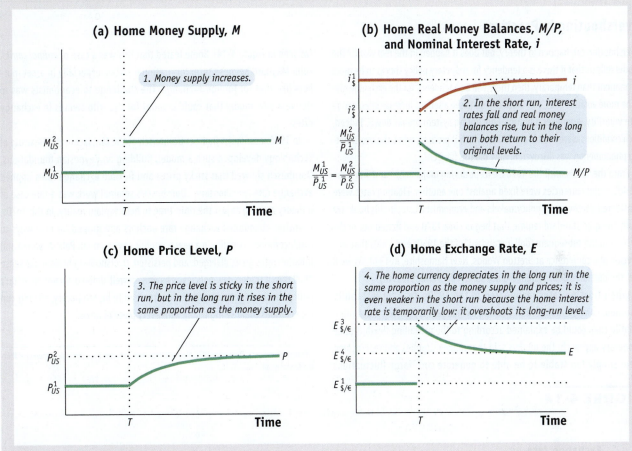

(a) Home Money Supply, M

1. Money supply increases.

(b) Home Real Money Balances, M/P, and Nominal Interest Rate, i

2. In the short run, interest rates fall and real money balances rise, but in the long run both return to their original levels.

(c) Home Price Level, P

3. The price level is sticky in the short run, but in the long run it rises in the same proportion as the money supply.

(d) Home Exchange Rate, E

4. The home currency depreciates in the long run in the same proportion as the money supply and prices; it is even weaker in the short run because the home interest rate is temporarily low: it overshoots its long-run level.

Responses to a Permanent Expansion of the Home Money Supply In panel (a), there is a one-time permanent increase in home (U.S.) nominal money supply at time T. In panel (b), prices are sticky in the short run, so there is a short-run increase in the real money supply and a fall in the home interest rate. In panel (c), in the long run, prices rise in the same proportion as the money supply. In panel (d), in the short run, the exchange rate overshoots its long-run value (the dollar depreciates by a large amount), but in the long run, the exchange rate will have risen only in proportion to changes in money and prices.

d. The exchange rate rises (depreciates) to a new higher level in the long run, rising in the same proportion as the nominal money supply. In the short run, however, the exchange rate rises even more, overshooting its long-run level, then gradually decreasing to its long-run level (which is still higher than the initial level).

The overshooting result adds yet another argument for the importance of a sound long-run nominal anchor: without it, exchange rates are likely to be more volatile, creating instability in the forex market and possibly in the wider economy. The wild fluctuations of exchange rates in the 1970s, at a time when exchange rate anchors were ripped loose, exposed these linkages with great clarity (see **Side Bar: Overshooting in Practice**). And new research provides evidence that the shift to a new form of anchoring, inflation targeting, might be helping to bring down exchange rate volatility in recent years.[3]

[3] Andrew K. Rose, 2007, "A Stable International Monetary System Emerges: Inflation Targeting Is Bretton Woods, Reversed," *Journal of International Money and Finance*, 26(5), 663–681.

Overshooting in Practice

Overshooting can happen in theory, but does it happen in the real world? The model tells us that if there is a tendency for monetary policy shocks to be more permanent than temporary, then there will be a tendency for the exchange rate to be more volatile. Thus, we might expect to see a serious increase in exchange rate volatility whenever a nominal anchoring system breaks down. Indeed, such conditions were seen in the 1970s, which is precisely when the overshooting phenomenon was discovered. How did this happen?

From the 1870s until the 1970s, except during major crises and wars, the world's major currencies were fixed against one another. Floating rates were considered anathema by policymakers and economists. Later in this book, we study the gold standard regime that began circa 1870 and fizzled out in the 1930s and the subsequent "dollar standard" of the 1950s and 1960s that was devised at a conference at Bretton Woods, New Hampshire, in 1944. As we'll see, the Bretton Woods system did not survive for various reasons.

When floating rates reappeared in the 1970s, fears of instability returned. Concern mounted as floating exchange rates proved much more volatile than could be explained according to the prevailing flexible-price monetary approach: the models said that money supplies and real income were simply too stable to be able to generate such large fluctuations

(as seen in Figure 4-14). Some feared that this was a case of *animal spirits*, John Maynard Keynes's term for irrational forces, especially in asset markets like that for foreign exchange. The challenge to economists was to derive a new model that could account for the wild swings in exchange rates.

In 1976, economist Rudiger Dornbusch of the Massachusetts Institute of Technology developed such a model. Building on Keynesian foundations, Dornbusch showed that sticky prices and flexible exchange rates implied exchange rate overshooting.[*] Dornbusch's seminal work was a rare case of a theory arriving at just the right time to help explain reality. In the 1970s, countries abandoned exchange rate anchors and groped for new ways to conduct monetary policy in a new economic environment. Policies varied and inflation rates grew, diverged, and persisted. Overshooting helps make sense of all this: if traders saw policies as having no well-defined anchor, monetary policy shocks might no longer be guaranteed to be temporary, so long-run expectations could swing wildly with every piece of news.

---

[*] Rudiger Dornbusch, December 1976, "Expectations and Exchange Rate Dynamics," *Journal of Political Economy*, 84, 1161–1176.

FIGURE 4-14

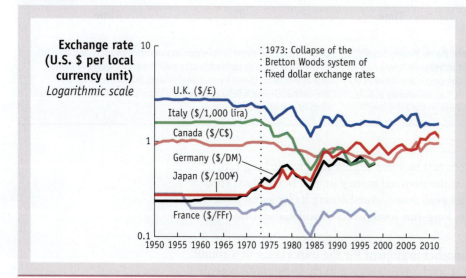

Exchange Rates for Major Currencies Before and After 1973 Under the Bretton Woods system of fixed but adjustable dollar pegs, exchange rates were mostly stable from 1950 until 1970. The system was declared officially dead in 1973. From then on, all of these currencies have fluctuated against the dollar.

Data from: IMF, International Financial Statistics.

5 Fixed Exchange Rates and the Trilemma

We have developed a complete theory of exchange rates, based on the assumption that market forces in the money market and the forex market determine exchange rates. Our models have the most obvious application to the case of floating exchange rate regimes. But as we have seen, not every country floats. Can our theory also be applied to the equally important case of fixed exchange rate regimes and to other intermediate regimes? The answer is yes, and we conclude this chapter by adapting our existing theory for the case of fixed regimes.

What Is a Fixed Exchange Rate Regime?

To understand the crucial difference between fixing and floating, we contrast the polar cases of tight fixing (hard pegs including narrow bands) and free floating, and ignore, for now, intermediate regimes. We also set aside regimes that include controls on arbitrage (*capital controls*) because such extremes of government intervention render our theory superfluous. Instead, we focus on the case of a fixed rate regime without controls so that capital is mobile and arbitrage is free to operate in the forex market.

Here, the government itself becomes an actor in the forex market, and uses intervention in the market to influence the market rate. Exchange rate intervention takes the form of the central bank buying and selling foreign currency at a fixed price, thus holding the market exchange rate at a fixed level, denoted $\bar{E}$.

We can explore the implications of that policy in the short run and the long run using the familiar building blocks of our theory. To give a concrete flavor to these analyses, we replace the United States and the Eurozone (whose currencies float against each other) with an example of an actual fixed exchange rate regime. In this example, Foreign remains the Eurozone, but Home is now Denmark.

We examine the implications of Denmark's decision to peg its currency, the krone, to the euro at a fixed rate $\bar{E}_{DKr/\euro}$.[4]

In the long run, fixing the exchange rate is one kind of nominal anchor. Yet even if Denmark allowed the krone to float but had *some* nominal anchor, Denmark's monetary policy would still be constrained in the long run by the need to achieve its chosen nominal target. We have seen that any country with a nominal anchor faces long-run monetary policy constraints of some kind. *What we now show is that a country with a fixed exchange rate faces monetary policy constraints not just in the long run but also in the short run.*

Pegging Sacrifices Monetary Policy Autonomy in the Short Run: Example

By assumption, equilibrium in the krone–euro forex market requires that the Danish interest rate be equal to the Eurozone interest rate plus the expected rate of depreciation of the krone. But under a peg, the expected rate of depreciation is zero.

Here uncovered interest parity reduces to the simple condition that the Danish central bank must set its interest rate equal to $i_\euro$, the rate set by the ECB:

$$i_{DKr} = i_\euro + \underbrace{\frac{E^e_{DKr/\euro} - E_{DKr/\euro}}{E_{DKr/\euro}}}_{\substack{\text{Equals zero} \\ \text{for a credible} \\ \text{fixed exchange rate}}} = i_\euro$$

Denmark has lost control of its monetary policy: it cannot independently change its interest rate under a peg.

The same is true of money supply policy. Short-run equilibrium in Denmark's money market requires that money supply equal money demand, but once Denmark's interest rate is set equal to the Eurozone interest rate $i_\euro$, there is only one feasible level for the money supply, as we see by imposing $i_\euro$ as the Danish interest rate in money market equilibrium:

$$M_{DEN} = \bar{P}_{DEN} L_{DEN}(i_{DKr}) Y_{DEN} = \bar{P}_{DEN} L_{DEN}(i_\euro) Y_{DEN}$$

The implications are striking. The final expression contains the euro interest rate (exogenous, as far as the Danes are concerned), the fixed price level (exogenous by assumption), and output (also exogenous by assumption). No variable in this expression is

---

[4] The actual arrangement is a "narrow band" centered on 7.46038 DKr/€ and officially of width ±2.25%, according to the ERM arrangement between Denmark and the Eurozone that has been in effect since 1999. In practice, the peg is much tighter and the krone usually stays within ±0.5% of the central rate.

under the control of the Danish authorities in the short run, and this is the only level of the Danish money supply consistent with equilibrium in the money and forex markets at the pegged rate $\bar{E}_{DKr/\text{€}}$. If the Danish central bank is to maintain the peg, then in the short run it must choose the level of money supply implied by the last equation.

What's going on? Arbitrage is the key force. For example, if the Danish central bank tried to supply more krone and lower interest rates, it would be foiled by arbitrage. Danes would want to sell krone deposits and buy higher-yield euro deposits, applying downward pressure on the krone. To maintain the peg, whatever krone the Danish central bank had tried to pump into circulation, it would promptly have to buy them back in the forex market.

Thus, *our short-run theory still applies, but with a different chain of causality*:

- Under a float, the home monetary authorities pick the money supply M. In the short run, the choice of M determines the interest rate i in the money market; in turn, via UIP, the level of i determines the exchange rate E. The money supply is an input in the model (an exogenous variable), and the exchange rate is an output of the model (an endogenous variable).

- Under a fix, this logic is reversed. Home monetary authorities pick the fixed level of the exchange rate E. In the short run, a fixed E pins down the home interest rate i via UIP (forcing i to equal the foreign interest rate i^*); in turn, the level of i determines the level of the money supply M necessary to meet money demand. The exchange rate is an input in the model (an exogenous variable), and the money supply is an output of the model (an endogenous variable).

This reversal of short-run causality is shown in a new schematic in the top part of Figure 4-15.

Pegging Sacrifices Monetary Policy Autonomy in the Long Run: Example

As we have noted, choosing a nominal anchor implies a loss of long-run monetary policy autonomy. Let's quickly see how that works when the anchor is a fixed exchange rate.

Following our discussion of the standard monetary model, we must first ask what the nominal interest rate is going to be in Denmark in the long run. But we have already answered that question; it is going to be tied down the same way as in the short run, at the level set by the ECB, namely $i_\text{€}$. We might question, in turn, where *that* level $i_\text{€}$ comes from (the answer is that it will be related to the "neutral" level of the nominal interest rate consistent with the ECB's own nominal anchor, its inflation target for the Eurozone). But that is beside the point: all that matters is that $i_\text{€}$ is as much out of Denmark's control in the long run as it is in the short run.

Next we turn to the price level in Denmark, which is determined in the long run by PPP. But if the exchange rate is pegged, we can write long-run PPP for Denmark as

$$P_{DEN} = \bar{E}_{DKr/\text{€}}P_{EUR}$$

Here we encounter another variable that is totally outside of Danish control in the long run. Under PPP, pegging to the euro means that the Danish price level is a fixed multiple of the Eurozone price level (which is exogenous, as far as the Danes are concerned).

With the long-run nominal interest rate and price level outside of Danish control, we can show, as before, that monetary policy autonomy is out of the question. We just substitute $i_{DKr} = i_\text{€}$ and $P_{DEN} = \bar{E}_{DKr/\text{€}}P_{EUR}$ into Denmark's long-run money market equilibrium to obtain

$$M_{DEN} = P_{DEN}L_{DEN}(i_{DKr})Y_{DEN} = \bar{E}_{DKr/\text{€}}P_{EUR}L_{DEN}(i_\text{€})Y_{DEN}$$

FIGURE 4-15

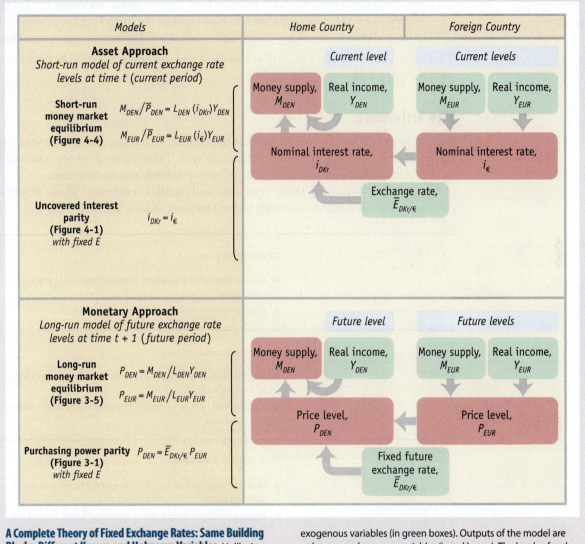

A Complete Theory of Fixed Exchange Rates: Same Building Blocks, Different Known and Unknown Variables Unlike in Figure 4-10, the home country is now assumed to fix its exchange rate with the foreign country. Inputs to the model are known exogenous variables (in green boxes). Outputs of the model are unknown endogenous variables (in red boxes). The levels of real income and the fixed exchange rate determine the home money supply levels, given outcomes in the foreign country.

The final expression contains the long-run euro interest rate and price levels (exogenous, as far as the Danes are concerned), the fixed exchange rate level (exogenous by assumption), and long-run Danish output (also exogenous by assumption). Again, no variable in the final expression is under the control of the Danish authorities in the long run, and this is the only level of the Danish money supply consistent with equilibrium in the money and forex market at the pegged rate of $\bar{E}_{DKr/\text{€}}$.

Thus, *our long-run theory still applies, just with a different chain of causality*:

■ Under a float, the home monetary authorities pick the money supply M. In the long run, the growth rate of M determines the interest rate i via the Fisher effect and also the price level P; in turn, via PPP, the level of P determines the exchange rate E. The money supply is an input in the model (an exogenous variable), and the exchange rate is an output of the model (an endogenous variable).

■ Under a fix, this logic is reversed. Home monetary authorities pick the exchange rate E. In the long run, the choice of E determines the price level P via PPP, and also the interest rate i via UIP; these, in turn, determine the necessary level of the money supply M. The exchange rate is an input of the model (an exogenous variable), and the money supply is an output of the model (an endogenous variable).

This reversal of long-run causality is also shown in the new schematic in the bottom part of Figure 4-15.

The Trilemma

Our findings lead to the conclusion that policymakers face some tough choices. Not all desirable policy goals can be simultaneously met. These constraints are summed up in one of the most important principles in open-economy macroeconomics.

Consider the following three equations and parallel statements about desirable *policy goals*. For illustration we return to the Denmark–Eurozone example:

1. $\dfrac{E^e_{DKr/\euro} - E_{DKr/\euro}}{E_{DKr/\euro}} = 0$

   A fixed exchange rate

   ■ May be desired as a means to promote stability in trade and investment
   ■ Represented here by zero expected depreciation

2. $i_{DKr} = i_\euro + \dfrac{E^e_{DKr/\euro} - E_{DKr/\euro}}{E_{DKr/\euro}}$

   International capital mobility

   ■ May be desired as a means to promote integration, efficiency, and risk sharing
   ■ Represented here by uncovered interest parity, which results from arbitrage

3. $i_{DKr} \neq i_\euro$

   Monetary policy autonomy

   ■ May be desired as a means to manage the home economy's business cycle
   ■ Represented here by the ability to set the home interest rate independently of the foreign interest rate

For a variety of reasons, as noted, governments may want to pursue all three of these policy goals. But they can't: formulae 1, 2, and 3 show that it is a *mathematical impossibility* as shown by the following statements:

■ 1 and 2 imply not 3 (1 and 2 imply interest equality, contradicting 3).
■ 2 and 3 imply not 1 (2 and 3 imply an expected change in E, contradicting 1).
■ 3 and 1 imply not 2 (3 and 1 imply a difference between domestic and foreign returns, contradicting 2).

This result, known as the **trilemma**, is one of the most important ideas in international macroeconomics.[5] It tells us that the three policy goals just outlined are mutually incompatible: you cannot have all three at once. You must choose to drop one of the three (or, equivalently, you must adopt one of three pairs: 1 and 2, 2 and 3, or 3 and 1). Sadly, there is a long history of macroeconomic disasters stemming from the failure of some policy that ignored this fundamental lesson.

---

[5] A definition: "Trilemma *noun* 1. a quandary posed by three alternative courses of action" (*Collins English Dictionary* online).

FIGURE 4-16

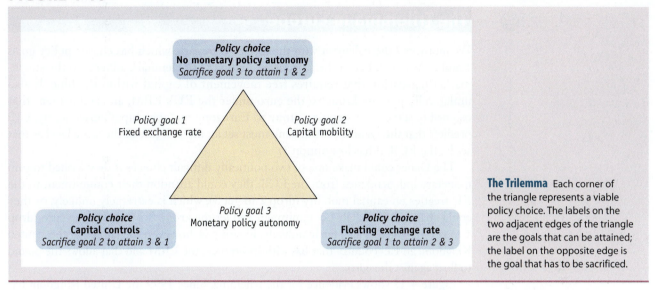

Policy choice
No monetary policy autonomy
Sacrifice goal 3 to attain 1 & 2

Policy goal 1
Fixed exchange rate

Policy goal 2
Capital mobility

Policy goal 3
Monetary policy autonomy

Policy choice
Capital controls
Sacrifice goal 2 to attain 3 & 1

Policy choice
Floating exchange rate
Sacrifice goal 1 to attain 2 & 3

The Trilemma Each corner of the triangle represents a viable policy choice. The labels on the two adjacent edges of the triangle are the goals that can be attained; the label on the opposite edge is the goal that has to be sacrificed.

The trilemma can be illustrated graphically as in Figure 4-16. Each corner of the triangle represents a viable policy regime choice. For each corner, the label on the opposite edge of the triangle indicates the goal that has been sacrificed, while the labels on the two adjacent edges show the two goals that can be attained under that choice (see **Side Bar: Intermediate Regimes**).

SIDE BAR

Intermediate Regimes

The lessons of the trilemma most clearly apply when the policies are at the ends of a spectrum: a hard peg or a float, perfect capital mobility or immobility, complete autonomy or none at all. But sometimes a country may not be fully in one of the three corners: the rigidity of the peg, the degree of capital mobility, and the independence of monetary policy could be partial rather than full.

For example, in a band arrangement, the exchange rate is maintained within a range of ±X% of some central rate. The significance of the band is that some expected depreciation (i.e., a little bit of floating) is possible. As a result, a limited interest differential can open up between the two countries. For example, suppose the band is 2% wide (i.e., ±1% around a central rate). To compute home interest rates, UIP tells us that we must add the foreign interest rate (let's suppose it is 5%) to the expected rate of depreciation (which is ±2% if the exchange rate moves from one band edge to the other). Thus, Home may "fix" this way and still have the freedom to set 12-month interest rates in the range between 3% and 7%. But the home country cannot evade the trilemma forever: on average, over time, the rate of depreciation will have to be zero to keep the exchange rate within the narrow band, meaning that the home interest rate must track the foreign interest rate apart from small deviations.

Similar qualifications to the trilemma could result from partial capital mobility, in which barriers to arbitrage could also lead to interest differentials. And with such differentials emerging, the desire for partial monetary autonomy can be accommodated.

In practice, once these distinctions are understood, it is usually possible to make some kind of judgment about which corner best describes the country's policy choice. For example, in 2007 both Slovakia and Denmark were supposedly pegged to the euro as members of the EU's Exchange Rate Mechanism (ERM). But the similarities ended there. The Danish krone was operating in ERM bands of official width ±2.25%, but closer to ±0.5% in practice, a pretty hard peg with almost no movement. The Slovak koruna was operating with ±15% bands and at one point even shifted that band by appreciating its central rate by 8.5% in March 2007. With its perpetual narrow band, Denmark's regime was clearly fixed. With its wide and adjustable bands, Slovakia's regime was closer to managed floating.[*]

---

[*] Note that Slovakia adopted the euro in 2009.

APPLICATION

The Trilemma in Europe

We motivated the trilemma with the case of Denmark, which has chosen policy goals 1 and 2. As a member of the European Union (EU), Denmark adheres to the single-market legislation that requires free movement of capital within the bloc. It also unilaterally pegs its krone to the euro under the EU's ERM, an arrangement that ostensibly serves as a stepping-stone to Eurozone membership. Consequently, UIP predicts that the Danish central bank must set an interest rate at the same level as that set by the ECB; it has lost option 3.

The Danes could make one of two politically difficult choices if they wished to gain monetary independence from the ECB: they could abandon their commitment to the EU treaties on capital mobility (drop 2 to get 3), which is extremely unlikely, or they could abandon their ERM commitment and let the krone float against the euro (drop 1 to get 3), which is also fairly unlikely. Floating is, however, the choice of the United Kingdom, an EU country that has withdrawn from the ERM and that allows the pound to float against the euro.

Figure 4-17 shows evidence for the trilemma. Since 1999 the United Kingdom has had the ability to set interest rates independently of the ECB. But Denmark has not: since 1999 the Danish interest rate has tracked the ECB's rate almost exactly. (Most of the departures from equality reflect uncertainty about the euro project and Denmark's peg at two key moments: at the very start of the euro project in 1999, and during the credibility crisis of the Eurozone since the crisis of 2008.)

FIGURE 4-17

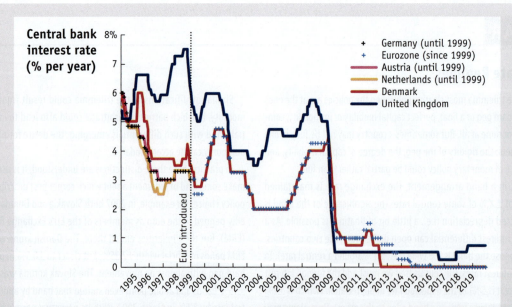

The Trilemma in Europe The figure shows selected central banks' base interest rates for the period 1994 to 2015 with reference to the German mark and euro base rates. In this period, the British made a policy choice to float against the German mark and (after 1999) against the euro. This permitted monetary independence because interest rates set by the Bank of England could diverge from those set in Frankfurt. No such independence in policymaking was afforded by the Danish decision to peg the krone first to the mark and then to the euro. Since 1999 the Danish interest rate has moved almost exactly in line with the ECB rate. Similar forces operated pre-1999 for other countries pegging to the mark, such as the Netherlands and Austria. Until they joined the Eurozone in 1999, their interest rates, like that of Denmark, closely tracked the German rate.

Data from: Websites of central banks.

These monetary policy ties to Frankfurt even predate the euro itself. Before 1999 Denmark, and some countries such as Austria and the Netherlands, pegged to the German mark with the same result: their interest rates had to track the German interest rate, but the U.K. interest rate did not. The big difference is that Austria and the Netherlands have formally abolished their national currencies, the schilling and the guilder, and have adopted the euro—an extreme and explicit renunciation of monetary independence. Meanwhile, the Danish krone lives on, showing that a national currency can suggest monetary sovereignty in theory but may deliver nothing of the sort in practice.

6 Conclusions

In this chapter, we drew together everything we have learned so far about exchange rates. We built on the concepts of arbitrage and equilibrium in the forex market in the short run, taking expectations as given and applying uncovered interest parity. We also relied on the purchasing power parity theory as a guide to exchange rate determination in the long run. Putting together all these building blocks provides a complete and internally consistent theory of exchange rate determination.

Exchange rates are an interesting topic in and of themselves, but at the end of the day, we also care about what they mean for the wider economy, how they relate to macroeconomic performance, and the part they play in the global monetary system. That is our goal in the next chapters, in which we apply our exchange rate theories in a wider framework to help us understand how exchange rates function in the national and international economy.

The theory we've developed in the past three chapters is the first tool that economists and policymakers pick up when studying a problem involving exchange rates. This theory has served well in rich and poor countries, whether in periods of economic stability or turbulence. Remarkably, it has even been applied in wartime, and to round off our discussion of exchange rates, we examine some colorful applications of the theory from conflicts past and present.

APPLICATION

News and the Foreign Exchange Market in Wartime

Our theory of exchange rates places expectations at center stage, but demonstrating the effect of changing expectations empirically is a challenge. However, wars dramatically expose the power of expectations to change exchange rates. War raises the risk that a currency may depreciate in value rapidly in the future, possibly all the way to zero. For one thing, the government may need to print money to finance its war effort, but how much inflation this practice will generate may be unclear. In addition, there is a risk of defeat and a decision by the victor to impose new economic arrangements such as a new currency; the existing currency may then be converted into the new currency at a rate dictated by the victors, or, in a worst-case scenario, it may be declared totally worthless, that is, not legal tender. Demand for the currency will then collapse to nothing, and so will its value. Investors in the forex market are continually updating their forecasts about a war's possible outcomes, and, as a result, the path of an exchange rate during wartime usually reveals a clear influence of the effects of news.

The U.S. Civil War, 1861–65 For four years, beginning April 12, 1861, a war raged between Union (Northern) and Confederate (Southern) forces. An important economic dimension of this conflict was the decision by the Confederate states to issue their own currency, the Confederate dollar, to help gain economic autonomy from the North and finance their war effort. The exchange rate of the Confederate dollar against the U.S. dollar is shown in Figure 4-18.

How should we interpret these data? The two currencies differed in one important respect. If the South had won, and the Confederate states had gained independence, they would have kept their Confederate dollar, and the Northern United States would have kept their U.S. dollar, too. Instead, the South was defeated, and, as expected in these circumstances, the U.S. dollar was imposed as the sole currency of the unified country; the Confederate dollar, like all liabilities of the Confederate nation, was repudiated by the victors and, hence, became worthless.

War news regularly influenced the exchange rate.[6] As the South headed for defeat, the value of the Confederate dollar shrank. The overall trend was driven partly by inflationary war finance and partly by the probability of defeat. Major Northern victories marked "N" tended to coincide with depreciations of the Confederate dollar. Major Southern victories marked "S" were associated with appreciations or, at least, a slower depreciation. The key Union victory at Gettysburg, July 1–3, 1863, and the near simultaneous fall of Vicksburg on July 4 were followed by a dramatic depreciation of the Confederate dollar. By contrast, Southern victories (in the winter of 1862 to 1863 and the spring of 1864) were periods when the Southern currency held steady or even appreciated. But by the fall of 1864, and particularly after Sherman's March, the writing was on the wall, and the Confederate dollar began its final decline.

FIGURE 4-18

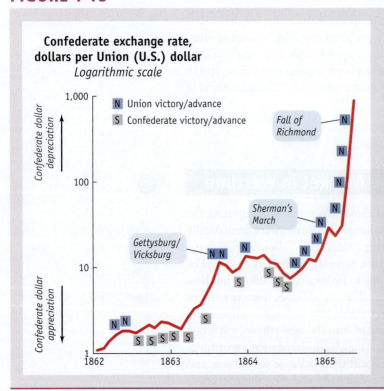

Exchange Rates and News in the U.S. Civil War The value of the Confederate dollar fluctuated against the U.S. dollar and is shown on a logarithmic scale. Against the backdrop of a steady trend, victories and advances by the North (N) were generally associated with faster depreciation of the Confederate currency, whereas major Southern successes (S) usually led to a stronger Confederate currency.

Data from: Wesley C. Mitchell, 1908, Gold, Prices, and Wages Under the Greenback Standard (Berkeley, Calif.: University of California Press), Table 2; George T. McCandless, Jr., 1996, "Money, Expectations, and the U.S. Civil War," American Economic Review, 86(3), 661–671.

---

[6] This correlation was noted by Wesley Mitchell in 1903 (*A History of the Greenbacks*; Chicago: University of Chicago Press). For recent econometric studies that examine this phenomenon, see George T. McCandless, Jr., 1996, "Money, Expectations, and U.S. Civil War," *American Economic Review*, 86(3), 661–671; and Kristen L. Willard, Timothy W. Guinnane, and Harvey S. Rosen, 1996, "Turning Points in the Civil War: Views from the Greenback Market," *American Economic Review*, 86(4), 1001–1018.

Currency traders in New York did good business either way. They were known to whistle "John Brown's Body" after a Union victory and "Dixie" after Confederate success, making profits as they traded dollars for gold and vice versa. Abraham Lincoln was not impressed, declaring, "What do you think of those fellows in Wall Street, who are gambling in gold at such a time as this? . . . For my part, I wish every one of them had his devilish head shot off."

The Iraq War, 2002–03 The Civil War is not the only example of such phenomena. In 2003, Iraq was invaded by a U.S.-led coalition of forces intent on overthrowing the regime of Saddam Hussein, and the effects of war on currencies were again visible.[7]

Our analysis of this case is made a little more complicated by the fact that at the time of the invasion there were *two* currencies in Iraq. Indeed, some might say there were two Iraqs. Following a 1991 war, Iraq had been divided: in the North, a de facto Kurdish government was protected by a no-fly zone enforced by the Royal Air Force and U.S. Air Force; in the South, Saddam's regime continued. The two regions developed into two distinct economies, and each had its own currency. In the North, Iraqi dinar notes called "Swiss" dinars circulated.[8] In the South, a new currency, the "Saddam" or "print" dinar, was introduced.[9]

Figure 4-19 shows the close correlation between wartime news and exchange rate movements for this modern episode. We can compare exchange rate movements with well-known events, but panel (a) allows another interesting comparison. In 2002, a company called TradeSports Exchange allowed bets on Saddam's destiny by setting up a market in contracts that paid $1 if he was deposed by a certain date, and the prices of these contracts are shown using the left scale. After he was deposed, contracts that paid out upon his capture were traded, and these are also shown. If such a contract had a price of, say, 80¢, then this implied that "the market" believed the probability of overthrow or apprehension was 80%.

In panel (b), we see the exchange rates of the Swiss dinar against the U.S. dollar and the Saddam dinar from 2002 to 2003. The Kurds' Swiss dinar–U.S. dollar rate had held at 18 per U.S. dollar for several years but steadily appreciated in 2002 and 2003 as the prospect of a war to depose Saddam became more likely. By May 2003, when the invasion phase of the war ended and Saddam had been deposed, it had appreciated as far as 6 to the dollar. The war clearly drove this trend: the more likely the removal of Saddam, the more durable would be Kurdish autonomy, and the more likely it was that a postwar currency would be created that respected the value of the Kurds' Swiss dinars. Notice how the rise in the value of the Swiss dinar tracked the odds of regime change until mid-2003.

After Baghdad fell, the coalition sought to capture Saddam, who had gone into hiding. As the hunt wore on, and a militant/terrorist insurgency began, fears mounted that he would never be found and his regime might survive underground and reappear. The odds on capture fell, and, moving in parallel, so did the value of the Swiss dinar. The Kurds now faced a rising probability that the whole affair would end badly for them and their currency. (However, when Saddam Hussein was captured on December 14, 2003, the Swiss dinar appreciated again.)

Currencies in wartime: A Confederate 2 dollar note of 1864 issued in Richmond; an Iraqi Swiss 25 dinar from the Kurdish region; a widely forged post-1991 Iraqi Saddam 25 dinar note; a post-2003 250 new Iraqi dinar note.

---

[7] This case study draws on Mervyn King, May 2004, "The Institutions of Monetary Policy," *American Economic Review*, 94(2), 1–13.

[8] The notes were printed in Britain using plates of Swiss manufacture. The Kurds issued no new notes of their own; indeed, they had no means to do so and simply used this legacy currency after 1991. No new Swiss dinars were issued after 1989 in the South, either.

[9] Once economic sanctions were imposed after the 1991 war, Baghdad had no access to the high-security technology and papers used to make modern banknotes. Instead, the Swiss dinar was retired, and the Saddam regime issued new legal tender notes in a form that it *could* print by using low-technology offset litho techniques that your local printer might use. These were the so-called Saddam or print dinars. Circulation of these notes exploded: a large volume of notes were printed by the Iraqi Central Bank and counterfeits added to this number. For these reasons, the northern currency, the Swiss dinar, was much more stable in the 1990s than the Saddam dinar.

FIGURE 4-19

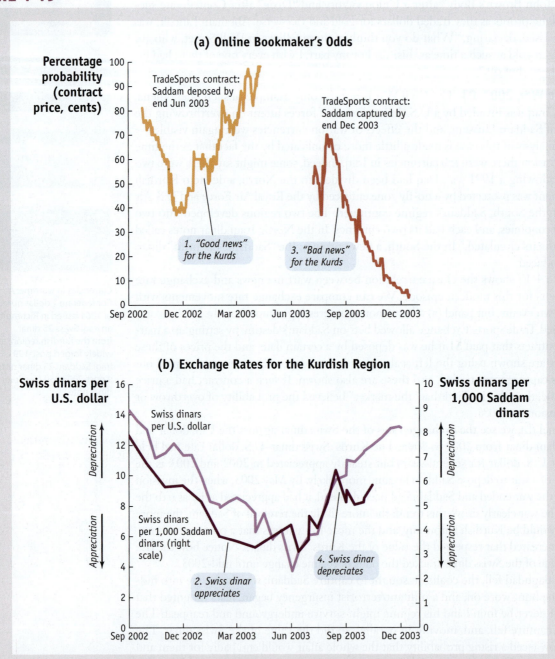

(a) Online Bookmaker's Odds

Percentage probability (contract price, cents)

TradeSports contract: Saddam deposed by end Jun 2003

TradeSports contract: Saddam captured by end Dec 2003

1. "Good news" for the Kurds

3. "Bad news" for the Kurds

Sep 2002   Dec 2002   Mar 2003   Jun 2003   Sep 2003   Dec 2003

(b) Exchange Rates for the Kurdish Region

Swiss dinars per U.S. dollar

Swiss dinars per 1,000 Saddam dinars

Depreciation

Appreciation

Swiss dinars per U.S. dollar

Swiss dinars per 1,000 Saddam dinars (right scale)

2. Swiss dinar appreciates

4. Swiss dinar depreciates

Sep 2002   Dec 2002   Mar 2003   Jun 2003   Sep 2003   Dec 2003

Exchange Rates and News in the Iraq War As regime change looked more likely from 2002 to 2003, as reflected in panel (a), the Swiss dinar, the currency used by the Kurds, appreciated against the U.S. dollar and the Saddam dinar, the currency used in the south, as shown in panel (b). When the U.S. invasion ended, the difficult postwar transition began. Insurgencies and the failure to find Saddam Hussein became a cause for concern, as reflected in panel (a). The Swiss dinar

depreciated against the dollar until December 2003, as shown in panel (b).

Notes: Panel (a) shows two contract prices: the value in cents of a TradeSports contract that paid 100¢ if Saddam were deposed by the end of June 2003 and 0 otherwise, and the value in cents of a contract that paid 100¢ if Saddam were captured by the end of December 2003 and 0 otherwise.

Data from: Mervyn King, 2004, "The Institutions of Monetary Policy," American Economic Review, 94(2), 1–13.

We can also track related movements in the Swiss dinar against the Saddam or print dinar. Before and during the war, while the Swiss dinar was appreciating against the U.S. dollar, it was also appreciating against the Saddam dinar. It strengthened from around 10 Swiss dinars per 1,000 Saddam dinars in early 2002 to about 3 Swiss per 1,000 Saddam in mid-2003. Then, as the postwar operations dragged on, this trend was reversed. By late 2003, the market rate was about 6 Swiss per 1,000 Saddam. Again, we can see how the Kurds' fortunes appeared to the market to rise and fall.

What became of all these dinars? Iraqis fared better than the holders of Confederate dollars. A new dinar was created under a currency reform announced in July 2003 and implemented from October 15, 2003, to January 15, 2004.[10] Exchange rate expectations soon moved into line with the increasingly credible official conversion rates and U.S. dollar exchange rates for the new dinar.

KEY POINTS

1. Our theory of exchange rates builds on two ideas: arbitrage and expectations. First, we developed the theory for the case of floating exchange rates.

2. In the short run, we assume prices are sticky and the asset approach to exchange rates is valid. Interest-bearing accounts in different currencies may offer different rates of nominal interest. Currencies may be expected to depreciate or appreciate against one another. There is an incentive for arbitrage: investors will shift funds from one country to another until the expected rate of return (measured in a common currency) is equalized. Arbitrage in the foreign exchange (forex or FX) market determines today's spot exchange rate, and the forex market is in equilibrium when the uncovered interest parity condition holds. To apply the uncovered interest parity (UIP) condition, however, we need a forecast of the expected exchange rate in the long run.

3. In the long run, we assume prices are flexible and the monetary approach to exchange rates is valid. This approach states that in the long run, purchasing power parity (PPP) holds so that the exchange rate must equal the ratio of the price levels in the two countries. Each price level, in turn, depends on the ratio of money supply to money demand in each country. The monetary approach can be used to forecast the long-run future expected exchange rate, which, in turn, feeds back into short-run exchange rate determination via the UIP equation.

4. Putting together all of these ingredients yields a complete theory of how exchange rates are determined in the short run and the long run.

5. This model can be used to analyze the impact of changes to monetary policy, as well as other shocks to the economy.

6. A temporary home monetary expansion causes home interest rates to fall and the home exchange rate to depreciate. This temporary policy can be consistent with a nominal anchor in the long run.

7. A permanent home monetary expansion causes home interest rates to fall and the home exchange rate to depreciate and, in the short run, overshoot what will eventually be its long-run level. This permanent policy is inconsistent with a nominal anchor in the long run.

8. The case of fixed exchange rates can also be studied using this theory. Under capital mobility, interest parity becomes very simple. In this case, the home interest rate equals the foreign interest rate. Home monetary policy loses all autonomy compared with the floating case. The only way to recover it is to impose capital controls. This is the essence of the trilemma.

---

[10] Under this reform, all the Swiss and Saddam notes were retired and a newly designed, secure currency for Iraq was brought into circulation nationally. As long as this currency reform was seen as credible, and the market believed it would successfully take place, the market rate would have to converge to the fixed rate set in advance by the authorities for note replacement. As the reform date approached, this convergence occurred, except for what appears to be a small "forgery risk premium" on the Saddam notes—detecting a fake among these notes was by no means simple.

KEY TERMS

asset approach to exchange rates,
  p. 99
fundamental equation of the asset
  approach to exchange rates, p. 101

FX market diagram, p. 102
nominal rigidity, p. 107

overshooting, p. 124
trilemma, p. 130

PROBLEMS

1. **Discovering Data** In this question we will be
testing an assumption of our model of exchange
rate determination. In particular, you will be
showing that the PPP assumption often fails in
the short run, emphasizing the importance of the
unifying approach discussed in this chapter. Go
to the website of Federal Reserve Economic Data
(FRED) at https://research.stlouisfed.org/fred2/
and download annual data for Consumer Price
Indices for the United States, Japan, and Canada.
In addition, download annual data for the U.S.
dollar exchange rate with the Canadian dollar and
Japanese yen going back to 1971. Put each data
series into a separate column in a new spreadsheet.

   a. We will want to check our assumption for *relative*
   PPP (that the difference in inflation between
   each of these countries and the United States
   should equal the change in the exchange rate).
   To do this you must first calculate the percent
   change in the spot exchange rate for each year.
   Do this for Japan and Canada with respect to the
   United States. In both cases, when did the largest
   appreciation occur? The largest depreciation?

   b. Now check relative PPP as stated in
   Equation (3-2). Compute the difference in annual
   rate of inflation in these two pairs of countries
   (Canada and the United States, and Japan and the
   United States) and see if it is equal to the annual
   change in the exchange rate for the pair. Create
   a new column showing the magnitude of the
   deviation from relative PPP. Next, compute the
   mean and standard deviation (of this deviation)
   for each country pair over the sample period. Are
   the means what you would expect them to be if
   PPP holds in the long run? What is the largest
   deviation from our PPP assumption?

   c. Create a line graph showing the deviations from
   relative PPP plotted against time in each case.
   Does it appear that these deviations are trend-
   ing toward zero over time? What appears to be
   the longest time before a deviation from PPP
   returns to zero?

WORK IT OUT   Achieve | interactive activity

2. Use the money market and FX diagrams to answer the following questions about the relationship between the British pound
(£) and the U.S. dollar ($). The exchange rate is in U.S. dollars per
British pound $E_{\$/£}$. We want to consider how a change in the U.S.
money supply affects interest rates and exchange rates. On all
graphs, label the initial equilibrium point A.

   a. Illustrate how a *temporary* increase in the U.S. money supply affects the money and FX markets. Label your short-run
   equilibrium point B and your long-run equilibrium point C.

   b. Using your diagram from (a), state how each of the following
   variables changes in the *short run* (increase/decrease/no change):
   U.S. interest rate, British interest rate, the exchange rate $E_{\$/£}$, the
   expected exchange rate $E^e_{\$/£}$, and the U.S. price level P_{US}.

   c. Using your diagram from (a), state how each of the following
   variables changes in the *long run* (increase/decrease/no change
   relative to their initial values at point A): U.S. interest rate, British
   interest rate, the exchange rate $E_{\$/£}$, the expected exchange rate
   $E^e_{\$/£}$, and U.S. price level P_{US}.

3. Use the money market and FX diagrams to answer
the following questions. This question considers
the relationship between the Indian rupee (Rs) and
the U.S. dollar ($). The exchange rate is in rupees
per dollar, $E_{Rs/\$}$. On all graphs, label the initial
equilibrium point A.

   a. Illustrate how a *permanent* decrease in India's
   money supply affects the money and FX markets. Label your short-run equilibrium point B
   and your long-run equilibrium point C.

   b. By plotting them on a chart with time on the
   horizontal axis, illustrate how each of the following variables changes over time (for India):
   nominal money supply M_{IN}, price level P_{IN}, real
   money supply M_{IN}/P_{IN}, interest rate i_{Rs}, and the
   exchange rate $E_{Rs/\$}$.

   c. Using your previous analysis, state how each
   of the following variables changes in the *short
   run* (increase/decrease/no change): India's
   interest rate i_{Rs}, the exchange rate $E_{Rs/\$}$,
   expected exchange rate $E^e_{Rs/\$}$, and price
   level P_{IN}.

d. Using your previous analysis, state how each of the following variables changes in the *long run* (increase/decrease/no change relative to their initial values at point A): India's interest rate i_{Rs}, the exchange rate $E_{Rs/\$}$, the expected exchange rate $E^e_{Rs/\$}$, and India's price level P_{IN}.

e. Explain how overshooting applies to this situation.

4. Is overshooting (in theory and in practice) consistent with purchasing power parity? Consider the reasons for the usefulness of PPP in the short run versus the long run and the assumption we've used in the asset approach (in the short run versus the long run). How does overshooting help to resolve the empirical behavior of exchange rates in the short run versus the long run?

5. Use the money market and FX diagrams to answer the following questions. This question considers the relationship between the euro (€) and the U.S. dollar ($). The exchange rate is in U.S. dollars per euro, $E_{\$/€}$. Suppose that with financial innovation in the United States, real money demand in the United States decreases. On all graphs, label the initial equilibrium point A.

a. Assume this change in U.S. real money demand is temporary. Using the FX/money market diagrams, illustrate how this change affects the money and FX markets. Label your short-run equilibrium point B and your long-run equilibrium point C.

b. Assume this change in U.S. real money demand is permanent. Using a new diagram, illustrate how this change affects the money and FX markets. Label your short-run equilibrium point B and your long-run equilibrium point C.

c. Illustrate how each of the following variables changes over time in response to a permanent reduction in real money demand: nominal money supply M_{US}, price level P_{US}, real money supply M_{US}/P_{US}, U.S. interest rate $i_\$$, and the exchange rate $E_{\$/€}$.

6. This question considers how the FX market will respond to changes in monetary policy in South Korea. For these questions, define the exchange rate as South Korean won per Japanese yen, $E_{won/¥}$. Use the FX and money market diagrams to answer the following questions. On all graphs, label the initial equilibrium point A.

a. Suppose the Bank of Korea permanently increases its money supply. Illustrate the short-run (label equilibrium point B) and long-run effects (label equilibrium point C) of this policy.

b. Now, suppose the Bank of Korea announces it plans to permanently increase its money supply but doesn't actually implement this policy. How will this affect the FX market in the short run if investors believe the Bank of Korea's announcement?

c. Finally, suppose the Bank of Korea permanently increases its money supply, but this change is not anticipated. When the Bank of Korea implements this policy, how will this affect the FX market in the short run?

d. Using your previous answers, evaluate the following statements:

■ If a country wants to decrease the value of its currency, it can do so (temporarily) without lowering domestic interest rates.

■ The central bank can increase both the domestic price level and value of its currency in the long run.

■ The most effective way to decrease the value of a currency is through surprising investors.

7. In the late 1990s, several East Asian countries used limited flexibility or currency pegs in managing their exchange rates relative to the U.S. dollar. This question considers how different countries responded to the East Asian currency crisis (1997–1998). For the following questions, treat the East Asian country as the home country and the United States as the foreign country. Also, for the diagrams, you may assume these countries maintained a currency peg (fixed rate) relative to the U.S. dollar. Also, for the following questions, you need consider only the short-run effects.

a. In July 1997, investors expected that the Thai baht would depreciate. That is, they expected that Thailand's central bank would be unable to maintain the currency peg with the U.S. dollar. Illustrate how this change in investors' expectations affects the Thai money market and FX market, with the exchange rate defined as baht (B) per U.S. dollar, denoted $E_{B/\$}$. Assume the Thai central bank wants to maintain capital mobility and preserve the level of its interest rate, and abandons the currency peg in favor of a floating exchange rate regime.

b. Indonesia faced the same constraints as Thailand—investors feared Indonesia would be forced to abandon its currency peg. Illustrate how this change in investors' expectations affects the Indonesian money market and FX market, with the exchange rate defined as rupiahs (Rp) per U.S. dollar, denoted $E_{Rp/\$}$. Assume that the Indonesian central bank wants to maintain capital mobility and the currency peg.

c. Malaysia had a similar experience, except that it used capital controls to maintain its currency peg and preserve the level of its interest rate. Illustrate how this change in investors' expectations affects the Malaysian money market and FX market, with the exchange rate defined as ringgit (RM) per U.S. dollar, denoted $E_{RM/\$}$. You need show only the short-run effects of this change in investors' expectations.

d. Compare and contrast the three approaches just outlined. As a policymaker, which would you favor? Explain.

8. Several countries have opted to join currency unions. Examples include those in the euro area, the CFA franc union in West Africa, and the Caribbean currency union. This involves sacrificing the domestic currency in favor of using a single currency unit in multiple countries. Assuming that once a country joins a currency union, it will not leave, do these countries face the policy trilemma discussed in the text? Explain.

9. During the Great Depression, the United States remained on the international gold standard longer than other countries. This effectively meant that the United States was committed to maintaining a fixed exchange rate at the onset of the Great Depression. The U.S. dollar was pegged to the value of gold, along with other major currencies, including the British pound, French franc, and so on. Many researchers have blamed the severity of the Great Depression on the Federal Reserve and its failure to react to economic conditions in 1929 and 1930. Discuss how the policy trilemma applies to this situation.

10. On June 20, 2007, John Authers, investment editor of the *Financial Times*, wrote the following in his column "The Short View":

> The Bank of England published minutes showing that only the narrowest possible margin, 5–4, voted down [an interest] rate hike last month. Nobody foresaw this. . . . The news took sterling back above $1.99, and to a 15-year high against the yen.

Can you explain the logic of this statement? Interest rates in the United Kingdom had remained unchanged in the weeks since the vote and were still unchanged after the minutes were released. What news was contained in the minutes that caused traders to react? Explain using the asset approach.

11. We can use the asset approach to both make predictions about how the market will react to current events and understand how important these events are to investors. Consider the behavior of the Union/Confederate exchange rate during the Civil War. How would each of the following events affect the exchange rate, defined as Confederate dollars per Union dollar, $E_{C\$/\$}$?

a. The Confederacy increases the money supply by 2,900% between July and December 1861.

b. The Union Army suffers a defeat in Battle of Chickamauga in September 1863.

c. The Confederate Army suffers a major defeat with Sherman's March in the autumn of 1864.

5

National and International Accounts: Income, Wealth, and the Balance of Payments

Money is sent from one country to another for various purposes: such as the payment of tributes or subsidies; remittances of revenue to or from dependencies, or of rents or other incomes to their absent owners; emigration of capital, or transmission of it for foreign investment. The most usual purpose, however, is that of payment for goods. To show in what circumstances money actually passes from country to country for this or any of the other purposes mentioned, it is necessary briefly to state the nature of the mechanism by which international trade is carried on, when it takes place not by barter but through the medium of money.

John Stuart Mill, 1848

Questions to Consider

1   How do economists measure a nation's expenditure, income, and product?

2   How do we measure international transactions involving goods, services, income, and assets, as well as transfers between countries?

3   How do all these relate to a nation's wealth and how it changes over time?

In Chapter 2, we encountered George, the hypothetical American tourist in Paris. We learned about how he traded some of his assets (such as dollars converted into euros, or charges on his debit card against his bank account) for goods and services (hotel, food, wine, etc.). Every day households and firms routinely trade goods, services, and assets, but when such transactions occur between countries they link the home economy with the rest of the world. In the upcoming chapters, we study economic transactions between countries, how they are undertaken, and the impact they have on the macroeconomy.

The first task of any macroeconomist is to measure economic transactions. The collection and analysis of such data can help improve research and policy-making. In a closed economy, interest often centers on important aggregate flows such as national output, consumption, investment, and so on. When an economy is open to transactions with the rest of the world, there are many other additional economic transactions that take place across borders. In today's world economy

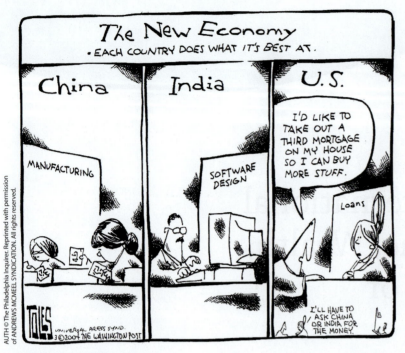

International transactions involve goods, services, and financial assets.

these international flows of trade and finance have reached unprecedented levels. Cross-border flows of goods, services, and capital are measured in various ways and are increasingly important subjects of discussion for economists, policymakers, businesses, and well-informed citizens. What do all these measures mean, and how are they related? How does the global economy actually function?

The goals of this chapter are to explain the international system of trade and payments, to discover how international trade in *goods and services* is complemented and balanced by a parallel trade in *assets*, and to see how these transactions relate to national income and wealth. In the remainder of the book, we use these essential tools to understand the macroeconomic links between nations.

1 Measuring Macroeconomic Activity: An Overview

To understand macroeconomic accounting in an open economy, we build on the principles used to track payments in a closed economy. As you may recall from previous courses in economics, a closed economy is characterized by a *circular flow of payments*, in which economic resources are exchanged for payments as they move through the economy. At various points in this flow, economic activity is measured and recorded in the **national income and product accounts**. In an open economy, however, such measurements are more complicated because we have to account for resource and payment flows between nations. These cross-border flows are recorded in a nation's **balance of payments accounts**. In the following section, we survey the principles behind these two sets of measurements. In later sections, we define the measurements more precisely and explore how they work in practice.

The Flow of Payments in a Closed Economy: Introducing the National Income and Product Accounts

Figure 5-1 shows how payments flow in a closed economy. We can start to follow the flow at the top with **gross national expenditure (GNE)**, the total expenditure on final goods and services by home consumers, businesses, and government in any given period (usually a calendar year, unless otherwise noted). GNE is the sum of three variables: personal consumption C, investment I, and government spending G.

When GNE is spent, where do the payments flow next? The spending counted in GNE constitutes all payments for final goods and services within the nation's borders. Because the economy is closed, the nation's expenditure must be spent on the final goods and services produced within the same nation. More specifically, a country's **gross domestic product (GDP)** is the value of all *intermediate* and *final* goods and services produced as output by home firms, minus the value of all intermediate goods and services purchased as inputs by home firms. (GDP is also known as *value added*.) GDP is a product measure, in contrast to GNE, which is an expenditure measure. In a closed economy, intermediate sales must equal intermediate purchases, so in

FIGURE 5-1

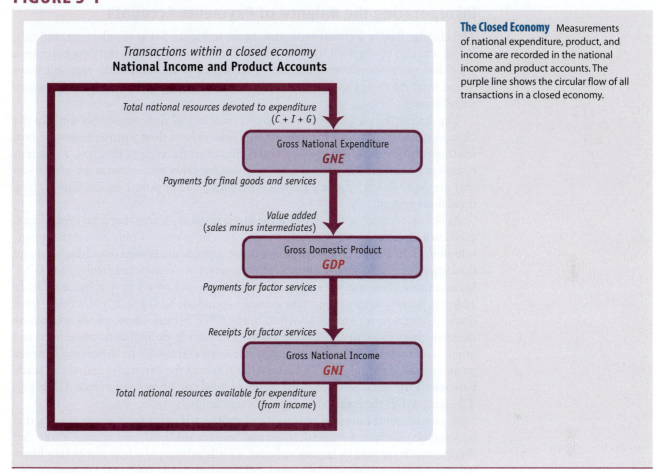

Transactions within a closed economy
National Income and Product Accounts

Total national resources devoted to expenditure
$(C + I + G)$

Gross National Expenditure
GNE

Payments for final goods and services

Value added
(sales minus intermediates)

Gross Domestic Product
GDP

Payments for factor services

Receipts for factor services

Gross National Income
GNI

Total national resources available for expenditure
(from income)

The Closed Economy Measurements of national expenditure, product, and income are recorded in the national income and product accounts. The purple line shows the circular flow of all transactions in a closed economy.

GDP these two terms cancel out, leaving only the value of final goods and services produced, which equals the expenditure on final goods and services, or GNE. Thus, GDP equals GNE.

When GDP is sold, where do the payments flow next? GDP measures the value of firm outputs sold minus the cost of firm inputs bought. This remaining flow, equal to sales minus costs, is left over to be paid by firms as income to the factors of production employed by the firms. The factor owners receiving this income are the owners of labor (who receive wages, salaries, etc.), the owners of capital (who receive profits, interest, etc.), and the owners of land (who receive rent, etc.). The factors may be owned by households, government, or firms, but exactly who owns the factors is not important. The key thing in a closed economy is that all such income is paid to domestic entities. The total income of an economy is **gross national income (GNI)**. At this point in our circular flow, we can see that in a closed economy the expenditure on total goods and services, GNE, equals GDP, which is then paid as income to the factors of production in the form of GNI.

Once GNI is received by factors, where do the payments flow next? Clearly, there is no way for a closed economy to finance expenditure except out of its own income, so total income is, in turn, spent and must be the same as total expenditure. This is shown by the loop that flows back to the top of Figure 5-1.

What we have seen in our tour around the circular flow is that *in a closed economy*, all the economic aggregate measures are equal: GNE equals GDP, which equals GNI, which equals GNE. *In a closed economy, expenditure is the same as product, which is the same as income.* Our understanding of the circular flow in a closed economy is complete.

The Flow of Payments in an Open Economy: Incorporating the Balance of Payments Accounts

The circular flow in a closed economy shown in Figure 5-1 is simple, neat, and tidy. When a nation opens itself to trade with other nations, however, the flow becomes a good deal more complicated. Figure 5-2 incorporates all of the extra payment flows to and from the rest of the world, which are recorded in a nation's *balance of payments (BOP) accounts*.

The circulating purple arrows on the left side of this figure resemble those in the closed-economy case seen in Figure 5-1. These arrows flow within the purple box, which represents the home country, and do not cross the edge of that box, which represents the international border. The cross-border flows that occur in an open economy are represented by green arrows. There are five key points on the figure where these flows appear.

As before, we start at the top with the home economy's gross national expenditure, GNE, which is the sum of consumption C plus investment I plus government consumption G. In an open economy, some home expenditure is used to purchase foreign final goods and services. At point 1, these *imports* are subtracted from home GNE because those goods are not sold by domestic firms and *are not* part of home GDP. In addition, some foreign expenditure is used to purchase final goods and services from home. These *exports* must be added to home GNE because those goods are sold by domestic firms and *are* part of home GDP. (The same logic applies to any exports and imports of intermediate goods, which is left as an exercise.) The difference between payments made for imports and payments received for exports is called the **trade balance (TB)**, and it equals net payments to domestic firms due to trade. GNE plus TB equals GDP, the total value of production in the home economy.

At point 2, some home GDP is paid to foreign entities for *factor service imports*, that is, domestic payments to capital, labor, and land owned by foreign entities. Note that this income *is not* paid to factors at home, so it is subtracted when computing home income, because it *is not* part of home GNI. Similarly, some foreign GDP may be paid to domestic entities as payment for *factor service exports*, that is, foreign payments to capital, labor, and land owned by domestic entities. Note that this income *is* paid to factors at home, so it is added when computing home income, because it *is* part of home GNI. The value of factor service exports minus factor service imports is known as **net factor income from abroad (NFIA)**. Thus GDP plus NFIA equals GNI, the total income earned by domestic entities from all sources, domestic and foreign.

At point 3, we see that the home country may not retain all of its earned income GNI. Why? Domestic entities might give some of it away—for example, as foreign aid or remittances by migrants to their families back home. Similarly, domestic entities might receive gifts from abroad. Such gifts may take the form of income transfers or may be "in kind" transfers of goods and services. They are considered nonmarket transactions, and are referred to as *unilateral transfers*. **Net unilateral transfers (NUT)** equals the value of unilateral transfers the country receives from the rest of the world minus those it gives to the rest of the world. These net transfers are added to GNI to calculate **gross national disposable income (GNDI)**. Thus GNI plus NUT equals GNDI, which represents the total income resources available to the home country.

The balance of payments accounts collect together the trade balance, net factor income from abroad, and net unilateral transfers and report their sum as the **current account (CA)**, an important tally of all international transactions in goods, services, and income that occur through market transactions or transfers. The current account is not, however, a complete picture of international transactions. Goods, services, and income are not the only items that flow between open economies. Financial assets such as stocks, bonds, or real estate are also traded across international borders.

FIGURE 5-2

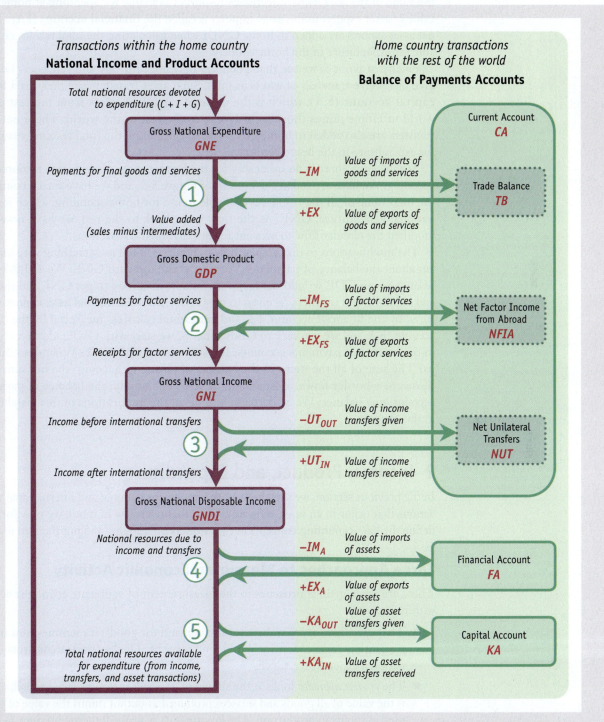

The Open Economy Measurements of national expenditure, product, and income are recorded in the national income and product accounts, with the major categories shown on the left. Measurements of international transactions are recorded in the balance of payments accounts, with the major categories shown on the right. The purple line shows the flow of transactions within the home economy; the green lines show all cross-border transactions.

At point 4, we see that a country's capacity to spend is not restricted to be equal to its GNDI, but instead can be increased or decreased by the export or import of assets to or from other countries. When foreign entities acquire assets from home entities, the value of these *asset exports* increases resources available for spending at home. Conversely, when domestic entities acquire assets from the rest of the world, the value of the *asset imports* decreases resources available for spending at home. The value of asset exports minus asset imports is called the **financial account (FA).** These net asset exports are added to home GNDI when calculating the total resources available for expenditure in the home country.

Finally, at point 5, we see that a country may not only buy and sell assets but also give or receive transfers of assets as gifts. Such asset transfers are measured by the **capital account (KA),** which is the value of capital transfers from the rest of the world to Home minus those from Home to the rest of the world. These net asset transfers are also added to home GNDI when calculating the total resources available for expenditure in the home country.

At this point, there is no other way for the home country to generate resources for spending. We have arrived at the bottom of Figure 5-2, and we have finally computed the total value of all the resources available to use for home spending, which is gross national expenditure, GNE. As the flow loops back to the top, we have now fully modified the circular flow to account for international transactions.[1]

The modifications to the circular flow in Figure 5-2 tell us something very important about the balance of payments. We start at the top with GNE. We add the trade balance to get GDP, we add net factor income from abroad to get GNI, and then we add net unilateral transfers received to get GNDI. We then add net asset exports measured by the financial account, FA, and net capital transfers measured by the capital account, KA, and we get back to GNE. That is, we start with GNE, add in *everything* in the balance of payments accounts, and still end up with GNE. What does this tell us? The sum of all the items in the balance of payments account, the net sum of all those cross-border flows, must add up to zero! Put simply: the balance of payments account *must* balance. We explore in more detail the implications of this insight later in this chapter.

2 Income, Product, and Expenditure

In the previous section, we sketched out the important national and international transactions that occur in an open economy. With that overview in mind, we now formally define the key accounting concepts in the two sets of accounts and put them to use.

Three Approaches to Measuring Economic Activity

There are three main approaches to the measurement of aggregate economic activity within a country:

- The *expenditure approach* looks at the demand for goods: it examines how much is spent on demand for final goods and services. The key measure is gross national expenditure, GNE.

- The *product approach* looks at the supply of goods: it measures value added, which is the value of all goods and services produced as output minus the value of goods used as inputs in production. The key measure is gross domestic product, GDP.

- The *income approach* focuses on payments to owners of factors and tracks the amount of income they receive. The key measures are gross national income, GNI, and gross national disposable income, GNDI (which includes net transfers).

---

[1] In the past, both the financial account, FA, and capital account, KA, were added up and jointly known as "the capital account." This change should be kept in mind not only when consulting older documents but also when listening to contemporary discussion because not everyone cares for the new (and somewhat confusing) paymenclature. Indeed, in some countries this older terminology is still in official use today.

It is crucial to note that in a closed economy the three approaches generate the same number. In a closed economy, $GNE = GDP = GNI = GNDI$. In an open economy, however, this is not true.

From GNE to GDP: Accounting for Trade in Goods and Services

We can start with gross national expenditure, or GNE, which is *by definition* the sum of consumption C, investment I, and government consumption G. Formally, these three elements are defined, respectively, as follows:

- *Personal consumption expenditure* (usually called "consumption") equals total spending by private households on final goods and services, including nondurable goods such as food, durable goods such as a television, and services such as window cleaning or gardening.

- *Gross private domestic investment* (usually called "investment") equals total spending by firms or households on final goods and services to make additions to the stock of capital. Investment includes construction of a new house or a new factory, the purchase of new equipment, and net increases in inventories of goods held by firms (i.e., unsold output).

- *Government consumption expenditure and gross investment* (often called "government consumption") equals spending by the public sector on final goods and services, including spending on public works, national defense, the police, and the civil service. It does *not* include any transfer payments or income redistributions, such as Social Security or unemployment insurance payments—these are *not* purchases of goods or services, just rearrangements of private spending power.

As for gross domestic product, or GDP, it is *by definition* the value of all goods and services produced as output by firms, minus the value of all intermediate goods and services purchased as inputs by firms. It is thus a product measure, in contrast to the expenditure measure GNE. Because of trade, not all of the GNE payments go to GDP, and not all of GDP payments arise from GNE.

To adjust GNE and find the contribution going into GDP, we *subtract* the value of final goods imported (home spending that goes to foreign firms) and *add* the value of final goods exported (foreign spending that goes to home firms). In addition, we can't forget about intermediate goods: we *subtract* the value of imported intermediates (in GDP they also count as Home's purchased inputs) and *add* the value of exported intermediates (in GDP they also count as Home's produced output).[2] So, adding it all up, to get from GNE to GDP, we add the value of *all* exports denoted *EX* and subtract the value of *all* imports *IM*. Thus,

$$\underbrace{GDP}_{\substack{\text{Gross} \\ \text{domestic} \\ \text{product}}} = \underbrace{C + I + G}_{\substack{\text{Gross} \\ \text{national} \\ \text{expenditure} \\ GNE}} + \underbrace{\left(\underbrace{EX}_{\substack{\text{All exports,} \\ \text{final \& intermediate}}} - \underbrace{IM}_{\substack{\text{All imports,} \\ \text{final \& intermediate}}} \right)}_{\substack{\text{Trade balance} \\ TB}} \qquad (5\text{-}1)$$

This formula for GDP says that *gross domestic product equals gross national expenditure (GNE) plus the trade balance (TB).*

---

[2] Note that intermediate inputs sold by home firms and purchased by other home firms cancel out in GDP, in both closed and open economies. For example, suppose there are two firms A and B, and Firm A makes a $200 table (a final good) and buys $100 in wood (an intermediate input) from Firm B, and there is no trade. Total sales are $300; but GDP or value added is total sales of $300 minus the $100 of inputs purchased; so GDP is equal to $200. Now suppose Firm B makes and exports $50 of extra wood. After this change, GDP is equal to $250. You can see here that GDP *is not equal to* the value of final goods produced in an economy (although it is quite often claimed, mistakenly, that this is a definition of GDP).

It is important to understand and account for intermediate goods transactions properly because trade in intermediate goods has surged in recent decades due to globalization and outsourcing. For example, according to the 2010 *Economic Report of the President*, one-third of the growth of world trade from 1970 to 1990 was driven by intermediate trade arising from the growth of "vertically specialized" production processes (outsourcing, offshoring, etc.). More strikingly, as of 2010—and probably for the first time in world history—a higher percentage of total world trade now consists of trade in intermediate goods (60%) than in final goods (40%).

The trade balance, TB, is also called *net exports*. Because it is the net value of exports minus imports, it may be positive or negative.

If *TB* > 0, exports are greater than imports and we say a country has a *trade surplus*.
If *TB* < 0, imports are greater than exports and we say a country has a *trade deficit*.

In 2019 the United States had a trade deficit because exports X were \$2,504 billion and imports M were \$3,136 billion. Thus, the U.S. trade balance or *TB* was –\$632 billion.

From GDP to GNI: Accounting for Trade in Factor Services

Trade in factor services occurs when, say, the home country is paid income by a foreign country as compensation for the use of labor, capital, and land owned by home entities but in service in the foreign country. We say the home country is exporting factor services to the foreign country and receiving factor income in return.

An example of a labor service export is a home country professional temporarily working overseas, say, a U.S. architect freelancing in London. The wages she earns in the United Kingdom are factor income for the United States. An example of trade in capital services is *foreign direct investment*. For example, U.S.-owned factories in Ireland generate income for their U.S. owners; Japanese-owned factories in the United States generate income for their Japanese owners. Other examples of payments for capital services include income from overseas *financial* assets such as foreign securities, real estate, or loans to governments, firms, and households.

These payments are accounted for as additions to and subtractions from home GDP. Some home GDP is paid out as *income payments* to foreign entities for factor services imported by the home country IM_{FS}. In addition, domestic entities receive some income payments from foreign entities as *income receipts* for factor services exported by the home country EX_{FS}.

After accounting for these income flows, we see that gross national income, GNI, the total income earned by domestic entities, is GDP plus the factor income arriving from overseas EX_{FS}, minus the factor income going out overseas IM_{FS}.[3] The last two terms, income receipts minus income payments, are the home country's *net factor income from abroad*, $NFIA = EX_{FS} - IM_{FS}$. This may be a positive or negative number, depending on whether income receipts are larger or smaller than income payments.

With the help of the GDP expression in Equation (5-1), we obtain the key formula for GNI that says the *gross national income equals gross domestic product (GDP) plus net factor income from abroad (NFIA)*.

$$GNI = \underbrace{\underbrace{C + I + G}_{\substack{\text{Gross national} \\ \text{expenditure} \\ GNE}} + \underbrace{(EX - IM)}_{\substack{\text{Trade balance} \\ TB}}}_{GDP} + \underbrace{(EX_{FS} - IM_{FS})}_{\substack{\text{Net factor income} \\ \text{from abroad} \\ NFIA}} \qquad (5\text{-}2)$$

---

[3] GNI is the accounting concept formerly known as GNP, or *gross national product*. The term GNP is still often used, but GNI is technically more accurate because the concept is a measurement of income rather than product. Note that taxes and subsidies on production and imports are counted in GNE (both) and GDP (production taxes only). This treatment ensures that the tax income paid to the home country is properly counted as a part of home income. We simplify the presentation in this textbook by assuming there are no taxes and subsidies.

In 2019 the United States received income payments from foreigners EX_{FS} of $1,158 billion and made income payments to foreigners IM_{FS} of $863 billion. Thus, the U.S. net factor income from abroad or *NFIA* was +$296 billion.

APPLICATION

Celtic Tiger or Tortoise?

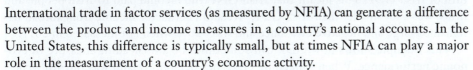

International trade in factor services (as measured by NFIA) can generate a difference between the product and income measures in a country's national accounts. In the United States, this difference is typically small, but at times NFIA can play a major role in the measurement of a country's economic activity.

In the 1970s, Ireland was one of the poorer countries in Europe, but over the next three decades it experienced speedy economic growth with an accompanying investment boom now known as the Irish Miracle. From 1980 to 2007, Irish real GDP per person grew at a phenomenal rate of 4.1% per year—not as rapid as in some developing countries but extremely rapid by the standards of the rich countries of the European Union (EU) or the Organization for Economic Cooperation and Development (OECD). Comparisons with fast-growing Asian economies—the "Asian Tigers"—soon had people speaking of the "Celtic Tiger" when referring to Ireland. Despite a large recession after the 2008 crisis, real GDP per person in Ireland is still almost three times its 1980 level.

But did Irish citizens enjoy all of these gains? No. Figure 5-3 shows that in 1980 Ireland's annual net factor income from abroad was virtually nil—about €120 per

FIGURE 5-3

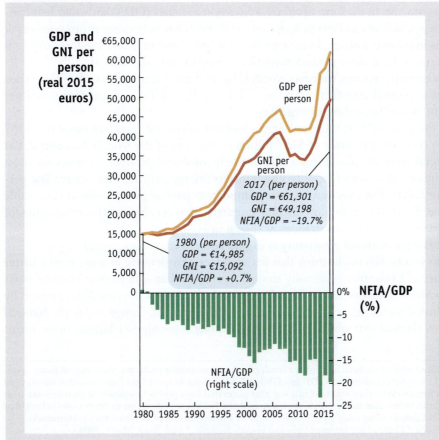

A Paper Tiger? The chart shows trends in GDP, GNI, and NFIA in Ireland from 1980 to 2011. Irish GNI per capita grew more slowly than GDP per capita during the boom years of the 1980s and 1990s because an ever-larger share of GDP was sent abroad as net factor income to foreign investors. Close to zero in 1980, this share had risen to around 15% of GDP by the year 2000 and has remained at approximately that level ever since.

Data from: World Bank, World Development Indicators.

person (in year 2000 real euros) or +0.9% of GDP. Yet by 2000, and in the years since, around 15% to 20% of Irish GDP was being used to make net factor income payments to foreigners who had invested heavily in the Irish economy by buying stocks and bonds and by purchasing land and building factories on it. (By some estimates, 75% of Ireland's industrial-sector GDP originated in foreign-owned plants in 2004.) These foreign investors expected their big Irish investments to generate income, and so they did, in the form of net factor payments abroad amounting to almost one-fifth of Irish GDP. This meant that Irish GNI (the income paid to Irish people and firms) was a lot smaller than Irish GDP.[4] Ireland's net factor income from abroad has remained large and negative ever since and was −20% when last measured in 2017.

This example shows how GDP can sometimes be a misleading measure of economic performance. When ranked by GDP per person, Ireland was the 4th richest OECD economy in 2004; but when ranked by GNI per person, it was only 17th richest.[5] The Irish outflow of net factor payments is certainly an extreme case, but it serves to underscore an important point about income measurement in open economies. Any country that relies heavily on foreign investment to generate economic growth is not getting a free lunch. Irish GNI per person grew at "only" 3.6% from 1980 to the peak in 2007, and this was 0.5% per year less than the growth rate of GDP per person over the same period. By any measure the Irish economy grew impressively, to be sure, but the more humble GNI figures may give a more accurate measure of what the Irish Miracle actually meant for the Irish.

From GNI to GNDI: Accounting for Transfers of Income

So far, we have fully described market transactions in goods, services, and income. However, many international transactions take place outside of markets. International nonmarket transfers of goods, services, and income include such things as foreign aid by governments in the form of *official development assistance* (ODA) and other help, private charitable gifts to foreign recipients, and income remittances sent to relatives or friends in other countries. These transfers are "gifts" and may take the form of goods and services (food aid, volunteer medical services) or income transfers.

If a country receives transfers worth UT_{IN} and gives transfers worth UT_{OUT}, then its net unilateral transfers, NUT, are $NUT = UT_{IN} - UT_{OUT}$. Because this is a net amount, it may be positive or negative.

In the year 2019, the United States had net unilateral transfers equal to −$167 billion (i.e., a net transfer of $167 billion to the rest of the world). In general, net unilateral transfers play a small role in the income and product accounts for most high-income countries (net outgoing transfers are typically no more than a few percent of GNI). But they can be a very important part of gross national disposable income (GNDI) in many low-income countries that receive significant amounts of foreign aid or migrant remittances, as shown in Figure 5-4.

Measuring national generosity is highly controversial and a recurring theme of current affairs. You might think that net unilateral transfers are in some ways a better measure of a country's generosity toward foreigners than official development assistance, which is but one component. For example, looking at the year 2010, a report by the United States Agency for International Development, *Foreign Aid in the National Interest*, claimed that while the U.S. ODA budget was only $11 billion, other forms

---

[4] Irish GDP might have been inflated as a result of various accounting problems. Some special factors exacerbated the difference between GDP and GNI in Ireland, such as special tax incentives that encouraged foreign firms to keep their accounts in a way that generated high profits "on paper" at their low-tax Irish subsidiaries rather than in their high-tax home country. For these reasons, many economists believe that Irish GNI, despite being more conservative, might be a truer measure of the economy's performance.

[5] Joe Cullen, "There's Lies, Damned Lies, and Wealth Statistics," *Irish Times*, May 1, 2004.

FIGURE 5-4

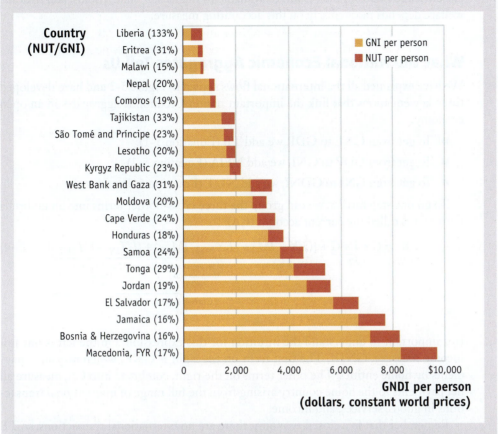

Major Transfer Recipients The chart shows average figures for the decade 2001 to 2010 for all countries in which average net unilateral transfers exceeded 15% of GNI. Many of the countries shown were heavily reliant on foreign aid, including some of the poorest countries in the world, such as Liberia, Eritrea, Malawi, and Nepal. Some countries with higher incomes also have large transfers because of substantial migrant remittances from a large number of emigrant workers overseas, for example, Tonga, El Salvador, Honduras, and Cape Verde.

Data from: World Bank, World Development Indicators.

of U.S. government assistance (such as contributions to global security and humanitarian assistance) amounted to $19 billion, and assistance from private U.S. citizens totaled somewhere between $55 and $70 billion—for total foreign assistance equal to $85 to $100 billion, about 8 to 10 times the level of ODA (and most of it not even counted in *NUT*).

To include the impact of aid and all other transfers in the overall calculation of a country's income resources, we add net unilateral transfers to gross national income. Using the definition of GNI in Equation (5-2), we obtain a full measure of national income in an open economy, known as gross national disposable income (GNDI), henceforth denoted *Y*:

$$\underbrace{Y}_{GNDI} = \underbrace{\underbrace{(C + I + G)}_{GNE} + \underbrace{(EX - IM)}_{\substack{\text{Trade balance} \\ TB}} + \underbrace{(EX_{FS} - IM_{FS})}_{\substack{\text{Net factor income} \\ \text{from abroad} \\ NFIA}}}_{GNI} + \underbrace{(UT_{IN} - UT_{OUT})}_{\substack{\text{Net unilateral} \\ \text{transfers} \\ NUT}} \quad (5\text{-}3)$$

In general, economists and policymakers prefer to use GNDI to measure national income. Why? GDP is not a true measure of income because, unlike GNI, it does not include net factor income from abroad. GNI is not a perfect measure either because it leaves out international transfers. GNDI is a preferred measure because it most closely corresponds to the resources available to the nation's households, and national welfare depends most closely on this accounting measure.

What the National Economic Aggregates Tell Us

We have explained all the international flows shown in Figure 5-2 and have developed three key equations that link the important national economic aggregates in an open economy:

- To get from GNE to GDP, we add TB (Equation 5-1).
- To get from GDP to GNI, we add NFIA (Equation 5-2).
- To get from GNI to GDNI, we add NUT (Equation 5-3).

To go one step further, we can group the three cross-border terms into an umbrella term that is called the current account (CA):

$$\underbrace{Y}_{GNDI} = \underbrace{C + I + G}_{GNE} + \{\underbrace{(EX - IM)}_{\substack{\text{Trade balance} \\ TB}} + \underbrace{(EX_{FS} - IM_{FS})}_{\substack{\text{Net factor income} \\ \text{from abroad} \\ NFIA}} + \underbrace{(UT_{IN} - UT_{OUT})}_{\substack{\text{Net unilateral} \\ \text{transfers} \\ NUT}}\} \qquad (5\text{-}4)$$

$$\underbrace{\phantom{(EX - IM) + (EX_{FS} - IM_{FS}) + (UT_{IN} - UT_{OUT})}}_{\substack{\text{Current account} \\ CA}}$$

It is important to understand the intuition for this expression. On the left is our full income measure, GNDI. The first term on the right is GNE, which measures payments by home entities. The other terms on the right, combined into CA, measure all net payments to the home country arising from the full range of international transactions in goods, services, and income.

Remember that in a closed economy, there are no international transactions, so TB and NFIA and NUT (and hence CA) are all zero. Therefore, in a closed economy, the four main aggregates GNDI, GNI, GDP, and GNE are exactly equal. In an open economy, however, each of these four aggregates can differ from the others.

Understanding the Data for the National Economic Aggregates

Now that we've learned how a nation's principal economic aggregates are affected by international transactions in theory, let's see how this works in practice. In this section, we take a look at some data from the real world to see how they are recorded and presented in official statistics.

Table 5-1 shows data for the United States in 2019 reported by the Bureau of Economic Analysis in the official national income and product accounts.

Lines 1 to 3 of the table show the components of gross national expenditure GNE. Personal consumption expenditures C were $14,563 billion, gross private domestic investment I was $3,744 billion, and government consumption G was $3,753 billion. Summing up, GNE was $22,060 billion, shown on line 4.

Line 5 shows the trade balance, TB, the net export of goods and services, which was −$632 billion. (Net exports are negative because the United States imported more goods and services than it exported.) Adding this to GNE gives gross domestic product GDP of $21,428 billion on line 6. Next we account for net factor income from abroad NFIA, +$296 billion on line 7. Adding this to GDP gives gross national income GNI of $21,723 billion on line 8.

Finally, to get to the bottom line, we account for the fact that the United States received net unilateral transfers from the rest of the world of −$167 billion (i.e., made

TABLE 5-1

U.S. Economic Aggregates in 2019 The table shows the computation of GDP, GNI, and GNDI in 2019 in billions of dollars using the components of gross national expenditure, the trade balance, international income payments, and unilateral transfers.

Line	Category	Symbol	$ billions
1	Consumption (personal consumption expenditures)	C	14,563
2	+ Investment (gross private domestic investment)	I	13,744
3	+ Government consumption (government expenditures)	G	3,753
4	= Gross national expenditure	GNE	22,060
5	+ Trade balance	TB	−632
6	= Gross domestic product	GDP	21,428
7	+ Net factor income from abroad	NFIA	296
8	= Gross national income	GNI	21,723
9	+ Net unilateral transfers	NUT	−167
10	= Gross national disposable income	GNDI	21,577

Note: Details may not add to totals because of rounding.

Data from: U.S. Bureau of Economic Analysis, NIPA Tables 1.1.5 and 4.1, using the NIPA definition of the United States. Data revised as of March 26, 2020.

net transfers to the rest of the world of $167 billion) on line 9. Adding these negative transfers to GNI results in a GNDI of $21,557 billion on line 10.

Some Recent Trends Figures 5-5 and 5-6 show recent trends in various components of U.S. national income. Examining these breakdowns gives us a sense of the relative economic significance of each component.

In Figure 5-5, GNE is shown as the sum of consumption (C), investment (I), and government consumption (G). C accounts for about 70% of GNE, while G accounts for about 15%. Both of these components are relatively stable. Investment accounts

FIGURE 5-5

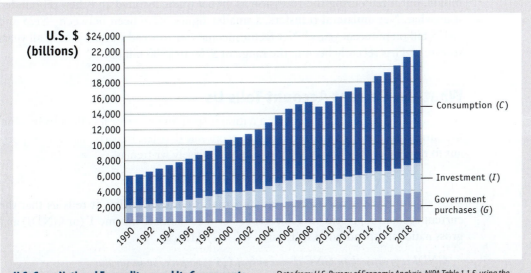

U.S. Gross National Expenditure and Its Components, 1990–2019 The figure shows U.S. consumption (C), investment (I), and government purchases (G), in billions of dollars.

Data from: U.S. Bureau of Economic Analysis, NIPA Table 1.1.5, using the NIPA definition of the United States, which excludes U.S. territories. Data revisions as of March 26, 2020.

FIGURE 5-6

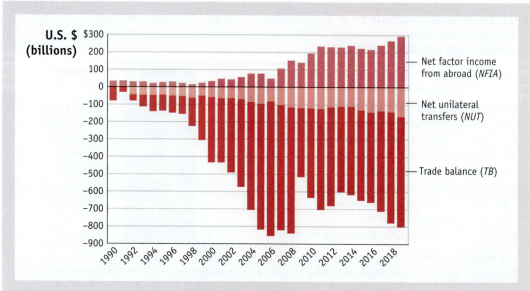

U.S. Current Account and Its Components, 1990–2019
The figure shows the U.S. trade balance (TB), net factor income from abroad (NFIA), and net unilateral transfers (NUT), in billions of dollars.

Data from: U.S. Bureau of Economic Analysis, NIPA Table 4.1, using the NIPA definition of the United States, which excludes U.S. territories. Data revisions as of March 26, 2020.

for the rest (about 15% of GNE), but *I* tends to fluctuate more than *C* and *G* (e.g., it fell steeply after the Great Recession in 2008–10). Over the period shown, GNE grew from around $6,000 billion to around $22,000 billion in current dollars.

Figure 5-6 shows the trade balance (TB), net factor income from abroad (NFIA), and net unilateral transfers (NUT), which constitute the current account (CA). In the United States, the trade balance is the dominant component in the current account. For the entire period shown, the trade balance has been in deficit and has grown larger over time. From 2005 to 2008, the trade balance was between –$700 and –$800 billion, but it fell during the recession as global trade declined and then rebounded somewhat. Net unilateral transfers, a smaller figure, have been between –$125 and –$175 billion in recent years.[6] Net factor income from abroad was positive in all years shown, and has recently been in the range of $200 to $300 billion.

What the Current Account Tells Us

Because it tells us, in effect, whether a nation is spending more or less than its income, the current account plays a central role in economic debates. In particular, it is important to remember that Equation (5-4) can be concisely written as

$$Y = C + I + G + CA \tag{5-5}$$

This equation is the open-economy **national income identity**. It tells us that the current account represents the difference between national income *Y* (or GNDI) and gross national expenditure GNE (or *C* + *I* + *G*). Hence,

GNDI is greater than GNE if and only if CA is positive, or in surplus.
GNDI is less than GNE if and only if CA is negative, or in deficit.

---

[6] In 1991 the United States was in the unusual position of being a net recipient of unilateral transfers: this was a result of transfer payments from other rich countries willing to help defray U.S. military expenses in the Gulf War.

Subtracting $C + G$ from both sides of the last identity, we can see that the current account is also the difference between **national saving** ($S = Y - C - G$) and investment:

$$\underbrace{S}_{Y - C - G} = I + CA \qquad (5\text{-}6)$$

where national saving is defined as income minus consumption minus government consumption. This equation is called the **current account identity** even though it is just a rearrangement of the national income identity. Thus,

S is greater than I if and only if CA is positive, or in surplus.
S is less than I if and only if CA is negative, or in deficit.

These last two equations give us two ways of interpreting the current account, and tell us something important about a nation's economic condition. A current account deficit measures how much a country spends in excess of its income or—equivalently—how it saves too little relative to its investment needs. (Surpluses mean the opposite.) We can now understand the widespread use of the current account deficit in the media as a measure of how a country is "spending more than it earns" or "saving too little" or "living beyond its means."

APPLICATION

Global Imbalances

We can apply what we have learned to study some remarkable features of financial globalization in recent years, including the explosion in *global imbalances:* the widely discussed current account surpluses and deficits that have been of great concern to policymakers.

Figure 5-7 shows trends from the 1970s to the early 2010s in saving, investment, and the current account for four groups of industrial countries. All flows are expressed as ratios relative to each region's GDP. Some trends stand out. First, in all four cases, saving and investment have been on a marked downward trend for almost 50 years. From its peak, the ratio of saving to GDP fell by about 8 percentage points in the United States, about 15 percentage points in Japan, and about 6 percentage points in the Eurozone and other countries. Investment ratios typically followed a downward path in all regions, too. In Japan, this decline was steeper than the decline in savings, but in the United States, there was hardly any decline in investment.

These trends reflect the recent history of the industrialized countries. The U.S. economy grew rapidly after 1990 and the Japanese economy grew very slowly, with other countries in between. The fast-growing U.S. economy generated high investment demand, while in slumping Japan investment collapsed; other regions maintained middling levels of growth and investment. Decreased saving in all the countries reflects the demographic shift toward aging populations. That is, higher and higher percentages of these nations' populations are retired, are no longer earning income, and are living on funds they saved in the past.

The current account identity tells us that CA equals S minus I. Thus, investment and saving trends have a predictable impact on the current accounts of industrial countries. Because saving fell more than investment in the United States, the current account moved sharply into deficit, a trend that was only briefly slowed in the early 1990s. By 2003–05 the U.S. current account was at a record deficit level, close to −6% of U.S. GDP, only to fall later in the Great Recession. In Japan, saving fell less than investment, so the opposite happened: a very big current account surplus opened

FIGURE 5-7

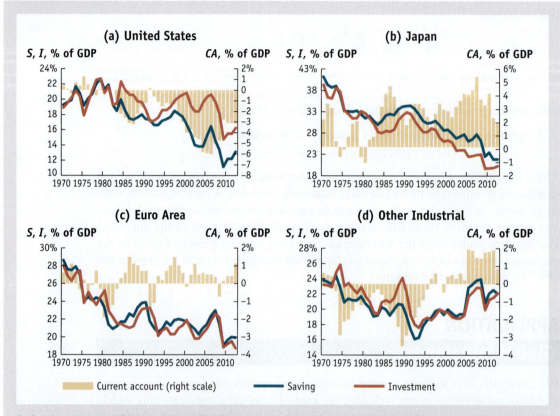

(a) United States

(b) Japan

(c) Euro Area

(d) Other Industrial

Current account (right scale)   Saving   Investment

Saving, Investment, and Current Account Trends: Industrial Countries The charts show saving, investment, and the current account as a percent of each subregion's GDP for four groups of advanced countries. The United States has seen both saving and investment fall since 1980, but saving has fallen further than investment, opening up a large current account deficit approaching 6% of GDP in recent years. Japan's experience is the opposite: investment has fallen further than saving, opening up a large current account surplus of about 3% to 5% of GDP, which has narrowed somewhat since the 2008 crisis and recession. The Euro area has also seen saving and investment fall but has been closer to balance overall. Other advanced countries (e.g., non-Euro area EU countries, Canada, Australia, etc.) have tended to run large current account deficits, which have recently moved toward balance.

Data from: IMF, World Economic Outlook, September 2005, and updates.

up in the 1980s and 1990s, also closing recently. In the euro area and other industrial regions, the difference between saving and investment was fairly steady, so their current accounts were closer to balance.

To uncover the sources of the trends in total saving, Figure 5-8 examines two of its components, public and private saving. We define **private saving** as the part of *after-tax* private sector disposable income that is *not* devoted to private consumption C. After-tax private sector disposable income, in turn, is national income Y minus the net taxes T paid by households to the government. Hence, private saving S_p is

$$S_p = Y - T - C \qquad (5\text{-}7)$$

Private saving can be a positive number, but if the private sector consumption exceeds after-tax disposable income, then private saving is negative. (Here, the private sector includes households and private firms, which are ultimately owned by households.)

FIGURE 5-8

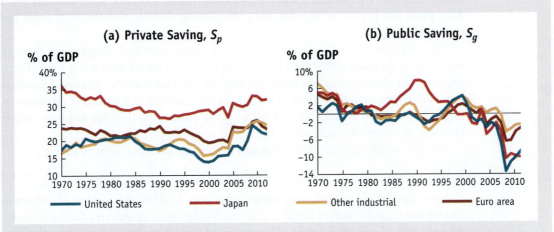

(a) Private Saving, S_p

(b) Public Saving, S_g

Legend: United States — Japan — Other industrial — Euro area

Private and Public Saving Trends: Industrial Countries The chart on the left shows private saving and the chart on the right public saving, both as a percent of GDP. Private saving has been declining in the industrial countries, especially in Japan (since the 1970s) and in the United States (since the 1980s). Private saving has been more stable in the Euro area and other countries. Public saving is clearly more volatile than private saving. Japan has been mostly in surplus and massively so in the late 1980s and early 1990s. The United States briefly ran a government surplus in the late 1990s but then returned to a deficit position. All advanced countries have moved sharply toward lower public saving (in fact, larger deficits) and higher private savings since the 2008 crisis and recession.

Data from: IMF, World Economic Outlook, September 2005, and updates.

Similarly, we define **government saving** or **public saving** as the difference between tax revenue T received by the government and government purchases G.[7] Hence, public saving S_g equals

$$S_g = T - G \qquad (5\text{-}8)$$

Government saving is positive when tax revenue exceeds government consumption $(T > G)$ and the government runs a *budget surplus*. If the government runs a *budget deficit*, however, government consumption exceeds tax revenue $(G > T)$, and public saving is negative.

If we add these last two equations, we see that private saving plus government saving equals total national saving

$$S = Y - C - G = \underbrace{(Y - T - C)}_{\text{Private saving}} + \underbrace{(T - G)}_{\text{Government saving}} = S_p + S_g \qquad (5\text{-}9)$$

In this last equation, taxes cancel out and do not affect saving in the aggregate because they are a transfer from the private sector to the public sector.

One striking feature of the charts in Figure 5-8 is the smooth path of private saving compared with the volatile path of public saving. Public saving is government tax revenue minus spending, and it fluctuates greatly as economic conditions change. The most noticeable feature is the very large public surpluses run up in Japan in the boom of the 1980s and early 1990s, which then disappeared during the long slump in the mid- to late 1990s and early 2000s. In other cases, surpluses in the 1970s soon gave way to deficits in the 1980s, and despite occasional improvements in the fiscal balance

---

[7] Here, the government includes all levels of government: national/federal, state/regional, local/municipal, and so on.

(as in the late 1990s), deficits have been the norm in the public sector. The United States witnessed a particularly sharp move from surplus to deficit after the year 2000. All regions saw private saving rise and public saving decline after the 2008 crisis and up to 2012.

Do government deficits cause current account deficits? Sometimes they go together: in the early 2000s the U.S. government went into deficit when it was fighting two wars (Afghanistan and Iraq) and implemented tax cuts. At the same time there was a large increase in the current account deficit, as seen in Figure 5-7. Sometimes, however, the "twin deficits" do not occur at the same time; they are not inextricably linked, as is sometimes believed. Why?

We can use the equation just given and the current account identity to write

$$CA = S_p + S_g - I \qquad\qquad (5\text{-}10)$$

Now suppose the government lowers your taxes by $100 this year and borrows to finance the resulting deficit but also says you will be taxed by an extra $100 plus interest next year to pay off the debt. The theory of *Ricardian equivalence* asserts that you and other households will save the tax cut to pay next year's tax increase, so that any fall in public saving will be fully offset by a rise in private saving. In this situation, the current account (as seen in Equation 5-10) would be *unchanged*. However, empirical studies do not support this theory: private saving does not fully offset government saving in practice.[8]

How large is the effect of a government deficit on the current account deficit? Research suggests that a change of 1% of GDP in the government deficit (or surplus) coincides with a 0.2% to 0.4% of GDP change in the current account deficit (or surplus), a result consistent with a partial Ricardian offset.

A second reason why the current account might move independently of saving (public or private) is that during the same time period there may be a change in the level of investment in the last equation. A comparison of Figures 5-7 and 5-8 shows this effect at work. For example, we can see from Figure 5-7 that the large U.S. current account deficits of the early to mid-1990s were driven by an investment boom, even though total saving rose slightly, driven by an increase in public saving seen in Figure 5-8. Here, there was no correlation between government deficit (falling) and current account deficit (rising). Shifts after the 2008 recession illustrate multiple factors at work: U.S. investment collapsed and private saving rose as recession fears increased. The combined effects of lower investment and higher private saving more than offset the decline in public saving, and so overall the current account deficit started to decline.

Finally, Figure 5-9 shows global trends in saving, investment, and the current account for advanced countries, emerging and developing economies, and the world economy since 1980. Because the U.S. economy accounts for a large part of the world economy, in aggregate, the industrial countries have shifted into current account deficit over this period, a trend that has been offset by a shift toward current account surplus in the developing countries. The industrialized countries all followed a trend of declining investment and saving ratios, but the developing countries saw the opposite trend: rising investment and saving ratios. For the developing countries, however, the saving increase was larger than the investment increase, allowing a current account surplus to open up. Overall, the industrial country trend of lower saving and investment drove the world trend of lower saving and investment in the 1980s and 1990s. But since the 2000s, the rising share of high-saving emerging and developing countries in the world economy has caused the world

---

[8] Menzie D. Chinn and Hiro Ito, 2007, "Current Account Balances, Financial Development and Institutions: Assaying the World 'Saving Glut,'" *Journal of International Money and Finance*, 26(4), 546–569.

FIGURE 5-9

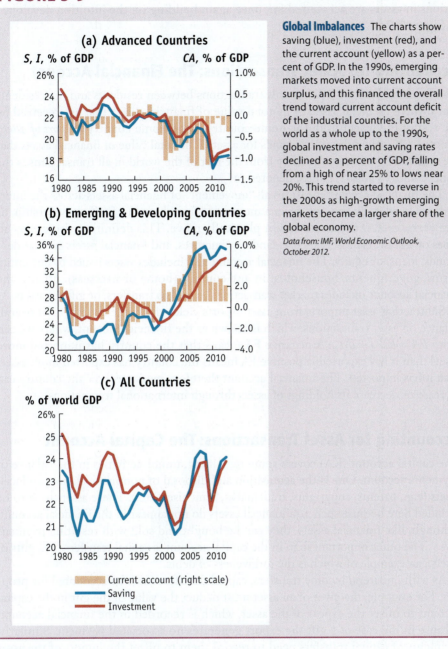

(a) Advanced Countries

S, I, % of GDP   *CA, % of GDP*

(b) Emerging & Developing Countries

S, I, % of GDP   *CA, % of GDP*

(c) All Countries

% of world GDP

Current account (right scale)
Saving
Investment

Global Imbalances The charts show saving (blue), investment (red), and the current account (yellow) as a percent of GDP. In the 1990s, emerging markets moved into current account surplus, and this financed the overall trend toward current account deficit of the industrial countries. For the world as a whole up to the 1990s, global investment and saving rates declined as a percent of GDP, falling from a high of near 25% to lows near 20%. This trend started to reverse in the 2000s as high-growth emerging markets became a larger share of the global economy.

Data from: IMF, World Economic Outlook, October 2012.

trends to reverse. Saving and investment have been on the rise in recent years, but the effects have been felt very unevenly across the globe, leading to the imbalances we have studied.

3 The Balance of Payments

In the previous section, we saw that the current account summarizes the flow of all international market transactions in goods, services, and factor services plus nonmarket transfers. In this section, we look at what's left: international transactions in assets. These transactions are of great importance because they tell us how the current account is financed and, hence, whether a country is becoming more or less indebted to the rest of the world. We begin by looking at how transactions in assets are accounted for, once again building on the intuition developed in Figure 5-2.[9]

Accounting for Asset Transactions: The Financial Account

The financial account (FA) records transactions between residents and nonresidents that involve financial assets. The total value of financial assets that are received by the rest of the world from the home country is the home country's *export of assets*, denoted EX_A (the subscript A stands for asset). The total value of financial assets that are received by the home country from the rest of the world in all transactions is the home country's *import of assets*, denoted IM_A.

The financial account measures all "movement" of financial assets across the international border. By this, we mean a movement from home to foreign ownership, or vice versa, even if the assets do not physically move. This definition also covers all types of assets: real assets such as land or structures, and financial assets such as debt (bonds, loans) or equity. The financial account also includes assets issued by any entity (firms, governments, households) in any country (home or overseas). Finally, the financial account includes market transactions as well as transfers, or gifts of assets.

Subtracting asset imports from asset exports yields the home country's net overall balance on asset transactions, which is known as the financial account, where we can write $FA = EX_A - IM_A$. A negative FA means that the country has imported more assets than it has exported; a positive FA means the country has exported more assets than it has imported. The financial account therefore measures how the country can increase or decrease its holdings of assets through international transactions.

Accounting for Asset Transactions: The Capital Account

The capital account (KA) covers some remaining, minor activities in the balance of payments account. One is the acquisition and disposal of nonfinancial, nonproduced assets (e.g., patents, copyrights, trademarks, franchises, etc.). These assets have to be included here because such nonfinancial assets do not appear in the financial account, although, like financial assets, they can be bought and sold with resulting payment flows. The other important item in the capital account is capital transfers (i.e., gifts of assets), an example of which is the forgiveness of debts.[10]

As with unilateral income transfers, capital transfers must be accounted for properly. For example, the giver of an asset must deduct the value of the gift in the capital account to offset the export of the asset, which is recorded in the financial account, because in the case of a gift the export generates no associated payment. Similarly, recipients of capital transfers need to record them to offset the import of the asset recorded in the financial account.

Using similar notation to that employed with unilateral transfers of income, we denote capital transfers received by the home country as KA_{IN} and capital transfers given by the home country as KA_{OUT}. The capital account, $KA = KA_{IN} - KA_{OUT}$, denotes net capital transfers received. A negative KA indicates that more capital transfers were given by the home country than it received; a positive KA indicates that the home country received more capital transfers than it made.

---

[9] Officially, following the 1993 revision to the System of National Accounts by the U.N. Statistical Office, the place where international transactions are recorded should be called "rest of the world account" or the "external transactions account." The United States calls it the "international transactions account." However, the older terminology was the "balance of payments account," and this usage persists, so we adopt it here.

[10] The capital account does *not* include involuntary debt cancellation, such as results from unilateral defaults. Changes in assets and liabilities due to defaults are counted as capital losses, or valuation effects, which are discussed later in this chapter.

The capital account is a minor and technical accounting item for most developed countries, usually close to zero. In some developing countries, however, the capital account can at times play an important role because in some years nonmarket debt forgiveness can be large, whereas market-based international financial transactions may be small.

Accounting for Home and Foreign Assets

Asset trades in the financial account can be broken down into two types: assets issued by home entities (home assets) and assets issued by foreign entities (foreign assets). This is of economic interest, and sometimes of political interest, because the breakdown makes clear the distinction between the location of the asset issuer and the location of the asset owner, that is, who owes what to whom.

From the home perspective, a foreign asset is a claim on a foreign country. When a home entity holds such an asset, it is called an **external asset** of the home country because it represents an obligation owed to the home country by the rest of the world. Conversely, from the home country's perspective, a home asset is a claim on the home country. When a foreign entity holds such an asset, it is called an **external liability** of the home country because it represents an obligation owed by the home country to the rest of the world. For example, when a U.S. firm invests overseas and acquires a computer factory located in Ireland, the acquisition is an external asset for the United States (and an external liability for Ireland). When a Japanese firm acquires an automobile plant in the United States, the acquisition is an external liability for the United States (and an external asset for Japan). A moment's thought reveals that all other assets traded across borders have a nation in which they are located and a nation by which they are owned—this is true for bank accounts, equities, government debt, corporate bonds, and so on. (For some examples, see **Side Bar: The Double-Entry Principle in the Balance of Payments**.)

If we use superscripts H and F to denote home and foreign assets, we can break down the financial account, FA, as the sum of the net exports of each type of asset:

$$FA = \underbrace{\left(EX_A^H - IM_A^H\right)}_{\substack{\text{Net export of} \\ \text{home assets}}} + \underbrace{\left(EX_A^F - IM_A^F\right)}_{\substack{\text{Net export of} \\ \text{foreign assets}}} = \underbrace{\left(EX_A^H - IM_A^H\right)}_{\substack{\text{Net export of} \\ \text{home assets} \\ = \\ \text{Net additions to} \\ \text{external liabilities}}} - \underbrace{\left(IM_A^F - EX_A^F\right)}_{\substack{\text{Net import of} \\ \text{foreign assets} \\ = \\ \text{Net additions to} \\ \text{external assets}}} \quad (5\text{-}11)$$

In the last part of this formula, we use the fact that net imports of foreign assets are just *minus* net exports of foreign assets, allowing us to change the sign. This reveals to us that FA equals *the additions to external liabilities* (the home-owned assets moving into foreign ownership, net) *minus the additions to external assets* (the foreign-owned assets moving into home ownership, net). This is our first indication of how flows of assets have implications for changes in a nation's wealth, a topic to which we return shortly.

How the Balance of Payments Accounts Work: A Macroeconomic View

To further understand the links between flows of goods, services, income, and assets, we have to understand how the current account, capital account, and financial account are related and why, in the end, the balance of payments accounts must balance as seen in the open-economy circular flow (Figure 5-2).

Recall from Equation (5-4) that gross national disposable income (GNDI) is

$$Y = GNDI = GNE + TB + NFIA + NUT = \underbrace{GNE + CA}_{\substack{\text{Resources available to home} \\ \text{country from income}}}$$

Does this expression represent all of the resources that are available to the home economy to finance expenditure? No. It represents only the income resources, that is, the resources obtained from the market sale and purchase of goods, services, and factor services and from nonmarket transfers. In addition, the home economy can free up (or use up) resources in another way: by engaging in net sales (or purchases) of assets. We can calculate these extra resources using our previous definitions:

$$\underbrace{(\underbrace{EX_A}_{\substack{\text{Value of}\\\text{all assets}\\\text{exported}}} - \underbrace{KA_{OUT}}_{\substack{\text{Value of}\\\text{all assets}\\\text{exported}\\\text{as gifts}}})}_{\substack{\text{Value of all assets}\\\text{exported via sales}}} - \underbrace{(\underbrace{IM_A}_{\substack{\text{Value of}\\\text{all assets}\\\text{imported}}} - \underbrace{KA_{IN}}_{\substack{\text{Value of}\\\text{all assets}\\\text{imported}\\\text{as gifts}}})}_{\substack{\text{Value of all assets}\\\text{imported via purchases}}} = EX_A - IM_A + KA_{IN} - KA_{OUT} = \underbrace{FA + KA}_{\substack{\text{Extra resources}\\\text{available to the}\\\text{home country due}\\\text{to asset trades}}}$$

Adding the last two expressions, we arrive at the value of the total resources available to the home country for expenditure purposes. This total value must equal the total value of home expenditure on final goods and services, that is, gross national expenditure (GNE):

$$\underbrace{GNE + CA}_{\substack{\text{Resources available}\\\text{to home country}\\\text{due to income}}} + \underbrace{FA + KA}_{\substack{\text{Extra resources available}\\\text{to the home country}\\\text{due to asset trades}}} = GNE$$

We can cancel GNE from both sides of this expression to obtain the important result known as the balance of payments identity or **BOP identity**:

$$\underbrace{CA}_{\text{Current account}} + \underbrace{KA}_{\text{Capital account}} + \underbrace{FA}_{\text{Financial account}} = 0 \qquad \text{(5-12)}$$

The balance of payments sums to zero: it does balance!

How the Balance of Payments Accounts Work: A Microeconomic View

We have just found that at the macroeconomic level, $CA + KA + FA = 0$, a very simple equation that summarizes, in three variables, every single one of the millions of international transactions a nation engages in. This is one way to look at the BOP accounts.

Another way to look at the BOP is to look behind these three variables to the specific flows we saw in Figure 5-2, and the individual transactions within each flow.

$$CA = (EX - IM) + (EX_{FS} - IM_{FS}) + (UT_{IN} - UT_{OUT})$$
$$KA = (KA_{IN} - KA_{OUT}) \qquad \text{(5-13)}$$
$$FA = (EX_A^H - IM_A^H) + (EX_A^F - IM_A^F)$$

Written this way, the components of the BOP identity allow us to see the details behind why the accounts must balance. As you can observe from these equations, there are 12 transaction types (each preceded by either a plus or minus sign) and 3 accounts (CA, KA, FA) in which they can appear.

If an item has a plus sign, it is called a balance of payments credit, or **BOP credit**. Six types of transactions receive a plus (+) sign as follows:

Current account (CA):	Exports of goods and services ($+EX$);
	Exports of factor services ($+EX_{FS}$);
	Unilateral transfers received ($+UT_{IN}$).
Capital account (KA):	Capital transfers received ($+KA_{IN}$).
Financial account (FA):	Exports of home and foreign assets $\left(+EX_A^H, +EX_A^F\right)$.

If an item has a minus sign, it is called a balance of payments debit, or **BOP debit**. Six types of transactions receive a minus (−) sign as follows:

Current account (CA):	Imports of goods and services ($-IM$);
	Imports of factor services ($-IM_{FS}$);
	Unilateral transfers given ($-UT_{OUT}$).
Capital account (KA):	Capital transfers given ($-KA_{OUT}$);
Financial account (FA):	Imports of home and foreign assets ($-IM_A^H, -IM_A^F$).

Now, to see why the BOP accounts have to balance overall, we only need to understand one simple principle: *Every market transaction (whether for goods, services, factor services, or assets) has two parts. If party A engages in a transaction with a counterparty B, then A receives from B an item of a given value, and in return B receives from A an item of equal value.*[11]

Thus, whenever a transaction generates a credit somewhere in the BOP account, it must also generate a corresponding debit somewhere else in the BOP account. Similarly, every debit generates a corresponding credit. (For more detail on this topic, see **Side Bar: The Double-Entry Principle in the Balance of Payments**.)

SIDE BAR

The Double-Entry Principle in the Balance of Payments

We can make the double-entry principle more concrete by looking at some (mostly) hypothetical international transactions and figuring out how they would be recorded in the U.S. BOP accounts.

1. Recall from Chapter 2 that our friend George was in Paris. Suppose he spent $110 (€100) on French wine one evening. This is a U.S. import of a foreign service. George pays with his American Express card. The bar is owed $110 (or €100) by American Express (and AMEX is owed by George). The United States has exported an asset to France: the bar now has a claim against American Express. From the U.S. perspective, this represents an increase in U.S. assets owned by foreigners. The double entries in the U.S. BOP appear in the current account and the financial account:

CA: Drinks in Paris bar	$-IM$	−$110
FA: Bar's claim on AMEX	$+EX_A^H$	+$110

2. George was in the bar to meet his Danish cousin Georg. They both work as wine merchants. After a few bottles of Bordeaux, George enthuses about Arkansas chardonnay and insists Georg give it a try. Georg counters by telling George he should really try some Jutland rosé. Each cousin returns home and asks his firm to ship a case of each wine (worth $36) to the other. This barter transaction (involving no financial activity) would appear solely as two entries in the U.S. current account:

CA: Arkansas wine exported to Denmark	EX	+$36
CA: Jutland wine imported to United States	$-IM$	−$36

3. Later that night, George met a French entrepreneur in a smoky corner of the bar. George vaguely remembers the story: the entrepreneur's French tech

company was poised for unbelievable success with an upcoming share issue. George decides to invest $10,000 to buy the French stock; he imports a French asset. The stock is sold to him through the French bank BNP, and George sends them a U.S. dollar check. BNP then has a claim against Citibank, an export of a home asset to France. Both entries fall within the financial account:

FA: George's French tech stocks	$-IM_A^F$	−$10,000
FA: BNP claim against Citibank	$+EX_A^H$	+$10,000

4. Rather surprisingly, George's French stocks do quite well. Later that year they have doubled in value. George makes a $5,000 donation to charity. His charity purchases U.S. relief supplies that will be exported to a country suffering a natural disaster. The two entries here are entirely in the U.S. current account. The supplies are a nonmarket export of goods offset by the value of the unilateral transfer:

CA: Relief supplies exported	EX	+$5,000
CA: George's charitable gift	$-UT_{OUT}$	−$5,000

5. George was also pleased to see that some poor countries were benefiting from another kind of foreign assistance, debt forgiveness. The U.S. secretary of state announced that the United States would forgive $1 billion of debt owed by a developing country. This would decrease U.S.-owned assets overseas. The United States was exporting the developing country's assets: it hands the canceled debts back, a credit in the financial account. The double entries would be seen in the capital and financial accounts:

KA: U.S. grant of debt relief	$-KA_{OUT}$	−$1,000,000,000
FA: Decline in U.S. external assets	$+EX_A^F$	+$1,000,000,000

---

[11] This principle applies not only to market transactions but also to nonmarket transactions such as gifts or foreign aid that enter into the BOP accounts either as "net unilateral transfers" or in the capital account. For example, a $100 export of food aid is not a market transaction, but appears as a credit item in total exports. This credit is offset in the BOP accounts by a −$100 debit in net unilateral transfers. In this way, nonmarket gifts, for which nothing is offered in return, are properly recorded and yet leave the BOP accounts in balance.

It might not be obvious where the offsetting item is, but it must exist somewhere *if* the accounts have been measured properly. As we shall see shortly, this is a big "if": mismeasurement can sometimes be an important issue.

Understanding the Data for the Balance of Payments Account

To illustrate all the principles we've learned, let's look at the United States' balance of payments account. Table 5-2 shows an extract of the U.S. BOP accounts for 2019.[12]

In the current account, in the top part of the table, we look first at the trade in goods and services on lines 1 and 3. Overall exports *EX* were +$2,498 billion (line 1, a credit), and imports *IM* were –$3,114 billion (line 3, a debit). In the summary items,

TABLE 5-2

The U.S. Balance of Payments in 2019 The table shows U.S. international transactions in 2019 in billions of dollars. Major categories are in bold type.

Major Account	Line	Category or Subcategory	Symbol	$ billions
	1	**Exports of goods and services**	$+EX$	**2,498**
	1a	Of which: Goods		1,653
	1b	Services		845
	2	**Income receipts** [= exports of factor services]	$+EX_{FS}$	**1,123**
Current Account	3	**Imports of goods and services** (–)	$-IM$	**–3,114**
	3a	Of which: Goods (–)		–2,519
	3b	Services (–)		–595
	4	**Income payments** [= imports of factor services (–)]	$-IM_{FS}$	**–866**
	5	**Net unilateral transfers**	NUT	**–139**
	6	**Capital account** net	KA	**0**
	7	**U.S.-owned assets abroad** net increase (–) [= net imports of ROW assets or financial outflow (–)]	$+EX_A^F - IM_A^F$	**–427**
Capital and Financial Account	7a	Of which: U.S. official reserve assets		–5
	7b	Other assets		–422
	8	**Foreign-owned assets in U.S.** net increase (+) [= net exports of U.S. assets or financial inflow (+)]	$+EX_A^H - IM_A^H$	**823**
	8a	Of which: Foreign official assets		92
	8b	Other assets		731
Statistical Discrepancy	9	**Statistical discrepancy** (sum of 1 to 8, sign reversed)	SD	**102**
		Balance on current account (lines 1, 2, 3, 4, and 5)	CA	**–498**
		Of which: Balance on goods and services (lines 1 and 3)	TB	–616
Summary Items		Balance on income (lines 2 and 4)	$NFIA$	257
		Balance on financial account (lines 7 and 8)	FA	**395**
		Of which: Official settlements balance (lines 7a and 8a)		97
		Nonreserve financial account (lines 7b and 8b)		298

Notes: Details may not add to totals because of rounding. The statistical discrepancy shown here includes financial derivatives not otherwise counted.

Data from: U.S. Bureau of Economic Analysis, ITA Tables 1.1 and 9.1, using the ITA definition of the United States. This includes U.S. territories, so these figures are slightly different from those in Table 5-1. Data as of March 19, 2020.

---

[12] The BOP account is published each year as the "international transactions account (ITA)" by the BEA. Note that the ITA uses a different geographical definition of the United States territory than the national income and product accounts (NIPA), so the figures mentioned below and in Table 5-2 do not exactly match those discussed earlier in this chapter and in Table 5-1.

we see that the balance on goods and services, the trade balance *TB*, was −$616 billion (line 1 plus line 3, or exports minus imports). Exports and imports and the trade balance are also broken down even further into goods and service components (shown on lines 1ab and 3ab, and in the summary items).

The next part of the current account on lines 2 and 4 deals with trade in factor services, also known as the *income account* (referring to the income paid to those factors). Income receipts for factor service exports, EX_{FS}, generated a credit of +$1,123 billion and income payments for factor service imports, IM_{FS}, generated a debit of −$866 billion. Adding these two items resulted in net factor income from abroad *NFIA* equal to +$257 billion (line 2 plus line 4), a net credit, also shown in the summary items.

Coming to the last item in the current account, we see that net unilateral transfers *NUT* were −$139 billion, a net debit (line 5); the United States was a net donor as measured by the net transfer of goods, services, and income to the rest of the world. (Typically, in summary tables like these, unilateral transfers are shown only in net form.)

Overall, summing lines 1 through 5, the 2019 U.S. current account balance *CA* was −$498 billion, that is, a deficit of $498 billion, as shown in the summary items at the foot of the table.

A country with a current account surplus is called a **(net) lender**. By the BOP identity, we know that it must have a deficit in its asset accounts, so like any lender, it is, on net, buying assets (acquiring IOUs from borrowers). For example, China is a large net lender. A country with a current account deficit is called a **(net) borrower**. By the BOP identity, we know that it must have a surplus in its asset accounts, so like any borrower, it is, on net, selling assets (issuing IOUs to lenders). As we can see, the United States is a large net borrower.

Now we move to the capital and financial accounts. Typically, in summary tables like these, the capital account is shown only in net form. The United States in 2019 had a negligible capital account *KA* of $0 billion (line 6), when rounded to the nearest billion. In most years *KA* is small and close to, if not exactly equal to, zero.

Lastly, we move to the financial account. As explained, this account can be broken down in terms of the exports and imports of two kinds of assets: U.S. assets (U.S. external liabilities) and rest-of-the-world assets (U.S. external assets). In this summary the net trades are shown for each kind of asset.

We see that the United States was engaged in the net import of foreign assets, so that external assets (U.S.-owned assets abroad) increased by $427 billion. This net import of foreign assets is recorded as a debit of −$427 billion (line 7). Note that the minus sign maintains the convention, even for assets, that imports are debits.

At the same time, the United States was engaged in the net export of U.S. assets to the rest of the world so that external liabilities (foreign-owned assets in the United States) increased by $823 billion; the net export of U.S. assets is duly recorded as a credit of +$823 billion (line 8).

The sum of lines 7 and 8 gives the financial account balance, *FA*, of +$395 billion, which is also recorded in the summary items.

To provide further information on interventions by central banks and other official entities, financial account transactions are often also broken down into reserve and nonreserve components. Changes in reserves arise from official intervention in the forex market—for example, purchases and sales by home and foreign monetary and other authorities. The balance on all reserve transactions is called the *official settlements balance*, and the balance on all other asset trades is called the *nonreserve financial account*. These two balances are also shown in the summary items. We see here that U.S. authorities intervened a little: a net import of $5 billion of U.S. official reserves (line 7a) means that the Federal Reserve and/or Treasury bought $5 billion in foreign (i.e., nondollar) exchange reserves. At the same time, foreign central banks often intervene quite a lot; but in 2019, in contrast to their accumulations in past years, they increased their holdings by $9 billion in U.S. dollar reserve assets (line 8a).

Adding up the current account, the capital account, and the financial account (lines 1 through 8), we find that the total of the three accounts in 2019 was –$102 billion (–$498 + $0 + $395, allowing for rounding errors), which was a very large discrepancy by historical standards. The BOP accounts are supposed to balance by adding to zero—in reality, they never do. Why not? Because the statistical agencies tasked with gathering BOP data find it impossible to track every single international transaction correctly, due to measurement errors and omissions. Some problems result from the smuggling of goods or trade tax evasion. Larger errors are likely due to the mismeasured, concealed, or illicit financial income flows and asset movements (e.g., due to money laundering or tax evasion).

The Statistical Discrepancy To "account" for this error, statistical agencies create an accounting item, the *statistical discrepancy* (SD) equal to minus the error $SD = -(CA + KA + FA)$. With that "correction," the amended version of the BOP identity will hold true in practice, sweeping away the real-world measurement problems. In the table, the statistical discrepancy is shown on line 9.[13] Once the statistical discrepancy is included, the balance of payments accounts always balance.

Some Recent Trends in the U.S. Balance of Payments Figure 5-10 shows recent trends in various components of the U.S. balance of payments. The sharp downward trend of the current account is as previously shown in Figure 5-6, so for the balance of payments identity to hold, there must be an offsetting upward trend in other parts of the BOP accounts. This is indeed the case. We can see that the United States has been financing its growing deficit on the current account primarily by running an expanding surplus on the financial account. In the mid-1990s, there was close to a $100 billion current account deficit and a comparable financial account surplus. A decade later, both figures were in the region of $800 billion, with a substantial decline seen in the period since the global financial crisis of 2008 and up to 2012.

What the Balance of Payments Account Tells Us

The balance of payments accounts consist of the following:

- The current account (CA), which measures external transactions in goods, services, factor services, and unilateral transfers.
- The financial account (FA) and the capital account (KA), which measure external transaction in assets.

Using the principle that market transactions must consist of a trade of two items of equal value, we find that the balance of payments accounts really do balance.

Surpluses on the current account side of the BOP accounts must be offset by deficits on the asset side. Similarly, deficits on the current account must be offset by surpluses on the asset side. By telling us how current account imbalances are financed, the balance of payments connects a country's income and spending decisions to the evolution of that country's wealth, an important connection we develop further in the final section of this chapter.

---

[13] Prior to 2007, the U.S. statistical discrepancy included unmeasured financial derivatives transactions. Starting in 2007, the BEA estimates these transactions, but they are not as yet broken down in detail into home and foreign assets. For clarity, they are not reported here and are included in the statistical discrepancy in Table 5-2.

FIGURE 5-10

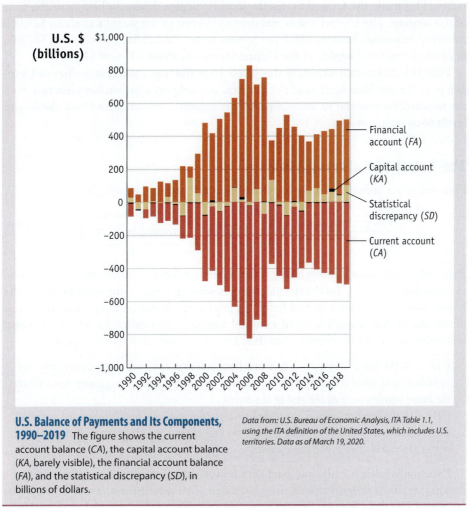

U.S. Balance of Payments and Its Components, 1990–2019 The figure shows the current account balance (*CA*), the capital account balance (*KA*, barely visible), the financial account balance (*FA*), and the statistical discrepancy (*SD*), in billions of dollars.

Data from: U.S. Bureau of Economic Analysis, ITA Table 1.1, using the ITA definition of the United States, which includes U.S. territories. Data as of March 19, 2020.

4 External Wealth

The measurement of a nation's income flow is not the only important economic variable that must be adapted to the open-economy environment. Economists, policymakers, and the general public also care about a nation's stock of *wealth*. And so, probably, do you.

For example, Anne has income and expenditures of $50,000 each year and savings in the bank of $10,000. But she also has a credit card debt of $20,000. Beth's life is identical to Anne's in almost every respect: she has income and expenditures of $50,000 each year and savings of $10,000, but she has no credit card debt. Who is better off? Clearly, Beth is. Her income is the same as Anne's. But Anne's wealth or "net worth" is –$10,000 (savings of $10,000 minus debt of $20,000), whereas Beth has a net worth of +$10,000. Anne's wealth is –20% of her income; Beth's wealth is +20% of her income.

Just as a household is better off with higher wealth, all else equal, so is a country. We can calculate a home country's "net worth" or **external wealth** with respect to the rest of the world (ROW) by adding up all of the home assets owned by ROW (foreigners' claims against home) and then subtracting all of the ROW assets owned by the home country (home claims against foreigners). Doing this for the United States at the end of year 2018 (the latest year for which we have data), we would find that the

United States had an external wealth of about –$9,592 billion, according to BEA estimates. This made the United States the world's biggest debtor in history at the time of this writing. The United States' net debt to the rest of the world was about $29,000 for every American. Because GDP per person in the United States was about $63,000 in 2018, the external wealth of the United States was about –47% of GDP.

Why is U.S. external wealth at this level? How did it get there, and what will happen next? In this final section of the chapter, we build on what we have learned from the national income and balance of payments accounts to understand how the wealth levels of countries evolve.

The Level of External Wealth

First, we give a definition of the level of a country's external wealth (W):

$$\underbrace{\text{External wealth}}_{W} = \underbrace{\begin{bmatrix} \text{ROW assets} \\ \text{owned by home} \end{bmatrix}}_{A} - \underbrace{\begin{bmatrix} \text{Home assets} \\ \text{owned by ROW} \end{bmatrix}}_{L} \qquad (5\text{-}14)$$

External wealth equals the value of total external assets (A) minus the value of total external liabilities (L). Total external assets is what the rest of the world owes to the home country, and total external liabilities is what the home country owes to the rest of the world. A country's level of external wealth is also called its *net international investment position* or *net foreign assets*. It is a stock measure, not a flow measure.

> If $W > 0$, *the home country is a* **net creditor** *country: external assets exceed external liabilities, and what the rest of the world owes the home country is greater than what the home country owes to the rest of the world.*
>
> If $W < 0$, *the home country is a* **net debtor** *country: external liabilities exceed external assets, and what the home country owes to the rest of the world is greater than what the rest of the world owes to the home country.*

External wealth is only one part of a nation's total wealth. The other part of a nation's wealth is *internal wealth*, the total value of all nonfinancial assets in the home country. (The links between external wealth and total wealth are explored further in the appendix to this chapter.)

Because we are focusing on international economic relationships, our main emphasis is on external wealth because it measures the outstanding obligations of one country to another. Those obligations, and when and how they are paid, can be the source of great economic and political stress. Moreover, the net debts of nations, like those of individuals, ultimately carry a cost. To understand external wealth, let's look at how it is measured and how it evolves.

Changes in External Wealth

There are two reasons a country's level of external wealth changes over time.

1. *Financial flows:* As a result of asset trades, the country can increase or decrease its external assets and liabilities. How? Net exports of foreign assets cause an equal decrease in the level of external assets and hence a corresponding decrease in external wealth. Net exports of home assets cause an equal increase in the level of external liabilities and hence a corresponding decrease in external wealth. For example, if net exports of assets (whether home or foreign) are +$1 billion, then the change in external wealth is –$1 billion. The net export of assets of all kinds is measured by the financial account (FA), and this has a *negative* effect on external wealth in any period.

2. *Valuation effects:* The value of existing external assets and liabilities may change over time because of capital gains or losses. In the case of external wealth, this change in value could be due to price effects or exchange rate effects. For example, suppose a U.S. citizen buys 100 shares of BP on the London Stock Exchange at £7 each. Suppose the exchange rate is $1.5 per pound. These U.S. external assets are worth $10.50 each (1.5 times 7), for a total of $1,050. Suppose the price of these shares then falls to £6, and the exchange rate stays the same. Each share is now worth $9.00 (1.5 times 6) and the 100 shares are valued at $900. Their value has fallen in dollar terms by $150 (£1 times 1.5 times 100), which is a capital loss. This is an example of a price effect. Now suppose the exchange rate rises to $1.6 per pound. Each share is still worth £6 in U.K. currency but $9.60 in U.S. currency (1.6 times 6), so the total value of the shares rises to $960, which, relative to the $900 they were previously worth, implies a capital gain of $60. This is an example of an exchange rate effect. Similar effects can change the value of external liabilities.

Adding up these two contributions to the change in external wealth (ΔW), we find

$$\underbrace{\left[\begin{array}{c}\text{Change in} \\ \text{external wealth}\end{array}\right]}_{\substack{\Delta W}} = -\underbrace{\left[\begin{array}{c}\text{Financial} \\ \text{account}\end{array}\right]}_{\substack{\text{Net export of assets} \\ = \\ FA}} + \underbrace{\left[\begin{array}{c}\text{Capital gains on} \\ \text{external wealth}\end{array}\right]}_{\substack{\text{Valuation effects} \\ = \\ \text{Capital gains minus} \\ \text{capital losses}}} \qquad (5\text{-}15)$$

We gain a deeper understanding of this expression if we recall the BOP identity: the current account plus the capital account plus the financial account equals zero. Hence, *minus* the financial account equals the current account plus the capital account, or $-FA = CA + KA$. Substituting this identity into Equation (5-15), we obtain

$$\underbrace{\left[\begin{array}{c}\text{Change in} \\ \text{external wealth}\end{array}\right]}_{\substack{\Delta W}} = \underbrace{\left[\begin{array}{c}\text{Current} \\ \text{account}\end{array}\right]}_{\substack{CA \\ = \\ \text{Unspent} \\ \text{income}}} + \underbrace{\left[\begin{array}{c}\text{Capital} \\ \text{account}\end{array}\right]}_{\substack{KA \\ = \\ \text{Net capital} \\ \text{transfers received}}} + \underbrace{\left[\begin{array}{c}\text{Capital gains on} \\ \text{external wealth}\end{array}\right]}_{\substack{\text{Valuation effects} \\ = \\ \text{Capital gains} \\ \text{minus capital losses}}} \qquad (5\text{-}16)$$

This fundamental formula tells us that a country can increase its external wealth in one of only three ways:

- Through its own thrift (a CA surplus, so expenditure is less than income)
- By the charity of others (a KA surplus, by receiving net gifts of wealth)
- With the help of windfalls (having positive capital gains)

Similarly, a country can reduce its external wealth by doing any of the opposites.

Understanding the Data on External Wealth

To track external wealth accurately, statisticians apply Equation (5-15). They face the challenge of not only keeping tabs on every trade in assets but also correctly assessing the impact of changing financial market conditions around the world on the value of the country's external assets and liabilities.

Measures of levels and changes in national external wealth are recorded in an account known as the net international investment position. To illustrate, a simplified version of this account for the United States appears in Table 5-3. The latest detailed data for the year 2018 show a clear distinction between the contribution of financial flows (net trade in assets) to changes in external wealth, in column (a), and the impact of various kinds of valuation effects—columns (b), (c), and (d).

TABLE 5-3

U.S. External Wealth in 2017–18 The table shows changes in the U.S. net international investment position during the year 2018 in billions of dollars. The net result in row 3 equals row 1 minus row 2.

Category	Position, end 2017 ($ billions)	Financial Flows (a)	Price Changes (b)	Exchange Rate Changes (c)	Other Changes (d)	Total (a+b+c+d)	Position, end 2018 ($ billions)
			CHANGES IN POSITION DURING 2018 ($ BILLIONS)				
				VALUATION EFFECTS			
1. External Assets	26,212	311	−2,036	−1,719	−19	−2,463	23,749
= U.S.-owned assets abroad:							
2. External Liabilities	33,993	736	−1,646	−56	315	−651	33,342
= Foreign-owned assets in the United States							
3. External Wealth	−7,781	−425	−390	−663	−334	−1,811	−9,592
= (Line 1 minus line 2) = U.S. net international investment position							
Symbol	W (end 2017)	−FA		Capital gains		ΔW	W (end 2018)

Note: Financial derivatives are excluded. Totals may not add up due to rounding.

Data from: U.S. Bureau of Economic Analysis, IIP Table 1.3. Data revised as of March 31, 2020.

Table 5-3, line 3, column (a), shows that in 2018 the United States, on net, exported $425 billion in assets (the minus sign denotes a net export since this column records *minus* the financial account; asset exports of $736 billion on line 2, minus asset imports of $311 billion on line 1). On their own, these financial flows would have changed U.S. external wealth by −$425 billion in just one year. Yet the total change in external wealth shown on line 3 was −$1,811 billion in that year due to combined valuation effects and "other changes" in columns (b), (c), and (d), which lowered U.S. external wealth even more over the same period. The valuation effects were driven by $390 billion in price change effects offset and −$663 billion in exchange rate effects. "Other" changes are recorded as −$334 billion. Thus, while the United States borrowed, on net, an additional $425 billion from the rest of the world in 2018, its external wealth actually fell by $1,811 billion, about four times as much.

So what happened in 2018 to explain the valuation effects? Three main factors were at work. Equity values were down in the United States and worldwide as the Fed signaled tighter policy near the year end. The U.S. dollar also strengthened on this news. U.S. external assets include a larger share of equities than U.S. external liabilities, which consist of a great deal of U.S. debt. This difference in the composition of the two portfolios meant that falling equity markets tended to lower the value of U.S. external assets and lower the value of U.S. external liabilities (column b). Recall that U.S. external liabilities include vast foreign holdings of U.S. Treasury securities, held either as foreign official assets in central banks or as low-risk assets by foreign investors. These assets' prices changed little in dollar terms and did not experience any exchange rate valuation effects because they are denominated in dollars. But as the U.S. dollar strengthened in 2018 against most foreign currencies, the value of the large share of U.S. external assets denominated in foreign currencies fell dramatically in value (column c).

Some Recent Trends Over the longer run, the changes in external wealth in Equation (5-16) gradually add up. In the case of the United States, for the past three decades, the financial account has almost always been in surplus, reflecting a net export of assets to the rest of the world to pay for chronic current account deficits (the capital account has been negligibly small).

If there were no valuation effects, then Equation (5-15) would make a simple prediction. The change in the level of external wealth between two dates should equal the cumulative net import of assets (minus the financial account) over the intervening period. For example, if we had taken the U.S. external wealth level at the end of 1988 and added to that level all subsequent financial flows for the next 30 years until the end of 2018, we would have estimated U.S. external wealth in 2018 at about −$1 trillion. In reality, the actual 2018 figure shown in Table 5-3 was a bit smaller, at "only" −$9.5 trillion.

Why? Valuation effects or capital gains generated the difference of about $1.5 trillion in external wealth over the period, and from 1988 to 2018 these effects reduced U.S. net external indebtedness in 2018 by almost 15% compared with the level that financial flows alone would have predicted. The flip side of these valuation effects is that the rest of the world outside the United States suffered an equal and opposite capital loss over the same period. Why? Capital gains always have a "zero sum" property—by symmetry, an increase in the dollar value of the home country's external assets is simultaneously an increase in the dollar value of the rest of the world's external liabilities. As these calculations show, at least for the United States, these effects can be large on an annual basis, and can cumulate to large amounts over several decades.

What External Wealth Tells Us

External wealth data tell us the net credit or debit position of a country with respect to the rest of the world. They include data on external assets (foreign assets owned by the home country) and external liabilities (home assets owned by foreigners). A creditor country has positive external wealth, a debtor country negative external wealth.

What drives external wealth? The current account told us about the imbalances in a country's external flows of goods, services, factor services, and income. The balance of payments accounts told us how these imbalances require offsetting financial flows of assets between countries. Countries with a current account surplus (deficit) must be net buyers (sellers) of assets. This buying and selling of assets has implications for external wealth. An increase in a country's external wealth results from every net import of assets; conversely, a decrease in external wealth results from every net export of assets. In addition, countries can experience capital gains or losses on their external assets and liabilities that cause changes in external wealth. All of these changes are summarized in the statement of a country's net international investment position.

5 Conclusions

The science of macroeconomics would be impossible without data, and the vast majority of the data we employ emerge from the efforts of official statisticians around the world. Despite all the statistical discrepancies, and even the occasional errors of omission and commission (see **Side Bar: Beware of Greeks Bearing Statistics**), we would be lost without these measures of macroeconomic activity.

This chapter has illustrated some important accounting concepts and has highlighted some unusual and intriguing features of the current international economic system. We have seen how a consistent system of national income and product accounts allows countries to track international trade flows (including trade in intermediate goods), cross-border factor income flows, and unilateral transfers. We have also seen how these net resource flows of goods and services can be matched against a parallel set of net payment activities involving assets in the balance of payments accounts. Finally, we have seen how the flow of trades in assets can be combined with capital gains and losses to track the evolution of a nation's stock of external wealth, an important part of its total wealth, as recorded in the statement of the net international investment position.

In the remainder of the book, we make extensive use of the concepts introduced in this chapter to develop theories that explore the global macroeconomic linkages between nations.

SIDE BAR

Beware of Greeks Bearing Statistics

It is important, but rather sad, to note that when it comes to national statistics, we cannot believe everything we read. Over the years numerous governments have been suspected of fiddling with their official data for various purposes, as indicated by the following examples:

- *Greece.* In 2001 Greece was allowed to join the Eurozone. One of the criteria it had to meet in order to join was that its budget deficit could not be over 3% of its GDP. Greece met this requirement according to its official statistics. In November 2004, after it had been allowed to join the Eurozone, Greece admitted that its 2003 budget deficit was really 3.4%, twice as large as it had previously claimed. In fact, the budget deficit had not been below 3% since 1999. The EU was not amused. Greece continued to publish incorrect or manipulated data (including a 25% upward adjustment to GDP to take into account "black economy" activity such as prostitution). By inflating its GDP, Greece made its budget deficit position look better than it was, which may have allowed Greece to borrow from other countries on favorable terms. When the euro crisis hit in 2008–09, the full horror of Greece's weak economic and fiscal position became clear, by which point the fiasco forced other Eurozone nations and the IMF to provide emergency funding in 2010. Greece eventually defaulted in 2011 and went into a deeper depression, and the economic and political ramifications (e.g., austerity policies, the collapse of the Cyprus banking system in 2013, and undermined confidence in other weak economies) have continued to threaten the survival of the euro project itself.

- *Italy.* In 1987 Italy was considered much poorer than northern European countries. But its statisticians also decided to increase GDP by 15% after some guesswork to account for the black economy. Instantly, Italians had a higher official GDP per person than the British, an event known as *il sorpasso.* Not that this made any Italians actually feel richer.

- *Argentina.* After its 2001 crisis, a new populist government took over but faced problems with high and persistent inflation. To "solve" this problem, the government "reorganized" its official statistical bureau, which then started publishing much lower, and highly suspicious, inflation data into the next decade. As the *Economist* reported in 2012, "Since 2007, when Guillermo Moreno, the secretary of internal trade, [told] the statistics institute, INDEC, that their figures had better not show inflation shooting up, prices and the official record have parted ways. Private-sector economists and . . . provincial government [statistics] show inflation two to three times higher than INDEC's number."[14] Lower inflation also helped the government avoid larger costs of indexed benefits and allowed the government to claim it had solved the inflation problem. Few believed these published data were true.

- *China.* As part of the International Comparison Project (ICP) by the World Bank, China's own estimate of its yuan price level came in much higher than had been expected. This had various implications: dividing nominal yuan income by the price level made China look quite a bit poorer. And higher prices made China's real exchange rate less undervalued, or even overvalued. Since poorer countries usually have lower price levels, both of these impacts had the effect of making China's exchange rate look more fairly valued, given its standard of living. This came about at a time when China was under considerable political pressure to appreciate its currency. But skeptics doubted whether the data were totally plausible, because the change in the yuan price level since the previous ICP was much larger than that implied by China's own official inflation data over the same period.

---

[14] "Argentina's inflation problem: The price of cooking the books," *The Economist,* February 25, 2012.

1. National flows of expenditure, product, income, and wealth, and international flows of goods, services, income, and assets, together measure important aspects of a country's economic performance and describe its economy's relationship to economies in the rest of the world. The records kept in the national income and product accounts, the balance of payments account, and the net international investment position track these data.

2. The key measures of economic activity are:

   - Gross national expenditure (GNE) measures an economy's total spending on final goods and services. It is the sum of consumption, investment, and government consumption: $GNE = C + I + G$.

   - Gross domestic product (GDP) measures total production (value of all output minus value of all purchased inputs).

   - Gross national income (GNI) measures the total payments to an economy's domestic factors.

   - Gross national disposable income (GNDI, also denoted Y) measures an economy's disposable income, including transfers.

3. In a closed economy, $GNE = GDP = GNI = GNDI$. In an open economy, GDP need not equal GNE. When nations can trade, the sum of goods and services demanded by domestic residents need not be the same as the sum of goods and services supplied by domestic firms. The difference between GDP and GNE is the trade balance: TB: $GDP = GNE + TB$. The trade balance is the difference between a nation's imports and exports of goods and services.

4. In an open economy, GDP need not equal GNI because imports and exports of factor services (measured by net factor income from abroad or NFIA) imply that factor income received by domestic residents need not be the same as factor payments made by domestic firms. Thus, $GNI = GDP + NFIA$.

5. In an open economy, the true level of disposable income is best measured by gross national disposable income or $Y = GNDI$. GNDI need not equal GNI because net unilateral transfers (NUT) to foreigners may be positive, due to foreign aid and other nonmarket gifts. Thus, $Y = GNDI = GNI + NUT$.

6. The sum of all the aforementioned international transactions, $TB + NFIA + NUT$, is called the current account (CA).

7. From the relationships just outlined, we find that $Y = C + I + G + CA$. This expression is known as the *national income identity*.

8. National saving S is defined as $Y - C - G$. From the national income identity, we can derive the current account identity: $S = I + CA$. The current account equals saving minus investment. Movements in saving or investment, all else equal, feed directly into the current account.

9. All international trades in goods and services and in assets are recorded in an account known as the balance of payments (BOP). As a result of double-entry bookkeeping, and allowing for gifts and transfers, the BOP must sum to zero.

10. The BOP contains the following:

    - Net exports of goods and services, TB, called the trade balance

    - Net exports of factor services, NFIA, called the net factor income from abroad

    - Net unilateral transfers received, NUT, called the net unilateral transfers

    - Net transfers of assets received, KA, called the capital account

    - Net exports of assets, FA, called the financial account

11. The first three items are the current account CA. Since the BOP accounts sum to zero, this implies the balance of payments identity: $CA + FA + KA = 0$.

12. External wealth is a measure of a country's credit or debt position versus the rest of the world. It equals external assets—rest of world (ROW) assets owned by home—minus external liabilities (home assets owned by ROW). The net export (import) of assets lowers (raises) a country's external wealth. External wealth is one part of a country's total wealth.

13. External wealth can change for one of two reasons: the export or import of assets (called financial flows) or changes in the value of existing assets due to capital gains or losses (called valuation effects). Both of these channels affect net external wealth.

KEY TERMS

national income and product accounts, p. 142

balance of payments accounts, p. 142

gross national expenditure (GNE), p. 142

gross domestic product (GDP), p. 142

gross national income (GNI), p. 143

trade balance (TB), p. 144

net factor income from abroad (NFIA), p. 144

net unilateral transfers (NUT), p. 144

gross national disposable income (GNDI), p. 144

current account (CA), p. 144

financial account (FA), p. 146

capital account (KA), p. 146

national income identity, p. 154

national saving, p. 155

current account identity, p. 155

private saving, p. 156

government saving, p. 157

public saving, p. 157

external asset, p. 161

external liability, p. 161

BOP identity, p. 162

BOP credit, p. 162

BOP debit, p. 163

(net) lender, p. 165

(net) borrower, p. 165

external wealth, p. 167

net creditor, p. 168

net debtor, p. 168

PROBLEMS

1. **Discovering Data** In this question you will study the official macroeconomic statistics reported in your country. These can be found by searching the web for "National Accounts" and your country's name. In the United States, these can be found at http://www.bea.gov and by accessing the National Income and Product Account (NIPA) tables 1.1.5 and 4.1.

   a. Using annual data, compute GDP, GNE, and GNDI in the most recent year.

   b. Was your country's GDP higher or lower than its GNE in the past year? Interpret this finding.

   c. Was your country's GNI higher or lower than its GDP? Interpret this finding.

   d. Was your country a net giver or receiver of unilateral transfers?

2. To the right is a partial table of OECD member countries using data from the World Bank, with the countries ranked according to their GDP per capita in 2014 (these numbers are reported in current U.S. dollars). Compute the ratio of GNI to GDP in each case. What does this imply about net factor income from abroad in each country? Compute the GNI rankings of these countries. Are there any major differences between the GDP and GNI rankings? What do these differences imply?

		GDP per Person	GNI per Person
1	Luxembourg	$116,613	$75,960
2	Norway	$97,300	$103,620
3	Switzerland	$85,617	$84,720
4	Australia	$61,980	$64,600
5	Denmark	$60,718	$61,330
6	Sweden	$58,899	$61,570
7	United States	$54,630	$55,230
8	Ireland	$54,339	$46,520
9	Netherlands	$52,138	$51,630
10	Austria	$51,122	$49,600
11	Canada	$50,231	$51,630
12	Finland	$49,842	$48,440
13	Germany	$47,774	$47,590
14	Belgium	$47,328	$47,240
15	United Kingdom	$46,297	$43,390
16	New Zealand	$44,342	$41,070
17	France	$42,726	$42,950
18	Israel	$37,206	$35,320
19	Japan	$36,194	$42,000
20	Italy	$35,223	$29,390
21	Spain	$29,721	$29,390
22	South Korea	$27,971	$27,090
23	Slovenia	$24,002	$23,580
24	Portugal	$22,124	$21,360
25	Greece	$21,673	$22,810
26	Czech Republic	$19,502	$18,350
27	Estonia	$20,147	$19,010
28	Poland	$14,082	$13,680
29	Hungary	$14,027	$13,340
30	Turkey	$10,515	$10,830
31	Mexico	$10,325	$9,870

3. Note the following accounting identity for gross national income (GNI):

$$GNI = C + I + G + TB + NFIA$$

Using this expression, show that in a closed economy, gross domestic product (GDP), gross national income (GNI), and gross national expenditures (GNE) are the same. Show that domestic investment is equal to domestic savings.

4. Show how each of the following would affect the U.S. balance of payments. Include a description of the debit and credit items, and in each case identify which specific account is affected (e.g., imports of goods and services, IM; exports of assets, EX_A; and so on). (For this question, you may find it helpful to refer to the Appendix.)

   a. A California computer manufacturer purchases a $50 hard disk from a Malaysian company, paying the funds from a bank account in Malaysia.

   b. A U.S. tourist to Japan sells his iPod to a local resident for yen worth $100.

   c. The U.S. central bank purchases $500 million worth of U.S. Treasury bonds from a British financial firm and sells pound sterling foreign reserves.

   d. A U.S. owner of Sony shares receives $10,000 in dividend payments, which are paid into a Tokyo bank.

   e. The central bank of China purchases $1 million of export earnings from a firm that has sold $1 million of toys to the United States, and the central bank holds these dollars as reserves.

   f. The U.S. government forgives a $50 million debt owed by a developing country.

WORK IT OUT   ▨ Achieve | interactive activity

5. In 2016 the country of Ikonomia has a current account deficit of $1 billion and a nonreserve financial account surplus of $700 million. Ikonomia's capital account is in a $150 million surplus. In addition, Ikonomian factories located in foreign countries earn $700 million. Ikonomia has a trade deficit of $600 million. Assume Ikonomia neither gives nor receives unilateral transfers. Ikonomia's GDP is $9.4 billion.

   a. What happened to Ikonomia's net foreign assets during 2016? Did it acquire or lose foreign assets during the year?

   b. Compute the official settlements balance (OSB). Based on this number, what happened to the central bank's (foreign) reserves?

   c. How much income did foreign factors of production earn in Ikonomia during 2016?

   d. Compute net factor income from abroad (NFIA).

   e. Using the identity $BOP = CA + FA + KA$, show that $BOP = 0$.

   f. Compute Ikonomia's gross national expenditure (GNE), gross national income (GNI), and gross national disposable income (GNDI).

6. To answer this question, you must obtain data from the Bureau of Economic Analysis (BEA), http://www .bea.gov, on the U.S. balance of payments (BOP) tables. Go to interactive tables to obtain *annual* data for 2015 (the default setting is for quarterly data). It may take you some time to become familiar with how to navigate the website. *You need only refer to Table 1 on the BOP accounts.* Using the BOP data, compute the following for the United States:

   a. Trade balance (TB), net factor income from abroad (NFIA), net unilateral transfers (NUT), and current account (CA)

   b. Financial account (FA)

   c. Official settlements balance (OSB), referred to as "U.S. official reserve assets" and "Foreign official assets in the U.S."

   d. Nonreserve financial account (NRFA)

   e. Balance of payments (BOP). Note that this may not equal zero because of statistical discrepancy. Verify that the discrepancy is the same as the one reported by the BEA.

7. Continuing from the previous question, find nominal GDP for the United States in 2015 (you can find it elsewhere on the BEA site). Use this information along with your previous calculations to answer the following:

   a. Compute gross national expenditure (GNE), gross national income (GNI), and gross national disposable income (GNDI).

   b. In macroeconomics, we often assume the U.S. economy is a closed economy when building models that describe how changes in policy and shocks affect the economy. Based on the previous data (BOP and GDP), do you think this is a reasonable assumption to make? Do international transactions account for a large share of total transactions (involving goods and services, or income) involving the United States?

8. During the 1980s, the United States experienced "twin deficits" in the current account and government budget. Since 1998 the U.S. current account deficit has grown steadily along with rising government budget deficits. Do government budget deficits lead to current account deficits? Identify other possible sources of the current account deficits. Do current account deficits necessarily indicate problems in the economy?

9. Consider the economy of Opulenza. In Opulenza, domestic investment of $400 million earned $15 million in capital gains during 2009. Opulenzans purchased $160 million in new foreign assets during the year; foreigners purchased $120 million in Opulenzan assets. Assume that the valuation effects total $5 million in capital gains.

   a. Compute the change in domestic wealth in Opulenza.

   b. Compute the change in external wealth for Opulenza.

   c. Compute the total change in wealth for Opulenza.

   d. Compute domestic savings for Opulenza.

   e. Compute Opulenza's current account. Is the CA in deficit or surplus?

   f. Explain the intuition for the CA deficit/surplus in terms of savings in Opulenza, financial flows, and its domestic/external wealth position.

   g. How would an appreciation in Opulenza's currency affect its domestic, external, and total wealth? Assume that foreign assets owned by Opulenzans are denominated in foreign currency.

10. This question asks you to compute valuation effects for the United States in 2018, using the same methods mentioned in the chapter. Use the bea.gov website to collect the data needed for this question: look under the "International" heading.

    Visit the BEA's balance of payments data page and obtain the U.S. balance of payments for 2018 in billions of dollars. Be sure to get the correct year, and annual data, not quarterly.

    Visit the BEA's net international investment position data page and obtain the U.S. net international investment position for end 2017 to end 2018.

    a. What was the U.S. current account for 2018?

    b. What was the U.S. financial account for 2018?

    c. What was the U.S. change in external wealth for 2018?

    d. What was the U.S. total valuation effect for 2018?

    e. Does the answer to part (c) equal the answer to part (b) plus the answer to part (d)? Why?

    f. What do the BEA data indicate was the U.S. valuation effect due to exchange rate changes for 2018?

11. Go to the UN website and find out what the Millennium Development Goals are (http://www .un.org/millenniumgoals). Go to the Gleneagles summit documents and examine the promises made (http://www.g8.utoronto.ca/summit/2005gleneagles /index.html). Use the web to check up on how well these G8 promises are being kept, such as the UN goal of 0.7% of GDP in official development assistance, the promise to eradicate export subsidies, and the aim to double aid by 2010. It is now more than ten years on from 2010: has anything improved since then in terms of these commitments? (*Hint:* Search for Internet sites such as Oxfam or the Jubilee Debt Campaign, or look for the World Bank Tools for Monitoring the Millennium Development Goals.)

APPENDIX
External Wealth and Total Wealth

In this chapter, we studied external wealth, but individuals and countries care about their total wealth. How does external wealth relate to total wealth?

External wealth is only part of a country's *total wealth*, the sum of the home capital stock (all nonfinancial assets in the home economy, denoted K) plus amounts owed to home by foreigners (A) minus amounts owed foreigners by home (L):

$$\text{Total wealth} = \underbrace{K}_{\substack{\text{Home nonfinancial} \\ \text{assets}}} + \underbrace{(A-L)}_{\text{External wealth}}$$

In this definition, note that we deliberately exclude financial assets owed by one home entity to another home entity because in the aggregate these cancel out and form no part of a country's total wealth.

Changes in the value of total wealth can then be written as follows:

$$\begin{bmatrix} \text{Change in} \\ \text{total wealth} \end{bmatrix} = \underbrace{\begin{bmatrix} \text{Additions} \\ \text{to } K \end{bmatrix} + \begin{bmatrix} \text{Additions} \\ \text{to } A-L \end{bmatrix}}_{\text{Additions (acquisitions minus disposals)}} + \underbrace{\begin{bmatrix} \text{Capital gains} \\ \text{on } K \end{bmatrix} + \begin{bmatrix} \text{Capital gains} \\ \text{on } A-L \end{bmatrix}}_{\text{Valuation effects (gains minus losses)}}$$

There are two kinds of terms in this expression. The total value of wealth (of a person or a country) may change due to *additions* of assets (such as purchases, sales, or net gifts) or due to valuation effects (capital gains—or, if they are negative, capital losses—arising from changes in the prices of assets).

The previous equation can be simplified by two observations. First, additions to the domestic capital stock K have a simpler expression: they are known as investment, denoted I. (Strictly, this is the gross addition to the capital stock; the net addition would require the subtraction of depreciation, and in the previous notation that would be accounted for under valuation effects since depreciating assets fall in value.)

Second, additions to external wealth, $A - L$, also have a simpler expression: they are equal to net additions to external assets minus net additions to external liabilities, and as we saw in the main chapter, these are equal to *minus* the financial account, $-FA$.

Substituting, we can rewrite the last equation as

$$\begin{bmatrix} \text{Change in} \\ \text{total wealth} \end{bmatrix} = \underbrace{I}_{\substack{\text{Additions to } K \\ = \\ \text{Additions to} \\ \text{assets in the} \\ \text{home economy}}} + \underbrace{(-FA)}_{\substack{\text{Additions to} \\ A-L \\ = \\ \text{Net import of} \\ \text{assets into the} \\ \text{home economy}}} + \underbrace{\begin{bmatrix} \text{Capital gains} \\ \text{on } K \end{bmatrix} + \begin{bmatrix} \text{Capital gains} \\ \text{on } A-L \end{bmatrix}}_{\text{Valuation effects (gains minus losses)}}$$

Now, using the BOP identity, we know that $CA + KA + FA = 0$ so that minus the financial account $-FA$ must equal $CA + KA$; hence, we can rewrite the last equation as

$$\begin{bmatrix} \text{Change in} \\ \text{total wealth} \end{bmatrix} = I + CA + KA + \underbrace{\begin{bmatrix} \text{Capital gains} \\ \text{on } K \end{bmatrix} + \begin{bmatrix} \text{Capital gains} \\ \text{on } A-L \end{bmatrix}}_{\text{Valuation effects (gains minus losses)}}$$

Notice what has happened here. The BOP identity makes the connection between external asset trade and activity in the current account. We take the connection one step further using the current account identity, $S = I + CA$, which allows us to write

$$\begin{bmatrix} \text{Change in} \\ \text{total wealth} \end{bmatrix} = S + KA + \underbrace{\begin{bmatrix} \text{Capital gains} \\ \text{on } K \end{bmatrix} + \begin{bmatrix} \text{Capital gains} \\ \text{on } A - L \end{bmatrix}}_{\text{Valuation effects (gains minus losses)}}$$

The message of this expression is clear. As we all probably know from personal experience, there are only three ways to get more (or less) wealthy: do more (or less) saving (S), receive (or give) gifts of assets (KA), or enjoy the good (bad) fortune of capital gains (losses) on your portfolio. What is true about individuals' wealth is also true for the wealth of a nation in the aggregate.

6

Balance of Payments I: The Gains from Financial Globalization

Save for a rainy day.

Make hay while the sun shines.

Don't put all your eggs in one basket.

Questions to Consider

1 How can countries use the balance of payments to make consumption smoother?

2 How can countries use the balance of payments to make more efficient investments?

3 How can countries use the balance of payments to better diversify against risk?

How does your household cope with economic shocks and the financial challenges they pose? Let's take an extreme example. Suppose you are self-employed and own a business. A severe storm appears and a flood overwhelms your town. This is bad news on several fronts. As people recover from the disaster, businesses, including yours, suffer and your income is lower for several months. If your business premises are damaged, you must also plan to make new investments to repair the damage.

If you have no financial dealings with anyone, your household, as a little closed economy, faces a difficult trade-off as your income falls. Your household income has to equal its consumption plus investment. Would you try to maintain your level of consumption, and neglect the need to invest in repairs? Or would you invest, and let your household suffer as you cut back drastically on consumption? Faced with an emergency like this, most of us look for help beyond our own household, if we can: we might hope for transfers (gifts from friends and family, or emergency relief payments from the government or a charity), or we might rely on financial markets (dip into savings, apply for a loan, rely on an insurance payout, etc.).

What does this story have to do with international economics? If we redraw the boundaries of this experiment and expand from the household unit to the local, regional, and finally national level, the same logic applies. Countries face shocks all the time, and how they are able to cope with them depends on whether they are open or closed to economic interactions with other nations.

To get a sense of how countries can deal with shocks, we can look at data from Caribbean and Central American countries that have faced the same kinds of shock as the household we just described. Every year many tropical storms, some of them of hurricane strength, sweep through this region. The storms are large—hundreds of miles across—and most countries in the region are much smaller in size, some no more than little islets. For them, a hurricane is the town flood blown up to a national scale. The worst storms cause widespread destruction and loss of life.

Hurricanes are tragic human events, but they provide an opportunity for research. Economists study them because such an "act of God"—in economics jargon, a "natural experiment"—provides a laboratory-like test of economic theory. Figure 6-1 shows the average macroeconomic response in these countries after they were hit by a hurricane. In the aftermath, these countries do some of the things we would expect households to do: accept nonmarket gifts (transfers from foreign countries) and borrow (by running a current account deficit). If we subtract nonmarket transfers and examine market behavior alone, the patterns are striking. Measured as a fraction of GDP, investment is typically 3% to 6% higher than normal in the three years during and after a hurricane, and saving is 1% to 5% lower (excluding transfers). Combining the two effects, the current account (saving minus investment) falls dramatically and is 6% to 10% more in deficit than normal.

Hurricanes are extreme examples of economic shocks. They are not representative of the normal fluctuations that countries experience, but the size and randomness of the hurricanes allow us to look at nations' macroeconomic responses to such shocks. These responses illustrate some of the financial mechanisms that help open economies cope with all types of shocks, large and small, natural or human in origin.

In this chapter, we see how financially open economies can, in theory, benefit from financial globalization. We first look at the factors that limit international borrowing and lending. Then, in the remaining sections of the chapter, we see how a nation's ability to use international financial markets allows it to accomplish three different goals:

- consumption smoothing (maintaining stable consumption as income fluctuates);
- efficient investment (borrowing to build productive capital); and
- diversification of risk (by trading of stocks between countries).

FIGURE 6-1

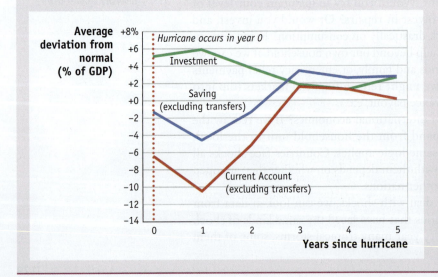

The Macroeconomics of Hurricanes The figure shows the average response (excluding transfers) of investment, saving, and the current account in a sample of Caribbean and Central American countries in the years during and after severe hurricane damage. The responses are as expected: investment rises (to rebuild) and saving falls (to limit the fall in consumption); hence, the current account moves sharply toward deficit.

Note: Transfers are excluded from saving and the current account, and the saving measure is calculated as $S - NUT = I + CA - NUT$.

Data from: John C. Bluedorn, 2005, "Hurricanes: Intertemporal Trade and Capital Shocks," Oxford Economics Working Paper No. 2005-241.

Along the way, we look at how well the theoretical gains from financial globalization translate into reality and find that many of these gains have yet to be realized. In advanced countries, the gains from financial globalization appear to be large and easier to obtain, but in poorer countries the gains may be smaller and harder to realize. We want to understand why these differences exist, and what risks may arise for poor countries that attempt to capture the gains from financial globalization.

1 The Limits on How Much a Country Can Borrow: The Long-Run Budget Constraint

Our introductory examples show how borrowing can help countries (like households) better cope with shocks. But, also like households, there is a limit to how much a country can borrow and how much lenders will lend. Understanding the constraints on how countries might borrow and lend to each other is our first task in this chapter. With this understanding we can then examine how financial globalization shapes the economic choices available to a country as economic conditions change over time. The ability to borrow in times of need and lend in times of prosperity has profound effects on a country's well-being.

Hurricane Mitch battered Central America from October 22, 1998, to November 5, 1998. It was the deadliest hurricane in more than 200 years and the second deadliest ever recorded.

When we study an economy as it evolves over time, we are taking a *dynamic* (or *intertemporal*) approach to macroeconomics—rather than a *static* approach, which looks at the state of the economy at one specific time. One key to the dynamic approach is that we must keep track of how a country manages its wealth to see if it is doing so in a way that is sustainable in the long run. The intertemporal approach makes use of the key lessons from the end of the last chapter, which taught us how to account for the change in a nation's external wealth from one period to the next. Recall that a home country's external wealth (or net worth) with respect to the rest of the world (ROW) is all of the ROW assets owned by the home country (home claims against foreigners) minus all of the home assets owned by ROW (foreigners' claims against Home).

In this section, we use changes in an open economy's external wealth to determine its **long-run budget constraint (LRBC)**, the limit to how much a nation can borrow in the long run. The LRBC tells us precisely how and why a country must, in the long run, "live within its means." A country's ability to adjust its external wealth through borrowing and lending provides a buffer against economic shocks, but the LRBC places a limit on the use of this buffer.

To develop some intuition, let's look at a simple household analogy. This year (year 0) you borrow $100,000 from the bank at an interest rate of 10% annually. You have no other wealth and inflation is zero. There are two possible ways in which you can deal with your debt in each subsequent year.

Case 1 *A debt that is serviced.* Every year you pay the 10% interest due on the principal amount of the loan, $10,000, but you never pay any principal. At the end of each year, the bank renews (or rolls over) the loan, and your wealth remains constant at −$100,000.

Case 2 *A debt that is not serviced.* You pay neither interest nor principal and ask the bank to roll over the principal *plus* the interest due on it each year. In year 1, the overdue 10% interest is $10,000, and your debt grows by 10% to $110,000. In year 2, the overdue interest is 10% of $110,000, or $11,000, and your debt grows by 10% again to $121,000. Assuming this process goes on and on, your level of debt grows by 10% every year.

Case 2 is not sustainable. If the bank allows it, your debt level will explode to infinity as it grows by 10% every year forever. In the long run, lenders will simply not allow the debt to grow indefinitely without any servicing. Indeed, the requirement that a debt be serviced is the essence of the LRBC, as we see in the next section.

How the Long-Run Budget Constraint Is Determined

As is usual when building an economic model, we start with a basic model that makes a number of simplifying assumptions, but yields lessons that can be extended to more complex cases. Here are the assumptions we make about various conditions that affect our model of the long-run budget constraint:

- Prices are perfectly flexible. Under this assumption, all analysis in this chapter can be conducted in terms of real variables, and all monetary aspects of the economy can be ignored. (To adjust for inflation and convert to real terms, we could divide all nominal quantities by an index of prices.)

- The country is a **small open economy**. The country trades goods and services with the rest of the world through exports and imports and can lend or borrow overseas, but only by issuing or buying debt (bonds). Because it is small, the country cannot influence prices in world markets for goods and services.

- All debt carries a real interest rate r^*, the **world real interest rate**, which we assume to be constant. Because the country is small, it takes the world real interest rate as given, and we assume the country can lend or borrow an unlimited amount at this interest rate.

- The country pays a real interest rate r^* on its start-of-period debt liabilities L and is paid the same interest rate r^* on its start-of-period debt assets A. In any period, the country earns net interest income payments (i.e., factor income for owners of financial capital) equal to r^*A minus r^*L or, more simply, r^*W, where W is external wealth $(A - L)$ at the start of the period, and external wealth may vary over time.

- Thus, r^*W here corresponds to net factor income from abroad (NFIA) as recorded in the current account, because for simplicity we assume that there is no cross-border income to labor or other factors. We will also further assume that there are no unilateral transfers ($NUT = 0$), no capital transfers ($KA = 0$), and no capital gains on external wealth. Under the assumptions we have made, there are only two nonzero items in the current account: the trade balance (TB) and net factor income from abroad, r^*W. If r^*W is positive, the country is earning interest, and in this case it must be a lender/creditor with positive external wealth W. Similarly, if r^*W is negative, the country is paying interest and must be a borrower/debtor with negative external wealth W.

Calculating the Change in Wealth Each Period In Chapter 5, we saw that the change in a country's external wealth is the sum of three terms: the current account, the capital account, and capital gains on external wealth. In the special case we are studying, we have assumed that the last two terms are zero. We have also assumed that the country's current account is the sum of just two terms: TB, its trade balance, plus r^*W, the net interest payments the country receives on the external wealth it held at the end of the last period.

Mathematically, we can write the change in external wealth from end of year $N - 1$ to end of year N as follows (where subscripts denote periods, here years):

$$\Delta W_N = \underbrace{W_N - W_{N-1}}_{\substack{\text{Change in external} \\ \text{wealth this period}}} = \underbrace{TB_N}_{\substack{\text{Trade balance} \\ \text{this period}}} + \underbrace{r^*W_{N-1}}_{\substack{\text{Interest paid/received on} \\ \text{last period's external wealth}}}$$

In this simplified world, a nation's external wealth can change for only two reasons: changes in the current-period trade balance, or changes in interest received or paid on last period's external wealth (net factor income).

Calculating Future Wealth Levels Now that we have a formula for wealth changes, and assuming we know the initial level of wealth in year $N - 1$, we can compute the level of wealth at any time in the future by repeated application of the formula.

To find wealth at the end of year N, we rearrange the preceding equation:

$$\underbrace{W_N}_{\substack{\text{External wealth at}\\\text{the end of this period}}} = \underbrace{TB_N}_{\substack{\text{Trade balance}\\\text{this period}}} + \underbrace{(1+r^*)W_{N-1}}_{\substack{\text{Last period's external wealth}\\\text{plus interest paid/received}}}$$

This equation shows a key result: *wealth at the end of a period* is the sum of two terms: the *trade balance this period* TB_N (which captures the addition to wealth from net exports, exports minus imports) plus *wealth at the end of last period* $(1+r^*)$ *times* W_{N-1} (which captures the wealth from last period plus the interest earned on that wealth). The examples in the following sections will help us understand the changes in a country's external wealth and the role that the trade balance plays.

The Budget Constraint in a Two-Period Example

Let's put what we've learned about changes in external wealth to work in a simplified two-period example. Suppose we start in year 0, so $N = 0$. Suppose further that a country has some initial external wealth from year –1 (an inheritance from the past), and can borrow or lend in the present period (year 0). We also impose the following limit: by the end of year 1, the country must pay off what it has borrowed from other countries and must call in all loans it has made to other countries. That is, the country must end year 1 with zero external wealth.

As we saw in the formula given earlier, $W_0 = (1+r^*)W_{-1} + TB_0$. Wealth at the end of year 0 depends on two things. At the end of year 0, the country carries over from the last period (year –1) its initial wealth level, plus any interest accumulated on it. In addition, if the country runs a trade deficit, it has to run its external wealth down by adding liabilities (borrowing) or cashing in external assets (dissaving); conversely, if the country runs a trade surplus, it lends that amount to the rest of the world.

That's the end of year 0. But where do things stand at the end of year 1? We have stated that the country must have zero external wealth at the end of year 1, so how will it achieve that goal?

Applying the preceding formula to year 1, we know that $W_1 = 0 = (1+r^*)W_0 + TB_1$. We can then substitute $W_0 = (1+r^*)W_{-1} + TB_0$ into this formula to find that

$$W_1 = 0 = (1+r^*)^2 W_{-1} + (1+r^*)TB_0 + TB_1$$

This equation shows that two years later at the end of year 1 the country has accumulated wealth equal to the trade balance in years 0 and 1 $(TB_0 + TB_1)$, plus one year of interest earned (or paid) on the year 0 trade balance (r^*TB_0), plus the two years of interest and principal earned (or paid) on its initial wealth $(1+r^*)^2 W_{-1}$.

Because we have stated that the final wealth level W_1 must be zero, the right-hand side of the last equation must be zero, too. For that to be the case, the trade balances in year 0 (TB_0) and in year 1 (TB_1) (plus any accumulated interest) must be equal and opposite to initial wealth (W_{-1}) (plus any accumulated interest):

$$-(1+r^*)^2 W_{-1} = (1+r^*)TB_0 + TB_1$$

This equation is the *two-period budget constraint*. This is a special case of the long-run budget constraint, one which assumes that no wealth (or debt) is carried forward for any later periods. It tells us that a creditor country with positive initial wealth (left-hand-side negative) will run trade deficits "on average" in present and future periods, to run down its assets; conversely, a debtor country (left-hand-side positive) will run trade surpluses "on average" in present and future periods, to pay off its debts.

Present Value Form Dividing the previous equation by $(1+r^*)$ gives us another useful way to express the two-period budget constraint:

$$\underbrace{-(1+r^*)W_{-1}}_{\substack{\text{Minus the present value} \\ \text{of wealth from last period}}} = \underbrace{TB_0 + \frac{TB_1}{(1+r^*)}}_{\substack{\text{Present value of all present} \\ \text{and future trade balances}}}$$

Every element in this statement of the two-period budget constraint represents a quantity expressed in present value terms.

The **present value** of X in period N is the amount that would have to be set aside now so that, with accumulated interest, X is available N periods from now. If the interest rate is r^*, then the present value of X is $X/(1+r^*)^N$. For example, if you are told that you will receive \$121 in the future at the end of year 2 and the interest rate is 10%, then the present value of that \$121 today, in year 0, is \$100 because \$100 × 1.1 (interest earned in year 1) × 1.1 (interest earned in year 2) = \$121.

A Two-Period Example Let's put some numbers into the last equation. Suppose a country starts in debt, with a wealth level of –\$100 million at the end of year–1: W_{-1} = –\$100 million. Question: at a real interest rate of 10%, how can the country satisfy the two-period budget constraint that it must have zero external wealth at the end of year 1? Answer: to pay off the \$110 million (initial debt plus the interest accruing on this debt during period 0) on the left-hand side, the country must ensure that the present value of future trade balances TB is +\$110 million on the right-hand side.

The country can do this in many ways.

- It can pay off its debt at the end of period 0 by running a trade surplus of \$110 million in period 0 and then have balanced trade in period 1.

- It can wait to pay off the debt until the end of period 1 by having balanced trade in period 0 and then running a trade surplus of \$121 million in period 1.

- It can pay off the debt and its accumulated interest through any other combination of trade balances in periods 0 and 1, as long as external wealth at the end of period 1 is zero and the budget constraint is satisfied.

Extending the Theory to the Long Run By extending the two-period model to N periods, and allowing N to run to infinity, we can transform the two-period budget constraint into the long-run budget constraint. Repeating the two-period logic N times, external wealth after N periods is initial wealth and accumulated interest on that wealth (whether positive or negative) plus all intervening trade balances and accumulated interest on those positive or negative trade balances. If external wealth is to be zero at the end of N periods, then the sum of the present values of N present and future trade balances must equal minus the present value of external wealth. If N runs to infinity, we get an infinite sum and arrive at the equation of the LRBC:[1]

---

[1] To get this result, we can take the basic equation for the change in external wealth, $W_0 = (1+r^*)W_{-1} + TB_0$, and apply it N times with repeated substitution to obtain wealth at the end of period N:

$$W_N = (1+r^*)^{N+1}W_{-1} + (1+r^*)^N TB_0 + (1+r^*)^{N-1}TB_1 + (1+r^*)^{N-2}TB_2 + \cdots + (1+r^*)TB_{N-1} + TB_N$$

We can then work toward the LRBC in the text if we divide the previous equation by $(1+r^*)^N$:

$$\frac{W_N}{(1+r^*)^N} = (1+r^*)W_{-1} + TB_0 + \frac{TB_1}{(1+r^*)} + \frac{TB_2}{(1+r^*)^2} + \cdots + \frac{TB_N}{(1+r^*)^N}$$

As we saw earlier, external wealth W_N explodes, growing by a factor $(1+r^*)$ every period. To prevent this, external wealth W_N (whether positive or negative) must grow more slowly in the long run than the factor $(1+r^*)^N$. In this case, as N approaches infinity, the left-hand side of the above equation will approach zero. When this is the case, the right-hand side must also approach zero. This tendency of the right-hand side to go to zero in the limit leads directly to the LRBC Equation (6-1) in the text.

$$\text{LRBC: } \underbrace{-(1+r^*)W_{-1}}_{\substack{\text{Minus the present}\\\text{value of wealth}\\\text{from last period}}} = \underbrace{TB_0 + \frac{TB_1}{(1+r^*)} + \frac{TB_2}{(1+r^*)^2} + \frac{TB_3}{(1+r^*)^3} + \frac{TB_4}{(1+r^*)^4} + \cdots}_{\text{Present value of all present and future trade balances}} \qquad (6\text{-}1)$$

This expression for the LRBC says that a debtor country must have future trade balances that are positive in present value terms so that they offset the country's initially negative wealth. Conversely, a creditor country must have future trade balances that are negative in present value terms so that they offset the country's initially positive wealth. The LRBC is key to our analysis of how countries can lend or borrow because it imposes a condition that rules out choices that would lead to exploding positive or negative external wealth.

A Long-Run Example: The Perpetual Loan

The following example helps us understand the long-run budget constraint, and we can apply it to various cases that we present in the rest of the chapter. It shows us how countries that take out an initial loan must make payments to service that loan in the future.

Suppose that today is year 0 and a country is to pay (e.g., to its creditors) a constant amount X every year starting next year, year 1. What is the present value (PV) of that sequence of payments (X)?

$$PV(X) = \frac{X}{(1+r^*)} + \frac{X}{(1+r^*)^2} + \frac{X}{(1+r^*)^3} + \cdots$$

This expression for $PV(X)$ is an infinite sum. If we multiply this equation by $(1+r^*)$, we obtain

$$PV(X)(1+r^*) = X + \frac{X}{(1+r^*)} + \frac{X}{(1+r^*)^2} + \frac{X}{(1+r^*)^3} + \cdots$$

To find a simple expression for $PV(X)$, we subtract the first equation from the second, cancel out all of the terms on the right except X, then rearrange the remaining equation $r^*PV(X) = X$ to arrive at:

$$\underbrace{\frac{X}{(1+r^*)} + \frac{X}{(1+r^*)^2} + \frac{X}{(1+r^*)^3} + \cdots}_{PV(X)} = \frac{X}{r^*} \qquad (6\text{-}2)$$

This formula helps us compute $PV(X)$ for any stream of constant payments, something we often need to do to verify the long-run budget constraint.

For example, if the constant payment is $X = 100$ and the interest rate is 5% ($r^* = 0.05$), Equation (6-2) says that the present value of a stream of payments of 100 starting in year 1 is $100/0.05 = 2,000$:

$$\frac{100}{(1+0.05)} + \frac{100}{(1+0.05)^2} + \frac{100}{(1+0.05)^3} + \cdots = \frac{100}{0.05} = 2,000$$

This example, which we will often revisit later in this chapter, shows the stream of interest payments on a **perpetual loan** (i.e., an interest-only loan or, equivalently, a sequence of loans for which *only* the principal is refinanced or rolled over every year). If the amount loaned by the creditor is $2,000 in year 0, and this principal amount is outstanding forever, then the interest that must be paid each year to service the debt is 5% of $2,000, or $100. If the loan payments are always fully serviced, the present value of the future interest payments equals the value of the amount loaned in year 0 and the LRBC is satisfied.

Implications of the LRBC for Gross National Expenditure and Gross Domestic Product

In economics, a budget constraint always tells us something about the limits to expenditure, whether for a person, firm, or government. The LRBC is no different—it tells us that in the long run, a country's expenditure (GNE) is limited by how much it produces (GDP).

To see why this is true, recall from Chapter 5 that the trade balance is the difference between gross domestic product and gross national expenditure, $TB = GDP - GNE$. If we insert this expression into the LRBC equation (6-1) and collect terms, we see that

$$\underbrace{\underbrace{(1+r^*)W_{-1}}_{\substack{\text{Present value of} \\ \text{wealth from} \\ \text{last period}}} + \underbrace{GDP_0 + \frac{GDP_1}{(1+r^*)} + \frac{GDP_2}{(1+r^*)^2} + \cdots}_{\text{Present value of present and future GDP}}}_{\text{Present value of the country's resources}} \qquad (6\text{-}3)$$

$$= \underbrace{GNE_0 + \frac{GNE_1}{(1+r^*)} + \frac{GNE_2}{(1+r^*)^2} + \cdots}_{\substack{\text{Present value of present and future GNE} \\ = \\ \text{Present value of the country's spending}}}$$

The left side of this equation is the present value of the country's resources in the long run: the present value of any inherited wealth plus the present value of present and future product as measured by GDP. The right side is the present value of all present and future spending ($C + I + G$) as measured by GNE.

We have arrived at the following, very important, result: *the long-run budget constraint (LRBC) says that in the long run, in present value terms, a country's expenditures (GNE) must equal its production (GDP) plus any initial wealth.* The LRBC states that an economy must live within its means in the long run.

Summary

The key lesson of our intertemporal model is that a closed economy is subject to a tighter budget constraint than an open economy. In a closed economy, "living within your means" requires a country to have balanced trade each and every year. In an open economy, "living within your means" requires only that a country must maintain a balance between its trade deficits and surpluses that satisfies the long-run budget constraint—they must balance only in a present value sense, rather than year by year.

This conclusion implies that an open economy should be able to do better (or at least no worse) than a closed economy in achieving its desired pattern of expenditure over time. This is the essence of the theoretical argument that there are gains from financial globalization.

In the next section, we examine this argument in greater detail and consider under what circumstances it is valid in the real world. First, however, we consider some situations in which the assumptions of the model might need to be modified.

APPLICATION

The Favorable Situation of the United States

Two assumptions greatly simplified our intertemporal model. We assumed that the same real rate of interest r^* applied to income received on assets and income paid on liabilities, and we assumed that there were no capital gains on external wealth. However, these assumptions do not hold true for the United States.

"Exorbitant Privilege" Since the 1980s, the United States has been the world's largest-ever net debtor with $W = A - L < 0$. Under the model's simplifying assumptions, negative external wealth would lead to a deficit on net factor income from abroad with $r^*W = r^*(A - L) < 0$. And yet as we saw in the last chapter, U.S. net factor income from abroad has been positive throughout this period! How can this be?

The only way a net debtor can earn positive net interest income is by receiving a higher rate of interest on its assets than it pays on its liabilities. The data show that this has been consistently true for the United States since the 1960s. The interest the United States has received on its assets has been higher by about 1.5 to 2 percentage points per year on average (with a slight downward trend) than the interest it pays on its liabilities.

To develop a framework to make sense of this finding, suppose the United States receives interest at the world real interest rate r^* on its external assets but pays interest at a lower rate r^0 on its liabilities. Then its net factor income from abroad is $r^*A - r^0L = r^*W + (r^* - r^0)L$. The final term, the interest rate difference times total liabilities, is an income bonus the United States earns as a "banker to the world"—like any other bank, it borrows low and lends high.

Understandably, the rest of the world may resent this state of affairs from time to time. In the 1960s French officials complained about the United States' "exorbitant privilege" of being able to borrow cheaply by issuing external liabilities in the form of reserve assets (Treasury debt) while earning higher returns on U.S. external assets such as foreign equity and foreign direct investment. This conclusion is not borne out in the data, however. U.S. Bureau of Economic Analysis (BEA) data suggest that most of the interest rate difference is due not to the low interest paid on Treasury debt, but to the low interest rate on U.S. equity liabilities (i.e., low profits earned on foreign investment in the United States).[2]

"Manna from Heaven" The difference between interest earned and interest paid isn't the only deviation from our simple model that benefits the United States. BEA statistics reveal that the country has long enjoyed positive capital gains, KG, on its external wealth. This gain, which started in the 1980s, comes from a difference of two percentage points between large capital gains on several types of external assets and smaller capital losses on external liabilities.

It is hard to pin down the source of these capital gains because the BEA data suggest that these effects are not the result of price or exchange rate effects, and they just reflect capital gains that cannot be otherwise measured. As a result, the accuracy and meaning of these measurements are controversial. Some skeptics call these capital gains "statistical manna from heaven." Others think these gains are real and may reflect the United States acting as a kind of "venture capitalist to the world." As with the "exorbitant privilege," this financial gain for the United States is a loss for the rest of the world.[3]

---

[2] John Kitchen, 2007, "Sharecroppers or Shrewd Capitalists? Projections of the U.S. Current Account, International Income Flows, and Net International Debt," *Review of International Economics*, 15(5), 1036–1061; Barry Bosworth, Susan M. Collins, and Gabriel Chodorow-Reich, 2007, "Returns on FDI: Does the US Really Do Better?" *Brookings Trade Forum*, 177–210.

[3] William R. Cline, 2005, *The United States as a Debtor Nation* (Washington, D.C.: Institute for International Economics and Center for Global Development); Pierre-Olivier Gourinchas and Hélène Rey, 2007, "From World Banker to World Venture Capitalist: US External Adjustment and the Exorbitant Privilege," in *G7 Current Account Imbalances: Sustainability and Adjustment*, ed. Richard Clarida (Chicago: University of Chicago Press).

Summary When we add the 2% capital gain differential to the 1.5% interest differential, we end up with a U.S. total return differential (interest plus capital gains) of about 3.5% per year on average since the 1980s. For comparison, in the same period, the total return differential was close to zero in every other G7 country.

To include the effects of the total return differential in our model, we have to incorporate the effect of the extra "bonuses" on external wealth as well as the conventional terms that reflect the trade balance and interest payments:

$$\underbrace{\Delta W_N = W_N - W_{N-1}}_{\substack{\text{Change in}\\\text{external wealth}\\\text{this period}}} = \underbrace{\underbrace{TB_N}_{\substack{\text{Trade}\\\text{balance}\\\text{this period}}} + \underbrace{r^*W_{N-1}}_{\substack{\text{Interest paid/received}\\\text{on last period's}\\\text{external wealth}}}}_{\text{Conventional effects}} + \underbrace{\underbrace{(r^* - r^0)L}_{\substack{\text{Income due to}\\\text{interest rate}\\\text{differential}}} + \underbrace{KG}_{\substack{\text{Capital gains}\\\text{on external}\\\text{wealth}}}}_{\text{Additional effects}}$$

Too Good to Be True? With this equation, the implications of the final two terms become clearer for the U.S. economy. When positive, they offset wealth losses due to trade deficits. Thus, if these terms increase in value by 1% of GDP, for example, then the United States could run an additional 1% of GDP in trade deficit forever and still satisfy its LRBC.

As Figure 6-2 shows, the United States has benefited greatly from these offsets in recent years, with their contributions to external wealth averaging 1.8% of GDP per year in the period 1985–94 and as much as 2.5% of GDP in 2005–14. These large offsets have led some economists to take a relaxed view of the swollen U.S. trade deficit

---

FIGURE 6-2

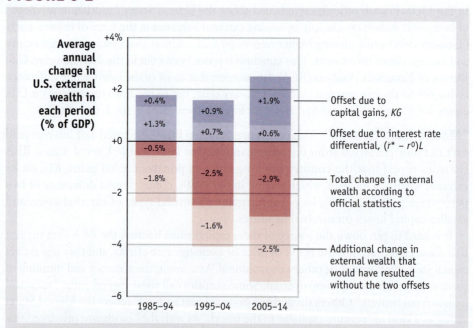

How Favorable Interest Rates and Capital Gains on External Wealth Help the United States The total average annual change in U.S. external wealth each period is shown by the dark red columns. Negative changes were offset in part by two positive effects. One effect was due to the favorable interest rate differentials on U.S. assets (high) versus liabilities (low). The other effect was due to favorable rates of capital gains on U.S. assets (high) versus liabilities (low). Without these two offsetting effects, the declines in U.S. external wealth would have been much bigger.

Note: Interest rate differential effects are computed assuming that counterfactual liability yields would have been equal to asset yields. Capital gains are computed as the difference between financial flows and changes in external wealth.

Data from: U.S. Bureau of Economic Analysis, Balance of Payments Accounts, and Net International Investment Position.

because the offsets finance a large chunk of the country's trade deficit—with luck, in perpetuity.[4] However, we may not be able to count on these offsets forever: longer-run evidence suggests that they are not stable and may be diminishing over time.[5]

Others warn that, given the likely presence of errors in these data, we really have no idea what is going on. In 2006 economist Daniel Gros calculated that the United States had borrowed $5,500 billion over 20 years, even though its external wealth had fallen by "only" $2,800 billion. Have $2.7 trillion dollars been mislaid? Gros argued that most of this difference can be attributed to poor U.S. measurement of the assets foreigners own and investment earnings foreigners receive. Correcting these errors would make all of the additional offset terms disappear—and roughly double the estimated current level of U.S. net indebtedness to the rest of the world.[6]

APPLICATION

The Difficult Situation of the Emerging Markets

The previous application showed that the simple intertemporal model may not work for the United States. In this section, we see that its assumptions may also not work for emerging markets and developing countries.

As in the U.S. example, the first assumption we might question is that these nations face the same real interest rate on assets and liabilities. The United States borrows low and lends high. For most poorer countries, the opposite is true. Because of country risk, investors typically expect a risk premium before they will buy any assets issued by these countries, whether government debt, private debt or equity, or foreign direct investments.

Figure 6-3 plots historical government credit ratings, from the rating agency Standard & Poor's (S&P), against public debt levels, as a share of GDP, for a large sample of countries. These data are for years prior to the financial crisis of 2008 and the Great Recession, but the example shows that bond ratings are correlated with risk premiums. At the top of the figure are the advanced countries whose bonds were then rated AA or better. Before the financial crisis, almost all the advanced countries had very high credit ratings and moderate debt levels; after the financial crisis and Great Recession, this rapidly changed for some advanced countries as debt rapidly ballooned and credit ratings fell, with some starting to resemble emerging markets.

In previous years, all advanced-country bonds carried very-small-risk premiums because investors were confident that these countries would repay their debts. In addition, the risk premiums did not increase markedly even as these countries went further into debt, as shown by the line of best fit for this subsample. In the bottom half of the figure, we see that emerging markets and developing countries inhabited a very different world. They had worse credit ratings and correspondingly higher-risk premiums. Only about half of the government bonds issued by these countries were considered investment grade (BBB– and above); the rest were considered junk bonds. Investors demanded extra profit as compensation for the perceived risks of investing in many of these countries.

Figure 6-3 also shows that in poorer countries ratings deteriorated rapidly as debt levels rose, an effect that was much stronger than in the advanced countries, as

---

[4] Ricardo Hausmann and Federico Sturzenegger, "'Dark Matter' Makes the US Deficit Disappear," *Financial Times*, December 7, 2005.
[5] Christopher M. Meissner and Alan M. Taylor, 2008, "Losing Our Marbles in the New Century? The Great Rebalancing in Historical Perspective," in *Global Imbalances and the Evolving World Economy*, ed. J. S. Little (Boston: Federal Reserve Bank of Boston).
[6] Daniel Gros, "Discrepancies in US Accounts Hide Black Hole," *Financial Times*, June 14, 2006.

FIGURE 6-3

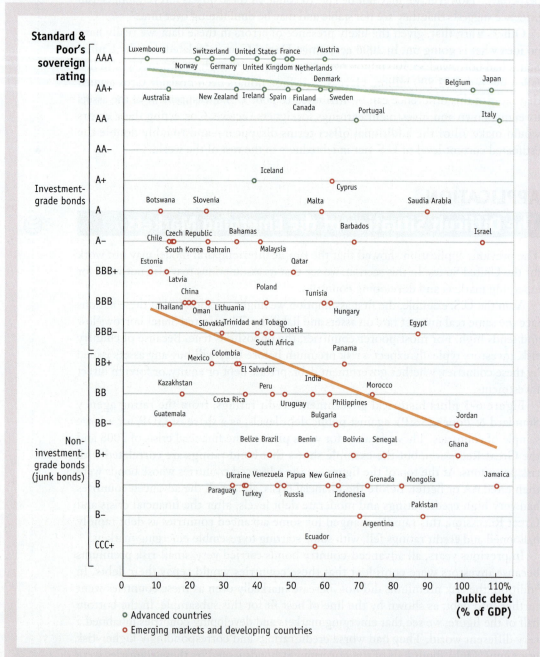

Sovereign Ratings and Public Debt Levels: Advanced Countries Versus Emerging Markets and Developing Countries The data shown are for the period from 1995 to 2005. The advanced countries (green) are at the top of the chart. Their credit ratings (vertical axis) do not drop very much in response to an increase in debt levels (horizontal axis). And ratings are always high investment grade. The emerging markets and developing countries (orange) are at the bottom of the graph. Their ratings are low or junk, and their ratings deteriorate as debt levels rise.

Note: The data shown are from the period before the global financial crisis. Since that event, many advanced countries have seen large increases in public debt and ratings downgrades, and in some cases the impacts have been serious, e.g., Iceland, Ireland, Portugal, and Spain.

Data from: Inter-American Development Bank, 2006, "How to Live with Debt," Ideas for Development in the Americas 11 (September–December), Figure 2.

revealed by the steeper line of best fit. These observations illustrate the more stringent limits to borrowing that typically face poorer countries: as debt levels rise, perceived creditworthiness drops off quickly, and the cost of borrowing becomes prohibitive, if it is possible at all.

This brings us to the other assumption of the simple model that sometimes fails to hold in poorer countries, the assumption that the country can borrow or lend as much as it wants at the prevailing world real interest rate. On the lending side, it usually isn't a problem to save as much as you want. On the borrowing side, however, lenders often tell borrowers that they have reached a debt limit and can borrow no more. When that happens, access to external credit ceases, and anything additional a country wants to consume or invest has to be taken out of its own income.

Figure 6-4 illustrates the remarkable frequency with which emerging market countries experience this kind of isolation from global capital markets. Research by economists Guillermo Calvo and Carmen Reinhart has focused attention on the sometimes fickle "stop-start" nature of external finance, especially in emerging markets.[7] In a **sudden stop**, a borrower country sees its financial account surplus rapidly shrink (suddenly nobody wants to buy any more of its domestic assets) and so the current account deficit also must shrink (because there is now no way to finance a trade imbalance). Reaching a debt limit can be a jolting macroeconomic shock for any economy, because it requires sudden and possibly large adjustments to national expenditure and its composition. Most seriously, output may drop if domestic investment is curtailed as a result of lack of access to external credit. As the constraints arising from hitting a debt limit start to bite, the upside of financial globalization recedes, and the downside of macroeconomic and financial instability may take its place. In later chapters, we examine why credit market disruptions happen by looking in more detail at financial problems, crises, and default (the latter is discussed in the supplementary online Chapter 11).

FIGURE 6-4

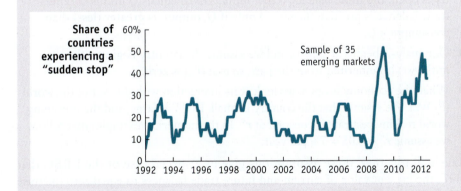

Sudden Stops in Emerging Markets On occasion, capital flows can suddenly stop, meaning that those who wish to borrow anew or roll over an existing loan will be unable to obtain financing. These capital market shutdowns occur frequently in emerging markets.

Data from: Guillermo A. Calvo, Alejandro Izquierdo, and Luis-Fernando Mejía, 2004, "On the Empirics of Sudden Stops: The Relevance of Balance-Sheet Effects," NBER Working Paper No. 10520, and subsequent updates from the authors.

---

[7] On the disruptions and costs caused by sudden stops, see Guillermo Calvo and Carmen M. Reinhart, 2000, "When Capital Inflows Suddenly Stop: Consequences and Policy Options," in *Reforming the International Monetary and Financial System*, ed. Peter B. Kenen and Alexander K. Swoboda (Washington, D.C.: International Monetary Fund), pp. 175–201; Pablo E. Guidotti, Federico Sturzenegger, and Agustín Villar, 2004, "On the Consequences of Sudden Stops," *Economía*, 4(2), 171–214; Michael M. Hutchison and Ilan Noy, 2006, "Sudden Stops and the Mexican Wave: Currency Crises, Capital Flow Reversals and Output Loss in Emerging Markets," *Journal of Development Economics*, 79(1), 225–248.

2 Gains from Consumption Smoothing

In the next two sections of this chapter, we bring together the long-run budget constraint and a simplified model of an economy to see how gains from financial globalization can be achieved in theory. First, we focus on the gains that result when an open economy uses external borrowing and lending to eliminate undesirable fluctuations in aggregate consumption.

The Basic Model

We retain all of the assumptions we made when developing the long-run budget constraint (LRBC). There are no international transfers of income or capital, and the price level is perfectly flexible, so all nominal values are also real values, and so on. We also adopt some additional assumptions. These hold whether the economy is closed or open.

- The economy's GDP or output is denoted Q. It is produced each period using labor as the only input. Production of GDP may be subject to shocks; depending on the shock, the same amount of labor input may yield different amounts of output.

- Households, which consume, are identical. This means we can think of a representative household, and use the terms "household" and "country" interchangeably. The country/household prefers a level of consumption C that is constant over time, or smooth. This level of smooth consumption must be consistent with the country/household's LRBC.

- To keep the rest of the model simple—for now—we assume that consumption is the only source of demand, and that both investment I and government spending G are zero. Under these assumptions, GNE equals personal consumption expenditures C. In this simple case, if the country is open, the trade balance (GDP minus GNE) equals Q minus C. The trade balance is positive (negative) only if Q, output, is greater (less) than consumption C.

- Our analysis begins at time 0, and we assume the country begins with zero initial wealth inherited from the past, so that W_{-1} is zero.

- When the economy is open, we look at its interaction with the rest of the world (ROW). We assume that the country is small, ROW is large, and the prevailing world real interest rate is constant at r^*. In the numerical examples that follow, we assume $r^* = 0.05 = 5\%$ per year.

Taken all together, these assumptions give us a special case of the LRBC that requires the present value of current and future trade balances to equal zero (because initial wealth is zero):

$$\underbrace{0}_{\text{Initial wealth is zero}} = \text{Present value of } TB = \underbrace{\text{Present value of } Q}_{\text{Present value of GDP}} - \underbrace{\text{Present value of } C}_{\text{Present value of GNE}}$$

or equivalently,

$$\underbrace{\text{Present value of } Q}_{\text{Present value of GDP}} = \underbrace{\text{Present value of } C}_{\text{Present value of GNE}} \tag{6-4}$$

Remember, this equation says that the LRBC will hold, and the present value of current and future TB will be zero, if and only if the present value of current and future Q equals the present value of current and future C.

Consumption Smoothing: A Numerical Example and Generalization

Now that we've clarified the assumptions for our model, we can explore how countries smooth consumption by examining two cases:

- A closed economy, in which $TB = 0$ in all periods, external borrowing and lending are not possible, and the LRBC is automatically satisfied
- An open economy, in which TB does not have to be zero, borrowing and lending are possible, and we must verify that the LRBC is satisfied

Let's begin with a numerical example that illustrates the gains from consumption smoothing. We will generalize the result later.

Closed Versus Open Economy: No Shocks Table 6-1 provides a numerical example for our model economy when it is closed and experiences no shocks. Output Q is 100 units in each period, and all output is devoted to consumption. The present value of 100 in each period starting in year 0 equals the present value of 100 in year 0, which is simply 100, plus the present value of 100 in every subsequent year, which is $100/0.05 = 2,000$ [using Equation (6-2), from the case of a perpetual loan]. Thus, the present value of present and future output is 2,100.

If this economy were open rather than closed, nothing would be different. The LRBC is satisfied because there is a zero trade balance at all times. Consumption C is perfectly smooth: every year the country consumes all 100 units of its output, and this is the country's preferred consumption path. There are no gains from financial globalization because this open country prefers to consume only what it produces each year, thus has no need to borrow or lend to achieve its preferred consumption path.

Closed Versus Open Economy: Shocks The smooth path for the closed economy cannot be maintained if it suffers shocks to output, such as one of the hurricanes discussed at the start of the chapter. Suppose there is a temporary unanticipated output shock of −21 units in year 0. Output Q falls to 79 in year 0 and then returns to a level of 100 thereafter. The change in the present value of output is the drop of 21 in year 0. The present value of output falls from 2,100 to 2,079, a drop of 1%.

Over time, will consumption in an open economy respond to this shock in the same way closed-economy consumption does? In the closed economy, there is no doubt what happens. Because all output is consumed and there is no possibility of a trade imbalance, consumption necessarily falls to 79 in year 0 and then rises back to 100 in year 1 and stays there forever. The path of consumption is no longer smooth, as shown in Table 6-2.

TABLE 6-1

A Closed or Open Economy with No Shocks Output equals consumption. Trade balance is zero. Consumption is smooth.

				Period					Present Value
		0	1	2	3	4	5	...	($r^* = 0.05$)
Output *GDP*	*Q*	100	100	100	100	100	100	...	2,100
Expenditure *GNE*	*C*	100	100	100	100	100	100	...	2,100
Trade balance	*TB*	0	0	0	0	0	0	...	0

Note: All variables take the same values from period 1 onward.

TABLE 6-2

A Closed Economy with Temporary Shocks Output equals consumption. Trade balance is zero. Consumption is volatile.

		Period							Present Value
		0	1	2	3	4	5	...	($r^* = 0.05$)
Output *GDP*	*Q*	79	100	100	100	100	100	...	2,079
Expenditure *GNE*	*C*	79	100	100	100	100	100	...	2,079
Trade balance	*TB*	0	0	0	0	0	0	...	0

Note: All variables take the same values from period 1 onward.

In the open economy, however, a smooth consumption path is still attainable because the country can borrow from abroad in year 0, and then repay over time. The country can't afford its original smooth consumption path of 100 every period, because the present value of output is now less. So what smooth consumption path can it afford?

In the first section of this chapter, we spent some time deriving the LRBC. Now we can see why: the LRBC, given by Equation (6-4), is the key to determining a smooth consumption path in the face of economic shocks. Once we establish the present value of output, we know the present value of consumption, because these must be the same; from this fact we can figure out how to smooth consumption.

In this example, the present value of output Q has fallen 1% (from 2,100 to 2,079), so the present value of consumption must also fall by 1%. How should the country achieve this? Consumption can remain smooth, and satisfy the LRBC, if it falls by 1% (from 100 to 99) in every year. To double-check this logic, we compute the present value of C, using the perpetual loan formula again: $99 + 99/0.05 = 99 + 1,980 = 2,079$. Because the present value of C and the present value of Q are equal, the LRBC is satisfied.

Table 6-3 shows the path of all the important macroeconomic aggregates for the open economy. In year 0, the country runs a trade balance of $TB = -20$ (a deficit), because output Q is 79 and consumption C is 99. In subsequent years, when output is 100, the country keeps consumption at 99, and has a trade balance $TB = +1$ (a surplus). Offsetting this +1 trade balance, the country must make net factor payments

TABLE 6-3

An Open Economy with Temporary Shocks A trade deficit is run when output is temporarily low. Consumption is smooth.

		Period							Present Value
		0	1	2	3	4	5	...	($r^* = 0.05$)
Output *GDP*	*Q*	79	100	100	100	100	100	...	2,079
Expenditure *GNE*	*C*	99	99	99	99	99	99	...	2,079
Trade balance	*TB*	−20	+1	+1	+1	+1	+1	...	0
Net factor income from abroad	*NFIA*	0	−1	−1	−1	−1	−1	...	—
Current account	*CA*	−20	0	0	0	0	0	...	—
External wealth	*W*	−20	−20	−20	−20	−20	−20	...	—

Note: All variables take the same values from period 1 onward.

NFIA = −1 in the form of interest paid. The country must borrow 20 in year 0, and then make, in perpetuity, 5% interest payments of 1 unit on the 20 units borrowed.

In year 0, the current account *CA* (= *TB* + *NFIA*) is −20. In all subsequent years, net factor income from abroad is −1 and the trade balance is +1, implying that the current account is 0, with no further borrowing. The country's external wealth *W* is therefore −20 in all periods, corresponding to the perpetual loan taken out in year 0. External wealth is constant at −20; it does not explode because interest payments are made in full each period and no further borrowing is required.

The lesson is clear. When output fluctuates, a closed economy cannot smooth consumption, but an open one can.

Generalizing The lesson of our numerical example applies to any situation in which a country wants to smooth its consumption when confronted with shocks. Suppose, more generally, that output *Q* and consumption *C* are initially stable at some value with *Q* = *C* and external wealth of zero. The LRBC is satisfied because the trade balance is zero at all times.

Now suppose output unexpectedly falls in year 0 by an amount Δ*Q*, and then returns to its prior value for all future periods. The loss of output in year 0 reduces the present value of output (*GDP*) by the amount Δ*Q*. To meet the LRBC, the country must lower the present value of consumption by the same amount. A closed economy has to accomplish this by lowering its consumption by the whole amount of Δ*Q* in year 0, here again, because that is its only option! An open economy, however, as before, can lower its consumption uniformly in every period by a smaller amount, given by Δ*C* < Δ*Q*. But how big a reduction is needed to meet the LRBC?

Because consumption falls less than output in year 0, the country will run a trade deficit of Δ*Q* − Δ*C* < 0 in year 0. The country must borrow from other nations an amount equal to this trade deficit, and external wealth falls by the amount of that new debt. In subsequent years, output returns to its normal level but consumption stays at its reduced level, so trade surpluses of Δ*C* are run in all subsequent years.

Because the LRBC requires that these surpluses be large enough to service the debt, we know how large the drop in consumption must be. A loan of Δ*Q* − Δ*C* in year 0 requires interest payments of $r^*(\Delta Q - \Delta C)$ in later years. If the subsequent trade surpluses of Δ*C* are to cover these interest payments, then we know that Δ*C* must be chosen so that

$$\underbrace{r^* \times \underbrace{(\Delta Q - \Delta C)}_{\substack{\text{Amount} \\ \text{borrowed in} \\ \text{year 0}}}}_{\text{Interest due in subsequent years}} = \underbrace{\Delta C}_{\substack{\text{Trade surplus} \\ \text{in subsequent} \\ \text{years}}}$$

To find out how big a cut in consumption is necessary, we rearrange and find that

$$\Delta C = \frac{r^*}{1 + r^*} \Delta Q$$

Note that the fraction in the above equation is between zero and 1. Thus, the generalized lesson is that an open economy only needs to lower its steady consumption level by a *fraction* of the size of the temporary output loss. (For instance, in the previous numerical example, Δ*C* = (0.05/1.05) × (21) = 1, so consumption had to fall by 1 unit.)

Smoothing Consumption When a Shock Is Permanent We just showed how an open economy uses international borrowing to smooth consumption in response to a temporary shock to output. When the shock is permanent, however, the outcome is different. With a permanent shock, output will be lower by ΔQ in all years, so the only way either a closed or open economy can satisfy the LRBC while keeping consumption smooth is to cut consumption by $\Delta C = \Delta Q$ in all years. This is optimal, even in an open economy, because consumption remains smooth, although at a reduced level.

Comparing the results for a temporary shock and a permanent shock, we see an important point: consumers can smooth out temporary shocks—they have to adjust a bit, but the adjustment is far smaller than the shock itself—but they must adjust immediately and fully to permanent shocks. For example, if your income drops by 50% just this month, you might borrow to make it through this month with minimal adjustment in spending; however, if your income is going to remain 50% lower in every subsequent month, then you need to cut your spending permanently.

Summary: Save for a Rainy Day

Financial openness allows countries to "save for a rainy day." This section's lesson has a simple household analogy. If you cannot use financial institutions to lend (save) or borrow (dissave), you have to spend what you earn each period. If you have unusually low income, you have little to spend. If you have a windfall, you have to spend it all. Borrowing and lending to smooth consumption fluctuations makes a household better off. The same applies to countries.

In a closed economy, consumption must equal output in every period, so output fluctuations immediately generate consumption fluctuations. In an open economy, the desired smooth consumption path can be achieved by running a trade deficit during bad times and a trade surplus during good times. By extension, deficits and surpluses can also be used to finance extraordinary and temporary emergency spending needs, such as the costs of war (see **Side Bar: Wars and the Current Account**).

SIDE BAR

Wars and the Current Account

Our theory of consumption smoothing can take into account temporary and "desired" consumption shocks. The most obvious example of such a shock is war.

Although we assumed zero government spending above, in reality, countries' consumption includes private consumption C and public consumption G. It is simple to augment the model to include G as well as C. Under this circumstance, the constraint is that the present value of GNE $(C+G)$ must equal the present value of GDP. A war means a temporary increase in G.

Borrowing internationally to finance war-related costs goes back centuries. Historians have long argued about the importance of the creation of the British public debt market as a factor in the country's rise to global leadership compared with powerful continental rivals like France. From the early 1700s (which saw rapid financial development led by major financiers like the Rothschilds) to the end of the Napoleonic Wars in 1815, the British were able to maintain good credit; they could borrow domestically and externally cheaply and easily (often from the Dutch) to finance the simultaneous needs of capital formation for the Industrial Revolution and high levels of military spending.

In the nineteenth century, borrowing to finance war-related costs became more commonplace. In the 1870s the defeated French issued bonds in London to finance a reparation payment to the triumphant Germans. World War I and World War II saw massive lending by the United States to other Allied countries. More recently, when the United States went to war in Afghanistan (2001) and Iraq (2003), there was a sharp increase in the U.S. current account deficit and in external debt due in part to war-related borrowing.

Better at raising armies than managing finance, the French fought with one hand tied behind their back.

APPLICATION

Consumption Volatility and Financial Openness

Does the evidence show that countries avoid consumption volatility by embracing financial globalization? A simple test might be to compute the ratio of consumption volatility to output volatility (where volatility equals the standard deviation of the growth rate). If consumption smoothing is achieved, the computed ratio ought to be low. In fact, in our simple model of a small, open economy that can borrow or lend without limit, and that prefers a perfectly smooth path of consumption, this ratio should fall to zero because the economy can take advantage of financial globalization by borrowing and lending to other countries. In practice, this ratio will not be zero if all countries are affected by common global shocks. For example, if every country suffers a negative shock, every country will want to borrow, but that will not be possible: if all countries want to borrow, no countries will want to lend. In practice, however, not all shocks are global, so countries ought to be able to achieve some reduction in consumption volatility through external finance. (We consider the importance of local and global shocks later in this chapter.)

With this in mind, Figure 6-5 presents some discouraging evidence. On the horizontal axis, countries are sorted into 10 groups (deciles) from those that participate least in financial globalization (are least financially liberalized) to those that participate most. On the left are the less financially open countries with tight capital controls (generally poorer countries), and on the right are the more financially

FIGURE 6-5

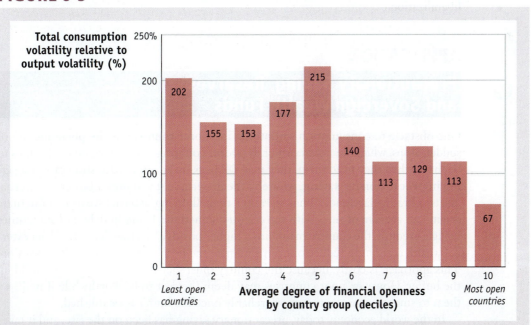

Consumption Volatility Relative to Output Volatility For a very large sample of 166 countries over the period 1990 to 2010, we compute the ratio of consumption volatility to output volatility, expressed as a percentage. A ratio of less than 100% indicates that some consumption smoothing has been achieved. Countries are then assembled into 10 groups (deciles), ordered from least financially open (1) to most financially open (10). The average volatility in each group is shown. Only

the most financially open countries have volatility ratios of less than 100%. The high ratios in groups 1 to 9 show, perversely, that consumption is even more volatile than output in these countries.

Data from: Volatility is measured by the standard deviation of real output growth rates and total consumption growth rates from the Penn World Table 8.1. Index of financial openness is from Sebastian Edwards, "Capital Controls, Sudden Stops and Current Account Reversals," in Sebastian Edwards, ed., 2007, International Capital Flows (Chicago: University of Chicago Press).

open countries that permit free movement of capital (mostly advanced countries). For all these countries, we assess their ability to smooth total consumption ($C + G$) in the period from 1990 to 2010 using annual data. In closed countries, we would expect that the volatility of consumption would be similar to the volatility of output (GDP) so that the ratio of the two would be close to 100%. But if an open country were able to smooth consumption in line with our simple model, this ratio ought to be lower than 100%.

The figure shows that most groups of countries have an average consumption-to-output volatility ratio of well above 100%. Moreover, as financial liberalization increases, this ratio shows little sign of decrease until fairly high levels of liberalization are reached (above the fifth decile). Indeed, until we get to the tenth decile, all of these ratios are above 100%. Similar findings have been found using a variety of tests, and it appears that only at a very high level of financial liberalization does financial globalization deliver modest consumption-smoothing benefits.[8]

Why are these findings so far from the predictions of our model? In poorer countries, some of the relatively high consumption volatility must be unrelated to financial openness—it is there even in closed countries. In the real world, households are not identical and global capital markets do not reach every person. Some people and firms do not or cannot participate in even domestic financial markets, perhaps because of backward financial systems. Other problems may stem from the way financial markets operate (e.g., poor transparency and regulation) in emerging market countries that are partially open and/or have partially developed their financial systems.

The evidence may not imply a failure of financial globalization, but it does not provide a ringing endorsement either. Consumption-smoothing gains may prove elusive for emerging markets until they advance further by improving poor governance and weak institutions, developing their financial systems, and pursuing further financial liberalization.

APPLICATION

Precautionary Saving, Reserves, and Sovereign Wealth Funds

One obstacle to consumption smoothing in poorer countries is the phenomenon of sudden stops, which we noted earlier. If poorer countries can't count on credit lines to be there when they need them, they may fall back on an alternative strategy of engaging in **precautionary saving**, whereby the government acquires a buffer of external assets, a "rainy day fund." That is, rather than allowing external wealth to fluctuate around an average of zero, with the country sometimes being in debt and sometimes being a creditor, the country maintains a higher positive "average balance" in its external wealth account to reduce or even eliminate the need to go into a net debt position. This approach is costly, because the country must sacrifice consumption to build up the buffer. However, poor countries may deem the cost to be worthwhile if it allows them to smooth consumption more reliably once the buffer is established.

In the world economy today, precautionary saving has been on the rise, and it takes two forms. The first is the accumulation of **foreign reserves** by central banks. Foreign reserves are safe assets denominated in foreign currency, like U.S. Treasury securities and other low-risk debt issued by governments in rich, solvent countries. They can be used not only for precautionary saving but also for other purposes, such as maintaining a fixed exchange rate. As external assets on the nation's balance sheet, these

---

[8] M. Ayhan Kose, Eswar S. Prasad, and Marco E. Terrones, 2007, "How Does Financial Globalization Affect Risk Sharing? Patterns and Channels," IZA Discussion Papers 2903, Institute for the Study of Labor (IZA).

reserves can be deployed during a sudden stop to cushion the blow to the domestic economy. Many economists argue that much of reserve accumulation in recent years in emerging markets is driven by this precautionary motive.[9]

The second form of precautionary saving by governments is through what are called **sovereign wealth funds**, state-owned asset management companies that invest some government savings (possibly including central bank reserves) overseas. Often, the asset management companies place the government savings in safe assets; increasingly, however, the funds are being placed in riskier assets such as equity and FDI. Some countries, such as Norway (which had an oil boom in the 1970s), use such funds to save windfall gains from the exploitation of natural resources for future needs. Many newer funds have appeared in emerging markets and developing countries (such as Singapore, China, Malaysia, and Taiwan), but these funds have been driven more by precautionary saving than by resource booms.

As of March 2020, the countries with the biggest sovereign wealth funds were Norway ($1,187 billion), China ($941 billion), and Abu Dhabi ($697 billion), with other large funds in Saudi Arabia, Kuwait, Singapore, Qatar, Dubai, Australia, and South Korea.[10]

Most observers believe it is likely that sovereign wealth funds will continue to grow in size, and that their use will spread to other countries (see **Headlines: Copper-Bottomed Insurance**). It is interesting that, despite having a legitimate economic rationale, these funds may generate international tensions, as they already have, by attempting to acquire politically sensitive equity and FDI assets from advanced countries.

HEADLINES

Copper-Bottomed Insurance

Many developing countries experience output volatility. Sovereign wealth funds can buffer these shocks, by saving during good times to have a reserve of wealth available in bad times. Chile operates such a fund, which proved very useful in the 2008 crisis, and may well be needed again in the future.

SANTIAGO, Chile—During the emerging economies' commodities boom a few years back, Chilean Finance Minister Andrés Velasco was a wet blanket at the fiesta. Chile, the world's largest copper producer, was reaping a bonanza from the quadrupling in the metal's price. Mr. Velasco insisted on squirreling away a large chunk in a rainy-day fund.

As the savings swelled above $20 billion— more than 15% of Chile's economic output—Mr.

Velasco faced growing pressure to break open the piggy bank. In September, protesters barged into a presentation by Mr. Velasco, carrying an effigy of him and shouting, "The copper money is for the poor people."

The 48-year-old Mr. Velasco, wary that a flood of copper income could generate lending and consumption bubbles, stood his ground, even as the popularity of the center-left government withered. Latin American history, he cautioned,

was full of "booms that had been mismanaged and ended badly."

Today Mr. Velasco looks like a prophet. Since the onset of the global economic crisis, copper prices have fallen by 50%, in line with the sharp decline in other commodities. Emerging economies that got too giddy in the good years are now coping with nasty hangovers. Soybean-dependent Argentina is facing a possible debt default while oil-rich Russia has been

---

[9] Joshua Aizenman and Jaewoo Lee, 2005, "International Reserves: Precautionary Versus Mercantilist Views, Theory and Evidence," NBER Working Paper No. 11366; Romain Ranciere and Olivier Jeanne, 2006, "The Optimal Level of International Reserves for Emerging Market Countries: Formulas and Applications," IMF Working Paper No. 06/229; Ceyhun Bora Durdu, Enrique G. Mendoza, and Marco E. Terrones, 2007, "Precautionary Demand for Foreign Assets in Sudden Stop Economies: An Assessment of the New Mercantilism," NBER Working Paper No. 13123.

[10] Data from http://www.swfinstitute.org/fund-rankings/. The Hong Kong Monetary Authority Investment Portfolio ($540 billion) is excluded in the list here as it is not separate from, but part of, the central bank.

stuck bailing out banks and companies that got in over their heads in debt.

Thanks to Mr. Velasco's caution, Chile is now in a position to try to bootstrap its own recovery from the global recession. Mr. Velasco's preemptive moves have kept Chile's government from having to spend a single peso on bank bailouts. Having paid down foreign debt during the fat years, Chile is now a net creditor nation, with a debt rating that was upgraded by Moody's Investors Service in March. . . . As a result, economists expect the nation's annual economic output to decline a very slight 0.5% this year, compared with much steeper declines elsewhere. . . .

When Mr. Velasco left a professorship at Harvard University to become Ms. Bachelet's finance minister in 2006, he took office amid a historic surge in copper prices.

It was a minefield for a policy maker. When commodities are high, Mr. Velasco says, "a country seems very creditworthy, everyone wants to lend to you, capital flows in and consumption booms.". . . To avoid repeating history,

Mr. Velasco in 2006 pushed through a law requiring the annual budget to be based on an independent committee's estimate of the average copper price over the next 10 years—not on the current market price. Any copper income above the budgeted price goes into a savings fund maintained outside the country. . . . The program is "exactly what any household would do," Mr. Velasco says. "If you get some extra money, you will ask, 'Will I have this again next year?' If not you say, 'Well, I'll save part of it.'"

But a poll taken in May of 2006 revealed that two-thirds of Chileans wanted to spend the copper windfall, not save it. The Bachelet government increased spending at an 8% annual rate, expanding pension coverage and the day-care system. That wasn't enough to satisfy a populace with rising expectations. . . . Maligned for being passive during the boom, Mr. Velasco suddenly seemed to be everywhere all at once amid the bust. He flew to the U.S. in September to assess the financial damage first-hand. Then he began a series of meetings at home with leaders of big businesses and residents of small towns. And

the tightfisted finance minister started singing a new tune about the copper savings. "The savings aren't to keep behind a window but to spend if necessary," he said.

Mr. Velasco, who had problems in Congress in the past, was able to get the $4 billion stimulus package through both houses of Congress, with unanimous approval, in just nine days in January. Chile will endure a mild recession this year, economists say. But the effects will be eased by a stimulus representing two to three times the amount most other Latin American governments are enacting, relative to GDP. . . . Chile is putting $700 million into a huge infrastructure program designed to create at least 60,000 jobs in road paving, airport upgrades and housing construction. . . . One of the workers on the [housing] site is Roberto Urrutia. He had been unemployed since December, and had been so strapped for cash he'd had to cancel his telephone lines and borrow money for his children's schooling. "Putting my hard hat on is the greatest feeling in the world right now," he says.

Source: Republished with permission of Dow Jones & Company, Inc., from "Prudent Chile Thrives Amid Downturn," by Matt Moffett, Wall Street Journal, May 27, 2009; permission conveyed through Copyright Clearance Center, Inc.

3 Gains from Efficient Investment

Suppose an economy has opened up and is taking full advantage of the gains from consumption smoothing. Has it completely exploited the benefits of financial globalization? The answer is no, because openness delivers gains not only on the consumption side but also on the investment side by improving a country's ability to augment its capital stock and take advantage of new production opportunities.

The Basic Model

To illustrate these investment gains, we must refine the model we have been using by abandoning the assumption that output can be produced using only labor. We now assume that producing output requires labor and capital, which is created over time by investing output. When we make this change, the long-run budget constraint (LRBC) in Equation (6-4) must be modified to include investment I as a component of GNE. For simplicity, however, we still assume that government consumption G is zero. With this change, the LRBC becomes

$$\underset{\text{Initial wealth is zero}}{\underline{0}} = \text{Present value of } TB$$

Because the TB is output (Q) minus expenditure ($C + I$), we can rewrite this last equation in the following form:

$$\underbrace{\text{Present value of } Q}_{\text{Present value of } GDP} = \underbrace{\text{Present value of } C + \text{Present value of } I}_{\text{Present value of } GNE} \tag{6-5}$$

The LRBC will hold if and only if the present value of output Q equals the present value of expenditure $(C + I)$.

Using this modified LRBC, we now study investment and consumption decisions in two cases:

- A closed economy, in which external borrowing and lending are not possible, the trade balance is zero in all periods, and the LRBC is automatically satisfied

- An open economy, in which borrowing and lending are possible, the trade balance can be more or less than zero, and we must verify that the LRBC is satisfied

Efficient Investment: A Numerical Example and Generalization

Let's start with a country that has output of 100, consumption (C) of 100, no investment (I), a zero trade balance, and zero external wealth. If that state persisted, the LRBC would be satisfied, just as it was in the prior numerical example with consumption smoothing. This outcome describes the optimal path of consumption in both the closed and open economies when output is constant and there are no shocks; that is, nothing happens here that makes the country want to alter its output and consumption.

But now suppose there is a shock in year 0 that takes the form of a new investment opportunity. For example, it could be that in year 0 engineers discover that by building a new factory with a new machine, the country can produce a certain good much more cheaply than current technology allows. Or perhaps there is a resource discovery, but a mine must first be built to extract the minerals from the earth. What happens next? We turn first to a numerical example and then supply a more general answer.

We assume that the investment (in machines or factories or mines) would require an expenditure of 16 units, and that the investment will pay off in future years by increasing the country's output by 5 units in year 1 and all subsequent years (but not in year 0).

The country now faces some choices. Should it make this investment? And if it does, will it make out better if it is open or closed? We find the answers to these questions by looking at how an *open* economy would deal with the opportunity to invest and then showing why a country would make itself worse off by choosing to be closed, thereby relinquishing at least some of the gains the investment opportunity offers.

As in the previous example, the key to solving this problem is to work with the LRBC and see how the choices a country makes to satisfy it have to change as circumstances do. Before the investment opportunity shock, output and consumption were each 100 in all periods, and had a present value of 2,100. Investment was zero in every period, and the LRBC given by Equation (6-5) was satisfied. If the country decides to not act on the investment opportunity, this situation continues unchanged whether the economy is closed or open.

Now suppose an open economy undertakes the investment. First, we must calculate the difference this would make to the country's resources, as measured by the present value of output. Output would be 100 today and then 105 in every subsequent year. The present value of this stream of output is 100 plus 105/0.05 or 2,200. This is an increase of 100 over the old present value of output (2,100). The present value of the addition to output (of 5 units every subsequent period) is 100.

Can all of this additional output be devoted to consumption? No, because the country has had to invest 16 units in the current period to obtain this future stream of additional output. In this scenario, because all investment occurs in the current period, 16 is the present value of investment in the modified LRBC given by Equation (6-5).

Looking at that LRBC, we've calculated the present value of output (2,200), and now we have the present value of investment (16). We can see that the present value of consumption must equal 2,200 minus 16, or 2,184. This is 4% higher than it was without the investment. Even though some expenditure has to be devoted to investment, the resources available for consumption have risen by 4% in present value terms (from 2,100 without the investment, to 2,184 with it).

We can now find the new level of smooth consumption each period that satisfies the LRBC. Because the present value of C has risen by 4% from 2,100 to 2,184, the country can afford to raise consumption C in all periods by 4% from 100 to 104. (As a check, note that $104 + 104/0.05 = 2,184$.) Is the country better off if it makes the investment? Yes—not only does its consumption remain smooth, but it is also 4% higher in all periods.

Table 6-4 lays out the details of this case. In year 0, C is 104, I is 16, and GNE is 120. The trade balance is -20 because output Q is only 100. The country must borrow 20 units in year 0 to fund the investment of 16 *and* the 4 additional units of consumption the country can afford as a result of the investment. In all future years, C is 104, and because there is no subsequent investment, GNE is also 104. Output Q is 105, and the trade balance is $+1$.

The initial trade deficit of 20 in year 0 results in an external debt of 20. As a perpetual loan, with an interest rate of 5%, this debt of 20 must be serviced by net interest payments of -1 in each subsequent year if the LRBC is to be satisfied. The interest payment of -1 offsets the trade surplus of $+1$ each period forever. Hence, the current account is zero in all future years, with no further borrowing, and the country's external wealth is -20 in all periods. External wealth does not explode, and the LRBC is satisfied.

This outcome is preferable to any outcome a closed economy can achieve. To attain an output level of 105 from year 1 on, a closed economy would have to cut consumption to 84 in year 0 to free up 16 units for investment. Although the country would then enjoy consumption of 105 in all subsequent years, this is not a smooth consumption path! The open economy *could* choose this path (cutting consumption to 84 in year 0), because it satisfies the LRBC. It won't choose this path, however, because by making the investment in this way, it cannot smooth its consumption and cannot smooth it *at a higher level.* The open economy is better off making the investment *and* smoothing consumption, two goals that the closed economy cannot simultaneously achieve.

TABLE 6-4

An Open Economy with Investment and a Permanent Shock The economy runs a trade deficit to finance investment and consumption in period 0 and runs a trade surplus when output is higher in later periods. Consumption is smooth.

		Period							Present Value
		0	1	2	3	4	5	...	($r^* = 0.05$)
Output GDP	Q	100	105	105	105	105	105	...	2,200
Expenditure GNE {	C	104	104	104	104	104	104	...	2,184
	I	16	0	0	0	0	0	...	16
Trade balance	TB	−20	+1	+1	+1	+1	+1	...	0
Net factor income from abroad	NFIA	0	−1	−1	−1	−1	−1	...	—
Current account	CA	−20	0	0	0	0	0	...	—
External wealth	W	−20	−20	−20	−20	−20	−20	...	—

Note: All variables take the same values from period 1 onward.

Generalizing The lesson of our numerical example applies to any situation in which a country confronts new investment opportunities. Suppose that a country starts with zero external wealth, constant output Q, consumption C equal to output, and investment I equal to zero. A new investment opportunity appears requiring ΔK units of output in year 0. This investment will generate an additional ΔQ units of output in year 1 and all later years (but not in year 0).

Ultimately, consumers care about consumption. In an open economy, they can smooth their consumption, given future output. The constant level of consumption is limited only by the present value of available resources, as expressed by the LRBC. Maximizing the level of consumption is the same as maximizing the present value of consumption. Rearranging Equation (6-5), the LRBC requires that the present value of consumption must equal the present value of output minus the present value of investment. How is this present value maximized?

The increase in the present value of output $PV(Q)$ comes from extra output in every year but year 0, and the present value of these additions to output is, using Equation (6-2),

$$\text{Change in present value of output} = \frac{\Delta Q}{(1+r^*)} + \frac{\Delta Q}{(1+r^*)^2} + \frac{\Delta Q}{(1+r^*)^3} + \cdots = \frac{\Delta Q}{r^*}$$

The change in the present value of investment $PV(I)$ is simply ΔK.

This means the investment will increase the present value of consumption—and hence will be undertaken—if and only if $\Delta Q/r^* \geq \Delta K$. There are two ways to look at this conclusion. Rearranging, investment is undertaken when

$$\underbrace{\Delta Q}_{\substack{\text{Output increase in} \\ \text{subsequent periods}}} \geq \underbrace{r^* \times \Delta K}_{\substack{\text{Interest payment due in} \\ \text{subsequent periods to} \\ \text{finance initial investment}}}$$

The intuition here is that investment occurs up to the point at which the annual benefit from the marginal unit of capital (ΔQ) equals or exceeds the annual cost of borrowing the funds to pay for that capital ($r^*\Delta K$).

Putting it another way, dividing by ΔK, investment is undertaken when

$$\underbrace{\frac{\Delta Q}{\Delta K}}_{\substack{MPK \\ \text{Marginal product of capital}}} \geq \underbrace{r^*}_{\text{World real interest rate}} \qquad (6\text{-}6)$$

This is a standard formula for the optimal or efficient level of investment and may look familiar from other courses in economics. Firms will take on investment projects as long as the **marginal product of capital (MPK)** is at least as great as the real interest rate.

Summary: Make Hay While the Sun Shines

In an open economy, firms borrow and repay to undertake investment that maximizes the present value of output. Households also borrow and lend to smooth consumption, but these borrowing and lending decisions are separate from those of firms.

When investing, an open economy sets its MPK equal to the world real rate of interest. If conditions are unusually good (high productivity), it makes sense to invest more capital and produce more output. Conversely, when conditions turn bad (low productivity), it makes sense to lower capital inputs and produce less output. This strategy maximizes the present value of output minus investment. Households then address the separate problem of how to smooth the path of consumption when output changes. A closed economy must be self-sufficient. Any resources invested are resources not consumed. More investment implies less consumption. This creates a trade-off. When investment opportunities are good, the country wants to invest to generate higher output in the future. Anticipating that higher output, the country wants to consume more today, but it cannot—it must consume less to invest more.

Proverbially, financial openness helps countries to "make hay while the sun shines"—and, in particular, to do so without having to engage in a trade-off against the important objective of consumption smoothing. The lesson here has a simple household analogy. Suppose you find a great investment opportunity. If you have no financial dealings with the outside world, you would have to sacrifice consumption and save to finance the investment.

(See Appendix 2 at the end of the chapter for a detailed discussion of how these ideas apply to the question of economic growth and convergence between rich and poor countries.)

APPLICATION

Delinking Saving from Investment

The story of the Norwegian oil boom provides a good illustration of our theory about investment and financial openness. North Sea oil was discovered in the 1960s, but the mass exploitation of this resource was unprofitable because cheap and plentiful supplies of oil were being produced elsewhere, primarily in the Persian Gulf. Then came the first "oil shock" in the early 1970s, when the cartel of Oil Producing and Exporting Countries (OPEC) colluded to raise world oil prices dramatically, a shock that was (correctly) viewed as permanent. At these higher oil prices, it suddenly made sense to exploit North Sea oil. Starting in the early 1970s, oil platforms, pipelines, refineries, and terminals were sprouting offshore and along the coast of Norway, causing its capital stock to permanently increase in response to a new productive investment opportunity.

Figure 6-6 shows the path of saving (S) and investment (I) measured as ratios of GDP in Norway from 1965 to 1990. The oil boom is clearly visible in the investment

FIGURE 6-6

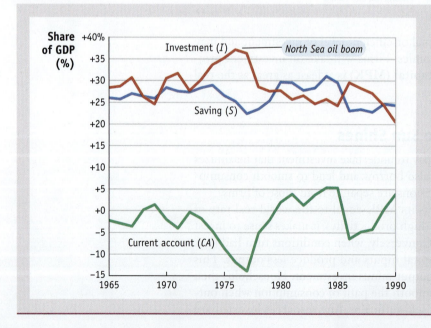

The Oil Boom in Norway Following a large increase in oil prices in the early 1970s, Norway invested heavily to exploit oil fields in the North Sea. Norway took advantage of openness to finance a temporary increase in investment by running a very large current account deficit, thus increasing its indebtedness to the rest of the world. At its peak, the current account deficit was more than 10% of GDP.

Data from: Alan M. Taylor, 2002, "A Century of Current Account Dynamics," Journal of International Money and Finance, 21(6), 725–748.

share of GDP, which in the 1970s rose about 10 percentage points above its typical level. Had Norway been a closed economy, this additional investment would have been financed by a decrease in the share of output devoted to public and private consumption. As you can see, no such sacrifice was necessary. Norway's saving rate was flat in this period or even fell slightly. In Norway's open economy, saving and investment were delinked and the difference was made up by the current account, $CA = S - I$, which moved sharply into deficit, approaching minus 15% of GDP at one point. Thus, all of the short-run increase in investment was financed by foreign investment in Norway, much of it by multinational oil companies.

Is Norway a special case? Economists have examined large international datasets to see whether there is general evidence that countries can delink investment decisions from saving decisions as the Norwegians did. One approach follows the pioneering work of Martin Feldstein and Charles Horioka.[11] They estimated what fraction β of each additional dollar saved tended to be invested in the same country. In other words, in their model, if saving rose by an amount ΔS, they estimated that investment would rise by an amount $\Delta I = \beta \Delta S$. In a closed economy, the "savings retention" measure β would equal 1, but they argued that increasing financial openness would tend to push β below 1.

For example, suppose one were to estimate β for the period 1980 to 2000 for three groups of countries with differing degrees of financial integration within the group: in a sample of countries in the European Union, where international financial integration had advanced furthest, the estimated value of β is 0.26, meaning that 26% of each additional dollar saved tended to be invested in the same country; in a sample of all developed countries with a somewhat lower level of financial integration, the estimate of β is 0.39; and in a sample of emerging markets, where financial integration was lower still, the estimate of β is 0.67.[12] These data thus indicate that financially open countries seem to have a greater ability to delink saving and investment, in that they have a much lower "savings retention" measure β.

4 Gains from Diversification of Risk

In the second section of this chapter, we studied consumption smoothing using a simplified model. We used a borrowing and lending approach, we considered a small open economy, we assumed that countries owned their own output, and we treated output shocks as given. We then saw how debt can be used to smooth the impact of output shocks on consumption. However, we also discussed the finding that in practice, countries seem to be unable to eliminate the effects of output volatility. The problems seem to be especially difficult in emerging markets and developing countries. We also saw that reliance on borrowing and lending may create problems because there may be limits to borrowing, risk premiums, and sudden stops in the availability of credit.

Are there other ways for a country to cope with shocks to output? Yes. In this final section, we show how **diversification**, another facet of financial globalization, can help smooth shocks by promoting risk sharing. With diversification, countries own not only the income stream from their own capital stock, but also income streams from capital stocks located in other countries. We see how, by using financial openness to trade such rights—for example, in the form of capital equity claims like stocks and shares—countries may be able to reduce the volatility of their incomes (and hence their consumption levels) without *any* net lending or borrowing whatsoever.

---

[11] Martin Feldstein and Charles Horioka, 1980, "Domestic Saving and International Capital Flows," *Economic Journal*, 90(358), 314–329.
[12] Author's calculations based on International Monetary Fund, International Financial Statistics, with investment and saving measured as a share of GDP.

Diversification: A Numerical Example and Generalization

To keep things simple and to permit us to focus on diversification, we assume there is no borrowing (the current account is zero at all times). To illustrate the gains from diversification, we examine the special case of a world with two countries, A and B, which are identical except that their respective outputs fluctuate asymmetrically; that is, they suffer equal and opposite shocks.

We now explore how this world economy performs in response to the output shocks. We examine the special case in which there are two possible "states of the world," which are assumed to occur with an equal probability of 50%. In terms of output levels, state 1 is a bad state for A and a good state for B; state 2 is a good state for A and a bad state for B.

We assume that all output is consumed and that there is no investment or government spending. As we know from the previous chapter, output is distributed to factors in the form of income. We assume output is divided 60–40 between labor income and capital income in each country. The key question for us is: who owns this income: domestic residents or foreigners?

Home Portfolios To begin, both countries are closed, and households in each country own the entire capital stock of their own country. Thus, A owns 100% of A's capital, and B owns 100% of B's capital. Under these assumptions, output (as measured by gross domestic product, GDP) is the same as income (as measured by gross national income, GNI) in A and B.

A numerical example is given in Table 6-5, panel (a). In state 1, A's output is 90, of which 54 units are payments to labor and 36 units are payments to capital; in state 2, A's output rises to 110, and factor payments rise to 66 for labor and 44 units for capital. The opposite is true in B: in state 1, B's output is higher than it is in state 2. Using our national accounting definitions, we know that in each closed economy, consumption, income GNI, and output GDP are equal. In both A and B, all of these quantities are volatile. GNI, and hence consumption, flips randomly between 90 and 110 in both countries. The variation of GNI about its mean of 100 is plus or minus 10 in each country. Because households prefer smooth consumption, this variation is undesirable.

World Portfolios Notice that when one country's capital income is up, the other's is down. World GDP equals world GNI and is always 200. World labor income is always 120 and world capital income is always 80.

It is apparent from Figure 6-7 that the two countries can achieve partial income smoothing if they diversify their portfolios of capital assets. For example, each country could own half of the domestic capital stock, and half of the other country's capital stock. Indeed, this is what standard portfolio theory says that investors should try to do. The results of this portfolio diversification are shown in Table 6-5, panel (b).

Now each country owns one-half of its own capital stock but sells the other half to the other country in exchange for half of the other country's capital stock.[13] Each country's output, or GDP, is still as it was described in panel (a). But now country incomes, or GNI, can differ from their outputs or GDP. Owning 50% of the world portfolio means that each country has a capital income of 40 every period. However, labor income still varies between 54 and 66 in the bad and good states, so total income (and hence consumption) varies between 94 and 106. Thus, as Table 6-5, panel (b), shows, capital income for each country is smoothed at 40 units, the average of A and B capital income in panel (a), as also illustrated in Figure 6-7.

How does the balance of payments work when countries hold the world portfolio? Consider country A. In state 1 (bad for A, good for B), A's income, or GNI,

---

[13] Note that this financial transaction would balance in the financial account, as a pure asset trade, so no borrowing or lending is needed and the current account remains zero, as we have assumed.

TABLE 6-5

Portfolio Diversification Choices: Diversifiable Risks In countries A and B, GDP is allocated 60% to labor income and 40% to capital income. There are two "states of the world": state 1 is bad for A and good for B; state 2 is the opposite. On average, GDP equals 100, but in the good state, GDP is 110, and in the bad state it is only 90. Thus, world GDP and GNI always equal 200, world labor income is always 120, and world capital income is always 80. When each country holds only its own assets as in panel (a), GNI equals GDP and is very volatile. When each country holds a 50% share of the world portfolio as in panel (b), GNI volatility decreases because capital income is now smoothed. When each country holds a portfolio made up only of the other country's capital as in panel (c), GNI volatility falls even further by making capital income vary inversely with labor income.

(a) When Countries Hold 100% Home Portfolios
Each country owns 100% of its own capital.

	COUNTRY A			COUNTRY B			WORLD		
	Capital Income	Labor Income	GDP = GNI	Capital Income	Labor Income	GDP = GNI	Capital Income	Labor Income	GDP = GNI
State 1	36	54	90	44	66	110	80	120	200
State 2	44	66	110	36	54	90	80	120	200
Variation about mean	∓4	∓6	∓10	±4	±6	±10	0	0	0

(b) When Countries Hold World Portfolios
Each country owns 50% A capital and 50% B capital with payoffs as in panel (a).

	COUNTRY A			COUNTRY B			WORLD		
	Capital Income	Labor Income	GNI	Capital Income	Labor Income	GNI	Capital Income	Labor Income	GDP = GNI
State 1	40	54	94	40	66	106	80	120	200
State 2	40	66	106	40	54	94	80	120	200
Variation about mean	0	∓6	∓6	0	±6	±6	0	0	0

(c) When Countries Hold 100% Foreign Portfolios
Each country owns 100% of the other country's capital with payoffs as in panel (a).

	COUNTRY A			COUNTRY B			WORLD		
	Capital Income	Labor Income	GNI	Capital Income	Labor Income	GNI	Capital Income	Labor Income	GDP = GNI
State 1	44	54	98	36	66	102	80	120	200
State 2	36	66	102	44	54	98	80	120	200
Variation about mean	±4	∓6	∓2	∓4	±6	±2	0	0	0

exceeds A's output, GDP, by 4 (94 – 90 = +4). Where does the extra income come from? The extra is net factor income from abroad of +4. Why is it +4? This is precisely equal to the difference between the income earned on A's external assets (50% of B's payments to capital of 44 = 22) and the income paid on A's external liabilities (50% of A's payments to capital of 36 = 18). What does A do with that net factor income? A runs a trade balance of –4, which means that A can consume 94, even when its output is only 90. Adding the trade balance of –4 to net factor income from abroad of +4 means that the current account is 0, and there is still no need for any net borrowing or lending, as assumed. These flows are reversed in state 2 (which is good for A, bad for B).

Note that after diversification, income, or GNI, varies in A and B by plus or minus 6 (around a mean of 100), which is less than the range of plus or minus 10 seen in Table 6-5, panel (a). This is because 40% of income is capital income and so 40% of the A income fluctuation of 10 can be smoothed by the portfolio diversification.

FIGURE 6-7

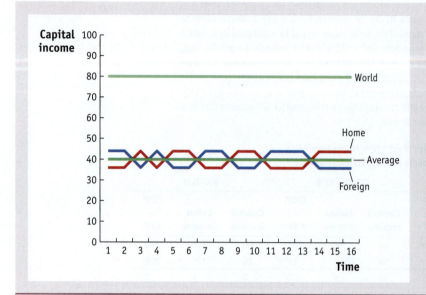

Portfolio Diversification and Capital Income: Diversifiable Risks The figure shows fluctuations in capital income over time for different portfolios, based on the data in Table 6-5. Countries trade claims to capital income by trading capital assets. When countries hold the world portfolio, they each earn a 50–50 split (or average) of world capital income. World capital income is constant if shocks in the two countries are asymmetrical and cancel out. All capital income risk is then fully diversifiable.

Generalizing Let us try to generalize the concept of capital income smoothing through diversification. Consider the volatility of capital income by itself, in the example we have just studied. Each country's payments to capital are volatile. A portfolio of 100% country A's capital or 100% of country B's capital has capital income that varies by plus or minus 4 (between 36 and 44). But a 50–50 mix of the two leaves the investor with a portfolio of minimum, zero volatility (it always pays 40).

This outcome is summed up in Figure 6-8, panel (a), which refers to either country, A or B. There is an identical high level of capital income volatility when the country holds either a 100% home portfolio or a 100% foreign portfolio. However, holding a mix of the two reduces capital income volatility, and a minimum volatility of zero can be achieved by holding the 50–50 mix of the world capital income portfolio.

To generalize this result to the real world, we need to recognize that not all shocks are asymmetric as we have assumed here. The outputs of countries A and B may not be equal and opposite (with correlation –1) as we have assumed here. In general, there will be some common shocks, which are identical shocks experienced by both countries. The impact of common shocks cannot be lessened or eliminated by any form of asset trade. For example, suppose we add an additional shock determined by two new states of the world, X and Y (these states of the world are independent of states of the world 1 and 2). We assume that in state X, the new shock adds five units to each country's output; in state Y, it subtracts five units from each. There is no way to avoid this shock by portfolio diversification. The X–Y shocks in each country are perfectly positively correlated (correlation +1). If this were the only shock, the countries' outputs would move up and down together and diversification would be pointless. This situation is shown in Figure 6-8, panel (b).

In the real world, any one country experiences some shocks that are correlated with those of other countries, either positively or negatively, and some that are uncorrelated. As long as some shocks are asymmetric, or country specific, and not common between the home and foreign country, then the two countries can take advantage of gains from the diversification of risk. In this more general case in which symmetric and asymmetric shocks are combined, as depicted in Figure 6-8, panel (c), holding a 100% portfolio of domestic (or foreign) assets generates a volatile income. But holding the 50–50 world portfolio will lower the volatility of income, albeit not all the way to zero (see Appendix 1 at the end of the chapter for a detailed discussion).

FIGURE 6-8

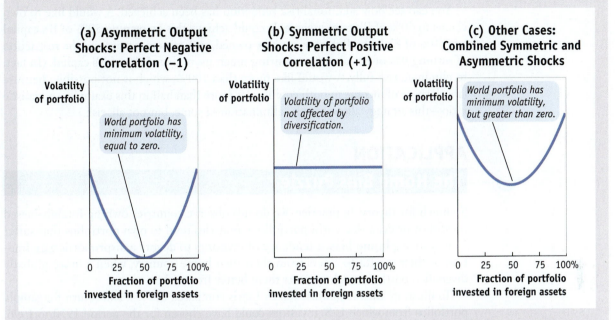

(a) Asymmetric Output Shocks: Perfect Negative Correlation (−1)

Volatility of portfolio

World portfolio has minimum volatility, equal to zero.

0   25   50   75   100%
Fraction of portfolio invested in foreign assets

(b) Symmetric Output Shocks: Perfect Positive Correlation (+1)

Volatility of portfolio

Volatility of portfolio not affected by diversification.

0   25   50   75   100%
Fraction of portfolio invested in foreign assets

(c) Other Cases: Combined Symmetric and Asymmetric Shocks

Volatility of portfolio

World portfolio has minimum volatility, but greater than zero.

0   25   50   75   100%
Fraction of portfolio invested in foreign assets

Return Correlations and Gains from Diversification The charts plot the volatility of capital income against the share of the portfolio devoted to foreign capital. The two countries are identical in size and experience shocks of similar amplitude. In panel (a), shocks are perfectly asymmetric (correlation = −1); capital income in the two countries is perfectly *negatively* correlated. Risk can be eliminated by holding the world portfolio, and there are large gains from diversification. In panel (b), shocks are perfectly symmetric (correlation = +1); capital income in the two countries is perfectly *positively* correlated. Risk cannot be reduced, and there are no gains from diversification. In panel (c), when both types of shock are present, the correlation is neither perfectly negative nor positive. Risk can be partially eliminated by holding the world portfolio, and there are still some gains from diversification.

Limits to Diversification: Capital Versus Labor Income As we saw in Table 6-5, panel (b), elimination of total income risk cannot be achieved by holding the world portfolio, even in the case of purely asymmetric shocks of capital assets. Why? Because labor income risk is not being shared. Admittedly, the same theory would apply if one could trade labor like an asset, but this is impossible because ownership rights to labor cannot be legally traded in the same way as one can trade capital or other property (that would be slavery).

Although it is true that labor income risk (and hence GDP risk) may not be diversifiable through the trading of claims to labor assets or GDP, this is not quite the end of our story—in theory at least. We saw in Table 6-5, panel (a), that capital and labor income in each country are perfectly correlated in this example: a good state raises both capital and labor income, and a bad state lowers both. This is not implausible—in reality, shocks to production do tend to raise and lower incomes of capital and labor simultaneously. This means that, as a risk-sharing device, trading claims to capital income can substitute for trading claims to labor income.

To illustrate this, imagine an unrealistic scenario in which the residents of each country own no capital stock in their own country but own the entire capital stock of the other country. As shown in Table 6-5, panel (c), owning only the other country's portfolio achieves more risk sharing than holding 50% of the world portfolio.

For example, when A is in the good state (state 2), A's labor income is 66 but A's capital income is 36 (assumed now to be 100% from B, which is in the bad state). This adds up to a portfolio of 102. In the bad state for A (state 2), A's labor income is 54, but A's capital income is 44 (from B, which is in a good state), for a total GNI of 98. So A's income (and consumption) vary by plus or minus 2, between 98 and 102 in panel (c).

Compare this fluctuation of ±2 around the mean of 100 to the fluctuations of ±10 (home portfolio) and ±6 (the world portfolio) in panels (a) and (b).

You can see how additional risk reduction has been achieved. A would like to own claims to 50% of B's total income. It could achieve this by owning 50% of B's capital and 50% of B's labor. But labor can't be owned, so A tries to get around the restriction of owning 0% of B's labor by acquiring much more than 50% of B's capital. (In fact, to eliminate risk fully, A would like more than 100%, which is not possible; because labor's share of income in both countries is more than half in this example—a realistic ratio—this strategy allows for the elimination of some, but not all, risk.)

APPLICATION

The Home Bias Puzzle

So much for theory. In practice, we do not observe countries owning foreign-biased portfolios or even the world portfolio. Countries tend to own portfolios that suffer from a strong **home bias**, a tendency of investors to devote a disproportionate fraction of their wealth to assets from their own home country, when a more globally diversified portfolio might protect them better from risk.

To illustrate this, economist Karen Lewis compared the risk and return for sample portfolios from which U.S. investors could have chosen for the period 1970 to 1996. In her experiment some assets are allocated to a domestic portfolio (the S&P 500) and the remainder to an overseas portfolio (Morgan Stanley's EAFE fund). In this stylized problem, the question is what weight to put on each portfolio, when the weights must sum to 100%. In reality, U.S. investors picked a weight of about 8% on foreign assets. Was this a smart choice?

Figure 6-9 shows the risk and return for every possible weight between 0% and 100%. Return is measured by the mean rate of return (annualized percent per year); risk is measured by the standard deviation of the return (its root mean square deviation from its mean).

With regard to returns, the foreign portfolio had a slightly higher average return than the home portfolio during this period, so increasing the weight in the foreign portfolio would have increased the returns: the mean return line slopes up slightly from left to right. What about risk? A 100% foreign portfolio (point E) would have generated higher risk than the home U.S. portfolio (point A); thus, E is above A. However, we know that some mix of the two portfolios ought to produce a lower volatility than either extreme because the two returns are not perfectly correlated. This minimum volatility will not be zero because there are some undiversifiable, symmetric shocks, but it will be lower than the volatility of the 100% home and 100% foreign portfolios: overseas and domestic returns are not perfectly correlated, implying that substantial country-specific diversifiable risks exist.

In fact, Lewis showed that a U.S. investor with a 0% weight on the overseas portfolio (point A) could have raised that weight to as much as 39% (point C), while simultaneously raising the average of her total return and lowering its risk. Even moving to the right of C (toward D) would make sense, though how far would depend on how the investor viewed the risk-return trade-off. Choosing a weight as low as 8% (point B) would seem to be a puzzle.

Broadly speaking, economists have had one of two reactions to the emergence of the "home bias puzzle" in the 1990s. One is to propose many different theories to explain it away: Perhaps it is costly to acquire foreign assets, or get information about them? Perhaps there are asymmetries between home and foreign countries' consumption patterns (due to nontraded goods or trade frictions or even tastes) that make domestic assets a better hedge against domestic consumption risk? Perhaps home investors worry about regulatory barriers and the problems of corporate governance

FIGURE 6-9

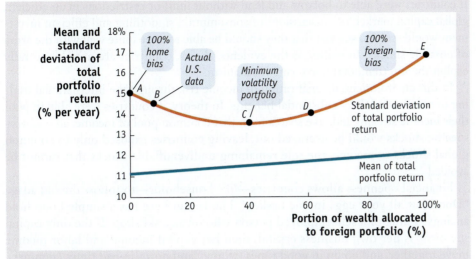

Portfolio Diversification in the United States The figure shows the return (mean of monthly return) and risk (standard deviation of monthly return) for a hypothetical portfolio made up from a mix of a pure home U.S. portfolio (the S&P 500) and a pure foreign portfolio (the Morgan Stanley EAFE) using data from the period 1970 to 1996. U.S. investors with a 0% weight on the overseas portfolio (point A) could have raised that weight as high as 39% (point C) and still raised the return and lowered risk. Even moving to the right of C (toward D) would make sense, though how far would depend on how the investor viewed the risk-return trade-off. The actual weight seen was extremely low at just 8% (point B) and was considered a puzzle.

Data from: Karen K. Lewis, 1999, "Trying to Explain Home Bias in Equities and Consumption," Journal of Economic Literature, 37(2), 571–608.

in foreign markets? These and many other solutions have been tried in extremely complex economic models, but none has been judged a complete success.

The other reaction of economists has been to look at the evidence of home bias in the period from the 1970s to the 1990s (the period of the Lewis study) as a legacy of the pronounced deglobalization of financial markets in the postwar period that might slowly disappear. Recent evidence suggests that this might be happening to some degree. There has been a dramatic increase in overseas equity investments in the last 40 years, with a very strong upward trend after 1985 in IMF data. For example, in the United States, the foreign share of the U.S. equity portfolio had risen to 12% by 2001 and 28% in 2010. Over the same period, the U.K. portfolio saw its foreign equity share rise from 28% to 50%. Furthermore, these figures might understate the true extent to which residents have diversified away from home capital because many large multinational firms have capital income streams that flow from operations in many countries. For example, an American purchasing a share of Intel or Ford, or a Briton purchasing a share of BP, or a Japanese person purchasing a share of Sony, is really purchasing shares of income streams from the globally diversified operations of these companies. Technically, Intel is recorded in the data as a 100% U.S. "home" stock, but this makes the home bias puzzle look much worse than it really is because investors do seem to invest heavily in firms such as these that provide an indirect foreign exposure.[14]

Recent trends in diversification within portfolios and within companies may mean that even if the puzzle cannot be explained away, perhaps it will gradually go away.

---

[14] On trends in home bias since 2001 see Christopher B. Philips, Francis M. Kinniry, Jr., and Scott J. Donaldson, 2012, "The Role of Home Bias in Global Asset Allocation Decisions," Vanguard Research. On the impact of multinationals see Fang Cai and Francis E. Warnock, 2006, "International Diversification at Home and Abroad," NBER Working Paper No. 12220.

Summary: Don't Put All Your Eggs in One Basket

If countries were able to borrow and lend without limit or restrictions in an efficient global capital market, our discussions of consumption smoothing and efficient investment would seem to suggest that they should be able to cope quite well with the array of possible shocks. In reality, as the evidence shows, countries are not able to fully exploit the intertemporal borrowing mechanism.

In this environment, diversification of income risk through the international trading of assets can deliver substantial benefits. In theory, if countries were able to pool their income streams and take shares from that common pool of income, all country-specific shocks would be averaged out, leaving countries exposed only to common global shocks to income, the sole remaining undiversifiable shocks that cannot be avoided.

Financial openness allows countries—like households—to follow the old adage "Don't put all your eggs in one basket." The lesson here has a simple household analogy. Think of a self-employed person who owns a ski shop. If the only capital she owns is her own business capital, then her capital income and labor income move together, and go up in good times (winter) and down in bad times (summer). Her total income could be smoothed if she sold some stock in her company and used the proceeds to buy stock in another company that faced asymmetric shocks (a surf shop, perhaps).

In practice, however, risk sharing through asset trade is limited. For one thing, the number of assets is limited. The market for claims to capital income is incomplete because not all capital assets are traded (e.g., many firms are privately held and are not listed on stock markets), and trade in labor assets is legally prohibited. Moreover, even with the traded assets available, investors have shown very little inclination to invest their wealth outside their own country, although that may be slowly changing in an environment of ongoing financial globalization.

5 Conclusions

If a firm or household were to retreat from the national financial markets by keeping its money in a bag in a closet and paying cash for all its purchases (house, cars, appliances, toothpaste, gum, etc.), we would regard it as a strange and potentially costly move. By allowing households to save and borrow, financial markets help households smooth consumption in the face of shocks to their income (such as a debilitating illness, the loss of a job, destruction of property by floods or other acts of nature). Likewise, financial markets allow firms to borrow to invest efficiently in productive projects and permit investors to diversify their portfolios across a wide range of assets.

On the global scale, the same principles apply in theory to countries, subject to the long-run budget constraint. They, too, face income shocks, new investment opportunities, and country-specific risks. We have seen how they can similarly benefit from access to an external capital market—the global capital market.

Theory proves to be far from reality, however: the extent to which countries make use of global financial markets is still limited. Even in the most financially open advanced countries, consumption shocks remain, investment is often financed out of domestic saving, and a home bias persists in investors' portfolios. In poorer countries, we see no consumption smoothing gains realized, and there is little scope for development based on external finance until current low productivity levels are improved.

Are global capital markets failing? To the criticism that financial globalization doesn't work, one could respond that it hasn't really been fully tried yet. Many emerging markets and most developing countries are still on the road to full financial liberalization, and large barriers remain. Even so, deeper institutional weaknesses in these countries may hinder the efficient operation of the mechanisms we have studied. One could argue that such weaknesses may be corrected or diminished by the stimulus to competition, transparency, accountability, and stability that financial openness may provide.[15] But without further institutional improvements, the benefits of financial globalization are likely to be much smaller for these countries, and any benefits must be weighed against potential offsetting costs, such as the risk of crises, which we discuss in later chapters.

KEY POINTS

1. Countries can use their external wealth as a buffer to smooth consumption in the face of fluctuations in output or investment. However, this process is not without its limits. The country must service its debts and must not allow debts to roll over and grow without limit at the real rate of interest.

2. The condition that guarantees that debts are serviced is the long-run budget constraint, or LRBC: the present value of future trade deficits must equal minus the present value of initial wealth.

3. The LRBC can be put another way: the present value of gross domestic product plus the present value of initial wealth (the country's resources) must equal the present value of gross national expenditure (the country's spending).

4. In a closed economy, the country must satisfy $TB = 0$ in every period as there is no external trade in goods or assets. In an open economy, the economy has to satisfy only the LRBC, which states that TB equals minus the present value of initial wealth. The former is a tighter constraint than the latter—implying that there can be gains from financial globalization.

5. The current account may be lower than normal in any period when there is unusually high private or public consumption (such as during a war), unusually low output (such as occurs after a natural disaster), or unusually high investment (such as that following a natural resource discovery).

6. If poor countries had the same productivity as rich countries, there would be substantial gains from investing in poor countries where the marginal product of capital, or MPK, would be much

higher. However, this is not the case, and there is little evidence of investment inefficiency at the global level as measured by MPK gaps between countries. What gaps there are may be due to risk premiums. Consequently, large-scale investment (and foreign aid) in poor countries may not accelerate economic growth.

7. In addition to lending and borrowing, a country can reduce its risk by the international diversification of income claims. In practice, only capital income claims (capital assets) are tradable. Labor is not a tradable asset.

8. When assets are traded internationally, two countries can eliminate the income risk arising from country-specific or idiosyncratic shocks; such risk is called diversifiable risk. However, they can do nothing to eliminate the global risk, the shocks common to both countries, called undiversifiable risk.

9. In practice, the use of the current account as a buffer and the extent of diversification fall far short of theory's prediction even in advanced countries. Consumption volatility persists, domestic investment is mostly financed from domestic saving, and portfolios display pronounced home bias.

10. In emerging markets and developing countries, financial openness has progressed more slowly and access to global capital markets is more limited and often on worse terms. The gains from financial openness appear weaker, and there is the downside risk of sudden stops and other crises. For gains to be realized, countries may require deeper institutional changes and further liberalization.

---

[15] M. Ayhan Kose, Eswar Prasad, Kenneth S. Rogoff, and Shang-Jin Wei, 2006, "Financial Globalization: A Reappraisal," NBER Working Paper No. 12484.

KEY TERMS

long-run budget constraint (LRBC), p. 181
small open economy, p. 182
world real interest rate, p. 182
present value, p. 184
perpetual loan, p. 185
sudden stop, p. 191
precautionary saving, p. 198

foreign reserves, p. 198
sovereign wealth funds, p. 199
marginal product of capital (MPK), p. 203
diversification, p. 205
home bias, p. 210
production function, p. 220
productivity, p. 220

convergence, p. 222
divergence, p. 224
technical efficiency, p. 224
social efficiency, p. 224
foreign aid, p. 227
World Bank, p. 227

PROBLEMS

1. **Discovering Data** Go the BEA website (bea.gov). Find the latest annual balance of payments data for the United States.

   a. Compute (1) income earned on external assets and (2) income paid on external liabilities.

   b. Find the latest net international investment position data for the United States. Compute (3) external assets and (4) external liabilities for the end of the prior year.

   c. Divide (1) by (3) and then divide (2) by (4) to find the implied rates of interest on external assets and liabilities. Is the United States still privileged?

2. Using the notation from the text, answer the following questions. You may assume that net labor income from abroad is zero, there are no capital gains on external wealth, and there are no unilateral transfers.

   a. Express the change in external wealth (ΔW_0) at the end of period 0 as a function of the economy's trade balance (TB), the real interest rate (a constant r^*), and initial external wealth (W_{-1}).

   b. Using (a), write an expression for the stock of external wealth at the end of period 0 (W_0). This should be written as a function of the economy's trade balance (TB_0), the real interest rate, and initial external wealth (W_{-1}).

   c. Using (a) and (b), write an expression for the stock of external wealth at the end of period 1 (W_1). This should be written as a function of the economy's trade balance (TB) each period, the real interest rate, and initial external wealth (W_{-1}).

   d. Using your answers from (a), (b), and (c), write an expression for the stock of external wealth at the end of period 2 (W_2). This should be written

as a function of the economy's trade balance (TB) each period, the real interest rate, and initial external wealth (W_{-1}).

   e. Suppose we require that W_2 equal zero. Write down the condition that the three trade balances (in periods 0, 1, and 2) must satisfy. Arrange the terms in present value form.

3. Using the assumptions and answers from the previous question, complete the following:

   a. Write an expression for the *future value* of the stock of external wealth in period N (W_N). This should be written as a function of the economy's trade balance (TB) each period, the real interest rate r^*, and initial external wealth.

   b. Using the answer from (a), write an expression for the *present value* of the stock of external wealth in period N (W_N).

   c. The long run budget constraint requires the present value of W_N to tend to zero as N gets large. Explain why this implies that the economy's initial external wealth is equal to the present value of future trade deficits.

   d. How would the expressions in parts (a) and (b) change if the economy had net labor income (positive or negative) to/from abroad or net unilateral transfers? Explain briefly.

4. *In this question assume all dollar units are real dollars in billions, so, for example, $150 means $150 billion. It is year 0. Argentina thinks it can find $150 of domestic investment projects with a marginal product of capital (MPK) equal to 10% (each $1 invested in year 0 pays off $0.10 in every later year). Argentina now invests $105 in year 0 by borrowing $105 from the rest of the world at*

a world real interest rate r^* of 5%. There is no further borrowing or investment after this.

Use the standard assumptions: Assume initial external wealth W (W in year -1) is 0. Assume $G = 0$ always; and assume $I = 0$ except in year 0. Also, assume $NUT = KA = 0$ and that there is no net labor income so $NFIA = r^*W$.

The projects start to pay off in year 1 and continue to pay off all years thereafter. Interest is paid in perpetuity, in year 1 and every year thereafter. In addition, assume that if the projects are *not* done, then $GDP = Q = C = \$200$ in all years, so that $PV(Q) = PV(C) = 200 + 200/0.05 = 4,200$.

a. Should Argentina fund the $105 worth of projects? Explain your answer.

b. Why might Argentina be able to borrow only $105 and not $150?

c. From this point forward, assume the projects totaling $105 are funded and completed in year 0. If the MPK is 10%, what is the total payoff from the projects in future years?

d. Assume this payoff is added to the $200 of GDP in all years starting in year 1. In dollars, what is Argentina's $Q = GDP$ in year 0, year 1, and later years?

e. At year 0, what is the new $PV(Q)$ in dollars? *Hint:* To ease computation, calculate the value of the increment in $PV(Q)$ due to the extra output in later years.

f. At year 0, what is the new $PV(I)$ in dollars? Therefore, what does the LRBC say is the new $PV(C)$ in dollars?

g. Assume that Argentina is consumption smoothing. What is the percent change in $PV(C)$? What is the new level of C in all years? Is Argentina better off?

h. For the year the projects go ahead, year 0, explain Argentina's balance of payments as follows: state the levels of CA, TB, NFIA, and FA.

i. What happens in later years? State the levels of CA, TB, NFIA, and FA in year 1 and every later year.

5. Continuing from the previous question, we now consider Argentina's external wealth position.

a. What is Argentina's external wealth W in year 0 and later? Suppose Argentina has a one-year debt (i.e., not a perpetual loan) that must be rolled over every year. After a few years, in year N, the world interest rate rises to 15%. Can Argentina

stick to its original plan? What are the interest payments due on the debt if $r^* = 15\%$? If $I = G = 0$, what must Argentina do to meet those payments?

b. Suppose Argentina decides to unilaterally default on its debt. Why might Argentina do this? State the levels of CA, TB, NFIA, and FA in year N and all subsequent years. What happens to the Argentine level of C in this case?

c. When the default occurs, what is the change in Argentina's external wealth W? What happens to the rest of the world's external wealth?

d. External wealth data for Argentina and the rest of the world are recorded in the account known as the net international investment position. Is this change in wealth recorded as a financial flow, a price effect, or an exchange rate effect?

6. This question refers to Appendix 2. Using production function and MPK diagrams, answer the following questions. For simplicity, assume there are two countries: a poor country (with low living standards) and a rich country (with high living standards).

a. Assuming that poor and rich countries have the same production function, illustrate how the poor country will converge with the rich country. Describe how this mechanism works.

b. In the data, countries with low living standards have capital-to-worker ratios that are too high to be consistent with the model used in (a). Describe and illustrate how we can modify the model used in (a) to be consistent with the data.

c. Given your assumptions from (b), what does this suggest about the ability of poor countries to converge with rich countries? What do we expect to happen to the gap between rich and poor countries over time? Explain.

Using the model from (b), explain and illustrate how convergence works in the following cases.

d. The poor country has a marginal product of capital that is higher than that of the rich country.

e. The marginal products in each country are equal. Then, the poor country experiences an increase in human capital through government funding of education.

f. The marginal products in each country are equal. Then, the poor country experiences political instability such that investors require a risk premium to invest in the poor country.

7. This question refers to Appendix 2. Assume that Brazil and the United States have different production functions $q = f(k)$, where q is output per worker and k is capital per worker. Let $q = Ak^{\frac{1}{3}}$. You are told that relative to the United States = 1, Brazil has an output per worker of 0.40 and capital per worker of 0.33. Can A be the same in Brazil as in the United States? If not, compute the level of A for Brazil. What is Brazil's MPK relative to the United States?

8. This question refers to Appendix 2. Use production function and MPK diagrams to examine Turkey and the European Union (EU). Assume that Turkey and the EU have different production functions $q = f(k)$, where q is output per worker and k is capital per worker. Let $q = Ak^{\frac{1}{3}}$. Assume that the productivity level A in Turkey is lower than that in the EU.

   a. Draw a production function diagram (with output per worker y as a function of capital per worker k) and an MPK diagram (*MPK* versus k) for the EU. (*Hint*: Be sure to draw the two diagrams with the production function directly above the MPK diagram so that the level of capital per worker k is consistent on your two diagrams.)

   b. For now, assume capital cannot flow freely in and out of Turkey. On the same diagrams, plot Turkish production function and *MPK* curves, assuming that the productivity level A in Turkey is half the EU level and that Turkish *MPK* exceeds EU *MPK*. Label the EU position in each chart *EU* and the Turkish position *T1*.

   c. Assume capital can now flow freely between Turkey and the EU and the rest of the world, and that the EU is already at the point where $MPK = r^*$. Label r^* on the vertical axis of the MPK diagram. Assume no risk premium. What will Turkey's capital per worker level k be? Label this outcome point *T2* in each diagram. Will Turkey converge to the EU level of q? Explain.

9. This question continues from the previous problem, focusing on how risk premiums explain the gaps in living standards across countries.

   a. Investors worry about the rule of law in Turkey and also about the potential for hyperinflation and other bad macroeconomic policies. Because of these worries, the initial gap between MPK in Turkey and r^* is a risk premium (RP). Label RP on the vertical axis of the MPK diagram. Now where does Turkey end up in terms of k and q?

   b. In light of (a), why might Turkey be keen to join the EU?

   c. Some EU countries are keen to exclude Turkey from the EU. What might be the *economic* arguments for that position?

10. In this chapter, we saw that financial market integration is necessary for countries to smooth consumption through borrowing and lending. Consider two economies: those of the Czech Republic and France. For each of the following shocks, explain how and to what extent each country can trade capital to better smooth consumption.

   a. The Czech Republic and France each experience an EU-wide recession.

   b. A strike in France leads to a reduction in French income.

   c. Floods destroy a portion of the Czech capital stock, lowering Czech income.

11. Assume that a country produces an output Q of 50 every year. The world interest rate is 10%. Consumption C is 50 every year, and $I = G = 0$. There is an unexpected drop in output in year 0, so output falls to 28 and is then expected to return to 50 in every future year. If the country desires to smooth consumption, how much should it borrow in period 0? What will the new level of consumption be from then on?

12. Assume that a country produces an output Q of 50 every year. The world interest rate is 10%. The country currently plans a consumption level C equal to 50 every year, and $I = G = 0$. There is then an unexpected war in year 0, which costs 22 units and is predicted to last one year. If the country desires to smooth consumption, how much should it borrow in period 0? What will the new level of consumption be from then on?

   The country wakes up in year 1 and discovers that the war is still going on and will eat up another 22 units of expenditure in year 1. If the country still desires to smooth consumption looking forward from year 1, how much should it borrow in period 1? What will the new level of consumption be from then on?

13. This question refers to Appendix 2. To learn more about the aid debate, download some of the conflicting arguments made by two prominent figures: Jeffrey Sachs and William Easterly (Hint: search online for "sachs easterly"). See, for example, their "Foreign Aid Face-off" in the *Los Angeles Times* (latimes.com, May 8,

2006). See also Nicholas Kristof, "Aid: Can It Work?" *New York Review of Books*, October 5, 2006. After weighing all these arguments, do you feel more or less optimistic about what aid can achieve?

14. Consider a world of two countries: Highland (H) and Lowland (L). Each country has an average output of 9 and desires to smooth consumption. All income takes the form of capital income and is fully consumed each period.

    a. Initially, there are two states of the world: Pestilence (P) and Flood (F). Each happens with 50% probability. Pestilence affects Highland and lowers the output there to 8, leaving Lowland unaffected with an output of 10. Flood affects Lowland and lowers the output there to 8, leaving Highland unaffected with an output of 10. Devise a table with two rows corresponding to each state (rows marked P and F). In three columns, show income to three portfolios: the portfolio of 100% H capital, the portfolio of 100% L capital, and the portfolio of 50% H + 50% L capital.

    b. Two more states of the world appear: Armageddon (A) and Utopia (U). Each happens with 50% probability but is uncorrelated with the P–F state. Armageddon affects both countries equally and lowers income in each country by a further four units, whatever the P–F state. Utopia leaves each country unaffected. Devise a table with four rows corresponding to each state (rows marked PA, PU, FA, and FU). In three columns, show income to three portfolios: the portfolio of 100% H capital, the portfolio of 100% L capital, and the portfolio of 50% H + 50% L capital.

    Compare your answers to parts (a) and (b), and consider the optimal portfolio choices. Does diversification eliminate consumption risk in each case? Explain.

APPENDIX 1
Common Versus Idiosyncratic Shocks

In reality, home and foreign incomes will not have a perfect inverse correlation as we have assumed in the text. Let us generalize a bit more for our two countries, and focus on capital income.

A More General Case Suppose the shocks to capital income are a and b, for countries A and B, respectively, and that these take a random value each period. The common shock is the *average shock* in the two countries: $\frac{1}{2}(a+b)$. In the chapter, we assumed the average shock was zero, so the shocks were equal and opposite. In the real world, however, this need not be the case.

We can define the A-specific shock as the shock a minus the average shock: $a-\frac{1}{2}(a+b)=\frac{1}{2}(a-b)$. Similarly, the B-specific shock is b minus the average shock: $b-\frac{1}{2}(a+b)=\frac{1}{2}(b-a)$. These *idiosyncratic shocks* are nonzero as long as the A shock is not the same as the B shock, that is, as long as a is not equal to b.

By doing this algebraic manipulation, the A shock can be written as the common shock plus the A-specific shock:

$$a = \underbrace{\frac{1}{2}(a+b)}_{\text{Common shock}} + \underbrace{\frac{1}{2}(a-b)}_{\text{A-specific shock}}$$

Similarly, the B shock can be written as the common shock plus the B-specific shock:

$$b = \underbrace{\frac{1}{2}(a+b)}_{\text{Common shock}} + \underbrace{\frac{1}{2}(b-a)}_{\text{B-specific shock}}$$

We see that the country-specific shocks are the exact opposites of each other: $\frac{1}{2}(a-b)$ and $\frac{1}{2}(b-a)$. The good news is that country-specific shocks are a *diversifiable* risk and satisfy the conditions of the simple case examined in the chapter. So the income risk they generate can be eliminated by diversification: in the world portfolio, the country-specific shocks cancel out, as we can see by adding up the last two equations.

But the common shock is $\frac{1}{2}(a+b)$. As long as this is nonzero, these shocks matter, that is, as long as the shocks are not equal and opposite, pure asymmetric country-specific shocks. The bad news is, the global shocks are an *undiversifiable* risk—no matter which assets you own, you get hit with the global shock, so asset trade offers no escape from these risks.

Numerical Example Figure 6-A1 (an extension of Figure 6-7) provides an illustration of the partial reduction in risk that can be achieved in this case. In Figure 6-7, each country owned 50% of the world portfolio, and there were two states, labeled 1 and 2. Recall that the capital incomes produced by the capital in each country, in each state, were *asymmetric* as follows: in state 1, A = 36, B = 44; in state 2, A = 44, B = 36. The occurrence of states 1 and 2 was random with 50–50 odds. If A and B diversified by each holding 50% of the world portfolio, they each ended up with stable capital income of 40 every period.

FIGURE 6-A1

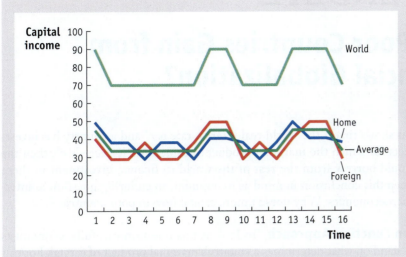

Portfolio Diversification and Capital Income: Undiversifiable Risks We take the example from Table 6-5 and Figure 6-7, and we add a common "global" shock to each country. With probability 50%, each country experiences a five-unit increase in capital income, and with probability 50% experiences a five-unit decrease in capital income. Holding half of the world portfolio reduces but does not eliminate capital income risk entirely because the global shock is an undiversifiable risk for the world as a whole.

In Figure 6-A1, we now add an extra "global" shock. This shock also has two states, labeled X and Y, that occur at random with 50–50 odds. However, the random X–Y shock is assumed to be *independent* of the 1–2 shock: and it is *symmetric* in the two countries, not asymmetric. We suppose that when the global shock is in state X, both countries receive 5 units more of capital income. When the global shock is in state Y, both countries receive 5 units less of capital income.

There are now four possible states of the world: 1X, 1Y, 2X, and 2Y. Each has a 25% chance of occurring. For the four states, the capital incomes of the portfolios are as follows:

1X	Home = 41	Foreign = 49	World = 90	Average = 45
2X	Home = 49	Foreign = 41	World = 90	Average = 45
1Y	Home = 31	Foreign = 39	World = 70	Average = 35
2Y	Home = 39	Foreign = 31	World = 70	Average = 35

From this table, and the example shown in Figure 6-A1, we see, as expected, that in this world, holding half of the world portfolio eliminates the risk associated with fluctuations between states 1 and 2. The best that each country can do is to have an income that fluctuates between 45 (half of 90, state X) and 35 (half of 70, state Y). In state X, all income risk associated with states 1 and 2 is gone. And in state Y, all income risk associated with states 1 and 2 is gone. But nothing can be done to eliminate the risk associated with fluctuations between states X and Y.

This more general result does not overturn our basic findings. Holding a 100% home portfolio generates a volatile capital income. So does holding a 100% foreign portfolio. Holding a mix of the two lowers the volatility of capital income, at least when some of the shocks are country-specific shocks, which is always the case in the real world.

APPENDIX 2

Can Poor Countries Gain from Financial Globalization?

Our analysis shows that if the world real interest rate is r^* and a country has investment projects for which the marginal product of capital MPK exceeds r^*, then the country should borrow from the rest of the world to finance investment in these projects. Keep this conclusion in mind as we examine an enduring question in international macroeconomics: Why doesn't more capital flow to poor countries?

Production Function Approach To look at this question carefully, economists must take a stand on what determines a country's marginal product of capital. For this purpose, economists usually employ a version of a **production function** that maps available capital per worker, $k = K/L$, and the prevailing level of **productivity** A to the level of output per worker, $q = Q/L$, where Q is gross domestic product (GDP).

A simple and widely used production function takes the form

$$\underbrace{q}_{\substack{\text{Output} \\ \text{per} \\ \text{worker}}} = \underbrace{A}_{\substack{\text{Productivity} \\ \text{level}}} \times \underbrace{k^{\theta}}_{\substack{\text{Capital} \\ \text{per worker}}}$$

where θ is a number between 0 and 1 that measures the contribution of capital to production.[16] Specifically, θ is the elasticity of output with respect to capital (i.e., a 1% increase in capital per worker generates a θ% increase in output per worker). In the real world, θ has been estimated to be approximately one-third, and this is the value we employ here.[17] An illustration is given in the top part of Figure 6-A2, panel (a), which graphs the production function for the case in which $\theta = \frac{1}{3}$ and the productivity level is set at a reference level of 1, so $A = 1$. Thus, for this case $q = k^{\frac{1}{3}}$.

With this production function, what is the marginal product of capital, MPK? It is the slope of the production function, the incremental change in output per worker Δq divided by the incremental change in capital per worker Δk. As we can see from the figure, capital's marginal product MPK (the extra output we get by increasing capital per worker) decreases as k increases. Indeed, from the preceding formula, we can find that MPK, or the slope of the production function, is given by

$$MPK = \frac{\Delta q}{\Delta k} = \underbrace{\theta A k^{\theta - 1}}_{\substack{\text{Slope of the} \\ \text{production function}}} = \theta \times \frac{q}{k}$$

Thus, in this special case, the *marginal product of capital* is proportional to output per worker divided by capital per worker (the output–capital ratio) or the *average product of capital*. The MPK for the case we are studying, in which $\theta = \frac{1}{3}$ and $A = 1$, is shown in the bottom part of Figure 6-A2, panel (a).

---

[16] This is called the Cobb–Douglas production function.

[17] Douglas Gollin, April 2002, "Getting Income Shares Right," *Journal of Political Economy*, 110(2), 458–474.

FIGURE 6-A2

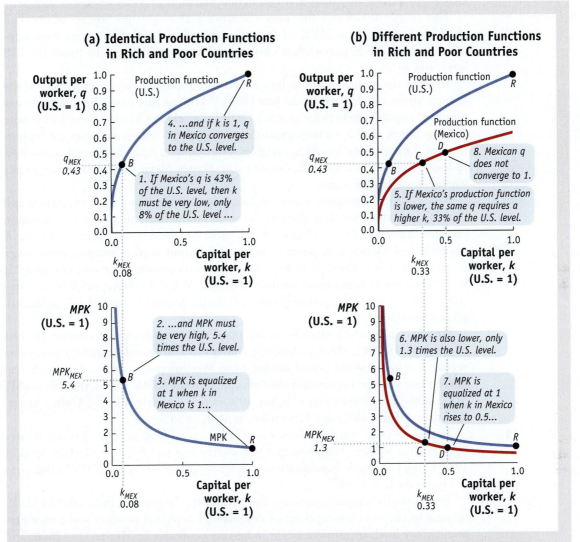

(a) Identical Production Functions in Rich and Poor Countries

Output per worker, q (U.S. = 1)

Production function (U.S.)

4. ...and if k is 1, q in Mexico converges to the U.S. level.

q_{MEX} 0.43

B

1. If Mexico's q is 43% of the U.S. level, then k must be very low, only 8% of the U.S. level ...

Capital per worker, k (U.S. = 1)

k_{MEX} 0.08

MPK (U.S. = 1)

2. ...and MPK must be very high, 5.4 times the U.S. level.

MPK_{MEX} 5.4

B

3. MPK is equalized at 1 when k in Mexico is 1...

MPK

R

Capital per worker, k (U.S. = 1)

k_{MEX} 0.08

(b) Different Production Functions in Rich and Poor Countries

Output per worker, q (U.S. = 1)

Production function (U.S.)

Production function (Mexico)

C   D

8. Mexican q does not converge to 1.

q_{MEX} 0.43

B

5. If Mexico's production function is lower, the same q requires a higher k, 33% of the U.S. level.

Capital per worker, k (U.S. = 1)

k_{MEX} 0.33

MPK (U.S. = 1)

6. MPK is also lower, only 1.3 times the U.S. level.

B

7. MPK is equalized at 1 when k in Mexico rises to 0.5...

MPK_{MEX} 1.3

C   D

R

Capital per worker, k (U.S. = 1)

k_{MEX} 0.33

Why Doesn't Capital Flow to Poor Countries? If poor and rich countries share the same level of productivity (a common production function), then MPK must be very high in poor countries, as shown in panel (a). For example, if B represents Mexico and R the United States, we would expect to see large flows of capital to poor countries, until their capital per worker k and, hence, output per worker q rise to levels seen in the rich world (movement from point B to point R). The result is convergence. This doesn't happen in reality. Poor and rich countries have different levels of productivity (different production functions) and so MPK may not be much higher in poor countries than it is in rich countries, as shown in panel (b). The poor country (Mexico) is now at C and not at B. Now investment occurs only until MPK falls to the rest of the world level at point D. The result is divergence. Capital per worker k and output per worker q do not converge to the levels seen in the rich country.

A Benchmark Model: Countries Have Identical Productivity Levels

To see how a country responds to the possibilities opened up by financial globalization, let's look at what determines the incentive to invest in small open economies of the type we are studying, assuming they all have access to the same level of productivity, $A = 1$.

To understand when such a country will invest, we need to understand how its MPK changes as k changes. For example, suppose the country increases k by a factor of 8. Because $q = k^{\frac{1}{3}}$, q increases by a factor of 2 (the cube root of 8). Let's suppose this brings the country up to the U.S. level of output per worker. Because $MPK = \theta \times (q/k)$

and because q has risen by a factor of 2, while k has risen by a factor of 8, MPK changes by a factor of $\frac{1}{4}$; that is, it falls to one-fourth its previous level.

This simple model says that poor countries with output per worker of one-half the U.S. level have an MPK of four times the U.S level. Countries with one-quarter $\left(\frac{1}{4}\right)$ the U.S. per-worker output level have an MPK of 16 times the U.S level, and so on.

To make the model concrete, let's see how well it applies to a comparison of the United States and Mexico in the late 1980s.[18] During this time, the United States produced approximately twice as much GDP per worker as Mexico. Now let's choose units such that all U.S. variables take the value 1, and Mexican variables are proportions of the corresponding U.S. variables. For example, with these units, q was 0.43 in Mexico in the late 1980s (i.e., output per worker in Mexico was 43% of output per worker in the United States).

Now consider the implications of assuming that the economies of Mexico and the United States were described by the same production function with a common productivity level, $A = 1$. In Figure 6-A2, panel (a), the United States is at point R (for rich) and Mexico is at point B, and its low output implies a capital per worker k that is only 8% of the U.S. level. What is Mexico's marginal product of capital? It is 5.4 times the U.S. marginal product of capital. Why? As above, MPK is θ (a constant for both countries equal to $\frac{1}{3}$) times q/k. In the United States, $q/k = 1$; in Mexico, $q/k = 0.43/0.08 = 5.4$.

We can think of the United States and other rich countries as representing the rest of the world (ROW), which collectively amount to a large and financially integrated region, that is, the world capital market, from Mexico's point of view. The world real interest rate r^* is the opportunity cost of capital for the ROW, that is, the rich world's MPK. If the real interest rate r^* is, say, 10% in rich countries like the United States, then their MPK is 10%, and Mexico has an MPK of 54%!

To take an even more dramatic example, we could look at India, a much poorer country than Mexico. India's output per worker was just 8.6% of the U.S. level in 1988. Using our simple benchmark model, we would infer that the MPK in India was 135 times the U.S. level![19]

To sum up, the simple model says that the poorer the country, the higher its MPK, because of the twin assumptions of diminishing marginal product and a common productivity level. Investment ought to be very profitable in Mexico (and India, and all poor countries). Investment in Mexico should continue until Mexico is at point R. Economists would describe such a trajectory for Mexico as **convergence**. If the world is characterized by convergence, countries can reach the level of capital per worker and output per worker of the rich country through investment and capital accumulation alone.

The Lucas Paradox: Why Doesn't Capital Flow from Rich to Poor Countries?
Twenty or thirty years ago, a widespread view among economists was that poor countries had access to exactly the same technologies as rich countries, given the flow of ideas and knowledge around a globalizing world. This led economists to assume that if policies shifted to allow greater international movement of capital, foreign investment would flood into poor countries because their very poverty implied that capital was scarce in these countries, and therefore its marginal product was high.

---

[18] In 1985 levels of GDP per worker were $23,256 in Mexico and $48,164 in the United States (in 1996 international dollars), according to the reference source for such data, the Penn World Tables. By 1995 this gap had widened a little. The data in this example are based on Robert E. Hall and Charles I. Jones, 1999, "Why Do Some Countries Produce So Much More Output per Worker Than Others?" *Quarterly Journal of Economics*, 114(1), 83–116.

[19] First solve for the relative level of capital per worker in India: $k_{IND}/k_{US} = [q_{IND}/q_{US}]^{1/\theta} = [0.086]^3 = 0.000636$. The relative MPK in India would then equal $[q_{IND}/q_{US}]/[k_{IND}/k_{US}] = [q_{IND}/q_{US}]^{1/\theta} = 0.086/[0.086]^3 = 1/[0.086]^2 = 135$.

But as Nobel laureate Robert Lucas wrote in his widely cited article "Why Doesn't Capital Flow from Rich to Poor Countries?":

> If this model were anywhere close to being accurate, and if world capital markets were anywhere close to being free and complete, it is clear that, in the face of return differentials of this magnitude, investment goods would flow rapidly from the United States and other wealthy countries to India and other poor countries. Indeed, one would expect no investment to occur in the wealthy countries. . . . The assumptions on technology and trade conditions that give rise to this example must be drastically wrong, but exactly what is wrong with them, and what assumptions should replace them?[20]

What was drastically wrong was the assumption of identical productivity levels A across countries, as represented by the single production function in Figure 6-A2, panel (a). Although this model is often invoked, it is generally invalid. Can we do better?

An Augmented Model: Countries Have Different Productivity Levels

To see why capital does not flow to poor countries, we now suppose that A, the productivity level, is different in the United States and Mexico, as denoted by country subscripts:

$$\underbrace{q_{US}}_{\substack{\text{Output per worker in} \\ \text{the United States}}} = \underbrace{A_{US}k_{US}^{\theta}}_{\text{U.S. production function}} \qquad \underbrace{q_{MEX}}_{\substack{\text{Output per worker} \\ \text{in Mexico}}} = \underbrace{A_{MEX}k_{MEX}^{\theta}}_{\text{Mexican production function}}$$

Countries have potentially different production functions and different MPK curves, depending on their relative levels of productivity, as shown in Figure 6-A2, panel (b). The Mexican curves are shown here as lower than the U.S. curves. We now show that this augmented model is a much better match with reality.

The earlier MPK equation holds for each country, so we can compute the ratios of country MPKs as

$$\frac{MPK_{MEX}}{MPK_{US}} = \frac{[\theta q_{MEX}/k_{MEX}]}{[\theta q_{US}/k_{US}]} = \frac{q_{MEX}/q_{US}}{k_{MEX}/k_{US}}$$

Using this equation, we can see the importance of allowing productivity levels to differ across countries. We know that $q_{MEX}/q_{US} = 0.43$, but we can also obtain data on capital per worker that show $k_{MEX}/k_{US} = 0.33$. If we plug these numbers into the last expression, we find that MPK in Mexico is not 5.4 times the U.S. level, as we had earlier determined, but only about 1.3 times (0.43/0.33) the U.S. level. The smaller multiple is due to the lower productivity level that our revised model reveals in Mexico.

Put another way, the data show that Mexico's capital per worker is about one-third ($\frac{1}{3}$) that of the United States. If the simple model were true, Mexico would have a level of output level per worker of $(\frac{1}{3})^{\frac{1}{3}} = 0.69$ or 69% of the U.S. level. However, Mexico's output per worker was much less, only 0.43 or 43% of the U.S. level. This gap can only be explained by a lower productivity level in Mexico. We infer that A in Mexico equals 0.43/0.69 = 0.63, or 63% of that in the United States.

This means that Mexico's production function and MPK curves are lower than those for the United States. This more accurate representation of reality is shown in Figure 6-A2, panel (b). Mexico is not at point B, as we assumed in panel (a); it is

---

[20] Robert E. Lucas, Jr., May 1990, "Why Doesn't Capital Flow from Rich to Poor Countries?" *American Economic Review*, 80(2), 92–96. Lucas presented the India example with the assumption that capital's share was 0.4 rather than one-third, and that India's output per worker was one-fifteenth of the U.S. level. In that case, India's MPK is "only" 58 times the U.S. level, an equally absurd conclusion.

at point C, on a different (lower) production function and a different (lower) MPK curve. The MPK gap between Mexico and the United States is much smaller, which greatly reduces the incentive for capital to migrate to Mexico from the United States.

The measured MPK differentials in the augmented model do not seem to indicate a major failure of global capital markets to allocate capital efficiently. But the augmented model has very different implications for convergence. Mexico would borrow only enough to move from point C to point D, where its MPK equals r^*. This investment would raise its output per worker a little, but it would still be far below that of the United States.

APPLICATION

A Versus k

In our previous calculations, we found that Mexico did not have a high level of MPK relative to the United States. Hence, we would not expect large flows of capital into Mexico but would expect Mexico to remain relatively poor even with access to global financial markets.

Is this conclusion true in general? What about other developing countries? Table 6-A1 repeats the same exercise we just did for many developing countries, including Mexico. In all cases, predicted gross domestic product (GDP) gains due to financial globalization are large with the benchmark model, but disappointingly small once we augment the model to correct for productivity differences. Moreover, if we were to allow for the fact that gross national income (GNI) gains are less than GDP gains as a result of factor payments to foreign capital that would be due on foreign investment, then the net GNI gains would be smaller still.

This is a profound result. Once we allow for productivity differences, investment will not cause poor countries to reach the same level of capital per worker or output per worker as rich countries. Economists describe this outcome as one of long-run **divergence** between rich and poor countries. Unless poor countries can lift their levels of productivity (raise A), access to international financial markets is of limited use. They may be able to usefully borrow capital, thereby increasing output per worker by some amount, but there are not enough opportunities for productive investment for complete convergence to occur.

In the developing world, global capital markets typically are not failing. Rather, low levels of productivity A make investment unprofitable, leading to low output levels that do not produce convergence. But what exactly does A represent?

An older school of thought focused on A as reflecting a country's **technical efficiency**, construed narrowly as a function of its technology and management capabilities. Today, many economists believe there is very little blocking the flow of such knowledge between countries, and that the problem must instead be one of implementation. These economists believe that the level of A may primarily reflect a country's **social efficiency**, construed broadly to include institutions, public policies, and even cultural conditions such as the level of trust. Low productivity might then follow from low levels of human capital (poor education policies) or poor-quality institutions (bad governance, corruption, red tape, and poor provision of public goods, including infrastructure). And indeed there is some evidence that, among poorer countries, more capital does tend to flow to the countries with better institutions.[21]

---

[21] James R. Lothian, April 2006, "Institutions, Capital Flows and Financial Integration," *Journal of International Money and Finance*, 25(3), 358–369; Laura Alfaro, Sebnem Kalemli-Ozcan, and Vadym Volosovych, 2008, "Why Doesn't Capital Flow from Rich to Poor Countries? An Empirical Investigation," *Review of Economics and Statistics*, 90(2), 347–368.

TABLE 6-A1

Why Capital Doesn't Flow to Poor Countries The table shows data on output and capital per worker (columns 1 and 2). Column 3 shows the level of productivity relative to the United States that is implied by the data. Productivity differences are large for poor countries. If these differences are assumed away, then the gains from financial globalization in poor countries could be large (columns 4, 5). But if they remain, the gains will be small (columns 6, 7).

	(a) Data		(b) Implied Productivity (U.S. = 1)	(c) Outcomes with Financial Globalization			
				With Productivity at the U.S. level, A_{US} Increase in		With Actual Productivity, A Increase in	
Country, Group, or Region	$\dfrac{q}{q_{US}}$	$\dfrac{k}{k_{US}}$	$\dfrac{A}{A_{US}}$	Capital k	Output q	Capital k	Output q
	(1)	(2)	(3)	(4)	(5)	(6)	(7)
Latin America							
Argentina	0.42	0.38	0.58	+163%	+139%	+15%	+5%
Brazil	0.32	0.24	0.51	+311	+214	+50	+15
Chile	0.26	0.26	0.41	+289	+280	+4	+1
Mexico	0.43	0.33	0.63	+207	+131	+53	+15
Asia							
China	0.06	0.05	0.17	+2,001	+1,569	+41	+12
India	0.09	0.04	0.24	+2,213	+1,064	+180	+41
Indonesia	0.11	0.09	0.24	+980	+805	+30	+9
Pakistan	0.13	0.04	0.37	+2,202	+679	+408	+72
Africa							
Congo	0.12	0.06	0.32	+1,677	+722	+218	+47
Kenya	0.06	0.03	0.18	+3,078	+1,674	+140	+34
Nigeria	0.05	0.04	0.14	+2,259	+1,970	+22	+7
South Africa	0.25	0.23	0.41	+334	+300	+13	+4
	Group Average			Based on Group Average			
Per Capita Income Quintiles							
1st (Poorest 20% of countries)	0.04	0.02	0.15	+5,371%	+2,474%	+210%	+46%
2nd (2nd Poorest 20%)	0.10	0.07	0.25	+1,426	+907	+86	+23
3rd (Middle 20%)	0.21	0.18	0.38	+463	+368	+32	+10
4th (2nd Richest 20%)	0.40	0.37	0.56	+167	+148	+12	+4
5th (Richest 20%)	0.75	0.85	0.80	+17	+32	−17	−6
Major Groups							
Developing	0.15	0.11	0.31	+836	+572	+65	+18
Emerging	0.29	0.23	0.48	+329	+241	+41	+12

Data from: Robert E. Hall and Charles I. Jones, February 1999, "Why Do Some Countries Produce So Much More Output per Worker Than Others?" Quarterly Journal of Economics, 114(1), 83–116.

More Bad News? The augmented model shows that as long as productivity gaps remain, investment will be discouraged, and, regrettably, poor countries will not see their incomes converge to rich levels. If we now take some other factors into account, the predictions of the model about convergence are even less optimistic.

■ The model makes no allowance for risk premiums. Suppose the MPK is 10% in the United States and 13% in Mexico. The differential may be a risk premium Mexico must pay to foreign lenders that compensates them for the risk of investing in an emerging market (e.g., risks of regulatory changes, tax changes, expropriation, and other political risks). In this case, no additional capital flows into Mexico. In Figure 6-A2, panel (b), Mexico stays at point *C* and its income does not increase at all.

■ Risk premiums may be large enough to cause capital to flow "uphill" from poor to rich. If world capital markets impose a risk premium higher than 3%, say, 7%, then capital would actually leave Mexico for the United States, moving from the higher to the lower MPK region, in search of a "safe haven" that provides higher risk-adjusted returns. In Figure 6-A2, panel (b), Mexico would move left of point *C* as capital flowed out, and per capita output would fall. Is this a relevant case? Yes. Figure 6-A3 shows that risk premiums can be substantial in emerging markets, including Mexico. And U.S. Treasury securities data indicate that from 1994 to 2015, U.S. holdings of Mexican assets rose from $52 billion to $166 billion, but Mexican holdings of U.S. assets rose from $6 billion to $157 billion. On net, capital has moved north, not south.

■ The model assumes that investment goods can be acquired at the same relative price in output terms everywhere. In fact, the model treats one unit of investment as the same as one unit of output. But in developing countries, it often costs much more than one unit of output to purchase one unit of capital goods.

FIGURE 6-A3

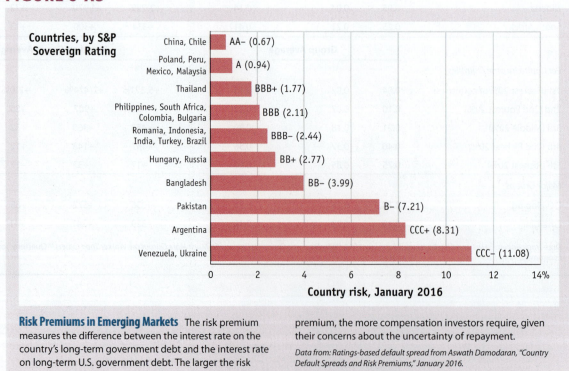

Risk Premiums in Emerging Markets The risk premium measures the difference between the interest rate on the country's long-term government debt and the interest rate on long-term U.S. government debt. The larger the risk premium, the more compensation investors require, given their concerns about the uncertainty of repayment.

Data from: Ratings-based default spread from Aswath Damodaran, "Country Default Spreads and Risk Premiums," January 2016.

Poor countries often are ill-equipped to efficiently supply nontraded capital goods (such as buildings or bridges), and their imported capital goods (such as machinery and equipment) are often quite expensive because of trade costs (such as tariffs and transport costs).[22]

- The model assumes that the contribution of capital to production is equal across countries. In our estimates, we used $\frac{1}{3}$ as the elasticity of output with respect to capital. But recent research suggests that capital's share may be much lower in many developing countries, where a large part of GDP is derived from natural resources with little use of physical capital. This lowers the MPK even more.[23]

- The model suggests that **foreign aid** may do no better than foreign investors in promoting growth. The model doesn't care where additional capital comes from. Investments paid for by transfers (aid or debt relief) rather than private investments face the same low MPK and the same divergence result holds. Economists dispute whether foreign aid can make a difference to long-term development and growth, or if it is only an act of charity to prop up the poor (or even a total waste of money). The argument also extends to non-market and preferential lending offered to poor countries by international financial institutions such as the **World Bank** (see **Side Bar: What Does the World Bank Do?**). In support of the case that aid can make a difference, aid proponents argue that aid can finance public goods that can provide externalities sufficient to jolt a poor country out of a bad equilibrium or "poverty trap"—goods that private markets cannot provide (such as infrastructure, public health, and education). Aid skeptics reply that the evidence for such effects is weak, either because the links are not there or because in practice aid is so bureaucratized and subject to so many diversions and misappropriations that very little of it actually gets spent wisely.

Some efforts are now being made to ensure that more aid is directed toward countries with better institutional environments: the U.S. Millennium Challenge

---

SIDE BAR

What Does the World Bank Do?

The World Bank (worldbank.org), based in Washington, D.C., is one of the Bretton Woods "twins" established in 1944 (the other is the International Monetary Fund). Its main arm, the International Bank for Reconstruction and Development, has 188 member countries. Its principal purpose is to provide financing and technical assistance to reduce poverty and promote sustained economic development in poor countries. A country's voting weight in the governance of the World Bank is based on the size of its capital contributions. The World Bank can raise funds at low interest rates and issue AAA-rated debt as good as that of any sovereign nation. It then lends to poor borrowers at low

rates. Because the borrower nations could not obtain loans on these terms (or even any terms) elsewhere, the loans are a form of aid or transfer. In return for the preferential rate, the bank may approve a loan for a particular development purpose (building infrastructure, for example) or to support a policy reform package. Controversially, conditions may also be imposed on the borrowing nation, such as changes in trade or fiscal policy. As a result of sovereignty, the implementation of the conditions and the use of the loans have in some cases not turned out as intended, although outright default on these preferential loans is almost unheard of.

---

[22] Alan M. Taylor, 1998, "On the Costs of Inward-Looking Development: Price Distortions, Growth, and Divergence in Latin America," *Journal of Economic History*, 58(1), 1–28; Jonathan Eaton and Samuel Kortum, 2001, "Trade in Capital Goods," *European Economic Review*, 45(7), 1195–1235.
[23] Francesco Caselli and James Feyrer, 2007, "The Marginal Product of Capital," *Quarterly Journal of Economics*, 122(2), 535–568.

Corporation has pursued this goal, as has the World Bank. But past evidence is not encouraging: an exhaustive study of aid and growth by economists Raghuram Rajan and Arvind Subramanian concluded: "We find little robust evidence of a positive (or negative) relationship between aid inflows into a country and its economic growth. We also find no evidence that aid works better in better policy or geographical environments, or that certain forms of aid work better than others. Our findings suggest that for aid to be effective in the future, the aid apparatus will have to be rethought."[24]

---

[24] Raghuram G. Rajan and Arvind Subramanian, 2008, "Aid and Growth: What Does the Cross-Country Evidence Really Show?" *Review of Economics and Statistics*, 90(4), 643–665.

7

Balance of Payments II: Output, Exchange Rates, and Macroeconomic Policies in the Short Run

If demand shifts from the products of country B to the products of country A, a depreciation by country B or an appreciation by country A would correct the external imbalance and also relieve unemployment in country B and restrain inflation in country A. This is the most favorable case for flexible exchange rates based on national currencies.

Robert Mundell, 1961

It is easy to understand the dislike . . . for a [fixed exchange rate] system which dictated that a slump must be aggravated by monetary reactions, although, doubtless, [people] had forgotten that the same system served to enhance booms.

Alec Ford, 1962

Questions to consider

1 How do the fluctuating economic forces of aggregate demand, operating through gross national expenditure and the trade balance, determine the equilibrium level of output in an economy in the short run?

2 In this setting, is it possible for fiscal and monetary policies to affect the short-run equilibrium outcome?

3 What are the pros and cons of using these policies to stabilize the economy, and how are the results of policy intervention shaped by the exchange rate regime?

Since the 2008 Global Financial Crisis, exchange rates have fluctuated a great deal, and they remain prominent in economic, financial, and political debates the world over. In early 2013, the head of the Deutsche Bundesbank, Jens Weidmann, used the term "currency war" as the euro gained strength against a weakening U.S. dollar. By 2019 the tables had turned in the United States, with President Donald Trump angrily tweeting about what he saw as a currency war against the United States by the Eurozone and China as their currencies weakened against the U.S. dollar. Why have exchange rate movements always caused such outbursts among political leaders and policymakers? Because the exchange rate matters for the performance of the economy as a whole.

Thus far our study of exchange rates has been largely disconnected from real activity and the rest of the economy. Chapters 2 through 4 developed a theory of exchange rates, in which the economy's level of output was taken as given. To gain a more complete understanding of how an open economy works, we now extend our theory to explore what happens when exchange rates and output fluctuate in the short run. To do this, we build on our balance of payments accounting framework to understand how macroeconomic aggregates (including output, income, consumption, investment, and the trade balance) move together and how they respond to shocks in an open economy.

The model we study is an open-economy variant of the IS–LM model that is widely used in the study of closed-economy macroeconomics. The key assumption of this type of Keynesian model is that prices are "sticky" in the short run so that output is determined by shifts in demand in the goods market. By the end of this chapter, we will have a model that explains the relationships among all the major macroeconomic variables in an open economy in the short run.

Such a model can shed light on many political economy issues, explaining why international tensions over flexible exchange rates keep erupting. We can also see how monetary and fiscal policies affect the economy, and discuss how they can be used to stabilize the economy and maintain full employment. One key lesson we learn in this chapter is that the feasibility and effectiveness of macroeconomic policies depend crucially on the type of exchange rate regime in operation.

1 Demand in the Open Economy

To understand macroeconomic fluctuations, we need to grasp how short-run disturbances affect three important markets in an economy: the goods market, the money market, and the forex market. In earlier chapters, we studied the forex market and the money market, so we will recap and apply here what we learned in those chapters. But what about the goods market? In the forex chapters, we assumed that output was fixed at a level $\bar{Y}$. We took this to be the full-employment level of output that would be expected to prevail in the long run, when all factor market prices have adjusted to ensure that all factors such as labor and capital are employed. *But these assumptions about output and employment are valid only in the long run.* To understand short-run fluctuations in economic activity, we now develop a short-run, sticky-price Keynesian model and show how fluctuations in demand can create fluctuations in real economic activity. To start building this model, we first make our assumptions clear and then look at how demand is defined and why it fluctuates.

Preliminaries and Assumptions

Our interest in this chapter is to study short-run fluctuations in a simplified, abstract world of two countries. Our main focus is on the home economy. We use an asterisk to denote foreign variables when we need them. For our purposes, the foreign economy can be thought of as "the rest of the world" (ROW). The key assumptions we make are as follows:

- Because we are examining the short run, we assume that home and foreign price levels, $\bar{P}$ and $\bar{P}^*$, are fixed due to price stickiness. As a result of price stickiness, expected inflation is fixed at zero, $\bar{\pi}^e = 0$. If prices are fixed, all quantities can be viewed as both real and nominal quantities in the short run because there is no inflation.

- We assume that government spending $\bar{G}$ and taxes $\bar{T}$ are fixed at some constant levels, which are subject to policy change.

- We assume that conditions in the foreign economy such as foreign output $\bar{Y}^*$ and the foreign interest rate $\bar{i}^*$ are fixed and taken as given. Our main interest is in the equilibrium and fluctuations in the home economy.

- We assume that income Y is equivalent to output: that is, gross domestic product (GDP) equals gross national disposable income (GNDI). From our study of the national accounts, we know that the difference between the two equals net factor income from abroad plus net unilateral transfers. The analysis in this chapter could easily be extended to include these additional sources of income, but this added complexity would not offer any additional significant insights. We further assume that net factor income from abroad (NFIA) and net unilateral transfers (NUT) are zero, which implies that the current account (CA) equals the trade balance (TB); for the rest of this chapter, we just refer to the trade balance.

Our main objective is to understand how output (income) is determined in the home economy in the short run. As we learned from the national accounts, total expenditure, or demand for home-produced goods and services, is made up of four components: consumption, investment, government consumption, and the trade balance. In the following section, we see how each component is determined in the short run, and use the fact that demand must equal supply to characterize the economy's short-run equilibrium.

Consumption

The simplest model of aggregate private consumption relates household **consumption** C to **disposable income** Y^d. As we learned in Chapter 5, disposable income is the level of total pretax income Y received by households minus the taxes paid by households $\overline{T}$, so that $Y^d = Y - \overline{T}$. Consumers tend to consume more as their disposable income rises, a relationship that can be represented by an increasing function, called the *consumption function:*

$$\text{Consumption} = C = C(Y - \overline{T})$$

A typical consumption function of this form is graphed in Figure 7-1; it slopes upward because consumption increases when disposable income increases.

This equation is known as the *Keynesian consumption function.* In some economic theories, consumption smoothing is both desirable and possible. That is, in any given year consumption need not depend on income in that year, but rather on total lifetime resources (wealth). In contrast, the Keynesian consumption function assumes that private consumption expenditure *is* sensitive to changes in current income. This assumption seems to be a more reasonable match with reality in the short run: research shows that there is not very much consumption smoothing at the household or national level in the short run.

FIGURE 7-1

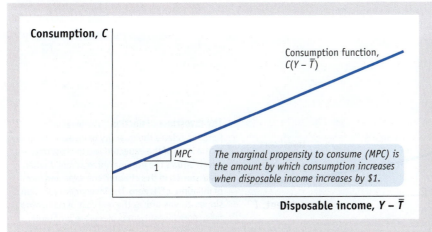

The marginal propensity to consume (MPC) is the amount by which consumption increases when disposable income increases by $1.

The Consumption Function The consumption function relates private consumption, C, to disposable income, $Y - \overline{T}$. The slope of the function is the marginal propensity to consume, MPC.

Marginal Effects The consumption function relates the level of consumption to the level of disposable income, but we are more often interested in the response of such variables to small changes in equilibrium, due to policy or other shocks. For that purpose, the slope of the consumption function is called the **marginal propensity to consume (MPC)**, and it tells us how much of every extra $1 of disposable income received by households is spent on consumption. We generally assume that MPC is between 0 and 1: when consumers receive an extra unit of disposable income (whether it's a euro, dollar, or yen), they will consume only part of it and save the remainder. For example, if you spend $0.75 of every extra $1 of disposable income you receive, your $MPC = 0.75$. The *marginal propensity to save (MPS)* is then given by $1 - MPC$. In this example $MPS = 0.25$, meaning that $0.25 of every extra $1 of disposable income is saved.

Investment

The simplest model of aggregate investment makes two key assumptions: firms can choose from many possible investment projects, each of which earns a different real return; and a firm will invest capital in a project only if the real returns exceed the firm's cost of borrowing capital. The firm's borrowing cost is the **expected real interest rate** r^e, which equals the nominal interest rate i minus the expected rate of inflation π^e: $r^e = i - \pi^e$. It is important to note that, in general, the expected real interest rate depends not only on the nominal interest rate but also on expected inflation. However, under our simplifying assumption that expected inflation is zero, the expected real interest rate equals the nominal interest rate, $r^e = i$.

When the expected real interest rate in the economy falls, we expect more investment projects to be undertaken. For example, at a real interest rate of 10%, there may be only $1 billion worth of profitable investment projects that firms wish to undertake; but if the real interest rate falls to 5%, there may now be $2 billion worth of profitable projects. Hence, our model assumes that investment I is a decreasing function of the real interest rate; that is, investment falls as the real interest rate rises.

$$\text{Investment} = I = I(i)$$

Remember that this is true only because when expected inflation is zero, the real interest rate equals the nominal interest rate. Figure 7-2 shows a typical investment function of this type. It slopes downward because as the real interest rate falls, the quantity of investment rises.

FIGURE 7-2

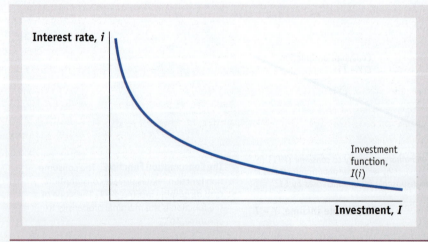

The Investment Function The investment function relates the quantity of investment, I, to the level of the expected real interest rate, which equals the nominal interest rate, i, when (as assumed in this chapter) the expected rate of inflation, π^e, is zero. The investment function slopes downward: as the real cost of borrowing falls, more investment projects are profitable.

Interest rate, i

Investment function, $I(i)$

Investment, I

The Government

To develop a basic model of economic activity in the short run, we assume that the government's role is simple. It collects an amount T of **taxes** from private households and spends an amount G on **government consumption** of goods and services.

Note that the latter includes only actual spending on goods and services bought by the public sector at all levels. For example, G includes military equipment and personnel, transport and infrastructure, public universities and schools, and so forth. Excluded from this concept are the often huge sums involved in government **transfer programs**, such as Social Security, medical care, or unemployment benefit systems, that redistribute income between households. Such transfers are excluded because we assume that *in the aggregate* they do not generate any change in the total expenditure on goods and services; they merely change who gets to engage in the act of spending. (Transfers are like negative taxes and, as such, can be seen as a part of T.)

In the unlikely event that $G = T$, government spending exactly equals taxes and we say that the government has a *balanced budget*. If $T > G$, the government is said to be running a *budget surplus* (of size $T - G$); if $G > T$, a *budget deficit* (of size $G - T$ or, equivalently, a negative surplus of $T - G$).

Fiscal policy is concerned with the levels of taxes and spending set by the government. In this chapter, we do not study in detail why or how governments make such policy choices; we make the simple assumption that in the short run the levels of taxes and spending are set exogenously at some fixed levels, denoted by an overbar:

$$\text{Government purchases} = G = \bar{G}$$
$$\text{Taxes} = T = \bar{T}$$

Policymakers may change these levels of taxes and spending at any time. We analyze the impact of such changes on the economy later in this chapter.

The Trade Balance

In the balance of payments chapter, we saw from an accounting standpoint that the trade balance (equal to exports minus imports) measures the impact of foreign trade on the demand for domestic output. To develop a model, however, we need to know what drives these flows, so in our simple model we now explore three key determinants of the trade balance: the real exchange rate, the level of home income, and the level of foreign income.

The Role of the Real Exchange Rate

What is the role of the real exchange rate? Recall George, the American tourist we met at the start of our study of exchange rates, who had to deal with a stronger dollar over the course of several years. If U.S. and French prices are sticky (constant in euro and U.S. dollar terms), then as the U.S. exchange rate appreciated, the prices of French goods and services became less and less expensive in dollar terms. In the end, George was ready to take a vacation in Paris instead of California. In the aggregate, when spending patterns change in response to changes in the real exchange rate, we say that there is **expenditure switching** from foreign purchases to domestic purchases.

Expenditure switching is a major factor in determining the level of a country's exports and imports. When learning about exchange rates in the long run, we saw that the real exchange rate is the price of goods and services in a foreign economy relative to the price of goods and services in the home economy. If Home's exchange rate is E, the home price level is $\bar{P}$ (fixed in the short run), and the foreign price level is $\bar{P}^*$ (also fixed in the short run), then the real exchange rate q of Home is defined as $q = E\bar{P}^*/\bar{P}$.

For example, suppose that the home country is the United States, and the reference basket costs \$100; suppose that in Canada the same basket costs C\$120 and the exchange rate is \$0.90 per Canadian dollar. In the expression $q = E\overline{P}^*/\overline{P}$, the numerator $E\overline{P}^*$ is the price of foreign goods converted into home currency terms, $\$108 = 120 \times 0.90$; the denominator $\overline{P}$ is the home currency price of home goods, \$100; the ratio of the two is the real exchange rate, $q = \$108/\$100 = 1.08$. This is the relative price of foreign goods in terms of home goods. In this case, Canadian goods are more expensive than U.S. goods.

A rise in the home real exchange rate (a real depreciation) signifies that foreign goods have become more expensive relative to home goods. As the real exchange rate rises, both home and foreign consumers will respond by *expenditure switching*: the home country will import less (as *home* consumers switch to buying home goods) and export more (as *foreign* consumers switch to buying home goods). These concepts are often seen in economic debates and news coverage (see **Headlines: The Curry Trade**), and they provide us with the following insight:

- *We expect the trade balance of the home country to be an increasing function of the home country's real exchange rate. That is, as the home country's real exchange rate rises (depreciates), it will export more and import less, and the trade balance rises.*

HEADLINES

The Curry Trade

In 2009, a dramatic weakening of the pound against the euro sparked an unlikely boom in cross-Channel grocery deliveries—a good example of how currency movements can lead to expenditure switching.

If carrying coals to Newcastle is judged a pointless exercise, then importing croissants, baguettes and bottles of claret into France might seem even more absurd. But, due to the strength of the euro against the pound, hundreds of Britons living in France are now using the internet to order their food, including many French specialties, from British supermarkets.

Simon Goodenough, the director of Sterling Shopping, a delivery firm based in Brackley, Northamptonshire, says his company has 2,500 British customers in France and is running five delivery vans full of food to France each week.

"We deliver food from Waitrose, Sainsbury's and Marks and Spencer, but by far the biggest is Asda," said Goodenough ". . . We sit in our depot sometimes looking at the things people have bought and just laugh at the craziness of it all. We have seen croissants and baguettes in people's shopping bags. And we have delivered bottles of Bergerac wine bought from Sainsbury's to a customer in Bergerac. We even have a few French customers who have now heard about what we do. They love things like curries and tacos, which they just can't get in France." . . .

Goodenough said many of his company's British customers hold pensions or savings in sterling rather than euros: "They have seen a 30% drop in their spending power over the past 18 months."

John Steventon owns La Maison Removals, a delivery company based in Rayleigh, Essex. It takes food from its warehouse to about 1,000 British customers in central France.

"We just can't cope with demand at the moment," he said. . . . "We found that friends in France were asking us to bring over British food for them so we just thought it made sense to set up a food delivery service. . . . The savings for buying food, in particular, are amazing due to the strength of the euro. Customers tell us that for every £100 they would spend in France buying food, they save £30 buying through us, even with our 15% commission. A lot of people are using us to get things they really miss, such as bacon and sausages."

Nikki Bundy, 41, has lived near Périgueux in the Dordogne with her family for four years. . . . "It's just so much cheaper for us to buy our food this way. . . . The food in France is lovely, but you can come out of a supermarket here with just two carrier bags having spent €100. I still try and buy my fresh fruit and veg in France, but most other things I now buy from Asda."

Source: Excerpted from Leo Hickman, "Expat orders for British supermarket food surge on strength of euro," The Guardian, June 9, 2010. Copyright Guardian News & Media Ltd 2010.

The Role of Income Levels The other determinant of the trade balance we might wish to consider is the income level in each country. As we argued earlier in our discussion of the consumption function, when domestic disposable income increases, consumers tend to spend more on all forms of consumption, including consumption of foreign goods. These arguments provide a second insight:

■ *We expect an increase in home income to be associated with an increase in home imports and a fall in the home country's trade balance.*

Symmetrically, from the standpoint of the ROW, an increase in ROW income ought to be associated with an increase in ROW spending on home goods, resulting in an increase in home exports. This is our third insight:

■ *We expect an increase in rest of the world income to be associated with an increase in home exports and a rise in the home country's trade balance.*

Combining the three insights above, we can write the trade balance as a function of three variables: the real exchange rate, home disposable income, and ROW disposable income:

$$TB = TB(\; \underbrace{E\bar{P}^*/\bar{P}}_{\substack{\text{Increasing}\\\text{function}}},\; \underbrace{Y - \bar{T}}_{\substack{\text{Decreasing}\\\text{function}}},\; \underbrace{Y^* - \bar{T}^*}_{\substack{\text{Increasing}\\\text{function}}}\;)$$

Figure 7-3 shows the relationship between the trade balance and the real exchange rate for the home country, all else equal—that is, holding home and foreign disposable income fixed. The trade balance is an *increasing* function of the real exchange rate $q = E\bar{P}^*/\bar{P}$. Thus, the relationship shown in Figure 7-3 is upward sloping. The reason is that an increase in the real exchange rate (a real depreciation) increases the trade balance by raising exports and lowering imports, implying a movement along the curve drawn.

The effect of the real exchange rate on the trade balance is now clear. What about the effects of changes in output? Figure 7-3 also shows the impact of an increase in home output on the trade balance. At any level of the real exchange rate, an increase in home output leads to more spending on imports, lowering the trade balance. This

FIGURE 7-3

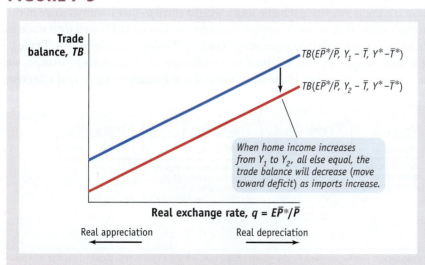

The Trade Balance and the Real Exchange Rate The trade balance is an increasing function of the real exchange rate, $E\bar{P}^*/\bar{P}$. When there is a real depreciation (a rise in q), foreign goods become more expensive relative to home goods, and we expect the trade balance to increase as exports rise and imports fall (a rise in TB). The trade balance may also depend on income. If home income levels rise, then some of the increase in income may be spent on the consumption of imports. For example, if home income rises from Y_1 to Y_2, then the trade balance will decrease, whatever the level of the real exchange rate, and the trade balance function will shift down.

change would be represented as a downward shift in the trade balance curve, that is, a reduction in the trade balance for a given level of $q = E\bar{P}^*/\bar{P}$.

Marginal Effects Once More The impact of changes in output on the trade balance can also be thought of in terms of the marginal propensity to consume. Suppose home output (which equals home income, because of the assumptions we've made) rises by an amount $\Delta Y = \$1$ and that, all else equal, this leads to an increase in home imports of $\Delta IM = \$MPC_F$, where $MPC_F > 0$. We refer to MPC_F as the *marginal propensity to consume foreign imports*. For example, if $MPC_F = 0.1$, this means that out of every additional \$1 of income, \$0.10 are spent on imports.

How does MPC_F relate to the MPC seen earlier? After a \$1 rise in income, any additional goods consumed have to come from somewhere, home or abroad. The fraction $\$MPC$ of the additional \$1 spent on all consumption must equal the sum of the incremental spending on home goods plus incremental spending on foreign goods. Let $MPC_H > 0$ be the *marginal propensity to consume home goods*. By assumption, $MPC = MPC_H + MPC_F$. For example, if $MPC_F = 0.10$ and $MPC_H = 0.65$, then $MPC = 0.75$; for every extra dollar of disposable income, home consumers spend 75 cents; 10 cents on imported foreign goods, and 65 cents on home goods (and they save 25 cents).[1]

APPLICATION

The Trade Balance and the Real Exchange Rate

Our theory assumes that the trade balance increases when the real exchange rate rises. Is there evidence to support this proposition? In Figure 7-4, we examine the evolution of the U.S. trade balance (as a share of GDP) in recent years as compared with the U.S. real exchange rate with the rest of the world (ROW).

By considering the home country to be the United States and the foreign "country" to be ROW, we cannot use data on the *bilateral* real exchange rate q for any individual foreign country. We need a composite or weighted-average measure of the price of goods in all foreign countries relative to the price of U.S. goods. To accomplish this, economists construct *multilateral* measures of real exchange rate movement.

The most common weighting scheme uses a weight equal to that country's share in the home country's trade. If there are N foreign countries, we can write Home's total trade as the sum of its trade with each foreign country: $\text{Trade} = \text{Trade}_1 + \text{Trade}_2 + \cdots + \text{Trade}_N$. Applying a trade weight to each bilateral real exchange rate's percentage change, we obtain the percentage change in Home's multilateral real exchange rate or **real effective exchange rate**:

$$\underbrace{\frac{\Delta q_{\text{effective}}}{q_{\text{effective}}}}_{\substack{\text{Real effective} \\ \text{exchange rate} \\ \text{change (in \%)}}} = \underbrace{\left(\frac{\text{Trade}_1}{\text{Trade}}\frac{\Delta q_1}{q_1}\right) + \left(\frac{\text{Trade}_2}{\text{Trade}}\frac{\Delta q_2}{q_2}\right) + \cdots + \left(\frac{\text{Trade}_N}{\text{Trade}}\frac{\Delta q_N}{q_N}\right)}_{\substack{\text{Trade-weighted average of} \\ \text{bilateral real exchange rate} \\ \text{changes (in \%)}}}$$

---

[1] A similar calculation can be applied to the export function, where exports will depend on the marginal propensity to consume imports in the foreign country.

FIGURE 7-4

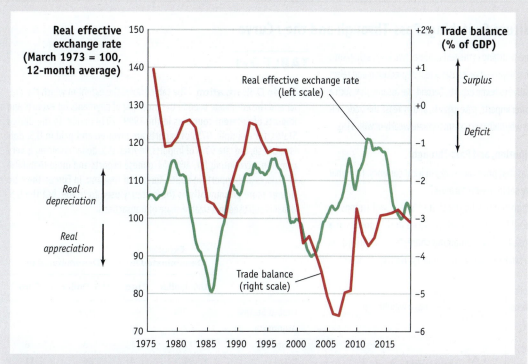

The Real Exchange Rate and the Trade Balance: United States, 1975–2018 Does the real exchange rate affect the trade balance in the way we have assumed? The data show that the U.S. trade balance is correlated with the U.S. real effective exchange rate index. Because the trade balance also depends on changes in U.S. and rest of the world disposable incomes (and other factors), and because it may respond with a lag to changes in the real exchange rate, the correlation is not perfect (as seen in the years 2000–08 when the United States had a spending boom).

Data from: Federal Reserve Economic Data (FRED).

For example, if we trade 40% with country 1 and 60% with country 2, and we have a real appreciation of 10% against 1 but a real depreciation of 30% against 2, then the change in our real effective exchange rate is $(40\% \times -10\%) + (60\% \times 30\%) = (0.4 \times -0.1) + (0.6 \times 0.3) = -0.04 + 0.18 = 0.14 = +14\%$. That is, we have experienced an effective trade-weighted real depreciation of 14%.

Figure 7-4 shows that the U.S. multilateral real exchange rate and the U.S. trade balance have been mostly positively correlated, as predicted by our model. In periods when the United States has experienced a real depreciation, the U.S. trade balance has tended to increase. Conversely, real appreciations have usually been associated with a fall in the trade balance. However, the correlation between the real exchange rate and the trade balance is not perfect. There appears to be a lag between, say, a real depreciation and a rise in the trade balance (as in the mid-1980s). Why? Import and export flows may react only slowly or weakly to changes in the real exchange rate, so the trade balance can react in unexpected ways (see **Side Bar: Barriers to Expenditure Switching: Pass-Through and the J Curve**). We can also see that the trade balance and real exchange rate did not move together as much during the years 2000 to 2008 because other factors, such as tax cuts and wartime spending, may have created extra deficit pressures that spilled over into the U.S. current account during this period.

SIDE BAR

Barriers to Expenditure Switching: Pass-Through and the J Curve

The basic analysis of expenditure switching in the text assumes two key mechanisms. First, we assume that a nominal depreciation causes a real depreciation and raises the price of foreign imports relative to home exports. Second, we assume that such a change in relative prices will lower imports, raise exports, and increase the trade balance. In reality, there are reasons why both mechanisms operate weakly or with a lag.

Trade Dollarization, Distribution, and Pass-Through

One assumption we made was that prices are sticky in local currency. But what if some *home* goods prices are set in *foreign* currency?

For example, let the foreign country be the United States and suppose a share d of the home-produced basket of goods is priced in U.S. dollars at a sticky *dollar* price $\overline{P}_1$. Suppose that the remaining share, $1-d$, is priced, as before, in local currency at a sticky *local currency* price $\overline{P}_2$. Hence,

$$\left.\begin{array}{c}\text{Price of foreign goods}\\ \text{relative to dollar-priced}\\ \text{home goods}\end{array}\right\} = \frac{E \times \overline{P}^*}{E \times \overline{P}_1} = \frac{\overline{P}^*}{\overline{P}_1} \text{ has a weight} = d$$

$$\left.\begin{array}{c}\text{Price of foreign goods}\\ \text{relative to local-currency-}\\ \text{priced home goods}\end{array}\right\} = \frac{E \times \overline{P}^*}{\overline{P}_2} \text{ has a weight} = 1-d$$

In this setup, what is the price of all foreign-produced goods relative to all home-produced goods (the real exchange rate)? It is the weighted sum of the relative prices of the two parts of the basket. Hence, we find

$$q = \text{Home real exchange rate} = d\frac{\overline{P}^*}{\overline{P}_1} + (1-d)\frac{E\overline{P}^*}{\overline{P}_2}$$

The first term with a weight d does not contain E because both numerator and denominator are dollar prices (already expressed in a common currency). Only the second term with a weight $(1-d)$ contains E, since the prices are in different currencies. Thus, a 1% increase in E will lead to only a $(1-d)$% increase in the real exchange rate.

When d is 0, all home goods are priced in local currency and we have our basic model; a 1% rise in E causes a 1% rise in q. There is full **pass-through** from changes in the nominal exchange rate to changes in the real exchange rate. But as d rises, pass-through falls. If d is 0.5, then a 1% rise in E causes just a 0.5% rise in q. The real exchange rate becomes less responsive to changes in the nominal exchange rate, and this means that expenditure switching effects will be muted.

It turns out that many countries around the world conduct a large fraction of their trade in a currency other than their own, such as U.S. dollars. The most obvious examples of goods with dollar prices are the major commodities: oil, copper, wheat, and so on. In some Persian Gulf economies, a nominal depreciation of the exchange rate does almost nothing to change the price of exports (more than 90% of which is oil priced in dollars) relative to the price of imports (again, overwhelmingly priced in dollars).

But dollar invoicing—and in Greater Europe, euro invoicing—extends around the world, as shown in Table 7-1. More than 90% of U.S. exports and imports are priced in dollars: all else equal, a U.S. depreciation will hardly

TABLE 7-1

Trade Dollarization The table shows the extent to which the dollar and the euro were used in the invoicing of payments for exports and imports of different countries in the 1999–2014 period. In the United States, for example, 97% of exports are invoiced and paid in U.S. dollars, but so, too, are 93% of imports. In Asia, U.S. dollar invoicing is very common, accounting for 50% of Japanese exports and more than 80% of exports and imports in South Korea and Thailand. In Europe the euro figures more prominently as the currency used for trade, but the U.S. dollar is still used in a sizable share of transactions.

	Exports Denominated in		Imports Denominated in	
	U.S. Dollar	Euro	U.S. Dollar	Euro
United States	97%	—	93%	2%
Argentina	97	2	88	8
Australia	77	1	53	8
Brazil	94	4	84	11
Bulgaria	45	56	43	59
Canada	70	.	75	5
Colombia	99	0	99	0
Czech Republic	14	72	19	68
Denmark	23	31	25	32
Hungary	18	71	27	57
India	86	8	86	10
Indonesia	93	1	81	4
Israel	71	20	73	21
Japan	50	8	71	3
Malaysia	90	—	—	55
Norway	56	38	21	29
Pakistan	91	4	84	7
Poland	30	64	93	—
Romania	36	64	30	58
South Africa	52	17	31	67
South Korea	85	6	81	5
Sweden	27	22	25	36
Switzerland	19	35	13	53
Thailand	82	2	79	4
Turkey	46	41	59	31
Ukraine	76	7	75	16
United Kingdom	29	13	47	15
Euro Area:[*]				
France	40	50	47	45
Germany	24	62	35	55
Greece	61	35	63	33
Italy	32	61	51	44
Netherlands	36	50	47	42

	Exports Denominated in		Imports Denominated in	
	U.S. Dollar	Euro	U.S. Dollar	Euro
Portugal	35	55	43	52
Slovakia	4	95	22	77
Slovenia	12	81	30	66
Spain	34	58	41	54

For countries in the euro area the figures refer to imports and exports only with countries outside the monetary union.

Note: A dot means that the data are missing.

Data from: Averages for the years 1999–2014 for selected countries from Camila Casas, Federico Díez, Gita Gopinath, and Pierre-Olivier Gourinchas, "Dollar Pricing Redux," BIS Working Papers 653, Bank for International Settlements, 2017.

change the prices of these goods at all. Some Asian countries have trade flows that are over 80% dollarized. Much of this is intra-Asian trade; if, say, a Korean supplier sells to a Japanese manufacturer, very often they conduct the trade not in yen or won, but entirely in U.S. dollars, which is the currency of neither the exporter nor the importer! The table also shows that European countries have export and import trade heavily denominated in euros even when we look only at their trade with non-Eurozone countries.

Trade dollarization is not the only factor limiting pass-through in the real world. Even after an import has arrived at the port, it still has to pass through various intermediaries. The retail, wholesale, and other distribution activities all add a local currency cost or markup to the final price paid by the ultimate buyer. Suppose the markup is $100 on an import that costs $100 at the port, so the good retails for $200 in shops. Suppose a 10% depreciation of the dollar raises the port price to $110. All else equal, the retail price will rise to just $210, only a 5% increase at the point of final sale. Thus, expenditure switching by final users will be muted by the limited pass-through from port prices to final prices.

How large are these effects? A study of 76 developed and developing countries found that, over a period of one year, a 10% exchange rate depreciation resulted in a 6.5% rise in imported goods prices at the port of arrival but perhaps only a 4% rise in the retail prices of imported goods.[*]

The J Curve

Our model of the trade balance assumes that a real depreciation improves a country's trade balance by increasing exports and reducing imports. In reality, however, these effects may be slow to appear because orders for export and import goods are placed months in advance. Thus, at the moment of depreciation there will be no instantaneous change in export and import volumes.

What does this slow adjustment imply? Exports will continue to sell for a time in the same quantity and at the same domestic price, and so total export earnings remain fixed. What will change is the domestic price paid for the import goods. They will have become more expensive in domestic currency terms. If the same quantity of imports flows in but costs more per unit, then the home country's total import bill will rise.

As a result, if export earnings are fixed but import expenditures are rising, the trade balance will initially *fall* rather than rise, as shown in Figure 7-5. Only after time passes, and export and import orders adjust to the new relative prices, will the trade balance move in the positive direction we have assumed. Because of its distinctive shape, the curve traced out by the trade balance over time in Figure 7-5 is called the **J curve**. Some empirical studies find that the effects of the J curve last up to a year after the initial depreciation. Hence, the assumption that a depreciation boosts spending on the home country's goods may not hold in the very short run.

---

[*] Jeffrey A. Frankel, David C. Parsley, and Shang-Jin Wei, 2005, "Slow Passthrough Around the World: A New Import for Developing Countries?" National Bureau of Economic Research (NBER) Working Paper No. 11199.

FIGURE 7-5

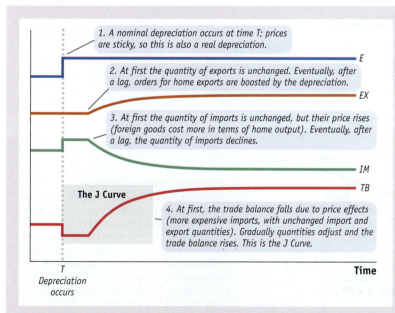

1. A nominal depreciation occurs at time *T*; prices are sticky, so this is also a real depreciation.

2. At first the quantity of exports is unchanged. Eventually, after a lag, orders for home exports are boosted by the depreciation.

3. At first the quantity of imports is unchanged, but their price rises (foreign goods cost more in terms of home output). Eventually, after a lag, the quantity of imports declines.

The J Curve

4. At first, the trade balance falls due to price effects (more expensive imports, with unchanged import and export quantities). Gradually quantities adjust and the trade balance rises. This is the J Curve.

T
Depreciation occurs

Time

The J Curve When prices are sticky and there is a nominal and real depreciation of the home currency, it may take time for the trade balance to move toward surplus. In fact, the initial impact may be toward deficit. If firms and households place orders in advance, then import and export quantities may react sluggishly to changes in the relative price of home and foreign goods. Hence, just after the depreciation, the value of home exports, *EX*, will be unchanged. However, home imports now cost more due to the depreciation. Thus, the value of imports, *IM*, would actually *rise* after a depreciation, causing the trade balance $TB = EX - IM$ to fall. Only after some time would exports rise and imports fall, allowing the trade balance to rise relative to its pre-depreciation level. The path traced by the trade balance during this process looks vaguely like a letter *J*.

Exogenous Changes in Demand

We have already treated as given, or exogenous, the changes or *shocks* in demand that originate in changes to government purchases or taxes. However, other exogenous changes in demand can affect consumption, investment, or the trade balance, and it is important to know how to analyze these, too. Examples of such changes are illustrated in Figure 7-6.

FIGURE 7-6

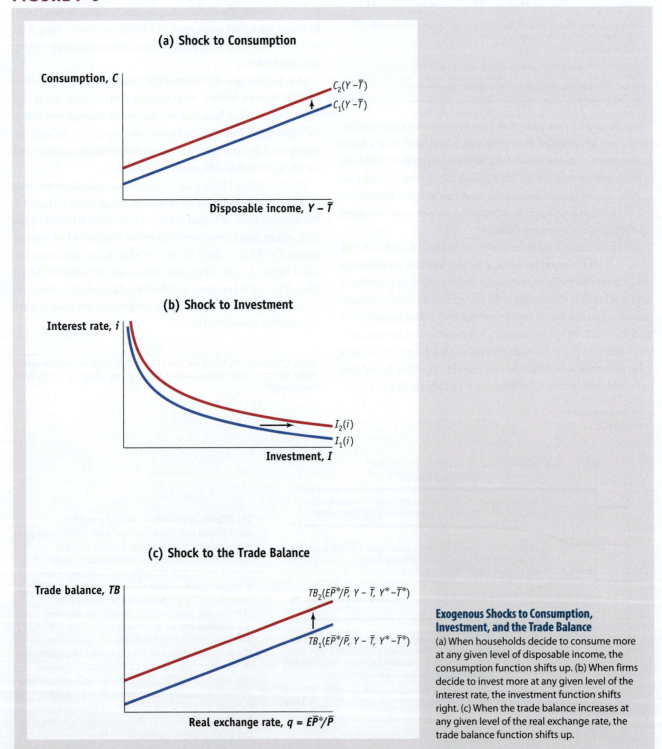

(a) Shock to Consumption

Consumption, C

$C_2(Y - \bar{T})$

$C_1(Y - \bar{T})$

Disposable income, $Y - \bar{T}$

(b) Shock to Investment

Interest rate, i

$I_2(i)$

$I_1(i)$

Investment, I

(c) Shock to the Trade Balance

Trade balance, TB

$TB_2(E\bar{P}^*/\bar{P}, \, Y - \bar{T}, \, Y^* - \bar{T}^*)$

$TB_1(E\bar{P}^*/\bar{P}, \, Y - \bar{T}, \, Y^* - \bar{T}^*)$

Real exchange rate, $q = E\bar{P}^*/\bar{P}$

Exogenous Shocks to Consumption, Investment, and the Trade Balance
(a) When households decide to consume more at any given level of disposable income, the consumption function shifts up. (b) When firms decide to invest more at any given level of the interest rate, the investment function shifts right. (c) When the trade balance increases at any given level of the real exchange rate, the trade balance function shifts up.

- *An exogenous change in consumption.* Suppose that at any given level of disposable income, consumers decide to spend more on consumption. After this shock, the consumption function would shift up as in Figure 7-6, panel (a). For example, an increase in household wealth following a stock market or housing market boom (as seen in expansions since 1990) could lead to a shift of this sort. This is a change in consumption demand unconnected to disposable income.

- *An exogenous change in investment.* Suppose that at any given level of the interest rate, firms decide to invest more. After this shock, the investment function would shift right as in Figure 7-6, panel (b). For example, a belief that high-technology companies had great prospects for success led to a large surge in investment in this sector in many countries in the 1990s. This is a change in investment demand unconnected to the interest rate.

- *An exogenous change in the trade balance.* Suppose that at any given level of the real exchange rate, export demand rises and/or import demand falls. After one of these shocks, the trade balance function would shift up as in Figure 7-6, panel (c). Such a change happened in the 1980s when U.S. consumers' tastes shifted away from the large domestic automobiles made in Detroit toward smaller fuel-efficient imported cars manufactured in Japan. This is a switch in demand away from U.S. and toward Japanese products that is unconnected with the real exchange rate.

2 Goods Market Equilibrium: The Keynesian Cross

We have now studied the determinants of each component of demand. We next put all the components together and show that the goods market is in equilibrium when total demand from all these components is equal to total supply.

Supply and Demand

The total aggregate *supply* of final goods and services is equal to total national output measured by GDP. Given our assumption that the current account equals the trade balance, gross national income equals GDP:

$$\text{Supply} = GDP = Y$$

Aggregate demand, or just "demand," consists of all the possible sources of demand for this supply of output. In the balance of payments chapter, we studied the expenditure side of the national income accounts and saw that supply is absorbed into different uses according to the national income identity. This accounting identity *always* holds true. But an identity is not an economic model. A model must explain how, in equilibrium, the observed demands take on their desired or planned values and still satisfy the accounting identity. How can we construct such a model?

We may write total demand for GDP as

$$\text{Demand} = D = C + I + G + TB$$

We can substitute the formulae for consumption, investment, and the trade balance presented in the first section of this chapter into this total demand equation to obtain

$$D = C(Y - \overline{T}) + I(i) + \overline{G} + TB(E\overline{P}^*/\overline{P}, Y - \overline{T}, Y^* - \overline{T}^*)$$

Finally, in an equilibrium, demand must equal supply, so from the preceding two equations we can see that the **goods market equilibrium condition** is

$$Y = \underbrace{C(Y - \overline{T}) + I(i) + \overline{G} + TB(E\overline{P}^*/\overline{P}, Y - \overline{T}, Y^* - \overline{T}^*)}_{D} \qquad \text{(7-1)}$$

Determinants of Demand

The right-hand side of Equation (7-1) shows that many factors can affect demand: home and foreign output (Y and Y^*), home and foreign taxes (T and T^*), the home nominal interest rate (i), government spending ($\bar{G}$), and the real exchange rate ($E\bar{P}^*/\bar{P}$). Let us examine each of these in turn. We start with home output (Y), and assume that all other factors remain fixed.

A rise in output Y (all else equal) will cause the right-hand side to increase. For example, suppose output increases by $\Delta Y = \$1$. This change causes consumption spending C to increase by $+\$MPC$. The change in imports will be $+\$MPC_F$, causing the trade balance to change by $-\$MPC_F$. So the total change in D will be $\$(MPC - MPC_F) = \$MPC_H > 0$, a positive number. This is an intuitive result: an extra \$1 of output generates some spending on home goods (an amount $\$MPC_H$), with the remainder either spent on foreign goods (an amount $\$MPC_F$) or saved (an amount $\$MPS$).

Using this result, Figure 7-7, panel (a), plots demand D, the right-hand side of Equation (7-1), as a function of income or output Y only. For the moment, we hold

FIGURE 7-7

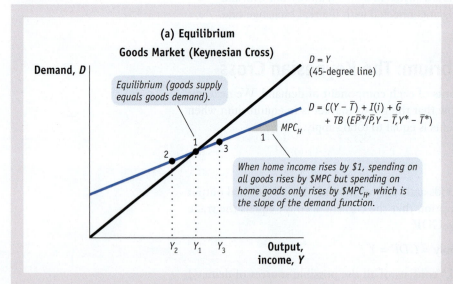

(a) Equilibrium
Goods Market (Keynesian Cross)

Demand, D

$D = Y$
(45-degree line)

Equilibrium (goods supply equals goods demand).

$D = C(Y - \bar{T}) + I(i) + \bar{G}$
$+ TB (E\bar{P}^*/\bar{P}, Y - \bar{T}, Y^* - \bar{T}^*)$

MPC_H

When home income rises by \$1, spending on all goods rises by $\$MPC$ but spending on home goods only rises by $\$MPC_H$, which is the slope of the demand function.

Y_2 Y_1 Y_3 Output, income, Y

Panel (a): The Goods Market Equilibrium and the Keynesian Cross   Equilibrium is where demand, D, equals real output or income, Y. In this diagram, equilibrium is at point 1, at an income or output level of Y_1. The goods market will adjust toward this equilibrium. At point 2, the output level is Y_2 and demand, D, exceeds supply, Y; as inventories fall, firms expand production and output rises toward Y_1. At point 3, the output level is Y_3 and supply Y exceeds demand; as inventories rise, firms cut production and output falls toward Y_1.

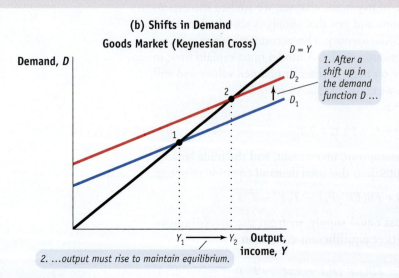

(b) Shifts in Demand
Goods Market (Keynesian Cross)

Demand, D

$D = Y$

D_2
D_1

1. After a shift up in the demand function D ...

Y_1 ⟶ Y_2 Output, income, Y

2. ...output must rise to maintain equilibrium.

Panel (b): Shifts in Demand   The goods market is initially in equilibrium at point 1, at which demand and supply both equal Y_1. An increase in demand, D, at all levels of real output, Y, shifts the demand curve up from D_1 to D_2. Equilibrium shifts to point 2, where demand and supply are higher and both equal Y_2. Such an increase in demand could result from changes in one or more of the components of demand: C, I, G, or TB.

fixed all other determinants of D. Because D increases as Y increases, the demand function has a positive slope MPC_H, a number between 0 and 1.

Also drawn is the 45-degree line, which represents Y, the left-hand side of Equation (7-1). The 45-degree line has a slope of 1, so it is steeper than the demand function.

This diagram is often called the **Keynesian cross**. It depicts the goods market equilibrium: the goods market is in equilibrium at point 1 where the two lines intersect, for that is the unique point where $D = Y$. This corresponds to an income or output level of Y_1.

Why does the goods market adjust to an equilibrium at this point? It must be that to the right of point 1, output tends to fall; to the left of point 1, output tends to rise. But why is that the case? The Keynesian adjustment process under the assumption of sticky prices centers on quantity adjustment by firms. At point 2, the output level is Y_2 and demand D exceeds supply Y; as their inventories fall, firms risk running out of goods to sell, so they move to expand production and output rises toward Y_1. At point 3, the output level is Y_3 and supply Y exceeds demand; as inventories rise, firms have too many goods unsold, so they move to cut production and output falls toward Y_1. Only at point 1 are firms in an equilibrium in which production levels are stable in the short run.

Note that the crucial assumptions in this model are that prices are fixed and firms are willing to adjust their production and employment to meet whatever the desired level of demand happens to be. These assumptions may be realistic in the short run, but they do not apply in the long run, when prices can adjust and output and employment are determined by the economy's ability to fully employ its technology and resources.

Factors That Shift the Demand Curve

The Keynesian cross also allows us to examine the impact of the other factors in Equation (7-1) on goods market equilibrium. Let's look at five important cases:

- *A change in government spending.* An exogenous rise in government purchases $\bar{G}$ (all else equal) increases demand at every level of output, as seen in Equation (7-1). More government purchases directly add to the total demand in the economy. This change causes an upward shift in the demand function D, as in Figure 7-7, panel (b). Goods market equilibrium shifts from point 1 to point 2, to an output level Y_2.

The lesson: any exogenous change in G (due to changes in the government budget) will cause the demand curve to shift.

- *A change in taxes (or other factors affecting consumption).* A fall in taxes $\bar{T}$ (all else equal) increases disposable income. When consumers have more disposable income, they spend more on consumption. This change raises demand at every level of output Y, because C increases as disposable income increases. This is seen in Equation (7-1) and in Figure 7-7, panel (b). Thus, a fall in taxes shifts the demand function upward from D_1 to D_2, as shown again in Figure 7-7, panel (b). The increase in D causes the goods market equilibrium to shift from point 1 to point 2, and output rises to Y_2.

The lesson: any exogenous change in C (due to changes in taxes, tastes, etc.) will cause the demand curve to shift.

- *A change in the home interest rate (or other factors affecting investment).* A fall in the interest rate, i, (all else equal) will lead to an increase in I, as firms find it profitable to engage in more investment projects, and spend more. This change leads to an increase in D at every level of output. The demand function shifts upward, as seen in Figure 7-7, panel (b). The increase in demand causes the goods market equilibrium to shift from point 1 to point 2, and output rises to Y_2.

The lesson: any exogenous change in I (due to changes in interest rates, the expected profitability of investment, changes in tax policy, etc.) will cause the demand curve to shift.

■ *A change in the home exchange rate.* A rise in the nominal exchange rate, E, (all else equal) implies a rise in the real exchange rate EP^*/P (due to sticky prices). This is a real depreciation, and through its effects on the trade balance via expenditure switching, it will increase demand at any given level of home output. For example, spending switches from foreign goods to American goods when the U.S. dollar depreciates. This change causes the demand function to shift up, as seen again in Figure 7-7, panel (b).

The lesson: any change in the exchange rate will cause the demand curve to shift.

■ *A change in the home or foreign price level.* If prices are flexible, then a *rise* in foreign prices or a *fall* in domestic prices causes a home real depreciation, raising $q = E\overline{P}^*/\overline{P}$. This real depreciation causes the trade balance to rise and, all else equal, it will increase demand at any given level of home output. For example, spending switches from foreign goods to American goods when the U.S. prices fall. This change causes the demand function D to shift up, as seen yet again in Figure 7-7, panel (b).

The lesson: any change in P^* or P will cause the demand curve to shift.

Summary

An increase in output Y causes a move along the demand curve (and similarly for a decrease). But any increase in demand that is *not* due to a change in output Y will instead cause the demand curve itself to shift upward in the Keynesian cross diagram, as in Figure 7-7, panel (b). Similarly, any contraction in demand not due to output changes will cause the demand function to shift downward.

To conclude, the main factors that shift the demand curve up are as follows:

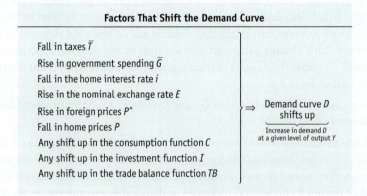

Factors That Shift the Demand Curve

Fall in taxes $\overline{T}$
Rise in government spending $\overline{G}$
Fall in the home interest rate i
Rise in the nominal exchange rate E
Rise in foreign prices P^* $\Rightarrow$ Demand curve D
Fall in home prices P shifts up
Any shift up in the consumption function C Increase in demand D
Any shift up in the investment function I at a given level of output Y
Any shift up in the trade balance function TB

The opposite changes lead to a decrease in demand and shift the demand curve down.

3 Goods and Forex Market Equilibria: Deriving the IS Curve

We have made an important first step in our study of the short-run behavior of exchange rates and output. Our analysis of demand shows how the level of output adjusts to ensure a goods market equilibrium, given the levels of each component of demand. Each component, in turn, has its own particular determinants, and we have examined how shifts in these determinants (or in other exogenous factors) might shift the level of demand and, hence, change the equilibrium level of output.

But there is more than one market in the economy, and a *general equilibrium* requires equilibrium in all markets—that is, equilibrium in the goods market, the money market, and the forex market. We need to bring all three markets into the analysis, and we do that next by developing a tool of macroeconomic analysis known as the IS–LM diagram. A version of this may be familiar to you from the study of closed-economy macroeconomics, but in this chapter we develop a variant of this approach for an open economy.

Analyzing equilibria in three markets simultaneously is a difficult task, but it is made more manageable by proceeding one step at a time using familiar tools. Our first step builds on the Keynesian cross depiction of goods market equilibrium developed in the last section and then adds on the depiction of forex market equilibrium that we developed in the earlier exchange rate chapters.

Equilibrium in Two Markets

We begin by defining the **IS curve**, which is one part of the IS–LM diagram.

The IS curve shows combinations of output Y and the interest rate i for which the goods and forex markets are in equilibrium.

In Figure 7-8, panel (b), we derive the IS curve by using the Keynesian cross in panel (a) to analyze goods market equilibrium. In panel (c), we impose the uncovered interest parity (UIP) relationship that ensures the forex market is in equilibrium.

Before we continue, let's take a closer look at why the various graphs in this figure are oriented as they are. The Keynesian cross in panel (a) and the IS diagram in panel (b) share a common horizontal axis, the level of output or income. Hence, these figures are arranged one above the other so that these common output axes line up.

The forex market in panel (c) and the IS diagram in panel (b) share a common vertical axis, the level of the domestic interest rate. Hence, these figures are arranged side by side so that these common interest rate axes line up.

We thus know that if output Y is at a level consistent with demand equaling supply, shown in the Keynesian cross in panel (a), and if the interest rate i is at a level consistent with UIP, shown in the forex market in panel (c), then the result in panel (b) is that we must have a combination of Y and i consistent with equilibrium in both goods and forex markets.

Forex Market Recap

In earlier chapters we learned that the forex market is in equilibrium when the expected returns expressed in domestic currency are the same on foreign and domestic interest-bearing (money market) bank deposits. Equation (2-3) described this condition, known as UIP, which we can write here as:

$$\underbrace{\underbrace{i}_{\text{Domestic interest rate}}}_{\text{Domestic return}} = \underbrace{\underbrace{i^*}_{\text{Foreign interest rate}} + \underbrace{\left(\frac{E^e}{E} - 1\right)}_{\substack{\text{Expected rate of depreciation} \\ \text{of the domestic currency}}}}_{\text{Foreign return}}$$

The expected return on the foreign deposit *measured in home currency* equals the foreign interest rate plus the expected rate of depreciation of the home currency.

Taking the foreign interest rate i^* and expectations of the future exchange rate E^e as given, we know that the right-hand side of this expression decreases as E increases: the intuition for this is that the more expensive it is to purchase foreign currency today, the lower the expected return must be, all else equal.

The inverse relationship between E and the expected foreign return on the right-hand side of the previous equation is shown by the downward-sloping *FR*

FIGURE 7-8

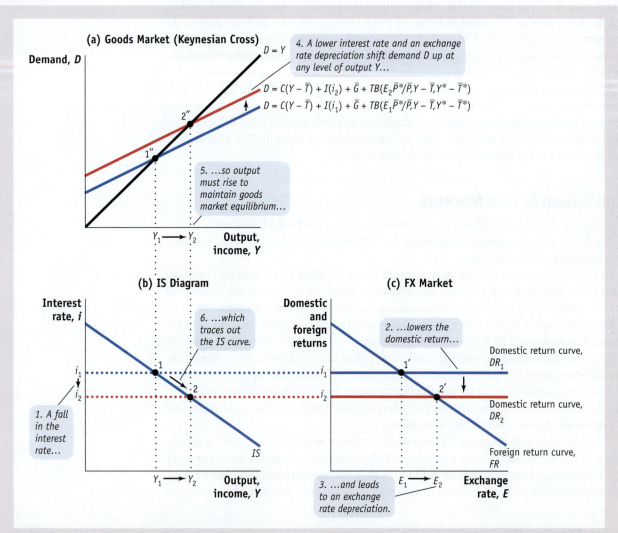

Deriving the IS Curve The Keynesian cross is in panel (a), IS curve in panel (b), and forex (FX) market in panel (c). The economy starts in equilibrium with output Y_1; interest rate i_1; and exchange rate E_1. Consider the effect of a decrease in the interest rate from i_1 to i_2, all else equal. In panel (c), a lower interest rate causes a depreciation; equilibrium moves from 1' to 2'. A lower interest rate boosts investment and a depreciation boosts the trade balance. In panel (a), demand shifts up, the equilibrium moves from 1" to 2", and output rises from Y_1 to Y_2. In panel (b), we go from point 1 to point 2. The IS curve is thus traced out, a downward-sloping relationship between the interest rate and output. When the interest rate falls from i_1 to i_2, output rises from Y_1 to Y_2. The IS curve describes all combinations of i and Y consistent with goods and FX market equilibria in panels (a) and (c).

(foreign return) line in panel (c) of Figure 7-8. The domestic return DR is the horizontal line corresponding to the level of the domestic interest rate i.

Deriving the IS Curve

Using the setup in Figure 7-8, we can now derive the shape of the IS curve by considering how changes in the interest rate affect output *if the goods and forex markets are to remain in equilibrium.*

Initial Equilibrium Let us suppose that the goods and forex markets are initially in equilibrium at an interest rate i_1, an output or income level Y_1, and an exchange rate E_1.

In panel (a) by assumption, at an output level Y_1, demand equals supply, so the output level Y_1 must correspond to the point 1″, which is at the intersection of the Keynesian cross, and the figure is drawn accordingly.

In panel (c) by assumption, at an interest rate i_1 and an exchange rate E_1, the domestic and foreign returns must be equal, so this must be the point 1′, which is at the intersection of the DR_1 and FR curves, and the figure is drawn accordingly.

Finally, in panel (b) by assumption, at an interest rate i_1 and an output level Y_1, both goods and forex markets are in equilibrium. Thus, the point 1 is on the IS curve, *by definition*.

Lines are drawn joining the equal output levels Y_1 in panels (a) and (b). The domestic return line DR_1 traces out the home interest rate level from panel (b) across to panel (c).

A Fall in the Interest Rate   Now in Figure 7-8, let us suppose that the home interest rate falls from i_1 to i_2. What happens to equilibria in the goods and forex markets?

We first look at the forex market in panel (c). From our analysis of UIP in earlier chapters we know that when the home interest rate falls, domestic deposits have a lower return and look less attractive to investors. To maintain forex market equilibrium, the exchange rate must rise (the Home currency must depreciate) until domestic and foreign returns are once again equal. In our example, when the home interest rate falls to i_2, the exchange rate must rise from E_1 to E_2 to equalize FR and DR_2 and restore equilibrium in the forex market at point 2′.

How do the changes in the home interest rate and the exchange rate affect demand? As shown in panel (a), demand will increase (shift up) for two reasons, as we learned earlier in this chapter.

First, when the domestic interest rate falls, firms are willing to engage in more investment projects, and their increased investment augments demand. The increase in investment, all else equal, *directly* increases demand D at any level of output Y.

Second, the exchange rate E has risen (depreciated). Because prices are sticky in the short run, this rise in the nominal exchange rate E also causes a rise in the real exchange rate, $E\bar{P}^*/\bar{P}$. That is, the nominal depreciation causes a real depreciation. This increases demand D via expenditure switching. At any level of output Y consumers switch expenditure from relatively more expensive foreign goods toward relatively less expensive domestic goods. Thus, the fall in the interest rate *indirectly* boosts demand via exchange rate effects felt through the trade balance.

One important observation is in order: in an open economy, the phenomenon of expenditure switching operates as an additional element in demand that is not present in a closed economy. *In an open economy, lower interest rates stimulate demand through the traditional closed-economy investment channel and through the trade balance. The trade balance effect occurs because lower interest rates cause a nominal depreciation, which in the short run is also a real depreciation, which stimulates external demand via the trade balance.*

To summarize, panel (a) shows clearly that in response to a decrease in the interest rate, the demand curve D has shifted up and the Keynesian cross goods market equilibrium is restored by a rise in output to Y_2, which corresponds to point 2″.

In panel (b), we can now derive the shape of the IS curve. At an interest rate i_1 and output level Y_1, and at an interest rate i_2 and an output level Y_2, both the goods and forex markets are in equilibrium.

We have now derived the shape of the IS curve, which describes goods and forex market equilibrium. When the interest rate falls from i_1 to i_2, output rises from Y_1 to Y_2. The IS curve is downward-sloping, which illustrates the negative relationship between the interest rate i and output Y.

Factors That Shift the IS Curve

In deriving the IS curve, we treated various demand factors as exogenous, including fiscal policy, price levels, and the exchange rate. If any factors other than the interest rate and output change, the position of the IS curve will have to change. These effects are central in any analysis of changes in an economy's equilibrium. We now explore several changes that result in an increase in demand, that is, an upward shift in the demand curve in Figure 7-9, panel (a). (A decrease in demand would result from changes in the opposite direction.)

■ *A change in government spending.* If demand shifts up because of a *rise in $\bar{G}$*, a fiscal expansion, all else equal, what happens to the IS curve? The initial equilibrium point (Y_1, i_1) would no longer be a goods market equilibrium: if the interest rate is unchanged at i_1, then I is unchanged, as are the exchange rate E and hence, trade balance (TB). Yet demand has risen due to the change in G. That demand has to be satisfied somehow, so more output has to be produced. Some—but not all—of that extra output will be consumed, but the rest can meet the extra demand generated by the rise in government

---

FIGURE 7-9

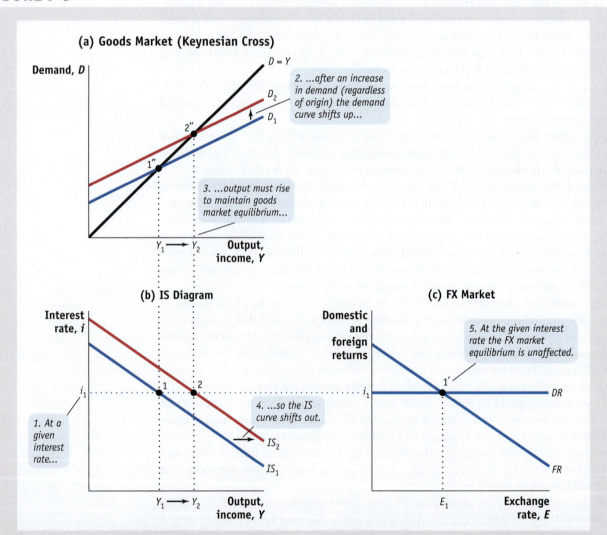

Exogenous Shifts in Demand Cause the IS Curve to Shift In the Keynesian cross in panel (a), when the interest rate is held constant at i_1, an exogenous increase in demand (due to other factors) causes the demand curve to shift up from D_1 to D_2 as shown, all else equal. This moves the equilibrium from 1″ to 2″, raising output from Y_1 to Y_2. In the IS diagram in panel (b), output has risen, with no change in the interest rate. The IS curve has therefore shifted right from IS_1 to IS_2. The nominal interest rate and hence the exchange rate are unchanged in this example, as seen in panel (c).

spending. At the interest rate i_1, output must rise to Y_2 for the goods market to once again be in equilibrium. Thus, the IS curve must shift right as shown in Figure 7-9, panel (b).

The lesson: a rise in government spending shifts the IS curve out.

■ *A change in taxes.* Suppose taxes were to decrease. With all other factors remaining unchanged, this tax cut makes demand shift up by boosting private consumption, all else equal. We assume that the interest rate i_1, the exchange rate E_1, and government's spending policy are all fixed. Thus, neither I nor TB nor G change. With an excess of demand, supply has to rise, so output must again increase to Y_2 and the IS curve shifts right.

The lesson: a reduction in taxes shifts the IS curve out.

■ *A change in the foreign interest rate or expected future exchange rate.* A *rise* in the foreign interest rate i^* or a *rise* in the future expected exchange rate E^e causes a depreciation of the home currency, all else equal (recall that in the forex market, the FR curve shifts out because the return on foreign deposits has increased; if the home interest rate is unchanged, E must rise). A rise in E causes the real exchange rate to depreciate, because prices are sticky. As a result, TB rises via expenditure switching, and demand increases. Because C, I, and G do not change, there is an excess of demand, and supply has to rise to restore equilibrium. Output Y increases, and the IS curve shifts right.

The lesson: an increase in the foreign return (via i^* or E^e) shifts the IS curve out.

■ *A change in the home or foreign price level.* If prices are flexible, then a *rise* in foreign prices or a *fall* in domestic prices causes a home real depreciation, raising $q = E\bar{P}^*/\bar{P}$. This real depreciation causes TB to rise and, all else equal, demand will rise to a position like D_2. With an excess of demand, supply has to rise to restore equilibrium. Output Y must increase, and the IS curve shifts right.

The lesson: an increase in P^* or a decrease in P shifts the IS curve out.

These examples show that the position of the IS curve depends on various factors that we treat as given (or exogenous). We may write this observation using the notation

$$IS = IS(G, T, i^*, E^e, P^*, P)$$

There are many other exogenous shocks to the economy that can be analyzed in a similar fashion—for example, a sudden exogenous change in consumption, investment, or the trade balance. How will the IS curve react in each case? You may have detected a pattern from the preceding discussion.

The general rule is as follows: *any type of shock that increases demand at a given level of output will shift the IS curve to the right; any shock that decreases demand will shift the IS curve down.*

Summing Up the IS Curve

When prices are sticky, the IS curve summarizes the relationship between output Y and the interest rate i necessary to keep the goods and forex markets in short-run equilibrium. The IS curve is downward-sloping. Why? Lower interest rates stimulate demand via the investment channel and, through exchange rate depreciation, via the trade balance. Higher demand can be satisfied in the short run only by higher output. Thus, when the interest rate falls, output rises, and the economy moves along the IS curve.

As for shifts in the IS curve, we have found that any factor that increases demand D at a given home interest rate i must cause the demand curve to shift up, leading to higher output Y and, as a result, an outward shift in the IS curve.

To conclude, the main factors that shift the IS curve out can be summed up as follows, and they comprise a list of factors that raise demand *for a given level of the home interest rate*:

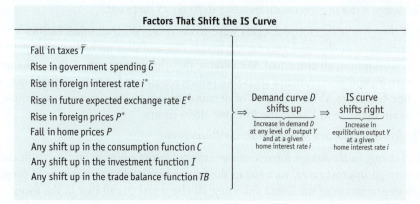

Factors That Shift the IS Curve

Fall in taxes $\bar{T}$
Rise in government spending $\bar{G}$
Rise in foreign interest rate i^*
Rise in future expected exchange rate E^e
Rise in foreign prices P^*
Fall in home prices P
Any shift up in the consumption function C
Any shift up in the investment function I
Any shift up in the trade balance function TB

$\Rightarrow$ Demand curve D shifts up
Increase in demand D at any level of output Y and at a given home interest rate i

$\Rightarrow$ IS curve shifts right
Increase in equilibrium output Y at a given home interest rate i

The opposite changes lead to a decrease in demand and shift the demand curve down and the IS curve to the left.

4 Money Market Equilibrium: Deriving the LM Curve

The IS curve links the forex market and the goods market as depicted by the Keynesian cross. It summarizes combinations of Y and i at which goods demand equals goods supply in a way that is consistent with forex market equilibrium. We have now taken care of equilibria in two out of three markets, so there is only one market left to worry about. In this section, we derive a set of combinations of Y and i that ensures equilibrium in the money market, a concept that can be represented graphically as the **LM curve**.

The LM curve is more straightforward to derive than the IS curve for a couple of reasons. First, the money market is something we have already studied in earlier chapters, so we already have all the tools we need to build the LM curve. Second, unlike the IS curve, the open-economy LM curve is no different from the closed-economy LM curve, so there will be no new material here if you have previously studied the closed-economy IS–LM model in another course.

Money Market Recap

In our earlier study of the money market, we assumed that the level of output or income Y was given. In deriving the LM curve, we now face a new question: What happens in the money market when an economy's output changes?

In the short run, the price level is assumed to be sticky at a level $\bar{P}$, and the money market is in equilibrium when the demand for real money balances $L(i)Y$ equals the real money supply $M/\bar{P}$:

$$\underbrace{\frac{M}{\bar{P}}}_{\substack{\text{Real} \\ \text{money} \\ \text{supply}}} = \underbrace{L(i)Y}_{\substack{\text{Real} \\ \text{money} \\ \text{demand}}} \tag{7-2}$$

Figure 7-10, panel (a), shows that real money demand MD varies inversely with the nominal interest rate. As a result of this relationship, the demand curve for real money balances slopes downward. The real money supply MS is assumed to be fixed for now. Initially, the level of output is at Y_1 and the money market is in equilibrium at $1'$, where real money demand is on MD_1 at $M/\bar{P} = L(i_1)Y_1$.

FIGURE 7-10

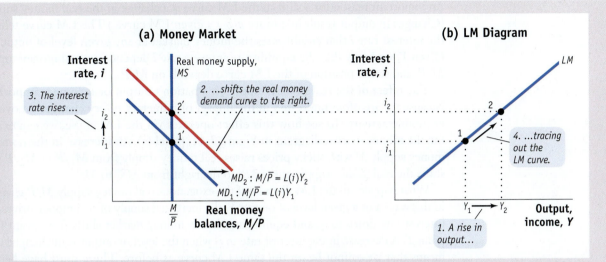

(a) Money Market

(b) LM Diagram

Interest rate, i

Real money supply, MS

3. The interest rate rises ...

2. ...shifts the real money demand curve to the right.

i_2

2′

i_1

1′

$MD_2 : M/\overline{P} = L(i)Y_2$

$MD_1 : M/\overline{P} = L(i)Y_1$

$\frac{M}{\overline{P}}$

Real money balances, M/P

Interest rate, i

LM

i_2

2

1

i_1

4. ...tracing out the LM curve.

Y_1 → Y_2

Output, income, Y

1. A rise in output...

Deriving the LM Curve If there is an increase in real income or output from Y_1 to Y_2 in panel (b), the effect in the money market in panel (a) is to shift the demand for real money balances to the right, all else equal. If the real supply of money, MS, is held fixed at $M/\overline{P}$, then the interest rate rises from i_1 to i_2 and money market equilibrium moves from point 1′ to point 2′. The relationship thus described between the interest rate and income, all else equal, is known as the LM curve and is depicted in panel (b) by the shift from point 1 to point 2. The LM curve is upward-sloping: when the output level rises from Y_1 to Y_2, the interest rate rises from i_1 to i_2. The LM curve in panel (b) describes all combinations of i and Y that are consistent with money market equilibrium in panel (a).

If output changes, the real money demand curve shifts. For example, if output rises to Y_2 and the real money supply $M/\overline{P}$ remains fixed, then real money demand increases because more output implies a larger number of transactions in the economy for which money is needed. The real money demand curve shifts right to MD_2. To keep money supply and demand equal, $M/\overline{P} = L(i)Y_2$, the interest rate rises from $i = i_1$ to $i = i_2$. Equilibrium moves from 1′ to 2′.

Deriving the LM Curve

This exercise can be repeated for any level of output Y. Doing so will generate a combination of interest rates i and outputs Y for which the money market is in equilibrium. This set of points, called the LM curve, is drawn in Figure 7-10, panel (b).

For example, if the real money supply is fixed at $M/\overline{P}$, an increase in output from Y_1 to Y_2 generates a rise in the nominal interest rate from i_1 to i_2 in panel (a), as we have just seen. This change can also be depicted as a move from point 1 to point 2 along the LM curve, as shown in panel (b).

We have now derived the shape of the LM curve, which describes money market equilibrium. When output rises from Y_1 to Y_2, the interest rate rises from i_1 to i_2. The LM curve is an upward-sloping relationship between the interest rate i and output Y.

The two ways of depicting the money market equilibrium are entirely equivalent. The money market diagram shows the relationship between real money balances demanded and supplied at different interest rates, holding output fixed. The LM curve diagram shows the relationship between output and the interest rate holding real money balances as fixed. Because the LM curve does *not* hold output fixed, it is important to developing our model of how output, interest rates, and exchange rates fluctuate in the short run.

Factors That Shift the LM Curve

An important reason for a shift in the LM curve is a change in the real money supply. (Changes in output result in a move *along* a given LM curve.) The LM curve tells us the interest rate i that equilibrates the money market at any given level of output Y. Given Y, we know that the equilibrium interest rate i depends on real money supply $M/\overline{P}$, and so the position of the LM curve depends on $M/\overline{P}$.

The effect of the real money supply on a nation's output or income is important because we are often interested in the impact of monetary policy changes on overall economic activity. To see how this effect operates via the LM curve, we can examine the money market diagram in Figure 7-11, panel (a). An increase in the nominal money supply M with sticky prices raises real money supply from $M_1/\overline{P}$ to $M_2/\overline{P}$ and shifts the real money supply curve MS to the right from MS_1 to MS_2.

What happens in the LM diagram if the exogenous real money supply $M/\overline{P}$ changes in this way? For a given level of output Y, the increased supply of real money drives the interest rate down to i_2, and equilibrium in the money market shifts from point 1′ to point 2′. A decrease in the interest rate to i_2 when the level of output is unchanged at Y means that we cannot be on the same LM curve as before. There must have been a downward shift of the LM curve from LM_1 to LM_2, as shown in Figure 7-11, panel (b).

We have shown the following: *an increase in real money supply shifts the LM curve down or to the right; a decrease in the real money supply shifts the LM curve up or to the left.*

Thus, the position of the LM curve is a function of real money supply:

$$LM = LM(M/\overline{P})$$

Remember that in this short-run model of the economy, prices are sticky and treated as given, so any change in the real money supply in the short run is caused by changes in the nominal money supply M, which for now we take as given or exogenous.

Other factors can influence the position of the LM curve. In addition to changes in the money supply, exogenous changes in real money demand will also cause the LM

FIGURE 7-11

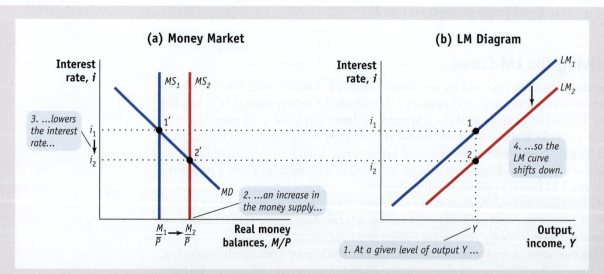

(a) Money Market

(b) LM Diagram

3. ...lowers the interest rate...

2. ...an increase in the money supply...

4. ...so the LM curve shifts down.

1. At a given level of output Y ...

Change in the Money Supply Shifts the LM Curve In the money market, shown in panel (a), we hold fixed the level of real income or output, Y, and hence real money demand, MD. All else equal, we show the effect of an increase in money supply from M_1 to M_2. The real money supply curve moves out from MS_1 to MS_2. This moves the equilibrium from 1′ to 2′, lowering the interest rate from i_1 to i_2. In the LM diagram, shown in panel (b), the interest rate has fallen, with no change in the level of income or output, so the economy moves from point 1 to point 2. The LM curve has therefore shifted down from LM_1 to LM_2.

curve to shift. For example, for a given money supply, a decrease in the demand for real money balances (a decrease in the L function) at a given level of output Y will tend to lower the interest rate, all else equal, which would be depicted as a shift down or to the right in the LM curve.

Summing Up the LM Curve

When prices are sticky, the LM curve summarizes the relationship between output Y and interest rate i necessary to keep the money market in short-run equilibrium for a given level of the real money supply. The LM curve is upward-sloping. Why? In a money market equilibrium, if real money supply is constant, then real money demand must also be constant. If output rises, real money demand rises and to maintain equilibrium, real money demand must contract. This contraction in real money demand is accomplished by a rise in the interest rate. Thus, on the LM curve, when output rises, so, too, does the interest rate.

The following factors shift the LM curve:

Factors That Shift the LM Curve

Rise in (nominal) money supply M
Any shift left in the money demand function L $\Biggr\} \Rightarrow$ LM curve shifts down or right

<u>Decrease in equilibrium home interest rate i at given level of output Y</u>

The opposite changes lead to an increase in the home interest rate and shift the LM curve up or to the left.

5 The Short-Run IS–LM–FX Model of an Open Economy

We are now in a position to fully characterize an open economy that is in equilibrium in goods, money, and forex markets, as shown in Figure 7-12. This IS–LM–FX figure combines the goods market (the IS curve), the money market (the LM curve), and the forex (FX) market diagrams.

The IS and LM curves are both drawn in panel (a). The goods and forex markets are in equilibrium if and only if the economy is on the IS curve. The money market is in equilibrium if and only if the economy is on the LM curve. Thus, all three markets are in equilibrium if and only if the economy is at point 1, where IS and LM intersect.

The forex market, or FX market, is drawn in panel (b). The domestic return (DR) in the forex market equals the money market interest rate. Equilibrium is at point 1′ where the foreign return (FR) is equal to the domestic return.

Understanding the Model While it is useful to have a simple graphical depiction of our model, it is also important to keep in mind the three key underlying equilibrium concepts that the IS–LM–FX diagram actually describes. In *any* state of equilibrium in this model the following conditions must *all* be true in the home economy:

Forex market equilibrium: UIP holds for given i^* and E^e:

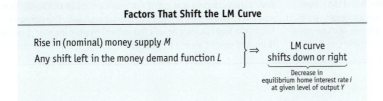

$$\underbrace{\underset{\text{Domestic interest rate}}{i}}_{\text{Domestic return}} = \underbrace{\underset{\text{Foreign interest rate}}{i^*} + \underbrace{\left(\frac{E^e}{E} - 1 \right)}_{\substack{\text{Expected rate of depreciation} \\ \text{of the domestic currency}}}}_{\text{Foreign return}}$$

FIGURE 7-12

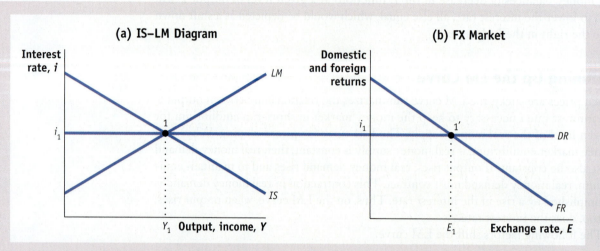

(a) IS–LM Diagram

Interest rate, *i*

LM

1

*i*₁

IS

*Y*₁ Output, income, *Y*

(b) FX Market

Domestic and foreign returns

*i*₁

1′

DR

FR

*E*₁   Exchange rate, *E*

Equilibrium in the IS–LM–FX Model In panel (a), the IS and LM curves are both drawn. The goods and forex markets are in equilibrium when the economy is on the IS curve. The money market is in equilibrium when the economy is on the LM curve. Both markets are in equilibrium if and only if the economy is at point 1, the unique point of intersection of IS and LM. In panel (b), the forex (FX) market is shown. The domestic return, DR, in the forex market equals the money market interest rate. Equilibrium is at point 1′ where the foreign return FR equals domestic return.

Money market equilibrium: money supply equals demand for given M and $\overline{P}$;

$$\underbrace{\frac{M}{\overline{P}}}_{\substack{\text{Real} \\ \text{money} \\ \text{supply}}} = \underbrace{L(i)Y}_{\substack{\text{Real} \\ \text{money} \\ \text{demand}}}$$

Goods market equilibrium: goods markets clear for given $\overline{P}, \overline{P}^*, \overline{T}$, and $\overline{G}$;

$$Y = \underbrace{C(Y - \overline{T}) + I(i) + \overline{G} + TB(E\overline{P}^*/\overline{P}, Y - \overline{T}, Y^* - \overline{T}^*)}_{D}$$

Implications of the Model As we can see, the IS–LM–FX diagram only keeps track of three home variables—those displayed on the axes, namely, the interest rate, output, and the exchange rate. These *are* important economic outcomes that we want to understand and keep track of. But what if, for example, we also want to understand how home variables like consumption C, investment I, or the trade balance TB would react to any change in the model's equilibrium? To see how other variables of interest (C, I, TB) behave in a way consistent with IS–LM–FX equilibrium, we need to use the final goods market equilibrium equation, shown above. Only in this way can we understand how changes in each of the constituent parts of demand are determined as a function of interest rates, output, and the exchange rate. Even though these effects are not apparent from looking at the diagram alone, the goods market equilibrium equation can, with a little thought, allow us to derive these further implications in a straightforward manner. (*Hint*: For a helpful worked example, consult the Work It Out question at the end of this chapter.)

Applying the Model In the remainder of this chapter, and in the rest of this book, we make extensive use of this two-panel IS–LM–FX diagram of the open-economy equilibrium to analyze the short-run response of an open economy to various types of shocks. In particular, we focus on how government policies affect the economy and the extent to which they can be employed to enhance macroeconomic performance and stability.

Macroeconomic Policies in the Short Run

Now that we understand the open-economy IS–LM–FX model and all the factors that influence an economy's short-run equilibrium, we can use the model to look at how a nation's key macroeconomic variables (output, exchange rates, trade balance) are affected in the short run by changes in government macroeconomic policies.

We focus on the two main policy actions: changes in **monetary policy**, implemented through changes in the money supply, and changes in **fiscal policy**, involving changes in government spending or taxes. Of particular interest is the question of whether governments can use such policies to insulate the economy from fluctuations in output.

We will see that the impact of these policies is profoundly affected by a nation's choice of exchange rate regime, and we will consider the two polar cases of fixed and floating exchange rates. Many countries are on some kind of flexible exchange rate regime and many are on some kind of fixed regime, so considering policy effects under both fixed and floating systems is essential.

The key assumptions of this section are as follows. The economy begins in a state of long-run equilibrium. We then consider policy changes in the home economy, assuming that conditions in the foreign economy (i.e., the rest of the world) are unchanged. The home economy is subject to the usual short-run assumption of a sticky price level at home *and* abroad. Furthermore, we assume that the forex market operates freely and unrestricted by capital controls and that the exchange rate is determined by market forces.

Temporary Policies, Unchanged Expectations Finally, we examine only *temporary* changes in policies. We will assume that long-run expectations about the future state of the economy are unaffected by the policy changes. In particular, the future expected exchange rate E^e is held fixed. The reason for studying temporary policies is that we are primarily interested in how governments use fiscal and monetary policies to handle temporary shocks and business cycles in the short run, and our model is applicable only in the short run.[2]

The key lesson of this section is that policies matter and can have significant macroeconomic effects in the short run. Moreover, their impacts depend in a big way on the type of exchange rate regime in place. Once we understand these linkages, we will better understand the contentious and ongoing debates about exchange rates and macroeconomic policies, including the never-ending arguments over the merits of fixed and floating exchange rates (a topic covered in detail in the next chapter).

Monetary Policy Under Floating Exchange Rates

In this policy experiment, we consider a temporary monetary expansion in the home country when the exchange rate is allowed to float. Because the expansion is not permanent, we assume there is no change in long-run expectations so that the expected future exchange rate remains steady at E^e. This means that there is no change in the expected foreign return curve in the forex market.

Figure 7-13 illustrates the predictions of the model. In panel (a) in the IS–LM diagram, the goods and money markets are initially in equilibrium at point 1. The

---

[2] Moreover, permanent changes may not be truly feasible given realistic constraints on governments. For example, a permanent increase in money supply, all else equal, would lead to a permanent increase in the price level, violating a money, exchange rate, or inflation target (the nominal anchor). A permanent increase in government spending, with no increase in taxes, would not be feasible given the government's long-run budget constraint.

FIGURE 7-13

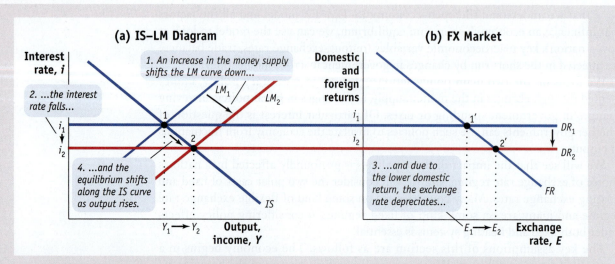

Monetary Policy Under Floating Exchange Rates In panel (a) in the IS–LM diagram, the goods and money markets are initially in equilibrium at point 1. The interest rate in the money market is also the domestic return, DR_1, that prevails in the FX market. In panel (b), the FX market is initially in equilibrium at point 1′. A temporary monetary expansion that increases the money supply would shift the LM curve down in panel (a) from LM_1 to LM_2, causing the interest rate to fall from i_1 to i_2. DR falls from DR_1 to DR_2. In panel (b), the lower interest rate implies that the exchange rate must depreciate, rising from E_1 to E_2. As the interest rate falls (increasing investment, I) and the exchange rate depreciates (increasing the trade balance), demand increases, which corresponds to the move down the IS curve from point 1 to point 2. Output expands from Y_1 to Y_2. The new equilibrium corresponds to points 2 and 2′.

interest rate in the money market is also the domestic return DR_1 that prevails in the forex market. In panel (b), the forex market is initially in equilibrium at point 1′.

A temporary monetary expansion that increases the money supply from M_1 to M_2 would shift the LM curve to the right in panel (a) from LM_1 to LM_2, causing the interest rate to fall from i_1 to i_2. In panel (b), the domestic return falls from DR_1 to DR_2. The lower interest rate would imply that the exchange rate must depreciate, rising from E_1 to E_2. As the interest rate falls (increasing investment I) and the exchange rate depreciates (increasing the trade balance), demand increases, which corresponds to the move down the IS curve from point 1 to point 2. Output expands from Y_1 to Y_2. The new equilibrium corresponds to points 2 and 2′.

The intuition for this result is as follows: monetary expansion tends to lower the home interest rate, all else equal. A lower interest rate stimulates demand in two ways. First, directly in the goods market, it causes investment demand I to increase. Second, indirectly, it causes the exchange rate to depreciate in the forex market, which in turn causes expenditure switching in the goods market, which causes the trade balance TB to increase. Both I and TB are sources of demand and both increase.

To sum up: a temporary monetary expansion under floating exchange rates is effective in combating economic downturns because it boosts output. It also lowers the home interest rate and causes a depreciation of the exchange rate. What happens to the trade balance cannot be predicted with certainty: increased home output will decrease the trade balance as the demand for imports will rise, but the real depreciation will increase the trade balance, because expenditure switching will tend to raise exports and diminish imports. In practice, economists tend to assume that the latter outweighs the former, so a temporary expansion of the money supply is usually predicted to increase the trade balance. (The case of a temporary contraction of monetary policy has opposite effects. As an exercise, work through this case using the same graphical apparatus.)

Monetary Policy Under Fixed Exchange Rates

Now let's look at what happens when a temporary monetary expansion occurs when the home country fixes its exchange rate with the foreign country at $\bar{E}$. The key to understanding this experiment is to recall the uncovered interest parity condition: *the home interest rate must equal the foreign interest rate under a fixed exchange rate.*

Figure 7-14 puts the model to work. In panel (a) in the IS–LM diagram, the goods and money markets are initially in equilibrium at point 1. In panel (b), the forex market is initially in equilibrium at point 1′.

A temporary monetary expansion that increases the money supply from M_1 to M_2 would shift the LM curve down and to the right in panel (a), and the interest rate would tend to fall, as we have just seen. In panel (b), the lower interest rate would imply that the exchange rate would tend to rise or depreciate toward E_2. This is inconsistent with the pegged exchange rate $\bar{E}$, so the policymakers cannot alter monetary policy and shift the LM curve in this way. They must leave the money supply equal to M_1, and the economy cannot deviate from its initial equilibrium.

This example illustrates a key lesson: under a fixed exchange rate, autonomous monetary policy is not an option. What is going on? Remember that under a fixed exchange rate, the home interest rate must exactly equal the foreign interest rate, $i = i^*$, according to the uncovered interest parity condition. Any shift in the LM curve would violate this restriction and break the fixed exchange rate.

To sum up: monetary policy under fixed exchange rates is impossible to undertake. Fixing the exchange rate means giving up monetary policy autonomy. In an earlier chapter, we learned about the trilemma: countries cannot simultaneously allow capital mobility, maintain fixed exchange rates, and pursue an autonomous monetary policy. We have now just seen the trilemma at work in the IS–LM–FX framework. By illustrating a potential benefit of autonomous monetary policy (the ability to use monetary policy to increase output), the model clearly exposes one of the major costs

FIGURE 7-14

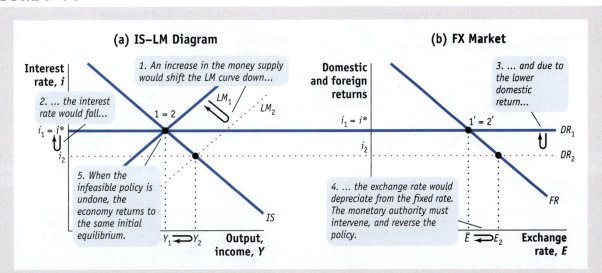

Monetary Policy Under Fixed Exchange Rates In panel (a) in the IS–LM diagram, the goods and money markets are initially in equilibrium at point 1. In panel (b), the FX market is initially in equilibrium at point 1′. A temporary monetary expansion that increases the money supply would shift the LM curve down in panel (a) from LM_1 to LM_2. In panel (b), the lower interest rate would imply that the exchange rate must depreciate, rising from $\bar{E}$ to E_2. This depreciation is inconsistent with the pegged exchange rate, so the policymakers cannot move LM in this way. They must leave the money supply unchanged, with the LM curve at LM_1. Implication: under a fixed exchange rate, autonomous monetary policy is not an option.

of fixed exchange rates. Monetary policy, which in principle could be used to influence the economy in the short run, is ruled out by a fixed exchange rate.

Fiscal Policy Under Floating Exchange Rates

We now turn to fiscal policy under a floating exchange rate. In this example, we consider a temporary increase in government spending from $\bar{G}_1$ to $\bar{G}_2$ in the home economy. Again, the effect is not permanent, so there are no changes in long-run expectations, and in particular the expected future exchange rate remains steady at E^e.

Figure 7-15 shows what happens in our model. In panel (a) in the IS–LM diagram, the goods and money markets are initially in equilibrium at point 1. The interest rate in the money market is also the domestic return DR_1 that prevails in the forex market. In panel (b), the forex market is initially in equilibrium at point 1′.

A temporary fiscal expansion that increases government spending from $\bar{G}_1$ to $\bar{G}_2$ would shift the IS curve to the right in panel (a) from IS_1 to IS_2, causing the interest rate to rise from i_1 to i_2. In panel (b), the domestic return rises from DR_1 to DR_2. The higher interest rate would imply that the exchange rate must appreciate, falling from E_1 to E_2. As the interest rate rises (decreasing investment) and the exchange rate appreciates (decreasing the trade balance), demand still tends to rise overall as government spending increases, which corresponds to the move up the LM curve from point 1 to point 2. Output expands from Y_1 to Y_2. The new equilibrium is at points 2 and 2′.

What is happening here? The fiscal expansion raises output as the IS curve shifts right. But the increases in output will raise interest rates, all else equal, given a fixed money supply. The resulting higher interest rates will reduce the investment component of demand, and this limits the rise in demand to less than the increase in government spending. This impact of fiscal expansion on investment is often referred to as *crowding out* by economists.

FIGURE 7-15

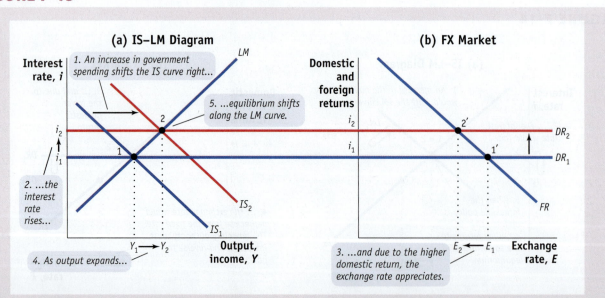

Fiscal Policy Under Floating Exchange Rates   In panel (a) in the IS–LM diagram, the goods and money markets are initially in equilibrium at point 1. The interest rate in the money market is also the domestic return, DR_1, that prevails in the FX market. In panel (b), the FX market is initially in equilibrium at point 1′. A temporary fiscal expansion that increases government spending would shift the IS curve to the right in panel (a) from IS_1 to IS_2, causing the interest rate to rise from i_1 to i_2. The domestic return shifts up from DR_1 to DR_2. In panel (b), the higher interest rate would imply that the exchange rate must appreciate, falling from E_1 to E_2. As the interest rate rises (decreasing investment, I) and the exchange rate appreciates (decreasing the trade balance), demand falls, which corresponds to the move along the LM curve from point 1 to point 2. Output expands from Y_1 to Y_2. The new equilibrium corresponds to points 2 and 2′.

The higher interest rate also causes the home currency to appreciate. As home consumers switch their consumption to now less expensive foreign goods, the trade balance will fall. Thus, the higher interest rate also (indirectly) leads to a *crowding out* of net exports, and this too limits the rise in output to less than the increase in government spending. Thus, in an open economy, fiscal expansion not only crowds out investment (by raising the interest rate) but also crowds out net exports (by causing the exchange rate to appreciate).

To sum up: a temporary expansion of fiscal policy under floating exchange rates is effective. It raises output at home, raises the interest rate, causes an appreciation of the exchange rate, and decreases the trade balance. (A temporary contraction of fiscal policy has opposite effects. As an exercise, work through the contraction case using the same graphical apparatus.)

Fiscal Policy Under Fixed Exchange Rates

Now let's see how the outcomes differ when the home country pegs its exchange rate with respect to the foreign country at $\bar{E}$. The key is to recall the parity condition: the home interest rate must remain exactly equal to the foreign interest rate for the peg to hold.

Figure 7-16 shows what happens in this case. In panel (a) in the IS–LM diagram, the goods and money markets are initially in equilibrium at point 1. The interest rate in the money market is also the domestic return DR_1 that prevails in the forex market. In panel (b), the forex market is initially in equilibrium at point 1'.

FIGURE 7-16

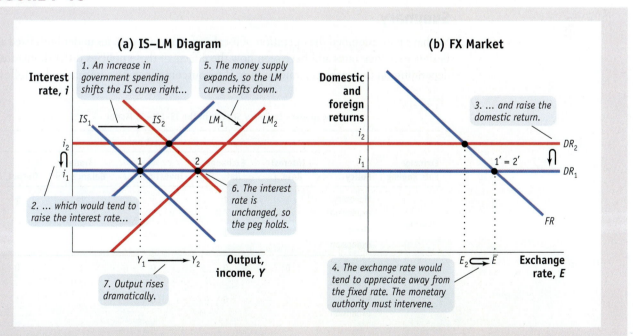

Fiscal Policy Under Fixed Exchange Rates   In panel (a) in the IS–LM diagram, the goods and money markets are initially in equilibrium at point 1. The interest rate in the money market is also the domestic return, DR_1, that prevails in the FX market. In panel (b), the FX market is initially in equilibrium at point 1'. A temporary fiscal expansion on its own increases government spending and would shift the IS curve to the right in panel (a) from IS_1 to IS_2, causing the interest rate to rise from i_1 to i_2. The domestic return would then rise from DR_1 to DR_2. In panel (b), the higher interest rate would imply that the exchange rate must appreciate, falling from $\bar{E}$ to E_2. To maintain the peg, the monetary authority must now intervene, shifting the LM curve down, from LM_1 to LM_2. The fiscal expansion thus prompts a monetary expansion. In the end, the interest rate and exchange rate are left unchanged, and output expands *dramatically* from Y_1 to Y_2. The new equilibrium corresponds to points 2 and 2'.

A temporary fiscal expansion that increases government spending from $\bar{G}_1$ to $\bar{G}_2$ would shift the IS curve to the right in panel (a) from IS_1 to IS_2, causing the interest rate to rise from i_1 to i_2. In panel (b), the domestic return would rise from DR_1 to DR_2. The higher interest rate would imply that the exchange rate must appreciate, falling from $\bar{E}$ to E_2. To maintain the peg, the monetary authority must intervene, shifting the LM curve to the right also, from LM_1 to LM_2. The fiscal expansion thus prompts a monetary expansion. In the end, the interest rate and exchange rate are left unchanged, and output expands *dramatically* from Y_1 to Y_2. The new equilibrium corresponds to points 2 and 2′.

What is happening here? From the last example, we know that there is appreciation pressure associated with a fiscal expansion if the currency is allowed to float. To maintain the peg, the monetary authority must immediately alter its monetary policy at the very moment the fiscal expansion occurs so that the LM curve shifts from LM_1 to LM_2. The way to do this is to expand the money supply; this generates pressure for depreciation and offsets the appreciation pressure. If the monetary authority pulls this off, the market exchange rate will stay at the initial pegged level, $\bar{E}$.

Thus, when a country is operating under a fixed exchange, fiscal policy is supereffective because any fiscal expansion by the government forces an immediate monetary expansion by the central bank to keep the exchange rate steady. The double, and simultaneous, expansion of demand by the fiscal and monetary authorities imposes a huge stimulus on the economy, and output rises from Y_1 to Y_2 (beyond the level achieved by the same fiscal expansion under a floating exchange rate).

To sum up: a temporary expansion of fiscal policy under fixed exchange rates raises output at home by a considerable amount. (The case of a temporary contraction of fiscal policy would have similar but opposite effects. As an exercise, work through this case using the same graphical apparatus.)

Summary

We have now examined the operation of fiscal and monetary policies under both fixed and flexible exchange rates and have seen how the effects of these policies differ dramatically depending on the exchange rate regime. The outcomes can be summarized as follows:

				Impact on:		
Exchange Rate Regime	**Policy**	**Interest Rate, _i_**	**Exchange Rate, _E_**	**Investment, _I_**	**Trade Balance, _TB_**	**Output, _Y_**
Floating	Monetary expansion	↓	↑	↑	↑?	↑
	Fiscal expansion	↑	↓	↓	↓	↑
Fixed	Monetary expansion	0	0	0	0	0
	Fiscal expansion	0	0	0	↓	↑

Responses to Policy Shocks in the IS–LM–FX Model

In this table, an up arrow ↑ indicates that the variable rises; a down arrow ↓ indicates that the variables falls; and a zero indicates no effect. The effects would be reversed for contractionary policies. The row of zeros for monetary expansion reflects the fact that it is not possible to use autonomous monetary policy when operating under a fixed exchange rate regime. In contrast, under a floating exchange rate regime, autonomous monetary policy and fiscal policy are both feasible. The power of monetary policy to expand demand comes from two forces in the short run: lower interest rates boost investment, and a depreciated exchange rate boosts the trade balance, all else equal. In the end, though, the trade balance will experience downward pressure from an import rise due to the increase in home output and income. The net effect on output and investment is positive, and the net effect on the trade balance is unclear—but in practice it, too, is likely to be positive.

Expansionary fiscal policy is also effective under a floating regime, even though the impact of extra spending is offset by crowding out in two areas: investment is crowded out by higher interest rates, and the trade balance is crowded out by an appreciated exchange rate. Thus, on net, investment falls and the trade balance falls, and the effect of the falling trade balance is unambiguously amplified by additional import demand arising from increased home output.

In a fixed exchange rate regime, monetary policy loses its power for two reasons. First, interest parity implies that the domestic interest rate cannot move independently of the foreign rate, so investment demand cannot be manipulated. Second, the peg means that there can be no movement in the exchange rate, so the trade balance cannot be manipulated by expenditure switching.

Only fiscal policy is feasible under a fixed regime. Tax cuts or spending increases by the government can generate additional demand. But fiscal expansion then requires a monetary expansion to keep interest rates steady and maintain the peg. Fiscal policy becomes ultra-powerful in a fixed exchange rate setting—the reason for this is that if interest rates and exchange rates are held steady by the central bank, investment and the trade balance are never crowded out by fiscal policy. Monetary policy follows fiscal policy and amplifies it.

6 Stabilization Policy

We now have seen that macroeconomic policies can affect economic activity in the short run. These effects open up the possibility that the authorities can use changes in policies to try to keep the economy at or near its full-employment level of output. This is the essence of **stabilization policy**. If the economy is hit by a temporary adverse shock, policymakers can use expansionary monetary and fiscal policies to prevent a deep recession. Conversely, if the economy is pushed by a shock above its full employment level of output, contractionary policies can tame the boom.

For example, suppose a temporary adverse shock such as a sudden decline in investment, consumption, or export demand shifts the IS curve to the left. Or suppose an adverse shock such as a sudden increase in money demand suddenly moves the LM curve up. Either shock would cause home output to fall. In principle, the home policymakers could offset these shocks by using fiscal or monetary policy to shift either the IS curve or LM curve (or both) to cause an offsetting increase in output. When used judiciously, monetary and fiscal policies can thus be used to stabilize the economy and absorb shocks.

The policies must be used with care, however. If the economy is stable and growing, an additional temporary monetary or fiscal stimulus may cause an unsustainable boom that will, when the stimulus is withdrawn, turn into an undesirable bust. In their efforts to do good, policymakers must be careful not to destabilize the economy through the ill-timed, inappropriate, or excessive use of monetary and fiscal policies.

APPLICATION

The Right Time for Austerity?

After the Great Recession in 2008–09, many observers would have predicted economic difficulties for Eastern Europe in the short run. Most countries had seen a rapid boom before 2008, with large expansions of credit, capital inflows, and high inflation of local wages and prices creating real appreciations: the same ingredients

FIGURE 7-17

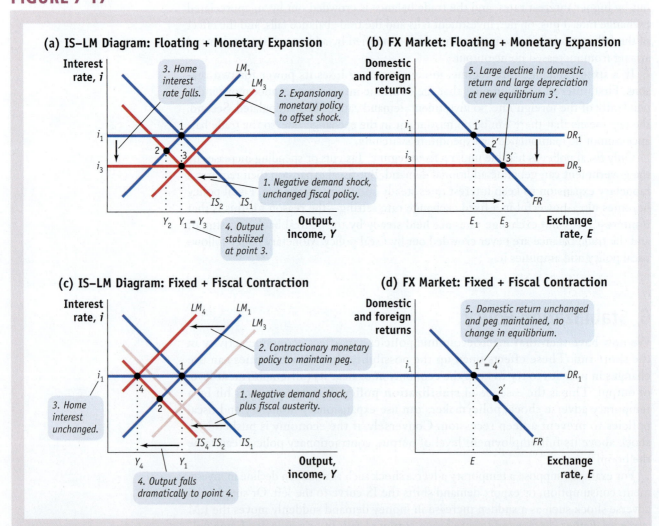

(a) IS–LM Diagram: Floating + Monetary Expansion

(b) FX Market: Floating + Monetary Expansion

(c) IS–LM Diagram: Fixed + Fiscal Contraction

(d) FX Market: Fixed + Fiscal Contraction

Examples of Policy Choices Under Floating and Fixed Exchange Rates In panels (a) and (c) in the IS–LM diagram, the goods and money markets are initially in equilibrium at point 1. The interest rate is also the domestic return, DR_1, that prevails in the FX market. In panels (b) and (d), the FX market is initially in equilibrium at point 1′. An exogenous negative shock to demand (e.g., a collapse in foreign income and/or a financial crisis at home) causes the IS curve to shift in from IS_1 to IS_2. Without further action, output and interest rates would fall and the exchange rate would tend to depreciate. In panels (a) and (b) we explore what happens when the central bank can stabilize output at its former level by responding with a monetary policy expansion, increasing the money supply and causing the LM curve to shift out from LM_1 to LM_3. The new equilibrium corresponds to points

3 and 3′. Output is now stabilized at the original level Y_1. The interest rate falls further from i_1 all the way to i_3. The domestic return falls from DR_1 to DR_3, and the exchange rate depreciates all the way from E_1 to E_3. In panels (c) and (d) we explore what happens when the exchange rate is fixed and the government pursues austerity and cuts government spending G. This causes the IS curve to shift in even further from IS_2 to IS_4. If the central bank does nothing, the home interest rate will fall further and the exchange rate will depreciate sharply at points 2 and 2′. To maintain the peg, as dictated by the trilemma, the home central bank must engage in contractionary monetary policy, decreasing the money supply and causing the LM curve to shift in all the way from LM_1 to LM_4. The new equilibrium corresponds to points 4 and 4′. The peg is preserved, but output collapses to the new level Y_4.

for a sharp postcrisis economic downturn that were seen in Greece, Spain, Portugal, and Ireland. Yet not all countries suffered the same fate. Here we use our analytical tools to look at two polar cases: Poland, which fared well, and Latvia, which did not.

In our framework, as the shocks first hit, the demand for Poland's and Latvia's exports declined as a result of a contraction in foreign output Y^* in their trading partners, mainly the rest of Europe. In addition, Poland and Latvia faced negative shocks to consumption and investment demand as consumers and investors cut back their expenditures in the face of uncertainty and tighter credit due to financial sector problems. These events would be represented by a leftward shift of Poland's and Latvia's IS curves from IS_1 to IS_2, which we show in Figure 7-17.

But the policy responses differed in each country, illustrating the contrasts between fixed and floating regimes. Because the Poles had a floating exchange rate, they were able to pursue strong monetary expansion and let their currency depreciate. They also maintained their plans for government spending in order to combat the decline in demand. Because the Latvians were pegging to the euro, they could not use monetary policy at all, and they had to pursue aggressive austerity and slash government spending in order to satisfy the demands of a European Union and International Monetary Fund assistance program. Our modeling framework makes some predictions about the consequences of these policy choices.

In Figure 7-17, panels (a) and (b), Poland first goes from point 1(1′) to point 2(2′), and the initial shock is partially offset by the induced depreciation of the Polish zloty and increased investment thanks to lower interest rates. In the end, demand would still be below its initial level and a recession would result with output falling from Y_1 to Y_2. However, the central bank responded with expansionary monetary policy, a shift out in the LM curve to LM_3. The economy shifted to point 3(3′): even lower interest rates amplified the depreciation of the zloty and stimulated demand through investment and expenditure-switching channels. In contrast, as shown in Figure 7-17, panels (c) and (d), Latvia cut government spending, so when its IS curve shifted in, it shifted *even farther* to IS_4. Bound by the trilemma, Latvia's LM curve had to follow those shifts in lockstep and move in to LM_4 in order to maintain the lat–euro peg. The Latvian economy moved from point 1(1′) to point 4(4′).

The model predicted that a recession might be avoided in Poland, but that there could be a very deep recession in Latvia. What actually happened? Check out the accompanying news item (see **Headlines: Poland Is Not Latvia**).

Problems in Policy Design and Implementation

In this chapter, we have looked at open-economy macroeconomics in the short run and at the role that monetary and fiscal policies can play in determining economic outcomes. The simple models we used have clear consequences. On the face of it, if policymakers were really operating in such an uncomplicated environment, they would have the ability to exert substantial control and could always keep output steady with no unemployed resources and no inflation pressure. In reality, life is more complicated for policymakers for a variety of reasons.

Policy Constraints Policymakers may not always be free to apply the policies they desire, sometimes due to other commitments that may seem of overriding importance. A fixed exchange rate rules out any use of monetary policy. Other firm monetary or fiscal policy rules, such as interest rate rules or balanced-budget rules, place limits on policy. The political economy of fiscal policy can be especially problematic for effective policy response, especially when parliaments or legislatures are divided. Even if policymakers want to act, other constraints may bind them. While it is always feasible to print money, it may not be possible (technically or politically) to raise the real resources necessary for

HEADLINES

Poland Is Not Latvia

Eastern Europe faced difficult times in the Great Recession. Yet not all countries suffered the same fate, as we see from this story and from the macroeconomic data presented and discussed in Figure 7-18.

. . . Poland and Latvia . . . inherited woefully deficient institutions from communism and have struggled with many of the same economic ills over the past two decades. They have also adopted staggeringly different approaches to the crisis, one of which was a lot more effective than the other.

. . . I don't think it's being radical to say that [since 2004] Poland's performance is both a lot better and a lot less variable and that if you were going to draw lessons from one of the two countries that it should probably be the country which avoided an enormous bubble and subsequent collapse. What is it that caused Poland's

economy to be so sound? Was it austerity? Was it hard money?

. . . Both Latvia and Poland actually ran rather substantial budget deficits during the height of the crisis, though Latvia's budgeting in the years preceding the crisis was more balanced and restrained than Poland's. . . . Poland's government

FIGURE 7-18

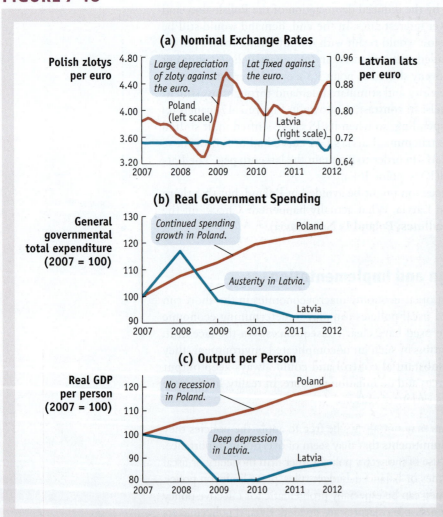

Macroeconomic Policy and Outcomes in Poland and Latvia, 2007–12 In the face of adverse demand shocks from outside and inside their economies, Poland and Latvia reacted differently. Panels (a) and (b) show that Poland pursued expansionary monetary policy, let its currency depreciate against the euro, and kept government spending on a stable growth path. Latvia maintained a fixed exchange rate with the euro and pursued an austerity approach with large government spending cuts from 2009 onward. Panel (c) shows that Poland escaped a recession, with positive growth in all years. In contrast, Latvia fell into a deep depression, and real GDP per capita fell 20% from its 2007 peak.

Data from: IMF, International Financial Statistics and World Economic Outlook. Exchange rates are 3-month moving averages; all other data are annual.

spending as a percentage of GDP was also noticeably higher than Latvia's both before the crisis and after it. . . . You can see how, starting in 2008, Latvia starts to make some sharp cuts while Poland continues its steady, modest increases.

So, basically, Poland is a country whose government habitually ran budget deficits before, during, and after the crisis, whose government spends a greater percentage of GDP than Latvia, and which did not cut spending in response to the crisis. Latvia, in contrast, ran balanced budgets, had a very small government as a percentage of GDP, and savagely cut spending in response to the crisis. While I don't think you can call Poland "profligate," if economics really were a morality play you'd expect the Latvians to come out way ahead since they've followed the austerity playbook down to the letter. However, in the real world, Poland's economic performance has been vastly, almost comically, superior to Latvia's despite the fact that the country didn't make any "hard choices."

All of this, of course, leaves out monetary policy. . . . Part of the reason that Latvia's economic performance has been so awful is that it has pegged its currency to the euro, a course of action which has made the lat artificially expensive and which made Latvia's course of "internal devaluation" necessary. . . . Poland did the exact opposite, allowing its currency, the zloty, to depreciate massively against the euro. . . .

Poland did not, in other words, "defend the zloty" because it realized that a devaluation of its currency would be incredibly helpful. And the Polish economy has continued to churn along while most of its neighbors have either crashed and burned or simply stagnated. . . .

There are plenty of lessons from Poland's economic success, including the need for effective government regulation (Poland never had an out-of-control bubble like Latvia), the need for exchange rate flexibility, and the extreme importance of a country having its own central bank. These lessons are neither left wing nor right wing, Poland's government is actually quite conservative. . . . Economics just isn't a morality play, and no matter how often the Latvians cast themselves as the diligent and upstanding enforcers of austerity their economic performance over the past five years has still been lousy.

Source: Excerpted from Mark Adomanis, "If Austerity Is So Awesome Why Hasn't Poland Tried It?" forbes.com, January 10, 2013. Reproduced with Permission of Forbes Media LLC © 2013

a fiscal expansion. Countries with weak tax systems or poor creditworthiness—problems that afflict developing countries—may find themselves unable to tax or borrow to finance an expansion of spending even if they wished to do so.

Incomplete Information and the Inside Lag Our models assume that the policymakers have full knowledge of the state of the economy before they take corrective action: they observe the economy's IS and LM curves and know what shocks have hit. In reality, macroeconomic data are compiled slowly, and it may take weeks or months for policymakers to fully understand the state of the economy today. Even then, it will take time to formulate a policy response (the lag between shock and policy actions is called the *inside lag*). On the monetary side, there may be a delay between policy meetings. On the fiscal side, it may take even more time to pass a bill through the legislature and then enable a real change in spending or taxing activity by the public sector.

Policy Response and the Outside Lag Even if they finally receive the correct information, policymakers then have to formulate the right response given by the model. In particular, they must not be distracted by other policies or agendas, nor subject to influence by interest groups that might wish to see different policies enacted. Finally, it takes time for whatever policies are enacted to have any effect on the economy through the spending decisions of the public and private sectors (the lag between policy actions and effects is called the *outside lag*).

Long-Horizon Plans Other factors may make investment and the trade balance less sensitive to policy. If the private sector understands that a policy change is temporary, then there may be reasons not to change consumption or investment expenditure. Suppose a firm can either build and operate a plant for several years or not build at all (e.g., the investment might be of an irreversible form). For example, a firm may not care about a higher real interest rate this year and may base its decision on the expected real interest rate that will affect its financing over many years ahead. Similarly, a temporary real appreciation may have little effect on whether a firm can profit in the long run from sales in the foreign market. In such circumstances, firms' investment and export activities may not be very sensitive to short-run policy changes.

Weak Links from the Nominal Exchange Rate to the Real Exchange Rate Our discussion assumed that changes in the nominal exchange rate lead to real exchange rate changes, but the reality can be somewhat different for some goods and services. For example, the Japanese yen appreciated from about 120 ¥/$ to 80 ¥/$ from 2008 to 2012, and then reversed and depreciated all the way back to 120 ¥/$ from 2012 to 2016, but during each of these episodes (with the exchange rate swinging up and down by 40% to 50%) the U.S. prices of Japanese-made cars, like some Toyotas, moved much less, changing only by small amounts, if at all. Why? There are a number of reasons for this weak pass-through phenomenon, including the dollarization of trade and the distribution margins that separate retail prices from port prices (as we saw in **Side Bar: Barriers to Expenditure Switching: Pass-Through and the J Curve**). The forces of arbitrage may also be weak as a result of noncompetitive market structures: for example, Toyota sells through exclusive dealers, and government regulation requires that cars meet different standards in Europe versus the United States. These obstacles allow a firm like Toyota to *price to market*: to charge a steady U.S. price even as the exchange rate moves temporarily. If a firm can bear (or hedge) the exchange rate risk, it might do this to avoid the volatile sales and alienated customers that might result from repeatedly changing its U.S. retail price list.

Pegged Currency Blocs Our model's predictions are also affected by the fact that for some major countries in the real world, their exchange rate arrangements are characterized—often not as a result of their own choice—by a mix of floating and fixed exchange rate systems with different trading partners. For most of the decade 2000–10, the dollar depreciated markedly against the euro, pound, and several other floating currencies, but in the emerging-market "Dollar Bloc" (China, India, and other countries), the monetary authorities have ensured that the variation in the value of their currencies against the dollar was small or zero. When a large bloc of other countries pegs to the U.S. dollar, this limits the ability of the United States to engineer a real effective depreciation.

Weak Links from the Real Exchange Rate to the Trade Balance Our discussion also assumed that real exchange rate changes lead to changes in the trade balance. There may be several reasons why these linkages are weak in reality. One major reason is transaction costs in trade. Suppose the exchange rate is $1 per euro and an American is consuming a domestic good that costs $100 as opposed to a European good costing €100 = $100. If the dollar appreciates to $0.95 per euro, then the European good looks cheaper on paper, only $95. Should the American switch to the import? Yes, if the good can be moved without cost—but there are few such goods! If shipping costs $10, it still makes sense to consume the domestic good until the exchange rate falls below $0.90 per euro. Practically, this means that expenditure switching may be a nonlinear phenomenon: it will be weak at first and then much stronger as the real exchange rate change grows larger. This phenomenon, coupled with the J curve effects discussed earlier, may cause the response of the trade balance in the short run to be small or even in the wrong direction.

APPLICATION

Macroeconomic Policies in the Liquidity Trap: From the Global Financial Crisis to the Coronavirus Recession

The last decade has seen monetary and fiscal authorities around the world struggling to respond to two of the largest recessions ever seen. First, one of the boldest experiments in macroeconomic policymaking began in 2008–10 in the major downturn that followed the Global Financial Crisis. It was characterized by two unusual features. First, central banks started running out of conventional policy space as interest rates approached zero. Second, fiscal policies that had not been used for decades as a major cyclical stabilization tools were suddenly dusted off and deployed. Now, at the time of writing, April 2020, the world economy is entering an even steeper collapse. The onset of the coronavirus pandemic set off public health interventions to slow infections, but lockdowns and travel restrictions have triggered a man-made recession. Economic policymakers are right back where they were ten years ago, with interest rates stuck at zero, and fiscal policy swinging into action on an even bigger scale.

How can we understand these economic policy choices? In this application, we look at the policy response and interpret events using the IS–LM–FX model of this chapter. Many of the problems we discuss had their earliest manifestation in Japan, where since the late 1990s nominal interest rates set by the Bank of Japan have been trapped at or near the **zero lower bound (ZLB)**. After the Great Recession of 2008, central banks in the United States, the Eurozone, Britain, and other economies found themselves in the same situation, and although some (like the Federal Reserve) were able to raise rates eventually, the fear was of a return to zero in the next recession. This has now come to pass.

Under ZLB conditions, policymakers came to the very rapid realization that monetary policy alone could not fully offset the magnitude of the shock to demand. In the context of our IS–LM–FX model, as consumption and investment fell for exogenous reasons, the shock moved the IS curve very far leftward. In 2008, one major source of the demand shock was that, as we saw in an earlier chapter, banks were very afraid of taking on risk and sharply reduced their lending to firms and households—and even when they did lend, they were still charging very high interest rates. Thus, even with very expansionary monetary policy, that is, large rightward shifts of the LM curve, low policy interest rates did not translate into cheap borrowing for the private sector. Once the U.S. Federal Reserve had brought its policy rate to zero in December 2008, there was little more it could do to stimulate demand using conventional monetary policies. A similar story unfolded in other economies at the time, and again in 2020, with financial conditions tight and few willing to borrow to spend on consumption or investment.

This peculiar situation is depicted by the blue lines in Figure 7-19 and differs from the normal IS–LM–FX setup we have seen so far. After the demand shock and the Fed's response to it, the IS curve has moved so far in (to IS_1) and the LM curve has moved so far out (to LM_1), that the IS and LM curves now intersect at a very low interest rate—so low that it is equal to zero. In the money market, nominal interest rates can't fall below zero, so another way of describing this situation is to say that the economy was at an IS–LM equilibrium at which the LM curve was absolutely flat and resting on the horizontal axis (at a 0% interest rate) in the diagram.

[Note that in the FX diagram this would place the domestic return DR at zero. Also, note that interest rates were by this time at zero in all developed countries for similar reasons. Thus, it is also appropriate to think of the foreign (e.g., euro) interest rate as also stuck at zero, which in the FX diagram would lower the foreign return FR.]

The situation just described is unusual in several ways. First, monetary policy is powerless in this situation: it cannot be used to lower interest rates because interest rates can't go any lower. In the diagram, moving the LM curve out to LM_2 does not dislodge the economy from the horizontal portion of the LM curve. We are still stuck on the IS_1 curve at a point 1 and a 0% interest rate. This unfortunate state of affairs is known as the *zero lower bound* (ZLB), already mentioned. It is also known as a *liquidity trap* because liquid money and interest-bearing assets have the same interest rate of zero, so there is no opportunity cost to holding money, and thus changes in the supply of central bank money have no effect on the incentive to switch between money and interest-bearing assets.

Can anything be done? Yes. The bad news is that fiscal policy is the only tool now available to increase demand. The good news is that fiscal policy has the potential to be super-powerful in this situation. The reason is that as long as interest rates are stuck at zero, and the monetary authorities keep them there, government spending will not crowd out investment or net exports, in contrast to the typical situation we studied earlier in this chapter. In other words, in this situation, a floating exchange

FIGURE 7-19

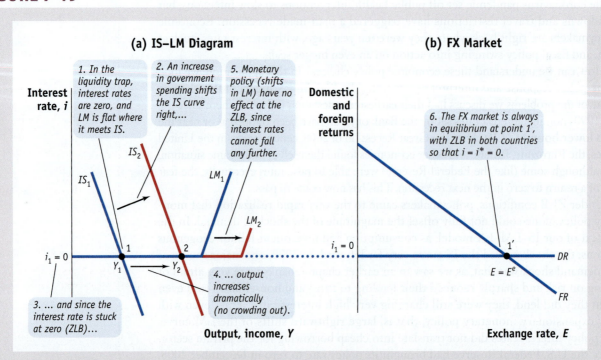

(a) IS–LM Diagram

(b) FX Market

1. In the liquidity trap, interest rates are zero, and LM is flat where it meets IS.

2. An increase in government spending shifts the IS curve right,...

5. Monetary policy (shifts in LM) have no effect at the ZLB, since interest rates cannot fall any further.

6. The FX market is always in equilibrium at point 1', with ZLB in both countries so that $i = i^* = 0$.

3. ... and since the interest rate is stuck at zero (ZLB)...

4. ... output increases dramatically (no crowding out).

Output, income, Y

Exchange rate, E

Macroeconomic Policies in the Liquidity Trap After a severe negative shock to demand, the IS curve may move very far to the left (IS_1). The nominal interest rate may then fall all the way to the zero lower bound (ZLB), with IS_1 intersecting the flat portion of the LM_1 curve at point 1, on the horizontal axis, in panel (a). Output is depressed at a level Y_1. In this scenario, monetary policy is impotent because expansionary monetary policy (e.g., a rightward shift from LM_1 to LM_2) cannot lower the interest rate any further. However, fiscal policy may be very effective, and a shift right from IS_1 to IS_2 leaves the economy still at the ZLB, but with a higher level of output Y_2. (The figure is drawn assuming the ZLB holds in both home and foreign economies, so the FX market is in equilibrium at point 1' with $E = E^e$ at all times.)

rate regime starts to look little different from a fixed exchange rate regime, with interest rates locked at the floor.[3]

Looking back over the last decade or more, from the Great Recession of 2008 through the Coronavirus Recession of 2020, we can gain some perspective on the path of the world economy towards this kind of policymaking environment. Figure 7-20 documents global monetary and fiscal policy responses each year around the world from 2007 to 2020. Panel (a) shows the path of monetary policy as given by the level of policy interest rates set by key central banks. Panel (b) shows the path of fiscal policy as given by the change in fiscal stance, measured by annual changes in the budget deficits $T - G$ of various countries or regions.

The paths of interest rates in panel (a) show a fairly common pattern among the central banks of the advanced economies. These rates were at what were considered normal positive levels in the mid-2000s. Only Japan was at zero, after a persistent slump dating back to the 1990s. Switzerland was at 1%, but all the others were in the 2% to 6% range. Outside Japan, with growth and inflation looking strong, these rates were raised somewhat just before the Great Recession of 2008. This was a possible contributing factor to that event given the large amount of household leverage that had built up. In the subsequent large recession, most of these central banks reduced rates to near, at, or even below zero. Absent strong enough fiscal policy responses—see next page— they also pursued many other unconventional policies to get further stimulus, like quantitative easing (buying public and private bonds) and forward guidance (promises to keep rates low) to ease credit conditions even with rates at the floor. One notable

[3] Note that, at the ZLB, the model resembles the fixed exchange rate model, not the floating exchange rate model, because being stuck at the ZLB pegs the interest rate (in this case at zero, rather than at i^*).

FIGURE 7-20

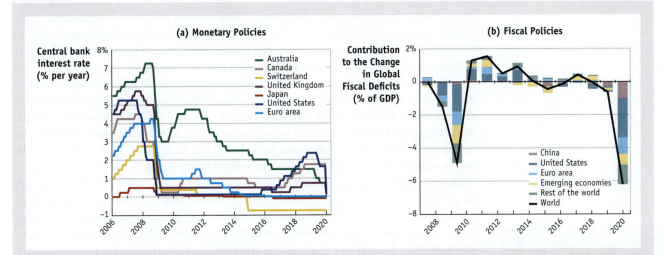

Monetary and Fiscal Policies from the Global Financial Crisis to the Coronavirus Recession In both recent downturns, monetary policy has hit the zero lower bound in the advanced economies, and fiscal policy has been deployed more aggressively than we have ever seen before in peacetime. Panel (a) shows selected central bank policy interest rates from 2006 to 2020. Panel (b) shows changes in government deficits scaled by global GDP from 2007 to 2020.

Data from: Central bank policy rates from Bank for International Settlements. Deficit data from IMF Fiscal Monitor.

exception was Australia, where strong underlying growth and inflation, supported by robust export demand from China, allowed the economy to escape a recession.

Later on, a rash decision by the ECB to prematurely raise rates in 2011 contributed to a double-dip Eurozone recession and a European debt crisis. Elsewhere rates were stuck near the ZLB for most of the 2010s decade, with only a few central banks (e.g., in the United States and Canada, and to a small degree in the United Kingdom) raising rates slowly in 2017–18. But these higher rates did not last long. The onset of the Coronavirus Recession prompted all central banks—including Australia—to aggressively cut rates again, all the way back to the ZLB by the end of March 2020. Once more, central banks started to activate unconventional measures, with the Fed (in tandem with the U.S. Treasury) again taking the lead to offer quasi-fiscal lending support to a wider range of credit markets on a massive scale, including not only mortgages but also corporate debt and even small business loans. Thus, from 2008 onwards, with only brief exceptions, virtually all central banks in advanced economies have spent more than a decade at the ZLB, with possibly much more to come as the damaging Coronavirus Recession drags on into the 2020s.

The paths of fiscal policies globally in panel (b) also show the imprint of the two great downturns and speak to an increasing, if reluctant, use of fiscal policy in the face of the ZLB. The chart shows contributions to the change in fiscal deficits (in % of world GDP). In 2008 and 2009 governments around the world allowed the routine operation of the so-called *automatic stabilizers* whereby deficits mechanically cushion the economy in a recession, as Y falls. To allow for this mechanism, our model would need some minor revision, but informally we would just acknowledge that, on the one hand, government spending G reacts positively to economic downturns (a negative correlation with Y), as welfare programs and unemployment insurance, for example, increase; and on the other hand, government tax revenues T react negatively to economic downturns (a positive correlation with Y), say, as income taxes decrease. In other words, this automatic deficit mechanism would offset the tendency of private demand to move pro-cyclically with the income level Y. But even in advanced countries this force is in general quite weak, in fact, and especially so in the United States, where tax rates are low, and state and local have self-imposed constraints in their borrowing. But the Great Recession of 2008 was so large that

Construction work on an interstate highway in Cleveland, Ohio, funded by government stimulus money through the ARRA.

more intervention was seen to be need than what the automatic stabilizers alone could provide. Around the world, the fiscal responses seen in 2008–09 were massive as governments enacted large temporary, discretionary *fiscal stimulus* programs. For example, in the United States, the $700 billion stimulus bill, known as the American Recovery and Reinvestment Act of 2009, spread over two years, raised spending on infrastructure and other programs and featured large tax cuts. (But this was not enough to support demand and prevent a massive U.S. recession, and for reasons well understood at the time: most of the tax cuts were saved, not spent, and the federal government spending increases were offset in dollar terms by harsh spending cuts by state and local governments.) On the world stage, the United States was by no means acting alone, and a concerted effort to pursue expansionary fiscal policy was agreed to at the 2009 G20 London Summit. The magnitude of these unprecedented peacetime fiscal policy actions is clearly seen in Figure 7-20, with a large negative (increasing deficit) spike associated with 2009. But this policy stance did not last and was unwound quickly in most countries within a couple of years. Some regions, notably in the Eurozone, reversed course into brutal austerity plans, helping to trigger a double-dip recession, especially in countries in deep downturns, like Spain, Portugal, Italy, Ireland and Greece, that were unable to borrow to fund continued fiscal stimulus. In China and many emerging economies, the stimulus was withdrawn more gradually, their growth rebounded more rapidly, financial crises were avoided, and these countries helped pull global growth back to speed.

The slow recovery dragged on for years, but the Coronavirus Recession of 2020 dramatically changed the course of events. Once more the ZLB limited what monetary policy could do, and governments again stepped in and spent huge sums, on an even larger scale than before, to keep their economies afloat, support households and business, and ramp up health systems and public health interventions. In the United States, a March 2020 fiscal stimulus package directed $2 trillion in spending increases, roughly *six times* the size of the package deployed in the previous downturn, with more to follow. But the virus was global, and many economies followed similar paths, with unprecedented financial commitments made by governments in the United Kingdom, Europe, Japan, Canada, and across the advanced economies. At the time of writing, emerging and developing economies—many with less ability to fund fiscal stimulus policies—faced the same macroeconomic challenge as the virus spread.

To sum up, the aggregate U.S. fiscal stimulus had four major weaknesses: it was rolled out too slowly, due to policy lags; the overall package was too small, given the magnitude of the decline in aggregate demand; the government spending portion of the stimulus, for which positive expenditure effects were certain, ended up being close to zero, due to state and local cuts; and this left almost all the work to tax cuts (automatic and discretionary) that recipients, for good reasons, were more likely to save rather than spend. With monetary policy impotent and fiscal policy weak and ill designed, the economy remained mired for a long time in its worst slump since the 1930s Great Depression.[4]

The Coronavirus Recession of 2020: Army Corps of Engineers constructs a field hospital at the Jacob K. Javits Convention Center in New York City, financed by federal government emergency funds.

Andrew Kelly/Reuters/Newscom

7 Conclusions

The analysis of macroeconomic policy is different in an open economy than in a closed economy. The trade balance generates an additional source of demand, and its fluctuations are driven by changes in output and the real exchange rate. Expenditure switching is a key mechanism at work here: as international relative prices change, demand shifts from foreign to home goods and vice versa.

The open economy IS–LM–FX framework is a workhorse model for analyzing the macroeconomic responses to shocks and to changes in monetary and fiscal policies. Exploring these responses, in turn, draws out some clear contrasts between the operation of fixed and flexible exchange rate regimes.

Under flexible exchange rates, monetary and fiscal policies can be used. Monetary expansions raise output and also lower the interest rate, which stimulates investment and causes a depreciation, which in turn stimulates the trade balance. Fiscal expansions raise output; raise the interest rate, which depresses investment; and cause an appreciation, which in turn lowers the trade balance.

With two policy tools available, the authorities have considerable flexibility. In particular, their ability to let the exchange rate adjust to absorb shocks makes a strong case for a floating exchange rate. Now we can understand the logic behind Robert Mundell's quote at the start of the chapter.

Under fixed exchange rates, monetary policy cannot be used because the home interest rate has to remain equal to the foreign interest rate in order for the exchange rate to remain fixed. But fiscal policy has great power under a fixed exchange rate. Fiscal expansions raise output and force the monetary authority to expand the money supply to prevent any rise in the interest rate and any appreciation of the exchange rate. In contrast to the floating case, in which interest rate increases and exchange rate appreciation put downward pressure on investment and the trade balance, the demand stimulus is even greater.

With only one policy tool available, the authorities in fixed rate regimes have much less flexibility. They also expose the economy to more volatility because any demand shock will entail an immediate and reinforcing monetary shock. The tendency of fixed exchange rate systems to amplify demand shocks helps us understand the logic behind Alec Ford's quote at the start of the chapter.

Whatever the regime, fixed or floating, our findings suggest that macroeconomic policy can *in principle* be used to stabilize an open economy when it suffers from external shocks. Under floating exchange rates, however, more policy options are available (monetary and fiscal policy responses are feasible) than under fixed exchange rates (only a fiscal policy response is feasible).

Despite these relatively simple lessons, real-world policy design is not straightforward. Policymakers have difficulty identifying shocks, devising the right response, and acting quickly enough to ensure that policy actions have a timely effect. Even then, under some conditions, the economy may respond in unusual ways. Both technical and political economy difficulties pose challenges to active macroeconomic policymaking.

KEY POINTS

1. In the short run, we assume prices are sticky at some preset level P. There is thus no inflation, and nominal and real quantities can be considered equivalent. We assume that output GDP equals income Y or GDNI and that the trade balance equals the current account (there are no transfers or factor income from abroad).

2. The Keynesian consumption function says that private consumption spending C is an increasing function of household disposable income $Y - T$.

3. The investment function says that total investment I is a decreasing function of the real or nominal interest rate i.

4. Government spending is assumed to be exogenously given at a level G.

5. The trade balance is assumed to be an increasing function of the real exchange rate EP^*/P, where P^* denotes the foreign price level.

6. The national income identity says that national income or output equals private consumption C, plus investment I, plus government spending G, plus the trade balance TB: $Y = C + I + G + TB$. The right-hand side of this expression is called *demand*, and its components depend on income, interest rates, and the real exchange rate. In equilibrium, demand must equal the left-hand side, supply, or total output Y.

7. If the interest rate falls in an open economy, demand is stimulated for two reasons. A lower interest rate directly stimulates investment. A lower interest rate also leads to an exchange rate depreciation, all else equal, which increases the trade balance. This demand must be satisfied for the goods market to remain in equilibrium, so output rises. This is the basis of the IS curve: declines in interest rates must call forth extra output to keep the goods market in equilibrium. Each point on the IS curve represents a combination of output Y and interest

rate i at which the goods and forex markets are in equilibrium. Because Y increases as i decreases, the IS curve is downward-sloping.

8. Real money demand arises primarily from transactions requirements. It increases when the volume of transactions (represented by national income, Y) increases, and decreases when the opportunity cost of holding money, the nominal interest rate i, increases.

9. The money market equilibrium says that the demand for real money balances L must equal the real money supply: $M/P = L(i)Y$. This equation is the basis for the LM curve: any increases in output Y must cause the interest rate to rise, all else equal (e.g., holding fixed real money M/P). Each point on the LM curve represents a combination of output Y and interest rate i at which the money market is in equilibrium. Because i increases as Y increases, the LM curve is upward-sloping.

10. The IS–LM diagram combines the IS and LM curves on one figure and shows the unique short-run equilibrium for output Y and the interest rate i that describes simultaneous equilibrium in the goods and money markets. The IS–LM diagram can be coupled with the forex market diagram to summarize conditions in all three markets: goods, money, and forex. This combined IS–LM–FX diagram can then be used to assess the impact of various macroeconomic policies in the short run.

11. Under a floating exchange rate, the interest rate and exchange rate are free to adjust to maintain

equilibrium. Thus, government policy is free to move either the IS or LM curves. The effects are as follows:

- Monetary expansion: LM shifts to the right, output rises, interest rate falls, exchange rate rises/depreciates.
- Fiscal expansion: IS shifts to the right, output rises, interest rate rises, exchange rate falls/appreciates.

12. Under a fixed exchange rate, the interest rate always equals the foreign interest rate and the exchange rate is pegged. Thus, the government is not free to move the LM curve: monetary policy must be adjusted to ensure that LM is in such a position that these exchange rate and interest rate conditions hold. The impacts are as follows:

- Monetary expansion: not feasible.
- Fiscal expansion: IS shifts to the right, LM follows it and also shifts to the right, output rises strongly, interest rate and exchange rate are unchanged.

13. The ability to manipulate the IS and LM curves gives the government the capacity to engage in stabilization policies to offset shocks to the economy and to try to maintain a full-employment level of output. This is easier said than done, however, because it is difficult to diagnose the correct policy response, and policies often take some time to have an impact, so that by the time the policy effects are felt, they may be ineffective or even counterproductive.

KEY TERMS

consumption, p. 231
disposable income, p. 231
marginal propensity to consume (MPC), p. 232
expected real interest rate, p. 232
taxes, p. 233
government consumption, p. 233

transfer programs, p. 233
expenditure switching, p. 233
real effective exchange rate, p. 236
pass-through, p. 238
J curve, p. 239
goods market equilibrium condition, p. 241

Keynesian cross, p. 243
IS curve, p. 245
LM curve, p. 250
monetary policy, p. 255
fiscal policy, p. 255
stabilization policy, p. 261
zero lower bound (ZLB), p. 267

PROBLEMS

1. **Discovering Data** In this chapter we discussed the weak link between the real exchange rate and the trade balance. We looked at a time series diagram showing these two variables for the United States in Figure 7-4, but what about other countries? Go to the online FRED database (https://fred.stlouisfed.org) and download the data for the real effective exchange rate, the

trade balance (in local currency), and GDP (in local currency) for China and Japan from 1995 to the present.

a. For each country make a chart, like Figure 7-4, that shows the real exchange rate and the trade balance as a percent of GDP on the same line graph. Use the left vertical axis for the real exchange rate and the right vertical axis for the trade balance as a percent of GDP.

b. For each country, do you find that these variables have a strong relationship? Is it what you would expect from this chapter? Explain why this relationship might fail or even go in the opposite direction of what we might expect.

2. In 2001, President George W. Bush and Federal Reserve Chairman Alan Greenspan were both concerned about a sluggish U.S. economy. They also were concerned about the large U.S. current account deficit. To help stimulate the economy, President Bush proposed a tax cut, while the Fed had been increasing U.S. money supply. Compare the effects of these two policies in terms of their implications for the current account. If policymakers are concerned about the current account deficit, discuss whether stimulatory fiscal policy or monetary policy makes more sense in this case. Then, reconsider similar issues for 2009–10, when the economy was in a deep slump, the Fed had taken interest rates to zero, and the Obama administration was arguing for a larger fiscal stimulus.

3. Suppose that American firms become more pessimistic and decide to reduce investment expenditure today in new factories and office space.

   a. How will this decrease in investment affect output, interest rates, and the current account?

   b. Now repeat part (a), assuming that domestic investment is very responsive to the interest rate so that U.S. firms will cancel most of their changes in investment plans if the interest rate falls. How will this affect the answer you gave previously?

WORK IT OUT | ≋ Achieᴠe | interactive activity

4. For each of the following situations, use the IS–LM–FX model to illustrate the effects of the shock. For each case, state the effect of the shock on the following variables (increase, decrease, no change, or ambiguous): Y, i, E, C, I, and TB. Note: In this question, assume the government allows the exchange rate to float and makes no policy response.

   a. Foreign output increases.

   b. Investors expect an appreciation of the home currency in the future.

   c. The home money supply decreases.

   d. Government spending at home decreases.

   Hint: In each case, make use of the goods market equilibrium condition to understand what happens to consumption, investment, and the trade balance in the shift from the old to the new equilibrium.

5. How would a decrease in the money supply of Paraguay (currency unit: the guaraní) affect its own output and its exchange rate with Brazil (currency unit: the real)? Do you think this policy in Paraguay might also affect output across the border in Brazil? Explain.

6. For each of the following situations, use the IS–LM–FX model to illustrate the effects of the shock and the policy response. For each case, state the effect of the shock on the following variables (increase, decrease, no change, or ambiguous): Y, i, E, C, I, and TB. Note: In this question (unlike in the Work It Out question), assume that the government allows the exchange rate to float but also responds by using monetary policy to stabilize output.

   a. Foreign output increases.

   b. Investors expect an appreciation of the home currency in the future.

   c. The home money supply decreases.

   d. Government spending at home decreases.

Hint: In each case, make use of the goods market equilibrium condition to understand what happens to consumption, investment, and the trade balance in the shift from the old to the new equilibrium.

7. Repeat the previous question, assuming the central bank responds in order to maintain a fixed exchange rate. In which case or cases will the government response be the same as in the previous question?

8. This question explores IS and FX equilibria in a numerical example.

   a. The consumption function is $C = 1.5 + 0.8(Y - T)$. What is the marginal propensity to consume? What is the marginal propensity to save?

   b. The trade balance is $TB = 5(1 - [1/E]) - 0.2(Y - 8)$. What is the marginal propensity to consume foreign goods? What is the marginal propensity to consume home goods?

   c. The investment function is $I = 3 - 10i$. What is investment when the interest rate i is equal to $0.10 = 10\%$?

   d. Assume government spending is G. Add up the four components of demand and write down the expression for D.

   e. Assume forex market equilibrium is given by $i = ([1/E] - 1) + 0.15$, where the two foreign return terms on the right are expected depreciation and the foreign interest rate. What is the foreign interest rate? What is the expected future exchange rate?

9. [More difficult] Continuing the last question, solve for the IS curve: obtain an expression for Y in terms of i, G, and T (eliminate E).

10. Assume that initially the IS curve is given by

$$IS_1: Y = 22 - 1.5T - 30i + 2G$$

and that the price level P is 1, and the LM curve is given by

$$LM_1: M = Y(1 - i)$$

The home central bank uses the interest rate as its policy instrument. Initially, the home interest rate equals the foreign interest rate of 10% or 0.1. Taxes and government spending both equal 2. Call this case 1.

a. According to the IS_1 curve, what is the level of output Y? Assume this is the desired full-employment level of output.

b. According to the LM_1 curve, at this level of output, what is the level of the home money supply?

c. Plot the IS_1 and LM_1 curves for case 1 on a chart. Label the axes and the equilibrium values.

d. Assume that forex market equilibrium is given by $i = ([1/E] - 1) + 0.10$, where the two foreign return terms on the right are expected depreciation and the foreign interest rate. The expected future exchange rate is 1. What is today's spot exchange rate?

e. There is now a foreign demand shock, such that the IS curve shifts left by 1.5 units at all levels of the interest rate, and the new IS curve is given by

$$IS_2: Y = 20.5 - 1.5T - 30i + 2G$$

The government asks the central bank to stabilize the economy at full employment. To stabilize and return output back to the desired level, according to this new IS curve, by how much must the interest rate be lowered from its initial level of 0.1? (Assume taxes and government spending remain at 2.) Call this case 2.

f. At the new lower interest rate and at full employment, on the new LM curve (LM_2), what is the new level of the money supply?

g. According to the forex market equilibrium, what is the new level of the spot exchange rate? How large is the depreciation of the home currency?

h. Plot the new IS_2 and LM_2 curves for case 2 on a chart. Label the axes and the equilibrium values.

i. Return to part (e). Now assume that the central bank refuses to change the interest rate from 10%. In this case, what is the new level of output? What is the money supply? And if the government decides instead to use fiscal policy to stabilize output, then according to the new IS curve, by how much must government spending be increased to achieve this goal? Call this case 3.

j. Plot the new IS_3 and LM_3 curves for case 3 on a chart. Label the axes and the equilibrium values.

11. In this chapter, we've studied how policy responses affect economic variables in an open economy. Consider each of the problems in policy design and implementation discussed in this chapter. Compare and contrast each problem as it applies to monetary policy stabilization versus fiscal policy stabilization.

APPENDIX 1

The Marshall–Lerner Condition

The model developed in this chapter assumes that a depreciation of a country's currency (a rise in q) will cause the trade balance to move toward surplus (a rise in TB). Is this assumption justified?

Let's look at a simple example. Consider a hypothetical two-country world in which trade is initially balanced, so $TB = 0$ or $EX = IM$. The question of how the trade balance changes then simplifies to a question of whether the change in exports is greater or less than the change in imports. Let us consider a small percentage change in the real exchange rate, say, $\Delta q/q = +1\%$, that is, a home real depreciation of 1%. Note that this is, approximately, a foreign real appreciation of 1%, since the foreign real exchange rate ($q^* = 1/q$) is simply the inverse of the home real exchange rate, implying that $\Delta q^*/q^* = -1\%$.

As we have argued, when home exports look cheaper to foreigners, the real value of home exports expressed in home units of output will *unambiguously* rise. This effect is described by the elasticity of home exports with respect to the home real exchange rate, denoted η, where

$$\frac{\Delta EX}{EX} = \eta \times \frac{\Delta q}{q} = \eta\%$$

That is, if the home country experiences a 1% real depreciation, its real exports (measured in home units) rise by $\eta\%$.

The same logic applies to the foreign country, with exports (EX^*), real exchange rate ($q^* = 1/q$), and elasticity (η^*), so that

$$\frac{\Delta EX^*}{EX^*} = \eta^* \times \frac{\Delta q^*}{q^*} = \eta^*\%$$

Now consider the trade link between the two countries. Foreign exports must equal home imports, measured in any consistent units. In home real output units

$$\begin{array}{c}\text{Home imports} \\ \text{in units of home output}\end{array} = \underbrace{IM(q)}_{\substack{\text{home imports} \\ \text{(real)}}}$$

$$\begin{array}{c}\text{Foreign exports} \\ \text{in units of home output}\end{array} = \underbrace{(1/P)}_{\substack{\text{Divide by home} \\ \text{price level to} \\ \text{convert to home} \\ \text{output units}}} \times \underbrace{\underbrace{E}_{\substack{\text{Exchange} \\ \text{rate converts} \\ \text{foreign to} \\ \text{domestic} \\ \text{currency}}} \times \underbrace{P^*}_{\substack{\text{Price of} \\ \text{foreign basket} \\ \text{in foreign} \\ \text{currency}}} \times \underbrace{EX^*(q^*)}_{\substack{\text{Foreign exports} \\ \text{(real)}}}}_{\substack{\text{Value of foreign exports in} \\ \text{foreign currency}}}$$

$$\underbrace{}_{\text{Value of foreign exports in home currency}}$$

Equating these two terms, we find that $IM(q) = (EP^*/P) \times EX^*(q^*)$. Thus,

$$IM(q) = q \times EX^*(q^*)$$

This expression makes intuitive sense for the stylized two-country world that we are studying. It states that *IM*, the quantity of home imports (measured in *home* output units), must equal the quantity of foreign exports EX^* (measured in *foreign* output units) multiplied by a factor q that converts units of foreign goods to units of home goods (since q is the relative price of foreign goods, that is, home goods per unit of foreign goods).

For a small change, we may write the percentage change in the previous equation as follows. On the left is the percentage change in imports; on the right is the percentage change in q times EX^*, which equals the percentage change in q plus the percentage change in EX^*:

$$\frac{\Delta IM}{IM} = \frac{\Delta q}{q} + \frac{\Delta EX^*}{EX^*} = \frac{\Delta q}{q} + [\eta^* \times \frac{\Delta q^*}{q^*}] = 1\% + [\eta^* \times (-1\%)] = (1 - \eta^*)\%$$

What is going on here? On the home import side, two effects come into play. Foreigners export a lower volume of their more expensive goods measured in foreign output units (a volume effect of $-\eta^*\%$), but those goods will cost more for home importers in terms of home output (a price effect of 1%). The price effect follows because the real exchange rate (the relative price of the foreign goods in terms of domestic goods) has increased (by 1%), and this makes every unit of imports cost more in real terms.

Starting from balanced trade with $EX = IM$, a 1% home real depreciation will cause EX to change by $\eta\%$ and IM to change by $1 - \eta^*\%$. The trade balance (initially zero) will increase (to become positive) if and only if the former impact on EX exceeds the latter impact on IM. This occurs if and only if $\eta > 1 - \eta^*$, or, equivalently,

$$\eta + \eta^* > 1$$

The last expression is known as the *Marshall–Lerner condition*: it says that the trade balance will increase after a real depreciation only if the responsiveness of trade volumes to real exchange rate changes is sufficiently large (or sufficiently elastic) to ensure that the volume effects exceed the price effects.

APPENDIX 2
Multilateral Real Exchange Rates

How do the predictions of our model change when a country trades with multiple countries or regions? Can our theory be extended to this more realistic case? Can we make a sensible aggregation of trade flows, trade balances, and real exchange rates across, say, N different countries?

Suppose that for trade with any foreign country (say, country 1), the fractional change in home exports (EX_1) and imports (IM_1) given a small change in the real exchange rate (q_1) is

$$\frac{\Delta EX_1}{EX_1} = \varepsilon \times \frac{\Delta q_1}{q_1}; \quad \frac{\Delta IM_1}{IM_1} = -\varepsilon \times \frac{\Delta q_1}{q_1}$$

The parameter $\varepsilon > 0$ is an *elasticity*. In this case, it is the elasticity of exports and imports with respect to the real exchange rate. When q rises by 1% (a real depreciation), exports rise by $\varepsilon\%$ and imports fall by $\varepsilon\%$. (A more complicated analysis is needed when the import and export elasticities differ; see Appendix 1.)

From these relationships, we find the following by rearranging:

$$\Delta TB_1 = \Delta EX_1 - \Delta IM_1 = \varepsilon \frac{\Delta q_1}{q_1} EX_1 + \varepsilon \frac{\Delta q_1}{q_1} IM_1$$

$$= \varepsilon \times (EX_1 + IM_1) \times \frac{\Delta q_1}{q_1}$$

$$= \varepsilon \times Trade_1 \times \frac{\Delta q_1}{q_1}$$

where $Trade_i = [EX_i + IM_i]$ is the total trade of the home country with country i.

Adding up this last equation across all countries, the change in the home trade balance is given by $\Delta TB = \Delta TB_1 + \Delta TB_2 + \cdots + \Delta TB_N$, which we can write as

$$\Delta TB = \varepsilon \times \left[Trade_1 \frac{\Delta q_1}{q_1} + Trade_2 \frac{\Delta q_2}{q_2} + \cdots + Trade_N \frac{\Delta q_N}{q_N} \right]$$

We normalize by total trade, where $Trade = Trade_1 + Trade_2 + \cdots + Trade_N$, to obtain

$$\Delta TB = \varepsilon \times Trade \times \underbrace{\left[\frac{Trade_1}{Trade} \frac{\Delta q_1}{q_1} + \frac{Trade_1}{Trade} \frac{\Delta q_2}{q_2} + \cdots + \frac{Trade_1}{Trade} \frac{\Delta q_N}{q_N} \right]}_{\text{Trade-weighted average of bilateral real exchange rate changes}}$$

The expression in brackets might look familiar. In Chapter 2, we introduced the concept of a *trade-weighted change in the nominal exchange rate*—the change in the value of a currency against a basket of currencies, where the change in each country-pair's nominal exchange rate was weighted by that particular country-pair's share of trade volume. The preceding expression is similar, only with nominal exchange rates replaced by real exchange rates. The expression shows that (with some assumptions) our model can be extended to more realistic scenarios with many countries by using the change in a trade-weighted real exchange rate covering all trading partners.

8

Fixed Versus Floating: International Monetary Experience

In truth, the gold standard is already a barbarous relic. All of us, from the Governor of the Bank of England downwards, are now primarily interested in preserving the stability of business, prices, and employment, and are not likely, when the choice is forced on us, deliberately to sacrifice these to the outworn dogma. . . . Advocates of the ancient standard do not observe how remote it now is from the spirit and the requirements of the age.

John Maynard Keynes, 1923

How many more fiascoes will it take before responsible people are finally convinced that a system of pegged exchange rates is not a satisfactory financial arrangement for a group of large countries with independent political systems and independent national policies?

Milton Friedman, 1992

The gold standard in particular—and even pegged exchange rates in general—have a bad name. But the gold standard's having lost her name in the 1920s and 1930s should not lead one to forget her 19th century virtues. . . . Can these lost long-term virtues be retrieved without the world again being in thrall to the barbarous relic? . . . In an integrated world economy, the choice of an exchange rate regime—and thus the common price level—should not be left to an individual country. The spillover effects are so high that it should be a matter of collective choice.

Ronald McKinnon, 2002

Questions to Consider

1 Why do some countries adopt a fixed exchange rate while others adopt a floating exchange rate regime?

2 How can we understand the costs and benefits of each type of regime?

3 Can the economic pros and cons help to explain the wide range of past and present policy choices?

A century ago, economists and policymakers may have had their differences of opinion, but—unlike today—almost all of them agreed that a fixed exchange rate was the ideal choice of exchange rate regime. Even if some countries occasionally adopted a floating rate, it was usually with the expectation that they would soon return to a fixed or pegged rate.

The preferred method for fixing the exchange rate was the **gold standard**, a system in which the value of a country's currency was fixed relative to an ounce of gold. As a result, the currency's value was also fixed against all other currencies that were also pegged to gold. The requirements of maintaining the gold standard were strict: although monetary authorities could issue paper money, they had to be willing and able to exchange paper currency for gold at the official fixed rate when asked to do so.

Figure 8-1 documents almost 150 years of exchange rate arrangements around the world. From 1870 to 1913, most of the world used the gold standard. At the peak in 1913, approximately 70% of the world's countries were part of the gold standard system; a few floated (about 20%) or used other metallic standards (about 10%). Since 1913 much has changed. Adherence to the gold standard weakened during World War I, waxed and waned in the 1920s and 1930s, then was never seen again. In the 1940s, John Maynard Keynes and policymakers from all over the world designed a new system of fixed exchange rates, the *Bretton Woods system*.

In the period after World War II, the figure shows that many currencies were pegged to the U.S. dollar in this system. Other currencies were pegged to the British pound, the French franc, the German mark, and the Soviet/Russian ruble. Because the pound, franc, and mark were all pegged to the dollar at this time, the vast majority of the world's currencies were directly or indirectly fixed to one another by what amounted to a "dollar standard" system. After 1970 the pound faded out as a peg choice, and around 1990 so did the ruble. After 1999 the euro replaced the franc and the mark.

Like the gold standard, the dollar-based system didn't endure. Beginning in the early 1970s, floating exchange rates became more common (more than 30% of all currency regimes in the 1980s and 1990s); in recent years, fixed exchange rates have risen again in prominence. Remember, however, that the data in the figure count all

FIGURE 8-1

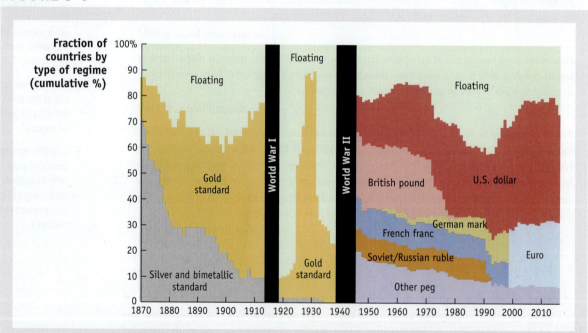

Exchange Rates Regimes of the World, 1870–2016 The shaded regions show the fraction of countries on each type of regime by year, and they add up to 100%. From 1870 to 1913, the gold standard became the dominant regime. During World War I (1914–18), most countries suspended the gold standard, and resumptions in the late 1920s were brief. After further suspensions in World War II (1939–45), most countries were fixed against the U.S. dollar (the pound, franc, mark, and ruble blocs were indirectly pegged to the dollar). Starting in the 1970s, more countries opted to float. In 1999 the euro replaced the franc and the mark as the base currency for many pegs.

Data from: Author's calculations based on Christopher M. Meissner, 2005, "A New World Order: Explaining the International Diffusion of the Gold Standard, 1870–1913," Journal of International Economics, 66(2), 385–406; Christopher M. Meissner and Nienke Oomes, 2009, "Why Do Countries Peg the Way They Peg? The Determinants of Anchor Currency Choice," Journal of International Money and Finance, 28(3), 522–547, and later updates; and extended with Ethan Ilzetzki, Carmen M. Reinhart, and Kenneth S. Rogoff, 2019, "Exchange Arrangements Entering the Twenty-First Century: Which Anchor Will Hold?" Quarterly Journal of Economics, 134(2), 599–646.

countries in an equal fashion, without any weighting for a nation's economic size (measured by GDP). In the larger economies of the world, and especially among the major currencies, floating regimes are more prevalent.

Why do some countries choose to fix and others to float? Why do they change their minds at different times? These are among the most enduring and controversial questions in international macroeconomics, and they have been the cause of conflicts among economists, policymakers, and commentators for many years. On one side of the debate are those like Milton Friedman (quoted at the start of this chapter), who in the 1950s argued against the prevailing orthodoxy, stating that floating rates are better because of their clear economic and political advantages. On the opposing side of the debate are figures such as Ronald McKinnon (also quoted above), who think that only a system of fixed rates can encourage cooperative policymaking, keep prices and output stable, and encourage international flows of trade and finance. In this chapter, we examine the pros and cons of different exchange rate regimes.

1 Exchange Rate Regime Choice: Key Issues

In previous chapters, we have examined the workings of the economy under fixed and floating exchange rates. One advantage of understanding the workings of these regimes in such detail is that it helps us to address a perennially important macro-economic policy question: What is the best exchange rate regime choice for a given country at a given time? In this section, we explore the pros and cons of fixed and floating exchange rates by combining the models we have developed with additional theory and evidence. We begin with an application about Germany and Britain in the early 1990s. This story highlights the choices policymakers face as they choose between fixed exchange rates (pegs) and floating exchange rates (floats).

APPLICATION

Britain and Europe: The Big Issues

One way to begin to understand the choice between fixed and floating regimes is to look at countries that have sometimes floated and sometimes fixed and to examine their reasons for switching. In this case study, we look at the British decision to switch from an exchange rate peg to floating in September 1992.

To begin, let's look at why Britain first adopted a peg. In 1973 Britain joined what would later become the European Union (EU), a membership that would endure until Brexit in 2020. Back in the 1970s, the European push toward a common currency was seen as the most ambitious part of a larger political and economic program that would eventually create a single market across Europe. Fixed exchange rates, and ultimately a common currency, were seen as a way to promote deeper integration and encourage trade and other forms of cross-border exchange by lowering transaction costs. In eventually agreeing to try a pegged exchange rate despite aversions to the political project, British policymakers were perhaps swayed by these ostensible benefits, and may have also felt that an exchange rate anchor could help keep British inflation low and stable. In political economy terms, narrow economic considerations loomed larger than bigger political concerns—at least back then.

The common currency (the euro) did not become a reality until 1999, when 11 countries began to use it. But the journey started in 1979 with the creation of a fixed exchange rate system called the *Exchange Rate Mechanism* (ERM). The ERM tied all member currencies together at fixed rates as a step on the way to the adoption of a single currency. In practice, however, the predominant currency in the ERM was the German mark or

Deutsche Mark (DM). This meant that in the 1980s and 1990s, the German central bank, the Bundesbank, largely retained its monetary autonomy and had the freedom to set its own money supply levels and nominal interest rates. Other countries in the ERM, or looking to join it, in effect had to *unilaterally* peg to the DM. The DM acted like the **base currency** or **center currency** (Germany was the *base country* or *center country*) in the ERM's fixed exchange rate system.[1]

In 1990, Britain joined the ERM. Based on our analysis of fixed exchange rates in the previous chapter, we can understand the implications of that choice using Figure 8-2. This figure shows the familiar one-country IS–LM–FX diagram for Britain and another IS–LM diagram for the center country, Germany. We treat Britain as the home country and Germany as the foreign country, and denote foreign variables with an asterisk.

Panel (a) shows an IS–LM diagram for Germany, with German output on the horizontal axis and the German DM interest rate on the vertical axis. Panel (b) shows the British IS–LM diagram, with British output on the horizontal axis. Panel (c) shows the British forex market, with the exchange rate in pounds per mark. The vertical axes of panels (b) and (c) show returns in pounds, the home currency.

Initially, we suppose the three diagrams are in equilibrium as follows. In panel (a), at point $1''$, German output is Y_1^* and the DM interest rate is i_1^*. In panel (b), at point 1, British output is Y_1 and the pound interest rate is i_1. In panel (c), at point $1'$, the pound is pegged to the DM at the fixed rate $\bar{E}$ and expected depreciation is zero. The trilemma tells us that monetary policy autonomy is lost in Britain: the British interest rate must equal the German interest rate, so there is uncovered interest parity with $i_1 = i_1^*$.

A Shock in Germany With the scene set, our story begins with a threat to the ERM from an unexpected source. The countries of Eastern Europe began their transition away from communism, a process that famously began with the fall of the Berlin Wall in 1989. After the wall fell, the reunification of East and West Germany was soon under way. Because the economically backward East Germany required significant funds to support social services, pay unemployment benefits, modernize infrastructure, and so on, the reunification imposed large fiscal costs on Germany, but West Germans were willing to pay these costs to see their country united. As we know from the previous chapter, an increase in German government consumption G^* can be represented as a shift to the right in the German IS curve, from IS_1^* to IS_2^* in panel (a). This shift would have moved the German economy's equilibrium from point $1''$ to point $3''$. All else equal, the model predicts an increase in German interest rates from i_1^* to i_3^* and a boom in German output from Y_1^* to Y_3^*.[2] This is indeed what started to happen.

The next chapter in the story involves the Bundesbank's response to the German government's expansionary fiscal policy. The Bundesbank was afraid that the boom in German output might cause an increase in German rates of inflation, and it wanted to avoid that outcome. Using its policy autonomy, the Bundesbank tightened its monetary policy by contracting the money supply and raising interest rates. This policy change is seen in the upward shift of the German LM curve, from LM_1^* to LM_2^* in panel (a). We suppose that the Bundesbank stabilizes German output at its initial level Y_1^* by raising German interest rates to the even higher level of i_2^*.[3]

---

[1] Officially, all currencies in the ERM were pegged to a basket of member currencies called the ecu (European currency unit).

[2] All else would not have been equal under this shift, given the ERM; Germany's interest rate increase would have been matched by other ERM members to preserve their pegs. For Germany, those shifts would be increases in the foreign interest rate (from Germany's perspective), and those responses would, in turn, have shifted Germany's IS curve a tiny bit farther to the right. These extra effects make no substantive difference to the analysis, so the extra shift is not shown here, for clarity.

[3] Interest rate responses in the ERM (described in footnote 2) would, in turn, have moved Germany's IS curve out yet farther, requiring a bit more tightening from the Bundesbank. Again, these indirect effects do not affect the analysis and are not shown, for clarity.

FIGURE 8-2

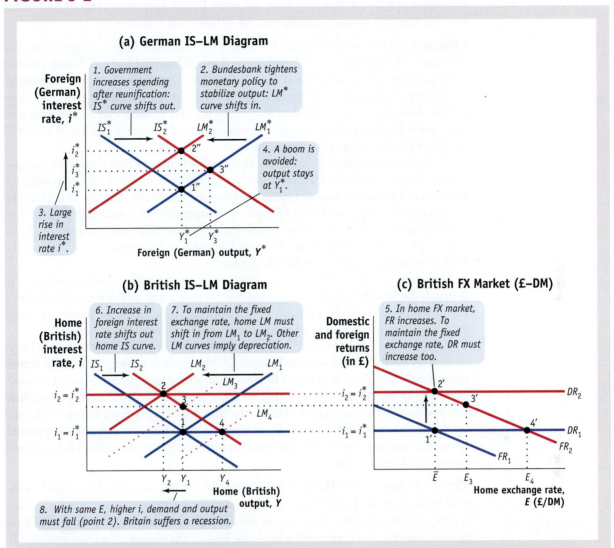

(a) German IS–LM Diagram

Foreign (German) interest rate, i^*

1. Government increases spending after reunification: IS^* curve shifts out.

2. Bundesbank tightens monetary policy to stabilize output: LM^* curve shifts in.

IS_1^* IS_2^* LM_2^* LM_1^*

2″

4. A boom is avoided: output stays at Y_1^*.

i_2^*
i_3^* 3″
i_1^* 1″

3. Large rise in interest rate i^*.

Y_1^* Y_3^*

Foreign (German) output, Y^*

(b) British IS–LM Diagram

Home (British) interest rate, i

6. Increase in foreign interest rate shifts out home IS curve.

7. To maintain the fixed exchange rate, home LM must shift in from LM_1 to LM_2. Other LM curves imply depreciation.

IS_1 IS_2 LM_2 LM_1

2
3 LM_3
$i_2 = i_2^*$
$i_1 = i_1^*$ 1 LM_4
4

Y_2 Y_1 Y_4

Home (British) output, Y

8. With same E, higher i, demand and output must fall (point 2). Britain suffers a recession.

(c) British FX Market (£–DM)

Domestic and foreign returns (in £)

5. In home FX market, FR increases. To maintain the fixed exchange rate, DR must increase too.

2′ DR_2
$i_2 = i_2^*$ 3′
$i_1 = i_1^*$ 1′ 4′ DR_1
FR_2
FR_1

$\bar{E}$ E_3 E_4

Home exchange rate, E (£/DM)

Off the Mark: Britain's Departure from the ERM in 1992
In panel (a), German reunification raises German government spending and shifts IS^* out. The German central bank contracts monetary policy, LM^* shifts up, and German output stabilizes at Y_1^*. Equilibrium shifts from point 1″ to point 2″, and the German interest rate rises from i_1^* to i_2^*. In Britain, under a peg, panels (b) and (c) show that foreign returns, FR, rise and so the British domestic return, DR, must rise to $i_2 = i_2^*$. The German interest rate rise also shifts out Britain's IS curve slightly from IS_1 to IS_2.

To maintain the peg, Britain's LM curve shifts up from LM_1 to LM_2. At the same exchange rate and a higher interest rate, demand falls and output drops from Y_1 to Y_2. Equilibrium moves from point 1 to point 2. If the British were to float, they could put the LM curve wherever they wanted. For example, at LM_4 the British interest rate holds at i_1 and output booms, but the forex market ends up at point 4′ and there is a depreciation of the pound to E_4. The British could also select LM_3 and stabilize output at the initial level Y_1, but the peg still has to break with E rising to E_3.

Choices for the Other ERM Countries What happened in the countries of the ERM that were pegging to the DM? We examine what these events implied for Britain, but the other ERM members faced the same problems. The IS–LM–FX model tells us that events in Germany have two implications for the British IS–LM–FX model. First, as the German interest rate i^* rises, the British foreign return curve FR shifts up in the British forex market (to recap: German deposits pay higher interest, all else equal). Second, as the German interest rate i^* rises, the British IS curve shifts out (to recap: at any given British interest rate, the pound has to depreciate more,

boosting British demand via expenditure switching). Now we only have to figure out how much the British IS curve shifts, what the British LM curve is up to, and hence how the equilibrium outcome depends on British policy choices.

Choice 1: Float and Prosper? First, let us suppose that in response to the increase in the German interest rate i^*, the Bank of England had left British interest rates unchanged at i_1, and suppose British fiscal policy had also been left unchanged. In addition, let's assume that Britain would have allowed the pound–DM exchange rate to float in the short run. For simplicity we also assume that in the long run, the expected exchange rate remains unchanged, so that the long-run future expected exchange rate E^e remains unchanged at $\bar{E}$.

With these assumptions in place, let's look at what happens to the investment component of demand: in Britain, I would be unchanged at $I(i_1)$. In the forex market in panel (c), the Bank of England, as assumed, holds the domestic return DR_1 constant at i_1. With the foreign return rising from FR_1 to FR_2 and the domestic return constant at DR_1, the new equilibrium would be at 4′ and the British exchange rate rises temporarily to E_4. Thus, if the Bank of England doesn't act, the pound would have to depreciate to E_4 against the DM; it would float, contrary to the ERM rules.

Now think about the effects of this depreciation on the trade balance component of demand: the British trade balance would rise because a nominal depreciation is also a real depreciation in the short run, given sticky prices.[4] As we saw in the previous chapter, British demand would therefore increase, as would British equilibrium output.

To sum up the result after all these adjustments occur, an increase in the foreign interest rate always shifts out the home IS curve, all else equal as shown in panel (b): British interest rates would still be at i_1, and British output would have risen to Y_4, on the new IS curve IS_2. To keep the interest rate at i_1, as output rises, the Bank of England would have had to expand its money supply, shifting the British LM curve from LM_1 to LM_4, and causing the pound to depreciate to E_4. If Britain were to float and depreciate the pound, it would experience a boom. But this would not have been compatible with Britain's continued ERM membership.

Choice 2: Peg and Suffer? If Britain's exchange rate were to stay pegged to the DM because of the ERM, however, the outcome for Britain would not be so rosy. In this scenario, the trilemma means that to maintain the peg, Britain would have to increase its interest rate and follow the lead of the center country, Germany. In panel (b), the pound interest rate would have to rise to the level $i_2 = i_2^*$ to maintain the peg. In panel (c), the domestic return would rise from DR_1 to DR_2 in step with the foreign return's rise from FR_1 to FR_2, and the new foreign exchange (forex or FX) market equilibrium would be at 2′. The Bank of England would accomplish this rise in DR by tightening its monetary policy and lowering the British money supply. In panel (b), under a peg, the new position of the IS curve at IS_2 would imply an upward shift in the British LM curve, as shown by the move from LM_1 to LM_2. So the British IS–LM equilibrium would now be at point 2, with output at Y_2. The adverse consequences for the British economy now become apparent. At point 2, as compared with the initial point 1, British demand has fallen. Why? British interest rates have risen (depressing investment demand I), but the exchange rate has remained at its pegged level $\bar{E}$ (so there is no change in the trade balance). To sum up, what we have shown in this scenario is that the IS curve may have moved right a bit, but the opposing shift in the LM curve would have been even larger. If Britain were to stay pegged and keep its membership in the ERM, Britain would experience a recession.

---

[4] This is true in a pure two-country model, and, from the British perspective, Germany is the "rest of the world." With many countries, however, the direction of change is still the same. All else equal, a British real depreciation against Germany will still imply a depreciation of the British real effective exchange rate against the rest of the world.

In 1992 Britain found itself facing a decision between these two choices. As we have noted, if the British pound had been floating against the DM, then leaving interest rates unchanged would have been an option, and Britain could have achieved equilibrium at point 4 with a higher output, Y_4. In fact, floating would have opened up the whole range of monetary policy options. For example, Britain could have chosen a mild monetary contraction by shifting the British LM curve from LM_1 to LM_3, moving the equilibrium in panel (b) to point 3, stabilizing U.K. output at its initial level Y_1, and allowing the FX market in panel (c) to settle at point 3' with a mild depreciation of the exchange rate to E_3.

What Happened Next? In September 1992, after an economic slowdown and after considerable last-minute dithering and turmoil, the British Conservative government finally decided that the benefits to Britain of being in ERM and the euro project were smaller than the costs suffered as a result of a German interest-rate hike in response to Germany-specific events. Two years after joining the ERM, Britain opted out.

Did Britain make the right choice? In Figure 8-3, we compare the economic performance of Britain with that of France, a large EU economy that maintained its ERM peg. After leaving the ERM in September 1992, Britain lowered interest rates in the short run, as shown in panel (a), and also depreciated its exchange rate against the DM, as shown in panel (b). In comparison, France never depreciated and had to maintain higher interest rates to keep the franc pegged to the DM until German monetary policy eased a year or two later. As our model would predict, the British economy boomed in subsequent years, as shown in panel (c). The French suffered slower growth, a fate shared by most of the other countries that stayed in the ERM.

Most Britons are opposed to the euro, some vehemently so.

The British choice stands to this day, but it is a political economy decision reflecting wider concerns than macroeconomics alone. Although the option to rejoin the

FIGURE 8-3

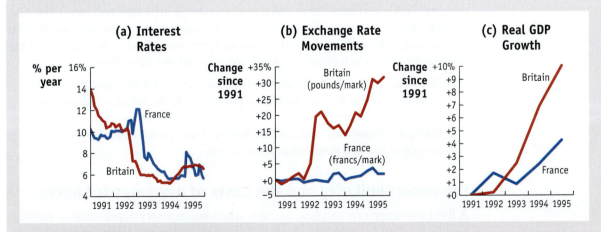

(a) Interest Rates

(b) Exchange Rate Movements

(c) Real GDP Growth

Floating Away: Britain Versus France After 1992 Britain's decision to exit the ERM allowed for more expansionary British monetary policy after September 1992. In other ERM countries that remained pegged to the mark, such as France, monetary policy had to be kept tighter to maintain the peg. Consistent with the model, the data show lower interest rates, a more depreciated currency, and faster output growth in Britain compared with France after 1992.

Note: Interest rates are three-month annualized London InterBank Offered Rates.

Data from: econstats.com; IMF, International Financial Statistics and World Economic Outlook databases.

ERM remained open after 1992, the idea of pegging to (much less joining) the euro was very unpopular in Britain. All subsequent British governments decided that the benefits of increased trade and economic integration with Europe were smaller than the associated costs of sacrificing British monetary autonomy. Eventually, in the 2016 Brexit referendum, the British voted to leave the EU, partly due to even broader concerns over sovereignty. On January 31, 2020, Britain left the EU project altogether.[5]

Key Factors in Exchange Rate Regime Choice: Integration and Similarity

We started this chapter with an application about the policy choice and trade-offs Britain faced in 1992 when it needed to decide between a fixed exchange rate (peg) and a floating exchange rate (float).

At different times, British authorities could see the potential benefits of participating fully in an economically integrated single European market and the ERM fixed exchange rate system. The fixed exchange rate, for example, would lower the costs of economic transactions among the members of the ERM zone. But, especially in 1992, the British could also see that there would be times when the monetary policy being pursued by authorities in Germany would be out of line with policy that was best for Britain. The fundamental source of this divergence between what Britain wanted and what Germany wanted was that each country faced different shocks. The fiscal shock that Germany experienced after reunification was not felt in Britain or any other ERM country.

To better understand these trade-offs, and the decision to fix or float, we now examine the issues that are at the heart of this decision: economic *integration* as measured by trade and other transactions, and economic *similarity*, as measured by the similarity of shocks.

Economic Integration and the Gains in Efficiency

The term **economic integration** refers to the growth of market linkages in goods, capital, and labor markets among regions and countries. By lowering transaction costs, a fixed exchange rate might promote integration and increase economic efficiency.

Trade is the clearest example of an activity that volatile exchange rates might discourage. Stable exchange rates and prices encourage arbitrage and lower the costs of trade. But trade is not the only type of international economic activity likely to be discouraged by exchange rate fluctuations. Currency-related transaction costs and uncertainty also act as barriers to cross-border capital and labor flows.

- ■ The lesson: *The greater the degree of economic integration between markets in the home country and the base country, the greater will be the volume of transactions between the two, and the greater will be the benefits the home country gains from fixing its exchange rate with the base country. As integration rises, the efficiency benefits of having a fixed exchange rate increase.*

Economic Similarity and the Costs of Asymmetric Shocks

A fixed exchange rate can lead to costs when one country experiences a country-specific shock or **asymmetric shock** that is not shared by the other country.

---

[5] Even the Liberal Democrats, for a long time pro-euro while just a small party perpetually in opposition, effectively dropped their stance once they had the opportunity to join a coalition government with the Conservatives in 2010.

The application on Britain and Germany showed why an *asymmetric* shock causes problems: it leads to a conflict between the policy goals of the two countries. In our example, German policymakers wanted to tighten monetary policy to offset a boom caused by a positive demand shock due to their expansionary fiscal policy. British policymakers did not want to implement the same policy because they had not experienced the same shock; following the German monetary policy would have caused a recession in Britain.

Similar or *symmetric* shocks do not cause such problems. Imagine that Germany and Britain experienced an identical expansionary demand shock. In this case, German and British monetary authorities would respond identically, raising interest rates by the same amount to stabilize output. This desired symmetric increase in interest rates would not conflict with Britain's fixed exchange rate commitment. If interest rates were initially set at a common level, $i_1 = i_1^*$, they would be raised to a new higher level, $i_2 = i_2^*$. By raising its rates, Britain could stabilize output *and* stay pegged because uncovered interest parity is still satisfied. The exchange rate $\bar{E}$ does not change, and even though Britain is pegging unilaterally to Germany, Britain has the interest rate it would choose even if it were floating and could make an independent monetary policy choice.

More generally, for any two home and foreign countries, when Home unilaterally pegs to Foreign, asymmetric shocks impose costs on Home in terms of undesired output volatility. When asymmetric shocks hit, the monetary policies that are best for Foreign and for Home will differ, and the peg means that Foreign's policy choice will automatically be imposed on Home. In contrast, symmetric shocks do not impose any costs because the monetary policies that Foreign and Home want to pursue will be the same, and Foreign's imposed choice will suit Home perfectly.

Real-world situations are more complex. Countries are not identical, and shocks may be a mix of large and small, symmetric and asymmetric.

■ The lesson: *The greater the degree of economic similarity between the home country and the base country (that is, if they face more symmetric shocks and fewer asymmetric shocks), then the smaller will be the economic stabilization costs to the home country of fixing its exchange rate to the base. As economic similarity rises, the stability costs of having a fixed exchange rate decrease.*

Simple Criteria for a Fixed Exchange Rate

We can now set out a theory of exchange rate regime choice by considering the *net benefits* (benefits minus the costs) of pegging versus floating. Our discussions about integration and similarity have shown the following:

■ *As integration rises, the efficiency benefits of a fixed exchange rate increase.*

■ *As symmetry rises, the stability costs of a fixed exchange rate decrease.*

Our theory says that if market integration or symmetry increases, the net benefits of a fixed exchange rate also increase. If the net benefits are negative, the home country should float if the decision is based solely on its economic interests. If the net benefits are positive, the home country should fix.

Figure 8-4 illustrates the theory in a **symmetry-integration diagram** in which the horizontal axis measures the degree of economic integration between a pair of locations, say, A and B, and the vertical axis measures the symmetry of the shocks experienced by the pair A and B.

We use the figure to see whether A should peg unilaterally to B (or vice versa). Suppose conditions change and the pair moves up and to the right, for example, from point 1 toward point 6. Along this path, integration and symmetry are both increasing,

FIGURE 8-4

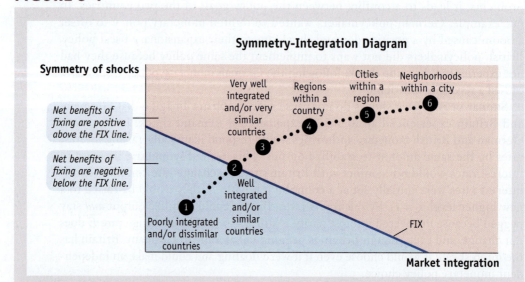

A Theory of Fixed Exchange Rates Points 1 to 6 in the figure represent a pair of locations. Suppose one location is considering pegging its exchange rate to its partner. If their markets become more integrated (a move to the right along the horizontal axis) or if the economic shocks they experience become more symmetric (a move up on the vertical axis), the net economic benefits of fixing increase. If the pair moves far enough up or to the right, then the benefits of fixing exceed costs (net benefits are positive), and the pair will cross the fixing threshold shown by the FIX line. Above the line, it is optimal for the region to fix. Below the line, it is optimal for the region to float.

so the net benefits of fixing are also increasing. At some critical point (point 2 in the graph), the net benefits turn positive. Before that point, floating is best. After that point, fixing is best.

Our argument is more general: whatever the direction of the path, as long as it moves up and to the right, it must cross some threshold like point 2 beyond which benefits outweigh costs. Thus, there will exist a set of points—a downward-sloping line passing through point 2—that delineates this threshold. We refer to this threshold as the FIX line. Points above the FIX line satisfy the economic criteria for a fixed exchange rate.

What might different points on this chart mean? If we are at point 6, we might think of A and B as neighborhoods in a city—they are very well integrated and an economic shock is usually felt by all neighborhoods in the city. If A and B were at point 5, they might be two cities. If A and B were at point 4, they might be the regions of a country, and still above the FIX line. If A and B were at point 3, they might be neighboring, well-integrated countries with few asymmetric shocks. Point 2 is right on the borderline. If A and B were at point 1, they might be less well-integrated countries with more asymmetric shocks and our theory says they should float.

The key prediction of our theory is this: *pairs of countries above the FIX line (more integrated, more similar shocks) will gain economically from adopting a fixed exchange rate. Those below the FIX line (less integrated, less similar shocks) will not.*

In a moment, we develop and apply this theory further. But first, let's see if there is evidence to support the theory's two main assumptions: Do fixed exchange rates deliver trade gains through integration? Do they impose stability costs by limiting monetary policy options?

APPLICATION

Do Fixed Exchange Rates Promote Trade?

The single most powerful argument *for* a fixed exchange rate is that it may boost trade by eliminating trade-hindering costs. The idea is an old one. In 1878, the United States had yet to re-adopt the gold standard following the Civil War. Policymakers were debating whether going back on gold made sense, and J. S. Moore, a U.S. Treasury official testifying before Congress, was questioned on the subject:

Question: Do you not think that the use of a common standard of value has a tendency to promote a free commercial interchange between the various countries using it?

Answer: If two countries, be they ever so distant from each other, should have the same standard of money . . . there would be no greater harmonizer than such an exchange.

Benefits Measured by Trade Levels As we have noted, this was the conventional wisdom among policymakers in the late nineteenth and early twentieth centuries, and research by economic historians has found strong support for their views: all else equal, two countries adopting the gold standard had bilateral trade levels 30% (or more) higher than comparable pairs of countries that were off the gold standard.[6] Thus, it appears that the gold standard *did* promote trade.

What about fixed exchange rates today? Do they promote trade? Economists have exhaustively tested this hypothesis using increasingly sophisticated statistical methods. We can look at some evidence from a recent study in which country pairs A–B were classified in four different ways:

a. The two countries are using a *common currency* (i.e., A and B are in a currency union or A has unilaterally adopted B's currency).

b. The two countries are linked by a *direct* exchange rate peg (i.e., A's currency is pegged to B's).

c. The two countries are linked by an *indirect* exchange rate peg, via a third currency (i.e., A and B have currencies pegged to C but not directly to each other).

d. The two countries are not linked by any type of peg (i.e., their currencies *float* against each other, even if one or both might be pegged to some other third currency).

Using this classification and trade data from 1973 to 1999, economists Jay Shambaugh and Michael Klein compared bilateral trade volumes for all pairs under the three pegged regimes (a) through (c) with the benchmark level of trade under a floating regime (d) to see if there were any systematic differences. They also used careful statistical techniques to control for other factors and to address possible reverse causality (that is, to eliminate the possibility that higher trade might have caused countries to fix their exchange rates). Figure 8-5 shows their key estimates, according to which currency unions increased bilateral trade by 38% relative to floating regimes. They also found that the adoption of a fixed exchange rate would promote trade, but only for the case of *direct* pegs. Adopting a direct peg increased bilateral trade by 21% compared with a floating exchange rate. Indirect pegs had a negligible and statistically insignificant effect.[7]

---

[6] J. Ernesto López Córdova and Christopher M. Meissner, March 2003, "Exchange Rate Regimes and International Trade: Evidence from the Classical Gold Standard Era, 1870–1913," *American Economic Review*, 93(1), 344–353; Antoni Estevadeordal, Brian Frantz, and Alan M. Taylor, May 2003, "The Rise and Fall of World Trade, 1870–1939," *Quarterly Journal of Economics*, 118(2), 359–407; Marc Flandreau and Mathilde Maurel, January 2005, "Monetary Union, Trade Integration, and Business Cycles in 19th Century Europe," *Open Economies Review*, 16(2), 135–152. The quotation is cited in an earlier draft of the paper by López Córdova and Meissner.

[7] Michael W. Klein and Jay C. Shambaugh, 2006, "Fixed Exchange Rates and Trade," *Journal of International Economics*, 70(2), 359–383.

FIGURE 8-5

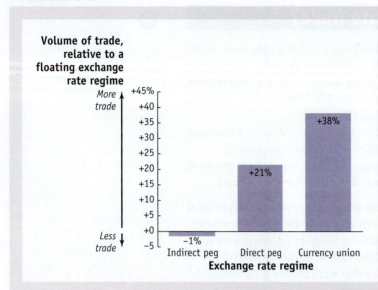

Volume of trade, relative to a floating exchange rate regime

Do Fixed Exchange Rates Promote Trade? The chart shows one study's estimates of the impact on trade volumes of various types of fixed exchange rate regimes, relative to a floating exchange rate regime. Indirect pegs were found to have a small but statistically insignificant impact on trade, but trade increased under a direct peg by 21%, and under a currency union by 38%, as compared with floating.

Note: Based on a gravity model of trade with binary controls for each type of exchange rate regime using country-pair fixed effects.

Data from: Author's calculations based on Michael W. Klein and Jay C. Shambaugh, 2006, "Fixed Exchange Rates and Trade," Journal of International Economics, 70(2), 359–383.

Benefits Measured by Price Convergence

The effect of exchange rate regimes on trade levels is one way to evaluate the impact of currency arrangements on international market integration, and it has been extensively researched. Another body of research examines the relationship between exchange rate regimes and price convergence. These studies use the law of one price (LOOP) and purchasing power parity (PPP) as criteria for measuring market integration. If fixed exchange rates promote trade by lowering transaction costs, then differences between prices (measured in a common currency) should be smaller among countries with pegged rates than among countries with floating rates. In other words, LOOP and PPP should be more likely to hold under a fixed exchange rate than under a floating regime. (Recall that price convergence underlies the gains-from-trade argument.)

Statistical methods can be used to detect how large price differences must be between two locations before arbitrage begins. Research on prices of baskets of goods shows that as exchange rate volatility increases (as it does when currencies float), price differences widen, and the speed at which prices in the two markets converge decreases. These findings offer support for the hypothesis that fixed exchange rates promote arbitrage and price convergence.[8]

Economists have also studied convergence in the prices of individual goods. For example, several studies focused on Europe have looked at the prices of various goods in different countries (e.g., retail prices of cars and TV sets, and the prices of Marlboro cigarettes in duty-free shops). These studies showed that higher exchange rate volatility is associated with larger price differences between locations. In particular, while price gaps still remain for many goods, the "in" countries (members of the ERM and now the Eurozone) saw prices converge much more than the "out" countries.[9]

---

[8] Maurice Obstfeld and Alan M. Taylor, 1997, "Nonlinear Aspects of Goods-Market Arbitrage and Adjustment: Heckscher's Commodity Points Revisited," *Journal of the Japanese and International Economies*, 11(4), 441–479.

[9] Marcus Asplund and Richard Friberg, 2001, "The Law of One Price in Scandinavian Duty-Free Stores," *American Economic Review*, 91(4), 1072–1083; Pinelopi Koujianou Goldberg and Frank Verboven, 2004, "Cross-Country Price Dispersion in the Euro Era: A Case Study of the European Car Market," *Economic Policy*, 19(40), 483–521; Jean Imbs, Haroon Mumtaz, Morten O. Ravn, and Hélène Rey, 2010, "One TV, One Price?" *Scandinavian Journal of Economics*, 112(4), 753–781.

APPLICATION

Do Fixed Exchange Rates Diminish Monetary Autonomy and Stability?

Probably the single most powerful argument *against* a fixed exchange rate is provided by the trilemma. An economy that unilaterally pegs to a foreign currency sacrifices its monetary policy autonomy.

We have seen the result many times now. If capital markets are open, arbitrage in the forex market implies uncovered interest parity. If the exchange rate is fixed, expected depreciation is zero, and the home interest rate must equal the foreign interest rate. The stark implication is that when a country pegs, it relinquishes its independent monetary policy: it has to adjust the money supply M at all times to ensure that the home interest rate i equals the foreign interest rate i^* (plus any risk premium).

The preceding case study of Britain and the ERM is one more example: Britain wanted to delink the British interest rate from the German interest rate. To do so, it had to stop pegging the pound to the German mark. Once it had done that, instead of having to contract the British economy as a result of unrelated events in Germany, it could maintain whatever interest rate it thought was best suited to British economic interests.

The Trilemma, Policy Constraints, and Interest Rate Correlations Is the trilemma truly a binding constraint? Economist Jay Shambaugh tested this proposition, and Figure 8-6 shows some evidence using his data. As we have seen, there are three main solutions to the trilemma. A country can do the following:

1. Opt for open capital markets, with fixed exchange rates (an "open peg").

2. Opt to open its capital market but allow the currency to float (an "open nonpeg").

3. Opt to close its capital markets ("closed").

In case 1, changes in the country's interest rate should match changes in the interest rate of the base country to which it is pegging. In cases 2 and 3, there is no need for the country's interest rate to move in step with the base.

Figure 8-6 displays evidence for the trilemma. On the vertical axis is the annual change in the domestic interest rate; on the horizontal axis is the annual change in the base country interest rate. The trilemma says that in an open peg the two changes should be the same and the points should lie on the 45-degree line. Indeed, for open pegs, shown in panel (a), the correlation of domestic and base interest rates is high and the line of best fit has a slope very close to 1. There are some deviations (possibly due to some pegs being more like bands), but these findings show that open pegs have very little monetary policy autonomy. In contrast, for the open nonpegs, shown in panel (b), and closed economies, shown in panel (c), domestic interest rates do not move as much in line with the base interest rate, the correlation is weak, and the slopes are much smaller than 1. These two regimes allow for some monetary policy autonomy.[10]

---

[10] The correlation isn't perfect for open pegs, nor is it zero for the other cases. This may not be surprising. Pegs are defined as fixed if they vary within a ±2% band. The band allows central banks a little flexibility with their exchange rates and interest rates that would be lacking in a strict peg (a band of zero width). As for nonpegs and closed countries, there may be reasons why their correlation with the base isn't zero. For example, they may have inflation targets or other monetary policy guidelines that cause their interest rates to follow paths similar to those of the base country. In other words, these countries may be able to change their interest rates a great deal, but how much they choose to change them is another matter.

FIGURE 8-6

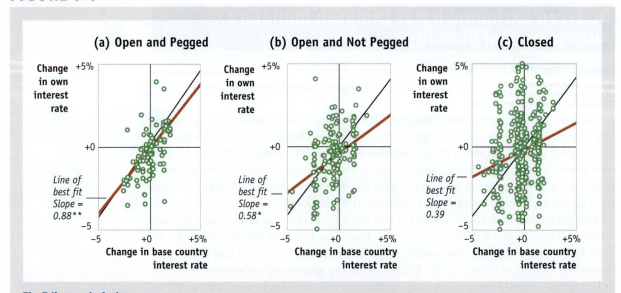

(a) Open and Pegged

Change in own interest rate

+5%

+0

−5

Line of best fit
Slope = 0.88**

−5   +0   +5%

Change in base country interest rate

(b) Open and Not Pegged

Change in own interest rate

+5%

+0

−5

Line of best fit
Slope = 0.58*

−5   +0   +5%

Change in base country interest rate

(c) Closed

Change in own interest rate

5%

+0

−5

Line of best fit
Slope = 0.39

−5   +0   +5%

Change in base country interest rate

The Trilemma in Action The trilemma says that if the home country is an open peg, it sacrifices monetary policy autonomy because changes in its own interest rate must match changes in the interest rate of the base country. Panel (a) shows that this is the case. The trilemma also says that there are two ways to get that autonomy back: switch to a floating exchange rate or impose capital controls. Panels (b) and (c) show that either of these two policies permits home interest rates to move more independently of the base country.

Notes: **Statistically significant at 1% level. *Statistically significant at 5% level. Hyper-inflations excluded.

Data from: Author's calculations based on Jay C. Shambaugh, 2004, "The Effect of Fixed Exchange Rates on Monetary Policy," Quarterly Journal of Economics, 119(1), 300–351.

Costs of Fixing Measured by Output Volatility The preceding evidence suggests that nations with open pegs have less monetary independence. But it does not tell us directly whether they suffer from greater output instability because their monetary authorities cannot use monetary policy to stabilize output when shocks hit. Some studies have found that, on average, the volatility of output growth *is* much higher under fixed regimes.[11] However, a problem in such studies is that countries often differ in all kinds of characteristics that may affect output volatility, not just the exchange rate regime—and the results can be sensitive to how one controls for all these other factors.[12]

In the search for cleaner evidence, some recent research has focused on a key prediction of the IS–LM–FX model: all else equal, an increase in the base-country interest rate should cause output to fall in a country that fixes its exchange rate to the base country. This decline in output occurs because countries that fix have to tighten their monetary policy and raise their interest rate to match that of the base country. In contrast, countries that float do not have to follow the base country's rate increase and can use their monetary policy autonomy to stabilize output, by lowering their interest rate and/or allowing their currency to depreciate. Economists Julian di Giovanni and Jay Shambaugh looked at changes in base-country interest rates (say, the U.S. dollar or euro rates) and examined the correlation of these base interest rate changes with changes in GDP in a large sample of fixed and floating nonbase countries. The results, shown in Figure 8-7, confirm the

[11]Atish R. Ghosh, Anne-Marie Gulde, Jonathan D. Ostry, and Holger C. Wolf, 1997, "Does the Nominal Exchange Rate Regime Matter?" NBER Working Paper 5874.
[12] See, for example, Eduardo Levy-Yeyati and Federico Sturzenegger, September 2003, "To Float or to Fix: Evidence on the Impact of Exchange Rate Regimes on Growth," *American Economic Review*, 93(4), 1173–1193; Kenneth Rogoff, Ashoka Mody, Nienke Oomes, Robin Brooks, and Aasim M. Husain, 2004, "Evolution and Performance of Exchange Rate Regimes," IMF Occasional Paper 229, International Monetary Fund.

FIGURE 8-7

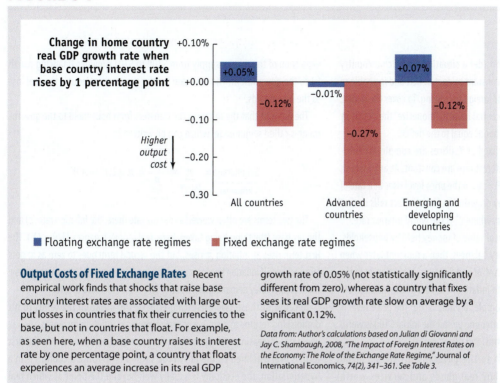

Output Costs of Fixed Exchange Rates Recent empirical work finds that shocks that raise base country interest rates are associated with large output losses in countries that fix their currencies to the base, but not in countries that float. For example, as seen here, when a base country raises its interest rate by one percentage point, a country that floats experiences an average increase in its real GDP growth rate of 0.05% (not statistically significantly different from zero), whereas a country that fixes sees its real GDP growth rate slow on average by a significant 0.12%.

Data from: Author's calculations based on Julian di Giovanni and Jay C. Shambaugh, 2008, "The Impact of Foreign Interest Rates on the Economy: The Role of the Exchange Rate Regime," Journal of International Economics, 74(2), 341–361. See Table 3.

theory's predictions: when a base country increases its interest rate, it spreads economic pain to those countries pegging to it, but not to the countries that float. These findings confirm that one cost of a fixed exchange rate regime is a more volatile level of output.

2 Other Benefits of Fixing

We began the chapter by emphasizing two key factors that influence the choice of fixed versus floating rate regimes: economic integration (market linkages) and economic similarity (symmetry of shocks). Other factors can play a role, however, and in this section, we explore some benefits of a fixed exchange rate regime that can be particularly important in emerging markets and developing countries.

Fiscal Discipline, Seigniorage, and Inflation

One common argument in favor of fixed exchange rate regimes in developing countries is that an exchange rate peg prevents the government from printing money to finance government expenditure. Under such a financing scheme, the central bank is called upon to *monetize* the government's deficit (i.e., give money to the government in exchange for debt). This process increases the money supply and leads to high inflation. The source of the government's revenue is, in effect, an inflation tax (called *seigniorage*) levied on the members of the public who hold money (see **Side Bar: The Inflation Tax**).

High inflation and hyperinflation (inflation in excess of 50% *per month*) are undesirable. If nothing else (such as fiscal discipline) can prevent them, a fixed exchange rate may start to look more attractive. Does a fixed exchange rate rule out inflationary

SIDE BAR

The Inflation Tax

How does the inflation tax work? Consider a situation in which a country with a floating exchange rate faces a constant budget deficit and is unable to finance this deficit through domestic or foreign borrowing. To cover the deficit, the treasury department calls on the central bank to "monetize" the deficit by purchasing an amount of government bonds equal to the deficit.

For simplicity, suppose output is fixed at Y, prices are completely flexible, and inflation and the nominal interest rate are constant. At any instant, money grows at a rate $\Delta M/M = \Delta P/P = \pi$, so the price level rises at a rate of inflation π equal to the rate of money growth. The Fisher effect tells us that the nominal interest rate is $i = r^* + \pi$, where r^* is the world interest rate.

This ongoing inflation erodes the real value of money held by households. If a household holds M/P in real money balances, then a moment later when prices have increased by an amount $\Delta M/M = \Delta P/P = \pi$, a fraction π of the real value of the original M/P is lost to inflation. The cost of the inflation tax to the household is $\pi \times M/P$. For example, if I hold $100, the price level is currently 1, and inflation is 1%, then after one period the initial $100 is worth only $99 in real (inflation-adjusted) terms, and prices are 1.01.

What is the inflation tax worth to the government? It can spend the extra money printed ΔM to buy real goods and services worth $\Delta M/P = (\Delta M/M) \times (M/P) = \pi \times (M/P)$. For the preceding example, the

expansion of the money supply from $100 to $101 provides financing worth $1 to the government. The real gain for the government equals the real loss to the households.

The amount that the inflation tax transfers from household to the government is called seigniorage, which can be written as

$$\underbrace{\text{Seigniorage}}_{\text{Inflation tax}} = \underbrace{\pi}_{\text{Tax rate}} \times \underbrace{\frac{M}{P}}_{\text{Tax base}} = \pi \times L(r^* + \pi)Y$$

The two terms are often viewed as the tax rate (here, the inflation rate π) and the tax base (the thing being taxed; here, real money balances $M/P = LY$). The first term rises as inflation π rises, but the second term goes to zero as π gets large because if inflation becomes very high, people try to hold almost no money; that is, real money demand given by $L(i)Y = L(r^* + \pi)Y$ falls to zero.

Because of these two offsetting effects, the inflation tax tends to hit diminishing returns as a source of real revenue: as inflation increases, the tax generates increasing real revenues at first, but eventually the rise in the first term is overwhelmed by the fall in the second term. Once a country is in a hyperinflation, the economy is usually well beyond the point at which real inflation tax revenues are maximized.

finance and the abuse of seigniorage by the government? In principle, yes, but this anti-inflationary effect is not unique to a fixed exchange rate. As we saw in an earlier chapter on the monetary approach to exchange rates, any nominal anchor (such as money, exchange rate, or inflation targets) will have the same effect.

If a country's currency floats, its central bank can print a lot or a little money, with very different inflation outcomes. If a country's currency is pegged, the central bank might run the peg well, with fairly stable prices, or it might run the peg so badly that a crisis occurs, the exchange rate collapses, and inflation erupts.

Nominal anchors imply a "promise" by the government to ensure certain monetary policy outcomes in the long run. However, these promises do not guarantee that the country will achieve these outcomes. All policy announcements including a fixed exchange rate are to some extent "cheap talk." If pressure from the treasury to monetize deficits gets too strong, the commitment to any kind of anchor could fail.

The debate over whether fixed exchange rates improve inflation performance cannot be settled by theory alone—it is an empirical question. What has happened in reality? Table 8-1 lays out the evidence on the world inflation performance from 1970 to 2019. Average inflation rates are computed for all countries and for subgroups of countries: for advanced economies (rich countries), and for emerging markets (middle-income countries integrated in world capital markets) and developing countries (other countries).

For all countries (column 1), we can see that average inflation performance appears largely unrelated to the exchange rate regime, whether the choice is a peg (11%), limited flexibility (10%), managed floating (13%), or freely floating (7%). Only the "freely falling" category (those economies with high inflation rates or hyperinflation)

TABLE 8-1

Inflation Performance and the Exchange Rate Regime Cross-country annual data from the period 1970 to 2019 can be used to explore the relationship, if any, between the exchange rate regime and the inflation performance of an economy. Floating was associated with slightly lower inflation in the world as a whole (7%) and in the advanced countries (4%) (columns 1 and 2). In emerging markets and developing countries (column 3), a fixed regime delivered lower inflation outcomes (10%).

	Annual Inflation Rate (%)		
Regime Type	World	Advanced Countries	Emerging Markets and Developing Countries
Fixed	11%	16%	10%
Limited flexibility	10	8	11
Managed floating	13	8	15
Freely floating	7	4	20
Freely falling	373	72	381

Data from: Based on Kenneth Rogoff, Ashoka Mody, Nienke Oomes, Robin Brooks, and Aasim M. Husain, 2004, "Evolution and Performance of Exchange Rate Regimes," IMF Occasional Paper 229, International Monetary Fund. Updated and expanded to 2019 using inflation data from International Monetary Fund, International Financial Statistics, and regime data from Ethan Ilzetzki, Carmen M. Reinhart, and Kenneth S. Rogoff, 2019, "Exchange Arrangements Entering the Twenty-First Century: Which Anchor Will Hold?" Quarterly Journal of Economics, 134(2), 599–646.

has astronomical rates of inflation (373%). Greater differences are seen within the subsamples of advanced countries (column 2) and for the emerging markets and developing countries (column 3). In advanced countries, floating is associated with lower inflation, suggesting that credible inflation targets have worked well on average. In emerging markets and developing countries, fixing is associated with lower inflation, suggesting that credibility was harder to attain outside of a peg. We may conclude that as long as monetary policy is guided by *some* kind of credible nominal anchor, the particular choice of fixed and floating may not matter that much.[13] But for different countries, the path to credibility may vary. In emerging markets and developing countries with histories of high inflation or even hyperinflation, people may need to see the government tie its own hands in a very open and verifiable way for expectations of perpetually high inflation to be lowered, and a peg is maybe the only way to do that.

■ The lesson: *Fixed exchange rates are neither necessary nor sufficient to ensure good inflation performance. Floating regimes can deliver low inflation in advanced economies. But in emerging and developing countries beset by a reputation for high inflation, an exchange rate peg may be the only way to a credible anchor.*

Liability Dollarization, National Wealth, and Contractionary Depreciations

As we learned in the balance of payments chapter, exchange rate changes can have a big effect on a nation's wealth. External assets and liabilities are never entirely denominated in local currency, so movements in the exchange rate can affect their value. For developing countries and emerging markets afflicted by the problem of *liability dollarization*, the wealth effects can be large and destabilizing, providing another argument for fixing the exchange rate.

Suppose there are just two countries and two currencies, Home and Foreign. Home has external assets A_H denominated in home currency (say, pesos) and A_F

---

[13] Kenneth Rogoff, Ashoka Mody, Nienke Oomes, Robin Brooks, and Aasim M. Husain, 2004, "Evolution and Performance of Exchange Rate Regimes," IMF Occasional Paper 229, International Monetary Fund, and author's updated calculations.

denominated in foreign currency (say, U.S. dollars). Similarly, it has external liabilities L_H denominated in home currency and L_F denominated in foreign currency. The nominal exchange rate is E (with the units being home currency per unit of foreign currency—here, pesos per dollar).

The value of Home's dollar external assets and liabilities can be expressed in pesos as EA_F and EL_F, respectively, using an exchange rate conversion. Hence, the home country's total external wealth is the sum total of assets minus liabilities expressed in local currency:

$$W = \underbrace{(A_H + EA_F)}_{\text{Assets}} - \underbrace{(L_H + EL_F)}_{\text{Liabilities}}$$

Now suppose there is a small change ΔE in the exchange rate, all else equal. This does not affect the values of A_H and L_H expressed in pesos, but it *does* change the values of EA_F and EL_F expressed in pesos. We can express the resulting change in national wealth expressed in pesos as

$$\Delta W = \underbrace{\Delta E}_{\substack{\text{Change in} \\ \text{exchange rate}}} \times \underbrace{\left[A_F - L_F \right]}_{\substack{\text{Net international credit (+) or debit (−)} \\ \text{position in dollar assets}}} \tag{8-1}$$

The expression is intuitive and revealing. After a depreciation ($\Delta E > 0$), the wealth effect is positive if foreign currency assets exceed foreign currency liabilities (the net dollar position in brackets is positive) and negative if foreign currency liabilities exceed foreign currency assets (the net dollar position in brackets is negative).

For example, consider first the case in which Home experiences a 10% depreciation, with assets of $100 billion and liabilities of $100 billion. What happens to Home wealth expressed in pesos if it has $50 billion of assets in dollars and no liabilities in dollars? It has a net credit position in dollars, so it ought to gain. Half of assets and all liabilities are expressed in pesos, so their value does not change. But the value of the half of assets denominated in dollars will rise in peso terms by 10% times $50 billion. In this case, a 10% depreciation increases national wealth expressed in pesos by 5% or $5 billion because it increases the peso value of a net foreign currency credit position.

Now look at the case in which Home experiences a 10% depreciation, as in the preceding example, with zero assets in dollars and $50 billion of liabilities in dollars. All assets and half of liabilities are expressed in pesos, so their value expressed in pesos does not change. But the value of the half of liabilities denominated in dollars will rise in peso terms by 10% times $50 billion. In this case, a depreciation decreases national wealth expressed in pesos by 5% or $5 billion because it increases the value of a net foreign currency debit position.

Destabilizing Wealth Shocks Why do these wealth effects have implications for stabilization policy? In the previous chapter, we saw that nominal exchange rate depreciation can be used as a short-run stabilization tool in the IS–LM–FX model. In the face of an adverse demand shock in the home country, for example, a depreciation will increase home aggregate demand by switching expenditure toward home goods. Now we can see that exchange rate movements can influence aggregate demand by affecting wealth expressed in local currency terms.

These effects matter because, in more complex short-run models of the economy, wealth affects the demand for goods. For example,

- Consumers might spend more when they have more wealth. In this case, the consumption function would become $C(Y - T, \text{Total wealth})$, and consumption would depend not just on after-tax income but also on wealth.

- Firms might find it easier to borrow if their wealth increases (e.g., wealth increases the net worth of firms, increasing the collateral available for loans). The investment function would then become $I(i, \text{Total wealth})$, and investment would depend on both the interest rate and wealth.

We can now begin to understand the importance of the exchange rate valuation effects summarized in Equation (8-1). This equation says that countries have to satisfy a special condition to avoid changes in external wealth whenever the exchange rate moves: the value of their foreign currency external assets must exactly equal foreign currency liabilities. If foreign currency external assets do not equal foreign currency external liabilities, the country is said to have a *currency mismatch* on its external balance sheet, and exchange rate changes will affect national wealth.

If foreign currency assets exceed foreign currency liabilities, then the country experiences an increase in wealth when the exchange rate depreciates. From the point of view of stabilization, this is likely to be beneficial: additional wealth will complement the direct stimulus to aggregate demand caused by a depreciation, making the effect of the depreciation *even more* expansionary. This scenario applies to only a few countries, most notably the United States.

However, if foreign currency liabilities exceed foreign currency assets, a country will experience a *decrease* in wealth when the exchange rate depreciates. From the point of view of stabilization policy, this wealth effect is unhelpful because the fall in wealth will tend to offset the conventional stimulus to aggregate demand caused by a depreciation. In principle, if the valuation effects are large enough, the overall effect of a depreciation can be contractionary! For example, while an interest rate cut might boost investment, and the ensuing depreciation might also boost the trade balance, such upward pressure on aggregate demand may well be offset partially or fully (or even outweighed) by decreases in wealth that put downward pressure on demand.

We now see that if a country has an adverse (i.e., negative) net position in foreign currency assets, then the conventional arguments for stabilization policy (and the need for floating) are weak. For many emerging market and developing economies, this is a serious problem. Most of these poorer countries are net debtors, so their external wealth shows a net debit position overall. But their net position in foreign currency is often just as much in debit, or even more so, because their liabilities are often close to 100% dollarized.

Evidence Based on Changes in Wealth When emerging markets experience large depreciations, they often suffer serious collapses in external wealth. To illustrate the severity of this problem, Figure 8-8 shows the impact of exchange rate valuation effects on wealth in eight countries. All the countries experienced exchange rate crises during the period in which the domestic currency lost much of its value relative to

FIGURE 8-8

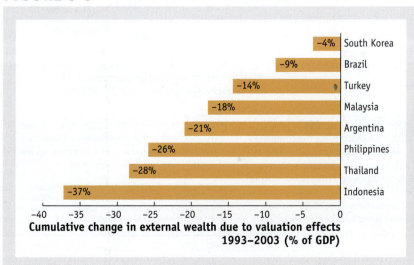

Exchange Rate Depreciations and Changes in Wealth The countries shown in the chart experienced crises and large depreciations of between 50% and 75% against the U.S. dollar and other major currencies from 1993 to 2003. Because large fractions of their external debt were denominated in foreign currencies, all suffered negative valuation effects causing their external wealth to fall, in some cases (such as Indonesia) quite dramatically.

Data from: IMF, World Economic Outlook, April 2005, Figure 3.6.

the U.S. dollar. Following the 1997 Asian crisis, South Korea, the Philippines, and Thailand saw their currencies depreciate by about 50%; Indonesia's currency depreciated by 75%. In 1998–99 the Brazilian real depreciated by almost 50%. In 2001 Turkey's lira depreciated suddenly by about 50%, after a long slide. And in Argentina, the peso depreciated by about 75% in 2002.

All of these countries also had large exposure to foreign currency debt with large levels of currency mismatch. The Asian countries had borrowed extensively in yen and U.S. dollars; Turkey, Brazil, and Argentina had borrowed extensively in U.S. dollars. As a result of the valuation effects of the depreciations and the liability dollarization, all of these countries saw large declines in external wealth, as Figure 8-8 shows. Countries such as Brazil and South Korea escaped lightly, with wealth falling cumulatively by only 5% to 10% of annual GDP. Countries with larger exposure to foreign currency debt, or with larger depreciations, suffered much more: in Argentina, the Philippines, and Thailand, the losses were 20% to 30% of GDP and in Indonesia almost 40% of GDP.

Evidence Based on Output Contractions Figure 8-8 tells us that countries with large liability dollarization suffered large wealth effects. But do these wealth effects cause so much economic damage that a country might reconsider its exchange rate regime?

Figure 8-9 suggests that wealth effects are associated with contractions and that the damage is fairly serious. Economists Michele Cavallo, Kate Kisselev, Fabrizio Perri, and Nouriel Roubini found a strong correlation between wealth losses on net foreign currency liabilities suffered during the large depreciations seen after an exchange rate

FIGURE 8-9

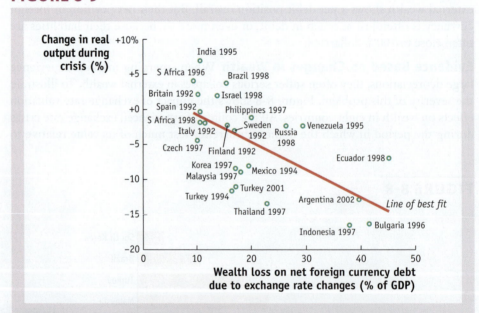

Foreign Currency Denominated Debt and the Costs of Crises This chart shows the correlation between a measure of the negative wealth impact of a real depreciation and the real output costs after an exchange rate crisis (a large depreciation). On the horizontal axis, the wealth impact is estimated by multiplying net debt denominated in foreign currency (as a fraction of GDP) by the size of the real depreciation. The negative correlation shows that larger losses on foreign currency debt due to exchange rate changes are associated with larger real output losses.

Data from: Michele Cavallo, Kate Kisselev, Fabrizio Perri, and Nouriel Roubini, "Exchange Rate Overshooting and the Costs of Floating," Federal Reserve Bank of San Francisco Working Paper Series, Working Paper 2005–07, May 2005.

crisis, and a measure of the subsequent fall in real output.[14] For example, after 1992 Britain barely suffered any negative wealth effect and, as we noted earlier, did well in its subsequent economic performance: Britain in 1992 sits in the upper left part of this scatterplot (very small wealth loss, no negative impact on GDP). At the other extreme (in the lower right part of this scatterplot) are countries like Argentina and Indonesia, where liability dollarization led to massive wealth losses after their crises in 2002 and 1997 (large wealth loss, large negative impact on GDP).

Original Sin Such findings have had a powerful influence among international macroeconomists and policymakers in recent years. Previously, external wealth effects were largely ignored and poorly understood. But now, after the adverse consequences of recent large depreciations, macroeconomists recognize that the problem of currency mismatch, driven by liability dollarization, is a key factor in the economic health of many developing countries and should be considered when choosing an exchange rate regime.

Yet these kinds of losses due to currency mismatch are an old problem. In the long history of international investment, one remarkably constant feature has been the inability of most countries—especially poor countries on the periphery of global capital markets—to borrow from abroad in their own currencies. In the late nineteenth century, such countries had to borrow in gold, or in a "hard currency" such as British pounds or U.S. dollars. The same is true today, as we can see in Table 8-2. In the world's financial centers and the Eurozone, only a small fraction of external liabilities is denominated in foreign currency. In other countries, the fraction is much higher; in developing countries, it is close to 100%.

Economists Barry Eichengreen, Ricardo Hausmann, and Ugo Panizza used the term "original sin" to refer to a country's inability to borrow in its own currency.[15] As

TABLE 8-2

Measures of "Original Sin" Only a few developed countries can issue external liabilities denominated in their own currency. In the financial centers and the Eurozone, the fraction of external liabilities denominated in foreign currency is less than 10%. In the remaining developed countries, it averages about 70%. In developing countries, external liabilities denominated in foreign currency are close to 100% on average.

	External Liabilities Denominated in Foreign Currency (average, %)
Financial centers (United States, United Kingdom, Switzerland, Japan)	8%
Eurozone countries	9
Other developed countries	72
Eastern European countries	84
Middle Eastern and African countries	90
Developing countries	93
Asia/Pacific countries	94
Latin American and Caribbean countries	100

Data from: Barry Eichengreen, Ricardo Hausmann, and Ugo Panizza, "The Pain of Original Sin," in Barry Eichengreen and Ricardo Hausmann, eds., 2005, Other People's Money: Debt Denomination and Financial Instability in Emerging-Market Economies (Chicago: University of Chicago Press).

---

[14] Michele Cavallo, Kate Kisselev, Fabrizio Perri, and Nouriel Roubini, May 2005, "Exchange Rate Overshooting and the Costs of Floating," Federal Reserve Bank of San Francisco Working Paper Series, Working Paper 2005–07.

[15] Barry Eichengreen, Ricardo Hausmann, and Ugo Panizza, 2005, "The Pain of Original Sin," in Barry Eichengreen and Ricardo Hausmann, eds., *Other People's Money: Debt Denomination and Financial Instability in Emerging-Market Economies* (Chicago: University of Chicago Press).

the term suggests, an historical perspective reveals that the "sin" is highly persistent and originates deep in a country's historical past. Countries with a weak record of macroeconomic management—often due to institutional or political weakness—have in the past been unable to follow prudent monetary and fiscal policies, so the real value of domestic currency debts was frequently eroded by periods of high inflation. Because creditors were mostly unwilling to hold such debt, domestic currency bond markets did not develop, and creditors would lend only in foreign currency, which promised a more stable long-term value.

Still, sinners can find redemption. One view argues that the problem is a global capital market failure: for many small countries, the pool of their domestic currency liabilities may be too small to offer any significant risk diversification benefits to foreign investors. In this case, multinational institutions could step in to create markets for securities in the currencies of small countries, or in baskets of such currencies. Another view argues that as such countries improve their institutional quality, design better policies, secure a low-inflation environment, and develop a better reputation, they will eventually free themselves from original sin and be able to issue domestic and even external debt in their own currencies. Many observers think this is already happening. Habitual "sinners" such as Mexico, Brazil, Colombia, and Uruguay have recently been able to issue some debt in their own currency. In addition, many emerging countries have been reducing currency mismatch: many governments have been piling up large stocks of foreign currency assets in central bank reserves and sovereign wealth funds, and both governments and in some cases the private sectors have been reducing their reliance on foreign currency loans. The recent trends indicate substantial progress in reducing original sin as compared with the 1990s.[16]

Yet any optimism must be tempered with caution. Only time will tell whether countries have really turned the corner and put their "sinful" ways behind them. Progress on domestic-currency borrowing is still very slow in many countries, and this still leaves the problem of currency mismatches in the private sector. While private sector exposure could be insured by the government, that insurance could, in turn, introduce the risk of abuse in the form of *moral hazard*, the risk that insured entities (here, private borrowers) will engage in excessive risk taking, knowing that they will be bailed out if they incur losses. This moral hazard could then create massive political problems, because it may not be clear who, in a crisis, would receive a public sector rescue, and who would not. Why can't the private sector simply hedge all its exchange rate risk? This solution would be ideal, but in many emerging markets and developing countries, currency derivative markets are poorly developed, many currencies cannot be hedged at all, and the costs are high.

If developing countries cannot avoid currency mismatches, they must try to cope with them. One way to cope is to reduce or stop external borrowing, but countries are not eager to give up all borrowing in world capital markets. A more feasible alternative is for developing countries to minimize or eliminate valuation effects by limiting the movement of the exchange rate. This is indeed what many countries are doing, and evidence shows that the larger a country's stock of foreign currency liabilities

Two Russian bonds: a 100 ruble bond of 1915 and a 1,000 U.S. dollar bond of 1916. Creditors knew the dollar value of the ruble bond could be eroded by ruble depreciation. Only default could erode the value of the dollar bond.

Stock Search International

---

[16] Barry Eichengreen and Ricardo Hausmann, 2005, "Original Sin: The Road to Redemption," in Barry Eichengreen and Ricardo Hausmann, eds., *Other People's Money: Debt Denomination and Financial Instability in Emerging-Market Economies* (Chicago: University of Chicago Press); John D. Burger and Francis E. Warnock, 2003, "Diversification, Original Sin, and International Bond Portfolios," International Finance Discussion Papers 755, Board of Governors of the Federal Reserve System; Camilo E. Tovar, 2005, "International Government Debt Denominated in Local Currency: Recent Developments in Latin America," *BIS Quarterly Review*, 109–118; Philip E. Lane and Jay C. Shambaugh, 2010, "Financial Exchange Rates and International Currency Exposures," *American Economic Review*, 100(1), 518–540.

relative to GDP, the more likely that country is to peg its currency to the currency in which the external debt is issued.[17]

■ The lesson: *In countries that cannot borrow in their own currency, floating exchange rates are less useful as a stabilization tool and may be destabilizing. Because this outcome applies particularly to developing countries, they will prefer fixed exchange rates to floating exchange rates, all else equal.*

Summary

We began the chapter by emphasizing the two key factors that influence the choice of fixed versus floating rate regimes: economic integration (market linkages) and economic similarity (symmetry of shocks). But we now see that many other factors can affect the benefits of fixing relative to floating.

A fixed exchange rate may have some additional benefits in some situations. It may be the only transparent and credible way to attain and maintain a nominal anchor, a goal that may be particularly important in emerging markets and developing countries with weak institutions, a lack of central bank independence, strong temptations to use the inflation tax, and poor reputations for monetary stability. A fixed exchange rate may also be the only way to avoid large fluctuations in external wealth, which can be a problem in emerging markets and developing countries with high levels of liability dollarization. These may be powerful additional reasons to fix, and they seem to apply with extra force in developing countries. Therefore, such countries may be less willing to allow their exchange rates to float—a situation that some economists describe as a **fear of floating**.

To illustrate the influence of additional costs and benefits, consider a home country thinking of pegging to the U.S. dollar as a base currency. Figure 8-10 shows that

FIGURE 8-10

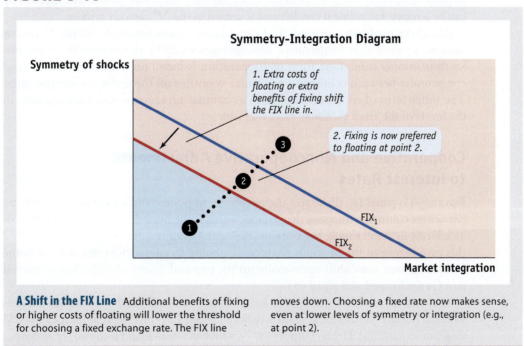

Symmetry-Integration Diagram

Symmetry of shocks

1. Extra costs of floating or extra benefits of fixing shift the FIX line in.

2. Fixing is now preferred to floating at point 2.

FIX₁

FIX₂

Market integration

A Shift in the FIX Line Additional benefits of fixing or higher costs of floating will lower the threshold for choosing a fixed exchange rate. The FIX line moves down. Choosing a fixed rate now makes sense, even at lower levels of symmetry or integration (e.g., at point 2).

[17] Ricardo Hausmann, Ugo Panizza, and Ernesto Stein, 2001, "Why Do Countries Float the Way They Float?" *Journal of Development Economics*, 66(2), 387–414; Christopher M. Meissner and Nienke Oomes, 2009, "Why Do Countries Peg the Way They Peg? The Determinants of Anchor Currency Choice," *Journal of International Money and Finance*, 28(3), 522–547.

a home country with a fear of floating would perceive additional benefits to a fixed exchange rate, and would be willing to peg its exchange at lower levels of integration and similarity. We would represent this choice as an inward shift of the FIX line from FIX_1 to FIX_2. Without fear of floating, based on FIX_1, the home country would float with symmetry-integration measures given by points 1 and 2, and fix at point 3. But if it had fear of floating, based on FIX_2, it would elect to fix at point 2 because the extra benefits of a fixed rate lower the threshold.

3 Fixed Exchange Rate Systems

So far, our discussion has considered only the simplest type of fixed exchange rate: a single home country that unilaterally pegs to a foreign base country. In reality there are more complex arrangements, called **fixed exchange rate systems**, which involve multiple countries. Examples include the global Bretton Woods system, in the 1950s and 1960s, and the European Exchange Rate Mechanism (ERM), to which all members have to adhere for at least two years as a precondition to euro entry.

Fixed exchange rate systems like these are based on a **reserve currency system** in which N countries $(1, 2, \ldots, N)$ participate. The Nth country, called the center country, provides the reserve currency, which is the base or center currency to which all the other countries peg. In the Bretton Woods system, for example, N was the U.S. dollar; in the ERM, N was the German mark until 1999, and is now the euro.

Throughout this chapter, we have assumed that a country pegs unilaterally to a center country, and we know that this leads to a fundamental asymmetry. The center country has monetary policy autonomy and can set its own interest rate i^* as it pleases. The other noncenter country, which is pegging, then has to adjust its own interest rate so that i equals i^* in order to maintain the peg. The noncenter country loses its ability to conduct stabilization policy, but the center country keeps that power. The asymmetry can be a recipe for political conflict and is known as the Nth *currency problem*.

Are these problems serious? And can a better arrangement be devised? In this section, we show that **cooperative arrangements** may be the answer. We study two kinds of cooperation. One form of cooperation is based on mutual agreement and compromise between center and noncenter countries on the setting of interest rates. The other form of cooperation is based on mutual agreements about adjustments to the levels of the fixed exchange rates themselves.

Cooperative and Noncooperative Adjustments to Interest Rates

Figure 8-11, panel (a), illustrates the possibility of policy conflict between center and noncenter countries. Suppose that Home, which is the noncenter country, experiences an adverse demand shock, but Foreign, the center country, does not. We have studied this case before in the previous chapter: the home IS curve shifts left and the home LM curve then must shift up to maintain the peg and ensure that the home interest rate i is unchanged and equal to i^*.

We now assume that these shifts have already occurred, and we start the analysis with the home equilibrium at point 1 (where IS_1 and LM_1 intersect) in Home's IS–LM diagram in panel (a). Home output is at Y_1, which is lower than Home's desired output Y_0. Foreign is in equilibrium at point 1′ (where IS_1^* and LM_1^* intersect) in Foreign's IS–LM diagram in panel (b). Because it is the center country, Foreign is assumed to have used stabilization policy and is therefore at its preferred output level Y_0^*. The home interest rate equals the foreign interest rate, $i_1 = i_1^*$, because Home is pegged to Foreign; this is the interest rate shown on both vertical axes.

FIGURE 8-11

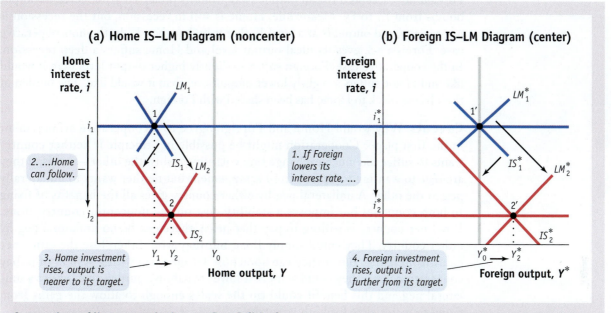

(a) Home IS–LM Diagram (noncenter)

(b) Foreign IS–LM Diagram (center)

Cooperative and Noncooperative Interest Rate Policies by the Center Country In panel (a), the noncenter home country is initially in equilibrium at point 1 with output at Y_1, which is lower than desired output Y_0. In panel (b), the center foreign country is in equilibrium at its desired output level Y_0^* at point 1′. Home and foreign interest rates are equal, $i_1 = i_1^*$, and the home country is unilaterally pegged to the foreign country. Foreign has monetary policy autonomy. If the center country makes no policy concession, this is the noncooperative outcome.

With cooperation, the foreign country can make a policy concession and lower its interest rate, and Home can do the same and maintain the peg. Lower interest rates in the other country shift each country's IS curve in, but the easing of monetary policy in both countries shifts each country's LM curve down. The net effect is to boost output in both countries. The new equilibria at points 2 and 2′ lie to the right of points 1 and 1′. Under this cooperative outcome, the foreign center country accepts a rise in output away from its desired level, from Y_0^* to Y_2^*. Meanwhile, home output gets closer to its desired level, rising from Y_1 to Y_2.

Because this is a unilateral peg, only Foreign, the center country, has monetary policy autonomy and the freedom to set nominal interest rates. Home is in recession (its output Y_1 is below its desired output Y_0), but Foreign has its desired output. If Foreign makes no policy concession to help Home out of its recession, this would be the noncooperative outcome. There would be no burden sharing between the two countries: Home is the only country to suffer.

Now suppose we shift to a cooperative outcome in which the center country makes a policy concession. How? Suppose Foreign lowers its interest rate from i_1^* to i_2^*. Home can now do the same, and indeed must do so to maintain the peg. How do the IS curves shift? A lower foreign interest rate implies that, *all else equal*, home demand is lower, so the home IS curve shifts in to IS_2; similarly, in panel (b), a lower home interest rate implies that, *all else equal*, foreign demand is lower, so the foreign IS* curve shifts in to IS_2^* in panel (b). However, the easing of monetary policy in both countries means that the LM curves shift down in both countries to LM_2 and LM_2^*.

What is the net result of all these shifts? To figure out the extent of the shift in the IS curve, we can think back to the Keynesian cross and the elements of demand that underlie points on the IS curve. The peg is being maintained. Because the nominal exchange rate is unchanged, the real exchange rate is unchanged, so neither country sees a shift in its Keynesian cross demand curve due to a change in the trade balance. But both countries do see a rise in the Keynesian cross demand curve, as investment demand rises thanks to lower interest rates. The rise in demand tells us that new equilibrium points 2 and 2′ lie to the right of points 1 and 1′: even though the IS curves have shifted in, the downward shifts in the LM curves dominate, and so output in each country will rise in equilibrium.

Compared with the noncooperative equilibrium outcome at points 1 and 1′, Foreign now accepts a rise in output away from its preferred stable level, as output booms from Y_0^* to Y_2^*. Meanwhile, Home is still in recession, but the recession is not as deep, and output is at a level Y_2 that is higher than Y_1. In the noncooperative case, Foreign achieves its ideal output level and Home suffers a deep recession. In the cooperative case, Foreign suffers a slightly higher output level than it would like and Home suffers a slightly lower output level than it would like. The burden of the adverse shock to Home has been shared with Foreign.

Caveats Why would Home and Foreign agree to a cooperative arrangement in the first place? Cooperation might be possible in principle if neither country wants to suffer too much exchange rate volatility against the other—that is, if they are *close* to wanting to be in a fixed arrangement but neither wants to unilaterally peg to the other. A unilateral peg by either country gives all the benefits of fixing to both countries but imposes a stability cost on the noncenter country alone. If neither country is willing to pay that price, there can be no unilateral peg by either country. They could simply float, but they would then lose the efficiency gains from fixing. But if they can somehow set up a peg with a system of policy cooperation, then they could achieve a lower instability burden than under a unilateral peg and this benefit could tip the scales enough to allow the gains from fixing to materialize for both countries.

Cooperation sounds great on paper. But the historical record casts doubt on the ability of countries to even get as far as announcing cooperation on fixed rates, let alone actually backing that up with true cooperative behavior. Indeed, it is rare to see credible cooperative announcements under *floating* rates, where much less is at stake. Why?

A major problem is that, at any given time, the shocks that hit a group of economies are typically asymmetric. A country at its ideal output level not suffering a shock may be unwilling to change its monetary policies just to help out a neighbor suffering a shock and keep a peg going. In theory, cooperation rests on the idea that my shock today could be your shock tomorrow, and we can all do better if we even out the burdens with the understanding that they will "average out" in the long run. But policymakers have to be able to make credible long-run commitments to make this work and suffer short-run pain for long-run gain. History shows that these abilities are often sadly lacking: shortsighted political goals commonly win out over longer-term economic considerations.

For example, consider the European ERM, which was effectively a set of unilateral pegs to the German mark, and now to the euro. The ERM was built around the idea of safeguarding gains from trade in Europe by fixing exchange rates, but the designers knew that it had to incorporate some burden-sharing measures to ensure that the burden of absorbing shocks didn't fall on every country but Germany. The measures proved inadequate, however, and in the crisis of 1992 the German Bundesbank ignored pleas from Italy, Britain, and other countries for an easing of German monetary policy as recessions took hold in the bloc of countries pegging to the German mark. When the test of cooperation came along, Germany wanted to stabilize Germany's output, and no one else's. Thus, even in a group of countries as geographically and politically united as the EU, it was tremendously difficult to make this kind of cooperation work. (This problem was supposed to be alleviated by true monetary union, with the arrival of the euro and the creation of the European Central Bank in 1999, but tensions still remain.)

The main lesson from history is that, in practice, the center country in a reserve currency system has tremendous autonomy, which it may be unwilling to give up, thus making cooperative outcomes hard to achieve consistently.

Cooperative and Noncooperative Adjustments to Exchange Rates

We have studied interest rate cooperation. Is there scope for cooperation in other ways? Yes. Countries may decide to adjust the level of the fixed exchange rate. Such an adjustment is (supposedly) a "one-shot" jump or change in the exchange rate at a particular time, which for now we assume to be unanticipated by investors. Apart from that single jump, at all times before and after the change, the exchange rate is left fixed and home and foreign interest rates remain equal.

Suppose a country that was previously pegging at a rate $\bar{E}_1$ announces that it will henceforth peg at a different rate, $\bar{E}_2 \neq \bar{E}_1$. By definition, if $\bar{E}_2 > \bar{E}_1$, there is a **devaluation** of the home currency; if $\bar{E}_2 < \bar{E}_1$, there is a **revaluation** of the home currency.

These terms are similar to the terms "depreciation" and "appreciation," which also describe exchange rate changes. Strictly speaking, the terms "devaluation" and "revaluation" should be used only when pegs are being adjusted; "depreciation" and "appreciation" should be used to describe exchange rates that float up or down. Note, however, that these terms are often used loosely and interchangeably.

A framework for understanding peg adjustment is shown in Figure 8-12. We assume now that both Home and Foreign are noncenter countries in a pegged exchange rate system and that each is pegged to a third center currency, say, the U.S. dollar.

(Why this change in the setup compared with the last section? Interest rate adjustment required us to study moves by the center country to help noncenter countries; with exchange rate adjustment, noncenter countries change their exchange rates relative to the center, so in this problem our focus shifts away from the center country.)

We assume that the center (the United States) is a large country with monetary policy autonomy that has set its interest rate at $i_\$$. Home is pegged to the U.S. dollar at $\bar{E}_{\text{home}/\$}$ and Foreign is pegged at $\bar{E}^*_{\text{foreign}/\$}$. In Home's IS–LM diagram in panel (a), equilibrium is initially at point 1 (where IS_1 and LM_1 intersect). Again, because of a prior adverse demand shock, home output is at Y_1 and is lower than Home's desired output Y_0. In Foreign's IS–LM diagram in panel (b), equilibrium is at Foreign's desired output level Y_0^* at point 1' (where IS_1^* and LM_1^* intersect). Because Home and Foreign peg to the center currency (here, the U.S. dollar), home and foreign interest rates equal the dollar interest rate, $i_1 = i_1^* = i_\$$.

Now suppose that in a cooperative arrangement, Home devalues against the dollar (and against Foreign) and maintains a peg at a new, higher exchange rate. That is, there is an unanticipated rise in $\bar{E}_{\text{home}/\$}$. The home and foreign interest rates remain equal to the dollar interest rate, $i_1 = i_1^* = i_\$$, because both countries still peg. We can think back to the IS–LM model, or back to the Keynesian cross that we used to construct the IS curve, if necessary, to figure out the effect of the change. Because the nominal depreciation by Home is also a real depreciation, Home sees demand increase: the home IS curve shifts out to IS_2. Furthermore, the real depreciation for Home is also a real appreciation for Foreign, so foreign demand *decreases*: the IS^* curve shifts in to IS_2^*. The outcome is cooperative because the burden of the adverse demand shock is being shared: home output at Y_2 is lower than the ideal Y_0 but not as low as at Y_1; and Foreign has accepted output lower at Y_2^* than its ideal Y_0^*.

Why might this kind of cooperation work? Home and Foreign could agree that Home would devalue a little (but not too much) so that both countries would jointly feel the pain. Some other time, when Foreign has a nasty shock, Home would "repay" by feeling some of Foreign's pain.

Now suppose we shift to a noncooperative outcome in which Home devalues more aggressively against the dollar. After a large real depreciation by Home, home demand is greatly boosted, and the home IS curve shifts out all the way to IS_3. Home's real

FIGURE 8-12

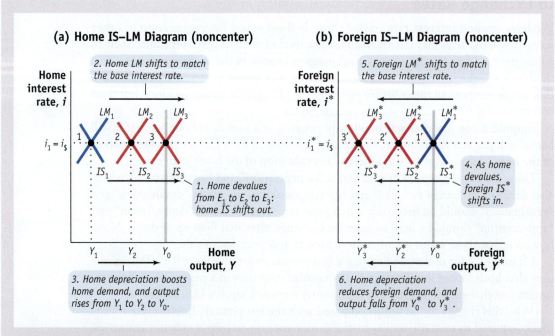

(a) Home IS–LM Diagram (noncenter)

2. Home LM shifts to match the base interest rate.

(b) Foreign IS–LM Diagram (noncenter)

5. Foreign LM* shifts to match the base interest rate.

1. Home devalues from E_1 to E_2 to E_3: home IS shifts out.

4. As home devalues, foreign IS* shifts in.

3. Home depreciation boosts home demand, and output rises from Y_1 to Y_2 to Y_0.

6. Home depreciation reduces foreign demand, and output falls from Y_0^* to Y_3^*.

Cooperative and Noncooperative Exchange Rate Adjustments by Noncenter Countries In panel (a), the noncenter home country is initially in equilibrium at point 1 with output at Y_1, which is lower than desired output Y_0. In panel (b), the noncenter foreign country is in equilibrium at its desired output level Y_0^* at point 1′. Home and foreign interest rates are equal to the base (dollar) interest rate and to each other, $i_1 = i_1^* = i_\$^*$, and the home country and the foreign country are unilaterally pegged to the base.

With cooperation, the home country devalues slightly against the dollar (and against the foreign country) and maintains a peg at a higher exchange rate. The home interest and foreign interest rates remain the same. But the home real depreciation causes home demand to increase: IS shifts out to IS_2. This is also a foreign real appreciation, so foreign demand decreases: IS^* shifts in to IS_2^*. Under this cooperative outcome at points 2 and 2′, the foreign country accepts a fall in output away from its desired level, from Y_0^* to Y_2^*. Meanwhile, home output gets closer to its desired level, rising from Y_1 to Y_2.

With noncooperation, the home country devalues more aggressively against the dollar. After a large home real depreciation, IS shifts out to IS_3 and IS^* shifts in to IS_3^*. Under this noncooperative outcome at points 3 and 3′, the home country gets its desired output Y_0 by "exporting" the recession to the foreign country, where output falls all the way to Y_3^*.

depreciation is also a large real appreciation for Foreign, where demand is greatly reduced, so the foreign IS* curve shifts in all the way to IS_3^*. The outcome is noncooperative: Home now gets its preferred outcome with output at its ideal level Y_0; it achieves this by "exporting" the recession to Foreign, where output falls all the way to Y_3^*.

There are two qualifications to this analysis. First, we have only considered a situation in which Home wishes to devalue to offset a negative demand shock. But the same logic applies when Home's economy is "overheating" and policymakers fear that output is above the ideal level, perhaps creating a risk of inflationary pressures. In that case, Home may wish to revalue its currency and export the overheating to Foreign.

Second, we have not considered the center country, here the United States. In reality, the center country also suffers some decrease in demand if Home devalues because the center will experience a real appreciation against Home. However, there is less to worry about in this instance: because the United States is the center country, it has policy autonomy, and can always use stabilization policy to boost demand. Thus, there may be a monetary easing in the center country, a secondary effect that we do not consider here.

Caveats We can now see that adjusting the peg is a policy that may be cooperative or noncooperative in nature. If noncooperative, it is usually called a **beggar-thy-neighbor**

policy: Home can improve its position at the expense of Foreign and without Foreign's agreement. When Home is in recession, and its policymakers choose a devaluation and real depreciation, they are engineering a diversion of some of world demand toward home goods and away from the rest of the world's goods.

This finding brings us to the main drawback of admitting noncooperative adjustments into a fixed exchange rate system. Two can play this game! If Home engages in such a policy, it is possible for Foreign to respond with a devaluation of its own in a tit-for-tat way. If this happens, the pretense of a fixed exchange rate system is over. The countries no longer peg and instead play a new noncooperative game against each other with floating exchange rates.

Cooperation may be most needed to sustain a fixed exchange rate system with adjustable pegs, so as to restrain beggar-thy-neighbor devaluations. But can it work? Consider continental Europe since World War II, under both the Bretton Woods system and the later European systems such as ERM (which predated the euro). A persistent concern of European policymakers in this period was the threat of beggar-thy-neighbor devaluations. For example, the British pound and the Italian lira devalued against the dollar and later the German mark on numerous occasions from the 1960s to the 1990s. Although some of these peg adjustments had the veneer of official multilateral decisions, some (like the 1992 ERM crisis) occurred when cooperation broke down.

APPLICATION

The Gold Standard

Our analysis in this section has focused on the problems of policy conflict in a reserve currency system in which there is one center country issuing a currency (e.g., the dollar or euro) to which all other noncenter countries peg. As we know from Figure 8-1, this is an apt description of most fixed exchange rate arrangements at the present time and going back as far as World War II. A key issue in such systems is the asymmetry between the center country, which retains monetary autonomy, and the noncenter countries, which forsake it.

Are there symmetric fixed exchange rate systems, in which there is no center country and the asymmetry created by the Nth currency problem can be avoided? In theory the ERM system worked this way before the advent of the euro in 1999, but, as the 1992 crisis showed, there was, in practice, a marked asymmetry between Germany and the other ERM countries. Historically, the only true symmetric systems have been those in which countries fixed the value of their currency relative to some commodity. The most famous and important of these systems was the gold standard, and this system had no center country because countries did not peg the exchange rate at $\bar{E}$, the local currency price of some base currency, but instead they pegged at $\bar{P}_g$, the local currency price of gold.

How did this system work? Under the gold standard, gold and money were seamlessly interchangeable, and the combined value of gold and money in the hands of the public was the relevant measure of money supply (M). For example, consider two countries, Britain pegging to gold at $\bar{P}_g$ (pounds per ounce of gold) and France pegging to gold at $\bar{P}_g^*$ (francs per ounce of gold). Under this system, one pound cost $1/\bar{P}_g$ ounces of gold, and each ounce of gold cost $\bar{P}_g^*$ francs, according to the fixed gold prices set by the central banks in each country. Thus, one pound cost $E_{par} = \bar{P}_g^*/\bar{P}_g$ francs, and this ratio defined the *par* exchange rate implied by the gold prices in each country.

The gold standard rested on the principle of free convertibility. This meant that central banks in both countries stood ready to buy and sell gold in exchange for paper money at these mint prices, and the export and import of gold were unrestricted. This allowed arbitrage forces to stabilize the system. How?

Suppose the market exchange rate in Paris (the price of one pound in francs) was E francs per pound and deviated from the par level, with $E < E_{\text{par}}$ francs per pound. This would create an arbitrage opportunity. The franc has appreciated relative to pounds, and arbitrageurs could change 1 ounce of gold into $\overline{P}_g^*$ francs at the central bank, and then into $\overline{P}_g^*/E$ pounds in the market, which could be shipped to London and converted into $\overline{P}_g^*/(E\overline{P}_g)$ ounces of gold, which could then be brought back to Paris. Because we assumed that $E < E_{\text{par}}$, $\overline{P}_g^*/(E\overline{P}_g) = E_{\text{par}}/E > 1$, and the trader ends up with more than an ounce of gold and makes a profit.

As a result of this trade, gold would leave Britain and the British money supply would fall (pounds would be redeemed at the Bank of England by the French traders, who would export the gold back to France). As gold entered France, the French money supply would expand (because the traders could leave it in gold form, or freely change it into franc notes at the Banque de France).

We can see again how arbitrage tends to stabilize the foreign exchange market (just as interest arbitrage did in the chapters on exchange rates). Here, the pound was depreciated relative to par and the arbitrage mechanism caused the British money supply to contract and the French money supply to expand. The arbitrage mechanism depended on French investors buying "cheap" pounds. This would bid up the price of pounds in Paris, so E would rise toward E_{par}, stabilizing the exchange rate at its par level.

Four observations are worth noting. First, the process of arbitrage was not really costless, so if the exchange rate deviated only slightly from parity, the profit from arbitrage might be zero or negative (i.e., a loss). Thus, there was a small band around the par rate in which the exchange rate might fluctuate without any arbitrage occurring. However, this band, delineated by limits known as the upper and lower "gold points," was typically small, permitting perhaps at most ±1% fluctuations in E on either side of E_{par}. The exchange rate was, therefore, very stable. For example, from 1879 to 1914, when Britain and the United States were pegged to gold at a par rate of $4.86 per pound, the daily dollar–pound market exchange rate in New York was within 1% of its par value 99.97% of the time (and within half a percent 77% of the time).[18]

Second, in our example we examined arbitrage in only one direction, but, naturally, there would have been a similar profitable arbitrage opportunity—subject to transaction costs—in the opposite direction if E had been above E_{par} and the franc had been depreciated relative to parity. (Working out how one makes a profit in that case, and what the net effect would be on each country's money supply, is left as an exercise.)

Third, gold arbitrage would enforce a fixed exchange rate at E_{par} (plus or minus small deviations within the gold points), thus setting expected depreciation to zero. Interest arbitrage between the two countries' money markets would equalize the interest rates in each country (subject to risk premiums). So our earlier approach to the study of fixed exchange rates remains valid, including a central principle, the trilemma.

Fourth, and most important, we see the inherent symmetry of the gold standard system when operated according to these principles. Both countries share in the adjustment mechanism, with the money supply contracting in the gold outflow country (here, Britain) and the money supply expanding in the gold inflow country (here, France). In theory, if these principles were adhered to, neither country would have the privileged position of being able to not change its monetary policy, in marked contrast to a center country in a reserve currency system. But in reality, the gold standard did not always operate quite so smoothly, as we see in the next section.

American Numismatic Association

"The best coin that has been struck for two thousand years" declared U.S. president Theodore Roosevelt, on the minting of this beautiful and intricate design to improve artistically on what he saw as the "atrocious hideousness" of American coinage. The U.S. gold parity was $20.67 per troy ounce from 1834 to 1933, so a $20 gold coin like this 1907 Saint Gaudens Double Eagle contained 20/20.67 = 0.9675 ounces of gold.

---

[18] Eugene Canjels, Gauri Prakash-Canjels, and Alan M. Taylor, 2004, "Measuring Market Integration: Foreign Exchange Arbitrage and the Gold Standard, 1879–1913," *Review of Economics and Statistics*, 86(4), 868–882.

4 International Monetary Experience

A vast diversity of exchange rate arrangements have been used throughout history. In the chapter that introduced exchange rates, we saw how different countries fix or float at present; at the start of this chapter, we saw how exchange rate arrangements have fluctuated over more than a century. These observations motivated us to study how countries choose to fix or float.

To better understand the international monetary experience and how we got to where we are today, we now apply what we have learned in the book so far.[19] In particular, we rely on the trilemma, which tells us that countries cannot simultaneously meet the three policy goals of a fixed exchange rate, capital mobility, and monetary policy autonomy. With the feasible policy choices thus set out, we draw on the ideas of this chapter about the costs and benefits of fixed and floating regimes to try to understand why various countries have made the choices they have at different times.

The Rise and Fall of the Gold Standard

As we saw in Figure 8-1, the history of international monetary arrangements from 1870 to 1939 was dominated by one story: the rise and fall of the gold standard regime. In 1870 about 15% of countries were on gold, rising to about 70% in 1913 and almost 90% during a brief period of resumption in the 1920s. But by 1939, only about 25% of the world was pegged to gold. What happened? The analysis in this chapter provides insights into one of the grand narratives of economic history.[20]

The period from 1870 to 1914 was the first era of globalization, with increasingly large flows of trade, capital, and people between countries. Depending on the countries in question, some of these developments were due to technological developments in transport and communications (such as steamships, the telegraph, etc.) and some were a result of policy change (such as tariff reductions). Our model suggests that as the volume of trade and other economic transactions between nations increase, there will be more to gain from adopting a fixed exchange rate (as in Figure 8-4). Thus, as nineteenth-century globalization proceeded, it is likely that more countries crossed the FIX line and met the economic criteria for fixing.

There were also other forces at work encouraging a switch to the gold peg before 1914. The stabilization costs of pegging were either seen as insignificant—because the pace of economic growth was not that unstable—or else politically irrelevant—because the majority of those adversely affected by business cycles and unemployment were from the mostly disenfranchised working classes. With the exception of some emerging markets, price stability was the major goal and the inflation tax was not seen as useful except in emergencies.

As for the question, why peg to gold? (as opposed to silver, or something else), note that once a gold peg became established in a few countries, the benefits of adoption in other countries would increase further. If you are the second country to go on the gold standard, it lowers your trade costs with one other country; if you are the 10th or 20th country to go on, it lowers your trade costs with 10 or 20 other countries; and so on. This can be thought of as a "snowball effect" (or *network externality*, as economists say), where only one standard can dominate in the end.[21]

[19] Barry Eichengreen, 1996, *Globalizing Capital: A History of the International Monetary System* (Princeton, NJ: Princeton University Press); Maurice Obstfeld and Alan M. Taylor, 2004, *Global Capital Markets: Integration, Crisis, and Growth* (Cambridge: Cambridge University Press).

[20] Lawrence Officer, October 1, 2001, "Gold Standard," *EH.Net Encyclopedia*, edited by Robert Whaples, http://eh.net/encyclopedia/article/officer.gold.standard.

[21] Christopher M. Meissner, 2005, "A New World Order: Explaining the International Diffusion of the Gold Standard, 1870–1913," *Journal of International Economics*, 66(2), 385–406.

Bryan's "cross of gold."

This is not to say that it was all smooth sailing before 1914. Many countries joined gold, only to leave temporarily because of a crisis. Even in countries that stayed on gold, not everyone loved the gold standard. The benefits were often less noticeable than the costs, particularly in times of deflation or in recessions. For example, in the United States, prices and output stagnated in the 1890s. As a result, many people supported leaving the gold standard to escape its monetary restrictions. The tensions reached a head in 1896 at the Democratic Convention in Chicago, when presidential candidate William Jennings Bryan ended his speech saying: "Having behind us the producing masses of this nation and the world, supported by the commercial interests, the laboring interests and the toilers everywhere, we will answer their demand for a gold standard by saying to them: You shall not press down upon the brow of labor this crown of thorns, you shall not crucify mankind upon a cross of gold." But Bryan lost, the pro-gold McKinley became president, the Gold Standard Act of 1900 buried any doubts, and tensions defused as economic growth and gold discoveries boosted output and prices.

These trends were upset by World War I. Countries participating in the war needed some way to finance their efforts. The inflation tax was heavily used, and this implied exit from the gold standard. In addition, once the war began in Europe (and later drew in the United States), the majority of global trade was affected by it: trade was almost 100% wiped out between warring nations, and fell by 50% between participants and neutral countries. This effect persisted long after the war ended, and was made worse by protectionism (higher tariffs and quotas) in the 1920s. By the 1930s, world trade had fallen to close to half of its 1914 level. All of these developments meant less economic integration—which in turn meant that the rationale for fixing based on gains from trade was being weakened.[22]

Then, from 1929 on, the Great Depression undermined the stability argument for pegging to gold. The 1920s and 1930s featured much more violent economic fluctuations than had been seen prior to 1914, raising the costs of pegging. Moreover, politically speaking, these costs could no longer be ignored so easily with the widening of the franchise over time. The rise of labor movements and political parties of the left started to give voice and electoral weight to constituencies that cared much more about the instability costs of a fixed exchange rate.[23]

Other factors also played a role. The Great Depression was accompanied by severe deflation, so to stay on gold might have risked further deflation given the slow growth of gold supplies to which all money supplies were linked. Deflation linked to inadequate gold supplies therefore undermined the usefulness of gold as a nominal anchor.[24] Many countries had followed beggar-thy-neighbor policies in the 1920s, choosing to re-peg their currencies to gold at devalued rates, making further devaluations tempting. Among developing countries, many economies were in recession before 1929 because of poor conditions in commodity markets, so they had another reason to devalue (as some did as early as 1929). The war had also left gold reserves distributed in a highly asymmetric fashion, leaving some countries with few reserves for intervention to support their pegs. As backup, many countries used major

---

[22] Reuven Glick and Alan M. Taylor, 2010, "Collateral Damage: Trade Disruption and the Economic Impact of War," *Review of Economics and Statistics*, 92(1), 102–127; Antoni Estevadeordal, Brian Frantz, and Alan M. Taylor, 2003, "The Rise and Fall of World Trade, 1870–1939," *Quarterly Journal of Economics*, 118(2), 359–407.

[23] Barry Eichengreen, 1992, *Golden Fetters: The Gold Standard and the Great Depression* (New York: Oxford University Press).

[24] World gold production more or less kept pace with output growth in the nineteenth century, but output grew much faster than gold stocks in the twentieth century. If gold gets scarcer, its relative price must rise. But if the money price of gold is pegged, the only way for the relative price of gold to rise is for all other prices to fall—that is, by economy-wide price deflation.

currencies as reserves, but the value of these reserves depended on everyone else's commitment to the gold peg, a commitment that was increasingly questionable.

All of these weaknesses undermined the confidence and credibility of the commitment to gold pegs in many countries, making the collapse of the pegs more likely. Currency traders would then speculate against various currencies, raising the risk of a crisis. In the face of such speculation, in 1931 both Germany and Austria imposed capital controls, and Britain floated the pound against gold. The gold standard system then unraveled in a largely uncoordinated, uncooperative, and destructive fashion.

In the language of the trilemma, with its three solution corners, the 1930s saw a movement by policymakers away from the "open capital market/fixed exchange rate" corner, and the other two corners came to dominate. Countries unwilling to close their capital markets by imposing controls opted to abandon the gold peg and moved to the open capital market/floating exchange rate solution, allowing them to regain monetary policy autonomy: Britain and the United States among others made this choice. Countries willing to adopt capital controls but unwilling to suffer the volatility of a floating rate moved to the "closed capital market/fixed exchange rate" solution, allowing them to regain monetary policy autonomy in a different way: Germany and many countries in South America made this choice. Gaining monetary autonomy gave all of these countries the freedom to pursue more expansionary monetary policies to try to revive their economies, and most of them did just that. Finally, a few countries (such as France and Switzerland) remained on the gold standard and did not devalue or impose controls, because they were not forced off gold (they had large reserves) and because they were worried about the inflationary consequences of floating. Countries that stuck with the gold standard paid a heavy price: compared with 1929, countries that floated had 26% higher output in 1935, and countries that adopted capital controls had 21% higher output, as compared with the countries that stayed on gold.[25]

Figure 8-13 shows these outcomes. To sum up: although many other factors were important, trade gains and an absence of (or political indifference to) stability costs helped bring the gold standard into being before 1914; reduced trade gains and stability costs that were higher (or more politically relevant) help explain the ultimate demise of the gold standard in the interwar period.

The 1930s Depression left deep economic and political scars in advanced countries. The longer central banks kept a hard peg to gold, the more monetary policy was slow and weak in responding to the crisis. Since that time economists have leaned against the idea of tying the hands of the central bank and giving up monetary policy autonomy by going back to such a hard peg regime. Despite the fringe enthusiasm of gold standard fanatics who periodically lobby for its return, the professional consensus has never wavered.

Bretton Woods to the Present

The international monetary system of the 1930s was chaotic. Near the end of World War II, allied economic policymakers gathered in the United States, at Bretton Woods, New Hampshire, to try to ensure that the postwar economy fared better. The architects of the postwar order, notably Harry Dexter White and John Maynard Keynes, constructed a system that preserved one key tenet of the gold standard regime—by keeping fixed rates—but discarded the other by imposing capital controls. The trilemma was resolved in favor of exchange rate stability to encourage the rebuilding

---

[25] Maurice Obstfeld and Alan M. Taylor, 2004, *Global Capital Markets: Integration, Crisis, and Growth* (Cambridge: Cambridge University Press). The output cost estimates are from page 143.

FIGURE 8-13

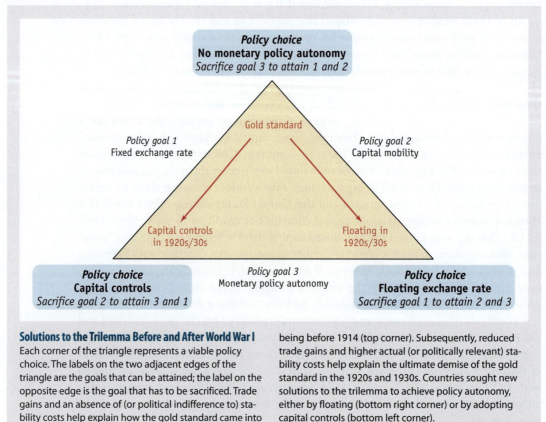

Solutions to the Trilemma Before and After World War I
Each corner of the triangle represents a viable policy choice. The labels on the two adjacent edges of the triangle are the goals that can be attained; the label on the opposite edge is the goal that has to be sacrificed. Trade gains and an absence of (or political indifference to) stability costs help explain how the gold standard came into being before 1914 (top corner). Subsequently, reduced trade gains and higher actual (or politically relevant) stability costs help explain the ultimate demise of the gold standard in the 1920s and 1930s. Countries sought new solutions to the trilemma to achieve policy autonomy, either by floating (bottom right corner) or by adopting capital controls (bottom left corner).

of trade in the postwar period. Countries would peg to the U.S. dollar; this made the U.S. dollar the center currency and the United States the center country. The U.S. dollar was, in turn, pegged to gold at a fixed price, a last vestige of the gold standard.

In Figure 8-14, the postwar period starts with the world firmly in the "closed capital market/fixed exchange rate" corner on the left. At Bretton Woods, the interests of international finance were seemingly dismissed, amid disdain for the speculators who had destabilized the gold standard in the 1920s and 1930s: U.S. Treasury Secretary Henry Morgenthau pronounced that the new institutions would "drive . . . the usurious money lenders from the temple of international finance." At the time, only the United States allowed full freedom of international capital movement, but this was soon to change.

It was obvious that to have trade one needed to have payments, so some kind of system for credit was needed, at least on a short-term basis. By the late 1950s, after getting by with half measures, many countries in Europe and elsewhere were ready to liberalize financial transactions related to current account transactions to free up the trade and payments system. At the same time, they sought to limit speculative financial transactions that were purely asset trades within the financial account (e.g., interest arbitrage by forex traders).

Unfortunately, in practice it proved difficult then (and has proved so ever since) to put watertight controls on financial transactions. Controls in the 1960s were very leaky and investors found ways to circumvent them and move money offshore from local currency deposits into foreign currency deposits. Some used accounting tricks such as over- or under-invoicing trade transactions to move money from one currency to another. Others took advantage of the largely unregulated offshore currency markets that had emerged in London and elsewhere in the late 1950s.

FIGURE 8-14

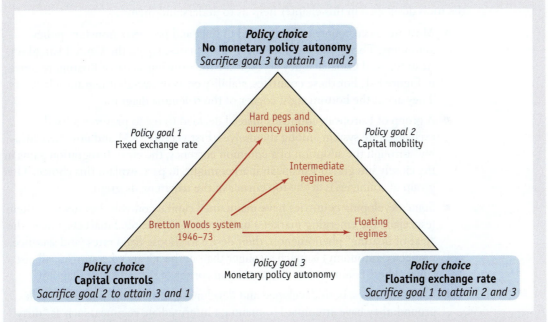

Solutions to the Trilemma Since World War II In the 1960s, the Bretton Woods system became unsustainable because capital mobility could not be contained. Thus, countries could no longer have fixed rates and monetary autonomy (bottom left corner). In the advanced countries, the trilemma was resolved by a shift to floating rates, which preserved autonomy and allowed for the present era of capital mobility (bottom right corner). The main exception was the currency union of the Eurozone. In developing countries and emerging markets, the "fear of floating" was stronger; when capital markets were opened, monetary policy autonomy was more often sacrificed and fixed exchange rates were maintained (top corner).

As capital mobility grew and controls failed to hold, the trilemma tells us that countries pegged to the dollar stood to lose their monetary policy autonomy. This was already a reason for them to think about exiting the dollar peg. With autonomy evaporating, the devaluation option came to be seen as the most important way of achieving policy compromise in a "fixed but adjustable" system. But increasingly frequent devaluations (and some revaluations) undermined the notion of a truly fixed rate system, made it more unstable, generated beggar-thy-neighbor policies, and—if anticipated—encouraged speculators.

The downsides became more and more apparent as the 1960s went on. Other factors included a growing unwillingness in many countries to peg to the U.S. dollar, after inflation in the Vietnam War era undermined the dollar's previously strong claim to be the best nominal anchor currency. It was also believed that this inflation would eventually conflict with the goal of fixing the dollar price of gold and that the United States would eventually abandon its commitment to convert dollars into gold, which happened in August 1971. By then it had become clear that U.S. policy was geared to U.S. interests, and if the rest of the world needed a reminder about asymmetry, they got it from U.S. Treasury Secretary John Connally, who in 1971 uttered the memorable words, "The dollar is our currency, but it's your problem."

Figure 8-14 tells us what must happen in an international monetary system once capital mobility reasserts itself, as happened to the Bretton Woods system in the 1960s. The "closed capital market/fixed exchange rate" corner on the left is no longer an option. Countries must make a choice: they can stay fixed and have no monetary autonomy (move to the top corner), or they can float and recover monetary autonomy (move to the right corner).

These choices came to the fore after the Bretton Woods system collapsed between 1971 and 1973. How did the world react? There have been a variety of outcomes, and the tools developed in this chapter help us to understand them:

- Most advanced countries have opted to float and preserve monetary policy autonomy. This group includes the United States, Japan, the United Kingdom, Australia, and Canada. They account for the growing share of floating regimes in Figure 8-1. For these countries, stability costs outweigh integration benefits. They are at the bottom right corner of the trilemma diagram.

- A group of European countries instead decided to try to preserve a fixed exchange rate system among themselves, first via the ERM and now "irrevocably" through the adoption of a common currency, the euro. Integration gains in the closely integrated European market might, in part, explain this choice. This group of countries is at the top corner of the trilemma diagram.

- Some developing countries have maintained capital controls, but many of them (especially the emerging markets) have opened their capital markets. Given the "fear of floating" phenomenon, their desire to choose fixed rates (and sacrifice monetary autonomy) is much stronger than in the advanced countries, all else equal. These countries are also at the top corner of the trilemma diagram.

- Some countries, both developed and developing, have camped in the middle ground: they have attempted to maintain intermediate regimes, such as "dirty floats" or pegs with "limited flexibility." India is often considered to be a case of an intermediate regime somewhere between floating or fixed. Such countries are somewhere in the middle on the right side of the trilemma diagram.

- Finally, some countries still impose some capital controls rather than embrace globalization. China has been in this position, although things are gradually starting to change and the authorities have suggested further moves toward financial liberalization in the future. These countries, mostly developing countries, are clinging to the bottom left corner of the trilemma diagram.

5 Conclusions

Exchange rate regimes have varied greatly across countries and across time and continue to do so. Explaining why this is the case and figuring out the optimal choice of exchange rate regime are major tasks in international macroeconomics.

We began this chapter by studying the main costs and benefits of fixed versus floating regimes. Fixing enhances the economic efficiency of international transactions. Floating allows authorities to stabilize an economy with monetary policy. The clash between these two goals creates a trade-off. Only with enough economic integration (more gains on transactions) and sufficiently symmetric shocks (less need for policy autonomy) do fixed exchange rates make sense, as shown in the symmetry-integration diagram.

However, other factors affect the trade-off, especially in emerging markets and developing countries: fixed exchange rates may provide the only credible nominal anchor after a high inflation, and they insulate countries with net foreign currency debt from the adverse wealth effects of depreciations.

Finally, we examined exchange rate systems in theory and in practice. Over the years, fixed rate systems such as the gold standard and the Bretton Woods system have come and gone, with collapses driven, at least in part, by failures of cooperation. That leaves us today with no real international monetary "system" at all, but rather many countries, and occasionally groups of countries, pursuing their own interests and trying to make the best choice of regime given their particular circumstances. As this chapter has shown, there may be good reasons why "one size fits all" will never apply to exchange rate regimes.

KEY POINTS

1. A wide variety of exchange rate regimes have been in operation throughout history to the present.

2. The benefits for the home country from a fixed exchange rate include lower transaction costs and increased trade, investment, and migration with the base or center country.

3. The costs to the home country from a fixed exchange rate arise primarily when the home and center countries experience different economic shocks and the home country would want to pursue monetary policies different from those of the base or center country.

4. The costs and benefits of fixing can be summed up on a symmetry-integration diagram. At high levels of symmetry and/or integration, above the FIX line, it makes sense to fix. At low levels of symmetry and/or integration, below the FIX line, it makes sense to float.

5. A fixed rate may confer extra benefits if it is the only viable nominal anchor in a high-inflation country and if it prevents adverse wealth shocks caused by depreciation in countries suffering from a currency mismatch.

6. Using these tools and the trilemma, we can better understand exchange rate regime choices in the past and in the present. Before 1914 it appears the gold standard did promote integration, and political concern for the loss of stabilization policies was limited. In the 1920s and 1930s, increased isolationism, economic instability, and political realignments undermined the gold standard. After 1945 and up to the late 1960s, the Bretton Woods system of fixed dollar exchange rates was feasible, with strict controls on capital mobility, and was attractive as long as U.S. policies were not at odds with the rest of the world. Since 1973 different countries and groups of countries have gone their own way, and today's diverse array of exchange rate regimes reflects the sovereign choice of each country.

KEY TERMS

gold standard, p. 279
base currency, p. 282
center currency, p. 282
economic integration, p. 286
asymmetric shock, p. 286

symmetry-integration diagram, p. 287
fear of floating, p. 301
fixed exchange rate systems, p. 302
reserve currency system, p. 302

cooperative arrangements, p. 302
devaluation, p. 305
revaluation, p. 305
beggar-thy-neighbor policy, p. 306

PROBLEMS

1. **Discovering Data** Visit the International Monetary Fund's website (http://www.imf.org) and locate the latest classification of exchange rate regimes in all countries around the world. How many countries are fixing, and how many are floating?

2. Using the IS–LM–FX model, illustrate how each of the following scenarios affects the home country. Compare the outcomes when the home country has a fixed exchange rate with the outcomes when the home currency floats.

   a. The foreign country increases the money supply.

   b. The home country cuts taxes.

   c. Investors expect a future appreciation in the home currency.

WORK IT OUT  Achieve | interactive activity

3. The Danish krone is currently pegged to the euro. Using the IS–LM–FX model for Home (Denmark) and Foreign (Eurozone), illustrate how each of the following scenarios affects Denmark:

   a. The Eurozone reduces its money supply.

   b. Denmark cuts government spending to reduce its budget deficit.

   c. The Eurozone countries increase their taxes.

4. Consider two countries that are currently pegged to the euro: Bulgaria and Comoros. Bulgaria is a member of the EU, allowing it to trade freely with other EU countries. Exports to the Eurozone account for the majority of Bulgaria's outbound trade, which mainly consists of manufacturing

goods, services, and wood. In contrast, Comoros is an archipelago of islands off the eastern coast of southern Africa that exports food commodities primarily to the United States and France. Comoros historically maintained a peg with the French franc, switching to the euro when France joined the Eurozone. Compare and contrast Bulgaria and Comoros in terms of their likely degree of integration symmetry with the Eurozone. Plot Comoros and Bulgaria on a symmetry-integration diagram as in Figure 8-4.

5. Use the symmetry-integration diagram as in Figure 8-4 to explore the evolution of international monetary regimes from 1870 to 1939—that is, during the rise and fall of the gold standard.

   a. From 1870 to 1913, world trade flows doubled in size relative to GDP, from about 10% to 20%. Many economic historians believe this was driven by exogenous declines in transaction costs, some of which were caused by changes in transport technology. How would you depict this shift for a pair of countries in the symmetry-integration diagram that started off just below the FIX line in 1870? Use the letter *A* to label your starting point in 1870 and use *B* to label the end point in 1913.

   b. From 1913 to 1939, world trade flows collapsed, falling in half relative to GDP, from about 20% back to 10%. Many economic historians think this was driven by exogenous increases in transaction costs from rising transport costs and increases in tariffs and quotas. How would you depict this shift for a pair of countries in the symmetry-integration diagram that started off just above the FIX line in 1913? Use the letter *B* to label your starting point in 1913 and use *C* to label the end point in 1939.

   c. Other economic historians contend that these changes in transaction costs arose endogenously. When countries went on the gold standard, they lowered their transaction costs and boosted trade. When they left gold, costs increased. If this is true, then do points *A*, *B*, and *C* represent unique solutions to the problem of choosing an exchange rate regime?

   d. Changes in other factors in the 1920s and 1930s had an impact on the sustainability of the gold standard. These included the following:
      i. An increase in country-specific shocks
      ii. An increase in democracy

      iii. Growth of world output relative to the supply of gold

      In each case, explain why these changes might have undermined commitment to the gold standard.

6. Many countries experiencing high and rising inflation, or even hyperinflation, will adopt a fixed exchange rate regime. Discuss the potential costs and benefits of a fixed exchange rate regime in this case. Comment on fiscal discipline, seigniorage, and expected future inflation.

7. In the late 1970s, several countries in Latin America, notably Mexico, Brazil, and Argentina, had accumulated large external debt burdens. A significant share of this debt was denominated in U.S. dollars. The United States pursued contractionary monetary policy from 1979 to 1982, raising dollar interest rates. How would this affect the value of the Latin American currencies relative to the U.S. dollar? How would this affect their external debt in local currency terms? If these countries had wanted to prevent a change in their external debt, what would have been the appropriate policy response, and what would be the drawbacks?

8. Home's currency, the peso, currently trades at an exchange rate of 1 peso per dollar. Home has external assets of $320 billion, 100% of which are denominated in dollars. It has external liabilities of $800 billion, 90% of which are denominated in dollars.

   a. Is Home a net creditor or debtor? What is Home's external wealth measured in pesos?

   b. What is Home's net position in dollar-denominated assets, measured in pesos? And what is it measured in U.S. dollars?

   c. If the peso depreciates to 1.2 pesos per dollar, what is the change in Home's external wealth measured in pesos?

9. Evaluate the empirical evidence on how currency depreciation affects wealth and output across countries. How does the decision of maintaining a fixed versus floating exchange rate regime depend on a country's external wealth position?

10. Home signs a free-trade agreement with Foreign, which lowers tariffs and other barriers to trade. Both countries are very similar in terms of economic shocks, as they each produce very similar goods. Use

a symmetry-integration diagram as in Figure 8-4 as part of your answer to the following questions:

a. Initially, trade rises. Does the rise in trade make Home more or less likely to peg its currency to Foreign's currency? Why?

b. In the longer run, freer trade causes the countries to follow their comparative advantage and specialize in producing very different types of goods. Does the rise in specialization make Home more or less likely to peg its currency to the foreign currency? Why?

11. Find the photo of the $20 gold coin on page 308 in this chapter and refer to the specifications in the adjoining caption. Calculate the U.S. dollar price of 1 ounce of gold under the pre-1913 gold standard. Now search the Internet to find details, including gold content, of a British gold sovereign coin worth £1 in the same era. Calculate the British pound price of 1 ounce of gold under the pre-1913 gold standard. Now compute the implied pound–dollar exchange rate. Check your answer against the value given in the text.

9

Exchange Rate Crises: How Pegs Work and How They Break

Global capital markets pose the same kinds of problems that jet planes do. They are faster, more comfortable, and they get you where you are going better. But the crashes are much more spectacular.

Lawrence Summers, U.S. Secretary of the Treasury, 1999

Either extreme: a fixed exchange rate through a currency board, but no central bank, or a central bank plus truly floating exchange rates; either of those is a tenable arrangement. But a pegged exchange rate with a central bank is a recipe for trouble.

Milton Friedman, Nobel laureate, 1998

Questions to Consider

1 How does a central bank manage its balance sheet to maintain a fixed exchange rate?

2 How can the use of central bank money for fiscal purposes lead to a currency crisis?

3 How can the possibilities of multiple equilibria and shifts in market sentiment lead to a currency crisis?

In the last chapter, we treated the question "fixed or floating?" as a one-time problem of exchange rate regime choice and assumed that, once the choice was made, the chosen regime would be stable and sustainable.

Unfortunately, the reality is different. The typical fixed exchange rate succeeds for a few years, only to break. One study found that the average duration of any peg was about five years, and the median duration was only two years.[1] When the break occurs, there is often a large, sudden depreciation accompanied by high economic and political costs. Such a collapse is known as an *exchange rate crisis*. When a country shifts from floating to fixed, the transition between the two is generally planned and smooth, but when a country shifts from fixed to floating the transition is typically unplanned and often catastrophic.

Despite the fragility exposed by recurrent crises, fixed exchange rate regimes are still in use. Typically, after a crisis, a country that prefers to have a fixed exchange rate

---

[1] Michael W. Klein and Jay C. Shambaugh, 2006, "The Nature of Exchange Rate Regimes," NBER Working Paper No. 12729. Since 1970, with the exception of some peculiar countries (the few destined to adopt the euro, oil exporters like Saudi Arabia and Bahrain, and tiny microstates like Bhutan and Kiribati), only a handful of pegs have lasted longer than a decade, and only one, Hong Kong's peg to the U.S. dollar, is still surviving. See also Maurice Obstfeld and Kenneth Rogoff, 1995, "The Mirage of Fixed Exchange Rates," *Journal of Economic Perspectives*, 9(4), 73–96.

will try to peg again: the cycle of crises may continue. Understanding exchange rate crises is a major goal of international macroeconomics because of the damage they do, not only to the country in which the crisis occurs but often to its neighbors and trading partners. In this chapter we learn about exchange rate crises, their causes, and their consequences.

1 Facts About Exchange Rate Crises

To understand the importance of exchange rate crises, let's examine what crises look like and the costs associated with them. We will now take a look at some of the most famous currency crisis episodes of the last 50 years, including cases in both advanced and emerging economies.

What Is an Exchange Rate Crisis?

A simple definition of an **exchange rate crisis** would be a "big" depreciation that occurs after a peg breaks.[2] But how big is big enough to qualify as a crisis? In practice, in an advanced country, a 10% to 15% depreciation might be considered large. In emerging markets, the bar might be set higher, say, 20% to 25%.[3] Examples of such crises are shown in Figure 9-1.

Panel (a) shows the depreciation of six European currencies against the German mark after 1992. Four currencies (the escudo, lira, peseta, and pound) were part of the European Exchange Rate Mechanism (ERM); the other two (the markka and krona) were not in the ERM but were pegging to the German mark. All six currencies lost 15% to 25% of their value against the mark within a year.

Panel (b) shows the depreciation of seven emerging market currencies against the U.S. dollar in various crises that occurred from 1994 to 2002. These depreciations, while also very rapid, were much larger than those in panel (a). These currencies lost 50% to 75% of their value against the dollar in the year following the crisis.

The figure illustrates two important points. First, exchange rate crises can occur in advanced countries as well as in emerging markets and developing countries. Second, the magnitude of the crisis, as measured by the subsequent depreciation of the currency, is often much greater in emerging markets and developing countries.

How Costly Are Exchange Rate Crises?

There is much evidence on the potentially damaging effects of exchange rate crises. The economic costs are often large, and the political costs can be even more dramatic (see **Side Bar: The Political Economy of Crises**).

Figure 9-2 presents some evidence of the effects of exchange rate crises. Annual rates of growth of GDP in years close to crises were compared with growth in other (i.e., "normal") years to obtain a measure of how growth differs during crisis periods. The figure shows that just before a crisis all countries have an annual economic growth rate that is between 0.5% and 1.0% below the growth rate in normal years.

---

[2] Economists sometimes use a broader concept of a *currency crisis* based on other criteria such as reserve losses. See Barry Eichengreen, Andrew K. Rose, and Charles Wyplosz, 1995, "Exchange Market Mayhem: The Antecedents and Aftermath of Speculative Attacks," *Economic Policy*, 10(21), 249–312.

[3] One widely used definition requires at least a 25% depreciation in one year to be sure that such a depreciation is beyond the limits of even a wide band, and a rate of depreciation that is at least 10% higher than in the previous year to ensure that the depreciation is not just part of a broken crawl. Jeffrey A. Frankel and Andrew K. Rose, 1996, "Currency Crashes in Emerging Markets: An Empirical Treatment," *Journal of International Economics*, 41(3-4), 351–366.

FIGURE 9-1

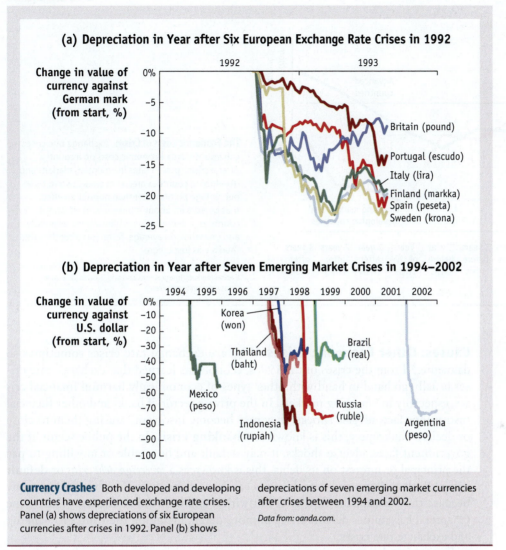

(a) Depreciation in Year after Six European Exchange Rate Crises in 1992

Change in value of
currency against
German mark
(from start, %)

Britain (pound)
Portugal (escudo)
Italy (lira)
Finland (markka)
Spain (peseta)
Sweden (krona)

(b) Depreciation in Year after Seven Emerging Market Crises in 1994–2002

Change in value of
currency against
U.S. dollar
(from start, %)

Korea
(won)
Thailand
(baht)
Brazil
(real)
Mexico
(peso)
Russia
(ruble)
Indonesia
(rupiah)
Argentina
(peso)

Currency Crashes Both developed and developing countries have experienced exchange rate crises. Panel (a) shows depreciations of six European currencies after crises in 1992. Panel (b) shows depreciations of seven emerging market currencies after crises between 1994 and 2002.

Data from: oanda.com.

After a typical exchange rate crisis, advanced countries and emerging markets react differently. Advanced countries tend to bounce back: growth accelerates and is above normal by the second and third years after the crisis. Emerging markets do not bounce back, and growth usually plummets: it is 2.5% to 3% below normal in the year of the crisis and the two subsequent years, and is still 1% below normal in the third year. All those reductions in growth add up to about a 10% decline in GDP relative to its typical trend three years after the crisis—a major recession.[4]

The major downturns in emerging markets often have serious economic and social consequences. For example, in the aftermath of the Argentina crisis of 2001 to 2002, news reports were filled with shocking tales of unemployment, financial ruin, rising poverty, hunger, and deprivation. After the Asian crisis of 1997, the recoveries were a little faster, but the economic misfortunes were still deep and painful. More recently, Argentina suffered another currency crisis in 2018–19, and economic distress is again on the rise.

---

[4] If we were to cumulate these effects over a seven-year time span, we would see that advanced countries typically experience a cycle in which they fall, at most, 3% below their normal real growth trend but then recover. Emerging markets and developing countries, however, typically suffer a deep downturn, with output at times more than 10% below its normal trend and stuck for some time at a persistently low level.

FIGURE 9-2

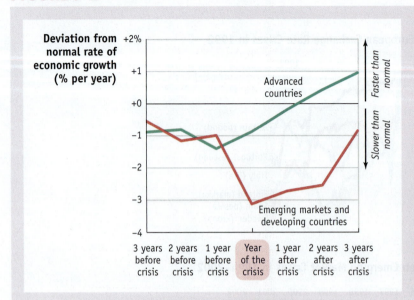

The Economic Costs of Crises Exchange rate crises can impose large economic costs on a country. After a crisis, growth rates in emerging markets and developing countries are, on average, two to three percentage points lower than normal, an effect that persists for about three years. In advanced countries, a depreciation is typically expansionary, and growth is, on average, faster just after the crisis than it was just before.

Data from: Maurice Obstfeld and Alan M. Taylor, 2004, Global Capital Markets: Integration, Crisis and Growth *(New York: Cambridge University Press).*

Causes: Other Economic Crises Why are exchange rate crises sometimes so damaging? From the crises of the 1990s, economists learned that exchange rate crises usually go hand in hand with other types of economically harmful financial crises, especially in emerging markets. In the private sector, if banks and other financial institutions face adverse shocks, they may become insolvent, causing them to close or declare bankruptcy: this is known as a **banking crisis**. In the public sector, if the government faces adverse shocks, it may default and be unable or unwilling to pay the principal or interest on its debts: this is known as a *sovereign debt crisis* or **default crisis**. Both banking and default crises can have damaging effects on the economy because they disrupt the flow of credit within and between countries. (The online Chapter 11 examines default crises in more detail, including their links to banking and exchange rate crises.)

International macroeconomists thus have three crisis types to consider: exchange rate crises, banking crises, and default crises. Evidence shows that they can occur one at a time, but they are also quite likely to occur simultaneously:

■ *The likelihood of a banking or default crisis increases significantly when a country is having an exchange rate crisis.* One study found that the probability of a banking crisis was 1.6 times higher during an exchange rate crisis (16% versus 10% on average). Another study found that the probability of a default crisis was more than 3 times higher during an exchange rate crisis (39% versus 12% on average).[5] Explanations for these findings focus on valuation effects. As we saw in the last chapter, a big depreciation causes a sudden increase in the local currency value of dollar debts (principal and interest). Because this change in value can raise debt burdens to intolerable levels, exchange rate crises are frequently accompanied by financial distress in the private and public sectors.

---

[5] Graciela L. Kaminsky and Carmen M. Reinhart, 1999, "The Twin Crises: The Causes of Banking and Balance-of-Payments Problems," *American Economic Review*, 89(3), 473–500; Carmen M. Reinhart, 2002, "Default, Currency Crises, and Sovereign Credit Ratings," *World Bank Economic Review*, 16(2), 151–170.

■ *The likelihood of an exchange rate crisis increases significantly when a country is having a banking or default crisis.* The same two studies just noted found that the probability of an exchange rate crisis was 1.5 times higher during a banking crisis (46% versus 29% on average). The probability of an exchange rate crisis was more than 5 times higher during a default crisis (84% versus 17% on average).

Explanations for these reverse effects center on the issuance of money by the central bank to bail out banks and governments. Banking crises can be horrendously costly. As can be seen in Table 9-1, countries have to cope not only with the direct fiscal costs of fixing a damaged banking sector (e.g., through the bailout and recapitalization

TABLE 9-1

Costly Banking Crises The table shows the estimated costs of major banking crises since 1991 in both advanced and emerging economies. Various measures are shown: the loss of output relative to trend, the direct costs to the government of repairing the banking system, and the change in the level of public debt.

Country	Starting Year of the Crisis	Output Loss (% of GDP)[1]	Direct Fiscal Costs (% of GDP)[2]	Increase in Public Debt (% of GDP)[3]
Argentina	2001	71.0%	9.6%	81.9%
Brazil	1994	0.0	13.2	−33.8
China	1998	19.4	18.0	11.2
Denmark	2008	36.0	3.1	24.9
Finland	1991	69.6	12.8	43.6
France	2008	23.0	1.0	17.3
Germany	2008	11.0	1.8	17.8
Greece	2008	43.0	27.3	44.5
Iceland	2008	43.0	44.2	72.2
Indonesia	1997	69.0	56.8	67.6
Ireland	2008	106.0	40.7	72.8
Italy	2008	32.0	0.3	8.6
Japan	1997	45.0	14.0	41.7
Korea	1997	57.6	31.2	9.9
Luxembourg	2008	36.0	7.7	14.6
Malaysia	1997	31.4	16.4	0.2
Mexico	1994	13.7	19.3	16.4
Netherlands	2008	23.0	12.7	26.8
Norway	1991	5.1	2.7	19.2
Portugal	2008	37.0	0.0	33.6
Russia	1998	—	0.1	−7.1
Russia	2008	0.0	2.3	6.4
Sweden	1991	32.9	3.6	36.2
Sweden	2008	25.0	0.7	11.1
Switzerland	2008	0.0	1.1	−0.2
Thailand	1997	109.3	43.8	42.1
Turkey	2000	37.0	32.0	15.3
United Kingdom	2007	25.0	8.8	24.4
United States	2007	31.0	4.5	23.6
Average		*36.9*	*14.8*	*25.6*

[1] Cumulative, actual relative to trend from crisis start year T until year $T + 3$.
[2] Restructuring costs including bank recapitalizations but excluding liquidity provision.
[3] From year before crisis starts $T − 1$ to year $T + 3$.

Data from: Peter Hooper, Michael Spencer, Torsten Sløk, and Thomas Mayer, 2013, "Financial Crises: Past and Present," Global Economic Perspectives, 15 May (Deutsche Bank, Markets Research, Global Economics); based on Fabian Valencia and Luc Laeven, 2012, "Systemic Banking Crises Database: An Update," IMF Working Paper 12/163, International Monetary Fund.

SIDE BAR

The Political Economy of Crises

Exchange rate crises don't simply have economic consequences—they often have political consequences, too. Figure 9-3 shows that exchange rate crises are often followed by personnel changes at the central bank or finance ministry and not infrequently by a change in a country's leadership, as well.

At first, this result might seem odd. As the economist Jeffrey Frankel said, speaking of the Indonesian crisis of 1997: "What is it about devaluation that carries such big political costs? How is it that a strong ruler like Indonesia's Suharto can easily weather 32 years of political, military, ethnic, and environmental challenges, only to succumb to a currency crisis?"*

In emerging markets, we know that the economic costs of exchange rate crises can be large, which helps explain how a Suharto could be undermined. There are many other examples: the Radical Party is the oldest political party in Argentina, but after the exchange rate crisis in 2001 to 2002 under the leadership of President Fernando de la Rúa and Economy Minister Domingo Cavallo, the party faced extinction, polling just 2.3% in the 2003 presidential election.**

Still, why do exchange rate crises carry large political costs in advanced countries where the exit from an exchange rate peg often allows for a depreciation and favorable growth performance? A pertinent example is

the decision by Britain's Conservative government to exit the ERM on "Black Wednesday," September 16, 1992. Chancellor Norman Lamont left his job within a year, and Prime Minister John Major tasted defeat at the next general election in 1997, despite faster economic growth after 1992.

The legacy of "Black Wednesday" haunted the Conservatives for years. On the question of economic competence, the polls gave the subsequent Labour government a massive lead for many years. It was not until 2010 that the Conservatives regained power, but only in a coalition, and under their fifth leader in 13 years, David Cameron (who had been a junior minister working under Lamont at the Treasury on that fateful day in 1992).

Even when a depreciation turns out to be good for the economy, the collapse of a peg typically destroys the reputations of politicians and policymakers for credibility and competence. Regaining the trust of the people can take a very long time.

* Jeffrey A. Frankel, 2005, "Mundell-Fleming Lecture: Contractionary Currency Crashes in Developing Countries," *IMF Staff Papers,* 52(2), 149–192.
** Cavallo had previously served the rival Peronist Party as economy minister in the Menem administration and had presided over the creation of the fixed exchange rate regime, as well as its collapse.

FIGURE 9-3

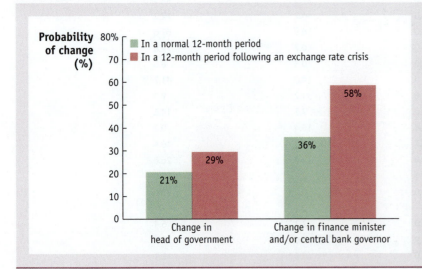

Probability of change (%)

- ◼ In a normal 12-month period
- ◼ In a 12-month period following an exchange rate crisis

Change in head of government: 21%, 29%
Change in finance minister and/or central bank governor: 36%, 58%

The Political Costs of Crises Exchange rate crises usually impose large political costs on those in power. Compared with what is likely to happen during normal, noncrisis times, it is 22% more likely that one of the two main officials with economic responsibilities (the finance minister and the central bank governor) will be out of a job the year following a crisis. It is also 9% more likely that the head of government (such as a president, prime minister, or premier) will have to depart for one reason or another.

Note: Data on heads of government are from 1971 to 2003, and data on finance ministers and central bank governors are from 1995 to 1999.

Data from: Jeffrey A. Frankel, 2005, "Mundell-Fleming Lecture: Contractionary Currency Crashes in Developing Countries," IMF Staff Papers, 52(2), 149–192.

of insolvent institutions) but also with typically very long and protracted recessions where output is significantly below trend. These slumps in turn create added cyclical drag on the government's fiscal position (lower taxes, higher spending), leading to a large runup in public debt. Such burdens might be handled purely via future fiscal adjustments, but they can sometimes endanger monetary policy and the nominal anchor. If a country is having a banking crisis, the central bank will be under pressure to extend credit or outright transfers to weak banks to prop them up. If a country is having a default crisis, the government will lose access to foreign and domestic loans and may pressure the central bank to lend to the government. This raises a key question: Why does the extension of credit by the central bank threaten an exchange rate peg? In this chapter, we show how a peg works—and how, if the central bank issues too much money to pay for bailouts and/or government deficits, it can place the peg at risk by causing a loss of reserves.

These findings show how crises are likely to happen in pairs, known as **twin crises**, or all three at once, known as **triple crises**, magnifying the costs of any one type of crisis.

Summary

Exchange rate crises have been a recurring fact of economic life for more than 100 years, and we have not seen the last of them. They can generate significant economic costs, and policymakers and scholars are seriously concerned about how to prevent them. What is it about fixed exchange rate regimes that makes them so fragile? Why and how do crises happen? And how can the risks of such crises be mitigated? These are the questions we address in the rest of this chapter.

2 How Pegs Work: The Mechanics of a Fixed Exchange Rate

To start, we must first understand how a pegged exchange rate works. Once we know what policymakers have to do to make a peg work, we will then be in a position to understand the factors that make a peg break.

To help us understand the economic mechanisms that operate in a fixed exchange rate system, we develop a simple model of what a central bank does. We then use the model to look at the demands placed on a central bank when a country adopts a fixed exchange rate.

Preliminaries and Assumptions

We consider a small open economy, the home country, in which the authorities are trying to peg to the currency of some foreign country. We make the following assumptions, some of which will be relaxed in later analyses:

- For convenience, and without implying that we are referring to any specific country, we assume that Home's currency is called the peso. The foreign currency to which Home pegs is the U.S. dollar. We assume the home authorities have been maintaining a fixed exchange rate, with E fixed at $\bar{E} = 1$ (one peso per U.S. dollar).

- The home central bank controls the peso money supply M by buying and selling assets in exchange for cash. The central bank trades only two types of assets: domestic bonds, often government bonds, denominated in local currency (pesos), and foreign assets, denominated in foreign currency (dollars).

- The home central bank intervenes in the foreign exchange (forex or FX) market to peg the exchange rate. It stands ready to buy and sell foreign exchange reserves at the fixed exchange rate $\bar{E}$. If it has no reserves, it cannot do this, the peg breaks, and the exchange rate is free to float.

- Unless stated otherwise, we assume that the peg is credible: everyone believes it will continue to hold. Uncovered interest parity then implies that the home and foreign interest rates are equal: $i = i^*$.

- We assume for now that Home's level of output or income is exogenous; that is, it is treated as given and denoted Y.

- There is a stable foreign price level $P^* = 1$ at all times. In the short run, Home's price level is sticky and fixed at a level $P = 1$. In the long run, if the exchange rate is kept fixed at 1, then Home's price level will be fixed at 1 as a result of purchasing power parity.

- As in previous chapters, Home's demand for real money balances M/P is determined by the level of output Y and the nominal interest rate i and takes the usual form, $M/P = L(i)Y$. The home money market must be in equilibrium, so money demand is always equal to money supply.

- We use the simplest model of a fixed exchange rate, where there is no financial system. The only money in Home is currency, also known as M0 or the monetary base. The monetary base (M0) and broad money (M1) are then the same, so the money supply is denoted M. This assumption allows us to examine the operation of a fixed exchange rate system by considering only the effects of the actions of a central bank.

- If there is no financial system in Home, we do not need to worry about the role of private banks in creating broad money through checking deposits, loans, and so on. A simple generalization would allow for banks by letting broad money be a constant multiple of the currency.[6] Still, the existence of a banking system is important, and even without formal theory, we will see later in the chapter how it can potentially affect the operation of a fixed exchange rate.

The Central Bank Balance Sheet

To understand how Home maintains the peg, we must understand how the home central bank manages its assets in relation to its sole liability, the money in circulation.

Suppose the central bank has purchased a quantity B pesos of domestic bonds. Because it is, in effect, loaning money to the domestic economy, the central bank's purchases are usually referred to as **domestic credit** created by the central bank. These purchases are also called the bank's *domestic assets*. Because the central bank purchases these assets with money, this purchase generates part of the money supply. The part of the home money supply created as a result of the central bank's issuing of domestic credit is denoted B.

Now suppose the central bank has also purchased a quantity R dollars of foreign exchange reserves, usually referred to as **reserves** or foreign assets, and that the exchange rate is pegged at a level $\bar{E} = 1$. The central bank also purchases its reserves with money. Thus, given that the exchange rate has always been 1 (by assumption), the part of the money supply created as a result of the central bank's purchase of foreign exchange reserves is $\bar{E}R = R$.[7]

Because the central bank holds only two types of assets, the last two expressions add up to the total money supply in the home economy:

$$\underbrace{M}_{\text{Money supply}} = \underbrace{B}_{\text{Domestic credit}} + \underbrace{R}_{\text{Reserves}} \tag{9-1}$$

This equation states that the money supply equals domestic credit plus reserves.

---

[6] Allowing that multiple (the money multiplier) to vary is also possible, but detailed analysis of that mechanism is beyond the scope of this chapter.

[7] In reality, central banks may have acquired reserves in the past at more or less favorable exchange rates, so the current peso value of reserves may be greater than or less than the peso value of the money spent to purchase them. In such cases, the central bank may have positive or negative net worth arising from capital gains or losses on previously purchased reserves (whether such gains are recorded on the central bank's balance sheet depends on its accounting practices and whether it marks reserves at book value or market value). We ignore this problem because it does not greatly affect the analysis that follows.

This expression is also useful when expressed not in levels but in changes:

$$\underbrace{\Delta M}_{\substack{\text{Change in} \\ \text{money supply}}} = \underbrace{\Delta B}_{\substack{\text{Change in} \\ \text{domestic credit}}} + \underbrace{\Delta R}_{\substack{\text{Change in} \\ \text{reserves}}} \tag{9-2}$$

This expression says that changes in the money supply must result from either changes in domestic credit or changes in reserves.

For example, if the central bank buys additional reserves $\Delta R = \$1,000$ dollars, then the money it spends adds $\Delta M = 1,000$ pesos to the money in circulation. If the central bank creates additional domestic credit of $\Delta B = 1,000$ pesos, then it buys 1,000 pesos of government debt, and this also adds $\Delta M = 1,000$ pesos to the money in circulation.

One common way of depicting Equation (9-1) is to write down each entry and construct the **central bank balance sheet**. The domestic debt and foreign reserves purchased by the central bank are its **assets**, $B + R$. The money supply issued by the central bank M makes up its **liabilities**.

Following is a hypothetical central bank balance sheet. The central bank has purchased 500 million pesos in domestic government bonds and 500 million pesos in foreign exchange reserves. The total money in circulation resulting from these purchases is 1,000 million pesos. As on any balance sheet, total assets equal total liabilities.

SIMPLIFIED CENTRAL BANK BALANCE SHEET (MILLIONS OF PESOS)			
Assets		**Liabilities**	
Reserves *R*	500	**Money supply *M***	1,000
Foreign assets (dollar reserves)		*Currency in circulation*	
Domestic credit *B*	500		
Domestic assets (peso bonds)			

Fixing, Floating, and the Role of Reserves

The crucial assumption in our simple model is that the central bank maintains the peg by intervening in the foreign exchange market by buying and selling reserves at the fixed exchange rate. In other words, our model supposes that if the central bank wants to fix the exchange rate, it must have some reserves it can trade to achieve that goal. We also assume, for now, that it holds reserves only for this purpose. Thus:

We assume that the exchange rate is fixed if and only if the central bank holds reserves; and the exchange rate is floating if and only if the central bank has no reserves.

These assumptions simplify our analysis by clarifying the relationship between the central bank balance sheet and the exchange rate regime. In reality, the relationship may be less clear, but the mechanisms in our model still play a dominant role.

For example, countries may adjust domestic credit as well as reserves, but they never try to maintain a peg by relying *solely* on domestic credit adjustments and zero reserves. Why? In the very short run, forex market conditions can change so quickly that only direct intervention in that market through reserve trading can maintain the peg. In addition, large adjustments to domestic credit may pose problems in an emerging market by causing instability in the bond market as the central bank buys or sells potentially large amounts of government bonds.

Countries can also float and yet keep some reserves on hand for reasons that we ignore in our model so as to keep it simple. They may want reserves on hand for future emergencies, such as war; or as a savings buffer in the event of a sudden stop to financial flows; or so they can peg at some later date.[8] Thus, the minimum level of reserves the

---

[8] Some of these functions may be provided by other reserve-holding agencies within the government (such as the treasury or a sovereign wealth fund). But often all reserves are held by the central bank, which frequently serves as the financial agent of the country.

central bank will tolerate on its balance sheet may not be at zero, but allowing for some other forms of reserves would not affect our analysis.

How Reserves Adjust to Maintain the Peg

We now turn to the key questions we need to answer to understand how a peg works. What level of reserves must the central bank have to maintain the peg? And how are reserves affected by changing macroeconomic conditions? If the central bank can maintain a level of reserves above zero, we know the peg will hold. If not, the peg breaks.

We can rearrange Equation (9-1) to solve for the level of reserves, with $R = M - B$. Why do we do that? It is important to remember that reserves are the unknown variable here: by assumption, reserves change as a result of the central bank's interventions in the forex market, which it must undertake to maintain the peg.

Because (in nominal terms) money supply equals money demand, given by $M = \bar{P}L(i)Y$, we can restate and rearrange Equation (9-1) to solve for the level of reserves:

$$\underbrace{R}_{\text{Reserves}} = \underbrace{\bar{P}L(i)Y}_{\text{Money demand}} - \underbrace{B}_{\text{Domestic credit}} \tag{9-3}$$

By substituting money demand for money supply, we can investigate how shocks to money demand (say, due to changes in output or the interest rate) or shocks to domestic credit affect the level of reserves.

We can solve this equation. Under our current assumptions, every element on the right-hand side is exogenous and known. The home price level is fixed, the output level is exogenous, interest parity tells us that the home interest rate equals the foreign interest rate, and we can treat domestic credit as predetermined by the central bank's purchases of domestic government debt.

Why is this answer for the reserve level correct and unique? Recall from the chapter on exchange rates in the short run how forex market equilibrium is attained. If the central bank bought more reserves than this, home money supply would expand and the home nominal interest rate would fall, the peso would depreciate, and the peg would break. To prevent this, the central bank would need to intervene in the forex market. The central bank would have to offset its initial purchase of reserves to keep the supply of pesos constant and keep the exchange rate holding steady. Similarly, if the central bank sold reserves for pesos, it would cause the peso to appreciate and the central bank would have to reverse course and buy back the reserves. The peg means that the central bank must keep the reserves at the level specified in Equation (9-3).

Graphical Analysis of the Central Bank Balance Sheet

Based on this toolkit, we show the mechanics of a pegged exchange rate in Figure 9-4, which illustrates the central bank balance sheet. On the horizontal axis is the money supply M and on the vertical axis is domestic credit B, both measured in pesos. Money demand is initially at the level M_1, and domestic credit is at B_1.

Two important lines appear in this figure. If reserves R are zero, then all of the money supply is due to domestic credit and Equation (9-1) tells us that $M = B$. The points where $M = B$ are on the 45-degree line. Points on this line, like point Z, correspond to cases in which the central bank balance sheet contains no reserves. By assumption, the country will then have a floating exchange rate, so we call this the **floating line**.

When the assets of the central bank include both reserves and domestic credit, then B and R are both greater than zero and they add up to M. The state of the central bank balance sheet must correspond to a point such as point 1 in this diagram,

FIGURE 9-4

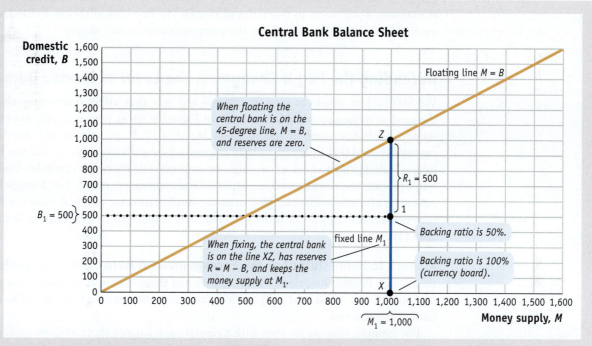

Central Bank Balance Sheet

Domestic credit, B

When floating the central bank is on the 45-degree line, M = B, and reserves are zero.

Floating line M = B

Z

$R_1 = 500$

$B_1 = 500$

1

When fixing, the central bank is on the line XZ, has reserves R = M − B, and keeps the money supply at M_1.

fixed line M_1

Backing ratio is 50%.

Backing ratio is 100% (currency board).

X

$M_1 = 1,000$

Money supply, M

The Central Bank Balance Sheet Diagram On the 45-degree line, reserves are at zero, and the money supply M equals domestic credit B. Variations in the money supply along this line would cause the exchange rate to float. There is a unique level of the money supply M_1 (here assumed to be 1,000) that ensures the exchange rate is at its chosen fixed value. To fix the money supply at this level, the central bank must choose a mix of assets on its balance sheet that corresponds to points on line XZ, points at which domestic credit B is less than money supply M. At point Z, reserves would be at zero; at point X, reserves would be 100% of the money supply. Any point in between on XZ is a feasible choice. At point 1, for example, domestic credit is $B_1 = 500$, reserves are $R_1 = 500$, and $B_1 + R_1 = M_1 = 1,000$.

somewhere on the vertical line XZ. We call this the **fixed line** because on this line the money supply is at the level M_1 necessary to maintain the peg.

If domestic credit is B_1, then reserves are $R_1 = M_1 − B_1$, the vertical (or horizontal) distance between point 1 and the 45-degree floating line. Hence, the distance to the floating line tells us how close to danger the peg is by showing how close the central bank is to the point at which reserves run out.[9] The point farthest from danger is X, on the horizontal axis. At this point, domestic credit B is zero and reserves R equal the money supply M. A fixed exchange rate that always operates with reserves equal to 100% of the money supply is known as a **currency board** system.[10]

To sum up: if the exchange rate is floating, the central bank balance sheet must correspond to points on the 45-degree floating line; if the exchange rate is fixed, the central bank balance sheet must correspond to points on the vertical fixed line.

---

[9] It is important to remember that under our assumptions, all other points in the figure (representing other balance sheet configurations) are ruled out. Floating means having zero reserves and being on the 45-degree line. Other points below the 45-degree line are ruled out because we assume that reserves imply pegging, and these other points would imply a higher or lower level of the money supply and hence an exchange rate other than the pegged rate $\bar{E}$. Points above the 45-degree line are also ruled out: they imply $B > M$ and $R < 0$, which is impossible because reserves cannot be negative.

[10] Strictly speaking, a currency board must satisfy certain other legal and procedural rules. It must own only low-risk interest-bearing foreign assets, not foreign liabilities. It must not perform any function except to exchange domestic currency for foreign currency at the fixed rate. It cannot lend to the domestic banking system to avert banking panics, for example. However, it may hold a bit more than 100% reserve backing, say, 105% to 110%, to guard against fluctuations in the value of its foreign assets.

The model is now complete, and with the aid of our key tools—the tables and graphs of the central bank balance sheet—we can see how a central bank that is trying to maintain a peg reacts to two types of shocks. We first look at shocks to the level of money demand and then shocks to the composition of money supply.

Defending the Peg I: Changes in the Level of Money Demand

We first look at shocks to money demand and how they affect reserves by altering the level of money supply M. As we saw in Equation (9-3), money supply is equal to money demand, as given by the equation $M = \overline{P}L(i)Y$. If the price level is fixed, then money demand will fluctuate only in response to shocks in output Y and the home interest rate i (which equals the foreign interest rate i^* if the peg is credible). For now, output is exogenous, and a rise in output will raise money demand. The foreign interest rate is also exogenous, and a rise in the foreign interest rate will raise the home interest rate and thus lower money demand. We assume all else is equal, so domestic credit is constant.

A Shock to Home Output or the Foreign Interest Rate
Suppose output falls or the foreign interest rate rises. We treat either of these events as an exogenous shock for now, all else equal, and suppose it decreases money demand by, say, 10% at the current interest rate.

For example, suppose we start with a central bank balance sheet as given earlier. Initially, money supply is $M_1 = 1,000$ million pesos. Suppose money demand then falls by 10%. This would lower money demand by 10% to $M_2 = 900$ million pesos. A fall in the demand for money would lower the interest rate in the money market and put depreciation pressure on the home currency. A floating exchange rate would allow the home currency to depreciate in these circumstances. To maintain the peg, the central bank must keep the interest rate unchanged. To achieve this goal, it must sell 100 million pesos ($100 million) of reserves, in exchange for cash, so that money supply contracts as much as money demand. The central bank's balance sheet will then be as follows:

**SIMPLIFIED CENTRAL BANK BALANCE SHEET AFTER MONEY DEMAND FALLS
(MILLIONS OF PESOS)**

Assets		Liabilities	
Reserves R	400	**Money supply M**	900
Foreign assets (dollar reserves)		Currency in circulation	
Domestic credit B	500		
Domestic assets (peso bonds)			

In Figure 9-5, we can trace the implications of the shock in a graph. The demand for money has fallen, so the *fixed line* is still vertical, but it shifts from the initial money demand level $M_1 = 1,000$ million pesos to a new lower level $M_2 = 900$ million pesos. There is no change to domestic credit, so it remains constant at the level $B_1 = 500$ million pesos. Thus, the central bank's balance sheet position shifts from point 1 to point 2. This shift takes the balance sheet position closer to the floating line in the diagram: reserves are falling. At point 2, reserves have fallen from $R_1 = \$500$ million to $R_2 = \$400$ million, as shown.

Figure 9-5 also shows what would happen with the opposite shock. If money demand increased by 10% from the initial money demand level $M_1 = 1,000$ million pesos to a new higher level $M_3 = 1,100$ million pesos, the central bank would need to prevent an interest rate rise and an appreciation by expanding the money supply by 100 million pesos. The central bank would need to intervene and increase the money

FIGURE 9-5

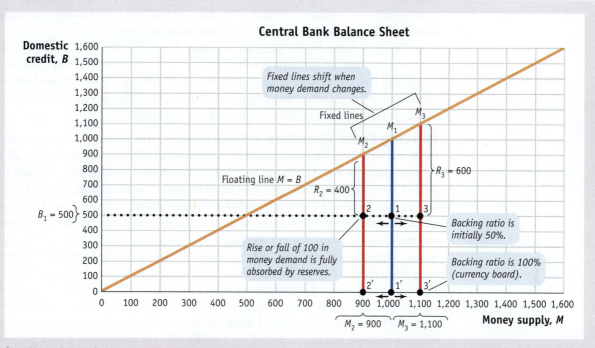

Shocks to Money Demand If money demand falls, interest rates tend to fall, leading to pressure for an exchange rate to depreciate. To prevent this, the central bank must intervene in the forex market and defend the peg by selling reserves, hence lowering the money supply to keep the interest rate fixed and thus ensuring that money supply equals money demand. As shown here, with the exchange rate fixed at 1 peso per dollar, we suppose that the money supply declines from $M_1 = 1,000$ million pesos to $M_2 = 900$ million pesos. If domestic credit is unchanged at $B_1 = 500$, the change in the central bank balance sheet is shown by a move from point 1 to point 2, and reserves absorb the money demand shock by falling from $R_1 = \$500$ million to $R_2 = \$400$ million. An opposite positive shock is shown by the move from point 1 to point 3, where $M_3 = 1,100$ million pesos and $R_3 = \$600$ million. In a currency board system, a country maintaining 100% reserves will be on the horizontal axis with zero domestic credit, $B = 0$. A currency board adjusts to money demand shocks by moving from point 1' to points 2' or 3'.

supply by purchasing $100 million of reserves. The central bank's balance sheet position would then shift from point 1 to point 3, moving away from the floating line, with reserves rising from $R_1 = 500$ million pesos to $R_3 = 600$ million pesos.

Equation (9-3) confirms these outcomes as a general result when domestic credit is constant (at B_1 in our example). We know that if the change in domestic credit is zero, $\Delta B = 0$, then any change in money supply must equal the change in reserves, $\Delta R = \Delta M$. This is also clear from Equation (9-2).

We have shown the following: *holding domestic credit constant, a change in money demand leads to an equal change in reserves.*

The Importance of the Backing Ratio In the first example above, money demand and money supply fell by 10% from 1,000 to 900, but reserves fell by 20% from 500 to 400. The proportional fall in reserves was greater than the proportional fall in money because reserves R were initially only 500 and just a fraction (one-half) of the money supply M, which was 1,000. When money demand fell by 100, reserves had to absorb all of the change, with domestic credit unchanged.

The ratio R/M is called the **backing ratio**, and it indicates the fraction of the money supply that is backed by reserves on the central bank balance sheet. It, therefore, tells us the size of the maximum negative money demand shock that the regime can withstand without running out of reserves *if* domestic credit remains unchanged. In our example, the backing ratio was 0.5 or 50% (reserves were 500 and money supply 1,000 initially), so the central bank could absorb up to a 50% decline in the money supply before all of its reserves run out. Because reserves were only 500 to start with, a shock of −500 to money demand would cause reserves to just run out.

In general, *for a given size of a shock to money demand, a higher backing ratio will better insulate an economy against running out of reserves, all else equal.*[11]

In Figure 9-5, the higher the backing ratio, the higher the level of reserves R and the lower the level of domestic credit B, for a given level of money supply M. In other words, the central bank balance sheet position on this figure would be closer to the horizontal axis and farther away from the floating line. This is a graphical illustration of the idea that a higher backing ratio makes a peg safer.

Currency Board Operation A 100% backing ratio puts the country exactly on the horizontal axis. This maximum backing ratio of 100% is maintained at all times by a currency board. In Figure 9-5, a currency board would start at point 1′, not point 1. Because reserves would then be 1,000 to start with, a shock of up to −1,000 to money demand could be accommodated without reserves running out. In the face of smaller shocks to money demand such as we have considered, of plus or minus 100, the central bank balance sheet would move to points 2′ or 3′, with reserves equal to money supply equal to money demand equal to 900 or 1,100. These points are as far away from the 45-degree floating line as one can get in this diagram, and they show how a currency board keeps reserves at a maximum 100%. A currency board can be thought of as the safest configuration of the central bank's balance sheet because with 100% backing, the central bank can cope with *any* shock to money demand without running out of reserves. Currency boards are considered a *hard peg* because their high backing ratio ought to confer on them greater resilience in the face of money demand shocks.

Why Does the Level of Money Demand Fluctuate? Our result tells us that to maintain the fixed exchange rate, the central bank must have enough reserves to endure a money demand shock without running out. A shock to money demand is not under the control of the authorities, but they must respond to it. Thus, it is important for policymakers to understand the sources and likely magnitudes of such shocks. Under our assumptions, money demand shocks originate either in shocks to home output Y or the foreign interest rate i^* (because under a credible peg $i = i^*$).

We have studied output fluctuations in earlier chapters, and one thing we observed was that output tends to be much more volatile in emerging markets and developing countries. Thus, the prudent level of reserves is likely to be much higher in these countries. Volatility in foreign interest rates can also be important, whether in U.S. dollars or in other currencies that form the base for pegs.

However, we must also confront a new possibility—that the peg is not fully credible and that simple interest parity fails to hold. In this case, the home interest rate will no longer equal the foreign interest rate, and additional disturbances to home money demand can be caused by the spread between the two. As we now see, this is a vital step toward understanding crises in emerging markets and developing countries.

---

[11] To see this, recall that the change in money supply equals the change in reserves, $\Delta M = \Delta R$; hence, for a given *proportional* size of money demand shock $\Delta M / M$, the proportional loss in reserves $\Delta R / R$ can be computed as

$$\% \text{ Change in reserves} = \frac{\Delta R}{R} = \frac{\Delta M}{R} = \frac{\Delta M / M}{R / M} = \frac{\% \text{ Change in money supply}}{\text{Backing ratio}}$$

The higher the backing ratio, the smaller the proportional loss of reserves $\Delta R / R$ for a given size of money demand shock $\Delta M / M$. In our example, the backing ratio was 0.5, so a 10% drop in money supply implied a 10%/0.5 = 20% drop in reserves.

APPLICATION

Risk Premiums in Advanced and Emerging Markets

So far in the book, we have assumed that uncovered interest parity (UIP) requires that the domestic return (the interest rate on home bank deposits) equals the foreign interest rate plus the expected rate of depreciation of the home currency. However, an important extension of UIP needs to be made when additional risks affect home bank deposits: a **risk premium** is then added to the foreign interest rate to compensate investors for the perceived risk of holding a home domestic currency deposit. This perceived risk is due to an aversion to exchange rate risk or a concern about default risk:

$$
\underbrace{i}_{\substack{\text{Peso} \\ \text{interest} \\ \text{rate}}} = \underbrace{i^*}_{\substack{\text{Dollar} \\ \text{interest} \\ \text{rate}}} + \underbrace{\frac{\Delta E^e_{\text{peso/\$}}}{E_{\text{peso/\$}}}}_{\substack{\text{Expected rate of} \\ \text{depreciation} \\ \text{of the peso}}} + \begin{bmatrix} \text{Exchange rate} \\ \text{risk premium} \end{bmatrix} + \begin{bmatrix} \text{Default} \\ \text{risk premium} \end{bmatrix} \quad (9\text{-}4)
$$

Interest rate spread
(equal to zero if peg is credible and there are no risk premiums)

The left-hand side is still the domestic return, but the right-hand side is now a *risk-adjusted foreign return*. The final three terms are the difference between home and foreign interest rates, and their sum total is known as the **interest rate spread**. What causes these spreads?

The first part of the interest rate spread is the **currency premium**:

$$
\text{Currency premium} = \frac{\Delta E^e_{\text{peso/\$}}}{E_{\text{peso/\$}}} + \begin{bmatrix} \text{Exchange rate} \\ \text{risk premium} \end{bmatrix}
$$

The currency premium should be zero for a credibly pegged exchange rate: the peso is not expected to change in value relative to the dollar. But if a peg is not credible, and investors suspect that the peg may break, there could be a premium reflecting both the size of the expected depreciation and the currency's perceived riskiness. The currency premium therefore reflects the credibility of monetary policy.

The second part of the interest rate spread is known as the **country premium**:

$$
\text{Country premium} = \begin{bmatrix} \text{Default} \\ \text{risk premium} \end{bmatrix}
$$

The country premium is compensation for perceived default risk. It will be greater than zero if investors suspect a risk of losses when they attempt to convert a home (peso) asset back to foreign currency (dollars) in the future. Such a loss might occur because of expropriation, bank failure, surprise taxation, delays, capital controls, other regulations, and so on. The country premium therefore reflects the credibility of property rights.

Why does all this matter? Fluctuations in currency and country premiums have the same effect in Equation (9-4) as fluctuations in the foreign interest rate i^*. Sudden increases in the interest rate spread raise the risk-adjusted foreign return and imply sudden increases in the domestic return, here given by the (peso) interest rate i. In some countries, these spreads can be large and volatile—and even more volatile than the foreign interest rate.

Figure 9-6 presents interest rate spreads for two countries with fixed exchange rates. Panel (a) shows an advanced country, Denmark, which has pegged to the euro since 1999; panel (b) shows an emerging market, Argentina, which pegged to the dollar from 1991 to 2001.

In Denmark, there was some spread in the early years of the euro from 1999 to 2002 (up to about 0.5% per year) and again some wider spreads in the 2009–10 crisis period,

FIGURE 9-6

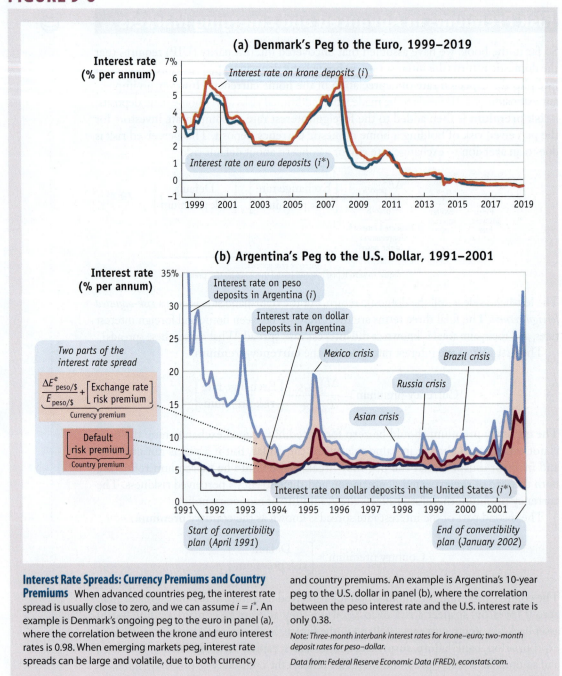

(a) Denmark's Peg to the Euro, 1999–2019

Interest rate
(% per annum)

Interest rate on krone deposits (*i*)

Interest rate on euro deposits (*i**)

(b) Argentina's Peg to the U.S. Dollar, 1991–2001

Interest rate
(% per annum)

Interest rate on peso
deposits in Argentina (*i*)

Interest rate on dollar
deposits in Argentina

Mexico crisis

Brazil crisis

Russia crisis

Asian crisis

Two parts of the
interest rate spread

$$\underbrace{\frac{\Delta E^e_{peso/\$}}{E_{peso/\$}} + \left[\begin{array}{c} \text{Exchange rate} \\ \text{risk premium} \end{array}\right]}_{\text{Currency premium}}$$

$$\underbrace{\left[\begin{array}{c} \text{Default} \\ \text{risk premium} \end{array}\right]}_{\text{Country premium}}$$

Interest rate on dollar deposits in the United States (*i**)

Start of convertibility
plan (April 1991)

End of convertibility
plan (January 2002)

Interest Rate Spreads: Currency Premiums and Country Premiums When advanced countries peg, the interest rate spread is usually close to zero, and we can assume *i* = *i**. An example is Denmark's ongoing peg to the euro in panel (a), where the correlation between the krone and euro interest rates is 0.98. When emerging markets peg, interest rate spreads can be large and volatile, due to both currency and country premiums. An example is Argentina's 10-year peg to the U.S. dollar in panel (b), where the correlation between the peso interest rate and the U.S. interest rate is only 0.38.

Note: Three-month interbank interest rates for krone–euro; two-month deposit rates for peso–dollar.

Data from: Federal Reserve Economic Data (FRED), econstats.com.

perhaps reflecting a worry that the krone–euro peg might not endure. Otherwise the spread was almost imperceptible (less than 0.1% per year). Overall, the simple correlation between the krone interest rate and the euro interest rate was very high, equal to 0.98. Investors came to see the peg as credible, eliminating the currency premium almost entirely. They also had no fear of default risk if they invested in Denmark, eliminating the country premium almost entirely. Thus one could assume at most times that *i* was approximately equal to *i** with no spread.

In Argentina the spreads were large: note the bigger vertical scale in panel (b). The annual peso and dollar interest rates were far apart, often differing by 2 or 3 percentage points and sometimes differing by more than 10 percentage points. Most striking is that changes in the spread were usually more important in determining the Argentine interest rate than were changes in the actual foreign (U.S. dollar) interest rate. Overall, the correlation between the peso interest rate i and the dollar interest rate i^* was low, equal to only 0.38. What was going on?

We can separately track currency risk and country risk because Argentine banks offered interest-bearing bank deposits denominated in both U.S. dollars and Argentine pesos. The lower two lines in panel (b) show the interest rate on U.S. dollar deposits in the United States (i^*) and the interest rate on U.S. dollar deposits in Argentina. Because the rates are expressed in the same currency, the difference between these two interest rates cannot be the result of a currency premium. It represents a pure measure of country premium: investors required a higher interest rate on dollar deposits in Argentina than on dollar deposits in the United States because they perceived that Argentine deposits might be subject to a default risk. (Investors were eventually proved right: in the 2001–02 crisis, many Argentine banks faced insolvency, some were closed for a time, capital controls were imposed at the border, and a "pesification" law turned many dollar assets into peso assets ex post, a form of expropriation and a contractual default.)

The upper line in panel (b) shows the interest rate on peso deposits in Argentina (i), which is even higher than the interest rate on U.S. dollar deposits in Argentina. Because these are interest rates on bank deposits in the same country, the difference between these two rates cannot be due to a country premium. It represents a pure measure of the currency premium. Investors required a higher interest rate on peso deposits in Argentina than on dollar deposits in Argentina because they perceived that peso deposits might be subject to a risk of depreciation, that is, a collapse of the peg. (Investors were eventually proved right again: in the 2001–02 crisis, the peso depreciated by 75% from $1 to the peso to about $0.25 to the peso, or four pesos per U.S. dollar.)

Summary Pegs in emerging markets are different from those in advanced countries. Because of fluctuations in interest rate spreads, they are subject to even greater interest rate shocks than the pegs of advanced countries, as a result of **credibility** problems. Currency premiums may fluctuate due to changes in investors' beliefs about the durability of the peg, a problem of the credibility of monetary policy. Country premiums may fluctuate due to changes in investors' beliefs about the security of their investments, a problem of the credibility of property rights.

Still, not every movement in emerging market spreads is driven by economic fundamentals. For example, in Argentina the figure shows that investors revised their risk premiums sharply upward when other emerging market countries were experiencing crises in the 1990s: Mexico in 1994, Asia in 1997, and later Russia and Brazil. With the exception of Brazil (a major trade partner for Argentina), there were no major changes in Argentine fundamentals during these crises. Thus, many economists consider this to be evidence of **contagion** in global capital markets, possibly even a sign of market inefficiency or irrationality, where crises in some parts of the global capital markets trigger adverse changes in market sentiment in faraway places.

APPLICATION

The Argentine Convertibility Plan Before the Tequila Crisis

The central bank balance sheet diagram helps us to see how a central bank manages a fixed exchange rate and what adjustments it needs to make in response to a shock in money demand.

FIGURE 9-7

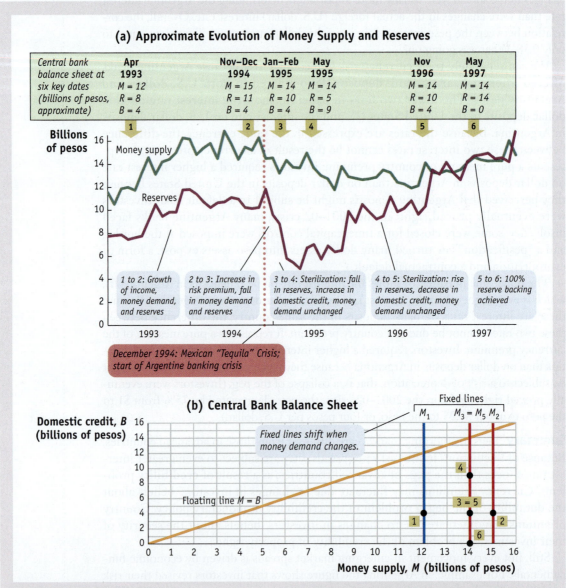

(a) Approximate Evolution of Money Supply and Reserves

Central bank balance sheet at six key dates (billions of pesos, approximate)	Apr 1993	Nov–Dec 1994	Jan–Feb 1995	May 1995	Nov 1996	May 1997
	M = 12	M = 15	M = 14	M = 14	M = 14	M = 14
	R = 8	R = 11	R = 10	R = 5	R = 10	R = 14
	B = 4	B = 4	B = 4	B = 9	B = 4	B = 0

1 to 2: Growth of income, money demand, and reserves

2 to 3: Increase in risk premium, fall in money demand and reserves

3 to 4: Sterilization: fall in reserves, increase in domestic credit, money demand unchanged

4 to 5: Sterilization: rise in reserves, decrease in domestic credit, money demand unchanged

5 to 6: 100% reserve backing achieved

December 1994: Mexican "Tequila" Crisis; start of Argentine banking crisis

(b) Central Bank Balance Sheet

Fixed lines shift when money demand changes.

Floating line M = B

Argentina's Central Bank Operations, 1993–97 In this period, one peso was worth one U.S. dollar. Panel (a) shows the money supply and reserves. The difference between the two is domestic credit. Six key dates are highlighted before, during, and after the Mexican Tequila Crisis. In panel (b), the balance sheet of the central bank at these key dates is shown. Prior to the crisis, domestic credit was essentially unchanged, and reserves grew from 8 billion to 11 billion pesos as money demand grew from M_1 to M_2 in line with rapid growth in incomes (move from point 1 to 2). After the crisis hit in December 1994, interest rate spreads widened, money demand fell from M_2 to M_3, but domestic credit stood still (to point 3) and $1 billion in reserves were lost. In 1995 there was a run on banks and on the currency, and the central bank sterilized by expanding domestic credit by 5 billion pesos and selling $5 billion of reserves as money demand remained constant (to point 4). Reserves reached a low level of $5 billion. By 1996 the crisis had passed and the central bank now replenished its reserves, reversing the earlier sterilization. Domestic credit fell by 5 billion pesos and reserves increased by $5 billion (to point 5, same as point 3). Further sterilized purchases of $4 billion of reserves brought the backing ratio up to 100% in 1997 (to point 6).

Data from: IMF, International Financial Statistics. Data compiled by Kurt Schuler.

We can put this analysis to use with a concrete example: the operation of Argentina's fixed exchange rate system (known as the Convertibility Plan), which began in 1991 and ended in 2002. In this plan, a peg was maintained as one peso per dollar. With the aid of Figure 9-7, we focus first on how the central bank managed its balance sheet during an early phase of the plan, in 1993 and 1994. (We will discuss later years shortly.)

Money Demand Shocks, 1993–94 The evolution of money supply and reserves is shown in panel (a). From point 1 to point 2 (April 1993 to November/December 1994), all was going well. Argentina had recovered from its hyperinflation in 1989 to 1990, prices were stable, the economy was growing, and so was money demand. Because money demand must equal money supply, the central bank had to increase the money supply. The central bank kept domestic credit more or less unchanged in this period at 4 billion pesos, so reserves had to expand (from 8 billion to 11 billion pesos) as the base money supply expanded (from 12 billion to 15 billion pesos). The backing ratio rose from about 67% (8/12) to about 73% (11/15). In the central bank balance sheet diagram in panel (b), this change is shown by the horizontal move from point 1 to point 2 as the money demand shock causes the fixed line to shift out from M_1 to M_2, so that higher levels of base money supply are now consistent with the peg.

Then an unexpected nasty shock happened: a risk premium shock occurred as a result of the so-called Tequila Crisis in Mexico in December 1994. Interest rate spreads widened for Argentina because of currency and country premiums, raising the home interest rate. Argentina's money demand fell. In panel (a), from point 2 to point 3 (November/December 1994 to January/February 1995), base money supply contracted by 1 billion pesos, and this was absorbed almost entirely by a contraction in reserves from 11 billion to 10 billion pesos. The backing ratio fell to about 71% (10/14). In panel (b), this change is shown by the horizontal move from point 2 to point 3 as the money demand shock causes the fixed line to shift in from M_2 to M_3.

To Be Continued Through all of these events, the backing ratio remained high and domestic credit remained roughly steady at around 4 billion pesos, corresponding to our model's assumptions so far. People wanted to swap some pesos for dollars, but nothing catastrophic had happened. However, this was about to change. The shock to Argentina's interest rate proved damaging to the real economy and especially the banking sector. Argentines also became nervous about holding pesos. Foreigners stopped lending to Argentina as the economic situation looked riskier. The central bank stepped in to provide assistance to the ailing banks. But we have yet to work out how a central bank can do this and still maintain a peg. After we complete that task, we will return to the story and see how Argentina managed to survive the Tequila Crisis.

Defending the Peg II: Changes in the Composition of Money Supply

So far we have examined changes to the level of money demand. We have assumed that the central bank's policy toward domestic credit was *passive*, and so B has been held constant up to now. In contrast, we now study shocks to domestic credit B, all else equal. To isolate the effects of changes in domestic credit, we assume that money demand is constant.

If money demand is constant, then so is money supply. Therefore, the key lesson of this section will be that, on its own, a change in domestic credit cannot affect the *level* of the money supply; it can only affect the *composition* in terms of domestic credit and reserves.

A Shock to Domestic Credit Suppose that the central bank increases domestic credit by an amount $\Delta B > 0$ from B_1 to B_2. This increase could be the result of an *open market operation* by the bank's bond trading desk to purchase bonds from private parties. Or it could be the result of a demand by the country's economics ministry that the bank directly finance government borrowing. For now we will not concern ourselves with the cause of this policy decision, and will not discuss whether it makes any sense. We just ask what implications it has for a central bank trying to maintain a peg, all else equal. We assume that domestic output and the foreign interest rate are unchanged.

For example, suppose we start with a central bank balance sheet with money supply at its initial level of $M_1 = 1,000$ million pesos. The bank then expands domestic credit from 500 to 600 million pesos by buying $\Delta B = 100$ million of peso bonds. All else equal, this action puts more money in circulation, which lowers the interest rate in the money market and puts depreciation pressure on the exchange rate. A floating rate would depreciate in these circumstances. To defend the peg, the central bank must sell enough reserves to keep the interest rate unchanged. To achieve that, it must sell 100 million pesos ($100 million) of reserves, in exchange for cash, so that the money supply remains unchanged. The central bank's balance sheet will then be as follows:

SIMPLIFIED CENTRAL BANK BALANCE SHEET AFTER EXPANSION OF DOMESTIC CREDIT (MILLIONS OF PESOS)			
Assets		**Liabilities**	
Reserves R	400	**Money supply M**	1,000
Foreign assets (dollar reserves)		Money in circulation	
Domestic credit B	600		
Domestic assets (peso bonds)			

What is the end result? Domestic credit B changes by +100 million pesos (rising to 600 million pesos), foreign exchange reserves R change by −100 million pesos (falling to 400 million pesos), and the money supply M remains unchanged (at 1,000 million pesos).

The bond purchases expand domestic credit but also cause the central bank to lose reserves as it is forced to intervene in the forex market. There is no change in monetary policy as measured by home money supply (or interest rates) because the sale and purchase actions by the central bank offset each other exactly. This type of central bank action is called **sterilization**, a sterilized intervention, or a sterilized sale of reserves.

In Figure 9-8, we show the implications of sterilization policies. On the vertical axis, domestic credit rises from B_1 to B_2. The balance sheet position of the central bank therefore shifts up the fixed line from point 1 to point 2. Reserves fall by ΔB from the initial level $R_1 = \$500$ million to a new level $R_2 = \$400$ million. The central bank has moved closer to point Z, the danger point of zero reserves on the 45-degree line. The backing ratio falls from 50% to 40%.

Figure 9-8 also shows what would happen with the opposite shock. If domestic credit fell by 100 million pesos to 400 million pesos at B_3, with an unchanged money demand, then reserves would rise by $100 million. The central bank's balance sheet ends up at point 3. Reserves rise from $R_1 = \$500$ million to $R_3 = \$600$ million. The backing ratio now rises from 50% to 60%.

We also see in Figure 9-8 that sterilization is impossible in the case of a currency board because a currency board requires that domestic credit always be zero and that reserves be 100% of the money supply at all times.

Equation (9-3) confirms this as a general result. We know that if the change in money demand is zero, then so is the change in money supply, $\Delta M = 0$; hence, the change in domestic credit, $\Delta B > 0$, must be offset by an equal and opposite change in reserves, $\Delta R = -\Delta B < 0$. This is also clear from Equation (9-2).

We have shown the following: *holding money demand constant, a change in domestic credit leads to an equal and opposite change in reserves, which is called a sterilization.*

Why Does the Composition of the Money Supply Fluctuate?   Our model tells us that sterilization has no effect on the level of money supply and hence no effect on interest rates and the rest of the economy. This prompts a question: if sterilization has no effect on these variables, why would central banks bother to do it? In the case of buying and selling government bonds, which is the predominant form of domestic credit, the effects are controversial but are generally thought to be small. The only

FIGURE 9-8

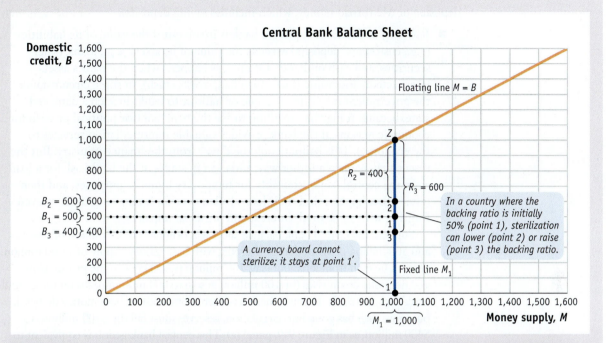

Sterilization If domestic credit rises, the money supply rises, all else equal, and interest rates tend to fall, putting pressure on the exchange rate to depreciate. To prevent this depreciation, keep the peg, and stay on the fixed line, the central bank must intervene and defend the peg by selling reserves to keep the money supply fixed. As shown here, with the exchange rate fixed at 1 peso per dollar, we suppose that the money supply is $M_1 = 1,000$ million pesos. If domestic credit increases from $B_1 = 500$ million pesos to $B_2 = 600$ million pesos, the central bank balance sheet moves from point 1 to point 2, and reserves fall from $R_1 = \$500$ million to $R_2 = \$400$ million. An opposite shock is shown by the move from point 1 to point 3, where $B_3 = 400$ million pesos and $R_3 = \$600$ million. If the country maintains 100% reserves, it has to stay at point 1′: a currency board cannot engage in sterilization.

possible effect would be indirect, via portfolio changes in the bond market. If the central bank absorbs some government debt, it leaves less peso debt for the private sector to hold, and this could change the risk premium on the domestic interest rate. But evidence for that type of effect is rather weak.[12]

However, there is another type of domestic credit that can have very important effects on the wider economy. This is domestic credit caused by a decision by the central bank to lend to private commercial banks in difficulty. Here, the central bank would be fulfilling one of its traditional responsibilities as the protector of the domestic financial system. This action has real effects because a domestic banking crisis, if allowed to happen, can cause serious economic harm by damaging the economy's payments system and credit markets.

In theory, when it comes to banks that are having difficulties, economists distinguish between banks that are illiquid and those that are insolvent. Let's see how loans from the central bank to private commercial banks affect the central bank balance

---

[12] This argument (which applies also to sterilized interventions under floating rates, which do not alter the level of the money supply) supposes that the central bank trades a large enough amount of the country's government debt that it can affect the default premium. If that were true, then an expansion of domestic credit would lower the amount of government debt that the private sector would have to hold and might convince private investors to tolerate a lower risk premium. This might then filter through into long- and short-term interest rates in the home economy, with beneficial effects. However, while this line of argument is true in theory, the evidence is often weak and inconsistent, and a source of ongoing controversy. See Maurice Obstfeld, 1982, "Can We Sterilize? Theory and Evidence," *American Economic Review*, 72(2), 45–50; Lucio Sarno and Mark P. Taylor, 2001, "Official Intervention in the Foreign Exchange Market: Is It Effective and, If So, How Does It Work?" *Journal of Economic Literature*, 39(3), 839–868.

sheet for these two cases. Note that for these cases we can no longer assume that M0 (currency or base money) is the same as M1 (narrow money, which includes checking deposits) or M2 (broad money, which includes saving deposits).

■ *Insolvency and bailouts.* A private bank is **insolvent** if the value of its liabilities (e.g., customers' deposits) exceeds the value of its assets (e.g., loans, other securities, and cash on hand). Often, this happens when the bank's assets unexpectedly lose value (loans turn bad, stocks crash). In some circumstances, the government may offer a rescue or **bailout** to banks in such a damaged state, because it may be unwilling to see the bank fail (for political or even for economic reasons, if the bank provides valuable intermediation services to the economy). This bailout could be direct from the finance ministry. But the rescue may happen another way, and even in stages, if the banks ask for a loan from the central bank ostensibly for temporary liquidity purposes, and then (after losses appear) find their loans rolled over for a very long time, or even forgiven with some or all interest and principal unpaid.

Suppose the central bank balance sheet was originally $500 million of reserves and 500 million pesos of domestic credit, with base money supply of 1,000 million pesos. The cash from a bailout (say, 100 million pesos) goes to the private bank and domestic credit rises (by 100 million pesos) to 600 million pesos on the central bank's balance sheet. Because there has been no increase in base money demand, but more cash has gone into circulation, reserves must fall (by $100 million) to $400 million, as in Figure 9-9, panel (a). This central bank action is equivalent to the central bank buying bonds worth 100 million pesos directly from the government (a sterilization, as we saw previously) and the government then bailing out the private bank with the proceeds. Bottom line: bailouts are very risky for the central bank because they cause reserves to drain, endangering the peg.

■ *Illiquidity and bank runs.* A private bank may be solvent, but it can still be **illiquid**: it holds some cash, but its loans cannot be sold (liquidated) quickly at a high price and depositors can withdraw at any time. If too many depositors attempt to withdraw their funds at once, the bank is in trouble if it has insufficient cash on hand: this is known as a **bank run**. In this situation, the central bank may lend money to commercial banks that are running out of cash. Suppose, for example, the monetary base is M0 and equals 1,000 million pesos as in the last example, but broad money is M2 (including bank deposits) and equals 2,000 million pesos. The difference of 1,000 million pesos is the value of bank checking and saving deposits (i.e., private bank–created money). If there is a run at a bank, and customers rush in and demand 100 million pesos in cash, the bank has to borrow 100 million pesos from somewhere to satisfy them. We suppose the bank is at zero cash or at the lowest level permitted by regulation—so it is constrained. Because every other bank is likewise constrained, fearful of lending to the troubled bank, or also experiencing a run, the problem cannot be solved by interbank lending. The central bank is then the **lender of last resort**. Crucially, in addition to the central bank expanding domestic credit (by 100 million pesos) to 600 million pesos, base money demand (demand for cash) also rises (by 100 million pesos) to 1,100 million pesos. Thus, we have a combination of the two types of shocks we have studied: an increase in domestic credit *and* an increase in (base) money demand, as shown in Figure 9-9, panel (b). Reserves do not change; they stay at $500 million. Why? The central bank is satisfying a demand for more cash, which absorbs the expansion of domestic credit. The situation will revert to normal when the run ends and the private bank pays back its loan to the central bank. Bottom line: providing liquidity to solvent banks is not risky for the central bank because there is no reserve drain to threaten the peg.

FIGURE 9-9

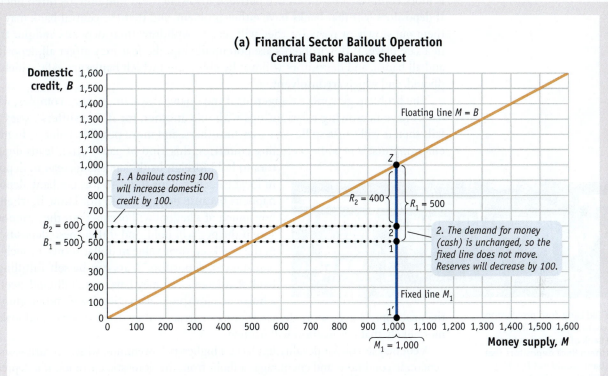

(a) Financial Sector Bailout Operation
Central Bank Balance Sheet

1. A bailout costing 100 will increase domestic credit by 100.

2. The demand for money (cash) is unchanged, so the fixed line does not move. Reserves will decrease by 100.

Floating line $M = B$

$R_2 = 400$

$R_1 = 500$

$B_2 = 600$
$B_1 = 500$

Fixed line M_1

$M_1 = 1,000$

Money supply, M

Domestic credit, B

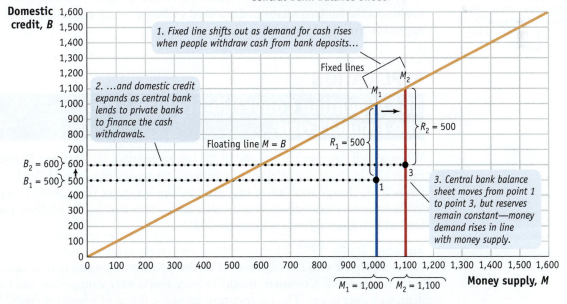

(b) Lender of Last Resort Operation
Central Bank Balance Sheet

1. Fixed line shifts out as demand for cash rises when people withdraw cash from bank deposits...

2. ...and domestic credit expands as central bank lends to private banks to finance the cash withdrawals.

Fixed lines

M_2

M_1

$R_2 = 500$

Floating line $M = B$

$R_1 = 500$

$B_2 = 600$
$B_1 = 500$

3. Central bank balance sheet moves from point 1 to point 3, but reserves remain constant—money demand rises in line with money supply.

$M_1 = 1,000$ $M_2 = 1,100$

Money supply, M

Domestic credit, B

The Central Bank and the Financial Sector In panel (a), a bailout occurs when the central bank prints money and buys domestic assets—the bad assets of insolvent private banks. There is no change in demand for base money (cash), so the expansion of domestic credit leads to a decrease of reserves. In panel (b), private bank depositors want to shift from holding deposits to holding cash. If the central bank acts as a lender of last resort and temporarily lends the needed cash to illiquid private banks, both the demand and supply of base money (cash) rise, so the level of reserves is unchanged.

This simple classification of banks as insolvent or illiquid is useful, but the reality is more complex. The difference between insolvency and illiquidity is often unclear. If depositors fear that banks have either problem, and that the central bank may bail them out slowly or partially, they will seek to withdraw their deposits and put them in a safe place. If the problems are potentially big, the fear may affect all depositors and all banks, and depositors will not be able to tell which banks are safe, which are illiquid, and which are insolvent.

The problem gets more dangerous if the financial system is more complex, when banks have borrowing relationships with one another, for if one suffers losses and fails then it will cause spillover losses for others, and more possible failures. In many emerging markets and developing countries, this kind of panic often leads depositors to hold foreign bank deposits instead of deposits in local currency. This flight to foreign bank deposits happens because depositors do not know if, when, or how much of a bailout will occur. Thus they cannot be sure if the peg will hold, and if their peso deposits will in the end keep their value in dollar terms. In such circumstances, depositors' fears can be self-fulfilling. A bank that faces a run may have to sell illiquid assets in a hurry at a low price, damaging itself and magnifying the problem. As depositors demand foreign currency, they drain reserves and make it more likely that devaluation will happen.

The Old Lady doth protest too much: In September 2007, the Bank of England assured Northern Rock depositors that the bank would not fail. The bank's balance sheet was widely believed to be healthy (solvent), but it was short of cash to fund mortgages (illiquid). Despite official assurances, there was a run on the bank because depositors preferred cash in hand to government promises.

A country at risk for devaluation faces a higher-risk premium, which in turn worsens economic conditions and encourages a flight from the domestic currency. If a depreciation happens, then banks and firms that have foreign currency liabilities will be in even worse shape, so running looks even better. And so the vicious circle continues.

To get a sense of the challenges faced by a central bank when confronted with difficulties in the banking sector under a fixed exchange rate, let us return to the case of Argentina after the Mexican Tequila Crisis.

APPLICATION

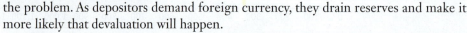

The Argentine Convertibility Plan After the Tequila Crisis

When we left Argentina at the end of the last application, the Mexican Tequila Crisis had just hit in December 1994, and Argentina's base money supply had fallen by a billion pesos. This change was shown in Figure 9-7 by the move from point 2 to point 3. With domestic credit steady, this meant that reserves also fell by a billion pesos to a level of 10 billion in January/February 1995.

Banking Crisis, 1995 Higher interest rates were reducing output as the private sector struggled with the high cost of credit. The government's budget deficit grew as tax revenues fell. Commercial bank balance sheets were damaged by bad loans and depressed asset prices. The country now faced the threat of a banking crisis.[13]

The central bank began extending loans, even to banks of questionable solvency. The loans became more abundant and for a much longer duration. Concerns grew that the

---

[13] See Laura D'Amato, Elena Grubisic, and Andrew Powell, 1997, "Contagion, Bank Fundamentals or Macroeconomic Shock? An Empirical Analysis of the Argentine 1995 Banking Problems," Working Paper No. 2, Central Bank of Argentina, Buenos Aires; Charles W. Calomiris and Andrew Powell, 2001, "Can Emerging Market Bank Regulators Establish Credible Discipline? The Case of Argentina, 1992–1999," in *Prudential Supervision: What Works and What Doesn't*, ed. Frederic S. Mishkin (Chicago: University of Chicago Press).

central bank had stepped up to, or over, the line between acting as a lender of last resort and bailing out insolvent institutions that could not repay.

People feared that banks would fail, but they could not easily tell the difference between a strong bank and a weak one. People withdrew checking and saving deposits, but the run made it only more likely that banks would fail. Contagion and uncertainty meant that the panic hit all banks, weak and strong alike. Dollar deposits caused an additional problem. If people wanted to withdraw pesos, the central bank's peso loans helped, but if they wanted to withdraw dollars, the peso loans would head right back to the central bank as the commercial banks demanded dollar reserves to satisfy the dollar claims.

Even as people started to run from bank deposits to cash, higher interest rates and lower output depressed the demand for cash. Reserves drained, casting more doubt on the viability of the fixed exchange rate, raising the currency premium, and draining more reserves. Given the fears of a banking crisis *and* an exchange rate crisis, cash and bank deposits were switched into dollars and moved to banks in Montevideo (Uruguay), Miami (Florida), or other offshore locations. People were now starting to run from the currency too.

The consequences for the central bank balance sheet were dramatic. Domestic credit expanded from 4 billion pesos to 9 billion pesos in the first half of 1995, as seen in Figure 9-7 at point 4 in panel (a), even as base money supply remained more or less steady near 14 billion pesos. Cash demand held up, but people were moving bank deposits into pesos and then offshore—and the central bank was providing the peso liquidity (to banks) and then the dollar liquidity (to people) to allow this capital flight to happen. As a result of this sterilization, reserves fell to a low of just 5 billion pesos, with the backing ratio collapsing to a low of about 36% (5/14). In the central bank balance sheet diagram in Figure 9-7, panel (b), the country was now moving vertically up to point 4 and getting perilously close to the floating line, the dangerous place where reserves run out.

Help from the IMF and Recovery In late 1994 Argentina was at the point of being cut off from further official lending by the **International Monetary Fund (IMF)** as a result of its failure to reduce its fiscal deficit and pursue other reforms. With private credit markets screeching toward a sudden stop after the Tequila Crisis, and the government running a large deficit, the situation looked bleak.

However, after the Tequila Crisis, the United States advanced a large assistance package to Mexico, and the IMF took a more lenient view of the Argentine situation, fearing the possibility of a global financial crisis if Argentina crashed too. IMF lending resumed. This was seen as "catalytic" in putting an end to the sudden stop, and a "Patriotic Bond" was issued in private capital markets. The loans provided desperately needed dollars. Some of the dollars could then be poured into the central bank. This replenished reserves, but it also revealed the scale of the bailing out. A substantial fund was set up to salvage insolvent commercial banks, a move that finally erased the stain of the bailouts from the central bank's balance sheet (bad commercial bank debt to the central bank was socialized and then turned into a government debt to foreigners).[14]

The Argentine authorities squeaked through a crisis, the economy recovered, capital flows resumed, and eventually the central bank's emergency loans were paid back. By 1996 economic growth had picked up, interest rate spreads eased, and confidence returned. The central bank reversed its earlier sterilization policies and replenished reserves by contracting domestic credit. By November 1996 domestic credit was back down to 4 billion pesos (its precrisis level), and by May 1997 the central bank had gone further and reduced domestic credit to zero. These steps are shown in the central bank balance sheet diagram in Figure 9-7, panel (b), by the moves from point 4 to point 5 to point 6.

---

[14] For a detailed account of Argentina's travails, see Paul Blustein, 2005, *And the Money Kept Rolling In (and Out): Wall Street, the IMF, and the Bankrupting of Argentina* (New York: Public Affairs).

Postscript Argentina's central bank ended up with a 100% backing ratio and was in a position to act as a strict currency board. However, it did not do so and in subsequent turbulent times continued to exercise discretion in its use of sterilization policies. The Convertibility Plan came to an end in 2001, however, when its room to maneuver finally ran out: the economy was in recession, the government was deeper in debt, the IMF and private creditors had reached their lending limits, and the government was reduced to raiding the banks and the central bank for resources. The details of that story, which are tied up with the Argentine 2001 default, are taken up in the online Chapter 11.

The Central Bank Balance Sheet and the Financial System

We can see from the experiences of Argentina and many other countries that the existence of a financial system affects the operations and balance sheet of the central bank. In particular, whether as a result of its own policy choices, formal laws and regulations, or political pressure, the typical central bank takes on the responsibility for monitoring, regulating, and—in an emergency—protecting a country's commercial banking system.

A More General Balance Sheet
As a result of its interactions with banks, the central bank's balance sheet is in reality more complicated than we have assumed in our simplified model. Typically, it looks something like this, with some hypothetical values inserted:[15]

GENERAL CENTRAL BANK BALANCE (MILLIONS OF PESOS)			
Assets		**Liabilities**	
Foreign assets	950	**Foreign liabilities**	50
of which:		of which:	
Foreign reserves (all currencies)	950	*Foreign currency debt issued by the*	50
Gold	0	*central bank*	
Domestic assets	500	**Domestic liabilities**	400
of which:		of which:	
Domestic government bonds bought	300	*Domestic currency debt issued by the*	400
Loans to commercial banks	200	*central bank*	
		Money supply M	1,000
		of which:	
		Currency in circulation	900
		Reserve liabilities to commercial banks	100

In the first row, the central bank's *net foreign assets* are worth 900 million pesos, given by 950 minus 50. We see that foreign assets can include other currencies besides the anchor currency (the dollar) and may also include gold. There may also be offsetting foreign liabilities if the central bank chooses to borrow. In this example, gold happens to be 0, foreign reserves are 950 million pesos, and foreign liabilities are 50 million pesos.

In the second row, *net domestic assets* are worth 100 million pesos, 500 minus 400. We see that domestic assets may be broken down into government bonds (here, 300 million pesos) and loans to commercial banks (here, 200 million pesos). All of these assets can be offset by domestic liabilities, such as debt issued in home currency by the central bank. In this example, the central bank has issued 400 million pesos in domestic debt, which we shall assume was used to finance the purchase of foreign reserves.

Finally, the money supply is a liability for the central bank worth 1,000 million pesos, as before. However, not all of that currency is "in circulation" (i.e., outside the central bank, in the hands of the public or in commercial bank vaults). Typically,

---

[15] For simplicity, we assume that the bank has zero net worth, so total assets equal total liabilities. In general, this will not be true from day to day as the central bank can make gains and losses on its assets and liabilities, and it may also have operating profits and losses. However, net worth is typically not very large and, over the longer run, any gains and losses are typically absorbed by the government treasury.

central banks place *reserve requirements* on commercial banks and force them to place some cash on deposit at the central bank. This is considered a prudent regulatory device. In this case, currency in circulation is 900 million pesos, and 100 million pesos is in the central bank as part of reserve requirements.

Despite all these refinements, the lessons of our simple model carry over. For example, in the simple approach, money supply (M) equaled foreign assets (R) plus domestic assets (B). We now see that, in general, money supply is equal to *net foreign assets* plus *net domestic assets*. The only real difference is the ability of the central bank to borrow by issuing nonmonetary liabilities, whether domestic or foreign.

Sterilization Bonds Why do central banks expand their balance sheets by issuing such liabilities? To see what the central bank can achieve by borrowing, consider what the preceding balance sheet would look like if the central bank had not borrowed to fund the purchase of reserves.

Without issuing domestic liabilities of 400 million pesos and foreign liabilities of 50 million pesos, reserves would be lower by 450 million pesos. In other words, they would fall from 950 million pesos to their original level of 500 million pesos seen in the example at the start of this chapter. Domestic credit would then be 500 million pesos, as it was in that earlier example, with money supply of 1,000 million pesos. Thus, what borrowing to buy reserves achieves is not a change in monetary policy (money supply and interest rates are unchanged, given the peg) but an increase in the backing ratio. Instead of a 50% backing ratio (500/1,000), the borrowing takes the central bank up to a 95% backing ratio (950/1,000).

But why stop there? What if the central bank borrowed, say, another 300 million pesos by issuing domestic debt and used the proceeds to purchase more reserves? Its domestic liabilities would rise from 400 to 700 million pesos (net domestic assets would fall from +100 to −200 million pesos), and on the other side of the balance sheet, reserves (foreign assets) would rise from 950 to 1,250 million pesos. Money supply would still be 1,000 million pesos, but the backing ratio would be 125%. This could go on and on. Borrow another 250 million pesos, and the backing ratio would rise to 150%.

As we have seen, these hypothetical operations are all examples of changes in the *composition* of the money supply—in terms of net foreign assets and net domestic assets—holding fixed the *level* of money supply. In other words, this is just a more general form of sterilization. And *sterilization is just a way to change the backing ratio, all else equal.*

What is new here is that the central bank's *net* domestic assets (assets minus liabilities) can be less than zero because the central bank is now allowed to borrow. Many central banks do just this, by issuing bonds—or **sterilization bonds** as they are fittingly described. This allows the backing ratio to potentially exceed 100%.

Looking back at Figure 9-8, we could depict this by allowing reserves R to represent *net* foreign assets, credit B to represent *net* domestic assets, and B to be less than zero. The key equation $M = R + B$ still holds, and the fixed and floating lines work as before, as long as we interpret zero *net* foreign assets as the trigger for a switch from fixed to floating.[16] So we can imagine that the fixed line in Figure 9-8 can extend down below the horizontal axis.

Going below the horizontal axis means that net domestic credit is negative, and the backing ratio is more than 100%. Why might countries want backing to be that high? As we saw, Argentina had high backing of more than 70% on the eve of the Tequila Crisis, but this would not have been enough for the peg to survive a major run from the financial system to dollars. In Figure 9-8, the zone below the horizontal axis would be an ultra-safe place, even farther from the floating line. Many countries have recently sought refuge in that direction (see **Side Bar: The Great Reserve Accumulation in Emerging Markets**).

---

[16] As we have argued, the precise level of that trigger may be arbitrary without affecting the insights from this analysis.

SIDE BAR

The Great Reserve Accumulation in Emerging Markets

An illustration of reserve buildup via sterilization is provided by the activities of the People's Bank of China, whose central bank balance sheet diagram is shown in Figure 9-10 in yuan (¥) units. The vertical distance to the 45-degree line represents net foreign assets R, which were essentially the same as foreign reserves because the bank had close to zero foreign liabilities.[*]

From 1995 to 2003 net domestic credit in China grew very slowly, from ¥1,409 billion to ¥2,218 billion, but rapid economic growth and financial development caused base money demand to grow rapidly, more than doubling, from ¥2,076 billion to ¥5,284 billion. Thus, most of the base money supply growth of ¥3,208 billion was absorbed by ¥2,399 billion of reserve accumulation. In this period, the backing ratio rose from 32% to 58%.

From 2003 to 2009 net domestic credit fell by ¥6,202 billion and eventually turned negative as the central bank sold large amounts of sterilization bonds. Money supply growth continued, rising from ¥5,284 billion to ¥14,399 billion, an increase of ¥9,115 billion. But the sterilization caused reserves to rise by almost twice as much, by ¥15,317 billion. The backing ratio rose from 58% to 128%. In the years 2009 to 2018, sterilization was not as much in play, and both reserves and domestic credit increased together; by 2018 money supply was ¥33,096 billion, with 65% backing in reserves of ¥21,582.

[*] In this period, foreign liabilities were just 1% of foreign assets.

FIGURE 9-10

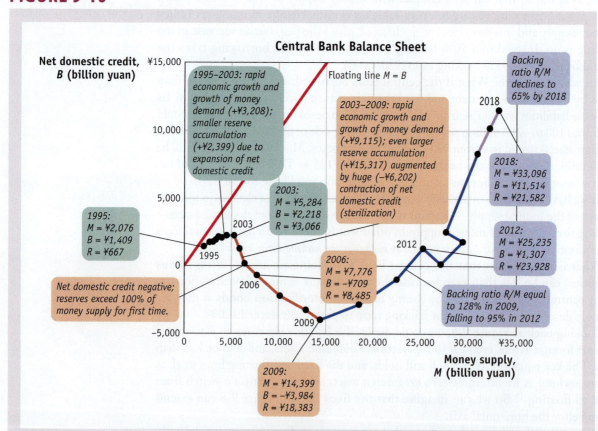

Central Bank Balance Sheet

Sterilization in China By issuing "sterilization bonds" central banks can borrow from domestic residents to buy more reserves. With sufficient borrowing of this kind, the central bank can end up with negative net domestic credit and reserves in excess of 100% of the money supply. The chart shows how this has happened in China in some recent years: from 1995 to 2003 net domestic credit in China was steady; reserve growth was almost entirely driven by money demand growth (movement to the right). From 2003 to 2009 sterilization (movement down) sent net domestic credit below zero; sterilization accounted for about 40% of the reserve growth in that period. In 2009–12 sterilization abated and the reserve backing ratio fell below 100% for the first time in seven years. By 2018 the reserve backing ratio was just 65%.

Data from: IMF, International Financial Statistics.

Given the country's economic (and political) importance, the Chinese case attracts a lot of attention—but it isn't the only example of this type of central bank behavior. Figure 9-11 shows the massive increase in reserves at central banks around the world in recent years: it started in about 1999, it mostly happened in Asia in countries pegging (more or less) to the dollar, and much of it was driven by large-scale sterilization. What was going on?

Causes of the Reserve Accumulation

Why are these countries, most of them poor emerging markets, accumulating massive hoards of reserves? There are various possible motivations for these reserve hoards, in addition to simply wanting greater backing ratios to absorb larger shocks to money demand.[**] For example, the countries may fear a sudden stop, when access to foreign capital markets dries up. Foreign creditors may cease to roll over short-term debt for a while, but if reserves are on hand, the central bank can temporarily cover the shortfall. This precautionary motive

---

[**] For a survey of the various possible explanations of the reserve buildup, see Joshua Aizenman, 2008, "Large Hoarding of International Reserves and the Emerging Global Economic Architecture," *Manchester School*, 76(5), 487–503; Olivier Jeanne, 2007, "International Reserves in Emerging Market Countries: Too Much of a Good Thing?" *Brookings Papers on Economic Activity*, 38(1), 1–80.

leads to policy guidelines or rules suggesting that an adequate and prudent level of reserves should be some multiple either of foreign trade or of short-term debt. In practice, such ratios usually imply reserve levels less than 100% of M0, the narrow money supply.

An alternative view, illustrated by the case of Argentina that we studied, would tend to focus on a different risk, the fragility of the financial sector. If there is a major banking crisis with a flight from local deposits to foreign banks, then a central bank may need a far greater level of reserves, adequate to cover some or all of M2, the broader measure of money that includes deposits and other liquid commercial bank liabilities. Because M2 can be several times M0, the reserve levels adequate for these purposes could be much larger and well over 100% of M0. Because reserves now far exceed traditional guidelines based on trade or debt levels, fears of financial fragility might be an important part of the explanation for the scale of the reserve buildup, with reserve backing in excess of 100% of M0. As economist Martin Feldstein pointed out after the Asian crisis, it is unrealistic to expect safe and crisis-free banking sector operations in emerging markets (in 2007 and 2008 we even saw bank runs in "developed countries" like the United Kingdom and the United States). But if countries are pegged, they then need to watch out

FIGURE 9-11

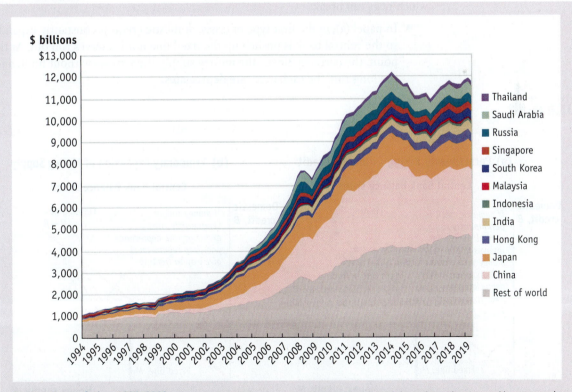

Reserve Accumulation, 1997–2019 By the end of 2013, reserve holdings worldwide exceeded $12,000 billion, about 12 times their level in 1994. They leveled off and remained close to this level through 2019. Most of the growth occurred in emerging markets, especially Asia. Much of these additional reserves were acquired through sterilization and have caused several countries' holdings of foreign exchange reserves to exceed 100% of the monetary base.

Data from: IMF, International Financial Statistics.

for the peg: ". . . Sufficient liquidity, either through foreign currency reserves or access to foreign credit, would let a government restructure and recapitalize its banks without experiencing a currency crisis. The more international liquidity a government has, the less depositors will feel that they must rush to convert their currency before the reserves are depleted. And preventing a currency decline can be the best way to protect bank solvency."[†]

Thus, current reserve levels can be seen as a reaction, in part, to the financial crises of the recent past: policymakers have taken a "never again"

stance, and have piled up a large war chest of reserves to guard against any risk of exchange rate crises. Is this wise? The benefits may seem clear, but many economists think this "insurance policy" carries too heavy an economic cost as countries invest in low-interest reserves and forsake investments with higher returns.

[†] See Martin S. Feldstein, March 1999, "A Self-Help Guide for Emerging Markets," *Foreign Affairs*, 78(2), 93–109.

Summary

In this section, we examined the constraints on the operations of the central bank when a fixed exchange rate is in operation. We focused on the central bank balance sheet, which in its simplest form describes how the narrow money supply (monetary base) is backed by foreign assets (reserves) and domestic assets (domestic credit). We have seen how, in response to money demand shocks, the central bank buys or sells reserves, to defend the peg. The central bank can also change the composition of the money supply through sterilization operations, which keep the money supply constant.

Two Types of Exchange Rate Crises When reserves go to zero, the country is floating, changes in domestic credit cause changes in the money supply, and the peg breaks. The central bank balance sheet diagrams in Figure 9-12 show two ways in which pegs can break:

- In panel (a), in the first type of crisis, domestic credit is constantly expanding, so the central bank is pushed up the fixed line until reserves run out. At this point, the currency floats, the money supply then grows without limit, and, in the long run, the exchange rate depreciates.

FIGURE 9-12

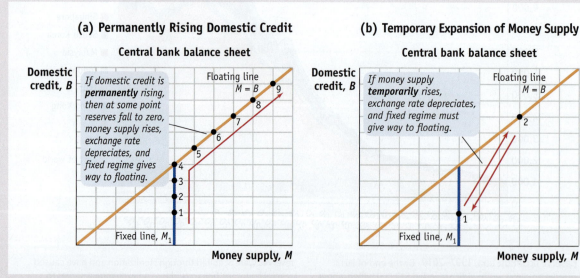

Two Types of Exchange Rate Crisis In our model, using the central bank balance sheet diagram, we can see what actions will cause the peg to break. Two types of crisis are highlighted here. In panel (a), a permanent and ongoing expansion of domestic credit is incompatible with a fixed exchange rate regime because, sooner or later, reserves will be reduced to zero, and then the money supply starts to expand. In panel (b), a temporary expansion of domestic credit and the money supply will lower interest rates and depreciate the exchange rate, even if a reversal of this policy is expected in the future. Both policies take the country off the fixed line and onto the floating line.

- In panel (b), in the second type of crisis, no long-run tendency exists for the money supply to grow, but there is a short-run temptation to expand the money supply temporarily, leading to a temporarily lower interest rate and a temporarily depreciated exchange rate.

In the next two sections, we develop models of these two types of crisis. Although the descriptions just given appear simple, a deeper examination reveals some peculiar features that illustrate the powerful role played by market expectations in triggering crises.

3 How Pegs Break I: Inconsistent Fiscal Policies

We begin with a so-called **first-generation crisis model** of inconsistent fiscal policies in a country with a fixed exchange rate, a model proposed by economist Paul Krugman.[17] This kind of crisis model has been successfully applied to many historical cases, including a series of Latin American crises in the 1980s.

The Basic Problem: Fiscal Dominance

In this model, the level of output plays no role, so we assume output is fixed at some level Y. However, the price level P plays an important role, and we allow the price level to be flexible and determined by purchasing power parity (PPP), as in the chapter on the long-run monetary model. For now we keep all our earlier assumptions from this chapter.

In this model, the government is running a persistent deficit (DEF) because of insufficient tax revenue, and the government's situation is so dire that it is unable to borrow from any creditor. It therefore turns to the central bank for financing. In this type of environment, economists speak of a situation of **fiscal dominance** in which the monetary authorities ultimately have no independence. The treasury hands over bonds in the amount DEF to the central bank, receives cash in the amount DEF in return, and uses the cash to fund the government deficit. As a result, domestic credit B increases by an amount $\Delta B = DEF$ every period. For simplicity, we assume that domestic credit B is growing at a constant positive rate of growth, $\Delta B/B = \mu$. For example, if $\mu = 0.1$, then domestic credit B is growing at 10% per period.

Given our previous graphical analysis of the central bank balance sheet, we can see that the fixed exchange rate is doomed. As in Figure 9-12, panel (a), every change in the level of domestic credit leads to an equal and opposite change in the level of reserves. This process can't go on forever because reserves must eventually run out. At that point, the peg breaks and the central bank shifts from a fixed exchange rate regime to a floating regime, in which the money supply equals domestic credit, $M = B$. We note a key point:

Once reserves run out, the money supply M, which was previously fixed, grows at the same rate of growth as domestic credit, $\Delta M/M = \Delta B/B = \mu$.

The reason the peg breaks in this situation is simple. There is an inconsistency between the authorities' commitment to a monetary policy of a fixed exchange rate and a fiscal policy of continuously monetizing deficits through an endless expansion of domestic credit. On the face of it, crisis results from elementary incompetence on the part of the authorities; to be more generous, we might say that the crisis happens because authorities are willing to let it happen because of overriding fiscal priorities.

---

[17] Paul Krugman, 1979, "A Model of Balance-of-Payments Crises," *Journal of Money, Credit and Banking*, 11(3), 311–325.

A Simple Model

In many ways, this situation is familiar. We have already seen the implications of long-run money growth. In the chapter on exchange rates in the long run, we learned what happens in response to an *unexpected* increase in the rate of money supply growth: if prices can adjust flexibly, then, after the increase, the economy ends up with all nominal values growing at the rate μ, the rate of growth of domestic credit. There will be inflation as the price level P grows at a rate μ, and depreciation as the exchange rate E also grows at a rate μ.

The Myopic Case Figure 3-14 (p. 87) described a case in which the rate of growth of the money supply unexpectedly increased by a fixed amount. We apply the same analysis here and assume that investors are *myopic* and do not see the crisis coming. (To be more realistic, we relax this assumption in a moment, but the myopic case provides useful insights.)

Drawing on what we know, Figure 9-13 describes this kind of crisis scenario, assuming that prices are stable in the foreign country, that the foreign interest rate is $i^* = 5\%$, and that all variables change continuously through time. For simplicity, we start with $M = P = E = 1$, and at all times we assume the foreign price level is 1, $P^* = 1$.

Starting at time 1, in the fixed regime, domestic credit is less than the money supply, $B < M$, and reserves are positive, $R > 0$. But because of the monetization of deficits, B is gradually rising, and, as a result, R is steadily falling. Eventually, reserves run out, and thereafter $B = M$ and $R = 0$. We assume for now that the regime change occurs at time 4. In the fixed regime, up to that point, money supply M is fixed, but when floating starts, M grows at a rate μ as shown in panel (a).

Because prices are flexible, the monetary model of exchange rates in the long run tells us that P will be fixed until time 4 and then it will grow at a rate μ. Thus, inflation rises by an amount μ at time 4. The Fisher effect tells us that an increase in the home inflation rate causes a one-for-one increase in the home interest rate. So the home interest rate i must rise and step up by an amount μ as we move from the fixed to the floating regime as shown in panel (b).

An increase in the home interest rate i at time 4 lowers the demand for real money balances, $M/P = L(i)Y$, because in the money demand function, L is a decreasing function of i. Thus, M/P "jumps" down as we change from fixed to floating. Because the money supply M does not change at time 4, the drop in M/P can be accommodated only by a jump in the flexible price level P at time 4. Because, by assumption, PPP holds continuously (and because $P^* = 1$), then we can just compute $E = P/P^* = P$. So the discontinuous rise in P also implies a discontinuous rise in E at time 4, and a depreciation of the home currency. Both E and P jump up and start to grow at rate μ at time 4, as shown in panel (c).

To sum up, in Figure 9-13, the exchange rate crisis occurs at time 4, but the exchange rate doesn't drift continuously away from its previous fixed level. It *jumps* away discontinuously. The new floating path of the exchange rate then rises at a growth rate μ, starting from a point that is above the old fixed rate at time 4.

For example, if the money growth rate is 10% after the crisis, as assumed, then there is a 10 percentage point increase in the interest rate from 5% to 15%. Now suppose this reduces real money demand by 20%, from 1.00 to 0.80. Because the nominal money supply M equals 1 just before and just after the crisis, it does not jump at time 4. To get M/P to fall from 1.00 to 0.80, P must jump up, from 1.0 to $(1/0.80) = 1.25$, implying an instantaneous 25% increase in P. To maintain purchasing power parity, there must also be a 25% increase in the exchange rate E, to 1.25, followed by growth at 10%.

One significant implication of the jump in nominal values is that anyone holding a peso that was worth 1 dollar will suddenly be left holding a peso that is worth only $1/1.25 = 0.80$ dollars. Investors holding pesos at the moment of crisis will suffer a capital loss (in dollar terms) if this model accurately describes their behavior.

FIGURE 9-13

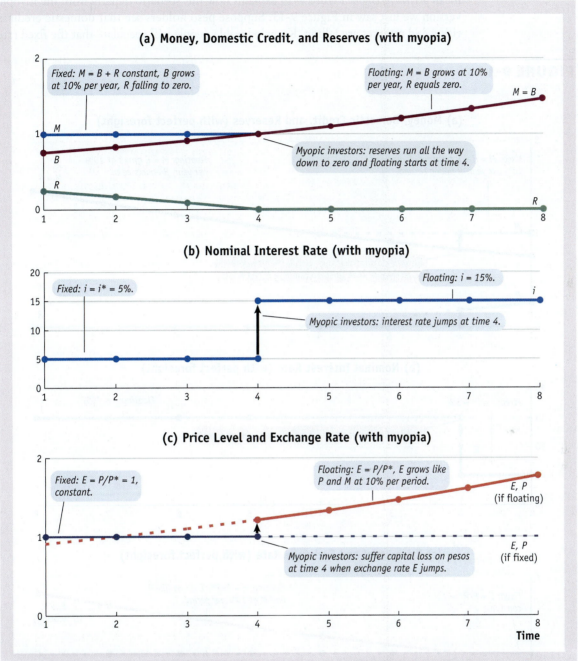

(a) Money, Domestic Credit, and Reserves (with myopia)

Fixed: M = B + R constant, B grows at 10% per year, R falling to zero.

Floating: M = B grows at 10% per year, R equals zero.

M = B

M

B

R

Myopic investors: reserves run all the way down to zero and floating starts at time 4.

R

(b) Nominal Interest Rate (with myopia)

Fixed: i = i* = 5%.

Floating: i = 15%.

i

Myopic investors: interest rate jumps at time 4.

(c) Price Level and Exchange Rate (with myopia)

Fixed: E = P/P* = 1, constant.

Floating: E = P/P*, E grows like P and M at 10% per period.

E, P
(if floating)

E, P
(if fixed)

Myopic investors: suffer capital loss on pesos at time 4 when exchange rate E jumps.

Time

An Exchange Rate Crisis Due to Inconsistent Fiscal Policies: Myopic Case In the fixed regime, money supply *M* is fixed, but expansion of domestic credit *B* implies that reserves *R* are falling to zero. Suppose the switch to floating occurs when reserves run out at time 4. Thereafter, the monetary model tells us that *M*, *P*, and *E* will all grow at a constant rate (here, 10% per period). The expected rates of inflation and depreciation are now positive, and the Fisher effect tells us that the interest rate must jump up at period 4 (by 10 percentage points). The interest rate increase means that real money demand $M/P = L(i)Y$ falls instantly at time 4. The money supply does not adjust immediately, so this jump in *M/P* must be accommodated by a jump in the price level *P*. To maintain purchasing power parity, *E* must also jump at the same time. Hence, myopic investors face a capital loss on pesos at time 4.

The Forward-Looking Case There is good reason to believe that investors will not be as shortsighted (myopic) as we have just assumed. It is usually well known when a government has a deficit that is being monetized, even if the authorities try to conceal the problem.

Let us move to the other extreme, *forward-looking* behavior, which for now we take to mean *perfect foresight*. Figure 9-14 explains how this scenario departs from the myopic version we just saw in Figure 9-13. Suppose peso holders see that domestic credit is rising and reserves are falling. Knowledgeable people will speculate that the fixed rate

FIGURE 9-14

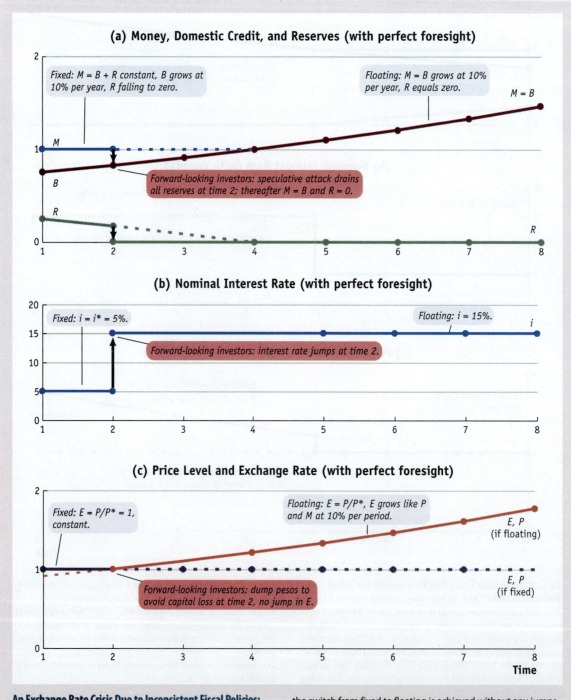

(a) Money, Domestic Credit, and Reserves (with perfect foresight)

Fixed: M = B + R constant, B grows at 10% per year, R falling to zero.

Floating: M = B grows at 10% per year, R equals zero.

M = B

M

B

Forward-looking investors: speculative attack drains all reserves at time 2; thereafter M = B and R = 0.

R

R

(b) Nominal Interest Rate (with perfect foresight)

Fixed: i = i* = 5%.

Floating: i = 15%.

i

Forward-looking investors: interest rate jumps at time 2.

(c) Price Level and Exchange Rate (with perfect foresight)

Fixed: E = P/P* = 1, constant.

Floating: E = P/P*, E grows like P and M at 10% per period.

E, P (if floating)

Forward-looking investors: dump pesos to avoid capital loss at time 2, no jump in E.

E, P (if fixed)

Time

An Exchange Rate Crisis Due to Inconsistent Fiscal Policies: Perfect-Foresight Case Compare this figure with Figure 9-13. If investors anticipate a crisis, they will seek to avoid losses by converting the pesos they are holding to dollars before period 4. The rational moment to attack is at time 2, the point at which the switch from fixed to floating is achieved without any jumps in E or P. Why? At time 2, the drop in money demand (due to the rise in the interest rate) exactly equals the decline in the money supply (the reserve loss), and money market equilibrium is maintained without the price level having to change.

is going to break in the near future. They will expect pesos to suddenly lose their dollar value if they hold them until the bitter end at time 4 when reserves would run out under myopia. They will therefore decide to dump pesos sooner. But when? And how?

When investors sell all their holdings of a particular currency, it is known as a **speculative attack**. When such an attack occurs, the economy must *immediately* switch to the floating regime we have already studied, since once it has zero reserves, the money supply M will always equal domestic credit B—which has been and will be growing at the constant rate μ. At that same time, the nominal interest rate will also jump up, when the Fisher effect kicks in, and there will be a jump down in both money demand (as the interest rise hits) and in the money supply (as the attack drains all remaining reserves).

In our example, the key lesson is that once an attack occurs, the economy completely switches over to the floating regime. Under myopia the switch occurred at time 4. But now, the switch happens well before time 4, and at the time of the attack the economy's inflation, exchange rates, prices, and interest rates all jump to their new (and rising) paths. This leaves one question: When does the speculative attack occur? From Figure 9-14, the answer must be at time 2. In this case, the path of the price level P and the exchange rate E are continuous as we switch from fixed to floating. Only then can the switch occur without any expected dollar gains or losses on holding pesos.

How does this pin down the attack at time 2? Suppose the attack were at any time later than 2, such as time 3. As we can see from the diagram, this requires a jump up in the exchange rate, a *discontinuous depreciation*. If peso holders wait to attack until time 3, they still suffer a capital loss because they have waited too long. What if the attack is before time 2, say, at time 1? An attack at time 1 implies a *discontinuous appreciation* of the peso. But if that happened, any individual peso holder would enjoy capital gains (in dollars) from holding on to pesos rather than exchanging them for reserves at the central bank at the prior fixed rate. They would therefore rather wait, let everyone else attack, and pocket the gains. But if one person thinks like that, all do, and the attack cannot materialize.

The speculative attack model teaches an important lesson. One moment, a central bank may have a pile of reserves on hand, draining away fairly slowly, giving the illusion that there is no imminent danger. The next moment, the reserves are all gone. The model can therefore explain why fixed exchange rates sometimes witness a sudden collapse rather than a long, lingering death.

APPLICATION

The Peruvian Crisis of 1986

An example of a crisis driven by inconsistent fiscal policies and excessive expansion of domestic credit is provided by the events in Peru from 1985 to 1986, illustrated in Figure 9-15.

In the early 1980s, Peru's political and economic conditions were highly unfavorable. The country had endured a period of social unrest and military rule in the 1970s, and the government had an enormous external debt burden. World commodity prices fell, exports and economic growth slowed, and government deficits grew. At the same time, world interest rates sharply increased.

The Peruvian government defaulted on its debt obligations and began negotiations with the IMF and other creditors. Denied fresh loans from world capital markets, and with low tax receipts that could not cover rising spending, government financing came to rely on money printing by the central bank—that is, the inflation tax. Domestic credit grew by 65% in 1982, 165% in 1983, and 93% in 1984—a rough doubling every year, on average. The dollar value of Peru's currency, the sol, rapidly sank.

FIGURE 9-15

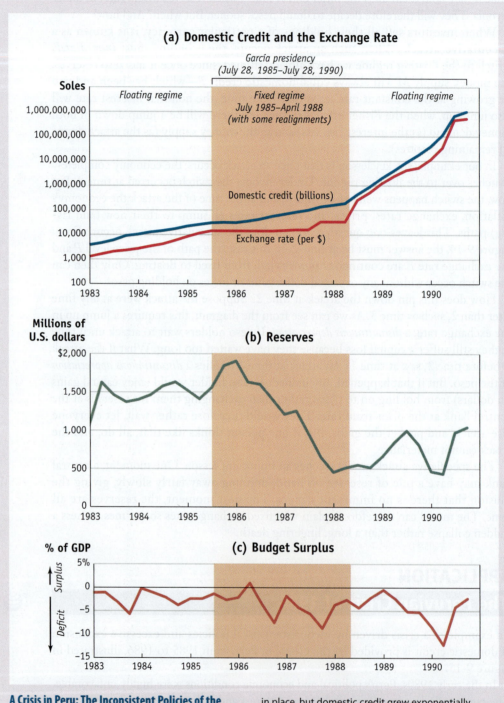

(a) Domestic Credit and the Exchange Rate

García presidency
(July 28, 1985–July 28, 1990)

Floating regime   *Fixed regime*
July 1985–April 1988
(with some realignments)   *Floating regime*

Soles

Domestic credit (billions)

Exchange rate (per $)

(b) Reserves

Millions of
U.S. dollars

(c) Budget Surplus

% of GDP

Surplus ↑
Deficit ↓

A Crisis in Peru: The Inconsistent Policies of the García Administration From 1985 to 1986 the Peruvian government implemented a fixed exchange rate regime, but government budget problems required significant monetization of budget deficits. Monetary and fiscal policies were inconsistent: a peg was in place, but domestic credit grew exponentially (note that the exchange rate and domestic credit are shown on logarithmic scales). The central bank lost three-quarters of its reserves in two years, and the peg had to be abandoned.

Data from: IMF, International Financial Statistics.

As economic conditions deteriorated further and political violence by guerilla groups intensified, President Alan García Pérez was elected to office in 1985. One important economic measure he instituted immediately was a fixed exchange rate. This stopped the depreciation and was intended to give Peru a firm nominal anchor. But, as we now know, its durability would depend on whether García's administration could solve its fiscal problems and put an end to the monetization of government deficits.

Some fiscal reform was attempted, and the economy recovered slightly: the government budget improved at first. But the administration could not get the government budget out of the red for long. The deficit fell from 2% to 3% of GDP to near zero in early 1986, but by mid-1986 it was growing again, averaging over 5% and peaking at 8% to 9% of GDP in late 1986 and 1987. The printing presses of the central bank kept running, and domestic credit grew 84% in 1985, 77% in 1986, and 146% in 1987—roughly doubling, on average, every year.

Under a fixed exchange rate regime, something had to give. With domestic credit exploding, the central bank was continually selling reserves to defend the peg.[18] Reserves fell from a peak of $2,000 million in early 1986 to $500 million in early 1988. The authorities gave up in April 1988 before the attack was complete and so avoided losing all their dollar reserves. The sol began to float and depreciation was rapid: the sol hit 250,000 sol/$ in September, 500,000 in November, and 1,200,000 by March 1989, and Peru was heading into a hyperinflation.[19]

The data closely match the predictions of the model. Under the peg, reserves drain as domestic credit grows, and the exchange rate is stable. Under the float, reserves are stable, and the exchange rate grows as domestic credit expands.

By the time García left office, Peru was in economic shambles. García's popularity sank. The 1990 presidential election was won by a political newcomer, Alberto Fujimori, who would struggle with the problems created by his predecessor (and problems of his own). Yet, remarkably, in 2006 Alan García Pérez was elected president of Peru for a second time. Twenty years is a long time in politics.

Expectations and the Critical Level of Reserves What determines the *critical level of reserves* R_c at which the crisis occurs? In the speculative attack model, the size of the sudden reserve loss, and hence the timing of the crisis, depend critically on market expectations about the future growth rate of domestic credit. The reserves R_c lost at the moment of crisis will depend on how much money investors want to convert into reserves when they attack. This, in turn, depends on how much money demand shrinks as we move from fixed to floating, and that is driven by the change in the interest rate.

Let's assume that each percentage point increase in the interest rate causes a ϕ% fall in real money balances.[20] At the moment of attack, the interest rate rises by an amount $\Delta i = \mu$, so the proportional fall in money demand is given by ϕ times that change. Thus, the change in money demand is given by $-\Delta M/M = \phi \times \mu$.

But we also know that the change in the money supply at the moment of attack $-\Delta M$ has to correspond exactly to the size of the reserve drain at the moment of attack, which equals the critical level of reserves R_c that are lost at that instant. Thus,

$$
\underbrace{\frac{R_c}{M}}_{\substack{\text{Critical} \\ \text{backing ratio} \\ \text{when attack occurs}}} = \frac{-\Delta M}{M} = \underbrace{\phi}_{\substack{\text{Responsiveness} \\ \text{of money demand} \\ \text{to interest rate changes}}} \times \underbrace{\mu}_{\substack{\text{Future} \\ \text{rate of growth of} \\ \text{domestic credit}}}
$$

This expression tells us the ratio of the critical level of reserves R_c to the money supply M. It depends on the sensitivity of money demand to the interest rate and on the *expected future rate of growth* of domestic credit μ (remember, investors are *forward-looking*).

---

[18] The peg spent most of its time close to 17,300 sol/$. Various realignments to 20,000 and then 33,000 sol/$ in late 1987 bought a little time at the end.

[19] A common currency unit is used throughout this case study for consistency and commensurability. In reality, there were two currency reforms in Peru as a result of inflationary finance. The inti replaced the sol on February 1, 1985, at 1 inti per 1,000 soles, and on July 1, 1991, the nuevo sol replaced the inti at a rate of 1,000,000 nuevos soles per inti.

[20] The constant parameter ϕ is called the *interest semi-elasticity of money demand*.

To illustrate, and continue our previous example, if the growth rate of domestic credit is expected to be $\mu = 10\%$, and if $\phi = 1.5$, then the fall in money demand and money supply at the moment of attack is 10% times 1.5, or 15%. Thus, when reserves have drained so far that the backing ratio falls to the critical level $R_c = 15\%$, the peg will break. But if μ rises to 20%, the critical level R_c will be twice as large, 30%.

We can now see that if people *expect* a fiscal problem to worsen (expect the deficit to increase, and thus domestic credit to grow faster to finance it), then reserves drain away faster, and the crisis hits sooner, at a higher critical level of reserves R_c. Thus, an increase in the *expected* rate of deficit monetization shortens the length of time that the peg will survive.

This result emphasizes the importance of market beliefs. Suppose a country has reserves well above the critical level. There is no imminent crisis. Then market beliefs change, perhaps because news or rumors emerge about a budget problem. Investors now expect a higher growth rate of domestic credit. Suppose that, as a result of this change in expectations, the critical level of reserves rises so much as to equal the current level of reserves. With the change in expectations, the time for a speculative attack is now. A crisis will happen immediately, *even though there has been no change in the economic situation as of today!*

Summary

The first-generation crisis model tells us that inconsistent fiscal policies can destroy a fixed exchange rate. Yet it is not actual fiscal policy that matters, but *beliefs* and *expectations* about future fiscal policy. Because beliefs about future deficits may or may not be justified, the model opens up the possibility that countries will be punished for crimes they do not intend to commit.

For example, some economists have argued that expected future deficits were a factor in the Asian currency crisis of 1997: the countries were affected by "crony capitalism" and the banking sectors were insolvent because of bad loans to insiders. Once the scale of these problems became known, investors believed that the monetary authorities would bail out the banks. Fears of a rapid future expansion of domestic credit thus undermined the pegs.[21]

4 How Pegs Break II: Contingent Monetary Policies

In the previous section, we found that inconsistent fiscal policies under a fixed exchange rate regime eventually cause an exchange rate crisis. However, the crises of the 1990s often did not conform to a model based on deficit monetization because budget problems were absent in many cases. In particular, the Exchange Rate Mechanism (ERM) crisis of 1992 affected developed countries in Europe, most of which were unlikely to monetize deficits. In countries with apparently sound economic policies, foreign currency speculators went for the attack and pegs broke.[22]

Economists therefore developed alternative models of crises, with the pioneering work on the **second-generation crisis model** being done by Maurice Obstfeld.

---

[21] See, for example, the discussion of Korea's precrisis weaknesses in the operation and regulation of the banking sector, and the central bank's willingness to furtively channel dollar reserves to bail out the banks, in Frederic Mishkin, 2006, *The Next Great Globalization: How Disadvantaged Nations Can Harness Their Financial Systems to Get Rich* (Princeton, N.J.: Princeton University Press). See also Craig Burnside, Martin Eichenbaum, and Sergio Rebelo, 2001, "Prospective Deficits and the Asian Currency Crisis," *Journal of Political Economy*, 109(6), 1155–1197.

[22] A helpful survey is provided by Sweta C. Saxena, 2004, "The Changing Nature of Currency Crises," *Journal of Economic Surveys*, 18(3), 321–350.

These types of models can explain how, even when policymaking is rational and purposeful—rather than incompetent and inconsistent—there may still be situations in which pegs break for no apparent reason.[23]

The Basic Problem: Contingent Commitment

The essence of the model is that policymakers are not committed to the peg under all circumstances. Defending the peg is therefore a **contingent commitment** (a slight oxymoron): if things get "bad enough," the government will let the exchange rate float rather than put the country through serious economic pain. The problem is that everyone—especially investors in the forex market—knows this and will adjust their expectations accordingly.

To develop some intuition, we return to Britain and Germany in 1992, the example we saw at the start of the previous chapter (on p. 281) when we studied fixed and floating regimes. Let's recap the basic story: the German central bank raised interest rates to deal with a domestic shock, the fiscal expansion arising from German unification after 1989. This left Britain with a higher interest rate and a lower output level than it wanted. What would Britain do in response?

If German interest rates are fairly low, so too are British interest rates, output costs in Britain are low, and nobody expects Britain to leave the peg. The peg is *credible*. But if German interest rates rise to high levels, output in Britain falls to an intolerably low level, and nobody expects Britain to stay on the peg for long. Instead, everyone thinks Britain will float and use expansionary monetary policy to boost output and depreciate the pound. The peg is *not credible*, and the market now expects a depreciation in the future.

The problem for Britain is that an expected depreciation will introduce a *currency premium*, as we saw earlier in this chapter. Investors will demand even higher interest rates in Britain to compensate for the imminent depreciation—and this will mean even lower output and even higher pain for Britain!

This creates a gray area. How? It is quite possible that the German interest rate can be at some "intermediate" level at which pegging is tolerable with no expected depreciation: people would expect the peg to hold and the peg would hold. But if there is an expected depreciation and a currency premium, pegging might be intolerable: people would expect the peg to fail and the peg would fail. Crucially, in both scenarios, ex ante market expectations are validated ex post, and hence would be considered "rational."

Based on these insights from the Britain–Germany example, we now develop an economic model with such *self-fulfilling expectations*. In this model we may not always find a single, unique equilibrium but rather **multiple equilibria**. Whether there is a crisis depends entirely on market sentiment, and not simply economic fundamentals.

A Simple Model

In this type of model, we need a measure of the cost of maintaining the peg. The simplest cost measure is the deviation of output Y in the short run below its full-employment level. To allow output to vary, we need to use the IS–LM–FX model introduced in the chapter on macroeconomic policy, which means that we reverse some of the assumptions we made before. From now on, output Y will be variable rather than

---

[23] Maurice Obstfeld, 1986, "Rational and Self-Fulfilling Balance-of-Payments Crises," *American Economic Review*, 76(1), 72–81.

FIGURE 9-16

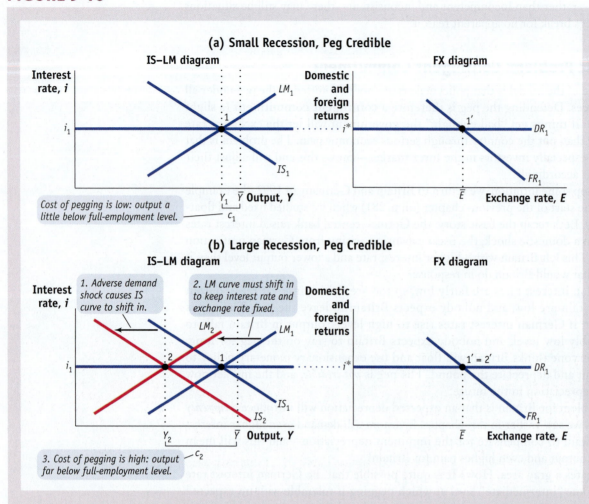

(a) Small Recession, Peg Credible

IS–LM diagram

Interest rate, i

LM_1

i_1 .... i^*

IS_1

Y_1 $\bar{Y}$ Output, Y

Cost of pegging is low: output a little below full-employment level. c_1

FX diagram

Domestic and foreign returns

DR_1

FR_1

$\bar{E}$ Exchange rate, E

(b) Large Recession, Peg Credible

IS–LM diagram

Interest rate, i

1. Adverse demand shock causes IS curve to shift in.

2. LM curve must shift in to keep interest rate and exchange rate fixed.

LM_2 LM_1

i_1 .... i^*

IS_1

IS_2

Y_2 $\bar{Y}$ Output, Y

3. Cost of pegging is high: output far below full-employment level. c_2

FX diagram

Domestic and foreign returns

$1' = 2'$ DR_1

FR_1

$\bar{E}$ Exchange rate, E

fixed, and it will be determined by the model. And from now on, prices will be sticky, not flexible, and treated as given.[24]

For simplicity, we assume there are *some* benefits from pegging, say, the gains from increased trade. Let these benefits be $b > 0$ and constant. Against the benefits of pegging, the government weighs costs c that equal the "output gap": full-employment $\bar{Y}$ output minus current output Y. If costs exceed benefits, we assume that the government will elect to float next period and use monetary policy to restore full-employment output. For simplicity, we assume each period lasts one year. (Restricting attention to this type of rule keeps things simple while illustrating the key trade-offs.)

In Figure 9-16, we use the home IS–LM–FX diagram to look at how outcomes under the peg can depend on both economic fundamentals and market expectations. We assume foreign output is fixed at Y^*, and we also assume there is no fiscal policy change, so we can focus only on home monetary policy choices. Most important, we assume that investors are aware of the contingent commitment to the peg.

---

[24] The reason for this change in assumptions is that at the heart of this model the crisis is not driven by a set of policies that will ultimately break the nominal anchor—inflation plays no role here, so prices can be assumed steady; instead, the key mechanism in this model is the desire *in certain circumstances* to stabilize output by using temporary shifts in monetary policy, which means that the exchange rate must be allowed to float.

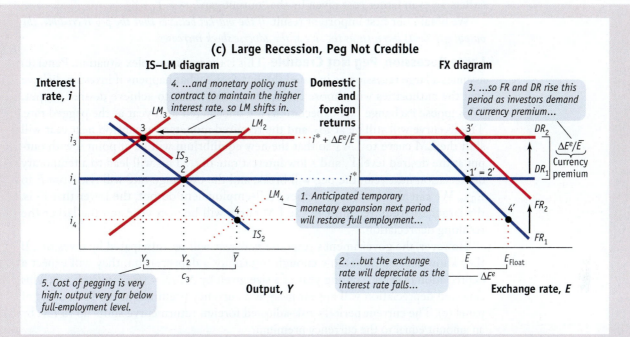

(c) Large Recession, Peg Not Credible

IS–LM diagram

Interest rate, i

4. ...and monetary policy must contract to maintain the higher interest rate, so LM shifts in.

LM_3

LM_2

i_3 — 3

IS_3

2

i_1

LM_4

i_4 — 4

IS_2

1. Anticipated temporary monetary expansion next period will restore full employment...

Y_3 Y_2 $\overline{Y}$

c_3

5. Cost of pegging is very high: output very far below full-employment level.

Output, Y

FX diagram

Domestic and foreign returns

3. ...so FR and DR rise this period as investors demand a currency premium...

3′ DR_2

$i^* + \Delta E^e/\overline{E}$

$\Delta E^e/\overline{E}$ Currency premium

1′ = 2′ DR_1

i^*

4′ FR_2

FR_1

2. ...but the exchange rate will depreciate as the interest rate falls...

$\overline{E}$ E_{Float}

ΔE^e

Exchange rate, E

Contingent Commitments and the Cost of Maintaining a Peg This figure describes how the IS–LM–FX equilibrium changes as demand shocks occur and as the credibility of the peg weakens. The economy is pegging at a fixed exchange rate $\overline{E}$. In panel (a), the economy is at IS–LM equilibrium at point 1, with the FX market at point 1′. Output is a little below desired output, so the cost of pegging c_1 is small. In panel (b), there is an adverse shock to domestic demand, and the IS curve shifts in. LM shifts in, too, to maintain the peg. The new IS–LM equilibrium occurs at point 2, with FX market equilibrium at point 2′ (same as 1′). The cost of pegging c_2 is higher. Panel (c) shows that if the country

wants to attain full-employment output next period, it must move to point 4, shifting the LM curve out and allowing the FX market to settle at point 4′ with the exchange rate depreciating to E_{float}. The peg would still be in operation today, but, by definition, it would no longer be credible if such a policy change were anticipated. Because of the lack of credibility, investors would insist on receiving a positive currency premium *today,* and the home interest rate would rise to i_3, squeezing demand even more and moving the IS–LM equilibrium to point 3 and the FX market to point 3′. Now the cost of pegging c_3 is even higher: having a noncredible peg is more costly than having a credible peg.

In this setup, it does not matter where adverse output shocks originate. They could result from increases in the foreign interest rate (as in the ERM example). Or they could be caused by a decline in the demand for home goods overseas. All that matters is that the home economy is in some kind of pain with output below the desired level.

Small Recession, Peg Credible Panel (a) shows a situation in which the pain is small. Initially, the IS_1 and LM_1 curves intersect at equilibrium point 1, and the home interest rate is $i_1 = i^*$ to maintain the peg. In the FX diagram, the domestic return is DR_1 and the foreign return FR_1. They intersect at point 1′ and the exchange rate is fixed at $E_1 = \overline{E}$. Home output is at Y_1, but we assume that the desired full-employment level of home output is $\overline{Y}$, slightly higher than Y_1. In this situation, when the peg is credible, the economy suffers a small cost given by the "output gap": $c_1 = \overline{Y} - Y_1$.

Large Recession, Peg Credible Panel (b) shows a situation in which the adverse shock to output is large. The IS_2 and LM_2 curves now intersect at equilibrium point 2. The IS curve has moved left by assumption: it is the source of the adverse shock. The LM curve has moved in to maintain the peg and preserve interest parity, so that the home interest rate remains at $i_1 = i^*$. In the FX diagram, the domestic return is still DR_1 and the foreign return is still FR_1, and they intersect at point 2′, the same as point $1'$, with $E_1 = \bar{E}$. Home output is now much lower at Y_2. Here, the economy suffers an even larger cost given by the "output gap": $c_2 = \bar{Y} - Y_2$.

We obtain our first important result: *if the market believes that the peg is credible, the output gap (cost) increases as the size of the adverse shock increases.*

Large Recession, Peg Not Credible

This is the most complex situation. Panel (c) assumes a large recession as in panel (b), but shows what happens if investors believe that the authorities will choose to depreciate next year to achieve desired output. We suppose exchange rate expectations are unchanged next year at the pegged rate. The IS curve will still be at IS_2, and the required monetary expansion next year will shift the LM curve to LM_4 so that the new equilibrium will be at point 4 with output at the desired level $\bar{Y}$, and a low interest rate of i_4. This will lead to a temporary depreciation next year, the peg will break, and the exchange rate will rise from $\bar{E}$ to E_{float}. We can also see that to achieve full-employment output, the lower that Y_2 is, the larger the required shift in the LM curve will be next year and the larger the resulting depreciation.

However, the government's response *next year* will be anticipated by investors. If they know that output is low enough to prompt a depreciation, they will expect a depreciation over the coming year of a size given by $\Delta E^e / \bar{E} = (E_{\text{float}} - \bar{E})/\bar{E} > 0$. This expected depreciation will appear *today* as a currency premium in the FX market of panel (c). The current period's risk-adjusted foreign return curve shifts up to FR_2 by an amount equal to the currency premium.

If the central bank wants to maintain the peg, even though it is not credible, it has to ensure forex market equilibrium at point $3'$, so it must raise the home interest rate to i_3. At today's pegged rate $\bar{E}$, uncovered interest parity now requires a higher home interest rate $i_3 = i^* + \Delta E^e / \bar{E}$. Graphically, this means the domestic return curve must also shift up (to DR_2) by an amount equal to the currency premium.

As we know from the earlier chapters on policy and regimes, this shift will depress home demand and lead to even lower home output today, which is shown at Y_3.

In more detail, today the IS curve moves out slightly to IS_3 due to expected depreciation, but the LM curve moves in a long way to LM_3 to defend the peg. The latter effect dominates, because we know that demand and output have to be lower today given the combination of the same exchange rate (no change in the trade balance) and a higher interest rate (lower investment demand). So the new IS–LM equilibrium is at point 3, to the *left* of point 2.

We also note that to achieve this monetary contraction, the central bank must sell reserves—and the drain can take the form of a speculative attack if the currency premium appears suddenly as a result of a switch in beliefs.

The loss of credibility makes a bad recession even worse. If the peg is not credible, a higher interest rate causes the costs of pegging to rise to $c_3 = \bar{Y} - Y_3$. Finally, we note that this cost will be higher when the output gap is higher, because a larger output gap implies a larger depreciation to restore full employment.

Our second important result: *if the forex market switches to believing that the peg is not credible, then reserves drain, the interest rate rises, and the output gap (cost) increases; also, the cost increases more if the output gap is larger to begin with.*

The Costs and Benefits of Pegging

Our IS–LM–FX analysis is now complete, and all we need to do is consider the implications.

Figure 9-17 sums up the cost–benefit analysis. The horizontal axis measures the output gap, or the cost of pegging, *when the peg is credible.* We denote these costs $c(\bar{E})$. This notation indicates that this is the cost c when the exchange rate is expected to be at $\bar{E}$ next period. The first of our results showed that this cost rises, and we move right along the horizontal axis, whenever the country suffers an adverse shock under the peg.

The vertical axis measures and compares the costs and benefits of pegging. Benefits are constant at b. The costs when the peg is credible are equal to $c(\bar{E})$ so these will fall on the 45-degree line, since $c(\bar{E})$ is measured on the horizontal axis.

Finally, the cost of pegging when the peg is not credible is denoted $c(E_{\text{float}})$. This notation indicates that this is the cost c when the exchange rate is expected to be at E_{float} next period.

The second of our results showed that the costs of pegging when the peg is not credible are always greater than the costs when the peg is credible, due to the rise in the currency premium associated with an expected depreciation. In other words, the $c(E_{\text{float}})$ line is above the $c(\bar{E})$ line, as shown. We also saw that the difference gets larger as the costs grow larger. In Figure 9-17, this means that the $c(E_{\text{float}})$ curve diverges from the $c(\bar{E})$ curve, as shown.

Corresponding to the previous analysis in Figure 9-16, point 1 (cost c_1) represents a small recession with a credible peg; point 2 (cost c_2) represents a large recession with a credible peg; point 3 (cost c_3) represents the same large recession with a non-credible peg.

With this basic apparatus, we can now analyze the "game" between the authorities and investors. To keep it simple, we suppose investors can choose from two beliefs about what the government will do: {peg, depreciate}. And we suppose the authorities then choose from two actions: {peg, depreciate}. Faced with this type of problem, economists search for what might be considered a rational outcome of the game. We look for a **self-confirming equilibrium**, that is, combinations of investor beliefs and government actions for which the ex post outcome validates the ex ante beliefs.

FIGURE 9-17

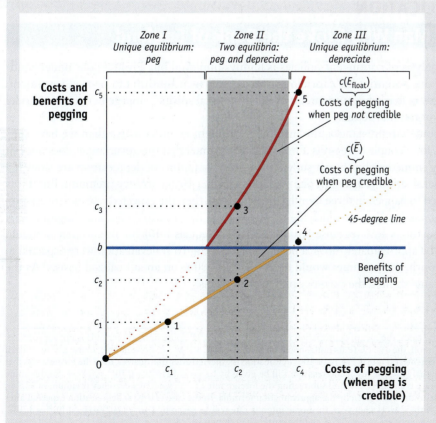

Contingent Policies and Multiple Equilibria
Building on Figure 9-16, this figure shows how the costs of pegging depend on whether the peg is credible, and how that affects the game between the authorities and investors. The costs of pegging when the peg is credible are shown on the horizontal axis. To measure these costs on the vertical axis, we can read off from the 45-degree line. We know that the costs of pegging when the peg is not credible will be even higher. Costs rise when investors do not believe in the peg. We assume the government believes the benefits of pegging (e.g., lower trade costs) are fixed and equal to B. In this world, the peg is always credible in Zone I, where benefits always exceed costs: the government never wants to depreciate and investors know it. The peg is always noncredible in Zone III, where costs always exceed benefits: the government always wants to depreciate and investors know it. Zone II is the gray area: if investors believe the peg is credible, costs are low and the peg will hold; if investors believe the peg is noncredible, costs are higher and the peg will break.

We can identify several such equilibria using Figure 9-17:

- In Zone I, $b > c(E_{\text{float}}) > c(\bar{E})$, so the benefits b of pegging always outweigh both kinds of costs, no matter what the market believes. The authorities will always choose to "peg." Anticipating this, the market belief will also be peg, and this is the only ex ante belief that will be validated ex post. Benefits are always given by b, and costs are always those of a credible peg $c(\bar{E})$. There is a unique self-confirming equilibrium: peg, with costs corresponding to the solid portion of the line $c(\bar{E})$. (Example: point 1.)

- In Zone III, $c(E_{\text{float}}) > c(\bar{E}) > b$, so both kinds of costs of pegging always outweigh the benefits b, no matter what the market believes. The authorities will always choose to "depreciate." Anticipating this, the market belief will also be depreciate, and this is the only ex ante belief that will be validated ex post. Benefits are then always given by b, and the costs are always those of a noncredible peg $c(E_{\text{float}})$. There is a unique self-confirming equilibrium: depreciate, with costs corresponding to the solid portion of the line $c(E_{\text{float}})$. (Example: point 5.)

- In Zone II, $c(E_{\text{float}}) > b > c(\bar{E})$. If the market belief is "depreciate," then the benefits b of pegging are less than the costs of the noncredible peg $c(E_{\text{float}})$; authorities will then choose depreciate, and market beliefs are validated for this case. Conversely, if the market belief is peg, then the benefits b of pegging are greater than the costs of a credible peg $c(\bar{E})$; authorities will then choose peg, and the market beliefs are also validated for this case. There are two self-confirming equilibria in this zone. Zone II is shown as a gray area in the diagram. And appropriately so! In this range, there is no unique equilibrium, and depending on market beliefs, costs may correspond to the solid portions of either line $c(\bar{E})$ or line $c(E_{\text{float}})$. (Examples: points 2 and 3.)

APPLICATION

The Man Who Broke the Bank of England

Our analysis of contingent policies is highly simplified but advances our understanding of the potential for capricious outcomes driven by shifts in market sentiment. Changes in market sentiment, often called "animal spirits," emerge here from a model based on rational actors.

In some circumstances, the instability problem is much worse than we have suggested, for a couple of reasons. First, we have assumed that the government does not exit the peg immediately when it suffers pain, so expectations of depreciation are slow. If a 10% devaluation is feared in one year, this causes a 10% currency premium. But if it is expected to happen in three months (next quarter), then the expected rate of depreciation on an *annualized* basis is much higher and is given by a fourfold compounding of a 10% increase: this is 46% (because 1.10 to the power 4 equals 1.46). So the currency premium would be approximately 46%, a heavy penalty. If the 10% devaluation were expected in one month, the premium would be more than 200% on an annualized basis.[25] As the time frame shrinks, the currency premium explodes!

---

[25] In these cases, the rate of depreciation is not small, so the UIP approximation formula is not appropriate. For precision, the exact UIP formula should be used: $1 + i = (1 + i^*)E^e/E$. For example, to use this formula, if the foreign interest rate is 2%, but a 10% devaluation is expected after one quarter, then the formula says that on an annual basis the home interest rate will be given by $1 + i = (1.02) \times (1 + 0.10)^4 = 1.4934$. So the home interest rate is about 49.3%, and subtracting the foreign rate of 2%, we find a currency premium of 47.3%, still close to the 46% given by the approximation formula. In the case of a 10% depreciation expected after 1 week, with 52 weeks per year, the home interest rate will be given by $1 + i = (1.02) \times (1 + 0.10)^{12} = 3.2012$, so the home interest rate is 220% and the currency premium is 218%.

For example, in 1992 Swedish interest rates climbed astronomically as investors speculated on the imminent demise of the krona's peg to the German mark. The annualized short-term (overnight) lending rate climbed to 75% on September 8 and 500% on September 19. Such an interest rate was not politically tenable for very long. Investors knew this, and they were proved right.

A second issue is how beliefs form in the first place. Suppose we are in Zone II at the "no crisis" self-confirming equilibrium, with beliefs and actions corresponding to "peg." A mass switch in beliefs to "depreciate" would also be a self-confirming equilibrium. How does the market end up in one equilibrium or the other?

If traders are a group of many individuals, spread diffusely throughout the market, then it is unclear how they could all suddenly coordinate a switch to a new set of beliefs. And if each trader can place only a small bet, then it would be irrational for any trader to switch beliefs—unless all traders switch, and without coordination the switch is not going to happen and the peg stands a chance of holding.

But what if there are only a few traders? Or even just one very large trader who can make very big bets? If that single trader changes beliefs, the entire market goes from believing "peg" (no bets) to believing "depreciate" (making as big a bet against the home currency as possible). The coordination problem is solved. This is illustrated by the British ERM crisis of 1992. The large trader was the Quantum Fund, owned by the famous (to some, infamous) investor George Soros, who likes to use the term "reflexivity" to describe how markets shape events, as well as vice versa.

Soros's firm placed one big bet after another, until he had borrowed billions of pounds and parked all the money in German mark deposits. "It was an obvious bet, a one-way bet," he later recalled.[26] If the pound held, he could convert his marks back to pounds, having paid a small interest cost (the difference between pound and mark interest rates for a few days); if the peg broke, he made billions as the pound fell. And who sold him the marks in exchange for pounds? The Bank of England, under orders from the U.K. Treasury, was intervening furiously, selling marks to prop up the pound at the limits of the ERM band.

The sudden increase in the currency premium was inducing a massive reserve drain. On the morning of September 16, 1992, the pressure on the pound became intense. The government made a feeble defense, raising the Bank's interest rates too little, too late, from 10% to 12% and, at the last gasp, to 15%. Pessimistic investors were unimpressed. With bearish sentiment so strong, reserve outflow was unlikely to halt without stronger measures, such as the Swedes had taken the week before. But with the British economy performing weakly, the government had little stomach for triple-digit interest rates—something investors well knew.

It was all over by lunchtime, with the bulk of the reserves lost, and an estimated £4 billion spent in a futile defense. The event has gone down in history as one more legendary British exchange rate fiasco.

George Soros: "Reflexivity is, in effect, a two-way feedback mechanism in which reality helps shape the participants' thinking and the participants' thinking helps shape reality."

Summary

Our results are striking. If government policies are contingent, then they will depend on market sentiment. But market sentiment, in turn, depends on what the market believes the government will do. If costs of pegging are "low," then pegs hold when they "should"—when the government has no desire to exit. If costs of pegging are "high," then crises happen when they "should"—when the government clearly wants to exit. But in between these extremes, an ambiguity arises in the form of multiple equilibria because for some "medium" range of costs, a crisis occurs if and only if the market expects a crisis.

---

[26] Ashley Seager, "Black Wednesday Still Haunts Britain," *Reuters*, September 16, 2002.

5 Conclusions

Fixed exchange rates exhibit no signs of disappearing. Despite all their potential benefits, however, history shows another persistent feature—the recurrent crises that mark
the collapse of fixed regimes.

In this chapter, we studied two kinds of crises. Adverse fiscal conditions can send
the money supply out of control. And changes in the real economy can weaken the
commitment to a peg. Expectations matter in each case—shifts in investor sentiment
can make the crises occur "sooner" (i.e., when economic fundamentals are better),
leading to worries that some crises are an unnecessary and undeserved punishment.

Can We Prevent Crises?

With these insights, we can now confront the major policy problem: How can these
crises be prevented? A number of solutions have been proposed that merit mention:

- *The case for capital controls.* Crises occur in the forex market when investors see
  an arbitrage opportunity in shifting from one currency to another. If a nation
  could shut down its forex market, the risk of a crisis occurring would be lower.
  However, experience shows that capital controls, which are used to limit or
  prevent cross-border arbitrage by investors, are hard to implement and never
  watertight. Empirically, there seems to be no consistent evidence that capital
  controls work to decrease crisis frequency or enhance growth. In addition,
  countries tend to want to maintain financial openness as a way to obtain some
  of the economic gains described in the chapter on financial globalization.
  Controls could be instituted as a temporary policy, but, given the speed with
  which crises can unfold, the controls often end up taking effect after the
  reserves have disappeared. In a few countries (Malaysia after 1997, Spain after
  1992), capital controls may have improved a crisis situation, but in many cases
  controls had only weak or negative effects.[27]

- *The case against intermediate regimes.* One lesson of the models presented in this
  chapter is that a change in market expectations today can trigger "unnecessary" crises, with no deterioration today in economic fundamentals (e.g., GDP,
  inflation, etc.). After the experience of the 1990s, many leading economists
  began to see that intermediate regimes (such as dirty floats and soft pegs) are
  very risky when fluid market expectations are taken into account. Under such
  regimes, the extent of the authorities' commitment to the exchange rate target
  would be seen as questionable, meaning that departures from the target to
  monetize deficits or pursue monetary autonomy might be suspected, leading
  to potentially self-fulfilling crises. How can a nation avoid this outcome? In
  the trilemma diagram, countries should get out of the middle and move to
  the corners. This view came to be known as the **corners hypothesis** or the
  missing middle. Given the prevailing view that controls are not a viable option,
  this reduces the trilemma to a dilemma: in this "bipolar" view, only the two
  extremes of a hard peg or a true float can be recommended (an idea dating back
  to Milton Friedman, quoted at the start of this chapter). Evidence has mounted

---

[27] See, for example, Sebastian Edwards and Jeffrey A. Frankel, eds., 2002, *Preventing Currency Crises in
Emerging Markets*, National Bureau of Economic Research Conference Report (Chicago: University of
Chicago Press); Sebastian Edwards, ed., 2007, *Capital Controls and Capital Flows in Emerging Economies:
Policies, Practices, and Consequences*, National Bureau of Economic Research Conference Report (Chicago:
University of Chicago Press); Reuven Glick, Xueyan Guo, and Michael Hutchison, 2006, "Currency Crises,
Capital-Account Liberalization, and Selection Bias," *Review of Economics and Statistics*, 88(4), 698–714; Rawi
Abdelal and Laura Alfaro, 2003, "Capital and Control: Lessons from Malaysia," *Challenge*, 46(4), 36–53.

that intermediate regimes have been more crisis-prone in the past (up to five times as likely to have a crisis than a hard peg, according to one study), but the move away from such regimes appears to be very slow.[28]

■ *The case for floating.* In a crisis, a peg breaks. If there isn't a peg, there is nothing to break. From that perspective, it might be desirable for all countries to float. However, in the chapter on fixed and floating regimes, we saw that there are powerful reasons to peg, especially in emerging markets and developing countries with *fear of floating*. And empirically, there is no overwhelming trend toward floating regimes in recent years. Thus, the floating corner has not attracted all that many countries in practice.

■ *The case for hard pegs.* If floating is out, then the "bipolar view" suggests that (short of dollarizing) countries should go the other way and adopt a really hard peg like a currency board. Only a few countries have ever taken this route, including such examples as Hong Kong (still operative), Estonia (now using the euro), and Argentina (until its 2001–2002 crisis). Not all of these regimes were *strict* currency boards, but they could all be considered hard pegs, with high reserve ratios and some rules to try to limit domestic credit. Did they work? Some worked very well. Although the Hong Kong Monetary Authority wasn't following the strict rules, the system has worked, and the massive reserves have kept the peg alive even in times of financial market turmoil. But hard pegs can also break like any other kind of government commitment, if the authorities deem it necessary, as they did in Argentina. The lesson: *all fixed exchange rates can be broken, no matter how strong they appear to be.*[29]

■ *The case for improving the institutions of macroeconomic policy and financial markets.* If hard pegs are not a panacea, then risks to pegged regimes might be minimized if the rest of the macroeconomic and financial structure in a country could be endowed with greater strength, increased stability, and enhanced transparency. Admittedly, these goals are always desirable no matter what the exchange rate regime, but they take on added importance when a country is pegging because fiscal and banking problems have emerged as the root cause of so many crises. The steps involved may be slow, incremental, bureaucratic, and unglamorous. But their defenders would claim that, although they lack the "quick-fix" appearance of currency boards and other schemes, these improvements are the foundations on which any successful fixed exchange rate regime must be built.

■ *The case for an international lender of last resort.* We have seen that the adequate level of reserves to avert a crisis can depend on market sentiment. Why not borrow more reserves? This solution is not possible if lenders worry about an imminent crisis and you face a sudden stop. This is where the IMF can help. The IMF may lend to countries in difficulty if it thinks they can restore stability in a timely fashion with the help of a loan. But making the right

---

[28] After Friedman, the corners hypothesis gained new life in the 1990s and became influential in the minds of leading international economists and policymakers, such as Andrew Crockett, Barry Eichengreen, Stanley Fischer, and Lawrence Summers. For surveys of the intellectual history and arguments for and against the bipolar views, see Morris Goldstein, 2002, *Managed Floating*, Policy Analyses in International Economics, No. 66 (Washington, D.C.: Peterson Institute for International Economics); Thomas D. Willett, 2007, "Why the Middle Is Unstable: The Political Economy of Exchange Rate Regimes and Currency Crises," *World Economy*, 30(5), 709–732. On crisis frequency and evidence for a trend away from the middle, see Andrea Bubula and Inci Otker-Robe, *The Continuing Bipolar Conundrum*, IMF Finance and Development, March 2004. Evidence of no such trend is given by Kenneth Rogoff, Ashoka Mody, Nienke Oomes, Robin Brooks, and Aasim M. Husain, 2004, "Evolution and Performance of Exchange Rate Regimes," IMF Occasional Paper No. 229.

[29] With few exceptions, most modern "currency boards" have violated the strict rule against using domestic credit and have not kept the backing ratio close to 100%.

After what happened in 1997, some Asian countries may not turn to the IMF again—and with their reserve accumulation, they may not need to.

judgments is far from easy. The IMF may impose unwelcome loan conditions that require policy change, including, for example, stricter control of budget deficits. If the conditions are ignored, the IMF may suspend the loan program. The IMF has also been criticized on occasion for being too hard (Korea in 1997) or too soft (Argentina in 2001). Moreover, its capacity to lend is limited and is increasingly dwarfed by private capital flows, causing concerns that future attacks may be too large for any IMF program to contain. Not that larger rescue capacity is necessarily good—at a basic level, many worry that the prospect of IMF bailouts, like any kind of insurance, may encourage lax behavior (*moral hazard*), which could worsen the crisis problem. Not surprisingly, the role of the IMF has been constantly questioned in the current era of globalization.[30]

■ *The case for self-insurance.* What if a country wants to peg, but none of the above ideas offers much comfort? What if capital controls are unattractive or porous, floating too risky, and currency boards too much of a straitjacket? What if a country knows that its domestic macroeconomic and financial architecture is still in a state of remodeling? What if the country looks back at the 1990s and worries that IMF programs will be too small, too late, too full of conditions, or not available when they are most needed? In some ways, this describes many of the Asian countries, and other emerging markets, in the 2000s. The vast reserve buildup of recent years seen in these countries may be an exercise in saving for a rainy day to protect themselves against unpredictable shifts in global financial market conditions.

KEY POINTS

1. An exchange rate crisis is a large and sudden depreciation that brings to an end a fixed exchange rate regime.

2. Such crises are common. The typical fixed exchange rate lasts only a few years. History shows that crises can affect all types of countries—advanced, emerging, and developing.

3. Crises have economic costs that tend to be very large in emerging markets and developing countries. Political costs are also large.

4. To avoid a crisis, the central bank in a country with a fixed exchange rate regime must have the ability to peg the exchange rate. In practice, this means the central bank needs foreign currency reserves, which can be bought or sold in the forex market at the fixed rate.

5. In a simple model of a central bank, the money supply consists of domestic credit and foreign reserves. Money demand is exogenous and is determined by interest rates and output levels that we assume

are beyond the control of the authorities when the exchange rate is pegged. In this model, reserves are simply money demand minus domestic credit.

6. If money demand rises (falls), holding domestic credit fixed, reserves rise (fall) by the same amount.

7. If domestic credit rises (falls), holding money demand fixed, reserves fall (rise) by the same amount and the money supply is unchanged. The combined result is called sterilization.

8. When the central bank gives assistance to the financial sector, it expands domestic credit. If it is a bailout, money demand is unchanged, and reserves drain. If it is a loan to satisfy depositors' demand for cash, then reserves stay constant.

9. A first-generation crisis occurs when domestic credit grows at a constant rate forever, usually due to the monetization of a chronic fiscal deficit. Eventually, reserves drain and the money supply grows at the same rate, causing inflation and depreciation.

---

[30] For a critical and nontechnical appraisal of IMF actions from 1994 to 2002, see Paul Blustein, 2001, *The Chastening: Inside the Crisis That Rocked the Global Financial System and Humbled the IMF* (New York: Public Affairs); and Paul Blustein, 2005, *And the Money Kept Rolling In (and Out): Wall Street, the IMF, and the Bankrupting of Argentina* (New York: Public Affairs).

Myopic investors do not anticipate the drain, and when reserves run out, they see a sudden jump (depreciation) in the exchange rate. Investors with foresight will try to sell domestic currency before that jump happens and by doing so will cause a speculative attack and a sudden drain of reserves.

10. A second-generation attack occurs when the authorities' commitment to the peg is contingent. If the domestic economy is suffering too high a cost from pegging, the authorities will consider floating and using expansionary monetary policy to boost output by allowing the currency to depreciate, thus breaking the peg. If investors anticipate that the government will break the peg, they will demand a currency premium, making interest even higher under the peg and raising the costs of pegging still further. In this setup, at some intermediate costs, the authorities will maintain the peg as long as investors find the peg credible, but they will allow their currency to depreciate if investors find the peg not credible. This creates multiple equilibria and self-fulfilling crises.

KEY TERMS

exchange rate crisis, p. 320
banking crisis, p. 322
default crisis, p. 322
twin crises, p. 325
triple crises, p. 325
domestic credit, p. 326
reserves, p. 326
central bank balance sheet, p. 327
assets, p. 327
liabilities, p. 327
floating line, p. 328
fixed line, p. 329
currency board, p. 329

backing ratio, p. 331
risk premium, p. 333
interest rate spread, p. 333
currency premium, p. 333
country premium, p. 333
credibility, p. 335
contagion, p. 335
sterilization, p. 338
insolvent, p. 340
bailout, p. 340
illiquid, p. 340
bank run, p. 340
lender of last resort, p. 340

International Monetary Fund (IMF), p. 343
sterilization bonds, p. 345
first-generation crisis model, p. 349
fiscal dominance, p. 349
speculative attack, p. 353
second-generation crisis model, p. 356
contingent commitment, p. 357
multiple equilibria, p. 357
self-confirming equilibrium, p. 361
corners hypothesis, p. 364

PROBLEMS

1. **📊 Discovering Data** From the information in Figure 2-4 identify three countries with fixed exchange rates. Now use the Internet to search for and visit the websites of each of these countries' central banks and download the latest balance sheet information. For each of the three central banks, answer the following questions.

   a. What is the size of the central bank's balance sheet in local currency (i.e., total assets or total liabilities)?

   b. On the liability side, what is the base money supply in local currency issued by the central bank (call it M_{base})?

   c. On the asset side, what is the quantity of foreign exchange reserves in local currency held by the central bank (call it R)?

   d. What is the central bank's backing ratio (R/M_{base})?

   Finally, given the balance sheet positions and backing ratios of these central banks, discuss their ability to defend their pegs.

2. The economic costs of currency crises appear to be larger in emerging markets and developing countries than they are in advanced countries. Discuss why this is the case, making reference to the interaction between the currency crisis and the financial sector. In what ways do currency crises lead to banking crises in these countries? In what ways do banking crises spark currency crises?

3. Using the central bank balance sheet diagrams, evaluate how each of the following shocks affects a country's ability to defend a fixed exchange rate.

   a. The central bank sells government bonds.

   b. Currency traders expect a depreciation in the home currency in the future.

c. An economic contraction leads to a change in home money demand.

d. The foreign interest rate falls.

4. Consider the central bank balance sheet for the country of Riqueza. Riqueza currently has 2,000 million escudos in its money supply, 1,200 million escudos of which is backed by domestic government bonds; the rest is backed by foreign exchange reserves. Assume that Riqueza maintains a fixed exchange rate of one escudo per dollar, the foreign interest rate remains unchanged, and money demand takes the usual form, $M/P = L(i)Y$. Assume prices are sticky.

   a. Show Riqueza's central bank balance sheet, assuming there are no private banks. What is the backing ratio?

   b. Suppose that Riqueza's central bank sells 400 million escudos in government bonds. Show how this affects the central bank balance sheet. Does this change affect Riqueza's money supply? Explain why or why not. What is the backing ratio now?

   c. Now, starting from this new position, suppose that there is an economic downturn in Riqueza, so that real income contracts by 10%. How will this affect money demand in Riqueza? How will forex traders respond to this change? Explain the responses in the money market and the forex market.

   d. Using a new balance sheet, show how the change described in part (c) affects Riqueza's central bank. What happens to domestic credit? What happens to Riqueza's foreign exchange reserves? Explain the responses in the money market and the forex market.

   e. How will the change above affect the central bank's ability to defend the fixed exchange rate? What is the backing ratio now? Describe how this situation differs from one in which the central bank buys government bonds, as in part (b).

5. What is a currency board? Describe the strict rules about the composition of reserves and domestic credit that apply to this type of monetary arrangement.

6. What is a lender of last resort, and what does it do? If a central bank acts as a lender of last resort under a fixed exchange rate regime, why are reserves at risk?

7. Suppose that a country has a local currency known as the dollar, its money supply is $1,500 million, and its domestic credit is equal to $1,000 million in the year 2020. The country maintains a fixed exchange rate, the central bank monetizes any government budget deficit, and prices are sticky.

   a. Compute total reserves for the year 2020 in dollars. Illustrate this situation on a central bank balance sheet diagram.

   b. Now, suppose the government unexpectedly runs a $200 million deficit in the year 2021 and the money supply is unchanged. Illustrate this change on your diagram. What is the new level of reserves?

   c. If the deficit is unexpected, will the central bank be able to defend the fixed exchange rate?

   d. Suppose the government runs a deficit of $200 million each year from this point forward. What will eventually happen to the central bank's reserves?

   e. In what year will the central bank be forced to abandon its exchange rate peg and why?

   f. What if the future deficits are anticipated? How does your answer to part (e) change? Explain briefly.

8. Consider two countries with fixed exchange rate regimes. In one country, government authorities exert fiscal dominance. In the other, they do not. Describe how this affects the central bank's ability to defend the exchange rate peg. How might this difference in fiscal dominance affect the central bank's credibility?

9. The government of the Republic of Andea is currently pegging the Andean peso to the dollar at $E = 1$ peso per dollar. Assume the following:

   In year 1 the money supply M is 2,700 pesos, reserves R are 1,500 pesos, and domestic credit B is 1,200 pesos. To finance spending, B is growing at 50% per year. Inflation is currently zero, prices are flexible, PPP holds at all times, and initially, $P = 1$. Assume also that the foreign price level is $P^* = 1$, so PPP holds. The government will float the peso if and only if it runs out of reserves. The U.S. nominal interest rate is 5%. Real output is fixed at $Y = 2,700$ at all times. Real money balances are $M/P = 2,700 = L(i)Y$, and L is initially equal to 1.

   a. Assume that Andean investors are myopic and do not foresee the reserves running out. Compute domestic credit in years 1, 2, 3, 4, and 5. At each date, also compute reserves, money supply, and the growth rate of money supply since the previous period (in percent).

b. Continue to assume myopia. When do reserves run out? Call this time T. Assume inflation is constant after time T. What will that new inflation rate be? What will the rate of depreciation be? What will the new domestic interest rate be? (*Hint:* Use PPP and the Fisher effect.)

c. Continue to assume myopia. Suppose that at time T, when the home interest rate i increases, then $L(i)$ drops from 1 to 2/3. Recall that Y remains fixed. What is M/P before time T? What will be the new level of M/P after time T, once reserves have run out and inflation has started?

d. Continue to assume myopia. At time T, what is the price level going to be right before reserves run out? Right after? What is the percentage increase in the price level? In the exchange rate? (*Hint:* Use the answer to part (c) and PPP.)

e. Suppose investors know the rate at which domestic credit is growing. Is the path described above consistent with rational behavior? What would rational investors want to do instead?

f. Given the data presented in the question so far, when do you think a speculative attack would occur? At what level of reserves will such an attack occur? Explain your answer.

10. A peg is not credible when investors fear depreciation in the future, despite official announcements. Why is the home interest rate always higher under a noncredible peg than under a credible peg? Why does that make it more costly to maintain a noncredible peg than a credible peg? Explain why nothing more than a shift in investor beliefs can cause a peg to break.

11. You are the economic advisor to Sir Bufton Tufton, the prime minister of Perfidia. The Bank of Perfidia is pegging the exchange rate of the local currency, the Perfidian albion. The albion is pegged to the wotan, which is the currency of the neighboring country of Wagneria. Until this week both countries have been at full employment. This morning, new data showed that Perfidia was in a mild recession, 1% below desired output. Tufton believes a downturn of 1% or less is economically and politically acceptable but a larger downturn is not. He must face the press in 15 minutes and is considering making one of three statements:

a. "We will abandon the peg to the wotan immediately."

b. "Our policies will not change unless economic conditions deteriorate further."

c. "We shall never surrender our peg to the wotan."

What would you say to Tufton concerning the merits of each statement?

12. What steps have been proposed to prevent exchange rate crises? Discuss their pros and cons.

10

The Euro: Economics and Politics

There is no future for the people of Europe other than in union.

Jean Monnet, a "founding father" of the European Union

This Treaty marks a new stage in the process of creating an ever closer union among the peoples of Europe, in which decisions are taken as closely as possible to the citizen.

Maastricht Treaty (Treaty on European Union), 1992, Title 1, Article A

Political unity can pave the way for monetary unity. Monetary unity imposed under unfavorable conditions will prove a barrier to the achievement of political unity.

Milton Friedman, Nobel laureate, 1997

Questions to consider

1 What are the costs and benefits of a currency union like the euro?

2 Why does the euro exist, and how does it actually function?

3 Is the euro experiment a success or a failure, and what does the future hold?

In 1961 the economist Robert Mundell wrote a paper discussing the idea of a *currency area*, also known as a **currency union** or *monetary union*, in which he considered the circumstances in which it might make economic sense for states or nations to replace their national monies with a single, common currency.

At the time, almost every country was a separate currency area, so Mundell, like many others, wondered whether his research was a hypothetical exercise of limited practical relevance: "What is the appropriate domain of a currency area? It might seem at first that the question is purely academic since it hardly appears within the realm of political feasibility that national currencies would ever be abandoned in favor of any other arrangement."[1]

But almost 40 years later, on January 1, 1999, 11 nations in Europe joined together to form such a currency area, now known as the *Euro area*, or **Eurozone**. Later that year, Mundell found himself the recipient of a Nobel Prize.

The Eurozone has since expanded and continues to expand. By 2020 it comprised 19 of the 27 member states of the European Union. They use the notes and coins bearing the name **euro** and the symbol €, which have taken the place of former national currencies (such as francs, marks, liras, and so on).

The euro remains one of the boldest experiments in the history of the international monetary system. It is a new currency that is used by more than 340 million people in

[1] Robert Mundell, 1961, "A Theory of Optimum Currency Areas," *American Economic Review*, 51, 657–665.

one of the world's most prosperous economic regions. The euro is having enormous economic impacts that will be felt for many years to come.

The goal of this chapter is to understand as fully as possible the political economy of the euro project: that is, its economic as well as political logic. We will study how the two have interacted, the evolving institutional forms, and how the euro actually operates in practice. We first examine the euro's economic logic by exploring and applying theories that seek to explain when it makes economic sense for different economic units (nations, regions, states) to adopt a common currency and when it makes economic sense for them to have distinct monies. To spoil the surprise: based on the current evidence, most economists judge that the Eurozone may not make sense from a purely economic standpoint, at least for now.

We then turn to the historical and political logic of the euro and discuss its distant origins and recent evolution within the larger political project of the European Union. Looking at the euro from these perspectives, we can see how the euro project unfolded as part of a larger enterprise. In this context, the success of the euro depends on assumptions that the European Union functions smoothly as a political union and adequately as an economic union—assumptions that are constantly under question.

The Ins and Outs of the Eurozone Before we begin our discussion of the euro, we need to familiarize ourselves a little with the European Union and the Eurozone, both of which may be unfamiliar ground. Way back at the start of the euro project several decades ago, policymakers imagined that the euro would end up as the single currency of *all* the member states of the **European Union (EU)**. The EU is a mainly economic, but increasingly political, union of countries that is in the process of extending across—and some might argue beyond—the geographical boundaries of Europe. The final impetus in the launching of the euro project came in 1992 with the signing of the *Treaty on European Union*, at Maastricht, in the Netherlands. Under this agreement, known as the **Maastricht Treaty**, the EU initiated a grand project of *Economic and Monetary Union (EMU)*. A major goal of EMU was to establish a currency union in the EU whose monetary affairs would be managed cooperatively by members through a new European Central Bank.[2]

Refer to the map in Figure 10-1, which shows the state of play at the time of this writing in mid-2020. The map depicts some of the EU's main political and monetary alignments. *The two are not the same*: different countries choose to participate in different aspects of economic and monetary integration, a curious feature of the EU project known as *variable geometry*. Here are some important facts now, with details to follow later:

- In mid-2020, the EU comprised 27 countries (*EU-27*). Of the 13 newest members, 10 had joined as part of a major enlargement in 2004; Romania and Bulgaria later joined in 2007, followed by Croatia in 2013. Five more official candidate countries were formally seeking to join the EU—Albania, North Macedonia, Montenegro, Serbia, and Turkey. One country, the United Kingdom, had just left the EU. This event (known as *Brexit*) took place on January 31, 2020, and stemmed from an earlier referendum in 2016.[3]

---

[2] Some very small non-EU, non-Eurozone states and territories also use the euro. Four micro-states outside the EU—Monaco, San Marino, Vatican City, and Andorra—have legal agreements allowing them to use the euro as their de jure currency (they had previously used the national currencies of their neighbors). All these countries except Andorra can mint their own euro coins. Some other economies also use the euro as their de facto currency, notably Montenegro and Kosovo, plus four French and one U.K. overseas dependent territory (Mayotte; Saint Barthélemy; Saint Pierre and Miquelon; the French Southern and Antarctic Lands; and Akrotiri and Dhekelia).

[3] Until the naming dispute with Greece was resolved, North Macedonia was often referred to in official communications as the Former Yugoslav Republic of Macedonia or, if you prefer acronyms, FYROM.

FIGURE 10-1

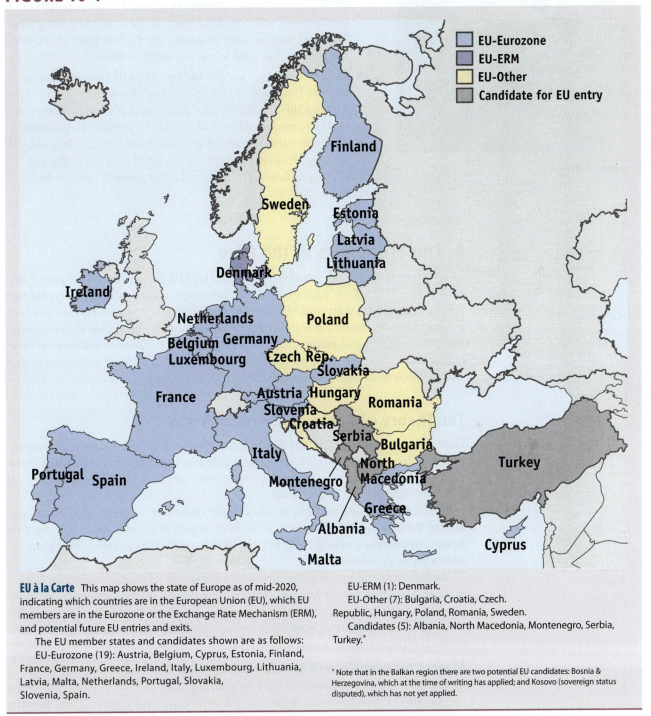

EU à la Carte This map shows the state of Europe as of mid-2020, indicating which countries are in the European Union (EU), which EU members are in the Eurozone or the Exchange Rate Mechanism (ERM), and potential future EU entries and exits.

The EU member states and candidates shown are as follows:

EU-Eurozone (19): Austria, Belgium, Cyprus, Estonia, Finland, France, Germany, Greece, Ireland, Italy, Luxembourg, Lithuania, Latvia, Malta, Netherlands, Portugal, Slovakia, Slovenia, Spain.

EU-ERM (1): Denmark.
EU-Other (7): Bulgaria, Croatia, Czech. Republic, Hungary, Poland, Romania, Sweden.
  Candidates (5): Albania, North Macedonia, Montenegro, Serbia, Turkey.*

* Note that in the Balkan region there are two potential EU candidates: Bosnia & Herzegovina, which at the time of writing has applied; and Kosovo (sovereign status disputed), which has not yet applied.

■ Note that a country can be in the EU but not in the Eurozone. It is important to remember who's "in" and who's "out" of the euro. At the launch of the euro in 1999, just 3 of 15 EU members opted to stay out of the Eurozone and keep their national currencies: these "out" countries were Denmark, Sweden, and the United Kingdom (which has now left the EU). The other 12 all went "in" by 2001. From then until 2013, a total of 13 new entrants joined the EU, with all of them initially "out" of the euro. Soon, the first of these countries, Slovenia (in 2007), became a member of the Eurozone, followed by Cyprus

Euro notes and coins.

and Malta (2008), Slovakia (2009), Estonia (2011), Latvia (2014), and Lithuania (2015). As of mid-2020, the remaining 6 new entrants still remained "out" of the Eurozone, along with Denmark and Sweden, so among the EU members there were a total of 19 "in" and 8 "out" of the Eurozone.

■ Most of the "outs" want to be "in." The official procedure to join the Eurozone requires that those who wish to get "in" must first peg their exchange rates to the euro in a system known as the *Exchange Rate Mechanism* (*ERM*) for at least two years and must also satisfy certain other qualification criteria. Only one country, Denmark, was part of the ERM as of 2020. We will discuss the ERM, the qualification criteria, and other peculiar rules of the Eurozone later in this chapter.

1 The Economics of the Euro

In the nineteenth century, economist John Stuart Mill thought it a "barbarism" that all countries insisted on "having, to their inconvenience and that of their neighbors, a peculiar currency of their own." Barbaric or not, national currencies have always been the norm, while currency unions are rare.[4] Economists presume that such outcomes reflect a deeper logic. A common currency may be more convenient and provide other benefits, but it also has some costs. For the "barbarism" of national currencies to persist, the costs must outweigh the benefits.

The Theory of Optimum Currency Areas

How does a country decide whether to join a currency union? To answer this question, let's see if one country, Home, should join a currency union with another country, Foreign. (Our analysis can be generalized to a case in which Foreign consists of multiple members of a larger currency union.)

If countries make a decision that best serves their self-interest—that is, an optimizing decision—when they form a currency union, then economists use the term **optimum currency area (OCA)** to refer to the resulting monetary union. How can such a decision be made?

To decide whether joining the currency union serves its economic interests, Home must evaluate whether the benefits outweigh the costs. This decision is similar to the decision to select a fixed or floating exchange rate, which we discussed in an earlier chapter. Two familiar ideas from that previous discussion can be applied and extended to the currency union decision.

Market Integration and Efficiency Benefits Adopting a common currency implies that the two regions will have an exchange rate fixed at 1. Hence, the same market integration criterion we used to discriminate between fixed and floating regimes can be applied to the case of an OCA:

If there is a greater degree of economic integration between the home region (A) and the other parts of the common currency zone (B), the volume of transactions between the two and the economic benefits of adopting a common currency due to lowered transaction costs and reduced uncertainty will both be larger.

---

[4] Many currency unions involve the unilateral adoption of a foreign currency by a country that plays no role in managing the common currency (e.g., Panama's use of the U.S. dollar). Even when a foreign country adopts a currency other than the dollar, this situation is often called *dollarization*. In only a few cases are currency unions multilateral in which all member countries participate in the monetary affairs of the union. The Eurozone is the most notable example of a multilateral currency union.

Economic Symmetry and Stability Costs When two regions adopt a common currency, each region will lose its monetary autonomy, and the monetary authorities who have control of the common currency will decide on a common monetary policy and set a common interest rate for all members. Hence, the similarity criterion we used to discriminate between fixed and floating regimes can be applied to the case of an OCA:

If a home country and its potential currency union partners are more economically similar or "symmetric" (they face more symmetric shocks and fewer asymmetric shocks), then it is less costly for the home country to join the currency union.

Simple Optimum Currency Area Criteria

We are now in a position to set out a theory of an OCA by considering the *net benefits* of adopting a common currency. The net benefits equal the benefits minus the costs. The two main lessons we have just encountered suggest the following:

- *As market integration rises, the efficiency benefits of a common currency increase.*
- *As symmetry rises, the stability costs of a common currency decrease.*

Summing up, the OCA theory says that if either market integration or symmetry increases, the net benefits of a common currency will rise. If the net benefits are negative, the home country would stay out based on its economic interests. If the net benefits turn positive, the home country would join based on its economic interests.

Figure 10-2 illustrates the OCA theory graphically, using the same symmetry-integration diagrams used for fixed and floating exchange rates in Chapter 8. The horizontal axis measures market integration for the Home–Foreign pair. The vertical axis measures the symmetry of the shocks experienced by the Home–Foreign pair. If the Home–Foreign pair moves up and to the right in the diagram, then the benefits increase, the costs fall, and so the net benefit of a currency union rises. At some point, the pair crosses a threshold, the OCA line, and enters a region in which it will be optimal for them to form a currency union based on their economic interests.

FIGURE 10-2

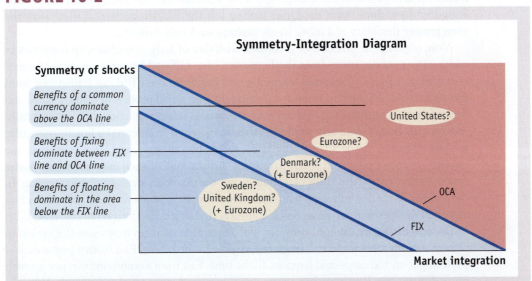

Stylized OCA Criteria Two regions are considering a currency union. If markets become more integrated (a move right on the horizontal axis), the net economic benefits of a currency union increase. If the economic shocks they experience become more symmetric (a move up the vertical axis), the net economic benefits of a currency union also increase. If a pair of regions move far enough up or to the right, benefits exceed costs, net benefits are positive, and they cross the OCA threshold. In the shaded region above the line, it is optimal for a pair of regions to form a currency union. In practice, the OCA line is likely to be above and to the right of the FIX line, as we expect the bar for joining a common currency to be higher than the bar for pegging to that same currency.

The figure looks familiar. The derivation of the OCA line here is identical to the derivation of the FIX line in Chapter 8, which raises an important question.

What's the Difference Between a Fixed Exchange Rate and a Currency Union?

If choosing to fix and choosing to form a currency union were identical decisions, then the FIX and OCA lines would be one and the same. In reality, we think they are likely to differ—and that the OCA line is likely to be above the FIX line, as drawn in Figure 10-2. Thus, when countries consider forming a currency union, the economic tests (based on symmetry and integration) set a higher bar than they set for judging whether it is optimal to fix.

Why might this be so? To give a concrete example, let's consider the case of Denmark, which we studied in an earlier chapter on exchange rates, as an example of the trilemma in Europe. The Danes are in the ERM, so the krone is pegged to the euro. But Denmark has spent a long time in the ERM and shows no signs of taking the next step into the Eurozone. This preference has been democratically expressed by the Danish people: proposals to join the Eurozone have been defeated by referendum. The Danish position looks slightly odd at first glance. Denmark appears to have ceded monetary autonomy to the European Central Bank because its interest rate tracks the euro interest rate closely. Yet the Danes do not gain the full benefits of a currency union because transactions between Denmark and the Eurozone still require a change of currency.

Even so, one can still make a logical case for Denmark to keep its own currency. By doing so, it better preserves the *option* to exercise monetary autonomy at some future date, even if the option is not being used currently. For one thing, even under the ERM, although the krone is pegged very tightly to the euro within ±2% by choice, the Danes could employ the full ±15% band allowed by ERM and give themselves much more exchange rate flexibility. (A ±15% band isn't a very hard peg—recall that the standard de facto threshold for a peg is no more than ±2% variation in one year.) And because they have only gone as far as pegging to—and not joining—the euro, the Danes are always free to leave the ERM at some future date (as Sweden and the United Kingdom have done, with the latter having left the EU altogether) if they want the even greater flexibility of a more freely floating exchange rate.

Now, contrast the position of Denmark with that of Italy, one of several countries in which rumors of departure from the Eurozone have surfaced from time to time (Greece is another example). Compared with a Danish exit from the ERM, an Italian exit from the euro would be messy, complicated, and costly. The actual process of retiring euros and reprinting and reintroducing new lira as money would be difficult enough. More seriously, however, all Italian contracts would have to be switched from euro to lira, in particular the private and public debt contracts. There would be a monumental legal battle over the implicit defaults that would follow from the "lirification" of such euro contracts. Some countries have tried these kinds of strategies, but the examples are not too encouraging. In the 1980s Liberia de-dollarized (and descended into economic crisis); in 2002 Argentina legislated the "pesification" of its dollar contracts (and descended into economic crisis).

Because the future cannot be known with certainty, countries may value the option to change their monetary and exchange rate regime in the future. Exit from a peg is easy— some might say too easy—and happens all the time. Exit from a common currency is much more difficult (the Eurozone has *no* exit procedure) and is expected to be costly. We conclude that because a country's options are more limited after joining a common currency than after joining a peg, the country will set tougher conditions for the former; thus, the smaller OCA region (above and to the right) must lie within the larger optimal fixing region (below and to the left), as shown in Figure 10-2. Put another way, the bar for joining a common currency is higher than the bar for pegging to that same currency.

Other Optimum Currency Area Criteria

Our simple model in Figure 10-2 illustrated two basic motives for joining a currency union, but there could be many other forces at work. These other considerations can still be examined using the same framework, which allows us to consider several additional arguments for joining a currency union.

Labor Market Integration In the analysis so far, the home and foreign countries trade goods and services, but labor is immobile between the two countries. But what if we suppose instead that Home and Foreign have an integrated labor market, so that labor is free to move between them? What effect will this have on the decision to form a currency union?

Labor market integration allows for an alternative adjustment mechanism in the event of asymmetric shocks. For example, suppose Home and Foreign initially have equal output and unemployment. Suppose further that a negative shock hits Home, but not Foreign. If output falls and unemployment rises in Home, then labor will start to migrate to Foreign, where unemployment is lower. If this migration can occur with ease, the impact of the negative shock on Home will be less painful. Furthermore, there will be less need for Home to implement an independent monetary policy response for stabilization purposes. With an excess supply of labor in one region, adjustment can occur through migration.

This reasoning suggests that the cost to Home of forming a currency union with Foreign, due to the loss of monetary policy autonomy, will be lower when the labor market integration between Home and Foreign is higher, because labor mobility provides another mechanism through which Home can adjust to the shock. All else equal, the possibility of gains of this sort would lower the OCA threshold, as reflected in the shift down of the OCA line from OCA_1 to OCA_2 in Figure 10-3. This shift expands the shaded zone in which currency union is preferred: countries are more likely to want to form a currency union when their labor markets are more integrated.

FIGURE 10-3

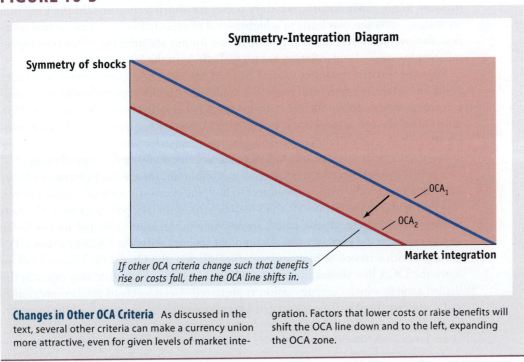

Symmetry-Integration Diagram

Symmetry of shocks

OCA_1

OCA_2

Market integration

If other OCA criteria change such that benefits rise or costs fall, then the OCA line shifts in.

Changes in Other OCA Criteria As discussed in the text, several other criteria can make a currency union more attractive, even for given levels of market integration. Factors that lower costs or raise benefits will shift the OCA line down and to the left, expanding the OCA zone.

Fiscal Transfers We have now examined two possible mechanisms through which countries in a currency union can cope with asymmetric shocks: monetary policy and labor markets, the key OCA trade-off emphasized by Robert Mundell. We have ignored fiscal policy. All else equal, one might argue that a country's fiscal policy is autonomous and largely independent of whether a country is inside or outside a currency union. But there is one important exception: fiscal policy will not be independent when a currency union is built on top of a federal political structure with fiscal mechanisms that permit interstate transfers—a system known as *fiscal federalism*, or a *fiscal union*.

If a region also has a fiscal union, then a third adjustment channel is available: when Home suffers a negative shock, the effects of the shock can be cushioned by fiscal transfers from Foreign, allowing more expansionary fiscal policy in Home than might otherwise be possible. For this argument to be compelling, however, the fiscal transfers must be large enough to make a difference. They must also help overcome some limit on the exercise of Home's fiscal policy; that is, the transfers must finance policies that Home could not finance in some other way (e.g., by government borrowing).

If these conditions are satisfied, then the presence of fiscal transfers will lower the costs of joining a currency union. We show the possibility of gains of this sort in Figure 10-3, where, all else equal, enhanced fiscal transfers mean a lower OCA threshold and a shift down from OCA_1 to OCA_2. This shift expands the shaded zone in which currency union is preferred: the better are the transfer mechanisms in the fiscal union, the more the countries are likely to want to form a currency union, an alternative but important OCA criterion stressed by the international economist Peter Kenen.[5]

Monetary Policy and Nominal Anchoring One important aspect of Home joining a currency union is that Home's central bank ceases to manage monetary policy (or ceases to exist altogether). Monetary policy is then carried out by a common central bank, whose policies and actions may be subject to different designs, objectives, and political oversight. This may or may not be a good thing, depending on whether the overall monetary policy performance of Home's central bank is (or is expected to be) as good as that of the common central bank.

For example, suppose that Home suffers from chronic high inflation that results from an **inflation bias** of home policymakers—the inability to resist the political pressure to use expansionary monetary policy for short-term gains. In the long run, on average, inflation bias leads to a higher level of expected inflation and actual inflation. But average levels of unemployment and output are unchanged because higher inflation is expected and inflation has no real effects in the long run.

Suppose that the common central bank of the currency union would be a more politically independent central bank that could resist political pressures to use expansionary monetary policy for short-term gains. It performs better by delivering low inflation on average, and no worse levels of unemployment or output. In this case, joining the currency union improves economic performance for Home by giving it a better nominal anchor: in this scenario, loss of monetary autonomy can be a good thing.

There is a possibility that this criterion was important for several Eurozone member states that historically have been subject to high inflation—for example, Italy, Greece, and Portugal. We can represent the possibility of monetary policy gains of this sort in Figure 10-3, where, all else equal, a worsening in the home nominal anchor (or an improvement in the currency union's nominal anchor) shifts the OCA line down. For countries with a record of high and variable inflation, the OCA threshold will fall, so again the OCA line moves down from OCA_1 to OCA_2. This shift also expands the shaded zone in which currency union is preferred: given levels of market integration and symmetry, high-inflation countries are more likely to want to join the currency

---

[5] Peter Kenen, 1969, "The Theory of Optimum Currency Areas: An Eclectic View," in *Monetary Problems in the International Economy*, ed. Robert A. Mundell and Alexander K. Swoboda (Chicago: University of Chicago Press), pp. 41–60.

union and the larger are the monetary policy gains of this sort. (Later on we consider the concerns of the low-inflation countries in this scenario.)

Political Objectives Finally, we turn to noneconomic gains and the possibility that countries will join a currency union even if it makes no pure economic sense for them to do so. For instance, one can imagine that Home's "political welfare" may go up, even if pure economic welfare goes down. How?

Suppose a state or group of states is in a situation in which forming a currency union has value for political, security, strategic, or other reasons. For example, when the United States expanded westward in the nineteenth century, it was accepted, without question, that new territories and states would adopt the U.S. dollar. In recent times, eastward expansion of the EU comes with an assumption that, in the end, accession to the union will culminate in monetary union. These beliefs, assumptions, and accords did not rest very much, if at all, on any of the economic OCA criteria we have discussed so far. Instead, they were an act of political faith, of a belief in the states' common political future, a statement about destiny. For example, during and after the Great Recession of 2008, commentators and politicians speaking about states in the Baltics and Eastern Europe argued that these countries were willing to put up with the economic pain of being in the Eurozone during such an event because they had their eyes on the enduring political and security benefits that they hoped would accrue in their long-run post-Soviet existence.

Political benefits can also be represented in Figure 10-3 by the OCA line shifting down from OCA_1 to OCA_2. In this scenario, for countries between OCA_1 and OCA_2, there are *economic costs* to forming a currency union, but these are outweighed by the *political benefits*. The political dimension has played a significant role in EU and Eurozone history, and it is a major topic that plays a big part later in this chapter.

APPLICATION

Optimum Currency Areas: Europe Versus the United States

At first glance, the theory of OCAs helpfully sets out the important criteria by which we can judge whether it is in a country's interest to join a currency union. But while the OCA criteria work well in theory, in reality, the costs and benefits of a currency union cannot be measured with any great accuracy.

Recognizing this, we can try an alternative approach and use comparative analysis to shed some light on the issue by answering a slightly different question: How does Europe compare with the United States on each of the OCA criteria? Clearly, if one took the view that the United States works well as a common currency zone, and if we find that Europe performs as well as or better than the United States on the OCA criteria, then these findings would lend indirect support to the economic logic of the euro.

Goods Market Integration European countries trade a lot with one another. But as far as we can tell (the available data are not entirely comparable), the individual states within the United States trade even more with one another. For the 50 U.S. states shown in Figure 10-4, panel (a), trade flows between U.S. states are about 66% of U.S. GDP. Trade flows between the 17 Eurozone countries are only about 17% of Eurozone GDP. If the creation of a single EU market is still a work in progress (as we see in the next section), intra-EU trade flows will likely rise as the EU's internal market becomes more integrated. On this test, Europe is probably behind the United States for now.

Symmetry of Shocks A direct way to look at the symmetry of shocks is to compare the correlation of a state or country's GDP annual growth rate with the annual GDP growth of the entire zone. As shown in Figure 10-4, panel (b), in this test the Eurozone countries compare more favorably with the U.S. states and regions on this test: for 50 U.S. states and 17 Eurozone countries, the average correlation

FIGURE 10-4

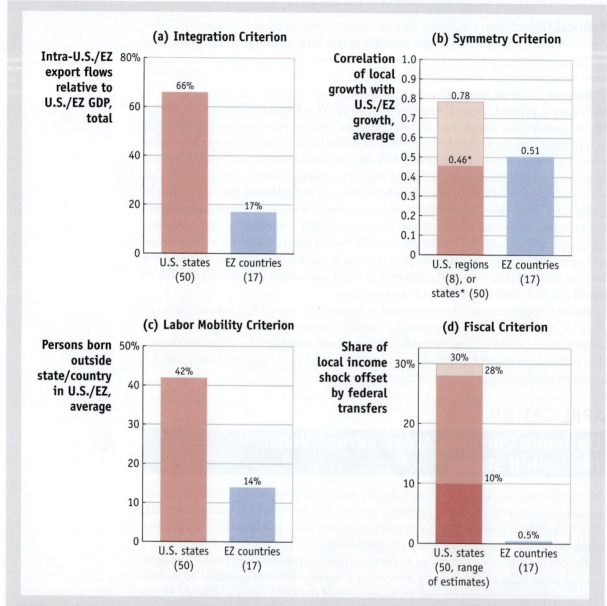

OCA Criteria for the Eurozone and the United States Most economists believe that the United States is much more likely to satisfy the OCA criteria than the Eurozone is. Why? Data in panel (a) show that interregional trade in the United States rises to levels much higher than those seen among Eurozone countries. Data in panel (b) show that U.S. and Eurozone shocks are comparably symmetric in terms of the correlation of macroeconomic shocks. Data in panel (c) show that U.S. labor markets are very integrated compared with those of the Eurozone. Data in panel

(d) show that three estimates of interstate fiscal stabilizers are large in the United States, but essentially nonexistent in the Eurozone.

Data from: Kevin H. O'Rourke and Alan M. Taylor, 2013, "Cross of Euros," Journal of Economic Perspectives, 27(3), 167–92. The data in this study cover the 17 member states that were in the Eurozone as of 2013. The eight U.S. census regions in panel (b) are Far West, Great Lakes, Mideast, New England, Plains, Rocky Mountain, Southeast, Southwest. In panel (d) upper and lower range of U.S. estimates are from multiple sources, with 28% figure based on federal income tax elasticities.

with the entire zone's GDP growth rate is close to 0.5 (the much larger eight U.S. census regions show a much higher correlation with the nation, of course). This result is not too surprising: there is no strong consensus that EU countries are more exposed to local shocks than the U.S. states. However, as we see in a moment, one potential problem for the EU is what happens in the future: one effect of greater EU goods market integration could be that EU countries start to specialize more, and thus become more dissimilar. If this occurs, the risk of asymmetric shocks will increase and the EU will be less likely to satisfy the OCA criteria.

Labor Mobility The data in Figure 10-4, panel (c), show what is well known: labor in Europe is much less mobile between states than it is in the United States. More than 40% of U.S. residents were born outside the state in which they live. In the Eurozone, only 14% of people were born in a different country than the one in which they live. There are obvious explanations for this: differences in culture and language present obstacles to intra-EU migration that are largely absent in the United States. In addition, although the EU is working to ease such frictions, the local regulatory environment and red tape may make it difficult for Europeans to live and work in another EU country, even if they have a legal right to do so. Finally, it is typically harder to hire and fire workers in Europe, a labor market characteristic that may dissuade workers from moving from one place to another in search of better opportunities. Economists have found that differences in unemployment across EU countries tend to be larger and more persistent than they are across the individual U.S. states. In short, the labor market adjustment mechanism is weaker in Europe. On this OCA criterion, Europe is far behind the United States.

Fiscal Transfers The data in Figure 10-4, panel (d), from a survey of the literature, show that when a U.S. state goes into a recession, for every $1 drop in that state's GDP, the federal government compensates with an offsetting transfer of between 10 cents and 30 cents (this range may be too low: the 28-cent figure is the most recent and is based on federal income tax variation alone). Stabilizing transfers of this kind are possible only when states agree to a fiscal union that gives substantial taxing-and-spending authority to a central authority. The United States has had a fiscal union with such stabilizing transfers for a long time, but the EU and the Eurozone have not, as yet, and there is no prospect for such a union any time soon. Although individual states in the Eurozone achieve similar results within their own borders, at the level of the Eurozone as a whole, the fiscal transfer mechanism is nonexistent, offsetting less than 1 cent for every €1 of a nation's GDP decline. (The EU budget is little more than 1% of EU GDP and is devoted to other purposes, notably agricultural subsidies, which do not vary much over the business cycle.)

Summary On the simple OCA criteria, the EU falls short of the United States as a successful OCA, as shown in Figure 10-5. Goods market integration is a little bit weaker, fiscal transfers are negligible, and labor mobility is very low. At best, one can note that economic shocks in the EU are fairly symmetric, but this fact alone gives only limited support for a currency union given the shortcomings in other areas.

Some economists argue that the economic stability costs are exaggerated: they have doubts about stabilization policy in theory (e.g., the Keynesian view that prices are sticky in the short run) or in practice (e.g., the caveats about policy activism noted in Chapter 7 on short-run macroeconomic policies). But most economists think there are still costs involved when a country sacrifices monetary autonomy. They worry that some, or all, Eurozone countries now have an inappropriate one-size-fits-all monetary policy that hinders the achievement of macroeconomic stability, especially when there is no fiscal union. Economists also worry that there are significant financial stability risks, not only because there is no well-defined and properly financed lender-of-last-resort mechanism to support the Eurozone banking system, but also because there is not even a *banking union*, a minimal fiscal union that fulfills

FIGURE 10-5

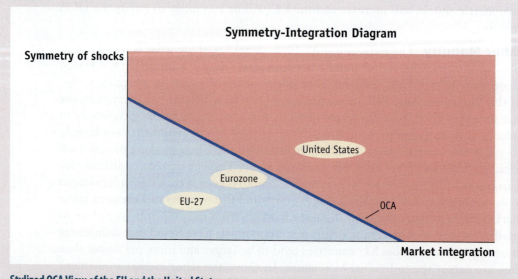

Stylized OCA View of the EU and the United States Most economists consider that the Eurozone and EU countries do not satisfy the OCA criteria—they have too little market integration and their shocks are too asymmetric. The Eurozone may be closer to the OCA line since integration runs deeper there, but it is still far behind the United States on the OCA criteria. If we expand to the EU of 27, it is likely that this larger zone fails to meet OCA criteria by an even larger margin, with lower integration and higher asymmetry than the current Eurozone.

the deposit insurance functions taken for granted in the United States and other advanced economies.

On balance, economists tend to believe that the EU, including the Eurozone within it, was not an OCA in the 1990s when the EMU project took shape and nothing much has happened since then to alter that judgment. Indeed, the crisis of 2008 and the Great Recession and its aftermath only strengthened their doubts.

Are the OCA Criteria Self-Fulfilling?

Our discussion so far has taken a fairly static view of the OCA criteria. Countries treat all of the conditions just discussed as given, and, assuming they have adequate information, they can then judge whether the costs of forming a currency union outweigh the benefits. However, another school of thought argues that some of the OCA criteria are not given (i.e., exogenous) and fixed in stone, but rather they are economic outcomes (i.e., endogenous) determined by, among other things, the creation of the currency union itself. In other words, even if the Eurozone isn't an OCA now, by adopting a common currency, it might become an OCA in the future.

Consider goods market integration, for example. The very act of joining a currency union might be expected to promote more trade by lowering transaction costs. Indeed, that is one of the main supposed benefits. In that case, if the OCA criteria were applied *ex ante* (before the currency union forms), then many countries might exhibit low trade volumes. Their low integration might mean that the OCA criteria are not met, and the currency union might not be formed based on those characteristics. However, if the currency union went ahead anyway, then it might be the case that *ex post* (after the currency union is up and running), countries would trade so much more that in the end the OCA criteria would indeed be satisfied.

This kind of argument is favored by euro-optimists, who see the EU single-market project as an ongoing process and the single currency as one of its crucial elements. This logic suggests that the OCA criteria can be self-fulfilling, at least for a group of

FIGURE 10-6

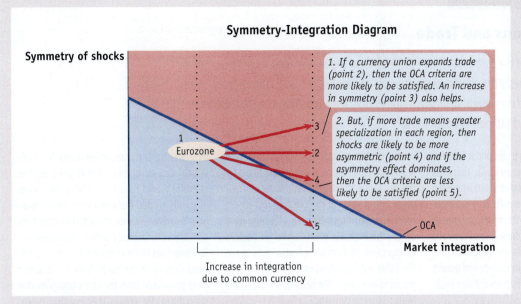

Symmetry-Integration Diagram

Symmetry of shocks

1. If a currency union expands trade (point 2), then the OCA criteria are more likely to be satisfied. An increase in symmetry (point 3) also helps.

2. But, if more trade means greater specialization in each region, then shocks are likely to be more asymmetric (point 4) and if the asymmetry effect dominates, then the OCA criteria are less likely to be satisfied (point 5).

Eurozone

1

2

3

4

5

OCA

Market integration

Increase in integration due to common currency

Self-Fulfilling OCA Criteria Euro-optimists believe that the OCA criteria can be self-fulfilling. Suppose the Eurozone is initially at point 1, but then the effects of EMU start to be felt. Eventually, there will be an increase in market integration (more trade, capital flows, migration), moving the zone to point 2. There may also be a greater synchronization of shocks in the Eurozone, moving the zone to point 3.

However, euro-pessimists note that market integration and more trade might also lead to more specialization by each country in the EU. In that case, the shocks to each country are likely to become more *asymmetric*, implying a move toward point 4 or point 5. In the case of point 5, the case for an OCA grows weaker, not stronger, after the long-run effects of the currency union have been worked out.

countries that are ex ante close to—but not quite—fulfilling the OCA requirements. For example, suppose the EU started out at point 1 in Figure 10-6, just below the OCA line. If the EU countries then formed a monetary union, they would wake up and discover that they had jumped to point 2 once the common currency had boosted trade among them, and, hey, presto: while monetary union didn't make sense beforehand, it does after the fact. Thus, even if the EU or the Eurozone does not look like an OCA now, it might turn out to be an OCA once it is fully operational. However, euro-pessimists doubt that this self-fulfilling effect will amount to much. Evidence is mixed, and the exact magnitude of this effect is subject to considerable dispute (see **Headlines: Currency Unions and Trade**).[6]

A further argument made by optimists is that greater integration under the EU project might also enhance other OCA criteria. For example, if goods markets are better connected, a case can be made that shocks will be more rapidly transmitted within the EU and will be felt more symmetrically. Thus, creating the Eurozone will not only boost trade but also increase the symmetry of shocks, corresponding to a shift from point 1 to point 3 in Figure 10-6. Such a process would strengthen the OCA argument even more.

Set against this optimistic view is the pessimistic prospect that further goods market integration might also lead to more specialization in production. According to this argument, once individual firms can easily serve the whole EU market, and not just their national market, they will exploit economies of scale and concentrate production. Some sectors in the EU might end up becoming concentrated in a few locations. Whereas in

---

[6] Some believe a common currency will have other effects, perhaps also encouraging labor and capital mobility within the Eurozone. These might also change the OCA calculus, but significant evidence on these effects has not been found as yet.

HEADLINES

Currency Unions and Trade

Did the introduction of the euro boost trade? Evidence from the decade following the start of the monetary union suggests the effects were not large, about +5% to +15%. A more recent meta-analysis that averaged over dozens of different studies from the years 2002 to 2016 came up with a similarly small impact estimate of about +12%.[*]

In the continuing controversies about Europe's bold experiment in monetary union, there has at least been some agreement about where the costs and benefits lie. The costs are macroeconomic, caused by forgoing the right to set interest rates to suit the specific economic conditions of a member state. The benefits are microeconomic, consisting of potential gains in trade and growth as the costs of changing currencies and exchange-rate uncertainty are removed.

A [2006] study[**] by Richard Baldwin, a trade economist at the Graduate Institute of International Studies in Geneva, scythes through [previous] estimates. He works out that the boost to trade within the euro area from the single currency is much smaller: between 5% and 15%, with a best estimate of 9%. Furthermore, the gain does not build up over time but has already occurred. And the three European Union countries that stayed out [of the Eurozone]—Britain, Sweden and Denmark—have gained almost as much as founder members, since the single currency has raised their exports to the euro zone by 7%.

Interest in the potential trade gains from the euro was primed . . . by a startling result from research into previous currency unions. In 2000 Andrew Rose, an economist at the University of California, Berkeley, reported that sharing a currency boosts trade by 235%.[†] Such a number looked too big to be true. It clashed with earlier research that found exchange-rate volatility reduced trade only marginally. . . .

Despite such worries, researchers continued to find large trade effects from currency unions. Mr. Baldwin explains why these estimates are unreliable. The main problem is that most of the countries involved are an odd bunch of small, poor economies that are in unions because of former colonial arrangements. Such is their diversity that it is impossible to model the full range of possible influences on their trade. But if some of the omitted factors are correlated with membership of a monetary union, the estimate of its impact on trade is exaggerated. And causality is also likely to run the other way: small, open economies, which would in any case trade heavily, are especially likely to share a currency. . . .

The intractable difficulties in working out the trade effect from previous currency unions means that previous estimates are fatally flawed. But the euro has now been in existence since the start of 1999, with notes and coins circulating since January 2002, so there is an increasing body of evidence based on its experience. That has certainly highlighted the macroeconomic disadvantages for its 12 member states. The loss of monetary sovereignty has hobbled first Germany and, more recently, Italy.

Despite these drawbacks, some studies have pointed to a substantial increase in trade within the euro area arising from monetary union, for example, by 20–25% in the first four years. As with the previous currency unions, however, many other explanatory influences might have come into play. Fortunately, unlike those earlier unions, there is a "control" group: the three countries that stayed out. This is particularly useful because they have shared other relevant aspects of membership of the EU, such as trade policy. It is on the basis of this that Mr. Baldwin reaches his best estimate of a 9% increase in trade within the euro area because of monetary union.

As important, he establishes that the boost to trade did not occur, as expected, by lowering the transaction costs for trade within the euro area. Had it done so, the stimulus would have been a fall in the prices of goods traded between euro-zone members relative to those traded with countries outside the currency union. However, Mr. Baldwin fails to find either this expected relative decline or the trade diversion it would have generated from the three countries that stayed out. He argues that another mechanism was at work. The introduction of the euro has in effect brought down the fixed cost of trading in the euro area. This has made it possible for companies selling products to just a few of the 12 member states to expand their market across more or all of them. This explains why the boost to trade has essentially been a one-off adjustment; and why countries that stayed out have benefited almost as much as those that joined.

[T]here is also an important lesson for the 12 members of the euro area. Even if their economies were insufficiently aligned to be best suited for a currency union, one hope has been that the euro would make them converge as they trade much more intensively with one another. The message from Mr. Baldwin's report is that this is too optimistic. Countries in the euro area will have to undertake more reforms, such as making their labour markets more flexible, if they are to make the best of life with a single monetary policy.

---

[*]Andrew K. Rose, 2016, "Why Estimates of the Trade Effects of the Eurozone Vary So Much," https://voxeu.org/article/why-estimates-trade-effects-eurozone-vary-so-much.
[**]Richard Baldwin, *In or Out: Does It Matter? An Evidence-Based Analysis of the Euro's Trade Effects* (London: Centre for Economic Policy Research, 2006).
[†]Andrew K. Rose, 2000, "One Money, One Market: The Effect of Common Currencies on Trade," *Economic Policy*, 30, 7–45.

---

the past trade barriers and other frictions allowed every EU country to produce a wide range of goods, in the future we might see more clustering (the United States provides many examples, such as the auto industry in Detroit, financial services in New York City, entertainment in Los Angeles, or technology in Silicon Valley and San Francisco). If specialization increases, each country will be less diversified and will face more asymmetric shocks. In Figure 10-6, this might correspond to a move from point 1 to point 4, where the case for OCA would strengthen, though not by much; or even a move to point 5, where the costs of asymmetric shocks are so large that they dominate the gains from market integration, so that the case for an OCA is weakened.

Some speculate that certain other OCA criteria could be affected by the adoption of the euro. Maybe the common currency will encourage greater labor and capital mobility? Maybe it will encourage more fiscal federalism? As with the arguments about the effects on trade creation and specialization, evidence for these claims is fuzzy. Economists cannot make a definitive judgment until the Eurozone experiment has run for many years and there are sufficient data to make reliable statistical inferences about the long-run outcome.

Summary

We have seen how a calculation of economic costs and benefits can help us decide whether a common currency makes sense. Based on these criteria alone, it appears that neither the Eurozone nor the larger EU is an OCA. Admittedly, this conclusion does not apply with equal force to every country in the Eurozone. Some subgroups of countries may satisfy the OCA criteria. For decades Luxembourg has, in fact, used the Belgian franc as a currency; and the Dutch guilder has been closely tied to the German mark. The BeNeLux countries, and maybe Austria too, have always been well integrated with Germany and are therefore stronger candidates for a currency union. Other countries also had strong criteria for joining: for Italy, perhaps, where monetary policy was often more erratic, a better nominal anchor might have outweighed other negatives.

So if the EU as a whole is not an OCA, then why does the euro exist? The euro project was seen as something bigger. This was a currency designed to unify a whole continent of disparate economies, to include France and Germany, Italy and the United Kingdom, to run from west to east, from Scandinavia to the Mediterranean—and it developed with very little reference to the OCA criteria. To understand why the euro happened, we need to study political logic, the topic of the next section.

2 The History and Politics of the Euro

The political origins of the European Union and the euro project can be found in the past. As long ago as 1861, the eminent French writer and statesman Victor Hugo could imagine that "a day will come in which markets open to commerce and minds open to ideas will be the sole battlefields." The timeline in Table 10-1 provides a summary of some of the most important events that have shaped European economic history since 1870. The course of events reveals a European project guided by politics as well as economics.

A Brief History of Europe

The table shows major political and economic events since 1870 and highlights the most important developments affecting monetary policy over the same period. The table is divided into two periods: panel (a) sketches the more distant history that shaped the creation of the EU and progress toward EMU, culminating in the

TABLE 10-1

(a) European Integration Through 1997 This table shows major political and economic events over the past century or more up to the creation of the euro.

	Major Political and Economic Events	Monetary Developments
1870–1914	Largely peaceful era; economic growth and stability.	The **gold standard** system of fixed exchange rates prevails.
1914–45	World Wars I and II; economic malaise, Great Depression.	Collapse of gold standard, floating exchange rates with instability; capital controls widespread.
1946	Period of postwar rapid growth begins, and will last until 1970s.	The **Bretton Woods system** of fixed exchange rates established.
1947–51	**Marshall Plan** reconstruction financed by United States and overseen by the **European High Authority.**	**European Payments Union** is created to free up the European payments system and facilitate trade.
1954–65	In 1954 France, West Germany, Italy, Belgium, Netherlands, Luxembourg form **European Coal and Steel Community** (ECSC). In 1957 they sign **Treaty of Rome** to form **European Economic Community** (EEC). In 1967 the **European Communities** (EC) merges EEC, ECSC, and Euratom; **Council of Ministers** and **European Commission** established.	
1971–73	**First enlargement:** Denmark, Ireland, and United Kingdom join (1973) to form an EC of 9 countries.	The **Bretton Woods system** of fixed exchange rates collapses.
1973–79	**European Parliament** directly elected (1979).	**European Monetary System** (EMS) of monetary cooperation creates a currency basket called the **ECU** (a precursor of euro) and the **Exchange Rate Mechanism** (ERM), a system of quasi-fixed exchange rates (1979). Belgium, Luxembourg, Denmark, Germany, France, Ireland, Italy, and Netherlands join EMS/ERM; United Kingdom joins EMS only.
1981–86	**Second and third enlargements:** Greece (1981), Portugal and Spain (1986) expand EC to 12 countries	Greece, Portugal, and Spain join EMS but not ERM.
1987–90	**Single European Act** (1987) has goal of EC "single market" by 1992.	Spain (1989) and United Kingdom (1990) join ERM.
1990	**German reunification** in 1990 creates new unified German state, adding former East Germany to the EC.	Capital controls abolished in EC.
1991	**Maastricht Treaty** transforms EC into **European Union** (EU); to take effect in 1993. EU citizenship and EU enlargement process established. Plan for **Economic and Monetary Union** (EMU) adopted.	Plan for EMU includes a common currency (Britain and Denmark retain right to opt out de jure). ERM set as the entry route to the euro. Rules for membership and **convergence criteria** established.
1992		Portugal joins ERM. **ERM crisis:** Britain exits ERM, as does Sweden, which will then de facto opt out of the euro; ERM bands eventually widened.
1993	EU sets out **Copenhagen Criteria,** the political and economic conditions that future EU applicants must satisfy.	Applicants expected to enter ERM/EMS and achieve requirements for monetary union in a given period.
1995	**Fourth enlargement:** Austria, Finland, and Sweden expand EU to 15 countries. **Treaty of Schengen** will create common border system, immigration policies, and free travel zone (Ireland and United Kingdom opt out; non-EU countries Iceland, Norway, and Switzerland opt in).	Austria, Finland, and Sweden join EMS. Austria (1995) and Finland (1996) join ERM.
1997	**Treaty of Amsterdam** addresses EU citizenship, rights, powers of European Parliament, employment, and common foreign and security policy.	**Stability and Growth Pact** is adopted to further enforce the Maastricht budgetary rules.

Maastricht Treaty and the preparations for the euro in the 1990s; panel (b) supplies more detail on important recent events affecting the EU and the EMU project starting from the creation of the euro.

The EU project emerged as a cooperative response to a history of noncooperation among nations on the continent, which twice in the twentieth century spilled over into violent military conflict, in World War I (1914–18) and World War II (1939–45). Even during the interwar years, political tensions ran high and economic cooperation

(b) European Integration Since 1998 This table shows major political and economic events in recent years since the creation of the euro.

	Major Political and Economic Events	Monetary Developments
1998	Eleven countries say they will adopt the euro: France, Germany, Italy, Belgium, Netherlands, Luxembourg, Ireland, Portugal, Spain, Austria, Finland.	The **European Central Bank** (ECB) is created. The 11 euro countries freeze their bilateral exchange rates on December 31.
1999		The **euro** is introduced as a unit of account on January 1. Euro notes and coins appear in 2002 and replace national currencies. Greece, Denmark join ERM.
2000–03		In Denmark and Sweden voters reject euro adoption in a referendum.
2001	**Treaty of Nice** addresses EU expansion, amends and consolidates Rome and Maastricht Treaties, and modifies voting procedures.	Greece becomes the 12th country to join the Eurozone.
2004	**Fifth enlargement:** Cyprus, the Czech Republic, Estonia, Hungary, Latvia, Lithuania, Malta, Poland, Slovakia, and Slovenia expand EU to 25 countries.	Estonia, Lithuania, and Slovenia join ERM.
2005	Ratification of EU **Constitutional Treaty** postponed indefinitely following rejection by voters in French and Dutch referenda. Controversial EU accession talks start for Turkey (candidate since 1999 and an associate member of EEC/EC/EU since 1963).	Cyprus, Latvia, Malta, and Slovakia join ERM. Twelve of 25 Eurozone members are in violation of the Stability and Growth Pact rules.
2007	**Sixth enlargement:** Bulgaria and Romania expand EU to 27 countries.	Slovenia becomes the 13th country to join the Eurozone.
2008–11	**Global Financial Crisis** (2008); peripheral countries (Greece, Ireland, Portugal, Spain) in deep recession and at risk of default (2009–); The troika (ECB/EU/IMF) **bailout programs** begin in crisis countries (2010).	Cyprus and Malta (2008), Slovakia (2009), and Estonia (2011) expand Eurozone to 17 countries; ECB (with the EU) takes extraordinary steps to support banks and governments.
2012–14	Fiscal contraction in EU and harsh **austerity** measures in periphery. Eurozone enters **double-dip** recession (2012). Unemployment climbs over 12%, youth unemployment over 24%; majority of people **distrust the EU** in 15 Eurozone countries; Croatia joins EU (2013).	ECB President Draghi promises (2012) to do **"whatever it takes"** to save the euro. Cyprus banking crisis (2013) is fifth troika program; de facto break in monetary union as **capital controls** imposed. Latvia joins the euro in 2014.
2015–16	In a 2015 referendum on the troika program, the **people of Greece reject austerity policies** but the Greek government capitulates to the terms after facing the threat of a banking crisis and ejection from the euro. In a 2016 **"Brexit"** referendum, the people of the United Kingdom vote to leave the EU. Multiple **terrorist attacks,** notably in France. **Migrant and refugee crisis** as people cross external EU border from Africa and Middle East. Rise of **populist** parties and movements in multiple countries, many of them hostile to free migration and also to the euro and/or the EU.	**Capital controls and seemingly indefinite troika program for Greece,** although IMF voices reluctance with status quo. Very **slow economic recovery** in Eurozone, and continued fiscal strains outside Germany. Some **banking distress** in many countries in 2016 after new "bail in" resolution rules go into effect.
2017–20	**Brexit**, the departure of the UK from the EU (2016 referendum, 2020 exit). Growth of **trade tensions** with the United States after the 2016 election of President Trump.	Stronger, centralized **banking supervision** by ECB in Frankfurt, replacing country-level efforts. Continued attempts, but failure to succeed in establishing a true **banking union** to create a common insurance pool covering all deposits across the Eurozone. Slow growth persists and interest rates stuck near zero, limiting policy space in the event of a new recession.

suffered. The situation was not helped by the punishing economic burdens placed on Germany by the Allied powers after World War I.[7] Matters only became worse during the severe economic downturn that was the Great Depression of the 1930s: protectionism surged again and the gold standard collapsed amid beggar-thy-neighbor devaluations (as discussed in the chapter on fixed and floating regimes).

---

[7] John Maynard Keynes, 1919, *The Economic Consequences of the Peace* (London: Macmillan).

A poster created by the Economic Cooperation Administration, an agency of the U.S. government, to promote the Marshall Plan in Europe.

In 1945, as a weak Europe emerged from the devastation of World War II, many feared that peace would only bring about a return to dire economic conditions. More economic suffering might also sow the seeds of more conflict in the future. At an extreme, some feared it would undermine the legitimacy of European capitalism, with the neighboring Soviet bloc all too eager to spread its alternative Communist model.

What could be done? In a speech in Zurich, on September 19, 1946, Winston Churchill presented his vision (see https://www.churchill-in-zurich.ch/en/):

> And what is the plight to which Europe has been reduced? . . . Over wide areas a vast quivering mass of tormented, hungry, care-worn and bewildered human beings gape at the ruins of their cities and their homes, and scan the dark horizons for the approach of some new peril, tyranny or terror. . . . That is all that Europeans, grouped in so many ancient states and nations . . . have got by tearing each other to pieces and spreading havoc far and wide. Yet all the while there is a remedy. . . . It is to recreate the European family, or as much of it as we can, and to provide it with a structure under which it can dwell in peace, in safety and in freedom. We must build a kind of United States of Europe.

Back from the Brink: Marshall Plan to Maastricht, 1945–91 Into this crisis stepped the United States, to offer what has gone down in history as the most generous and successful reconstruction plan ever undertaken, the **Marshall Plan** from 1948 to 1951.[8] Under this plan Americans poured billions of dollars' worth of aid into the war-torn regions of Western Europe to rebuild economic infrastructure (the Soviet bloc refused to take part in the plan).

The Marshall Plan required that the funds be allocated and administered by a European High Authority, composed of representatives of all countries, which encouraged collective action to solve common problems. Many cooperative arrangements were soon established: to smooth international payments and help trade (European Payments Union in 1950); to encourage trade and diminish rivalries in key goods like coal and steel (European Coal and Steel Community, or ECSC, in 1952); and to promote atomic and nuclear science without military rivalry (Euratom, in 1958).

In 1957 the **Treaty of Rome** was signed by six countries—France, West Germany, Italy, Belgium, Netherlands, and Luxembourg. They agreed to create the *European Economic Community*, or EEC, with plans for deeper economic cooperation and integration. In 1967 they went further and merged the EEC, the ECSC, and Euratom to create a new organization referred to as the *European Communities*, or EC. Within the EC, two major new entities were created: the *Council of Ministers*, an intergovernmental decision-making body formed of national heads of government, and a supranational administrative body, the *European Commission*.

The dropping of the word "economic" (in the move from EEC to EC) was significant. By the 1960s two future paths had emerged. Would the EC create just a zone of economic integration? Or would it go further and aspire to a political union or a federal system of states—and if so, how far? The question has been hotly debated ever since.

In the 1970s, two major challenges to the EC project emerged: problems of expansion and problems of monetary affairs. The expansion problem involved deciding when and how to admit new members. By 1973 the first enlargement added Denmark, Ireland, and the United Kingdom. The EC (i.e., the Council of Ministers) viewed

---

[8] George C. Marshall (1880–1959), American military leader during World War II and named U.S. Secretary of State in 1947, proposed the postwar reconstruction effort for Europe in a speech after he was awarded an honorary degree at Harvard University, on Thursday, June 5, 1947. The member countries set up the Organisation for European Economic Co-operation to allocate funds and deliver goods. It would later become the Organisation for Economic Co-operation and Development (OECD), which is still in operation today.

these states as the right type to gain entry—they had solid credentials in terms of economic development and stability, and all were established democracies. In contrast, the second and third enlargements included countries with weaker economic and political claims—but all the same, Greece (1981), Portugal (1986), and Spain (1986) were soon admitted to the growing club. The year 1975 also saw the first meeting of the *European Council*, the gathering of the heads of state or heads of government of all members. This body, which was only formalized in 2009, allows the highest-level elected representatives of each state to shape the EU-wide policy agenda and resolve major disputes at their regular EU summits. Its deliberations, typically lasting through the middle of the night, have played a major role in addressing Europe's increasingly frequent economic and political crises in recent years.

The problem of monetary affairs was precipitated by the collapse of the Bretton Woods system of fixed exchange rates in the early 1970s. As we saw in the fixed-floating chapter, the world had been operating since 1946 under a system of fixed dollar exchange rates with monetary autonomy, with the trilemma being resolved through the imposition of capital controls. In the 1970s, this system broke down and floating exchange rates became the norm in the advanced economies. At that time, except for wars and crises, Europe had spent roughly a century under some form of a fixed exchange rate system, and European policymakers worried that exchange rate instability might compromise their goals for economic union. Indeed, as early as 1970, the EC's visionary *Werner Report* anticipated a path via a transitional fixed exchange rate system toward a single currency within 10 years, although the process would take much longer than that. European leaders did take the first and fateful step down this road when they announced that they would create essentially a new mini–Bretton Woods of their own, the *European Monetary System*, or EMS, which began operation in 1979.

The centerpiece of the EMS was the **Exchange Rate Mechanism (ERM)**, a fixed exchange rate regime based on bands. The ERM defined each currency's central parity against a basket of currencies, the so-called *ECU* (European currency unit), the precursor to the euro. In practice, the non-German currencies ended up being pegged to the German mark, the central reserve currency in the system (just as the U.S. dollar had been the central reserve currency in the Bretton Woods system).

The ERM permitted a range of fluctuation on either side of the central value or *parity*: a narrow band of ±2.25% for most currencies (the escudo, lira, peseta, and pound were at times permitted a wider band of ±6%). In 1979 all EC countries except the United Kingdom joined the ERM; later, Spain joined in 1989, the United Kingdom in 1990, and Portugal in 1992. In principle, it was a "fixed but adjustable" system and the central parities could be changed, giving potential encouragement to speculators (also like Bretton Woods).

Crises and Opportunities: EMU and Other Projects, 1991–99 The EC entered the 1990s with the drive for further integration still going strong. Since 1979 a directly elected European parliament had been at work. In 1987 the Single European Act was passed with the goal of reducing further the barriers between countries through the creation of a "single market" by 1992.

If, within the EC, the political momentum was still strong, it was soon given another push by the end of the Cold War in 1989—although this push would end up taking the entire European project in somewhat new directions and often with unanticipated consequences. The Soviet Union disintegrated and Communist rule in Eastern Europe came to an end, symbolized by the fall of the Berlin Wall. What was the EC going to do in response? The Germans had no doubts—East and West Germany would be reunited quickly, to form Germany again. German reunification was formally completed on October 3, 1990. For the EC as a whole, though, there was the question of how to react to the new states on their eastern flank.

The countries of Eastern Europe were eager to move quickly and decisively away from communism and autocracy and toward capitalism and democracy, and they saw joining the EC as a natural means to that end, as we noted earlier. From a political and security standpoint, the EC could hardly say no to the former communist countries, and so plans for further eastern enlargement had to be made rather quickly. Other countries also waited in the wings. In the early 1990s wars broke out in the Balkans, forcing the EC to confront the big hole in its map between Italy and Greece. Did the former Yugoslav states and Albania belong in "Europe," too? And discussion of the eastern frontier of the EC soon brought to the fore the question of Turkey—a country that has had EC associate member status since 1963 and yet had to wait until 2005 for formal admission talks to begin, and whose possible admission to the EU has long been a matter of political friction (e.g., most recently in the Brexit referendum debate).

In the face of these political challenges, the EC needed to act with purpose, and the grandest treaty to date, the 1991 Treaty on European Union, or the Maastricht Treaty, was the response, reasserting more than ever the goal of creating an "ever closer union among the peoples of Europe." Adding more federal flavor, the treaty gave the EC a new name, the European Union, or EU, and created a notion of EU citizenship. The treaty also laid down the process for enlargement that would eventually take the EU, via three further enlargements, to 15 members in 1995, 25 in 2004, and 27 in 2007.

Later political developments in the 1990s built on Maastricht. The 1993 Copenhagen Criteria provided formal conditions for new members wanting admission, such as rule of law, human rights, democracy, and so on. The 1995 Schengen Treaty established a zone for the free movement of people (though Ireland and the United Kingdom opted out). The 1997 Amsterdam Treaty forged ahead in EU foreign and security policy and strengthened the rights of EU citizenship and the powers of the European parliament.

The most ambitious part of the Maastricht Treaty was its economic element: the EU-wide goal of **Economic and Monetary Union (EMU)**. The *economic union* would rest on the idea of a *single market*, a concept of an EU-wide, fully integrated economic area that would encompass goods and services markets, capital markets, and labor markets. To that end, the treaty established four indivisible central "pillars": the free movement of goods, free movement of services, free movement of capital, and free movement of people. The treaty also called on the European Commission to ensure that national laws and regulations did not stand in the way of these four freedoms.

Even more radical than all of this, however, was an ambitious fifth element in the treaty: the *monetary union*. This element would create a new currency (soon given the name "euro") that was envisaged as the future single currency for the entire EU. Indeed, for some of its adherents, the monetary union was seen as the necessary step to make the single market truly work. Under the plan for the euro, countries would transition at an appointed date from their pegged rates within the ERM into an *irrevocable peg* with the euro. Starting from 1992, constructing the four pillars of the single market proceeded gradually and smoothly, although problems would arise later on. But the plan for the monetary union almost immediately came into doubt and flirted with disaster.

The ERM proved to be a typically fragile fixed exchange rate system. As we saw in Chapter 9, its worst moment came in 1992. In the **ERM crisis**, several ERM countries suffered exchange rate crises and their pegs broke: the British pound, Italian lira, Portuguese escudo, and Spanish peseta. (Other non-ERM currencies, such as the Swedish krona and the Finnish markka pegged to the mark, also experienced crises and broken pegs.) Even the currencies that stayed within the ERM had to have their bands widened so much as to make their pegs look more like floats for a while. The whole system was reduced to a near shambles.

As we saw in the past two chapters, the fundamental cause of these crises was a tension between the macroeconomic objectives of the center country, Germany (tight monetary policy to prevent overheating after a large fiscal shock caused by reunification), and the objectives of the pegging countries (whose authorities wanted to use expansionary monetary policy to boost output during a period of global slowdown).

The ghosts of the 1992 crisis still roam today. Many countries rejoined the ERM, some at a new rate or with a wider band: Spain, Italy, and Portugal all regrouped, reentered ERM, and ultimately adopted the euro. But Britain permanently left the ERM and turned its back on the common currency. Sweden, officially committed to the euro, has never shown any interest in joining even the ERM. Today, in both Britain and Sweden, public opposition to the euro remains high. And there is always the fear that another ERM-style crisis could again erupt in any EU members that peg to the euro.

Still, despite the exchange rate crisis in 1992, the ERM was patched up, and most countries remained committed to the plan to launch the euro. The ERM bands were widened in 1993 to a very slack ±15%, and most were happy to live within those limits and get ready for euro admission.

The Eurozone Is Launched: 1999 and Beyond The euro was launched in 11 countries on January 1, 1999, and administered by a newly created central bank, the **European Central Bank (ECB)**.[9] On that date the ECB took control of monetary policy in all Eurozone countries from each national central bank.[10] The national central banks still have responsibilities. They represent their country on the ECB Council, and still supervise and regulate their own country's financial system. The euro immediately became the unit of account in the Eurozone, and a gradual transition took place as euros began to enter circulation and national currencies were withdrawn.

Table 10-2 shows the history and current state of the EU at the time of this writing in 2020. The table shows the dates of membership in the EU, the ERM, and the Eurozone. Also shown are the fixed exchange rate parities of all ERM and euro members—for the latter, these were frozen upon euro entry and became obsolete once the national currencies were retired.[11]

As of 2020, 19 out of the 27 EU countries were in the Eurozone. Of the 8 "out" countries from the EU-27, there was only one country, Denmark, in the ERM and pegged to the euro, and it had chosen to be there for a long time. This left 7 "out" countries not in ERM. Six of them had floating exchange rates against the euro; Bulgaria was the exception, it has a non-ERM peg. Among the "out" countries, only Denmark can legally opt out of the euro indefinitely, although Sweden acts as if it can, too. (Both countries have popular opposition to the euro and are expected to stay out.) Beyond these cases, all the other "out" countries were officially obliged to join the ERM and then adopt the euro—at some point, although the timetable is not specific.

---

[9] The European Central Bank was established on June 1, 1998. It succeeded a prototype monetary authority, the European Monetary Institute (EMI), which for four and a half years had undertaken much of the groundwork for the euro project.

[10] All EU central banks cooperate as a group in the European System of Central Banks (ESCB). Within that group, the central banks of Eurozone member states (known, confusingly, as the Eurosystem banks) have a much closer relationship with the ECB. Only Eurosystem banks have representation on the ECB's Council.

[11] Since 1999 the original ERM has been replaced with a modified ERM II, with the euro replacing its predecessor, the ecu, as the base currency for pegging. Notwithstanding the Maastricht Treaty, all ERM members now operate in a de jure ±15% band (although, in practice, Denmark has stayed well inside the old, narrow ±2.25% band).

TABLE 10-2

The EU-27 and the Euro Project in 2020 This table shows the progress of each country through EU membership, ERM membership, and adoption of the euro (as of 2020). The euro parities of Eurozone members and ERM members are also shown, although the former have now abolished their national currencies. The dates for future ERM or euro membership are in most cases uncertain or unknown (shown by a question mark); or the dates are unlikely or not required (shown by a dash).

| | | Year Joined | | | | National Currency (Current or Former) |
		EU	ERM	Eurozone	Euro Parity (€1 =)	
Countries in the Eurozone	Austria	1995	1995	1999	13.7603	schilling
	Belgium	1959	1979	1999	40.3399	frank
	Cyprus	2004	2005	2008	0.585274	pound
	Estonia	2004	2004	2011	15.6466	kroon
	Finland	1995	1996	1999	5.94573	markka
	France	1959	1979	1999	6.55957	franc
	Germany	1959	1979	1999	1.95583	mark
	Greece	1981	1999	2001	340.75	drachma
	Ireland	1973	1979	1999	0.787564	pound
	Italy	1959	1979	1999	1936.27	lira
	Latvia	2004	2005	2014	0.702804	lat
	Lithuania	2004	2004	2015	3.4528	litas
	Luxembourg	1959	1979	1999	40.3399	franc
	Malta	2004	2005	2008	0.4293	lira
	Netherlands	1959	1979	1999	2.20371	guilder
	Portugal	1986	1992	1999	200.482	escudo
	Slovakia	2004	2005	2009	30.126	koruna
	Slovenia	2004	2004	2007	239.64	tolar
	Spain	1986	1989	1999	166.386	peseta
Countries in the ERM	Denmark*	1973	1999	—	7.46038	krone
Other EU Countries	Bulgaria	2007	?	?	?	lev
	Croatia	2013	?	?	?	kuna
	Czech Republic	2004	?	?	?	koruna
	Hungary	2004	?	?	?	forint
	Poland	2004	?	?	?	zloty
	Romania	2007	?	?	?	leu
	Sweden*	1995	—	—	?	krona

*Denmark can legally opt out of the euro. Sweden is opting out de facto by choosing not to join the ERM. All other countries are technically expected to join the euro at some point.

Summary

History shows that the countries of Europe have some deep tendency to prefer fixed exchange rates to floating rates. Apart from brief crisis episodes in times of turmoil (during wars, the Great Depression, and the early 1970s), most European countries have maintained pegged exchange rates against each other since the 1870s. They have now taken the additional step of adopting a common currency.

There have certainly been some economic changes in Europe that make it more likely to satisfy the OCA criteria now than at any time in the past. The EU project has pushed forward a process of deep economic integration, with major steps such as the EMU and Schengen treaties bringing Europe closer to the ideal of a single market. But integration is still very much a work in progress, and the OCA criteria are unlikely to be met soon.

Instead, European history leads us to the conclusion that the common currency fits as part of a political project rather than as a purely economic choice. To consider some of the implications of this conclusion, in the remainder of this chapter we consider some of the operational issues and problems faced by the Eurozone during its first two decades of existence.

3 Eurozone Tensions in Tranquil Times, 1999–2007

From its launch in 1999 until 2007 or so, the Eurozone was considered a success. Compared to what came next, this was a time of economic growth and stability for the Eurozone—a period with no recession and with the ECB untroubled by problems either with its explicit inflation target goal or its broader responsibility to support Eurozone economic and financial stability.

In this section we review this fortunate period, focusing on the way in which the ECB's monetary policy rules were devised, and the broader concerns about fiscal stability. This period will be remembered for a somewhat narrow and limited policy focus and a general complacency concerning some of the ultimately more dangerous macroeconomic trends that we discuss in the section that follows.

The European Central Bank

Suppose some German economists from the 1950s or 1960s, after having traveled forward in time to the present day, pop up next to you on a Frankfurt street corner, and say, "Take me to the central bank." They are surprised when you lead them to the new ECB building instead of the old Bundesbank building.

It is no coincidence that the European Central Bank is located in Frankfurt. It is a testament to the strong influence of German monetary policymakers and politicians in the design of the euro project, an influence they earned on account of the exemplary performance of the German economy, and especially its monetary policy, from the 1950s to the 1990s. To see how German influence has left its mark on the euro, we first examine how the ECB operates and then try to explain its peculiar goals and governance.

For economists, central banks have a few key features. To sum these up, we may ask: What policy instrument does the bank use? What is it supposed to do (goals) and not do (forbidden activities)? How are decisions on these policies made given the bank's governance structure? To whom is the bank accountable, and, subject to that, how much independence does the bank have? For the ECB, the brief answers are as follows:

- *Instrument and goals.* The instrument used by the ECB is the interest rate at which banks can borrow funds. According to its charter, the ECB's primary objective is to "maintain price stability" in the euro area. Its secondary goal is to "support the general economic policies in the Community with a view to contributing to the achievement of the objectives of the Community." (Many central banks have similar instruments and goals, but the ECB has a relatively strong focus on inflation.)

- *Forbidden activities.* To prevent the use of monetary policy for other goals, the ECB may not directly finance member states' fiscal deficits or provide bailouts to member governments or national public bodies. In addition, the ECB has no mandate to act as a lender of last resort by extending credit to financial institutions in the Eurozone in the event of a banking or financial crisis. (Most central banks are not so constrained, and they typically can buy their own government's debt and act as a lender of last resort to private banks or financial institutions.)

- *Governance and decision making.* Monetary policy decisions are made at meetings of the ECB's Governing Council, which consists of the central bank governors of the Eurozone national central banks and six members of the ECB's executive board. In practice, most policy decisions are made by consensus rather than by majority voting. Meetings are usually held twice each month.

- *Accountability and independence.* No monetary policy powers are given to any other EU institution. No EU institution has any formal oversight of the ECB, and the ECB does not have to report to any political body, elected or otherwise. The ECB does not release minutes of its meetings or details of any votes (but in 2015 it began to publish accounts of its meetings). The ECB has independence not only with respect to its instrument (it sets interest rates) but also with respect to its goal (it gets to define what "price stability" means). A small but growing number of central banks around the world has achieved some independence, but the ECB has more than most.

On all four points, the working of the ECB has been subject to strong criticisms.

Criticisms of the ECB   There is controversy over the price stability goal. The ECB chooses to define price stability as a Eurozone consumer price inflation rate of less than but "close to" 2% per year over the medium term. This target is vague (the notions of "close to" and "medium term" are not defined). The target is also asymmetrical (there is no lower bound to guard against deflation), a characteristic that became a particular worry as inflation rates fell toward zero during the Great Recession following the Global Financial Crisis of 2008. As global real interest rates have fallen to record low levels in recent years, the ECB, like other central banks, also now faces a much lower level for its "neutral" policy rate, which leaves little room for downward easing without hitting the zero lower bound for nominal interest rates—another problem with the ECB's choice of a low inflation target.

There is controversy over having only price stability as a goal. On paper, the ECB technically has a secondary goal of supporting and stabilizing the Eurozone economy. But in practice, the ECB has acted as if it places little weight on economic performance, growth, and unemployment, and where the real economy is in the business cycle. In this area, the ECB's policy preferences are different from, say, those of the U.S. Federal Reserve, which has a mandate from Congress not only to ensure price stability but also to achieve full employment. The ECB also differs from the Bank of England, whose former Governor Mervyn King once famously used the term "inflation nutter" to describe a policymaker with an excessive focus on price stability. The ECB's early obsessive focus on money and prices was thought to reflect a combination of its Germanic heritage and its relative lack of long-term reputation.

There is controversy over the ECB's way of conducting policy to achieve its goal. In addition to the "first pillar," which uses an economic analysis of expected price inflation to guide interest rate decisions, the bank has a "second pillar" in the form of a reference value for money supply growth (4.5% per annum). As we saw in the chapter on exchange rates in the long run, however, a fixed money growth rate can be consistent with an inflation target only by chance. For example, in the quantity theory model, which assumes a stable level of nominal interest rates in the long run, inflation equals the money growth rate minus the growth rate of real output. So the ECB's twin pillars will make sense only if real output just happens to grow at less than 2.5% per year, for only then will inflation be, at most, $4.5 - 2.5 = 2\%$ per year. Perhaps aware of the inconsistency of using two nominal anchors, the ECB has given the impression that most of the time it ignores the second pillar; nonetheless, concern about money supply growth is occasionally expressed.

There is controversy over the strict interpretation of the "forbidden activities" rules. What happens in the event of a large banking crisis in the Eurozone? When banking crises hit other nations, many central banks would choose to extend credit to specific troubled banks or to relax lending standards to the banking sector as a whole, and they could print money to do so. In the Eurozone, officially the ECB can print the money, but it cannot implement either type of additional lending; the national central banks of countries in the Eurozone can do the lending but can't print the money. National central banks can devise limited, local credit facilities or arrange private consortia to manage a small crisis, or they can hope for fiscal help from their national treasuries. Big crises could therefore prove more difficult to prevent or contain. (In a discussion that appears later in this chapter, we look at how the ECB reacted during and after the Global Financial Crisis of 2008 and how it was able to ease, or skirt, these rules somewhat.)

There is controversy over the decision-making process and lack of transparency. Votes are not formally required, and no votes of any kind are reported. Consensus decisions are preferred, but these may favor the status quo, causing policy to lag when it ought to move. Minutes are recorded but can be kept secret for 30 years, and their level of detail is not known. Some parts of meetings are private *without any record being kept at all*. Insistence on having all 19 central bank governors plus the 6 Executive Board members on the Council leads to a very large body; consensus can be hard to achieve, which, in turn, can make prompt action difficult to take. This design will become even more cumbersome should even more countries join the euro, but the structure of the Council is set in the Maastricht Treaty and is impossible to change without revising the treaty.

There is controversy over the ECB's lack of accountability. Because so much of its operation is secret and it answers to no political masters, some fear that people in the Eurozone will conclude that the ECB lacks legitimacy. Although the EU is a collection of democratic states, many of its decisions are made in places that are far from the people in these states. Many EU bodies suffer a perceived "democratic deficit," including the work of the unelected Commission and the treaties pursued at the intra-governmental level with no popular ratification and little consultation. The ECB can appear to be even further removed at a supra-governmental level. There is nothing akin to the U.S. requirement that the Federal Reserve chairman regularly answer questions from Congress. Rather, the ECB has a more informal dialogue and consultations with the Council, Commission, and Parliament. In response, the finance ministers of the Eurozone have ganged up to form the *Eurogroup*, which meets and opines about what is happening in the Eurozone and what the ECB is (or should be) doing. Occasionally, national heads of governments weigh in to attack the ECB's policy choices or to defend them. Along with the EU's commissioner for economic and monetary affairs, heads of government can make pronouncements and lobby, but they can do little more unless a treaty revision places the ECB under more scrutiny.

The German Model Some of these criticisms are valid and undisputed, but others are fiercely contested. Supporters of the ECB say that strong independence and freedom from political interference are exactly what is needed in a young institution that is struggling to achieve credibility and that the dominant problem in the Eurozone in the recent past has been inflation, not deflation. For many of these supporters, the ECB is set up the right way—almost a copy of the Bundesbank, with a strong focus on low inflation to the exclusion of other criteria and a complete separation of monetary policy from politics. Here, German preferences and German economic performance had been very different from those for the rest of the Eurozone, yet they prevailed. How can this be understood?

German preferences for a low-inflation environment have been extremely strong ever since the costly and chaotic interwar hyperinflation (discussed in the chapter on exchange rates in the long run). It was clear that the hyperinflation had been driven by reckless fiscal policy, which had led politicians to take over monetary policy and run the printing presses. After that fiasco, strong anti-inflation preferences, translated from the people via the political process, were reflected in the conduct of monetary policy by the Bundesbank from 1958 until the arrival of the euro in 1999. To ensure that the Bundesbank could deliver a firm nominal anchor, it was carefully insulated from political interference.

Today, as we learned when studying exchange rates in the long run, a popular recipe for sound monetary policy is a combination of central bank independence and an inflation target. Sometimes, the inflation target is set by the government, the so-called *New Zealand model*. But the so-called *German model* went further and faster: the Bundesbank was not only the first central bank to be granted full independence, it was also given both *instrument independence* (freedom to use interest rate policy in the short run) and *goal independence* (the power to decide what the inflation target should be in the long run). This became the model for the ECB, when Germany set most of the conditions for entering a monetary union with other countries where the traditions of central bank independence were weaker or nonexistent.

Monetary Union with Inflation Bias We can see where Germany's preferences came from. But how did it get its way? A deep problem in modern macroeconomics concerns the *time inconsistency* of policies.[12] According to this view, all countries have a problem with inflation bias under discretionary monetary policy. Policymakers would like to commit to low inflation, but without a credible commitment to low inflation, a politically controlled central bank has the temptation to use "surprise" monetary policy expansions to boost output. Eventually, this bias will be anticipated and built into inflation expectations, and hence, in the long run, real outcomes—such as output and unemployment—will be the same whatever the extent of the inflation bias. Long-run money neutrality means that printing money can't make an economy more productive or create jobs.

The inflation bias problem can be solved if we can separate the central bank from politics and install a "conservative central banker" who cares about inflation and nothing else. This separation was strong in Germany, but not elsewhere. Hence, a historically low-inflation country (e.g., Germany) might be worried that a monetary union with a high-inflation country (e.g., Italy) would lead to a monetary union with on average a tendency for middling levels of inflation—that is, looser monetary policies on average for Germany and tighter on average for Italy. In the long run, Germany and Italy would still get the same real outcomes (though in the short run, Germany might have a monetary-led boom and Italy a recession). But, while Italy might gain in the long run from lower inflation, Germany would lose from the shift to a high-inflation environment. Germany would need assurances that this would not happen, and because Germany was such a large and pivotal country in the EU, a Eurozone without Germany was unimaginable (based on simple OCA logic or on political logic). So Germany had a lot of bargaining power.

Essentially, the bargaining over the design of the ECB and the Eurozone boiled down to this: other countries were content to accept that in the long run their real outcomes would not be any different even if they switched to a monetary policy run by the ECB under the German model, and thus had to settle for less political manipulation of monetary policy.

Or so they said at the time. But how could one be sure that these countries did in fact mean what they said? One could take countries' word for it—trust them. Or one could make them prove it—test them. In a world of inflation bias, trust in monetary authorities is weak, so the Maastricht Treaty established some tests—that is, some rules for admission.

---

[12] Finn E. Kydland and Edward C. Prescott, 1977, "Rules Rather Than Discretion: The Inconsistency of Optimal Plans," *Journal of Political Economy*, 87, 473–492; Guillermo Calvo, 1978, "On the Time Consistency of Optimal Policy in a Monetary Economy," *Econometrica*, 46, 1411–1428; Robert J. Barro and David B. Gordon, 1983, "Rules, Discretion and Reputation in a Model of Monetary Policy," *Journal of Monetary Economics*, 12, 101–121.

TABLE 10-3

Rules of Euro Membership The Maastricht Treaty of 1991 established five conditions that aspiring members of the Eurozone must satisfy prior to entry. The last two fiscal rules are also supposed to be obeyed by members even after entry.

Rule (*prior to entry only)	Criterion
Exchange rate*	Two consecutive years in ERM band with no devaluation (no change in central parity).
Inflation rate*	No more than 1.5 percentage points above the level in the three member states with the lowest inflation in the previous year.
Long-term nominal interest rate*	No more than 2 percentage points above the level in the three member states with the lowest inflation in the previous year.
Government deficit	No more than 3% of GDP in previous financial year.[1]
Government debt	No more than 60% of GDP in previous financial year.[2]

Notes: The ERM bands in effect at the time of the Maastricht Treaty were narrow (±2.25% or ±6%); since 1993 they have been wide (±15%). The first rule is now applied using the wide bands. Escape clauses were included in the last two fiscal rules, as follows:

[1] *Or "the ratio must have declined substantially and continuously and reached a level close to 3% or, alternatively, must remain close to 3% while representing only an exceptional and temporary excess."*

[2] *Or "the ratio must have sufficiently diminished and must be approaching the reference value at a satisfactory pace."*

The Rules of the Club

The Maastricht Treaty established five rules for admission to the euro zone, as shown in Table 10-3. All five of these **convergence criteria** need to be satisfied for entry. Two of the five rules also serve as ongoing requirements for membership. The rules can be divided into two parts: three rules requiring convergence in nominal measures closely related to inflation and two rules requiring fiscal discipline to clamp down on the deeper determinants of inflation.

Nominal Convergence In the chapters on short- and long-run exchange rates, we explored some of the central implications of a fixed exchange rate, implications that also apply when two countries adopt a common currency (i.e., a fixed exchange rate of 1). Let's consider three implications:

- Under a peg, the exchange rate must be fixed or not vary beyond tight limits.
- Purchasing power parity (PPP) then implies that the two countries' inflation rates must be very close.
- Uncovered interest parity (UIP) then implies that the two countries' long-term nominal interest rates must be very close.

In fact, we may recall that the Fisher effect says that the inflation differential must equal the nominal interest rate differential—so if one is small, the other has to be small, too.

These three conditions all relate to the nominal anchoring provided by a peg, and they roughly correspond to the first three Maastricht criteria in Table 10-3.

The rules say that a country must stay in its ERM band (with no realignment) for two years to satisfy the peg rule.[13] It must have an inflation rate "close to" that of the three lowest-inflation countries in the zone to satisfy the inflation rule. And it must

---

[13] The two-year requirement for the ERM means a country can't cheat by stabilizing its currency at the last minute, possibly in an opportunistic way to get in at a favorable (depreciated) rate that boosts demand for the country's output. Still, as currently interpreted, the ERM rule means that a currency only has to stay within the wide (post-1993) ±15% ERM bands, so the constraint is not all that tight.

FIGURE 10-7

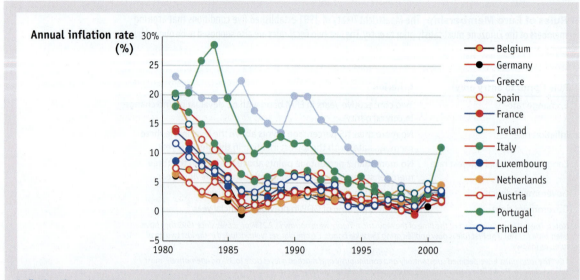

Inflation Convergence   To meet the Maastricht Treaty's convergence criteria, the first 12 members of the Eurozone had to reduce their inflation level below a moving target. This target was equal to average inflation in the three lowest-inflation countries in the bloc plus 1.5 percentage points. This process ensured that the Eurozone began with a low inflation rate. The countries currently in the ERM must pass the same test before they can adopt the euro.

Data from: European Economy, Statistical Annex, Autumn 2005.

have a long-term interest rate "close to" that in the three low-inflation countries.[14] All three tests must be met for a country to satisfy the admission criteria.

What is the economic sense for these rules? They appear, in some ways, superfluous because if a country credibly pegged to (or has adopted) the euro, theory says that these conditions would have to be satisfied in the long run anyway. For that reason they are also difficult to criticize—except to say that, if the rules are going to be met anyway, why not "just do it" and let countries join the euro without such conditions? The answer relates to our earlier discussion about inflation bias. If two countries with different inflation rates adopt a common currency, their inflation rates must converge—but to what level, high or low?

The way the rules were written forces countries to converge on the lowest inflation rates in the zone. We have argued that this outcome is needed for low-inflation countries to sign up, although it will require possibly painful policy change in the high-inflation countries. The Maastricht criteria ensure that high-inflation countries go through this pain and attain credibility by demonstrating their commitment to low inflation before they are allowed in. This process supposedly prevents governments with a preference for high inflation from entering the Eurozone and then trying to persuade the ECB to go soft on inflation. These three rules can thus be seen as addressing the credibility problem in a world of inflation bias. All current euro members successfully satisfied these rules to gain membership, and the end result was marked inflation convergence as shown in Figure 10-7. Current and future ERM members are required to go through the same test.

---

[14] The interest rate rule relates to the long-term interest rate for government borrowing, not the short-term rate that is central to UIP. Over the long run, the two move together and on average are generally separated by a positive *term premium*. Under a peg, then, countries will share identical *long-term* interest rates if and only if (1) there is no risk premium difference between them and (2) there is no term premium difference either. In practice, risk premiums and term premiums are higher for riskier borrowers, so in some ways this rule is also related to fiscal discipline (discussed in the next section).

Fiscal Discipline The Maastricht Treaty wasn't just tough on inflation; it was tough on the causes of inflation, and it saw the fundamental and deep causes of inflation as being not monetary, but fiscal. The other two Maastricht rules are openly aimed at constraining fiscal policy. They are applied not just as a condition for admission but also to all member states once they are in. The rules say that government debts and deficits cannot be above certain reference levels (although the treaty allows some exceptions). These levels were chosen somewhat arbitrarily: a deficit level of 3% of GDP and a debt level of 60% of GDP. However arbitrary these reference levels are, there still exist economic rationales for having some kinds of fiscal rules in a monetary union in which the member states maintain fiscal sovereignty.

Why might inflation ultimately be a fiscal problem? Consider two countries negotiating the treaty before the euro begins, one with low debt levels (e.g., Germany) and one with high debt levels (e.g., Italy). Germany has several possible fears in this case. One is that if Italy has high nominal debt (measured in lira at the time, but soon to be measured in euros), Italy will lobby for high inflation once in the union (because inflation destroys the real value of the government's debt). Another fear is that Italy has a higher default risk, which might result in political pressure for the ECB to break its own rules and bail out Italy in a crisis, which the ECB can do only by printing euros and, again, generating more inflation.

The main arguments for the fiscal rules are that any deal to form a currency union will require fiscally weak countries to tighten their belts and meet criteria set by fiscally strong countries in order to further ensure against inflation.

Criticism of the Convergence Criteria Because these rules constitute the main gatekeeping mechanism for the Eurozone, they have been carefully scrutinized and have generated much controversy.

First, these rules involve asymmetric adjustments that take a long time. In the 1980s and 1990s, they mostly involved German preferences on inflation and fiscal policy being imposed at great cost on other countries. Germany had lower inflation and larger surpluses than most countries, and the criteria were set close to the German levels, not surprisingly. To converge on these levels, tighter fiscal and monetary policies had to be adopted in countries like France, Italy, Portugal, and Spain while they tried to maintain the peg (to obey rule 1: staying in their ERM bands). As we saw in the chapter on output, exchange rates, and macroeconomic policy, fiscal contractions are even more contractionary under a peg than under a float. Such policies are politically costly, and hence the peg may not be fully credible. As we saw in the chapter on crises, foreign exchange traders often have doubts about the resolve of the authorities to stick with contractionary policies, and these doubts can increase the risk of self-fulfilling exchange rate crises, as happened in 1992. The same costs and risks now weigh on current Eurozone applicants seeking to pass these tests.

Second, the fiscal rules are seen as inflexible and arbitrary. The numerical targets have little justification: Why 3% for the deficit and not 4%? Why 60% and not 70% for the debt level? As for flexibility, the rules in particular pay no attention to the stage of the business cycle in a particular applicant country. A country in a recession may have a very large deficit even if on average the country has a government budget that is fairly balanced across the whole business cycle. In other words, the well-established arguments for the prudent use of countercyclical fiscal policy (including even nondiscretionary automatic stabilizers) are totally ignored by the Maastricht criteria. This is an ongoing problem, as we see in a moment.

Third, whatever good might result from the painful convergence process, it might be only fleeting. For example, the Greek or French governments of the 1990s may have subjected themselves to budgetary discipline and monetary conservatism. Had their preferences really changed, or did they just go along with the rules (or pretend to) merely as a way to get in? The same question applies to current Eurozone applicants.

The problems just noted do not disappear once countries are in the Eurozone. Countries continue to have their own fiscal policies as members of the Eurozone, and they all gain a share of influence on ECB policy through the governance structure of the central bank. Countries' incentives are different once the carrot of EMU membership has been eaten.

Sticking to the Rules

If "in" countries desire more monetary and fiscal flexibility than the rules allow, and being "in" means they no longer risk the punishment of being excluded from the Eurozone, then a skeptic would have to expect more severe budgetary problems and more lobbying for loose monetary policy to appear once countries had entered the Eurozone.

On this point, as we see, the skeptics were to some extent proved right, but the problems they identified were not entirely ignored in the Eurozone's design. On the monetary side, success (low and stable Eurozone inflation) would rest on the design of the ECB as an institution that could withstand political pressure and act with independence to deliver low inflation while ignoring pleas from member governments. In that respect, we have already noted the formidable efforts to make the ECB as independent as possible. On the fiscal side, however, success (in the shape of adherence to the budgetary rules) would rest on the mechanisms established to enforce the Maastricht fiscal criteria. This did not turn out quite so well.

The Stability and Growth Pact Within a few years of the Maastricht Treaty, the EU suspected that greater powers of monitoring and enforcement would be needed. Thus, in 1997 at Amsterdam, the EU adopted the **Stability and Growth Pact (SGP)**, which the EU website has described as "the concrete EU answer to concerns on the continuation of budgetary discipline in Economic and Monetary Union." In the end, this provided no answer whatsoever, and even before the ink was dry, naysayers were unkind enough to term it the "stupidity pact."

Throwing another acronym into the mix, the SGP was aimed at enforcing the 3% deficit rule and proposed the following to keep states in line: a "budgetary surveillance" process that would check on what member states were doing; a requirement to submit economic data and policy statements as part of a periodic review of "stability and convergence programs"; an "early warning mechanism" to detect any "slippage"; a "political commitment" that "ensures that effective peer pressure is exerted on a Member State failing to live up to its commitments"; and an "excessive deficits procedure" with "dissuasive elements" in the event of failure to require "immediate corrective action and, if necessary, allow for the imposition of sanctions."[15]

The shortcomings of the SGP, which became clear over time, were as follows:

- Surveillance failed because member states concealed the truth about their fiscal problems. Some hired private-sector accounting firms to make their deficits look smaller via accounting tricks (a suspiciously common deficit figure was 2.9%). In the case of Greece, the government simply falsified deficit figures for the purpose of gaining admission to the euro in 2001 and owned up once it was in.

- Punishment was weak, so even when "excessive deficits" were detected, not much was done about it. Peer pressure was ineffective, perhaps because so many of the governments were guilty of breaking the pact that very few had a leg to stand on. Corrective action was rare and states "did their best," which was often not very much. Formal SGP disciplining processes often started but never resulted in actual

---

[15] European Commission, Directorate General for Economic and Financial Affairs, "The Stability and Growth Pact." Published online. For a copy of this document, go to http://www.eubusiness.com/Finance/eu-stability-growth-pact/.

sanctions because heads of government, at summits of the European Council, proved very forgiving of each other and unwilling to dispense punishments.

- Deficit limits rule out the use of active stabilization policy, but they also shut down the "automatic stabilizer" functions of fiscal policy. Recessions automatically lower government revenues and raise spending, and the resulting deficits help boost aggregate demand and offset the recession. This makes deficit limits tough to swallow, even if monetary policy autonomy is kept as a stabilization tool. In a monetary union, where states have also relinquished monetary policy to the ECB, the pain of hard fiscal rules is likely to be intolerable.

- Once countries joined the euro, the main carrot enticing them to follow the SGP's budget rules (or to pretend to follow them) disappeared. Hence, surveillance, punishment, and commitment all quite predictably weakened once the euro was up and running.

These failures of the SGP came to light only gradually, but by 2003 the pact was in ruins, once it became clear that France and (ironically) Germany would be in breach of the pact and that no serious action would be taken against them.

As Figure 10-8 shows, after 1999 EU member states inside and outside the Eurozone saw their commitment to fiscal discipline weaken, in some cases dramatically

FIGURE 10-8

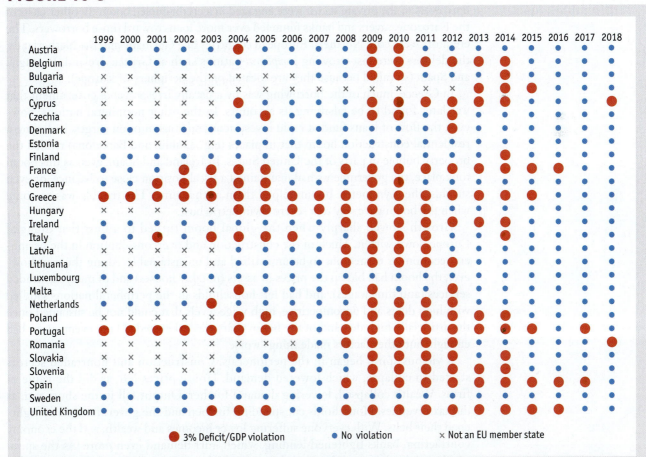

Breaking of Fiscal Rules The fiscal criteria laid down by the Maastricht Treaty for all EU members, and later affirmed by the Stability and Growth Pact, have been widely ignored. This figure shows how often each of the EU member states violated the 3% of GDP government deficit limit from 1999 to 2018. After the Global Financial Crisis and double-dip recession, the frequency of these violations increased even further. On average, member states violated this rule 36% of the time.

Data from: Eurostat.

so. On average, an EU member state was in violation of the deficit rule 36% of the time from 1999 to 2018. Enforcement was weak, and the European Commission had no serious disciplinary powers. The violation of fiscal rules in the Eurozone only got worse after the Great Recession began in 2008. The 60% debt limit will probably never be achieved again by many countries, and the 3% deficit rule is now also seen as empty of any meaning.

4 The Eurozone in Crisis, 2008–13

For almost 10 years, Eurozone policymaking focused on two main macroeconomic goals: the ECB's monetary policy credibility and inflation target, seen as a broad success given low and stable inflation outcomes; and the Eurozone governments' fiscal responsibility, seen as a failure given the general disregard for the SGP rules. However, policymakers (like their counterparts all over the world) failed to spot key macroeconomic and financial developments that were to plunge the Eurozone into crisis in 2008 and beyond.

Boom and Bust: Causes and Consequences of an Asymmetrical Crisis With a fanatical devotion to inflation targeting, the ECB (and its constituent central banks) paid insufficient attention to what was historically a primary responsibility of central banks, namely, financial stability. Within some parts of the Eurozone (as elsewhere) borrowers in the private sector were engaged in a credit-fueled boom. In other parts of the Eurozone, savers and banks funneled ever more loans toward those borrowers. The creditors were core Northern European countries like Germany and the Netherlands; the debtors were fast-growing *peripheral* nations such as Greece, Ireland, Portugal, and Spain (so called because they are located on the periphery of Europe).

In Greece, much of the borrowing was by a fiscally irresponsible government that was later found to be falsifying its accounts. In the other peripheral nations, however, the flow of loans funded rapid investment and consumption surges, including a residential construction boom that in places (e.g., Dublin and Barcelona) rivaled the property bubble in parts of the United States. In Ireland and Spain, even as this boom took place, the governments had maintained a fiscal position close to balance, or even surplus; the asymmetric boom helped them at that time. The trouble was to come when the boom gave way to a severe asymmetric bust.

Growth slowed sharply when the global boom turned to a bust that dragged Europe down with it. Much of the construction and overconsumption in the peripheral economies turned out to be unjustified and unsustainable. Along the way, however, the boom had bid up the prices of assets (notably houses) and of many nontraded services (and thus wages), and had left households in the peripheral nations saddled with high debts and uncompetitive, high wage levels that could not be sustained once the artificially high demand of the boom years was exhausted. These events were bad enough, but other factors made things worse.

A vicious spiral began in the peripherals. Construction and nontraded sectors started to collapse, which lowered demand. House prices fell, as did the value of firms. Wealth collapsed, lowering demand further. Output fell in the short run, as did tax revenues. Households cut spending further, and the governments also tightened their belts. With everyone suffering lower incomes and wealth, and the economy contracting, banks tightened lending, which hurt demand even more. As the spiral continued, banks found that their loans were often turning bad, and that many debts would be repaid only partially, if at all. Because much of the periphery's lending came from banks connected to the Northern European core, these developments triggered tighter credit everywhere in the Eurozone as banks turned cautious. Lending growth for the whole Eurozone was virtually frozen for five years.

The Policymaking Context The Eurozone faced hard choices after the crisis hit in 2008, but the policy measures taken were more timid and quickly reversed, as compared with actions in other countries.

Why? The choices made can potentially be explained by considering the unique features of the European monetary union. We highlight six points.

- **Limited Lender of Last Resort** The Eurozone is a monetary union and has a common central bank, but the ECB is highly inflation averse, is restricted from direct government finance, and is required not to engage in lender of last resort actions to banks lacking good collateral. It is therefore unwilling to intervene with emergency liquidity in weak local banks, except with strict guarantees from the local sovereign government; and it has been generally unwilling (with some exceptions) to intervene to ensure that weak sovereigns remain funded at sustainable interest rates.

- **No Fiscal Union** The Eurozone lacks a political-fiscal union, and has no fiscal policy tools, because there is no central budget that can be used to engage in cross-country stabilization of shocks. This is in large part due to the absence of a central European government (executive power) standing above the sovereigns (the member states). In contrast, in the United States, with a strong center, substantial federal-level automatic transfers between states act as a significant buffer. In fact, the Eurozone has the reverse problem: when the national sovereigns lose credit market access on reasonable terms, they must beg for assistance from the EU, the ECB, and the International Monetary Fund (IMF), the so-called *troika*. As a condition for granting assistance, these organizations have imposed harsh terms that require the countries to undertake fiscal contractions during their slumps, amplifying their business cycles. Overall, even for countries not in a rescue program, the EU authorities have sought even stricter fiscal rules and monitoring since the crisis, adding stringent new rules for all countries in addition to the Maastricht and SGP protocols. Greece has suffered the most extreme version of this external interference. In 2015 the troika imposed more harsh conditions, and even though a referendum rejected the terms, the Greek government felt it had no choice but to agree so as to avoid the threat of a forced exit from the euro ("Grexit") and the financial crisis that would follow.

- **No Banking Union** The Eurozone also lacks even the minimal political-fiscal cooperation to create a banking union, meaning that responsibility for supervising banks, and resolving or rescuing them when they are insolvent, rests with national sovereigns. In the United States, in contrast, the Federal Deposit Insurance Corporation and other institutions underpin a true federal-level banking union with a common pool of fiscal and monetary resources. Critically, the insurance of an individual U.S. state's banking system does not depend at all on the fiscal position of the state itself. Despite the EU's claims to have established a banking union in recent years, the actual structure is inadequate. The supervision and regulation of banks are run out of Frankfurt, but no common pool of fiscal resources at the Eurozone level has been created to back deposit insurance. Instead, from 2016 on, the "first loss" in the case of bank losses falls on "bailed in" equity holders, bondholders, and large depositors of the institution; any further loss then falls on the member state itself. There is no cross-country pooling of risk, mainly because strong countries understandably do not want to share risk with weak countries. But this unwillingness to create cross-country insurance, in turn, leads to a deeper problem: the doom loop.

- **Sovereign–Bank Doom Loop** Because there isn't a banking union or a political-fiscal union, a Eurozone country's national banks tend to hold the local national sovereign's debt; but, in turn, these sovereigns can end up bearing large fiscal costs to repair banking systems and protect depositors from losing their money, under the current rules just described. The banks and the sovereign can then enter into a so-called "doom loop": weak banks' losses can damage the sovereign's creditworthiness just when it may need funds to resolve a crisis; simultaneously, a weak sovereign's debt can decline in value, damaging the balance sheets of local banks where such local debt is predominantly held. In contrast, there is no local U.S. doom loop: an Illinois bank does not hold Illinois debt (so an Illinois default would not hurt Illinois banks), and an Illinois bank failure is handled by the federal authorities (and will not burden the state of Illinois itself).

■ **Labor Immobility** Because the Eurozone is especially weak on labor mobility (one of the OCA criteria), a local economic slump (say, in Spain) is likely to persist for longer because unemployed workers cannot migrate easily to another country where there are better opportunities. After the crisis, local long-term unemployment rates (especially among the youth) rose to very high levels in some countries, despite stronger economic conditions in the core Eurozone countries. The United States saw more labor migration between asymmetrically affected areas in its slump.

■ **Exit Risk** We know that after barely more than a decade, the credibility of the Eurozone as permanent, with no possibility of exit, is not 100% certain. Events have shown that the risk of a country's exit can put financial pressure on that country. If investors suspect that a country will exit the Eurozone, they will want to pull their money out of the country's banks and sell its debt to avoid potential losses. The result is capital flight to safe havens and higher risk premiums on local interest rates. These reflect the nonzero "redenomination risk" of local assets out of euro and into a new, and much depreciated, local currency, plus the risk of losses of depositors via bank restructuring. This dynamic was much in evidence in Cyprus in 2013, for example.

Many of the events in the timeline of 2008–13 can be better understood if we keep these six major points in mind. We now take a closer look at this period, with some key macroeconomic data present for reference in Figure 10-9.

Timeline of Events The first big problem occurred in April 2010 when Greece requested help as its country risk premium spiked and it could no longer borrow at sustainable rates, an action that roiled global financial markets. The EU/ECB/IMF troika jointly devised a plan to stave off the disaster of an uncontrolled default–cum–banking crisis. Together, the troika would provide €110 billion of loans that would give Greece two to three years of guaranteed funding. This help would only be provided under strict conditions that the Greek government radically cut its spending. Financial market turmoil continued, however, and the troika announced further measures for Greece on May 7, 2010.

To help other troubled nations (Ireland, Spain, Portugal, and Italy were all at risk), all EU countries established a fund to provide loans of up to €440 billion. This fund, now known as the *European Stability Mechanism* (ESM), was founded on the good credit of the other EU members and was backed by a once unimaginable bond-buying commitment from the ECB. In addition, funds of up to €60 billion from the EU budget provided a theoretical credit line of up to €500 billion. A further sum of €250 billion was pledged by the IMF. The troika believed that these funds would be large enough to cope with any financing problems that might arise in Ireland and Portugal. If financing problems had occurred in larger countries like Spain (or, even worse, Italy), the troika would have had to come up with more resources.

FIGURE 10-9

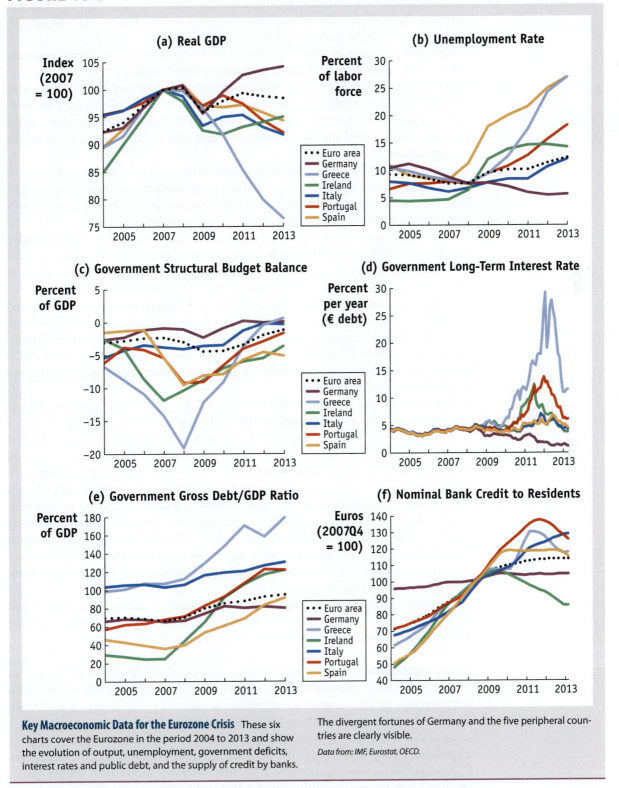

Key Macroeconomic Data for the Eurozone Crisis These six charts cover the Eurozone in the period 2004 to 2013 and show the evolution of output, unemployment, government deficits, interest rates and public debt, and the supply of credit by banks.

The divergent fortunes of Germany and the five peripheral countries are clearly visible.

Data from: IMF, Eurostat, OECD.

The announcement of these measures kept the panic under control only for a time. The risk premiums of the peripherals spiked again in November 2010, after EU leaders said they wanted to possibly impose losses on bondholders in any future rescues. When the EU leaders made this announcement, financial markets realized that they could suffer losses not only on their Greek bonds but also on their bonds issued by other weak countries on the periphery. Even though the EU officials backtracked, the financial markets continued to worry, and the borrowing costs for all peripherals started to climb. As their borrowing costs rose, they too lined up to seek official bail-out programs from the troika, often under some duress.

The troika thought its official funding would help keep the periphery countries' governments afloat until they could get back on their feet. But Greece's debt was so high that it eventually had to impose a partial default in February 2012. During May and June of 2012, many thought that Greece was on the verge of exiting the Eurozone, and there was further turmoil in financial and political circles. Greece remained in the Eurozone, but by 2013 the Greek unemployment rate was 27%; among youths, the unemployment rate was 58%.

By mid-November 2010, Ireland approached the troika to ask for an ESM program, which further shook confidence in the peripherals and in the euro itself. The Irish had a self-made problem. In 2008–09 Ireland guaranteed the safety of deposits in its private banks to prevent bank runs by bank debt holders, which would cause even more economic pain. This method of preventing bank failures did not solve the problem of the private losses; it just transferred the financial sector's massive losses to the government. By late 2010, the Irish government had to admit a loss of about 20% of GDP just to cover the banks' bad debts. The overall fiscal deficit for Ireland that year was an unheard-of 32% of GDP. Financial markets got scared, and the Irish government's interest rate climbed astronomically. It too was pushed into a program of harsh austerity involving public sector cuts and higher taxes. Unemployment rose from 4% in 2006 to 15% by 2012, and among youths it rose to 30%. Ireland was able to borrow affordably in financial markets again in July 2012, but the economy remained weak.

Spain also faced a banking crisis, and although the Spanish government did not intervene as quickly or as generously as did the Irish government, the losses could not be hidden forever, and the country's economy suffered. Banking systems in countries like Spain and Ireland have become so impaired that they do not lend much, and when they do, they do not pass on the ECB's low interest rates to local borrowers. The monetary policy transmission mechanism is broken as low ECB interest rates are not passed through to local firms and consumers. The banks may try to survive as "zombie banks," but they do not help the real economy very much. Similar banking stresses occurred in Portugal and Italy, and by 2013 the interest rates at which Spanish, Portuguese, and Italian firms could borrow from their countries' banks were 2 to 3 percentage points higher than the rates available to German or Austrian firms, causing even greater asymmetry.

Even though Portugal and Spain were not initially as damaged as Greece and Ireland, they shared in the collapse of economic growth in the Eurozone periphery. Spain's banking losses were continually revealed to be larger than previously admitted, and Portugal's growth rate—already bad before the crisis—got even worse. The continuing deterioration in fiscal conditions caused their lending rates to rise, so that in 2011 and 2012 Portugal and Spain, respectively, also reluctantly entered into bail-out programs. By 2013 Spanish unemployment reached 27% (56% among youths); in Portugal the rates reached 11% and 38%, respectively.

As of mid-2013, the latest country to enter an official bailout program was Cyprus, a small but telling example of how the Eurozone might cope with further distress. Cyprus had its own boom and bust, a housing bubble of sorts that had been fueled by an influx of foreign wealth (much of it Russian) seeking a safe, offshore tax haven. Cyprus's economy stalled in 2011 after its government credit rating had been down-graded. By 2012, banking problems in Cyprus were apparent: Cypriot banks still held significant Greek debt and were badly hit when the troika decided to allow a Greek default. As early as July 2012 Cyprus began months of confusing and contentious negotiations with the troika. As rumors emerged that bank depositors might suffer losses, a slow bank run developed in late 2012 and early 2013.

As it turns out, the rumors were well founded. On an extraordinary weekend in March 2013 the troika and the Cyprus government talked long into the night and finally made a deal that would impose significant "taxes" on all bank deposits, including those below the EU's legally guaranteed level of €100,000. All hell broke loose: angry protests began, people tried to get their money out of the banks and out of the country, parliament rejected the deal, and it took another weekend to sort out a different compromise that protected those with less than €100,000 in the bank but imposed losses on everyone else. Along the way, the government maneuvered around other laws and treaties: it imposed capital controls on banks and at the border, and also shunted aside the priority of depositors and creditors at Laiki Bank and the Bank of Cyprus (so that the ECB would be made a preferred creditor ex post; its loans to Laiki, secured with specific collateral, would be transferred whole, without losses, and the losses would be forced onto other secured and unsecured debts of the bank's large creditors, and, remarkably, those of the impaired-yet-acquiring Bank of Cyprus, too). Even though the entire operation was widely judged a political and economic disaster, the president of the Eurogroup (the organization of Eurozone finance ministers) described the outcome as a "template" for handling future crises, a view echoed by ECB president Mario Draghi some days later.

Who Bears the Costs? The view that countries should bear all of the pain for their crises is a consequence of the weak level of cooperation and collective burden-sharing in the Eurozone project. As we have noted, this is very different from the U.S. monetary union, where political, fiscal, and banking union structures work together to help spread risks and absorb shocks. The core countries of the Eurozone have made little effort to provide assistance to the peripherals, beyond lending them money, which will supposedly have to be paid back one day. The belief has been that every country is responsible for its own fiscal position.

But there is some inconsistency in the Eurozone's approach. Note that in principle the governments (and the banks) of the peripherals could have been allowed to default and resume operation in a more creditworthy state. Instead, the EU decided on a "moral hazard" or "bailout" approach of trying to ensure that no bank or government creditors were ever hurt. This controversial step had several motivations, many of them understandable, including the desire to protect core EU banks, to protect the collateral of the ECB, to avoid further contagion and panic in financial markets, and perhaps to defend the reputation of the euro as a serious global currency. These decisions cast aside the prior notion that every Eurozone country was responsible unto itself and the idea that the ECB would not go along in any bailouts. Politically, this course of action would bring about much greater centralization of power, with the European and/or IMF authorities dictating more and more terms on which periphery countries in official bailout programs could run their economic policies.

Because the EU leadership desperately wanted to prevent any country from defaulting, the ECB (like central banks in centuries past) became the only Eurozone institution willing and able to lend a hand. The ECB continued to lend to the private banks against the ever-weaker collateral of the peripheral governments' bonds. Prior to the crisis, the ECB had supposedly said it would refuse to lend against such government bonds when their ratings fell, but when push came to shove, the ECB relaxed its lending criteria again and again, because to do otherwise would have triggered a funding crisis for both the banks and their respective governments. By

2012, new ECB president Mario Draghi was promising to do "whatever it takes" to save the euro, but it isn't clear what he meant by that statement. We still do not know, for example, the exact scope and terms of the Outright Monetary Transactions program, a proposed ECB bond-buying program. But some Eurozone officials, such as German Bundesbank head Jens Weidmann, are not eager for the ECB to act as a backstop in government bond markets. He and others fear that undertaking such programs will lead to fiscal dominance, money printing, and inflationary budget financing.

From Double Dip to Brexit and Beyond ... To the skeptical, the Eurozone/ECB approach has been a giant "extend and pretend" refinancing scheme to postpone tough choices at the nexus of monetary, fiscal, and banking policies. Given the dismal growth path that is expected to continue into the future, the approach will likely fail unless it makes a plan to write down or restructure the underlying losses of banks and governments in the periphery, and even some in the core. The Eurozone needs to have plans and policies in place that will allow it to recapitalize failing banks and restore fiscal health to the governments.

The EU, ECB, IMF, and all of the Eurozone's member governments have been slow to understand (or even agree on) what is happening, and so it has been difficult for them to figure out what to do. As a result of this confusion, they send different signals to different program countries at different times. It remains unclear how these losses will be finally recognized. In addition, political and social unrest remains high, which is hardly surprising given the persistently high levels of unemployment and stagnant living standards, and, in recent years, rising public concerns in several countries about immigration and terrorism. In current and former troika program countries, debt-to-GDP levels remain high. Yet one way or another, through cuts in public spending, losses for depositors, levies for taxpayers, defaults or inflation for bondholders, or all of the above, some losses will eventually be felt and dealt with. We just don't know how the story will end yet.

A sudden growth miracle could quickly erase all of these problems. But many even doubt whether the current policies will be enough to maintain stability and prevent a continued long depression in the short to medium term. The ECB monetary policy stance changed little in 2010–13, but the governments of the Eurozone turned very hard in the direction of fiscal austerity, which led to a change in the total Eurozone government structural budget surplus of between 3 and 4 percentage points of GDP from 2010 to 2013.

Not coincidentally, in late 2011 the Eurozone went into a double-dip recession, and by early 2013 had recorded six straight quarters of negative growth. Measured from the last peak in output, the slump had dragged on in Europe for about as long as the Great Depression of the 1930s. To service their large euro-denominated debt, countries like Greece, Ireland, Portugal, Spain, and Cyprus needed to see their economies recover and their nominal GDP grow (as measured in euros). In the near term, however, growth for these economies was sluggish. A rise in net exports would have been the best hope, but this would normally require a real depreciation in a nation's currency. Because peripherals had no currencies to depreciate (they use the euro), the only way they could restore competitiveness and output was by a large decline in wages and costs, a tough process that is rarely successful and that was forced along by high unemployment. In addition to severe social and political pain, this harsh deflation kept nominal GDP low, causing the countries' debt burdens to grow ever larger as a fraction of income, despite their best efforts to cut government expenditures. By lowering demand and increasing unemployment, the austerity-under-duress undertaken by the peripherals may have been self-defeating.

The Eurozone faced stiff challenges, and its survival at times seemed uncertain, as soon as it was faced with its first major challenge, a financial crisis and then a large recession in the years 2008–12. Recessions and crises will happen again in the future, either from internal problems in Europe or because of an adverse external or global shock such as the 2020 global coronavirus pandemic underway at the time of this writing. So the vulnerability of the euro, due to its shaky policy frameworks, will need to be addressed. Sooner or later, in every big downturn similar problems are likely to arise over and over again.

The risk remains that in bad times one or more peripheral countries may default, or even exit the Eurozone. Core countries may also take large losses if they attempt to prop up the system, and they could balk at a "transfer union" to weaker countries to keep the single currency project going. Such an event would surely be a massive negative shock for the global economy and an incredibly serious crisis for Europe itself. Should a scenario like this unfold, tensions will rise, and the Eurozone in its present form might be in peril.

More broadly, even though calm had returned and the Eurozone economy had slowly grown in the years 2016 to 2020, a mood of more populist politics has been spreading across Europe, reflecting serious discontent among average voters at the economic and political malaise of the region since the start of the Great Recession. Parties on the far left and far right, standing on platforms often hostile to the euro or the EU, or critical of policies like free migration, have been gaining ground. Should these trends continue—and especially if economic hard times return—the institutions of the EU and the euro seem likely to face continued challenges for many years to come.

5 Conclusions: Assessing the Euro

The euro project must be understood at least as much in political terms as in economic terms. We have seen how the OCA criteria can be used to examine the logic of currency unions, but in the case of the EU these are not the whole story: Europe does not appear to satisfy the narrow definition of an OCA. In contrast, some of the most important criteria for the survival of the euro may relate to the non-OCA criteria that were included in the Maastricht Treaty. How well can the euro hold up in the future? Even after the crisis, both optimistic and pessimistic views persist.

Euro-Optimists For true optimists, the euro is already something of a success: it has functioned in a perfectly adequate way (apart from a crisis that has troubled many other countries too) and can be expected to become only more successful as time goes by. More countries are lining up to join the Eurozone. Even if there are costs in the short run, the argument goes, in the long run the benefits will become clear.

Optimists tend to stress that the OCA criteria might be self-fulfilling. In the long run, they believe the euro will create more trade in the Eurozone. It may also create more labor and capital mobility. They downplay the risk that shocks will become more asymmetric, or at least think this will be outweighed by greater market integration. This will enhance the Eurozone's claim to be an OCA. Since the euro is only a few years old, data are scarce, and these claims can be neither proved nor refuted decisively at present. However, the little evidence we have suggests that although labor mobility has not changed much, goods and services trade in the Eurozone is rising (even if no faster than outside) and capital market integration has perhaps improved

Paul Thomas/Daily Express/Mirrorpix

even more dramatically, as measured by the increase in cross-border asset trade and foreign direct investment flows in the Eurozone.[16]

Optimists also tend to believe that the ECB will prove to be a strong, credible, independent central bank that can resist political interference or the temptation to print money for the sake of expediency. On paper, the ECB certainly has such characteristics, with a very high degree of independence compared with other central banks. Again, the costs of a common currency may be large in the short run, but as long as the ECB can deliver on its low-inflation target, the optimists reckon it will, in the end, command the respect of the peoples and politicians of the Eurozone.

At a global level, optimists note that the euro is increasingly becoming a reserve currency for foreign central banks, a vehicle currency for trade, and is now the dominant currency used in international bond markets. These developments show the market's confidence in the currency and also augur well for the future, since trade and financing costs may be expected to fall as the euro becomes more widely used around the globe.

Finally, like the "father" of the EU, Jean Monnet, the optimists believe that the adoption of the euro, like entry to the EU itself, means "no going back": there is simply no imaginable political future for Europe apart from union. Neither the euro nor the EU has exit mechanisms. Perhaps such an idea was inconceivable to the institutional designers. For true believers, the EU project ultimately rests on a deep belief in the political logic of the process and in a presumed common destiny for the peoples of Europe. For them, the great crisis and economic suffering of the present are not a major concern: even if there are large costs to be shouldered in the short run, optimists believe that the long-run gains will make it all worthwhile.

Euro-Pessimists For true pessimists, the preceding arguments are not convincing. Market integration will not radically change because the impact of the euro on (already high) intra-EU trade levels will be small. Because cultural and linguistic barriers will persist, labor migration will be limited and held back even more by inflexible labor market institutions in most countries. In all markets, regulatory and other frictions will remain, and there is resistance to further economic integration. A 2005 EU directive to liberalize services proved unpopular and contributed to the failure of referenda on a proposed EU Constitutional Treaty in France and the Netherlands. Across the EU, the full implications of a single market in all dimensions (goods, services, capital, and labor) are only now being dimly understood by some stakeholders. As reality bites, the European Commission, national governments, political parties, and voters themselves increasingly disagree about how far and how fast this process should go.

If integration stops for lack of political support, a key economic rationale for the euro unravels. If political support for the EU stalls, then the political logic is weakened. If some countries press ahead for a closer, more highly integrated union of countries while others stand aside, the sense of a common destiny among all EU nations will be undermined.

On monetary policy, pessimists note that there is often wide divergence in the countries of the Eurozone. Low-growth, low-inflation countries tend to want looser monetary policy. High-growth, high-inflation countries tend to want tighter monetary policy. If different countries desire very different policies from the ECB, tensions may rise and governments may lose respect for the ECB's

---

[16] For an excellent survey, see Philip R. Lane, 2006, "The Real Effects of European Monetary Union," *Journal of Economic Perspectives*, 20(4), 47–66.

independence. The euro could also be threatened by fiscal problems. The rules say governments cannot lobby the ECB for low interest rates or high inflation to make their debt payments lower or to reduce the real value of their debts, nor can they urge a weaker euro to promote growth. But as history has typically shown, governments tend to trump central banks and will push them around if times get tough. Pessimists note that the Maastricht fiscal rules have evaporated and the SGP has been emptied of meaning. If some nations lobby for looser monetary or fiscal policies, the more fiscally prudent or inflation-averse nations may object, and the resulting fight will cause uncertainty and undermine the credibility of the euro and the ECB.

But the ECB is already in a protracted struggle. Prior to the crisis, the ECB was continually voicing its concerns about fiscal dangers. In November 2005 the ECB asserted its power to deny Eurozone banks the right to use government bonds as collateral if those bonds' credit rating fell too low; but after the 2008 crisis, the ECB caved in and continued to lend against peripheral country government debt of declining quality to prevent crises. The ECB then joined in the fiscal rescue of May 2010 by pledging to fund part of the troika's rescue program, thus stepping further away from its "no bailout" position. In 2012 the ECB said it would do "whatever it takes" to save the euro, launching the Outright Monetary Transaction bond-buying program under President Mario Draghi, a regime shift that finally brought calm to nervous financial markets.

Yet all is still not well, and a decade on from the crisis, the ECB remains stuck at the zero interest rate floor, and the economy struggles to grow. So there is practically no monetary policy space to fight the next recession, and austerity-minded governments may do little to help with fiscal policy either. Pessimists see no end to the monetary and fiscal policy tensions inherent in trying to impose a monetary union on a region with too many economic, political, cultural, and linguistic differences. At best, even if the euro survives, pessimists believe the region will suffer slow growth and ongoing internal policy conflicts. At worst, the tensions could cause the breakup of the Eurozone into blocs or the reintroduction of the former national currencies. The shock of the Brexit vote shows that European projects are not irreversible.

Summary On the upside, the political dimension of the EU might yet carry the day in the long run, despite current setbacks; in the medium run, the OCA criteria might turn out better than one might think; and even if they don't in the short run, the Eurozone can still survive and function, a workable albeit economically costly currency union.

On the downside, EU enlargement undercuts the OCA logic in the short run and could make the ECB's governance more cumbersome and make resolution of conflicts more difficult. As the member states of the Eurozone cope with severe fiscal problems, there is a significant risk of a clash between the fiscal goals of the governments and monetary goals of the ECB; and should the current crisis intensify (e.g., should any member country default or desire to leave the euro) the project would be in uncharted waters.

What do the people think? The results of successive Eurobarometer polls indicate that at the best of times only about 65% of the citizens of the Eurozone have thought that the euro has been beneficial for their own country, with that figure dipping to 50% or below in the Great Recession period. In some countries that figure is higher, in some lower. Since the crisis began, support has fallen from even these lukewarm levels, especially in the hard-hit peripheral countries. The euro remains an experiment—its arrival did not mark the end point of European monetary history, and its long-run fate is not entirely certain.

1. A currency union occurs when two or more sovereign nations share a common currency. Sometimes these arrangements are unilateral, such as when a country like Ecuador adopts the U.S. dollar. But some are multilateral, the most prominent example being the Eurozone.

2. The euro is (as of 2020) the currency of 19 European Union (EU) countries, and they manage it collectively by a common monetary authority, the European Central Bank (ECB). Most of the EU's 27 countries are expected to adopt the euro eventually.

3. According to the theory of optimum currency areas (OCAs), regions should employ a common currency only if they are well integrated and face fairly similar (symmetric) economic shocks. If these criteria are met, efficiency gains from trade should be large, and the costs of forgone monetary autonomy small.

4. A currency union is usually a more irreversible and costly step than simply fixing the exchange rate. The OCA threshold is therefore higher than the threshold for a fixed exchange rate.

5. Additional economic factors can strengthen the case for an OCA. If regions have high labor mobility or large fiscal transfers, these mechanisms may make the costs of a currency union smaller for any given asymmetric shock. In addition, countries with a poor nominal anchor may be eager to join a currency union with a country with a better reputation for inflation performance.

6. Political considerations can drive monetary unions, as when countries feel they have a common destiny and wish to treat monetary union as part of a broader goal of political union.

7. The Eurozone has fairly high trade integration, although not quite as high as that of the United States. The Eurozone might or might not pass this OCA test.

8. The Eurozone has fairly symmetric shocks for most countries. The Eurozone probably does pass this OCA test.

9. The Eurozone has very low labor mobility between countries. The Eurozone almost certainly fails this OCA test.

10. The OCA criteria may fail ex ante, but they may be self-fulfilling: thanks to the common currency, after some years, trade and labor mobility may increase, tipping the balance in favor of an OCA ex post. But increasing specialization due to trade may cause more asymmetric shocks, which would push in the opposite direction.

11. The lack of compelling economic arguments for the euro leads us to study its historical and political origins. The EU must be understood as a political project, and the euro is an important part of the conception of the EU. Although many EU citizens have trust in this project, polls show that such a view is held by only a bare majority.

12. The ECB plays the pivotal role in securing the future of the euro. If it can deliver low inflation and economic stability comparable with the German central bank, after which it was designed, the euro is more likely to succeed as a currency in the EU and as a global currency.

13. Attempts to exert political influence on the ECB continue, and the EU has often proved weak at punishing countries that break the rules of the Eurozone (the Maastricht criteria and the Stability and Growth Pact).

14. The Global Financial Crisis of 2008 and Great Recession were the first real test of the euro, and a stern test at that. Like other economies, the Eurozone suffered from excessive lending and financial bubbles in some countries, fiscal indiscipline in other countries, bailouts of banks, and (as a result) pressure on the central bank to deviate from established policies to support the real economy, banks, and governments. These problems were difficult to handle because they affected Eurozone countries in an asymmetric fashion. As a result, ECB and EU authorities struggled to devise effective policy responses based on broad cooperation except in the direst moments. The economic and political situation remains fragile, especially in the hard-hit peripheral economies of Greece, Ireland, Portugal, and Spain.

15. A double-dip recession began in 2011, making matters even worse: slow growth damaged fiscal positions, government ambitions were limited, and the ECB was reluctant to try aggressive or unconventional tactics (like quantitative easing) for several years.

16. A slow recovery followed, but fundamentals remain weak, public and private debt levels are high, and the European banking system remains fragile. Populist politics in many countries reflect a widespread mistrust of the current economic and political status quo, and the EU and Eurozone have faced growing criticism in many countries. New challenges (including a wave of external immigrants/refugees, a rise in terrorism, and trade tensions with the United States) have arisen in recent years. The 2020 exit of the United Kingdom from the EU dealt a blow to confidence in the supposedly deep and irreversible nature of the European project.

currency union, p. 371
Eurozone, p. 371
euro, p. 371
European Union (EU), p. 372
Maastricht Treaty, p. 372
optimum currency area (OCA),
    p. 374

inflation bias, p. 378
Marshall Plan, p. 388
Treaty of Rome, p. 388
Exchange Rate Mechanism (ERM),
    p. 389
Economic and Monetary Union
    (EMU), p. 390

ERM crisis, p. 390
European Central Bank (ECB),
    p. 391
convergence criteria, p. 397
Stability and Growth Pact (SGP),
    p. 400

PROBLEMS

1. **Discovering Data** Do some research on the Internet to construct an updated version of the map in Figure 10-1. You can find membership information on the websites of the European Union (europa.eu) and the European Central Bank (www.ecb.int). Since this book was written, have any new countries joined the European Union, applied to join, or left? Have any countries entered the Exchange Rate Mechanism, or exited from it? Have any new countries adopted the euro, or abandoned it?

2. One could view the United States as a currency union of 50 states. Compare and contrast the Eurozone and the United States in terms of the optimum currency area (OCA) criteria. Use charts to aid your explanation.

3. After German reunification and the disintegration of communist rule in Eastern Europe, most countries in that region sought to join the European Union (EU), including the Economic and Monetary Union (EMU). Many now use the euro. Why do you believe these countries were eager to integrate with Western Europe? Do you think policymakers in these countries believe that OCA criteria are self-fulfilling? Explain.

4. The Maastricht Treaty places strict requirements on government budget deficits and national debt. Why do you think the Maastricht Treaty called for fiscal discipline? If it is the central bank that is responsible for maintaining the fixed exchange rate, then why does fiscal discipline matter? How might this affect the gains/losses for joining a currency union?

5. The following figure shows some hypothetical OCA criteria with the Eurozone for selected countries. *Assume that these are based solely on economic criteria—that is, without reference to other political considerations.* Refer to the diagram in responding to the questions that follow. (Note: we also include the United Kingdom here so as to study its choices as well, prior to and contributing to its Brexit decision in 2020.)

Symmetry-Integration Diagram

a. Which of the countries satisfy the OCA criteria for joining a monetary union?

b. Compare Poland and the United Kingdom in terms of the OCA criteria regarding *market integration* with the Eurozone. Discuss one possible source of differences in integration (with the EU) in the two countries.

c. Compare Poland and the United Kingdom in terms of the OCA criteria regarding *symmetric versus asymmetric shocks* (relative to the Eurozone). Discuss one possible source of differences in symmetry (with the EU) in the two countries.

d. Suppose that policymakers in both Poland and the United Kingdom care only about being able to use policy in response to shocks. Which is more likely to seek membership in the EMU and why?

e. What did the ERM crises reveal about the preferences of the United Kingdom? Consider other costs and benefits not in the diagram, both economic and political. Does this help explain why the UK did not join the euro? Does this help explain why the UK eventually left the EU altogether?

f. What did membership of the Eurozone reveal about the preferences of Greece? Consider other costs and benefits not in the diagram, both economic and political.

6. Congress established the Federal Reserve System in 1914. Up to this point, the United States did not have a national currency; Federal Reserve notes are still the paper currency in circulation today. Earlier attempts at establishing a central bank were opposed on the grounds that a central bank would give the federal government a monopoly over money. This was a reflection of the historic debate between maintaining states' rights versus establishing a strong centralized authority in the United States. That is, the creation of the Fed and a national currency would mean that states would no longer have the authority to control the money supply on a regional level. Discuss the debate between states' rights versus centralized authority in the context of the EMU and the European Central Bank.

7. There have been reports that a group of six Gulf countries (Bahrain, Kuwait, Oman, Qatar, Saudi Arabia, and the United Arab Emirates) were considering the introduction of a single currency. Currently, these countries use currencies that are effectively pegged to the U.S. dollar. These countries rely heavily on oil exports to the rest of the world, and political leaders in these countries are concerned about diversifying trade. Based on this information, discuss the OCA criteria for this group of countries. What are the greatest potential benefits? What are the potential costs?

8. Compare and contrast the Fed and the European Central Bank in terms of their commitment to price stability and employment/output stability. Which central bank has more independence to pursue price stability as a primary objective? Explain.

9. Why do countries with less independent central banks tend to have higher inflation rates? Is it possible for the central bank to increase output and reduce unemployment in the long run? In the long run, is the German model a good one? Explain why or why not.

10. Compare the Maastricht Treaty convergence criteria with the OCA criteria. How are these convergence criteria related to the potential benefits and costs associated with joining a currency union? If you were a policymaker in a country seeking to join the EMU, which criteria would you eliminate and why?

Index

Balance of payments accounts, 142, 144–146, 145f
Baldwin, Richard, 384
Bands, 30
Bank(s)
  central. *See* Central bank(s); Central bank balance sheets; Central bank independence; *specific central banks*
  commercial, 36
  insolvency or illiquidity of, 340, 342
Banking crises, 322–323, 323t
Banking union, lack of, in Eurozone, 403
Bank of America, 36
Bank of England
  Northern Rock insolvency and, 342
  response to crisis of 2008-2009, 111
Barro, Robert J., 88n, 396n
Base currency, 29, 282
Base money, 68
Beggar-thy-neighbor policies, 306–307
Big Max Index, 66f, 67
Bilateral exchange rates, 26
Black markets, 37
Blanchard, Olivier, 92
Bluedorn, John C., 180n
Blustein, Paul, 343n, 366n
Bond(s)
  junk, 12
  sterilization, 345
  Treasury, U.S., 12
Bond ratings, 12
BOP credit, 162
BOP debit, 163
BOP identity, 162
Borrowers, net, 165
Bosworth, Barry, 187n
Brawling band, 32
Brazil
  country risk of, 12
  currency of, 298, 300
  exchange rate crisis of, 5
Bretton Woods conference, 311–312
Bretton Woods system, 280, 302, 314, 389
Brexit, 281, 285–286, 372
Britain. *See also* United Kingdom
  Brexit and, 281, 285–286, 372
  contingent commitment and, 357
  current account of, 196
  departure from ERM, 391
  exchange rate of, 29–30, 30f, 281–286, 283f, 311
  expenditure switching and, 234
Brooks, Robin, 292n, 365n
Bruno, Michael, 88n
Bryan, William Jennings, 310

Bubula, Andrea, 365n
Budget, 157–158, 233
  balanced, 233
Budget constraint, long-run. *See* Long-run budget constraint (LRBC)
Budget deficits, 157–158, 233
Budget surpluses, 157–158, 233
Burger, John D., 300n

C

CA. *See* Current account (CA)
Cagan, Philip, 78n
Cai, Fang, 211n
Calomiris, Charles W., 342n
Calvo, Guillermo, 191, 396n
Cameron, David, 324
Canada
  exchange rate of, 29–30, 30f
  following Great Recession, 269
  inflation in, 55–56
Canjels, Eugene, 308n
Capital, movement between countries. *See* Foreign direct investment (FDI)
Capital account (KA), 145f, 146, 160–161
Capital controls, 36–37, 364
Capital gains, 11
Caselli, Francesco, 227n
Cassel, Gustav, 55
Cavallo, Domingo, 324
Cavallo, Michele, 298, 299n
Celtic Tiger, 149
Center currency, 29, 282
Central bank(s), 69. *See also specific central banks*
  financial sector and, 340, 341f
  independence of, 92
  interest rate control by, 110–111
  as lender of last resort, 340
  open market operations of, 337
Central bank balance sheets, 326–327
  financial system and, 344–348
  sterilization bonds and, 345
  graphical analysis of, 328–330, 329f
Central bank independence, 92
CFA France zone, 32
CFP Franc zone, 32
Cheung, Yin-Wong, 120n
Chile
  default of, 11
  sovereign wealth fund of, 199–200
China
  capital controls in, 36
  following Great Recession, 269
  government manipulation of data in, 172
  reserve accumulation in, 346–347, 347f
  sovereign wealth fund of, 199

Chinn, Menzie D., 13n, 120n, 158n
Chodorow-Reich, Gabriel, 187n
Churchill, Winston, 388
CIP. *See* Covered interest parity (CIP)
Circular flow of payments, 142
Citi, 36
Civil War, U.S., foreign exchange and, 133–135, 134f
Cline, William R., 187n
Closed economies, flow of payments in, 142–143, 143f
Collins, Susan M., 187n
Colombia
  currency of, 300
  exchange rate of, 31f, 32
Commercial banks, 36
Common currency, 15
  comparing prices in using exchange rates, 26–28, 28t
Connally, John, 313
Consumption, 231–232
  disposable income related to, 231
  in GNE, 147
  government, 233
  in GNE, 147
Consumption function, 231, 231f
Consumption smoothing, 192–200
  basic model of, 192
  consumption volatility and financial openness and, 197–198
  numerical example of, 193–196
    in closed vs. open economy with no shocks, 193, 193t
    in closed vs. open economy with shocks, 193–195, 194t
  generalization of, 195
  precautionary saving, reserves, and sovereign wealth funds and, 198–199
  when a shock is permanent, 195–196
Contagion, 335
Contingent commitment, 357
Continuously linked settlement system, 34n
Convergence, 222
Convergence criteria, 397–400, 398f
Cooperative arrangements, 302
Copenhagen Criteria, 390
Corners hypothesis, 364
Coronavirus Recession
  fiscal stimulus and, 270
  interest rates and, 269
Corporations, 36
Costs
  of exchange rate crises, 320–325, 322f
    associated economic crises as, 322–325, 323t

of inflation, 88n
of pegging, 360–362, 361f
transaction
  deviations from purchasing power parity and, 64–65
  in foreign exchange markets, 35
Council of Ministers, 388
Country premiums, 333
Country risk, 12
Covered interest parity (CIP), 41–44
  evidence on, 43–44
Crawl, 32
Crawling peg, 32
Credibility, 335, 357, 359–361, 361f
Creditors, net, 168
Credit scores, 11–12
Crockett, Andrew, 365n
Cross rate, 39–40, 431f
Cullen, Joe, 150n
Currencies. *See also specific currencies*
  appreciation of. *See* Appreciation
  base (center), 29, 282
  common, 15
    comparing prices in using exchange rates, 26–28, 28t
  currency reform and, 78
  depreciation of. *See* Depreciation
  devaluation of, 305
  exchange rates and. *See* Exchange rate(s); Foreign exchange market
  overvaluation of, 59
  redenomination of, 78
  revaluation of, 305
  undervaluation of, 59
  vehicle, 40
Currency areas. *See* Currency unions; Eurozone; Optimum currency areas (OCAs)
Currency boards, 33–34, 329
  operation of, 332
Currency crises. *See* Exchange rate crises
Currency mismatch, liability dollarization and, 297–301
Currency premiums, 333, 357
Currency unions, 32, 371. *See also* Eurozone
Currency wars, 229
Current account (CA), 8–9, 144, 145f, 400f
  information provided by, 154–155
  wars and, 196
Current account identity, 155
Cyprus
  capital controls in, 36
  economic crisis in, 406–407